Bibliothèque
de la Faculté de Philosophie et Lettres
de l'Université de Liège

Bibliothèque de la Faculté de Philosophie et Lettres
de l'Université de Liège   Fascicule CLXXXI

Irène SIMON

THREE RESTORATION DIVINES

BARROW, SOUTH, TILLOTSON

Selected Sermons

1967

Société d'Edition « Les Belles Lettres »

36, rue de Fleurus, Paris

D/1967/0480/32

To James SUTHERLAND

Conformément au règlement de la « Bibliothèque de la Faculté de Philosophie et Lettres », le présent ouvrage a été examiné par une commission technique composée de M. J.R. Sutherland, professeur à l'Université de Londres, Mˡˡᵉ S.R.T.O. d'Ardenne, M. Ph. Devaux, M. L.-E. Halkin, M. A. Vandegans, professeurs à l'Université de Liège. Mˡˡᵉ S.R.T.O. d'Ardenne et M. J. Labarbe en ont assuré la révision et ont surveillé la correction des épreuves.

It is a pleasure to acknowledge the many debts I have incurred in preparing this edition. To the directors and staff of several libraries I wish to express my gratitude for their assistance and unfailing courtesy, particularly to the librarians of: the British Museum; the Bodleian Library; the Cambridge University Library; the Library of the University of London; Trinity College, Cambridge; Christ Church College, Oxford; the Library of the University of Liège; and to Mr. L.E. TANNER, Keeper of the Muniments and Library of Westminster Abbey.

Special thanks are due to my colleagues Professors S.R.T.O. D'ARDENNE and J. LABARBE and to Mme MAES-JELINEK for their help in correcting proofs, and to Professor Ch. FONTINOY for his comments on Barrow's Hebrew.

I have drawn a great deal upon the work of others. Specific obligations to published material are recorded in the footnotes. My greatest debt, for encouragement, criticism, and advice while the work was in progress, is recognized in the dedication.

CONTENTS

VOLUME I

PART I

PART II

VOLUME II

PART ONE

PART ONE

INTRODUCTION

Boswell relates that when Mr. Beauclerck's library was sold in 1781 John Wilkes expressed his surprise at finding that this gentleman owned so many sermons; to which Johnson replied: " Why, Sir, you are to consider that sermons make a considerable branch of literature; so that a library must be very imperfect if it has not a numerous collection of sermons. " [1] In the eighteenth century sermons indeed constituted an important part of publishers' lists, as they had done in earlier ages, [2] and they were still read by the educated public. Readers did not confine themselves to the works of their contemporaries, but frequently turned to sermons of earlier ages, that is, of the Restoration period and of the early eighteenth century, and many of these were reissued in handsome editions. No doubt some readers prized them not for their literary merits but for the 'sentiments' expressed in them, and expected from them edification rather than aesthetic pleasure: one remembers that the husband of Fielding's Amelia was converted by a series of sermons by Barrow in proof of the Christian religion. On the other hand, periodical essayists and grammarians often recommended the works of earlier divines as models of style and composition, while Blair paid special attention to them in his *Lectures on Rhetoric and Belles Lettres* (1783). Through their training in rhetoric as students, gentlemen would have become familiar with sermon literature, though not all would have summed up the advantages to be reaped from such study as Don Juan was to do:

> Much English I cannot pretend to speak,
> Learning that language chiefly from its preachers,

[1] *Boswell's Life of Johnson*, ed. G. Birkbeck Hill, revised by L.F. Powell, Oxford, 1934-50, IV, 105.

[2] It has been estimated that some 12,000 sermons were published in the Elizabethan period alone (see F.P. WILSON: *Seventeenth Century Prose*, Cambridge, 1960, p. 122); after the Restoration the chief readers were " the religious people, who, with their Sermons, their Treatises, and their Book Wars, kept the metropolitan Book Trade going. " (Edward ARBER: *The Term Catalogues*, London, 1903-6, I, xv.)

> Barrow, South, Tillotson, whom every week
> I study, also Blair, the highest reachers
> Of eloquence in piety and prose—[1]

In later years some of these gentlemen may have bought sermons with no other purpose than to display them in their libraries and impress their visitors, like Addison's Leonora earlier in the century. None the less, in the eighteenth century any well-stocked library would have contained a numerous collection of sermons, even if the owner was, like Mr. Beauclerck, a member of the gay world. For Johnson they made a considerable branch of literature, and he was not the man to judge by sheer numbers. Parson Adams discovered to his dismay that they were mere drugs on the market, but that booksellers were always willing to publish sermons " with the name of some great man ". Among such names those of several Restoration divines were certainly prominent : editions of the works of Barrow, Tillotson or Stillingfleet testify to the continued interest of the reading public, while references to, or praise of, other preachers such as South or Sherlock by eighteenth-century men of letters suggest that these too were still read with pleasure. Addison and Steele repeatedly commended Tillotson to their readers ; Pope owned a set of Barrow's Works [2] ; Fielding read South's sermons when he was a young man and returned to them in his later years [3] ; Boswell found the most lively account of wit in Barrow's sermon *Against Foolish Talking and Jesting* [4], while Johnson was once asked to give his opinion as to which were the best sermons for style [5]. Such a discussion of the comparative merits of pulpit orators is sufficient evidence that sermons were regarded as literature offering both profit and delight.

Men like Johnson would not have dreamt of dissociating the two ends of poetry when judging any literary work, but twentieth-century readers have tended to distrust works that purposely set out to edify, and many of them are likely to apply to all literature Keats' famous dictum on poetry that has a palpable design upon us. As a consequence sermons have fared badly with modern readers.

---

[1] *Don Juan*, II, clxv.
[2] See *The Correspondence of Alexander Pope*, ed. George Sherburn, Oxford, 1956, II, 81 (1721).
[3] See Allan WENDT : 'Fielding and South's " luscious morsel " ; A Last Word ', *N. & Q.*, N.S., IV (1957), 256-7.
[4] *Op. cit.*, IV, 105-6.
[5] *Op. cit.*, III, 247-8.

Though no student of English literature can ignore Burke's speech
On Conciliation with America, sermons have been allowed to fall
into oblivion, unless interest in them has been aroused by the
personality of the preacher and his contribution to other domains
of literature.   Donne is a case in point, but it is surely significant
that even T.S. Eliot's vindication of that other great Jacobean
preacher, Lancelot Andrewes, has so far failed to induce scholars
to edit his sermons [1] ; nor is Jeremy Taylor much better known,
except from the *Selected Passages* edited by Logan Pearsall Smith.
The publication of Donne's sermons has shown, however, how
misleading such selections can be, for the representative passages
tend to be purple patches, and their function and significance cannot be rightly assessed apart from the whole.   Neither the late-
eighteenth century *Beauties of South*, nor the twentieth-century
Golden Book of Tillotson, nor the *Selected Passages* from Donne's
sermons, can give the reader any inkling of the structure of the
whole, of the way the themes are developed, or of the full force
of the argument, and little idea of the contribution of the style to
the purpose in hand.

A more serious consequence of our neglect of sermon literature
is that some of the best prose stylists and most vigorous minds of
the past, such as Robert South, are virtually unknown to the student
of English literature, while every scrap of writing by some minor
poet is treasured carefully.   Coleridge was no doubt an omnivorous
reader, and he was deeply concerned with religious problems ;
still, his many annotations of seventeenth-century divines suggest
what an important place he intented to accord them in his projected
history of the development of English prose style.   Apart from
the intrinsic merits of individual pulpit orators, the Restoration
divines contributed through their sermons to the final triumph of
the new prose style and encouraged the taste for simpler structures
in literary compositions.   It is hard to define the part played by
each of the several converging forces in the gradual emergence
of the new tastes and standards, but pulpit oratory must have had
a far-reaching influence since from an early age many boys and
girls were expected to give their parents or teachers an account
of the sermons they heard.   From the testimonies of men and

---

[1] A selection of his sermons appeared when this book was already in the
press : Lancelot ANDREWES : *Sermons*, Selected and edited with an Introduction
by G.M. Story, Oxford, 1967.

women who in their youth or even childhood were trained to take
notes and memorize both the matter and the manner of sermons,
we gather that these were regarded not only as means of moral
edification, but as examples of composition from which the children
could learn. Such was the vogue of sermons in the Restoration
period that preachers often complained that many people considered
hearing sermons as the sum of religion, and that among these a
fair number were mainly interested in comparing the merits of the
several divines they went to hear ; but Evelyn's notes show that
devout men were also interested in, and sometimes criticized, the
preachers' style and manner. When the sermons were published,
they could be read for the same dual purpose, and their influence
on modes of thought and of style lasted well into the next century.

As Edward Arber pointed out in the preface to his edition of
The Term Catalogues,

> it was the religious people first, and the Scientists next,
> that made the fortunes of the London Book Trade. They
> often subscribed as much for the folios of a single writer,
> like Tillotson or Rushworth, Baxter or Ray, Manton or
> Bunyan, as would have bought a complete set of all the
> plays of that Time.[1]

The popularity of some preachers, with the polite audiences at
Whitehall or Westminster as well as with the sober congregations
of the City, also appears from several manuscript collections of
sermons that have come down to us : apparently some people
would copy whole sermons by hand, presumably from shorthand
notes, in order to read them again or to hand them round to friends.
Any account of the temper or intellectual climate of the age that
ignores these facts is therefore bound to be distorted. Nor can
the problem be dismissed by positing the existence of two cultural
groups and by assuming that the Dissenters alone were much concerned with religious issues. Dryden's *Religio Laici* is a private
meditation, but its style and manner are those of a man aware of
other men faced with the same difficulties, not those of the con-
templative worrying out the problems in his closet. Similarly, his
satiric mode in *Absalom and Achitophel* cannot be valued rightly
unless one remembers that his readers would have heard the story
of David expounded and applied to English history in sermon after
sermon.

[1] *Op. cit.*, III, vii.

One may wonder how close the printed versions were to the sermons delivered in the pulpit. This would depend on the method of delivery, which varied from preacher to preacher. Some divines read their sermons, while others preached *memoriter*; the former practice was discouraged by Charles II, and most divines complied, though Tillotson reverted to his earlier manner when he found that the effort to memorize his text was too great a strain. In both these cases the sermon was written out carefully before delivery; if the preacher was asked to print it as delivered, as was sometimes the case for sermons preached before the King, there would be few differences or none between the spoken and the printed version. But some divines, like Burnet, preached from notes and in such cases the discrepancy might be much greater. Moreover, when they prepared their sermons for the press some divines would revise them carefully, unless otherwise instructed; indeed they were sometimes asked to publish " what farther they had prepared to say ", as was usually the case for sermons preached before the Mayor and Aldermen of the City. They would then avail themselves of the opportunity to expand some passages, or they would compress the matter of successive sermons into one, or they would leave out passages which they had used elsewhere before. However interesting comparison of the two versions may be for the light the revisions throw on methods of composition and on individual authors' sense of style, the printed versions alone have a right to be treated as a branch of literature, not only because they alone were known to the wider reading public but because in revising their texts for publication the authors, like any other men of letters, wished to polish their work. They often had in mind the reading public, whose response could not be guided by the inflexions of the speaker's voice or by his gestures, but depended solely on the quality of the words on the page. In fact, they turned their sermons into literature.

The present selection purposes to make available to a wider public some of these Restoration sermons, which at present can only be found in the better libraries, and to place them in their historical context with regard to the developments in pulpit oratory in the seventeenth century and to the trends of thought which they reflect. The underlying assumption is that sermons were a considerable branch of literature in that period, and that they constitute a definite genre, whose success depends on the writer's ability to arouse and sustain his readers' interest, or to move them, or both. The interest will inevitably vary according as the reader is more or less concerned with the kind of problems expounded by the preacher, but it will also depend to a large extent on the preacher's way of handling his theme. One need not feel particularly concerned with the working of Providence in order to admire the magnificent structure of Bossuet's funeral orations, nor need one believe that " Unto God the Lord belong the issues of death " in order to be profoundly moved by Donne's *Deaths Duell.* The sermons in this collection do not achieve, or indeed attempt, such effects as Donne wrought on his audience and still works on his readers to-day. They will appeal not to those who, as T.S. Eliot said of Donne's readers, are " fascinated by ' personality ' in the romantic sense of the word ", but to those who value the craft of the artist in handling his theme and in making his words serve his purpose. These divines addressed an educated public, whether at Oxford or Cambridge or in the metropolis ; they set out to convince and persuade, not to arouse the passions. They did this in their several ways, each of which reveals the quality and scope of the mind at work in the composition.

CHAPTER ONE

THE REFORM OF PULPIT ORATORY
IN THE SEVENTEENTH CENTURY

In the sermon he preached at the funeral of his friend the Archbishop of Canterbury, Gilbert Burnet praised Tillotson for having set to himself a new pattern of preaching ; " such a one it was ", he said, " that 'tis hoped it will be long and much followed ". Tillotson, he explained, had always kept a due mean between a low flatness and the dresses of rhetoric, and he had retrenched all superfluities and needless enlargements ; in his sermons there was

> no affectation of learning, no squeezing of Texts, no super-
> ficial Strains, no false Thoughts nor bold Flights, all was
> solid yet lively, and grave as well as fine [1].

Though twentieth-century readers may not value Tillotson's sermons as highly as did the Bishop of Sarum, they will readily grant that he aptly defined the change that had come over pulpit oratory in England in the course of the seventeenth century. That the new style of preaching had come to stay appears from Thomas Birch's slight alteration to this passage, which he quoted in the Life of the Author prefixed to his folio edition of Tillotson's sermons in 1752 : " He formed therefore [a pattern] to himself, which has been justly considered as the best model for all succeeding ages " [2]. Birch then proceeded to give a brief sketch of the history of preaching since the Reformation, and ascribed the great corruption of pulpit oratory before the Restoration to Lancelot Andrewes, " whose reputation on other accounts gave a sanction to that vicious taste introduced by him several years before the death of Queen Elizabeth ". This taste, Birch said, was fostered

---

[1] Gilbert BURNET : *A Sermon Preached at the Funeral of the Most Reverend Father in God John, By Divine Providence, Lord Archbishop of Canterbury, Primate and Metropolitan of all England...*, London, 1694, p. 13 ; pp. 13-14.
[2] *The Works of John Tillotson, With the Life of the Author*, by Thomas BIRCH, London, 1820, I, xiii.

by the pedantry of King James's Court and resulted in " the dege-
neracy of all true eloquence, so that the most applauded preachers
of that time are now insupportable ; and all the wit and learning
of Dr. Donne cannot secure his sermons from universal neglect " [1].
However wrong-headed this view may appear to twentieth-century
readers, it is one that many people after the Restoration would
have endorsed.   On 15 July, 1683, Evelyn entered this note in his
diary :

> 15 A stranger preached on 6. *Jer*:8 : The not harkning to
> Instruction, portentous of desolation to a people : The old
> man preached much after Bish : *Andrews's* method, full of
> *Logical* divisions, in short, and broken periods, and latine
> sentences, now quite out of fashion in the pulpit ; grown
> into a far more profitable way, of plaine and practical, of
> which sort this *Nation* nor any other ever had greater
> plenty, and more profitable (I am confident) since the
> *Apostles* time [2].

The reform in pulpit oratory is only one aspect of the triumph of
' nature ' and ' sense ' which characterizes the neo-classical period,
and Birch's remark may be compared with Johnson's censure of
Donne's wit in the *Life of Cowley*.   With Tillotson, and particularly with his eighteenth-century imitators, the plain way of preaching may be thought to have triumphed with a vengeance, and we
may share Taine's amazement [3] at the popularity of such sermons,
although before ascribing the taste for them, as he does, to the
naturally dull temper of the English we had better inquire why
or how this new taste had developed.   This way of preaching
(together with other factors) may indeed have led to the utter
dessication of religious life in the eighteenth century and made the
Wesleyan revival imperative, but in the later seventeenth century
the need was obviously felt to restore something like the old
humanistic manner of preaching in order to curb the worst extravagances.   For this change in pulpit oratory reasons were not far
to seek, in the religious and political history of the times no less
than in the development of the literary tradition.

Though George Herbert advised country parsons not to follow

---

[1] *Ibid.*, p. xiv.
[2] John EVELYN : *Diary*, ed. E.S. de Beer, Oxford, 1955, IV, 330.
[3] *Histoire de la littérature anglaise*, Paris, 1921 [15], III, 265 ss.

" the other way of crumbling a text into small parts " [1], the method was characteristic of much witty preaching in the earlier seventeenth century and is best illustrated by Andrewes's sermons. These, it has been asserted [2], impressed his generation and may have set a fashion [3]. William Laud, Bishop of London and afterwards Arch-bishop of Canterbury, is usually numbered among the imitators of Andrewes, and his words on the scaffold are often quoted as evidence of his wit: " I am going apace, as you see, towards the Red Sea, and my feet are now upon the very brink of it ; an argument, I hope, that God is bringing me into the Land of Promise " [4]. Laud's sermons were published in his lifetime and reprinted during the Commonwealth [5], and they too may have exerted some influence on young divines, especially since his martyrdom enhanced his reputation. Yet, in few of these do we find examples of metaphysical wit. Nor does Laud ' squeeze ' his texts, though he may be a little too prone to find a king ' every way ' in them [6]. His style is Senecan and not unlike Andrewes's, but it is usually free of the agnominations which are one of the hallmarks of the latter's prose. Even when preaching before the King he seldom crumbles his text in order to expound the nicest points in it ; indeed, in such sermons as that on *Ps.* CXXII. 6,7, preached on 19 June, 1621, the division is as simple, and the overall plan as clear, as any later reformer of pulpit oratory could have wished. Other Anglican divines, such as Richard Corbet,

---

[1] *A Priest to the Temple, or The Country Parson*, (first published in 1652, but written before 1633 ; Herbert died in March 1632/3), in *Works*, ed. F.E. Hutchinson, Oxford, 1941, p. 235.

[2] See W.F. MITCHELL: *Pulpit Oratory from Andrewes to Tillotson*, London, 1932, p. 16.

[3] Lancelot Andrewes's sermons were published after his death, " by his Majesties special command ", by William Laud and John Buckeridge (*XCVI Sermons*, 1629). George Williamson quotes a remark by Bishop Felton (who died in 1626): " I had almost marred my own natural Trot by endeavouring to imitate his artificial Amble ". *The Senecan Amble*, A Study in Prose Form from Bacon to Collier, London, 1951, p. 231.

[4] Quoted by Mitchell, *op. cit.*, p. 157.

[5] See, for instance: *Seven Sermons Preached Upon Several Occasions*, London, 1651.

[6] See his *Sermon preached at White-Hall, on the 24 of March, 1621, being the day of the beginning of his Majesties most gracious Reigne* (on *Psal.* 21. 6,7), London, 1622 : " Now we can no sooner meet a *blessing* in the Text, but we presently find two Authors of it, *God* and the *King* : For there is *God Blessing* the King ; and the *King Blessing* the people. And a King is every way in the Text : For David the King set the Psalme for the People, and the People, they sing the Psalme rejoycing for the King ; And all this is, *that the King may rejoyce in thy strength, O Lord*, v. 1 And when this Psalme is sung in Harmonie, between the *King* and the *People*, then there is *Blessing* ", p. 48.

Bishop of Oxford, John Cosin, Bishop of Durham, Henry King,
Bishop of Chichester [1], or John Hacket, Bishop of Coventry and
Lichfield [2], had a reputation for witty preaching, while Joseph Hall,
' our English Seneca ', was called by Milton a ' tormentor of semi-
colons ' for the brevity of his style [3]. It is natural, therefore, that
this style of preaching should have been associated with the Anglo-
Catholic divines of the earlier seventeenth century, even though
some of them, notably Bishop Sanderson, did preach in a more
easy and natural manner [4]. The other great Anglican divine whose
fame in his time equalled that of Andrewes does not seem to have
been held responsible for the ' corruption ' of pulpit oratory. Birch
found that for all his wit and learning (or rather, because of it)
Donne deserved to be forgotten, but he only mentioned his sermons
as an instance of the ' vicious taste ' of James I and his Court.
Nor does any of the Restoration attacks against the oratory of
the former times refer to Donne specifically, though many of the
' vices ' censured might be illustrated from his sermons, particularly
the learned allusions, the conceits, or the play of wit. Yet Donne's
sermons were also in print [5] and might have exerted some influence
on prospective divines. True, one of the elegies prefixed to the
1633 edition of his *Poems*, which praises him as a second
Chrysostom, refers to the ' beetles ' that slighted in him " that
good, They could not see, and much less understood " :

---

[1] He is an imitator of Donne rather than of Andrewes, and indeed was
closely associated with the Dean of St Paul's.

[2] Mitchell (*op. cit.*, p. 166) quotes a characteristic example, the opening
of the third sermon Hackett preached on the text : ' Then was Jesus led up of
the Spirit into the wilderness to be tempted ' (*Matt.* IV. 1): " This text, you see,
will not let me go. I have been parting from it thrice, and still it invites me
to stay : As the Levite took farewell at Bethlem sundry times, and could not
get away, *Judg.* XIX. And now I have good cause to tarry, being led by the
leading of the spirit : whosoever shall compel thee to go a mile with him, go
with him twain, says *Christ, Matt.* V. 41, and if the spirit of God compel us to
go with him one sermon, we will go with him twain ; it cannot be irksome
or weary to follow such contemplations. "

[3] See *An Apology Against a Pamphlet*, in *Complete Prose Works*, New
Haven, 1953, I, 894. Hall's later sermons, however, are less terse.

[4] Birch recognizes this, but his views are slightly confused. It is not clear,
for instance, whether he means to praise Hall, and it is surely surprising that
he should think so highly of Jeremy Taylor, whose florid style of preaching
went out of fashion after the Restoration. It is only fair to add that Taylor,
being less knotty than the metaphysical preachers, would have struck an
eighteenth-century reader as more ' easy '.

[5] They were published by his son, John, in three folio volumes : *LXXX Sermons* (with Walton's Life), in 1640 ; *Fifty Sermons*, in 1649 ; *XXVI Sermons*,
in 1660.

'Tis true, they quitted him, to their poore power,
They humm'd against him ; And with face most sowre
Call'd him a strong lin'd man, a Macaroon,
And no way fit to speak to clouted shoone,
As fine words (truly) as you would desire,
But (verily) but a bad edifier.[1]

This, however, suggests no more than that Donne's eloquence was
not suited to the capacity of some hearers,—'clouted shoone' at
that ! But the increasing attacks on the blind mouths that scarce
themselves knew how to hold a sheep-hook while the sheep looked
up and were not fed, drew attention to the necessity for the
preacher to speak to the capacity of *all* his hearers. Donne and
Andrewes may well have felt that their sermons were 'seasonable'
to their audience, as the reformers were to claim that all sermons
should be ; only their audience was not the hungry sheep who
looked up to their pastor for doctrine and use. Donne certainly
seasoned his discourses to the taste of the critical congregation at
Lincoln's Inn, where he himself had been a student and where he
served as Reader in Divinity from 1616 to 1622, preaching twice
every Sunday in term time. Nor, if we are to believe Walton,
did his audience come away unedified by his sermons, whether at
St. Paul's Cathedral or at Court, for he preached the Word so,

> as shewed his own heart was possest with those very
> thoughts and joys that he laboured to distill into others :
> A Preacher in earnest ; weeping sometimes for his Auditory,
> sometimes with them : always preaching to himself, like an
> Angel from a cloud, but in none ; carrying some, as St *Paul*
> was, to Heaven in holy raptures, and inticing others by a
> sacred Art and Courtship to amend their lives : here pictur-
> ing a vice so as to make it ugly to those that practised it ;
> and a virtue so, as to make it be beloved even by those that
> lov'd it not ; and all this with a most particular grace and
> an unexpressible addition of comeliness [2].

That there were 'beetles' who could not see, and much less understand, 'that good he preached', we may readily grant. We may
also surmise that his references to the Church Fathers, as well as
his use of scientific or pseudo-scientific imagery, were not relished
by stricter members of his congregation, with whom he can hardly

---

[1] 'In Memory of Doctor *Donne* : By Mr R.B. ', ll. 39-44, in *The Poems
of John Donne*, ed. H.J.C. Grierson, Oxford, 1951, I, 386-7.
[2] Izaak WALTON : *The Lives of John Donne, Sir Henry Wotton, Richard
Hooker, George Herbert, and Robert Sanderson*, ed. G. Saintsbury, London,
1927, p. 49.

have been in favour after he preached, by command of the King,
a sermon justifying the *Instructions to Preachers* which James had
just issued to restrain Puritan preachers (1622). Still, in the literature dealing with the reform of pulpit oratory Donne never figures
as the arch-corrupter. Indeed, his name does not even appear
in the list of eminent English divines which John Wilkins gives in
Ecclesiastes (1646). Since in this part of his book (Part 2, Matter)
Wilkins is dealing with reference books, dictionaries, concordances,
commentaries on Scripture, books of controversy, etc., irrespective
of the particular denomination of the individual authors, or of their
way of handling their subject [1], there is no reason to assume that
he left out Donne on purpose. This surprising omission, by a
man who was familiar with Donne's works of controversy, makes
one wonder if the sermons of the Dean of St. Paul's—the last of
these, *Deaths Duell*, had impressed his audience so deeply that
it was published the year after his death with an elaborate title
recalling its impact upon his hearers [2]—were already falling into
oblivion. In any case, few preachers if any could have imitated
Donne, or even learned from him, while Andrewes's style could
have been easily taken as a model, even by preachers who did
not command comparable powers of exegetical analysis. It is
characteristic that Abraham Wright did not try his hand at a
sermon in Dr. Donne's way in his *Five Sermons in Five Several
Styles* (1656)[3], in which he gave imitations of different ways of
preaching. His imitation of Andrewes is close enough to make
one wonder if it *is* an imitation, though it may be significant that
he hardly uses agnominations since, as Evelyn's note shows,
Andrewes seems to have been remembered especially for 'crumbling his text'[4].

[1] Among English divines, he mentions Andrewes, Hall, and Taylor, whose
style of preaching he would hardly have recommended.
[2] *Deaths Duell, or, A Consolation To the Soule, Against the Dying Life,
and the Living Death of the Body... Being his last Sermon, and called by his
Majesties household The Doctors Owne Funerall Sermon*, London, 1632.
[3] The five ways of preaching he imitates are : Bishop Andrewes's, Bishop
Hall's, Dr. Mayne's and Mr. Cartwright's, The Presbyterian Way, and the
Independent Way. It appears from the preface, To the Christian Reader, that
the author's purpose was " to shew the difference betwixt Universitie and Citie-
breeding up of Preachers ; and to let the people know, that any one that hath
been bred a scholar is able to preach any way to the capacities and content
of any Auditorie " (sig. A² verso-A³). Given the date, the book must have
been prompted by the controversy about a learned ministry.
[4] South's ridicule of the jingle on *egress, ingress* and *regress* in his sermon
The Scribe Instructed clearly refers to Andrewes's practice.

The 'pedantry' of James I and his Court may indeed have fostered a 'vicious taste' in oratory. James, we know, prided himself on his knowledge of divinity no less than on his skill in poetry, and indeed was so much concerned with points of doctrine that he sent a delegation of English divines to the Synod of Dordt to defend the Calvinists against the claims of the Remonstrants. He certainly took delight in the "steady march of logic and passion "[1] with which Lancelot Andrewes edified the Court ; he may have prompted Donne's final decision to enter the priesthood by refusing to prefer him any other way[2] ; and he made William Laud Bishop of London. That James was generally regarded as the Solomon of his day appears not only from various comparisons[3], but from the title of the sermon preached at his funeral by John Williams, Bishop of Lincoln : *Great Britains Salomon*[4]. That he was himself witty we know from contemporary testimony[5], and he seems to have had a taste for witty conceits ; thus in a speech to Parliament advocating the Union of England and Scotland, he is reported to have said :

> I am the husband and the whole isle is my wife. I hope, therefore, that no man will be so unreasonable as to think that I, a Christian King, under the Gospel, should be the Polygamist and husband of two wives[6].

Before, however, we tax James with corrupting taste we should

[1] F.P. WILSON, *op. cit.*, p. 99.

[2] Whatever interpretation may be put on Donne's motives for taking holy orders, James's reply to Somerset's petition, as reported by Walton, shows him to have had a keen insight into the abilities of a man who had already signalled himself by his controversial treatises : " I know Mr. *Donne* is a learned man, has the abilities of a learned Divine ; and will prove a powerful Preacher, and my desire is to prefer him that way, and in that way, I will deny you nothing for him ", quoted in W.R. MUELLER : *John Donne Preacher*, London, 1962, pp. 24-25.

[3] For instance in the sermon preached by Laud on 19 June, 1621 : " And surely we have a *Jerusalem*, a State, and a Church to pray for, as well as they ; And this day was our *Salomon*, the very Peace of our *Jerusalem* borne." *Op. cit.*, p. 23.

[4] *Great Britains Salomon. A Sermon Preached at the Magnificent Funerall of the most high and mighty King, James..., by the Right Honorable, and Right Reverend Father in God, John, Lord Bishop of Lincolne...*, London, 1625.

[5] Thus Anthony Weldon, clerk of the kitchen to James I, in *The Court and Character of King James*, London, 1650 : " He was very witty, and had as many ready witty jests as any man living, at which he would not smile himselfe, but deliver them in a grave and serious manner." Reprinted in David Nichol SMITH : *Characters from the Histories and Memoirs of the Seventeenth Century*, Oxford, 1950, p. 6.

[6] Quoted in G.M. TREVELYAN : *England Under the Stuarts*, London, 1933[16], p. 107.

remember that metaphysical preaching had enjoyed considerable favour before his time. Thomas Playfere, who was Lady Margaret Professor of Divinity at Cambridge from 1596 to 1609, freely indulged in wordplay, in strange and often ludicrous similes, in balanced antitheses and antimetaboles [1], as much as in crumbling his text. Thus in a sermon delivered at Paul's Cross in 1593, and later dedicated to James I, he at one point compares the world's delights to the sirens against which Ulysses stopped his ears, and then says:

> Yea, we must binde our selves to the mast of the shippe, that is, to the Crosse of Christ, every one of us saying with our heavenly Ulysses, God forbid that I should delight in any thing, but in the Crosse of Christ, by which the world is crucified unto me, and I unto the world. For the world and all worldly delight is likened to a hedgehogge. A Hedgehog seemes to bee but a poore silly creature, not likely to doe any great harme, yet indeed it is full of bristles and prickles, whereby it may annoy a man very shrewdly. So worldly delight seemeth to bee little or nothing dangerous at the first, yet afterward as with bristles or pricks, it peaceth [= pierceth] through the very conscience with untollerable paines. Therefore wee must deale with this delight, as a man would handle a hedge hogge. The safest way to handle a hedge hogge is to take him by the heele [2].

Professor Williamson has reminded us that Thomas Nashe admired Playfere and could on occasion compliment him in kind [3], and that Lyly commended Lancelot Andrewes to Nashe even before he

---

[1] On Playfere's reputation for antimetaboles see WILLIAMSON, *op. cit.*, pp. 94-95. For examples, see next note.

[2] *Hearts Delight. A Sermon Preached at Paules Crosse in London in Easter Terme, 1593*, London, 1617, pp. 4-5. See also his comparison of the desires of the godly with the curtains of the tabernacle, because they are "coupled and tyed together, so that one desire draweth another, and all their desires draw together" (p. 25). Here are two examples of his use of antimetabole: "He that loves to desire God, (sayes Bernard) must also desire to love God" (p. 24); "But this he doth, as Augustine testifieth, Not by the love of error, but by the error of love" (p. 19); both show that there was precedent for this in patristic literature since Playfere is merely translating St Bernard's "qui amat desiderare, desiderat amare" and St Augustine's "Non erroris amore, sed amoris errore", which he quotes in the margin. There is little doubt that the Anglo-Catholic Divines' use of schemes was encouraged by their familiarity with the Fathers of the Church.

[3] *Op. cit.*, p. 95. Williamson quotes from Nashe's *Strange Newes* (1592): "Few such men speak out of Fames highest Pulpits, though out of her highest Pulpits speake the purest of all speakers."

became a well-known Court-preacher [1]. It would seem, then, that the taste for witty or metaphysical sermons developed at the same time, and from the same causes, as did the taste for metaphysical poetry.

Nor was this peculiar to England, and the blame attached to James I and his Court for encouraging this 'vicious taste' must be further tempered when we consider, for instance, the vogue of the *conception théologique* in France, which is best remembered from Boileau's censure of it in the *Art Poétique* [2]. As late as 1714 Fénelon was still denouncing the false taste for " jeux de mots affectés " in pulpit oratory [3], though Boileau considered it as extinct by 1674. In 1688 La Bruyère again inveighed against the florid or witty oratory which in some quarters was mistaken for wit :

> C'est avoir de l'esprit que de plaire au peuple dans un sermon par un style fleuri, une morale enjouée, des figures réitérées, des traits brillans et de vives descriptions ; mais ce n'est point en avoir assez. Un meilleur esprit néglige ces ornemens étrangers indignes de servir à l'Evangile ; il prêche simplement, fortement, chrétiennement [4].

He recognized that some of the worst ornaments had gone out of fashion at Court, but that this false taste still prevailed in town :

> Les citations profanes, les froides allusions, le mauvais pathétique, les antithèses, les figures outrées, ont fini : les portraits finiront, et feront place à une simple explication de l'Evangile, jointe aux mouvements qui inspirent la conversion.
>
> Cet homme que je souhaitais impatiemment, et que je ne daignais pas espérer de notre siècle, est enfin venu. Les courtisans, à force de goût et de connaître les bienséances, lui ont applaudi : ils ont, chose incroyable ! abandonné la chapelle du roi pour venir entendre avec le peuple la parole de Dieu annoncée par cet homme apostolique. La ville n'a

---

[1] *Ibid.*, p. 231. On the difference between Playfere and Andrewes, see J.W. BLENCH : *Preaching in England in the late Fifteenth and Sixteenth Centuries*, Oxford, 1964, pp. 64-70, 107-8.

[2] II, 121-2.

[3] *Lettre à M. Dacier sur les occupations de l'Académie* (1714), in FÉNELON : *De l'Existence et des Attributs de Dieu*, Paris, 1864, p. 485. Some thirty years before Fénelon had developed similar views in his *Dialogues sur l'éloquence* (written between 1681 and 1686). Since from 1697 he was virtually an exile from the polite world his *Lettre à M. Dacier* may reflect an outdated mode.

[4] De la chaire, in LA BRUYÈRE : *Les Caractères de Théophraste traduits du Grec. Avec les Caractères ou les Mœurs de ce Siècle*, Paris, 1700, II, 245.

pas été de l'avis de la cour. Où il a prêché, les paroissiens
ont déserté [1].

This was written thirty years after Furetière had shown, in his
*Nouvelle Allégorique, ou Histoire des derniers troubles arrivés au
Royaume d'Eloquence* (1658), how Queen Rhetoric, aided by her
prime minister Good Sense, succeeded in vanquishing her many
foes, such as false similes, conceits, puns and the like. But the
battle had to be fought again and again before the enemy was
finally driven from the field. Long before La Bruyère, too, Saint
Cyran, Le Maître de Sacy and others of Port-Royal had inveighed
against the gaudy conceits and vain trimmings which defaced the
Word of God. Bossuet, too, had emphasized that truth alone is
to be preached, and that the pomp of false ornaments only serves
to flatter the ear :

> Car les oreilles sont flattées par la cadence et l'arrangement
> des paroles ; l'imagination, réjouie par la délicatesse des
> pensées ; l'esprit, persuadé quelquefois par la vraisemblance
> du raisonnement : la conscience veut la vérité ; et comme
> c'est à la conscience que parlent les prédicateurs, ils doivent
> rechercher, mes sœurs, non des brillans qui égayent, ni une
> harmonie qui délecte, ni des mouvements qui chatouillent,
> mais des éclairs qui percent, un tonnerre qui émeuve, un
> foudre qui brise les cœurs [2].

The year after he preached this sermon Bossuet had occasion, in
his funeral oration for Father Bourgoing, Superior General of the
Oratory, to praise a true minister of God who disdained the artifices
of rhetoric and preached truth :

> La parole de l'Evangile sortait de sa bouche, vive, pénétrante,
> animée, toute pleine d'esprit et de feu... D'où lui venait cette
> force ? C'est, mes Frères, qu'il était plein de la doctrine
> céleste, c'est qu'il s'était nourri et rassasié du meilleur suc
> du Christianisme, c'est qu'il faisait régner dans ses sermons
> la vérité et la sagesse : l'éloquence suivait comme la servante,
> non recherchée avec soin, mais attirée par les choses mêmes.
> Ainsi « son discours se répandait à la manière d'un torrent ;
> et s'il trouvait en son chemin les fleurs de l'élocution, il les
> entraînait plutôt par sa propre impétuosité qu'il ne les
> cueillait pour se parer d'un tel ornement » : *Fertur quippe*

---

[1] *Ibid.*, pp. 241-2.
[2] Sermon sur la parole de Dieu (1661), in BOSSUET : *Œuvres Oratoires*,
ed. J. Lebarcq, Lille-Paris, 1891, III, 575.

impetu suo ; et elocutionis pulchritudinem, si occurrerit, vi
rerum rapit, non cura decoris assumit [1].

The discourse as a whole may be usefully compared with Burnet's
oration on the death of Archbishop Tillotson thirty years later,
since both praise the true pastor and develop similar points : the
need of preparation for the ministry, the nature of true Christian
eloquence, the value of prayer, the care for souls. Yet the differences too are striking : whereas Burnet enlarges on the works
of charity of Tillotson, Bossuet draws a veil over one of the main
tasks of his pastor, " la conduite des âmes ", and is content to
honour " par notre silence le mystérieux secret que Dieu a imposé
à ses ministres " [2] ; whereas Burnet's praise of Tillotson's style of
preaching is mainly negative, Bossuet stresses the *force, feu, lumière
ardente* of Bourgoing's sermons, and of course the two orations
themselves differ in style if not much in method. In fact, though
both preachers agree on what corrupts sacred eloquence, their
standards are altogether different : plain, solid, edifying sermons
for the one ; for the other " la parole de l'Evangile... vive, péné-
trante, animée, toute pleine d'esprit et de feu " [3]. True, the divine
whom Burnet was praising may be called a " practical preacher " [4],
while Father Bourgoing, a disciple of Berulle, is one of the
representative members of what has come to be known as " l'école
française de spiritualité " ; but the difference is also to be linked
with the diverging trends in pulpit oratory in England and in
France in the latter half of the century, and with the circumstances
from which these arose.

In England a change in the taste in pulpit oratory already
appears from the later sermons of Bishop Hall, which testify to
the gradual decline of the curt style. They are, indeed, " less terse,

[1] Oraison funèbre du Père Bourgoing (4 Dec., 1662), in BOSSUET : *Oraisons
Funèbres*, ed. Jacques Truchet, Paris, 1961, pp. 50-51.
[2] *Ibid.*, p. 52. Bossuet could hardly have enlarged on this point since he
had just reminded his hearers that Father Bourgoing had long been " confesseur
de feu Monseigneur le Duc d'Orléans, de glorieuse mémoire ", though as his
editor reminds us, " la mémoire de Gaston d'Orléans n'était pas fort glorieuse "
(n. 4, p. 51).
[3] George Herbert comes nearer to Bossuet's pattern when he advises country
parsons to move their hearers " by dipping, and seasoning all our words and
sentences in our hearts, before they come into our mouths, truly affecting, and
cordially expressing all that we say ; so that the auditors may plainly perceive
that every word is hart-deep ", *op. cit.*, p. 233.
[4] For attacks on Latitudinarians, particularly on Tillotson, as practical
preachers, see below.

less spasmodic, more continuous in style than his early sermons " [1] ;
they were praised by Sir Henry Wotton for the " pureness, plainness, and fulness " of their style [2], and by Hall's successor to the
see of Norwich, Edward Reynolds, for being " like the land of
Canaan, flowing with milk and honey " [3]. True, Reynolds argued
that wit " sanctified by grace, and fixed by humility " could be
of great use to the Church of God, and some of the examples he
gives, from the Fathers of the Church, show that he did not condemn " curious elegancies and paranomasias " ; but from his own
style it is clear that he did not favour the kind of witty preaching
that flourished in the third and fourth decades of the century.
In the sermons of Anglican divines, then, a more relaxed style
seems to have superseded the brief, jerky style which Andrewes's
method inevitably entailed [4], and Wotton's phrase 'fulness of style'
aptly characterizes the easier flow of the sentences in Hall's later
sermons.

With this went some of the schemes and figures of sound which
were part and parcel of Andrewes's exegesis, but not all ornaments
of style were discarded. In some preachers, notably Jeremy Taylor,
the easy and harmonious prose is enriched by the sensuous beauty
of the imagery. Taylor is indeed the great mellifluous preacher,
and for those who, like Coleridge, value sweetness and delicacy,
he is a source of endless delight. When discussing him, few
critics have forborne to refer to his magic, his haunting verbal
music ; indeed, as Logan Pearsall Smith said, one " is led captive
by a charm and spell which (one) cannot analyse " [5]. His rich
and often vivid imagery is sometimes marred by a certain quaint-
ness, which South ridiculed in a 1668 sermon. The felicity of his
diction is partly due to his use of unexpected or archaic words, or
of words in their Latin sense (though he advised his clergy to keep
to the common speech of the day). With Taylor ornate prose

---

[1] G. WILLIAMSON, op. cit., p. 247.

[2] Thomas FULLER : The Worthies of England, ed. John Freeman, London,
1952, p. 320.

[3] Edward REYNOLDS : The Pastoral Office, opened in a visitation sermon,
preached at Norwich, Oct. 10, 1662, in The Whole Works of the Right Rev.
Edward Reynolds, D.D., Lord Bishop of Norwich. Now first collected, ed. by
Alexander Chalmers, London, 1826, V, 403.

[4] Williamson quotes a Restoration parody of a sermon by Andrewes in
which his practice of division is ridiculed in the very title : 'The Ex-ale-tation
of Ale', op. cit., p. 249.

[5] The Golden Grove. Selected Passages from the Sermons and Writings
of Jeremy Taylor, ed. L. Pearsall Smith, Oxford, 1955, Introduction, p. xxx.

comes closest to poetry, instinct with emotion and sensuous rich-
ness, but many of the vices later condemned by the reformers of
pulpit oratory may be exemplified from his sermons. Such deco-
rativeness, no less than metaphysical wit, was soon to be out of
fashion.

How far these earlier models may have affected preachers after
the Restoration is hard to assess, but it is clear that they were
not entirely forgotten. For even those Anglicans who, at the
time of Laud's power, had resented his ceremonial innovations,
the excessive power of the bishops, and particularly the Court of
High Commission, were alarmed when the Anglican system as a
whole came under attack, and they looked back wistfully to the
days when the Church had been flourishing. The execution of
Laud and of Charles I inevitably confirmed their allegiance to the
old order and increased their admiration for the great Anglo-
Catholic divines of James's and Charles's time. After Cromwell
took power the Anglican clergy were mostly undisturbed, and many
of them conducted Prayer Book services if not openly at least
without being molested. A notable example is that of John Owen,
the Independent who became Dean of Christ Church and Vice-
Chancellor of Oxford University in 1650 and who

> suffered to meet quietly about three hundred Evangelicals
> every Lord's Day over against his own door, where they
> celebrated divine service according to the worship of the
> Church of England. And though he was often urged to it,
> yet he would never give them the least disturbance [1].

Besides, Anglicans " availed themselves of parishioners' power to
elect lecturers " [2], which the Puritans had early used to ensure the
'right' teaching of the Gospel, and which Parliament had confirmed by ordinance in 1641. Thus, besides those who, like Taylor
at Golden Grove, acted as private chaplains and taught little
congregations of loyalists, some Anglican divines went on preaching
during the Interregnum, particularly between 1650, when the laws
against them were relaxed, and 1656 when sterner measures were
taken against the sequestred clergy [3]. It is probable that the earlier

---

[1] From a contemporary account, quoted in V.H.H. GREEN : *Religion at
Oxford and Cambridge*, London, 1964, p. 147.
[2] Robert S. BOSHER : *The Making of the Restoration Settlement, 1642-1662*,
London, 1951, p. 12.
[3] *Ibid.*, p. 41.

mode of preaching was continued in some of these sermons [1].
When the Church was restored in 1660 the High-Church clergy
were active in shaping the religious policy which led to the Act
of Uniformity, and these churchmen of the old school may well
have revived the fashion for witty eloquence as well as for intolerance. Prominent among these was Thomas Pierce, as relentless
a defender of the old order as Peter Heylyn, and as 'witty' a
preacher as Andrewes. That the fashion lasted well into the
Restoration period may be gathered from the many references to
witty preaching by all the reformers of pulpit oratory, as well as
from Dryden's remark, in *The Dramatic Poetry of the Last Age*
(1672), that playing with words first ascended into the pulpit in
Sidney's time [2], " where (if you will give me leave to clench too)
it yet finds the benefit of its clergy ".

However important such men as Pierce may have been in
continuing or reviving the old style of preaching, we should not
forget that among the 'disaffected conformists' were men like
Jasper Mayne and Simon Patrick, and among the 'loyal conformists' men like Fuller and Edward Reynolds, both of whom
were to become bishops after the Restoration [3]. One of the legends
accredited by the High-Churchmen after the Restoration was that
their party had been oppressed and persecuted during the Interregnum, but this is flatly contradicted by many testimonies [4]. The

---

[1] Mitchell refers to Bishop Cosin's sermons, which " may be taken as a
proof that the Anglo-Catholic type of sermon was actually continued in some
quarters, more or less as a party badge ", *op. cit.*, p. 308.

[2] For Lyly's and Nashe's admiration for Playfere's wit, see above.

[3] The distinction is Bosher's. He quotes a passage from one of Fuller's
sermons justifying his submission to the new order, which aptly characterizes
the position of the moderate divines : " Not to dissemble in the sight of God
and man, I do ingeniously protest that I affect the Episcopal government... best
of any other... But I know that religion and learning hath flourished under
the Presbyterian government in France, Germany, The Low Countries... I know
the most learned and moderate English divines... have allowed the Reformed
Churches under Presbyterian discipline for sound and perfect in all essentials
necessary to salvation. If, therefore, denied my first desire, to live under that
Church government I best affected, I will contentedly conform to the Presbyterian
Government, and endeavour to deport myself quietly and comfortably under the
same. " *Op. cit.*, pp. 27-28.

[4] R.S. Bosher, who has done most to show how the Restoration settlement
was prepared by the Laudian clergy in exile and at home, warns us too :
" It would be misleading, however, to suggest that the history of the Church
of England during the Interregnum can be written exclusively in terms of this
minority party. The now well established tradition of depicting Anglicanism
as a persecuted underground movement began soon after the Restoration when
Laudian writers preferred to ignore the inconvenient truth that Anglican conformity to the Cromwellian Church was widespread. " *Op. cit.*, p. 24, n. 1.

survival of the vicious taste in pulpit oratory cannot, therefore, be wholly ascribed to the triumph of the Laudian clergy in 1662, any more than can the continued taste for metaphysical wit in some quarters long after it had been banished from the conversation of gentlemen [1].   Similarly, Thomas Birch's view about the corrupting influence of Anglo-Catholic divines may be regarded as an expression of eighteenth-century partiality for the Low Church, to which Coleridge referred in his notes on Stillingfleet [2].

It is tempting to ascribe the reform of pulpit oratory to the Puritans since their first avowed aim, from the days of Elizabeth, had been to provide a worthy preaching ministry for the people. The Marprelate tracts abound in accusations of sloth and ignorance against the clergy, which recall the attacks of Wycliff and of the early reformers and look forward to Milton's denunciation of the blind mouths. It is true, also, that " the greatest of all the Puritan writers, John Bunyan, habitually spoke to the capacity of his hearers in a prose as bare of ornaments as a dissenters' meeting-house, but with a single-minded conviction and a passionate earnestness that made his words shine with an almost unearthly light " [3]. Yet the crusade for a plain method and style of preaching in the later seventeenth-century was the work of Anglicans and mostly directed against the excesses of Puritan preaching. Nor should it be forgotten that one of the great admirers of Church ritual, George Herbert, could envisage an unlearned country audience and advised his parson to speak the kind of language they would understand :

> Sometimes he tells them stories, and sayings of others, according as his text invites him ; for them also men heed, and remember better then exhortations ; which though earnest, yet often dy with the sermon, especially with Country people ; which are thick, and heavy, and hard to raise to a poynt of Zeal, and fervency, and need a mountaine of fire to kindle them : but stories and sayings they will remember [4].

[1] See Dryden's reference to Clevelandism in the *Essay of Dramatic Poesy* (1668).

[2] S.T. COLERIDGE : *Notes on Stillingfleet*, ed. R. Garnett, Glasgow, 1875, p. 7. Coleridge finds St. superior to Chillingworth and attributes the high regard in which the latter is held to " the prevalency of the Low-Church Lockian Faction ".

[3] J.R. SUTHERLAND : *On English Prose*, Toronto-London, 1957, p. 63.

[4] *Op. cit.*, p. 233.

Baxter would have agreed with Herbert that the country parson
" is not witty, or learned, or eloquent, but Holy " [1], and would
have approved his method :

> The Parsons Method in handling a text consists of two
> parts ; first, a plain and evident declaration of the meaning
> of the text ; and secondly some choyce Observations drawn
> out of the whole text, as it lyes entire, and unbroken in the
> Scripture it self.   This he thinks naturall, and sweet, and
> grave [2].

Yet, when set beside Herbert's poem ' The Windows ', the following sentences of Baxter reveal the difference between the two men :

> Truth loves the Light, and is most Beautiful when most
> naked.   It is a Sign of an envious Enemy to hide the Truth ;
> and a Sign of an Hypocrite to do this under pretence of
> Revealing it :   And Therefore painted obscure Sermons (like
> the Painted Glass in the Windows that keep out the Light)
> are too oft the Marks of painted Hypocrites [3].

Behind such condemnation of eloquence there lurks " the same
horror of luxury that drove the Puritans to repudiate and destroy
rites and ceremonies, ecclesiastical vestments and painted windows " [4].   A comparison by another Anglican divine, Thomas Fuller,
will point up the difference :

> Reasons are the pillars of the fabrick of a Sermon ; but
> similitudes are the windows which give the best light [5].

Besides, not all Puritans preached in a plain style at the
beginning of the century.   The term ' Puritan ' is perhaps too loose
to be applied usefully to the Nonconformist Baxter on the one hand
and on the other to the Elizabethan Henry Smith and the Jacobean
Thomas Adams.   This last, however, was a strict Calvinist who
did not disdain the aids of rhetoric when preaching the Word of
God ;   his schemata, not unlike Andrewes's, recall the character-
writers, whom he often imitates in his sermons.   The following

---

[1] *Ibid.*   [2] *Ibid.*, pp. 234-5.
[3] Richard BAXTER : *Gildas Salvianus, The Reform'd Pastor*, (1656), in *The
Practical Works of the Late Rev^d and Pious, Mr. Richard Baxter*, London,
1707, IV, 358.
[4] J.R. SUTHERLAND, *op. cit.*, p. 62.
[5] *The Holy State* (1642), p. 84, quoted by Logan Pearsall SMITH, *op. cit.*,
p. xxxv.

example, from one of his sermons, is a moral exemplum " in the witty vein of Overbury " :

> His words are precise, his deeds concise ; he prays so long in the church, that he may with less suspicion prey on the church [1].

As to ' silver-tongued Smith ', the darling of the people, in spite of his strong Puritan sympathies he studded his sermons not only with homely proverbs but with vivid similes, which would bring home to his hearers the lesson he was teaching ; for instance :

> Our Fathers marvelling to see how suddenly men are, and are not, compared life to a dream in the night, to a bubble in the water, to a ship on the sea, to an arrow which never resteth till it fall, to a player, which speaketh his part upon the stage and straight he giveth place to another ; to a man which cometh to the market to buy one thing and sell another, and then is gone home again : so the figure of this World passeth away [2].

On the other hand, William Perkins, whose *Art of Prophesying* exerted a deep influence on the Puritans, recommended that ' a speech ' be " both simple and perspicuous, fit both for the people's understanding and to express the majesty of the spirit ", for it must be " spiritual and gracious " [3] ; it will be gracious if it expresses the grace of the heart, and it will be fit for the people's understanding if

> neither the words of art, nor Greek and Latin phrases and quirkes be intermingled in the sermon.
> 1 They disturb the mind of the auditors...
> 2 A strange word hindreth the understanding of those things that are spoken.   3 It draws the mind away from the purpose to some other matter [4].

Perkins does not censure similes and metaphors, but his condemnation of them may be inferred from his definition of style as

---

[1] *Sermons*, ed. John Brown, 1909, p. 227. Quoted by WILLIAMSON, *op. cit.*, p. 242.

[2] Henry SMITH : *The Godly Man's Request*, in *Sermons*, 1611, p. 276. Quoted by V.H.H. GREEN, *op. cit.*, p. 112.

[3] *The Art of Prophesying, or a Treatise concerning the sacred and true manner and method of preaching*. First written in Latin by Mr. William Perkins (1592) and now faithfully translated into English by Thomas Tuke, in William PERKINS : *Works*, London, 1631, II, 670.

[4] *Ibid.*, pp. 670-1.

well as from his repudiation of human skill. Yet he gives cautions
concerning sacred tropes in order to help preachers discover the
meaning of ' cryptical or hidden places ' in Scripture, that is, when
" the native (or natural) signification of the words do manifestly
disagree with either the analogy of faith, or very perspicuous places
in Scripture " [1], thereby acknowledging that the Word of God is
sometimes figurative. In view of later developments in Puritan
preaching, and of Restoration attacks against it, it is worth noting
that Perkins reaffirms what Tyndale among others had stressed,
that " There is onely one sense, and the same is literal " [2]. He
also emphasizes that human wisdom must be concealed both in the
matter and in the ' uttering ' of the sermon,

> because the preaching of the word is the Testimonie of God,
> and the profession of the knowledge of Christ, and not of
> humane skill. If any man think that by this means barbarism
> should be brought into pulpits ; he must understand that
> the minister may, yea and must, privately use all the libertie
> of the Arts, Philosophy, and vanity of reading, whilst he
> is in framing his sermon : but he ought in public to conceal
> all these from the people, and not to make the least
> ostentation. *Artis etiam est celare artem* [3].

Since Perkins shows that he had profited from the vanity of reading
Pagan authors, an uncharitable reader, like South, might be induced
to reverse Baxter's sentence and say : " It is a sign of an envious
enemy to hide the truth ; and a sign of a hypocrite to conceal his
learning under pretence of revealing the Spirit ". In any case,
unlike some mid-century Puritans, Perkins did not deny the use
of learning for a minister. Whether the method he recommends
would promote a plain way of preaching, i.e. one that is not only
simple and perspicuous in language but that eschews obscure notions
and needless controversies and presents clearly the essential points
of doctrine and of right practice, would depend on how preachers
interpreted Perkins's " right dividing of the word " (Chapter VI).
About this he says little more than that it comprises " resolution,
or partition, and application ", the former consisting in " resolving
the place propounded into sundry doctrines " by notation or by
collection. This left plenty of scope for interpretation.

---

[1] *Ibid.*, p. 654. As one might expect the example he gives is : " This is
my body which is broken for you. "
[2] *Ibid.*, p. 651.   [3] *Ibid.*, p. 670.

The impression one forms after reading the tracts of the reformers of pulpit oratory after the Restoration is that the influence
of earlier models was not so strong in corrupting the way of
preaching as the training prospective divines received at the
Universities and the method they were taught, particularly the
undue emphasis on the rhetoric of ornaments. In this respect the
Artes Concionandi and the various aids to elocution recommended
to students probably had more far-reaching effects than the printed
sermons of any masters of pulpit oratory. From John Eachard's
*Grounds and Occasions of the Contempt of the Clergy and Religion
Enquired into* (1670) we gather that schools and Universities were
to blame for the ignorance of the clergy, to which Eachard ascribes
their false way of preaching. The main faults are on the one hand
their " inconsiderate use of frightful metaphors " and " packing
their sermons full of similitudes ", and on the other " their common
method of preaching ", whether making the text " like something
or other ", dividing it so as to " make all fly into shivers ", deriving
strange observations from the text, choosing obscure texts or making
senseless use of concordances. Now, according to Eachard, these
derive from two chief heads : excessive use of storehouses of similes
and over-ingenuity instead of logic. He expatiates on the choiceness
of the authors out of which the clergy are furnished, particularly
on the treasuries of similitudes " ready fitted to most preaching
subjects, for the help of young beginners, who sometimes will not
make them hit handsomely " [1]. He does not trace their false
method to any particular cause, but the source of this may be
sought in some of the *Artes Concionandi* from which students
learnt the art of oratory.

From Wilkins's attempt in his manual *Ecclesiastes* (1646) to
teach a better way of preaching by outlining a clear method and
by defining the appropriate style for sermons [2], as well as from
Eachard's censure of the outstanding faults of the ignorant clergy,
it appears that the tradition of classical oratory favoured by the
humanists had been broken by undue emphasis on *some* aspects
of rhetoric. Neither of the more influential manuals on the art

---

[1] John EACHARD : *The Grounds and Occasions of the Contempt of the
Clergy and Religion Enquired into.* In a letter written to R.L. London, 1670,
in *An English Garner : Critical Essays and Literary Fragments*, ed. J. Churton
Collins, Westminster, 1903, p. 270.
[2] The manual went through at least 7 editions before the end of the century.

of preaching—Keckermann's *Rhetoreticae Ecclesiasticae* (Hanover, 1606) and the Puritan William Perkins's *Art of Prophesying* (published in Latin in 1592, translated into English in 1631)— encouraged ' crumbling the text ' or packing sermons with similitudes, but such later works as William Chappel's *The Preacher, or the Art and Method of Preaching* (1656) may have led to multiple division of the text.   On the other hand, the rhetorics of ornaments [1], i.e. those dealing exclusively with schemes and tropes, which began to multiply towards the end of the sixteenth century as Ramist logic and Talean rhetoric gained ground in England [2], certainly furnished ample storehouses of similes, which could be used, and no doubt were used, by some preachers without due regard to propriety.   They certainly put a premium on images and figures of all kinds, while Ramist logic emphasized that images are ' arguments ' [3].   Since Cambridge had early become a Ramist centre, the teaching of Ramist logic and Talean rhetoric must have influenced the training of young preachers, and one can easily guess what were the effects of such training on the verbal exegesis practised by young divines, or on the method of their sermons.

Moreover, the tendency to use ornaments in sermons was certainly encouraged by collections of images and figures gathered from the Bible.   Such a one is *Sacred Eloquence, or the Art of Rhetoric as it is laid down in Scripture* (1659), by the Oxford Puritan John Prideaux, who became Bishop of Worcester in 1641. The title tells its own tale : not only is the use of ornaments vindicated from the precedent of Scripture, but rhetoric is equated with ornament.   Though the author warns his readers that

> Divers aim to show how much they can say on a text with
> no regard at all how little their auditors can bear away ;
> as though they came into a Pulpit to open their store, not
> to feed their flocks ; and to beg applause of their con-

---

[1] For instance : Abraham Fraunce's *The Arcadian Rhetorike* (1588) and John Hoskins's *Directions for Speech and Style* (1599).

[2] By distinguishing the fields proper to dialectic (invention and disposition) and to rhetoric (elocution) Ramistic handbooks broke with the tradition of the old arts of rhetoric, which had included the methods for inventing and disposing the matter (see, for instance, Thomas Wilson's *Arte of Rhetorique*, 1560). Abraham Fraunce himself wrote a book of Ramist logic, *The Lawiers Logike* (1588).

[3] For the influence of Ramist logic and rhetoric on the development of metaphysical poetry, see Rosemond Tuve : *Elizabethan and Metaphysical Imagery*, Chicago, 1947 (Part II, Chapter XII).

gregations, that they are ready preachers, not to so lead
them that they may be profitable hearers [1],

his book must have been used by many as a ' magazine of phrases '.
Its main purpose, however, seems to have been to vindicate eloquence against the advocates of the bare style.

John Eachard, a Fellow of St. Catharine's College, Cambridge,
from 1658, must have been aware of the influence of such teaching
in his own University.   Moreover, he animadverted in his tract
on the harm done to future preachers by the disputations and other
academic exercises, because these fostered a spirit of contentiousness and levity, prejudiced students against sober sense, and disposed them to trifling and jingling.   This, one feels, must have
gone further to unfit them for the edification of their parishioners
than any model from former times, and this was precisely one of
the grounds of contempt for university training among the extreme
Puritans who were in favour of a godly rather than a learned
ministry.   In Eachard's view the two main evils of university
training lay in the absence of English exercises—whereas the
students were encouraged to produce ' dainty stuff ' for a Latin
entertainment out of their magazines of collected phrases—and
the practice of academic exercises.   To the latter, Eachard intimates,
can be traced all the evils which degrade pulpit oratory, and which
all the reformers condemned, whether squeezing or crumbling of
texts, improper observations from Scripture, fantastic phrases, Latin
or Greek tags, jingles, etc.   The whole passage, though long, may
be quoted if only because the tone no less than the content must
have incensed the sober bands who, misunderstanding Eachard's
purpose, felt it necessary to rebuke him for his attack on the
clergy :

> The second Inquiry that may be made is this : *Whether
> or not Punning, Quibbling, and that which they call Joquing*
> (joking), *and such delicacies of Wit*, highly admired in
> some Academic Exercises, *might not be very conveniently
> omitted ?*
> For one may desire but to know this one thing : in what
> Profession shall that sort of Wit prove of advantage ?   As
> for Law, where nothing but the most reaching subtility and
> the closest arguing is allowed of ; it is not to be imagined
> that blending now and then a piece of a dry verse, and

[1] p. 57.

wreathing here and there an odd Latin Saying into a dismal
jingle, should give Title to an estate, or clear out an obscure
evidence ! And as little serviceable can it be to Physic,
which is made up of severe Reason and well tried Experiments !

And as for Divinity, in this place I shall say no more,
but that those usually that have been Rope Dancers in the
Schools, ofttimes prove Jack Puddings in the Pulpit. For
he that in his youth has allowed himself this liberty of
Academic Wit ; by this means he has usually so thinned
his judgement, becomes so prejudiced against sober sense,
and so altogether disposed to trifling and jingling ; that,
so soon as he gets hold of a text, he presently thinks he
has catched one of his old School Questions ; and so falls
a flinging it out of one hand into another ! tossing it this
way, and that ! lets it run a little upon the line, then
" *tanutus* ! high jingo ! come again ! " here catching at a
word ! there lie nibbling and sucking at an *and*, a *by*, a *quis*
or a *quid*, a *sic* or a *sicut* ! and thus minces the Text so
small that his parishioners, until he *rendez-vous* (reassemble)
it again, can scarce tell, what is become of it [1].

Before we—like those who took up the cudgels to vindicate
the clergy—censure Eachard for fouling his own nest, we might
remember that another Cambridge man had criticized university
teaching in equally harsh terms almost thirty years before. In
The Reason of Church Government Urg'd against Prelaty (1641)
Milton had wondered how studious men came to write in defense
of prelacy while the liturgy of the Church of England itself confessed the service of God to be perfect freedom, and he had
found the answer in the false training that young men receive
in Universities : the hackney course of literature to dazzle the
ignorant, the fondness for 'metaphysical gargarisms' rather than
true and generous philosophy, the sophistry, and the fond over-
study of useless controversies [2]. Milton returned to the attack
eighteen years later in his *Considerations touching the likeliest
Means to Remove Hirelings out of the Church* (1659), urging
the vanity of university training as an argument against tithes :

And those theological disputations held there by Professors
and graduates are such as tend least of all to the edification
or capacitie of the people, but rather perplex and leaven

[1] *Op. cit.*, pp. 261-2.   [2] *Op. cit.*, I, 854.

pure doctrine with scholastical trash then enable any minister to the better preaching of the gospel [1].

Milton's view is no doubt biassed but no such charge can be preferred against Eachard, soon to become Master of St. Catharine's College. The irony is that the tendency to perplex the pure doctrine, as well as to argue from similitudes, may have been fostered by Ramist logic and rhetoric, which Milton highly valued [2]. As Miss Tuve remarked : " it is not mere chance that the two poets (Sidney and Milton) most indisputably connected with Ramist thought were Puritan in their sympathies " [3]. When in 1645 Parliamentary Commissioners were appointed to ensure ' godly and religious preaching ' at Cambridge they would hardly have objected to teaching based on the work of a Protestant martyr (whom Marlowe had celebrated in his *Massacre at Paris*). This is not to say that over-ingenuity, dividing the text and fantastic similes are to be laid at the door of the Puritans, though after the Restoration these vices came to be regarded as characteristic of ' fanatic ' preaching. The point is that while Anglo-Catholic divines of the earlier seventeenth century were later to be blamed for fostering a vicious taste, similar influences were at work in other quarters.

Strict Calvinists [4], in Britain as elsewhere, favoured closely reasoned arguments and emulated the logical coherence of their master, which led them to concentrate on dialectics rather than on rhetoric, to define dogmas and explicate their texts with the stern logic they had learnt from the *Institutes*. Many of them were remarkable for their dialectical skill, for their dry, scholastic method of arguing from a text. In the controversy with the Remonstrants and especially in the discourses at the Synod of Dordt they displayed their disputatious zeal for defining nice points of theology, so much so that, of the English divines who had intended to support their Calvinist brethren, many came back

---

[1] John MILTON : *Works*, New York, 1932, VI, 95.

[2] He wrote *A Fuller Institution of the Art of Logic, Arranged after the Manner of Peter Ramus* (1672).

[3] *Op. cit.*, p. 332. Miss Tuve reminds us that it was Sidney who aroused Abraham Fraunce's interest in Ramus.

[4] The term is as misleading as ' Puritan ' since the Church of England as such was, nominally at least, Calvinistic, that is, if the Thirty-Nine Articles are taken *stricto sensu*, (see Article XVI ' Of Predestination and Election '). " Anglicanism was indeed largely hammered out in the course of the [sixteenth]

sobered by the experience. One of them, John Hales of Eton [1], after attending the debates finally 'bade John Calvin good night '. If the barren controversies of the Lutherans opened a new scholastic period of dogmatic frivolity and led to the *rabies theologorum* which finally silenced the humanist Melanchton, the elaboration of Augustinianism at the hands of Calvin and his disciples issued in a system in which each proposition was argued with stern logical consecutiveness [2]. In sermons chains of syllogisms and explication of propositions nicely 'partitioned' from the text would result in fairly complicated arguments, which only a well-trained mind could follow. It is easy to understand that such arguments might also deteriorate into what Marvell was to call ' syllogistical legerdemain ' and sometimes lead to out-of-the way observations whose relation to the main design was most tenuous [3]. Such sermons, then, were often highly elaborate, though not ornate. William Prynne, " who preached not from the pulpit but from the press " [4], may be an extreme exponent of this heavy-going march of logic, but the syllogistic cast of his tracts is none the less characteristic of much Presbyterian eloquence. When the controversy over the discipline of the Church came to a head in England, Scripture was searched assiduously and texts expounded at great length to support the ' right' discipline. We need only turn to Milton's tracts to see with what zeal and contentiousness arguments from Scripture were

century, in part as a result of the intellectual collision between Puritan and Arminian at the Universities. It was perhaps one of the graver defects of Anglicanism that one of its formularies, the Thirty-Nine Articles, should have been drafted while its doctrinal teaching was still uncertain. It fastened on to the Church of England a set of doctrinal formulations which, intellectually impressive as they were and are, have rarely accorded with its actual teaching, and to which for long Anglican clergy have assented only in a general sense. Yet it is plain that for much of Elizabeth's reign Calvinism was the dominant theology at both Universities. Puritans and non-Puritans relied equally on the school of Geneva, albeit a reaction against Calvinism was beginning to set in by the end of the reign. " V.H.H. GREEN, *op. cit.*, p. 107. One of the most frequent accusations against Laud was that he was an Arminian (which he denied).

[1] Hales was not a member of the delegation, but as Chaplain to the Ambassador, Sir Dudley Carleton, he was an ' observer' at the Debates of the Synod.

[2] See John TULLOCH: *Rational Theology and Christian Philosophy in England in the Seventeenth Century*, Edinburgh, 1874, vol. I, ch. I.

[3] Eachard's censure of the ' cunning observations, doctrines, and inferences' in the common method of preaching probably refers to the practice inherited from some Puritan preachers.

[4] F.P. WILSON, *op. cit.*, p. 94.

marshalled in defence of reformation (or, for that matter, of divorce).

It should be remembered that at this point the other party began to answer in kind, and in their attempt to prove the divine origin of episcopacy Anglicans like Joseph Hall were led to argue in much the same manner as their opponents. In the circumstances one can understand the advice of the soberer divines to leave off all controversies and to confine preaching to the essential points of doctrine and use. True, these soberer minds usually came from the Anglican fold, who at the time had most to gain by the cessation of such controversies. Still, such pleas for toleration as Jeremy Taylor's *Discourse of the Liberty of Prophesying* (1647)[1] or John Hales's *Tract concerning Schism and Schismatics* (1642, but probably written about 1636)[2] are appeals to concord and charity directed against the hardening of differences which, to these men, were not religious differences at all yet were powerful enough to break the unity of common faith and worship. It is worth noting, too, that both defended private judgement and the freedom of rational inquiry[3], on grounds which look forward to the stand taken by the Anglicans after the Restoration. The same plea was made in a sermon preached by Jasper Mayne at Oxford in 1646 on *Rom.* XII. 18 *If it be possible, as much as lyeth in you, live peaceably with all men.* Mayne urged

> that we scholars, in those high mysterious points which have equal argument and proof on both sides, and which both sides (for ought I know) may hold, yet meet in heaven, doe factiously or peremptorily betake ourselves to neither ; but either lay them aside, as things of mere contemplation, not of practise or use ; or else speak of them to the people, only in that general sense wherein all sides agree, and as that general sense is laid down to us in the Scripture[4].

[1] As Logan Pearsall Smith remarks (*op. cit.*, p. xx), "The advantages of religious toleration were no doubt more apparent to Jeremy Taylor when he and his fellow-Anglicans were being persecuted, and when this book was written, than they appeared afterwards, when his own Church had regained power, and he himself, as one of its prelates, felt himself compelled to fall back on the secular arm to silence his opponents."

[2] William Laud was dissatisfied with this tract, which circulated in manuscript, and sent for Hales to try and argue him out of his tolerant position. See TULLOCH, *op. cit.*, ch. IV.

[3] This is even clearer in Hales's sermon *Of Enquiry and Private Judgement in Religion*, see John HALES : *Works*, Glasgow, 1765, vol. III.

[4] *A Sermon Concerning Unity and Agreement*, preached at Carfax Church in Oxford, August 9, 1646, by Jasper MAYNE, [Oxford], 1646, p. 34. Oxford had capitulated to the Parliamentary forces on 24 June, 1646.

If it be argued that Mayne was out to secure toleration for his own party, we need only turn to a sermon preached to the House of Commons on 31 March, 1647, and printed by their command, Ralph Cudworth's on *1 John* II. 3,4 *And hereby we do know that we know him, if we keep his Commandments. He that saith, I know him, and keepeth not his Commandments, is a liar, and the truth is not in him.* In his dedication Cudworth states again that the scope of his sermon

> was not to contend for *this* or *that opinion* ; but onely to perswade men to the *Life of Christ*, as the Pith and Kernel of all Religion. Without which, I may boldly say, all the severall *Forms* of *Religion* in the World, though we please our selves never so much in them, are but so many severall *Dreams*. And those many *Opinions* about *Religion*, that are every where so eagerly contended for on all sides, where *This* doth not lie at the Bottome, are but so many *Shadows* fighting with one another [1].

He compares those that

> spend all their zeal upon a violent obtruding of their own Opinions and Apprehensions upon others

to bellows that will blow a perpetual fire of discord, while

> these hungry, and starved *Opinions*, devoure all the Life and Substance of Religion [2].

The opening words of the sermon itself throw light on the endless disputations raging at the time, in the pulpit as well as in the press :

> We have much enquiry concerning knowledge in these latter times. The sonnes of Adam are now as busie as ever himself was, about *Tree of Knowledge* of good and evil, shaking the boughs of it, and scrambling for the fruit : whilest, I fear, many are too unmindfull of the *Tree of Life* [3].

Lest this be misunderstood for indifference to doctrine or for denial of the use of knowledge, it may be worth remembering that Cudworth ended his dedication with an appeal to the House of Commons " to promote ingenuous Learning ", and was careful to

---

[1] R. CUDWORTH : *A Sermon Preached before the Honourable House of Commons, At Westminster, March 31, 1647*, Cambridge, 1647. The Facsimile Text Society, New York, 1930, sig. 3 r. and v.
[2] *Ibid.*, sig. 3 v. and [4].   [3] *Ibid.*, p. 1.

add : " not that onely, which furnisheth the Pulpit, which you seem to be regardfull of ", but all that contributes to " the Noble and generous Improvement of an Understanding Faculty "[1]. From this, if from nothing else, we might gather that Cudworth disapproved of the prevalent disputations as much as did Jasper Mayne, and was far from allying himself with those who were soon to attack human learning and even to advocate the suppression of Universities. Yet, Cudworth had been appointed Master of Clare Hall, Cambridge, by the Parliamentary Visitors, and he was later on intimate terms with Cromwell's secretary, Thurloe. This only goes to show that men of different persuasions[2] were weary of the contentiousness which the pulpit as well as the press helped to foster, and that their plea for avoiding disputes was prompted by their desire both to establish concord and to promote the true Christian life. Unless we keep this in mind we cannot rightly assess the object of the reform of pulpit oratory, or its effect on the manner and matter of sermons in the succeeding age.

A little tract published in 1646 by John Geree[3], *The Character of an old English puritane or non-conformist*, may help us form a fair estimate of what the Puritans of an earlier generation expected of their sermons and what, no doubt, many of those who were not caught by the frenzy to argue or in thrall to the extremer Sects, continued to expect. The author, a " Preacher of the Word ", is obviously harking back to happier days : the old English Puritan, he tells us, was such a one that

> he esteemed that preaching best wherein was most of God, least of man, when vain flourishes of wit, and words were declined, and the demonstration of Gods power and spirit studied, yet could he distinguish between studied plainnesse and negligent rudenesse. He accounted perspicuitie the best grace of a Preacher. And that method best which was most helpful to understanding, affection, and memory. To which ordinarily he esteemed none so conducible as that by doctrine, reason and use[4].

---

[1] *Ibid.*, sig. A, A v.

[2] Cudworth cannot be regarded as a Puritan, but he was acceptable to the new rulers while Jasper Mayne was not.

[3] A Presbyterian minister. Geree is said to have been so horrified at the execution of Charles I that he died of the shock. See Christopher HILL : *Intellectual Origins of the English Revolution*, London, 1965, p. 5, n. 4.

[4] *The Character of an old English puritane or non-conformist*. By John Geree, M.A. and Preacher of the Word some time at Tewksbury, but now at

As to discipline, it is beyond argument :

> He thought God had left a rule in his word for discipline,
> and that Aristocraticall by Elders, not Monarchicall by
> bishops, nor democraticall by the people [1].

In true Puritan fashion the author then goes on :

> he disliked such Church-musicke as moved sensual delight,
> and was hinderance to spiritual enlargements. He accounted
> subjection to the Higher powers to be part of pure religion...
> Yet did he distinguish between Authority, and lust of
> Magistrates [2].

Given the varieties of Puritan as well as of Anglican preaching,
it would seem, then, that the distinguishing mark between the two
groups lay mainly in the use of ' carnal wisdom ' : to Geree preaching is best wherein is most of God, least of man. Even though
this may not always be a safe criterion, it certainly accounts for
the emphasis, in later discussions of pulpit oratory, on the use of
human learning as well as on the use of figurative language. As
we shall see, one of the central themes of Anglican divines after the
Restoration was the agreeableness of faith to reason, which to the
Puritans was anathema since they firmly held to the segregation
of the realms of nature and of grace. The Anglican reformers of
pulpit oratory advised preachers to make sparing use of quotations,
not because this was evil but because it was apt to be above the
capacity of their hearers, and was often no more than mere
ostentation of learning. On the other hand, the Word of God
being often figurative the Puritans did not discourage the use of
tropes provided they derived from the Bible ; nor did they discourage the use of familiar images which brought the Word of
God to the capacity of their hearers. This no doubt encouraged
the Puritans'—or rather, some extreme Sects'—use of cant, which
was ridiculed after the Restoration, notably by Robert South.

The older Puritans' slight on ' carnal wisdom ' had usually been
counterbalanced by their logical strictness, but after the Assembly
of Divines failed to establish a National Church the Sects began
to proliferate, and in many of them inspiration took the place of

Saint Albans. Published according to order. London, 1646, p. 2 (the tract
has 6 pages in all).
    [1] *Ibid.*, p. 4.   [2] *Ibid.*

dialectics. The spirit of enthusiasm was abroad. Just as in the social and political fields the more conservative Presbyterians tended to veer towards the old Loyalists, as they were to do in the Convention Parliament of 1659, so in the matter of preaching they would frown upon the extravagances of the ' fanatics ' no less than did the Anglicans, and Prynne thundered against the Sects with as much violence as he had against the Prelates. After the Restoration, however, attacks on the fanatics' jargon always imply that this was a characteristic of *all* Puritans. This blurring of differences no doubt made matters easier for those who wished to include them all in their opprobrium or ridicule ; it may also have reflected the view voiced by South in an anniversary sermon on the death of Charles I, that the Presbyterians were in fact responsible for letting loose the flood of enthusiasm no less than of republican feelings [1]. From then on the distinction seems to be clear-cut between Conformists' and Nonconformists' oratory ; or, at least, so the members of the Establishment would have us believe. But we should not allow ourselves to be guided by their prejudices. We need only turn to the sermons of Baxter or of Calamy to disprove this view. On reading, for instance, the Farewell Sermons [2] preached by the ministers who were ejected in 1662, one is struck by their reasonableness and by their moderate tone, and their language is just as ' sensible ' as any Anglican divine's. Among the former Presbyterians who did conform Edward Reynolds [3] may be accounted one of the best preachers of his time : the clear exposition and smooth development of the theme, the pregnant statement, the nervous yet easy style, together with the controlled feeling, suggest a mind of the first order. Indeed, on reading him one wonders whether in his brief career as Dean of Christ Church he did not contribute to mould the young divine whose sermons have the same vigour and pregnancy, Robert South.

Edward Reynolds, no less than Ralph Cudworth, highly valued

[1] Hobbes also thought that the Independents were ' a brood of Presbyterian hatching '.

[2] See, for instance, those of Edmund Calamy, Richard Baxter, and Mr. Bates, in *Farewell Sermons* Preached by Mr. Calamy, Dr. Manton..., London, 1663. The sermons were all preached on 17 August, 1662, and published from shorthand notes, i.e. not by the ministers themselves. By the Act of Uniformity ministers had to conform by 24 August, 1662, or leave the Church.

[3] Reynolds became Bishop of Norwich in 1661, i.e. before the Savoy Conference had failed to give satisfaction to the Presbyterians and before the Act of Uniformity was passed.

human learning, and for one of his sermons (preached in 1657) he chose as his text *Acts* VII. 22 *And Moses was learned in all the wisdom of the Egyptians, and was mighty in words and deeds* ; in it he argued that by the apostle Paul—who, he says, mentions it among his privileges, that he was brought up a scholar—" the Lord has given so much honour unto humane learning " [1]. He returned to the point in a sermon to his clergy on *The Pastoral Office* (1662), and asked the question which would inevitably have occurred to many of them : " how far forth a minister may make use of human wit or learning in the service of the Church ". In answer to which he stated clearly that learning is a gift of God, and " every good gift of God may be sanctified for the use of the Church " [2]. He did not hesitate to tell them that wit too " though it be naturally a proud and unruly thing, yet it may be so sanctified with grace, and fixed by humility, as to be of great use to the Church of God " [3] ; he warned them, however, not to indulge in it too much, " nor loosen the reins unto luxuriancy and fancy ", but to " proportion their ballast to their sail... so as they (might) render severe and solid truths the more amiable " [4].

Perkins also had recognized the use of profane learning for the preparation of sermons, provided it be concealed in the ' promulgation ' of them. By mid-century, however, the position had hardened in certain quarters. Milton's repudiation of university learning as unprofitable for preachers may be part of his tactical

---

[1] *A Sermon touching the use of humane learning*. Preached in Mercers' Chapel, at the Funeral of that learned Gentleman, Mr. John Langley, late school-master of Paul's School in London, on the 21st day of September, 1657, in *The Whole Works, op. cit.*, V, 33. The quality of this sermon is best assessed when compared with Tillotson's sermon at the funeral of Whichcote, his one-time master and predecessor at St. Lawrence Jewry. Reynolds was appointed Dean of Christ Church and Vice-Chancellor of Oxford University after the ejection of Samuel Fell by the Parliamentary Visitors in 1647 ; he lost both the deanery and the vice-chancellorship on his refusal to subscribe to the Engagement, which all heads of Colleges had to take by or before 1 January, 1650. The form of the Engagement was : " I do declare and promise, that I will be true and faithful to the Commonwealth of England, as the same is now Established, without a King or House of Lords " (*Resolves of Parliament Touching the Subscribing to an Engagment by or before the first of January next, and the names of the Refusers or Neglecters to be returned to the Parliament*. Die Jovis, 11 Octobr. 1649). Reynolds was succeeded by the Independent John Owen.

[2] *The Pastoral Office, opened in a visitation sermon preached at Ipswich,* Oct. 10, 1662, in *The Whole Works, op. cit.*, V, 402, 403. Reynolds' defence of wit once again reminds us of South.

[3] *Ibid.*   [4] *Ibid.*

game to gain his main point, the suppression of tithes [1] ; it is none the less characteristic of the extreme view held by some Puritans [2].   At one point he even goes so far as to state that " that which makes fit a minister, the scripture can best informe us to be only from above ", thus seemingly endorsing the view that all a minister needs is the inner light.   Sydrach Simpson, the Independent Master of Pembroke Hall, Cambridge, also asserted that human learning was not a preparation appointed by Christ, " either for the right understanding or right teaching of the Gospel " [3].   But some went even further, for instance, John Webster, a Cambridge graduate and a former Army Chaplain, who denied the use of learning altogether on the ground that preaching is by direct inspiration.   In two tracts published in 1653, *Academiarum Examen* (dedicated to Major General Lambert) and *The Saints Guide*, he argued that just as *poeta nascitur, non fit*, what the preacher needs is the divine afflatus, not art [4].   William Dell, a former Army Chaplain and then Master of Caius College, Cambridge, also denied the use of human learning in his *Confutation of Divers Gross and Antichristian Errors* (1654),

> For humane (as opposed to scriptural) learning mingled
> with divinity, or the Gospel of Christ understood accord-
> ing to Aristotle, hath begun, continued, and perfected the
> mysterie of iniquity in the outward Church [5].

He had already expounded this view the preceding year in *The Tryall of Spirits*, which can best be described as highly ' enthusiastic ' [6].   John Owen, Dean of Christ Church and Vice-Chancellor

---

[1] See Barbara KIEFER-LEWALSKI : ' Milton : Political Beliefs and Polemical Methods, 1659-60 ', *PMLA*, LXXIV (1959), 191-202.

[2] See, for instance, the Baptist Samuel How's *The Sufficiency of the Spirits Teaching, without Humane Learning*, London, 1640.   But this was a vexed question among the Puritans.   For the position, in the learned-ministry controversy, of the various groups within the Puritan party, see Barbara KIEFER-LEWALSKI : ' Milton on Learning and the Learned-Ministry Controversy ', *HLQ*, XXIV (1961), 267-81.

[3] Quoted by MITCHELL, *op. cit.*, p. 126.

[4] John WEBSTER : *Academiarum Examen, or the Examination of Academies*, London, 1653, p. 3 ; *The Saints Guide, or Christ the Rule and Ruler of Saints*, London, 1653.

[5] Quoted by V.H.H. GREEN, *op. cit.*, p. 138.

[6] William DELL : *The Tryall of Spirits, both in Teachers and Hearers, wherein is held forth the clear discovery and certain downfall of the carnall and antichristian Clergie of these times*, London, 1653.

of Oxford after Reynolds, though by no means ready to do away with houses of learning, also stressed the danger of mixing human learning in the explication of Scripture [1].

Such repudiation of human knowledge openly contradicted the injunctions of the *Directory for Public Worship* issued by ordinance of Parliament in 1644. Though the *Directory* ordered that the preacher should speak

> Plainly, that the meanest may understand, delivering the truth, not in the entising words of mans wisdome, but in demonstration of the Spirit and of power, least the Crosse of Christ should be made of none effect: abstaining also from unprofitable use of unknown Tongues, strange phrases, and cadences of sounds and words, sparingly citing sentences of Ecclesiastical, or other humane writers, ancient or moderne, be they never so elegant [2]

it also stated that

> It is presupposed (according to the Rules for Ordination) that the Minister of Christ is in some good measure gifted for so weighty a service, by his skill in the Originall Languages, and in such Arts and Sciences as are handmaids of Divinity, by his knowledge in the whole Body of Theology but most of all in the holy Scriptures [3].

The whole chapter of the *Directory* on 'The Preaching of the Word' in fact gives clear directions for avoiding most of the excesses which later reformers were to denounce, and some of these reformers were probably indebted to it, notably Wilkins. But by the fifties these directions were no longer heeded, and, as in the case of Reynolds, moderate Presbyterians had been replaced by Independents in many influential places (Dell and Simpson were both heads of Cambridge Houses). Not that the Independents were all *illuminati*; but Cromwell's policy of toleration allowed the Sects to worship and preach freely, and the Independents were loth to restrain them, as they themselves had been restrained by the 'new forcers of conscience'. Moreover, some of the Independents denied, contrary to the Presbyterians (and to the Anglicans), that

---

[1] John OWEN: *Of the Divine Originall, Authority, Self-Evidencing Light and Power of the Scripture*, Oxford, 1659.

[2] *A Directory for the Public Worship of God Throughout the Three Kingdoms of England, Scotland, and Ireland...*, London, 1644, p. 34.

[3] *Ibid.*, pp. 27-28.

special revelations had ceased ; hence, their readiness to allow for the gift of preaching under the guidance of the Spirit alone.

Whatever the defects of university training and their corrupting influence on preaching, which even Anglicans like Eachard denounced as late as 1670, only the extreme Puritans were out to suppress learning and advocated disendowment of Universities. " Cromwell himself had had no doubt that the Universities must serve as nurseries of ' godly ' learning. He would defend them against threatened disendowment by extremists of his own party, but he held sternly that their chief function was to supply pious teachers and ministers " [1]. Cudworth's appeal to the Commons in 1647 is significant in so far as he assumed that they would be careful of learning " which furnishes the pulpit ", but urged them also to further ' ingenuous learning '. The conflict between advocates of a learned and those of a godly ministry became sharper after the ordinance of March 1654 for regulating the selection of ministers. Commissioners or ' Triers ' were appointed to examine the qualification of the candidates : " Including Presbyterians, Independents, and Anabaptists, the Commission determined whether the applicant was of ' known godliness and integrity ' and of ' holy and good conversation '. It was not empowered to deal with questions of ordination or doctrine " [2]. The Triers were to be remembered bitterly by South [3], and no doubt in their proceedings they often put a premium on the godly deportment of men, whether sincere or feigned. The fear that men wholly unfit might be selected for the ministry prompted a number of defences of human learning by both Anglicans and moderate Puritans, who regarded it as a necessary part of the ministers' training.

Reynolds, as we saw, vindicated the use of learning in 1657. In a sermon he had prepared to preach on 4 December, 1655, and published in 1656 [4], Baxter warned the people against " Papists in garb of Sects ", who, to bring them back to Rome, were crying down tithes and maintenance of clergy, both of which were then usually justified partly by the need to repay ministers for the expense of their education and to allow them to prepare adequately

---

[1] V.H.H. GREEN, op. cit., p. 140. Cromwell, who had become Chancellor of Oxford University in 1650, gave manuscripts to the University.

[2] BOSHER, op. cit., p. 7.

[3] See The Scribe Instructed, in Sermons Preached upon Several Occasions, 6th ed., London, 1727, IV, Sermon I.

[4] He says he was " prevented by illness from preaching ".

for their task by further study. Baxter, however, not only insisted
on the necessity for the pastor to speak to the capacity of *all* men,
but advised him to use evidence and ornaments from Scripture
rather than from " Aristotle and the authority of men " ; " let
all writers, he said, have their due esteem, but compare none of
them with the Word of God " [1]. As early as 1647 Cudworth
strongly urged the Commons to promote learning at the Universities [2]. The Vice-Chancellor of Cambridge, Benjamin Whichcote [3],
also supported learning and to him Sedgewick dedicated his reply
to William Dell in 1653. Even Anthony Tuckney, the rigid
Calvinist Master of St. John's, Cambridge, is reported to have said,
at the time of electing fellows, that

> no one should have a greater regard to the godly than him-
> self ; but he was determined to choose none but *scholars*—
> adding very wisely, ' they may deceive me in their godliness,
> they cannot in their scholarship ' [4].

The Anglican Seth Ward published (anonymously) a tract
in reply to the attacks of William Dell and John Webster
(and Hobbes) and called it after the latter's pamphlet *Vindiciae
Academiarum* [5]. Another tract, also directed against William Dell,
is of particular interest because it shows to what fantastic use of
language the enthusiasts resorted as a consequence of being driven
by the Spirit alone. In 'ΕΠΙΣΚΟΠΟΣ ΔΙΔΑΚΤΙΚΟΣ (1653), which

---

[1] *Gildas Salvianus, The Reform'd Pastor, op. cit.*, p. 360.

[2] The sermon was preached on 31 March ; on 1 May, 1647, appeared an
ordinance of Parliament for the Visitation and Reformation of Oxford University,
which led to the ejection of the Vice-Chancellor, Samuel Fell, Dean of Christ
Church, and to the appointment of Edward Reynolds in his stead. It must
be remembered that when Oxford surrendered in 1646, the commander of the
Parliamentary forces, Fairfax, who was himself a cultured man and esteemed
learning, " included in the Articles of Surrender a clause to the effect that ' all
Churches, Chapels, Colleges, Halls, Libraries, Schools... shall be preserved from
defacing and spoil ' ". Thus was prevented the vandalism that wrecked so many
colleges in Cambridge. In 1644 Parliament passed an ordinance for the reformation of Cambridge University, " the execution of which was entrusted to the
Earl of Manchester, a not wholly unsympathetic governor ". V.H.H. GREEN,
op. cit., pp. 143, 142.

[3] No more than Cudworth can Whichcote be called a Puritan, though he
seems to have admired Cromwell. He did not, however, take the Covenant and
is said to have assisted Isaac Barrow (though unsuccessfully) in his application
for the Greek professorship. See TULLOCH, *op. cit.*, II, 88.

[4] Quoted by TULLOCH, *op. cit.*, II, 54.

[5] (Seth Ward): *Vindiciae Academiarum. Containing Some briefe Animadversions upon Mr Websters Book Stiled The Examination of Academies.
Together with an Appendix concerning what Mr Hobbs and Mr Dell have
published on this Argument*, Oxford, 1654.

he dedicated to Whichcote, Joseph Sedgewick, himself a Fellow of Christ's, Cambridge, repudiated Dell's assertion that to a gospel ministry learning, arts, and sciences are altogether unnecessary. He demonstrated that the text from St. Paul's Epistle to the Colossians (II, 8), which the supporters of a godly rather than a learned ministry always invoked, had been misunderstood by them :

> What learning St Paul speaks against, is condemned by learning itself. Philosophy, or the then-Philosophy, opposed reason as well as the Gospel. The place of *Col.* 2 answers itself. Philosophy according to the traditions of men and the principles of the world, the philosophy of the Sects, philosophical quirks and subtilties and ungrounded dreams and fancies concerning Angels and the like, is nothing to genuine Philosophy proceeding upon true principles of nature, that is, God's discovery of himself to our understandings by the light of reason and works of Creation [1].

Sedgewick published this tract together with a sermon he had preached at St. Mary's, Cambridge, on 1 May, 1653. The title of the book defines his object clearly enough : *A sermon preached at St Maries' in the University of Cambridge, May 1st, 1653. Or, An Essay to the Discovery of the Spirit of Enthusiasm and pretended Inspiration, that disturbs and strikes at the Universities. Together with an Appendix, wherein Mr Dell's Stumbling Stone* [2] *is briefly replied unto. And a fuller discourse of the use of Universities and Learning upon ecclesiasticall accounts, etc.* In the sermon he argues that it is contrary to the Apostle's words to despise the gifts of God, and that ministers must make use of their gifts [3]. In the answer to Dell he states emphatically that he should be

> ill-satisfied in an irrational gospel, and an opposition betwixt the discovery of God in natural light and post-revealed truth ; for the first is a divine revelation [4].

The point is of interest because it is a central tenet of Anglican

---

[1] Joseph SEDGEWICK : ʼΕΠΙΣΚΟΠΟΣ ΔΙΔΑΚΤΙΚΟΣ. *Learning's necessity to an able minister of the Gospel,* Cambridge, 1653, p. 55.

[2] William DELL : *The Stumbling Stone,* London, 1653.

[3] He rehearses the usual accusations against the learned clergy : that they speak Hebrew, Latin and Greek (this, he says, may sometimes be mere affectation ; but it does show that they can understand the original text); that they mix philosophical speculations with the Gospel and preach morality ; etc.

[4] *Op. cit.,* p. 20.

thought after the Restoration that the Word of God is a second revelation, the first being the natural notions implanted in the heart of man. Equally important is the fact that Sedgewick, who would not countenance an ' irrational Gospel ', was also horrified by the extravagant language of the enthusiasts. He thus makes clear the relation between ' enthusiasm '—even though limited, as in the case of some Independents, to belief that special revelations had not ceased—and the cant for which after the Restoration *all* Puritan preaching came to be branded. In enthusiasm, then, rather than in Puritanism as such, lies the source of the attacks on human learning as well as of the fantastic jargon which discredited the Saints. Having shown that St. Paul only meant to censure *vain* philosophy and the painted rhetoric of his times, Sedgewick went on to say :

> Yet true raisedness of expression, a majestical state, and artificial and genuine insinuations, with most pathetical captivatings of the mind, are obvious in Scripture : as obvious as fantastical cloud-reachings are affectedly frequent in our new formalists enthusiasm [1].

In his sermon at Carfax Church in 1646 Jasper Mayne had already attacked the dangerous error that universities, books, studies, and learning, are not necessary preparatories to make a preacher of the Gospel, and that

> any layman... if he find by himself that he is called by the Spirit of God, may put himself into orders and take the ministry upon him [2].

Though he was ready to grant that private inspiration was still possible, and that God might raise prophets now, yet he very much doubted whether God actually did so. In refuting the view that the Anglican clergy was unsanctified because the preacher did not claim to speak by the gift of the Spirit, he remarked on the new style of preaching and on the extravagances with which extempore—i.e. ' gifted '—preachers dazzled the people :

> Some pulpits have been thought unsanctified, because the preacher was not gifted, because he has not expressed himself in that light, fluent, running, passionate, zealous style, which should make him for that time appear religiously

[1] *Op. cit.*, p. 55.   [2] *Op. cit.*, p. 6.

distracted, or beside himself. Or because his prayer, or
Sermon hath been premeditated, and has not flown from
him in such an ex-tempore loose career of devout emptiness
and nothings, as serve only to entertain the people, as
bubbles do children, with a thin, unsolid, brittle, painted
blast of wind and air [1].

Beside this Sedgewick's denunciation of enthusiasm may well have
struck South as mere 'post-dated loyalty'.

By showing up the absurdity of preaching by the Spirit, and
the 'entertainment' it offered to the uneducated, Mayne had
indirectly defined one aspect of the 'rationalism' of the succeeding age, and also implied the class-distinction which marks off
enthusiastic writing from neo-classical literature. Conversely, one
may say that the stress on reason and good sense, premeditation
and control, which characterizes neo-classicism, was due, partly at
least, to the reaction against the excesses of enthusiasm in religion
in the preceding age [2]. It is surely no accident that the classical
temper is best defined in a sermon on extempore prayers by Robert
South (like Mayne, a Christ-Church man); nor that the patrician
scorn [3] of this Restoration preacher should be so often aimed at
the unthinking rabble that can be entertained by mere bubbles.
The clarity and sobriety of Restoration prose, the premium set on
perspicuity, the distrust of metaphorical language, the preference
for language such as men do use, may well have other sources than
this reaction against the turgid speeches which had caused such
revolutions in Church and State. But the revulsion from this
should also be taken into account. Similarly, the emphasis on order
and propriety in language and literature no less than in religion
and politics, appears as the natural reaction against the anarchy
of the closing years of the Interregnum. One need only turn to
the poems celebrating the return of Charles II to realize that the
promise of peace and order was welcomed with relief. And these
are the very qualities which the reformers of pulpit oratory advocated again and again : a clear method, a perspicuous and natural
style, a sober exposition of doctrine and use, and above all avoid-
ance of needless controversies. Though emphasis on these qualities

---

[1] *Op. cit.*, p. 38.
[2] See George WILLIAMSON : 'The Restoration Revolt against Enthusiasm',
SP, XXX (1933), 571-604.
[3] J.R. SUTHERLAND : 'Robert South', *Review of English Literature*, I, 1
(1960).

did in the long run foster the dullness of eighteenth-century preaching, though indeed by the end of the seventeenth century " the
great days of pulpit oratory are over " [1], it was an inevitable, and
on the whole a healthy, reaction against the excesses of the previous
age.   Together with other factors, it certainly encouraged a taste
for clear thinking and precise statement, for easy and natural
expression, for a mode of exposition that is at once persuasive and
undogmatic, and for a style that is both polished and free from
decoration.   It may also have contributed to bring home to the
poets that, as T.S. Eliot himself a great admirer of Dryden said,
verse should have the virtues of good prose.   The fact that for
mediocre writers poetry was hardly more than rhymed prose—and
not good prose at that—casts no reflection on the practice of men
like Dryden, whose prose and verse alike show to what varied uses
he could put the medium which the reformers had contributed to
shape.

On the other hand, the rationalism of Anglican theology after
the Restoration, however deeply rooted in the tradition of the
Church of England, was no doubt accentuated by the need to
resist attacks against reason on both fronts, from the Dissenters
and from the Romanists [2].   The Church's emphasis, after the
Restoration, on the agreeableness of faith and reason, her refusal
to be drawn into controversy over ' abstruse and speculative notions '
such as election and reprobation, her insistence upon catechetical
doctrines and upon their application to right practice [3], may be
regarded in the main as a return to the humanistic tradition, from

---

[1] F.P. WILSON, op. cit., p. 110.

[2] As we shall see, Baxter's warning against Papists in the garb of Sects
cannot be dismissed as a mere polemical gesture to frighten the true-blue
Protestants.

[3] This was laid down explicitly in the Directions Concerning Preachers
issued by the King in 1662 : " 2. That they be admonished not to spend their
time and study in the search of abstruse and speculative Notions, especially
in and about the deep points of Election and Reprobation, together with the
incomprehensible manner of the concurrence of Gods Grace, and mans Free
Will, and such other controversies as depend thereupon : But howsoever, that
they presume not positively and doctrinally to determine any thing concerning
the same... 4. But for the more edifying of the people in faith and godliness...
all Ministers and Preachers in their several respective Cures shall... in their
ordinary Sermons insist chiefly upon Catechetical Doctrines (wherein are contained
all the necessary and undoubted verities of Christian Religion) declaring with
all unto their Congregations what influences such Doctrines ought to have into
their lives and conversations, and stirring them up effectually, as well by their
Examples as their Doctrines, to the practice of such Religious and Moral Duties
as are the proper results of the said Doctrines... ".

which the subtle arguments of the Calvinists or the exegesis of the witty preachers no less than the extravagances of the Saints widely diverged. And the efforts of the reformers of pulpit oratory all bore in the same direction. It is surely no accident that the most influential of these, both through his treatise on preaching and through his own practice and life, should have called his manual for aspiring preachers *Ecclesiastes*. Such emphasis often resulted in 'mere moral preaching', an accusation that was often levelled at the Anglican clergy by the Dissenters [1] or even by the stricter members of their own congregations [2]; but it also ensured that the people should be edified in the central truths of Christianity, truths which, as the preachers repeatedly emphasized, are not merely speculative, but operative truths. And this very insistence was made the more necessary by the spread of Antinomianism as well as of infidelity and licentiousness. Given the circumstances, the reform of pulpit oratory was bound to be towards simplicity and perspicuity, and to emphasize the need for preachers to be trained in human as well as in divine knowledge.

*
* *

When we consider the chorus of divines who " by the third quarter of the century [are] pleading for the plain style and alluding contemptuously to fantastic wit or the squeezing of a text " [3], the most striking thing is that they all come from the Anglican fold, and that many of them distinctly refer the vices they censure to the Puritans' practice. This was not unnatural considering the excesses of the Saints and of some Calvinists, even though the Anglicans may have been a little too prone to fasten the blame on the other party. In the earlier part of the century, however, the attacks had usually come from the other side, from Puritans concerned that *all* the sheep be fed. Such was clearly one of the main purposes of the *Directory* issued by the Assembly of Divines in 1644, which among the reasons for abolishing the Book of Common Prayer, stated that

---

[1] See Pilgrim's visit to Vanity Fair.
[2] The parishioners of Tillotson at Keddington were dissatisfied because he did not 'preach Jesus Christ'. See BIRCH, *op. cit.*, p. xviii.
[3] F.P. WILSON, *op. cit.*, p. 101.

> Prelates and their Faction have laboured to raise the Estima-
> tion of it to such an Height... to the great hinderance of
> the Preaching of the Word, and (in some places, especially
> of late) to the justling it out, as unnecessary ; or (at best)
> as far inferiour to the Reading of Common-Prayer [1].

Both the method and the style recommended in their directions for
preaching are plain and perspicuous : the minister is to choose a
text ' holding forth some principle or head of Religion '; to give
a brief and perspicuous introduction from the text, or context, or
some parallel place ; if the text is long he is to give a brief summary,
if short a paraphrase, but

> In both, looking diligently to the scope of the Text, and
> pointing at the chief heads and grounds of Doctrine, which
> he is to raise from it [2].

This would have restrained the argumentative skill of preachers
apt to enlarge upon their text in order to bring in far-fetched
observations, as would the recommendation on how to " raise
doctrine from the text ", particularly

> that he chiefly insist upon those Doctrines which are prin-
> cipally intended, and make most for the edification of the
> hearers [3].

Division of the text according to words is to be eschewed, nor
must the members be so numerous that they burden the memory
of the hearers or entail the use of terms of art. The doctrine must
be plain, and the arguments solid ; all cavils are to be avoided.
The preacher is to apply the doctrine for instruction, to exhort or
dehort, to apply comfort or give ' notes of trial ' that the hearers
" may be able to examine themselves " [4]. He is neither to prosecute all the doctrines in the text nor to infer all the uses. And
the style is to be plain " that the meanest may understand ", free
from quotations in unknown tongues and from " cadences of sounds
and words " [5].

   Such a method would, on the whole, have suited most Anglican
reformers after the Restoration. And it is characteristic that the
sermon manual most influential in the next age was clearly based
on the *Directory*. This appears from Wilkins's subtitle to *Eccle-*

---

[1] *Directory, op. cit.*, Preface, p. 3.
[2] *Ibid.*, p. 29.   [3] pp. 29-30.   [4] p. 38.   [5] p. 24.

siastes, or *A Discourse Concerning the Gift of Preaching as it falls under the rules of art. Shewing the most proper rules and directions, for method, invention, books, expression, whereby a minister may be furnished with such abilities as may make him a Workman that needs not to be ashamed, but may save himself, and those that heare him* [1]. The last words (" a Workman that... ") reproduce *verbatim* the end of the first paragraph on preaching in the *Directory* and must have been recognizable to all readers. Besides, the *Directory* went on to say that certain abilities were 'presupposed' in all ministers, and Wilkins proposes to furnish them with such abilities. A reference in the preface To the Reader to " the vacancy of many places purged from scandalous ministers " may reveal the author's sympathies with the Puritans, unless he is merely using the cant of the time. Wilkins, who was later to become Bishop of Chester, could be all things to all men, and was eminently fit to act as a mediator ; he could rise above party, and he encouraged research and peaceful exchange of ideas at a time when controversies were raging [2]. In his sermon manual, as in his later dealings with men of opposite parties, he fostered that reasonable and equable temper that was his main quality. Though his was not, it seems, a mind of the first order, his interests—ranging from mechanics to the principles of a ' Universal Character ' and to divinity—were as many and as diverse as his sympathies were wide, and he is perhaps best described as an early Latitudinarian. His manual is intended to show to " those who pretend to the gift of preaching yet understand only their mother tongue... that great disadvantage in the want of academic education and learning ", for the gift of preaching is an art, and must be acquired, it is " no longer bestowed upon men by any special infusion " ; as he says : " A man may as well expect to be inspired with a gift of tongues, as with a gift of preaching " [3].

For all its dependence on the *Directory* Wilkins's method differs from that of the Presbyterian divines, and the differences, however slight, emphasize his own sobriety and reasonableness, just as the

---

[1] London, 1646.

[2] See Thomas SPRAT : *History of the Royal Society* (1667), ed. J.I. Cope and H.W. Jones, St. Louis-London, 1959, p. 53. On Wilkins, see also : J.G. CROWTHER : *Founders of British Science*, London, 1960, and *The Royal Society. Its Origins and its Founders*, ed. Sir Harold Hartley, London, 1960.

[3] *Ecclesiastes*, Preface.

reference books to which he directs aspiring preachers are characteristic of his own catholic taste and broad-mindedness. First he
gives a list of learned men, Protestant and others, who have written
on the subject, and he states that a preacher needs both ' spiritual '
and ' artificial ' abilities. The best method is ' by doctrine and use ';
the divine orator is to teach clearly, to convince strongly, and to
persuade powerfully ; hence the sermon is to consist of three parts :
explication, confirmation, and application. This is an important
simplification of the method propounded by Keckermann as well
as of the directions of the Assembly of Divines. Keckermann's
five-fold division—consideration of the text, division, explanation,
amplification, application, with the third and fourth constituting
the main body of the sermon—had usually entailed a highly coloured
story at the beginning (replacing the old exordium of classical
oratory); though he had advised preachers to divide their text
into few parts—over against the endless subdivisions of the schol-
astics, which many strict Calvinists were to imitate—he had also
envisaged explication as discussion of every word in the text, which
Andrewes and other Anglo-Catholic divines were to favour [1]. As
to the 1644 *Directory*, not only had it recommended a long extempore prayer before the sermon—which, as events proved, gave
occasion to many gospel preachers to show how ' ravished ' they
were—as well as another such prayer after the sermon, but it
proposed a plan consisting of : introduction to the text ; summary
or paraphrase of it ; analysis and division ; raising of doctrines ;
arguments and illustrations, together with (occasional) clearing of
doubtful places ; instruction, with confirmation of doctrine and
confutation of false doctrines ; and finally, dehortation, comfort
and (occasionally) aids to self-examination. This need not, but
often may, have entailed a more complex structure than that
envisaged by Wilkins. The *Directory*'s seven points reappear
when Wilkins explains how each of the three main parts " may
be further subdivided ", but by insisting on the simpler, three-fold,
division he was ensuring that the sermon should have a clear and
firm plan, free from all excrescences. And the advice he gave on
how to handle each part contributed to the same end.

First, for *Explication*. He advised preachers to avoid ingenious
interpretations :

[1] On Keckermann, see MITCHELL, *op. cit.*, pp. 95 ff.

> Beware of that vain affectation of finding something new
> and strange in every text, though never so plain. It will
> not so much shew our parts (which such men aim at) as
> our pride, and wantonness of wit. These new projectors
> in Divinity are the fittest matter out of which to shape, first
> a Sceptick, after that a Heretick, and then an Atheist[1].

While the first sentence reminds us of Bacon's denunciation of the
vain affectations of learning and of the cobwebs which the mind
of man spins out of its own substance, the second looks forward
to the insistence of Restoration divines on eschewing vain speculations because these are apt to raise doubts and to encourage
infidelity. Wilkins, we remember, was to be both the friend of
the new projectors in natural philosophy and a champion of faith,
who opposed the spread of infidelity by insisting on the agreeableness of natural and revealed religion[2]. As for division of the text,
he dismisses this in a few words ; it is needless, and the " common
practice of dissecting the words into minute parts " has too often
been the occasion of impertinency[3]. Next, the preacher should
unfold his text by inferring observations from it " by strong logical
consequence " for " the wrestling of Scripture unto improper truths,
may easily occasion the applying of them unto grosse falshoods " ;
the observations must be

> laid down in the most easie and perspicuous phrase that
> may be, not obscured by any theoretical or affected ex-
> pressions ; for if the hearers mistake in that, all that
> follows will be to little purpose[3].

In the second part, the *Confirmation*, the preacher is to use
arguments of two kinds, *quod sit* and *cur sit*. This is the usual
method recommended in all *artes concionandi*, but the grave
Assembly divines may well have frowned on reading that the
confirmation should be from testimony both human and divine, and
when Wilkins went on to state that

> testimonies of heathen men may be proper to shew a truth
> agreeable to natural light[4].

True, he did not say at this stage, as he was to say later in his

---

[1] *Op. cit.*, p. 9.
[2] See particularly : John WILKINS : *Of the Principles and Duties of Natural
Religion*, London, 1675 (edited by Tillotson).
[3] p. 12.   [4] p. 13.

Principles and Duties of Natural Religion, and as his friend and disciple Tillotson was to emphasize repeatedly, that natural religion, being implanted in the heart of man by God, is the fundament of revealed religion.   True, he was careful to warn his readers that

> to stuff a sermon with citations of authors, and the witty sayings of others, is to make a feast of vinegar and pepper, which may be delightful being used moderately as sauces, but must needs be very improper and offensive to be fed upon as diet [1];

but the difference from Perkins's injunction to conceal *all* human wisdom, as well as from the *Directory*, is one of great moment.

Equally important is his view that the third part, the *Application*, is " the life and soul of a sermon " [2].   Though he considers two kinds of applications, doctrinal and practical, he warns preachers that in the doctrinal part

> we ought to be specially careful that we manage these polemical discourses 1. with solid pressing arguments... 2. with much meeknesse and lenity in differences not funda- mental [3].

This meekness and lenity in differences not fundamental rather recalls the temper of the discussions at Great Tew in the preceding decade than the tone and style of the sermons and pamphlets in the year when Wilkins published his *Ecclesiastes.*   Though he was not associated with the men who gathered round Falkland, Wilkins may be regarded as a link between these sober and tolerant men and the Restoration divines in whom the gentle spirit of moderation prevailed, and who for that reason were called by the then opprobrious name ' Latitudinarians ' [4].

Wilkins's recommendations for *Expression*, in the third part of his manual, have been given due importance in all discussions of seventeenth-century prose because they must have contributed to the triumph of the plain prose that became the standard after the Restoration.   The phrase, Wilkins said, should be plain, full,

---

[1] p. 13.   [2] p. 14.   [3] p. 16.
[4] See (Edward FOWLER): *The Principles and Practices of Certain Moderate Divines of the Church of England (greatly misunderstood), Truly represented and defended ; Wherein (by the way) some controversies, of no mean import- ance, are succinctly discussed.   In a free discourse between two intimate friends.* In III Parts.   London, 1670.   Fowler, who was to become Bishop of Gloucester under William, refers to the ' long nick-name ' that has been fastened upon these divines (p. 9).

wholesome, and affectionate ; and in developing the first two
points [1] he described a mean between the extremes of brevity and
orotundity, and categorically repudiated all ornaments of speech,
invoking the authority of St. Paul, though others had shown, and
were to show, that the Apostle had only condemned *vain* rhetoric.
Wilkins, then, favoured bare rather than plain prose, and the
reason for this may be found in what he says on the next point,
wholesomeness :

> False opinions doe many times insinuate themselves by the
> use of suspicious phrases. And 'tis a dangerous fault when
> men cannot content themselves with the wholsome form of
> sound words, but do altogether affect new light and new
> language, which may in time destroy practical Godliness
> and the power of religion [2].

Like Jasper Mayne, Wilkins clearly feared the empty nothings
and far-fetched similitudes which dazzle the people and destroy
practical godliness. Though his own reasonable temper as well
as his interest in scientific experiments [3] may have made him
naturally averse from all metaphorical language, it is clear that

---

[1] " 1. It must be plain and natural, not being darkned with the affectation
of scholastical harshness, or rhetorical flourishes. Obscurity in the discourse
is an argument of ignorance in the mind. The greatest learning is to be seen
in the greatest plainnesse. The more clearly we understand anything ourselves,
the more easily can we expound it to others. When the notion itself is good,
the best way to set it off, is in the most obvious expression. St. Paul does
often glory in this, that his preaching was not in wisdom of words, or excellency
of speech, not with inticing words of mans wisdome, not as pleasing men, but
God who trieth the heart. A minister should speak as the orator of God,
1 *Pet.* 4.11. And it will not become the majesty of a divine embassage to be
garnished out with flaunting affected eloquence. How unsuitable is it to the
expectation of a hungry soul, who comes unto this ordinance with a desire
of spiritual comfort and instruction, and there to hear only a starched speech
full of puerile worded rhetorick ? How properly may such a deceived hearer
take up that of Seneca ? *Quid mihi lusoria ista proponis ?*... 'Tis a sign of
low thoughts and designs, when a mans chief study is about the polishing of
his phrase and words... such a one speaks only from his mouth, and not from
his heart.
2. It must be full, without empty and needless tautologies, which are to
be avoided in every solid businesse, much more in sacred. Our expression
should be so close, that they may not be obscure, and so plain, that they may
not seem vain and tedious. To deliver things in a crude, confused manner,
without digesting of them by previous meditation, will nauseate the hearers,
and is as improper for the edification of the mind, as raw meat is for the nourishment of the body. " *Op. cit.*, pp. 72-73.
[2] p. 73.
[3] R.F. Jones has argued that Wilkins's first two requirements for style
derived from the impact of the Baconian experimental philosophy. See ' Science
and English Prose Style, 1650-1675 ', *PMLA*, XLV (1930), reprinted in *Studies
in the Seventeenth Century*, Stanford (Cal.), 1951, pp. 75-111.

his main concern is with the corruption of doctrine that may result
from the imposture of words. A man whose temper and style
were as different as may be from Wilkins's, Robert South, was
to say no less of the absurd language that perverted people's
religion. What Wilkins recommends, then, is a clear and perspicuous style, free from needless amplifications and from 'flaunting
affected eloquence'. True, in his later *Discourse Concerning the
Gift of Prayer* (1653) Wilkins condemned both negligence and
affectation of wild 'mystical' phrases, both of which characterized
the enthusiasts' discourses. But his later work on a universal
character, i.e. a set of symbols which might figure ideas in an
unambiguous way and thus avoid the danger of confusion through
the metaphorical use of language, only accentuated his bent towards
mathematical plainness. However interesting his *Essay Towards
a Real Character and a Philosophical Language* (1668)—and
Newton devoted some time to similar research—such reduction of
words to mathematical symbols could only have resulted in something like the language used by the inhabitants of Swift's flying
island. But given the interest many people then took in reducing
language to method, such schemes were likely to appeal to men
like Sir William Petty, Evelyn, and other members of the Royal
Society, who, like Hobbes, were much concerned with the inconstant
signification of words.

The danger of Wilkins's emphasis on bareness is at once
apparent when one turns to his own sermons [1] : the style is indeed
plain and natural, and he certainly has not made it his chief study
to polish his phrases and words ; but after reading him one may
say with Pope : " We cannot blame indeed—but we may sleep ".
Such may well have been the opinion of the Merry Monarch, who
liked sermons to be short and plain, but pithy, and who relished
the sallies of Robert South. When we come to Wilkins's disciple
Tillotson we realize that, as Burnet said in his funeral oration, he
had profited from his work on the *Universal Character*, but we
may also agree with the late F.P. Wilson that " he has every
virtue and but one vice, the vice of being dull " [2].   More was

---

[1] *Sermons preached upon several occasions before the King at Whitehall,
By the Right Rev. Father in God, John Wilkins, Late Lord Bishop of Chester.
To which is added, A Discourse Concerning the Beauty of Providence, by the
same Author.* London, 1677 (edited by Tillotson).

[2] *Op. cit.*, p. 110.

needed than to retrench empty tautologies and rhetorical flourishes or to avoid scholastical harshness ; but at the time when Wilkins was writing his manual, closeness to the matter in hand must have appeared as devoutly to be wished [1]. And later reformers of pulpit oratory were to emphasize the point again and again.

To consider only the method and style of preaching recommended by Wilkins may be misleading if one ignores the second part of his book, dealing with matter. Though the minister is to avoid all affectation of learning in his sermons, he must command considerable knowledge to expound Scripture rightly. Wilkins takes it for granted that a minister has the Old and the New Testament both in the originals and in the most authentic translations, and he only lists reference books which will help him to interpret Scripture. These alone cover more than forty pages of his manual, ranging from dictionaries to ascertain the true meaning of Hebrew or Greek words, to commentaries on Scripture, to controversies about points of doctrine and of discipline, to studies on Jewish and pagan philosophy, on the writings of the Fathers, on ecclesiastical history, etc. Wilkins's undogmatic cast of mind best appears here, for he is content to list the reference works, and to say which side the writers defend, e.g. for or against episcopacy, for or against the Papists, for or against the Socinians, etc. True, he says that many of the controversies of the schoolmen are " but as cobwebs, fine for the spinning, but useless " [2]—after all Erasmus is his master—but he also acknowledges that writers such as Lombard and Aquinas will be useful. And, which is more daring at this date, he praises some Roman Catholic commentators for their " solid, pious matter " and the Jesuits for their " collections of former writers " [3]. Clearly a minister who followed the pattern laid down by Wilkins would not only be clear and perspicuous, but his teaching would be grounded on solid learning ; what is even more important, he would have inquired impartially into the

---

[1] The last of Wilkins's recommendations need not concern us here : expression must be " affectionate and cordial, as proceeding from the heart, and an experimental acquaintance with those truths which we deliver ", op. cit., p. 73. Though the different wording is surely significant, Wilkins's advice clearly derives from the Directory's recommendation that the minister deliver the Word of God " 6. With loving affection, that the people may see all coming from his godly zeale, and hearty desire to doe them good. And 7. As though of God, and perswaded in his owne heart, that all he teaches, is the truth of Christ ", op. cit., p. 35.

[2] p. 43.   [3] p. 49.

points of doctrine and discipline before he set up as a preacher.
In view of the stress laid by many Restoration divines on the need
for rational inquiry, Wilkins's contribution to what Dryden called
a sceptical method cannot be overemphasized. Perhaps this open-
ness of mind is more in evidence among the Latitudinarians than
among the High-Churchmen, but these too were to take their stand
on reason and freedom of inquiry.

If followers of Wilkins often sinned through dullness, no such
danger threatened the divinity students who took to heart the
sermon Robert South preached on 29 July, 1660, at St. Mary's,
Oxford, when the King's Commissioners met there for the visitation
of the University. This sermon, *The Scribe Instructed*, was not
published until the early eighteenth century, but since South was
a renowned preacher, Orator of Oxford University from 1660 and
a Canon of Christ Church from 1670, his influence is not to be
discounted [1], especially if we remember that his own college was

---

[1] Taking notes at sermons or even taking down whole sermons in shorthand
seems to have been fairly common in the seventeenth century. The practice
was favoured by the Puritans, and according to Anthony Wood note-taking at
sermons was ridiculed at Oxford after the Restoration (*Life and Times of
Anthony Wood*, ed. A. Clark, Oxford, 1891-95, I, 359). But what Aubrey
relates of his college friend Edward Davenant (whose uncle was Bishop of
Sarum) shows that such practices obtained elsewhere : "He had an excellent
way of improving his childrens memories, which was thus : he would make
one of them read a chapter or etc., and then they were (*sur le champ*) to
repeat what they remembred, which did exceedingly profitt them ; and so
for Sermons, he did not let them write notes (which jaded their memorie) but
gave an account vivâ voce. When his eldest son, John, came to Winton-schoole
(where the Boys were enjoyned to write Sermon-notes) he had not wrote ;
the Master askt him for his Notes—he had none, but sayd, If I doe not give
you as good an account of it as they doe, I am much mistaken." (*Brief Lives*,
ed. A. Clark, Oxford, 1898, I, 202-3). According to Aubrey Katherine Philips
could take down sermons *verbatim* when she was no more than ten ; but then
"she was when a child much against the Bishops" (*Ibid.*, II, 153). It will be
remembered that Pepys discovered that Paulina had left "many good notes of
sermons" (*Diary*, ed. H.B. Wheatley, London, 1962, VIII, 277). For similar
practices among Puritans, see Lucy HUTCHINSON's *Memoirs of the Life of Colonel
Hutchinson* (ed. J. Hutchinson, London, 1806); in the fragment of her autobiography Mrs. Hutchinson (b. 1620) relates that she was carried to sermons
when she was four years old and that when very young she could "remember
and repeat them exactly" (p. 16). See also G.H. HEALEY : *The Meditations
of Daniel Defoe*, Cummington (Mass.), 1946, Introduction, p. vii. In *Magnalia
Christi Americana* (1702) Cotton Mather says that John Winthrop did not take
notes but could repeat the sermons he heard. On the other hand, Benjamin
Franklin relates of his uncle Benjamin that "he was very pious, a great attender
of Sermons of the best Preachers, which he took down in his shorthand and
had with him many volumes of them". (*Autobiography*, ed. L.W. Labaree,
R.L. Ketcham, H.C. Boatfield, & H.H. Fineman, New Haven, 1964, p. 49).
Surreptitious editions of sermons were often set up from shorthand notes, and
some shorthand manuals were advertised as useful for those who wished to take

a seminary of young divines. On this occasion he took for his
text *Matt.* XIII. 52 *Then said he unto them, therefore every
Scribe which is instructed unto the Kingdom of Heaven, is like
unto a Man that is an Householder, which bringeth forth out of
his Treasure Things new and old*, and from this he showed what
qualifications are required of a minister of God, i.e. natural abilities
and abilities acquired by art or study. The three ' faculties ' the
scribe must be endowed with are *judicium*, to distinguish truth
from error ; memory, to treasure up his reading ; and ' invention ',
i.e. imagination. This last point, South knew, was apt to offend
many of his hearers, and he proceeds to vindicate this most decried
faculty not only as a gift of God which may be sanctified in the
work of the ministry [1], but as an " excellent endowment of the
mind, which gives a gloss and a shine to all the rest " [2].

South had said in his introduction that Christ, the great
preacher of righteousness, was furnished with a strain of heavenly
oratory, that in his sermons he used grace and ornament to gratify
his hearers and the advantages of rhetoric " so as to give [his
words] an easier entrance and admission into the mind and affections ". Here, then, was a defence of rhetoric, on the best of all
authorities. The minister is to preach truth, but he is to dress it
in a way that may be gratifying to his hearers ; grace and ornament are necessary for, as South says, " piety engages no man to
be dull, though lately, I confess, it passed with some for a mark
of regeneration ". He knew, however, that imagination was associated with enthusiasm, and therefore distinguished it from " a
conceited, curious, whimsical brain, which is apt to please itself
in strange, odd, and ungrounded notions ". The distinction is
an important one, especially as he himself was so often to ridicule
the flights of fancy and the unnatural jargon of the Puritans ; but
he had stated at the outset that preparation for the ministry is by
instruction, not by infusion. Indeed, the whole drift of the discourse is a defence of the learning necessary to ministers, and a
refutation of the arguments which had been advanced in the
previous years for the disendowment of Universities. South

---

notes at sermons ; see, for instance, the manual by Jeremiah RICH, ' Semiographer
to the Commonwealth ' : *Charactery or, a Most Easie and Exact Method of
Short and Swift Writing : Whereby Sermons and Speeches may be exactly
taken...*, London, 1646.

[1] Cp. with Edward Reynolds above.
[2] The sermon is printed in full below.

obviously took occasion of the Commissioners meeting to enter
this plea in favour of a learned ministry, of which the defence of
rhetoric is only a part. He recognized that a sermon must be
adapted to the circumstances, tempers, and apprehensions of the
hearers and therefore must " rise or fall in the degrees of its plainness, or quickness, according to their dullness, or docility "; the
preacher is to bring out of his treasure such entertainment as will
be answerable to his guests' palates as well as to the season of the
feast. Both propriety and grace are necessary. His ideal—and
he does say that he is giving a rule for the perfection to which
preachers ought to aspire—may be regarded as that of the classical
orators. The central notion is decorum, which governs the use of
ornament. Indeed, South ventures to give of Christ's sermons—
with a reverential acknowledgment of the differences—the testimony which Cicero gave of Demosthenes' orations. Like Cicero
he wishes the preacher not only to be furnished with imagination,
but to be trained in the use of it, that is, in rhetoric, for " as bare
words convey, so the propriety and elegancy of them gives force
and facility to the conveyance ". To him as to the Puritan John
Prideaux Scripture is not only a body of religion but " a system
of rhetoric ". He argues against the upholders of the bare style
that Scripture does not engage men to be dull, flat and slovenly
in their sermons, for this is to mistake the majesty of the matter.
Still, a caution is needed since some enemies of rhetoric have also
developed a new kind of figurative language, " their whole discourse being one continued meiosis to diminish, lessen, and debase
the great things of the Gospel ". The words of the text he is
expounding, South argues, mean nothing else but a plenty, or
fluent dexterity of the most suitable words, and pregnant arguments, to set off and enforce Gospel truths. He would have
agreed that ' True wit is nature to advantage dressed ', since he
had vindicated fancy on the ground that it is the

> power or ability of the mind, which suggests apposite and
> pertinent expressions, and handsome ways of clothing and
> setting off those truths, which the judgment has rationally
> pitched upon.

In all this one is struck by South's emphasis on the traditional
conception of rhetoric as an art of persuasion in aid of, and
grounded in, logic. He condemns both the whimsies of an unruly

fancy and the dry arguments of mere dialecticians, as well as all
slovenly language. Bacon himself would have agreed that rhetoric
is necessary to win assent, and he could have found nothing to
reprove in South's programme [1]. Discipline and control in the use
of ornament is what South advocates, and the elegancies will set
off the truths propounded. His defence of rhetoric is based, like
Bacon's, on the old faculty psychology : only " that which gives
a clear representation of a thing to the apprehension, makes a
suitable impression of it upon the will and affections ", therefore
the preacher is to give to men not universals but " a clear and lively
idea of particulars ". But he can also ground it on the authority
of St. Paul, who could not have insinuated himself so successfully
into both Jews and Gentiles if he had not been " a man of learning
and skill in the art and methods of rhetoric ".

The third part of the sermon—Inferences—defines the right
style of pulpit oratory as opposed to the two extremes : " indecent
levity " and the " coarse, careless, rude and insipid way ". Unlike
Wilkins, South is not content to define by means of negatives :
for him true wit is " a severe and manly thing ", it is consistent
with wisdom and in divinity is nothing else but " sacred truths
suitably expressed ", a definition which looks forward to Dryden's
' propriety of thoughts and words ' [2]. The passage is an epitome
of all the abuses in pulpit oratory in the seventeenth century, ranged
under the two main heads of indecent (i.e. inappropriate) wit and
of mean, insipid style [3] ; under the latter, however, he includes
the over-subtleties of the strict Calvinists and the extempore preaching of the enthusiasts, and he ascribes them both to the breathings
of the spirit. This, of course, is a flagrant distortion of the facts,
for the over-ingenious discourses of the Calvinists were the product
of their dialectical skill, not of the ' motions of the spirit '. But
South may well have lumped together the Presbyterians', the
Independents' and the Sects' ways of preaching for the sake of
argument, since the sermon ends on a violent diatribe against the
Puritans, typified by his ' Holderforth ', a nickname that was to
stick to them ever after.

---

[1] See Francis BACON : *Advancement of Learning*, in *Works*, ed. J. Spedding,
R.L. Ellis & D.D. Heath, London, 1857-74, III, 409-11 ; *De Augmentis Scientia-
rum*, VI. 3, ibid., I, 670-4.

[2] Unless it was inspired by it, since the text as we have it was first published
in 1715.

[3] It is too long to be quoted here, but see the sermon, below.

However much the picture South gives us of the oratory of the preceding years may be distorted by his partisan zeal, it is none the less interesting because it ranges from the excesses of the Anglo-Catholic divines to the absurdities of the tub-preachers. It should be remembered that South also censured the florid style of Jeremy Taylor—who had once committed what to South was the unpardonable sin, advocating accommodation with the Puritans, but had since persecuted them in his own diocese—in a sermon preached at Christ Church in 1668, shortly after Taylor's death. In this sermon, on *Luke* XXI. 15 *For I will give you a mouth and wisdom, which all your adversaries shall not be able to gainsay or resist*, South once more vindicates the need of learning for the ministry, as well as their claim to a due maintenance from the country, against those who believe that ministers should live " not only as spiritual persons, but as spirits "[1]. Christ promised to give his Apostles a mouth and wisdom, since

> it was highly requisite, that those, who were to be the inter-
> preters and spokesmen of Heaven, should have a rhetorick
> taught them from thence too[2].

Now, this ability of speech conferred on the Apostles had, South says, these three properties : clearness and perspicuity ; unaffected plainness and simplicity ; a suitable and becoming zeal or fervour. In developing these points South defined his own conception of plainness. Whereas in the earlier sermon he had vindicated the use of rhetoric, here the stress is on perspicuity. Some critics have tried to reconcile what seemed to them South's conflicting views of pulpit oratory[3] ; but in fact the two are perfectly con-sistent given the teachings of traditional rhetoric, which South had already recalled in his 1660 sermon through his reference to Cicero. Renaissance manuals of oratory and of poetry, like their classical Latin models, had treated imagery as conducive to ' clear-ness ', as means to illuminate or convey truths[4]. South stressed the necessity both to persuade and to convince ; he never con-sidered that the two could be divorced, though in one sermon he emphasized the need to reach the ' intellectual part ' through lively

---

[1] *Op. cit.*, V, 416.   [2] *Ibid.*, p. 430.
[3] See S. SPIKER : ' Figures of Speech in the Sermons of Robert South ', *RES*, XVI (1940), 444-55.
[4] See R. TUVE, *op. cit.*

particulars, and in the other that

> there could be no effectual Passage into the *Will*, but
> through the *Judgment*, nor any free admission into the
> *former*, but by a full passport from the *latter* [1].

The premium he set on perspicuity was intended to discourage
confused and disorderly thinking as well as obscurity of speech.
For all his reference to language as the dress of thought, South
did not envisage that the two could exist independently of each
other any more than did Pope or Johnson, for, as he said,

> all obscurity of Speech is resolveable into the Confusion
> and Disorder of the Speaker's Thoughts ; ... all Faults or
> Defects in a Man's *Expressions*, must presuppose the same
> in his *Notions* first [2].

His defence of plainness in the 1668 sermon cannot be rightly
assessed unless we view it in this perspective. When he argues
that the great truths Christ and his Apostles delivered would
support themselves without the aid of ornaments, that they were
proposed in the plainest and most intelligible language, he is attacking the preachers who ' amuse ' or astonish their auditories

> with difficult Nothings, Rabbinical whimsies, and remote
> Allusions, which no Man of Sense and solid Reason can
> hear without Weariness and Contempt [3].

Obscurity, whatever its form, defeats the purpose of the minister,
and South knew that " none are so transported and pleased with
it, as those, who least understand it " [4]. Hence, fustian bombast,
high-flown metaphors, scraps of Greek and Latin, and such ' insignificant trifles ' are to be banished from pulpit oratory, as are indeed
all ' affected schemes or airy fancies ', tropes and fine conceits,
' numerous and well-turned periods ', jests and witticisms, language
borrowed from ' plays and romances ', or starched similitudes ; in
Christ's sermons, he said, there is nothing

> of *the Fringes of the North-Star* ; nothing of *Nature's
> becoming unnatural*; nothing of the *Down of Angels Wings*;
> or *the beautiful Locks of Cherubims* : no starched similitudes,
> introduced with a *thus have I seen a cloud rolling in its airy
> Mansion*, and the like [5].

---

[1] *Op. cit.*, V, 432.   [2] *Ibid.*, p. 433.
[3] *Ibid.*, p. 432.   [4] p. 433.   [5] pp. 435-6.

These phrases had been used by the mellifluous Taylor and would have been recognized by South's hearers.

If South could then be rebuked for ridiculing the late Bishop of Down and Connor, he has been more often accused of sinning against his own precepts since he could never curb his wit, and indeed never tried to. But, as in *The Scribe Instructed*, South is here listing all the excesses against plainness which 'amuse' rather than edify the hearers ; he is not arguing for a bare style as such. As his own practice shows, he was as much averse to the rude insipid way as to all needless decoration and enlargements. If many of his sermons have the brilliancy of a cut diamond, it is because he set such store on clear thinking and vigorous expression. His own trenchant style closely adheres to his lucid thought and is made more lively by his apt images and his manly wit. He may indeed have inclined to a 'comical lightness of expression' whenever he was ridiculing the fanatics, though he might well have argued that he was keeping due decorum, if not to the sacred theme he was handling, at least to the particular matter in hand ; but he never resorted to the pitiful embellishments which only emasculate the thought. As he said in another sermon in his characteristic witty way, when once more referring to gifted preachers of the Geneva model,

> while such Persons are thus busied in *Preaching of Judgment*, it is much to be wished, that they would do it with *Judgment* too [1].

The main burden of his teaching is the need for discipline of thought and words, for restraint and orderliness, for concentration and forcefulness ; in his recommendations for preaching as well as in his own practice he is the champion of that clear shining beauty which is the product of a lively imagination generating the more fire as it is the better disciplined. South could have subscribed to Pope's view that " The winged courser, like a gen'rous horse, Shows most true mettle when you check his course ".

His defence of set prayers best defines the advantages to be reaped from control and premeditation. Extempore prayers he brands as rude, careless, incoherent, and confused ; they let the fancy run on impertinent subjects and in impertinent words, thereby encouraging loose talk and distracting the hearers from true

---

[1] *Op. cit.*, III, 430.

devotion : such negligence in addressing God not only argues a
profane lack of respect for Him but relaxes the tension and weakens
the feelings of the hearers. A set form of prayers, on the contrary,
far from stinting the spirit, ensures greater concentration on the
essential part of praying, ' affection ', and thereby intensifies
devotion :

> As for a Set form, in which the words are ready prepared
> to our hands, the Soul has nothing to do, but to attend to
> the work of raising the Affections and Devotions, to go
> along with those words : So that all the Powers of the Soul
> are took up in applying the *Heart* to this great Duty ; and
> it is the Exercise of the *Heart* (as has been already shown)
> that is truly and properly *a praying by the Spirit* [1].

No wonder that South should have championed brevity ; " when
the matter is not commensurate to the words ", he said, " all speaking is but tautology ", while compression enhances the energy of
the thought or feeling,

> Devotion so managed, being like Water in a Well, where
> you have Fullness in a little Compass ; which surely is
> much nobler, than the same carried out into many petit,
> creeping Rivulets, with *length* and *shallowness* together.
> Let him who prays, bestow all that Strength, Fervour and
> Attention, upon Shortness and Significance, that would
> otherwise run out, and lose itself in length and luxuriance
> of Speech to no purpose [2].

Brevity and force, then, are South's ideal of style, and in this
sense he does condemn all ' rhetorications '. His insistence that
the words must be commensurate with the matter may be similar
to the recommendations of the Royal Society that the scientists
" deliver so many *things*, almost in an equal number of *words* " [3],
though South was no friend of the natural philosophers ; his ideals
may indeed be " definitely Senecan " [4]; but neither the influence
of Senecan models nor of Baconian research is sufficient to account
for his true originality. In fact, South speaks like an artist, wishing to impart ' Life, force, and beauty ' to all he says. Though
he is an enemy of all pitiful embellishments, he feels no such horror
as Baxter does for the sensuous delight given by Church music or

---

[1] See *A Discourse against long Extemporary Prayers* below.
[2] *Ibid.* (second sermon).
[3] Thomas SPRAT : *History of the Royal Society*, Section XX, *op. cit*, p. 113.
[4] G. WILLIAMSON, *op. cit.*, p. 266.

tor the ornaments of the Church, for, he says, " I cannot persuade myself that God ever designed his Church for a rude, naked, unbeautiful lump " [1] ; the beauties of the heavens and of the earth fill him with wonder at the variety of the gifts of God, even as do the plumes of the peacock :

> certainly we might live without the Plumes of Peacocks, and the curious Colour of Flowers ; without so many different *Odours*, so many several *Tastes*, and such an infinite Diversity of *Airs* and *Sounds*. But where would then be the Glory and Lustre of the Universe ? The Flourish and Gaiety of Nature [1] ?

Clearly, we have moved a long way from Wilkins ; if South is to be accounted an apostle of plainness, it is plainness with a difference, such a difference as between the clear but insipid prose of Wilkins's sermons and Dryden's dedication of *The Assignation* to Sir Charles Sedley.

South's repeated denunciations of vicious pulpit oratory suggest how hard it was to purify the dialect of the tribe. In 1670 Eachard ascribed the contempt of the clergy to their way of preaching. Besides rousing protests from several fellow Anglicans, his tract provoked James Arderne, a graduate of Christ's College, Cambridge, who became a chaplain to Charles II and later Dean of Chester, to write his *Directions Concerning the Matter and Stile of Sermons* (1671). In his plea for a clear and plain way of preaching Arderne follows Wilkins fairly closely, and only a few of his points need be mentioned here. First, he tells his reader that the occasion of his letter is the tract in which Eachard " had laid together the most ridiculous passages of Sermons, gathered for the most part, either from Non-Conformists, or Divines of other times " [2], thus laying the vices censured at the door of the Puritans and of older models. Second, he is more specific about the common speech which the preacher is to use, and his words echo such views of language as are expressed in Evelyn's letter to Sir Peter Wyche [3]. Next, he censures all prying into the ' abstrusest secrets ' of God's

---

[1] See *The Christian Pentecost*, printed below.

[2] *Directions Concerning the Matter and Stile of Sermons, written to W.S., a Young Deacon*, by J.A., D.D., 1671 ; ed. John Mackay, Luttrell Reprints no. 13, Oxford, 1952, p. 1.

[3] See J.E. SPINGARN : *Critical Essays of the Seventeenth Century*, Oxford, 1957, II, 310-13.

Word, obviously expatiating on the *Directions for Preaching* issued
in 1662 by the King.   Finally, and here he diverges from Wilkins,
he mentions a ' variety of useful figures ' which may be ' pleasant ',
though he cautions his friend not to use too many in his discourse ;
he is aware that metaphors are " wholly rejected by some ", but
to him they are blameable only when " either they are boldly hal'd
to our purpose " or " pil'd and stack'd to the dimensions of a lusty
Allegory " [1].   For each figure he discusses he gives similar, sensible
advice, such as : not to use ' synonimie ' in stating the proposition,
because this is ' incongruous to shortness ' ; to use antithesis with
discretion ; to avoid the repetition of words of the same sound,
though he does not censure other schemes of words.   About
' periods and numbers in speech ' he has little to say except that
the preacher must not be " anxiously carefull, how a sentence will
fall into exact measures and proportions : this is too delicate and
effeminate " [2].   On the whole, then, what Arderne recommends
is a slightly modified form of Wilkins's plainness, though his
Directions are too brief for us to judge how far they could have
encouraged a more lively style.   Arderne's advice is sober and
moderate, favouring no excess, not even excessive plainness.

Joseph Glanvill's advocacy of a plain style was part of his
vindication of the Church [3], and he repeatedly returned to the
attack, with varied emphasis as occasion demanded.   A strong
supporter of the Royal Society, he not only defended the new
philosophy but shared the scientists' stylistic ideals.   His main
target was religious enthusiasm and the vices in oratory associated
with it [4].   In his two chief tracts on preaching, both published in
1678, *An Essay Concerning Preaching* and *A Seasonable Defence
of Preaching and the Plain Way of it*, he strongly censured the
fantastic style of the Nonconformists [5] and recommended a clear
perspicuous method and a plain style.   Since his main purpose
throughout his works was to show that faith was consistent with

---

[1] *Op. cit.*, p. 24.
[2] p. 29.
[3] See J.I. COPE : *Joseph Glanvill, Anglican Apologist*, St. Louis, 1956.
[4] See, for instance, ' Antifanatick Theologie, and Free Philosophy in a
Continuation of the New Atlantis ', the 7th essay, in *Essays on Several Important
Subjects in Philosophy and Religion*, London, 1676.
[5] In 1661 he had praised Baxter in a letter. See COPE, *op. cit.*, pp. 6-7 :
" Like More, Stillingfleet, Tillotson, and so many ' Latitudinarians ', Glanvill
saw in Baxter a learned spirit of conciliation from the other side of the Acts
for conformity. "

reason [1], he distrusted all appeals to the passions and the imagination through airy mystical phrases ; but he was even more concerned to further a reasonable way of preaching tending to give
instruction in faith and the good life, for

> when men once ramble in the way of *phrases*, *metaphors*,
> and *conceits*, as they lose themselves, so they perfectly dazle
> and amaze those others whom they should instruct [2].

What he advocated, in fact, was the sober, practical way of the
Latitudinarians, who were then accused of gentilism and heathen
worship because they preached morality.   Yet, Glanvill argued,
since the great design of religion is to perfect human nature and
since Christianity is the height and perfection of morality, to disparage moral preaching is merely to disgrace true godliness and
encourage atheism :

> By which we see how ignorantly, and dangerously those
> people talk, that disparage morality as a dull, lame thing
> of no account, or reckoning.   Upon this the religion of the
> second table is by too many neglected ; and the whole
> mystery of the new Godliness is laid in *frequent hearing*,
> and *devout seraphick talk*, *luscious fancies*, *new lights*,
> *incomes*, *manifestations*, *indwellings*, *sealings*, and such like.
> Thus *antinomianism* and all kinds of *fanaticism* have made
> their way by the disparagement of morality... Yea, through
> the indiscretions, and inconsiderateness of some preachers,
> the fantastry and vain babble of others, and the general
> disposition of the people to admire what makes a great shew,
> and pretends to more than ordinary spirituality ; things,
> in many places, come to that pass, that those who teach
> Christian virtue and religion, in plainness and simplicity,
> without senseless phrases, and fantastic affectations, shall
> be reckoned for dry moralists, and such as understand
> nothing of the life, and *power of godliness*.   Yea, those
> people have been so long used to gibberish and canting,
> that they cannot understand plain sense [3].

Though Glanvill animadverted more often on the cant of the

---

[1] See, for instance, his 1670 sermon : *Defence of Reason in the Affairs of
Religion*, revised as *Agreement of reason and religion*, the 5th essay in *Essays*
(1676).
[2] *Earnest Invitation to the Sacrament* (1672), quoted by COPE, *op. cit.*,
pp. 159-60.
[3] Sermon on *The Way of Happiness* (first published in 1670), in *Some
Discourses, Sermons and Remains of the Rev. Mr. Jos. Glanvill...*, published
by Ant. Horneck, London, 1681, pp. 73-74.

enthusiasts, he also censured the witty preachers whose vain affectations contributed to the contempt of the clergy. Thus in a sermon published in 1676, *The Churches prayer and complaint of contempt from prophane and fanatick Enemies*, he said :

> There is nothing by which some preachers have more exposed religion and themselves, than by propounding other ends, and such mean ones as gaining the reputation of being witty, eloquent, or learned : for when they miss their aim (as they always do with the wise) they fall under extreem contempt with them. The affectations of words, and meta-phors, and cadencies, and ends of Greek, and Latin, are now the scorn of the judicious, and as much despised and (almost) as generally as they deserve. They are banished from conversation, and are not endured in common matters ; for shame then let us not retain them in our pulpits and defile sacred subjects with them [1].

As one reads Glanvill's sermons one cannot help wishing that he had been granted time to revise them as he did many of his other works, which gained in plainness and cogency as the later versions became shorter [2]. As the above quotations must have made clear, this champion of plainness and perspicuity is fairly prolix, so that one wonders what he regarded as the due mean between fullness and closeness. Still, it is interesting to note that the crusade for retrenching all superfluities and affected phrases was mainly waged by men who were in touch with the educated circles of the metro-polis, where such flourishes had been banished from the con-versation of gentlemen. Glanvill's remark is not unlike that of La Bruyère about the false taste now out of fashion at Court but still relished by *le peuple*. The witty or the florid style of preach-ing must have lingered in some places, or the reformers would hardly have felt it necessary to refer so often to this false kind of eloquence. It is surely an ironic comment on the taste in oratory that Glanvill's *Discourses, Sermons and Remains* were published

---

[1] *Ibid.*, pp. 258-9.
[2] This is notably the case for *The Vanity of Dogmatizing*, published in 1661 ; revised as *Scepsis Scientifica* (1665), and later compressed into the first essay in *Essays on Several Important Subjects*, 1676. It has been argued that his gradual relinquishing of florid style testified to the impact of the Royal Society's recommendations for style. Yet, as one compares the three versions one also realizes that the gradual moving towards the essay form must have influenced the style. The same is true of *Plus Ultra*, first published in 1668 and later included in the *Essays*.

by Anthony Horneck, Preacher at the Savoy, who wrote a preface for this collection in a flowery and often absurd style. Glanvill's emphasis on plainness, however, results less from his taste in style than from his wish to instruct effectively: the preacher must be as plain as he can both in doctrine and in expressions; he must speak " in the proper, natural, easie way " so as to instruct " all sorts ", and his ' discoveries ' must be " in clear, facile, and distinct methods, not involved in confusions, nor spun out in divisions, or numerous particulars " [1]. This is the practical preacher speaking; one, we guess, who would hardly have understood South's theory of forcefulness, much less have shared his admiration for the plumes of the peacock. But Glanvill's audience at the Abbey Church at Bath, and his experience of preaching in the country, was also different from South's.

The *Essay Concerning Preaching* [2] rehearses the false tastes in pulpit oratory against which Glanvill sets his directions: polite and ingenious discourses with well-chosen words and even periods; witty sermons; new notions and learned observations; quotations and sentences out of the Fathers and the philosophers; numerous texts of Scripture; ' taking phrases ' and passionate outcries, or conversely dry arguments. To this he opposes his four-fold recommendation: that the sermon be plain, practical, methodical and affectionate [3]. Compared with Arderne's *Directions*, which obviously inspired Glanvill, and which, as we saw, slightly diverged from Wilkins's manual, Glanvill's tract is more detailed and more practical, and it grounds the—limited—use of rhetoric in the need to move the hearers' affections. His main purpose is to ensure instruction, by avoiding mysterious notions and speculations of theology; hence " plainness is for ever the best eloquence " [4]. By this he means a style free from hard words, deep and mysterious notions, affected rhetorications and phantastical phrases. Since the sermon ought to be practical the method must be natural and obvious, and not include too many particulars. In manner as well as in style proper the ideal is a due mean between ' tedious prolixity ' and ' too much conciseness '.

[1] *The Churches prayer, op. cit.*, pp. 259-60.
[2] (Joseph GLANVILL): *An Essay Concerning Preaching, Written for the Direction of a young divine and useful also for the people in order to profitable hearing*, London, 1678.
[3] Cp. with Wilkins's ' plain, full, wholesome, affectionate '.
[4] p. 25.

A sermon, however, is meant to move as well as to expound truths, and this will be achieved by means of " figures, and earnestness and passionate representations "[1]. For this use of rhetoric Glanvill finds precedent in God's own schemes of speech to raise our affections when He condescends to speak to our capacity. Compared with South's plea for rhetoric[2], Glanvill's defence of it sounds only half-hearted ; it is as though the preacher were to speak ' plainly' through most of his sermon, and suddenly become earnest and passionate in the application and exhortation. This is, in fact, what Glanvill does in his own sermons ; towards the conclusion of these, as J.I. Cope remarks, " the logical parade of propositions and recommendations which move so soporifically past the modern reader disappears, and the ' motive' comes on with a rush of rhetoric "[3]. South's conception is much closer to the Renaissance notion of ' clearness', it is in fact grounded in what one might call a unified or organic view of art, whereas Glanvill, the zealous defender of natural philosophy, envisages on the one hand, clear distinct ideas to strike the mind, and on the other, figures to move the affections. As such, Glanvill's rhetoric is much nearer to the rhetoric of ornaments, which South would not have countenanced. His—implicit—view that the two can work independently of each other reveals the danger lurking in the current phrase ' the dress of thought ', and suggests the rhymed commonplaces and false poetic diction which mediocre neo-classical poets—or critics—were apt to mistake for poetry[4].

This appears best in Glanvill's vindication of wit towards the end of the *Essay*, when he lists the various defects of preaching, among which he mentions ' witticizing' and its opposite, dullness or want of wit. Here he clearly paraphrases Hobbes on wit and fancy, but when he leaves his master he only succeeds in confusing

---

[1] p. 56.

[2] In a sermon preached in 1667 South said that " the grace of God is pleased to move us by ways suitable to our nature, and to sanctify these suitable inferior helps to greater and higher purposes " (*op. cit.*, I, 284).

[3] *Op. cit.*, p. 164.

[4] J.I. Cope draws attention to the shift from ' clearness' to ' perspicuity', mainly under the impact on literary theory of Hobbes's distinction between wit and fancy (*op. cit.*, p. 146). It is only fair to add, however, that Dryden no less than Pope, and to a lesser extent Johnson, were out to show that wit includes both judgement and fancy, or, to use Hobbes's terms, wit and fancy. Pope's refusal to alter the couplet which Dennis criticized for its ambiguity shows that the ambiguity was deliberate (see *An Essay On Criticism*, ed. E. Audra and Aubrey Williams, London, 1961, Introduction, p. 213).

the issues, and reveals his utter inability to grasp South's notion
of wit as a severe and manly thing :

> I do not by this reprehend all wit whatsoever in Preaching,
> nor anything that is truly such : for true wit is a perfection
> in our faculties, chiefly in the understanding and imagin-
> ation ; Wit in the understanding is a sagacity to find out
> the nature, relations, and consequences of things ; Wit in
> the imagination, is a quickness in the phancy to give things
> proper images ; now the more of these in sermons, the
> more of judgment and life ; and without wit of these kinds
> Preaching is dull, and unedifying. The Preacher should
> endeavour to speak sharp, and quick thoughts, and to set
> them out in lively colours ; this is proper, grave, and manly
> wit, but the other, that which consists in inversion of
> sentences, and playing with words, and the like, is vile
> and contemptible fooling...
> I have this to advertise more under this head, that even
> the wit that is true, that may be used, and ought to be
> endeavoured, should not be hunted after out of the road [1].

If for him wit that is true may be found ' out of the road ', then
decoration is not far away [2]. It may be surprising, too, to hear
this prolix writer recommend sharp and quick thoughts set out in
lively colours. The explanation is probably to be found in the
other tract he published the same year, *A Seasonable Defence of
Preaching. And the Plain Way of it.* Here Glanvill again contends that the plain way is the best, such as that used by " another
sort of learned men, whose design has been to study things ", i.e.
the natural philosophers, and whose learning and knowledge enable
them " to speak with the most judgment, propriety and plainness " [3].
His defence of preaching, however, is prompted by the fact that
it is hard for Anglican ministers to contend for an audience with
the Dissenting preachers, who draw large crowds through their
eloquence and fine language [4]. No wonder, then, if at the time
he could encourage a kind of liveliness that was obviously above
his own reach.

---

[1] *Op. cit.,* pp. 71-73.

[2] J.I. Cope interprets this passage as meaning that " ' wit ' welcomes imagination as a necessary vehicle for its full expression ", *op. cit.,* p. 165 ; but he
does not quote the second paragraph.

[3] *A Seasonable Defence of Preaching. And the Plain Way of it, A Dialogue,*
London, (1678) 1703, pp. 47-48.

[4] *Ibid.,* p. 41.

Glanvill's chief merit is to have contributed to convey ideas originating in better minds than his own. He could be at the same time a propagandist for the 'Platonic' philosophy, for the Royal Society, and for the Church. His views on pulpit oratory, though far from original and indeed often confusing [1], are the more characteristic of the general drift towards 'plainness', a term of praise which by then was used rather loosely to refer to the mathematical plainness recommended by the Royal Society as well as to the polished conversation of gentlemen.

It has been suggested that Glanvill's face-about on the use of rhetoric may have been due to the influence of Rapin's *Réflexions sur l'éloquence de ce temps* (1672) [2]. Though this seems unnecessary in view of Glanvill's wish to counter the attraction of the Dissenters, the eagerness with which Rapin's book was seized upon in England as soon as it appeared illumines one of the ways in which cross-fertilization works in literature. The whole movement for the reform of pulpit oratory in England had its roots in circumstances specifically English, and the evils it tried to eradicate had been aggraved by religious developments which had no counterpart in France. Yet, when the *Réflexions* appeared in 1672, it must have seemed to be expressing just what many people in England were feeling—even though it did so in a more polished form than many of them had been able or willing to achieve. In the same year two independent translations were published [3], one version obviously hurried through the press in order to meet the demand of the public before the other appeared [4]. If the teachings of the French Jesuit had been heeded by preachers in England they would certainly have conduced to a more polished and graceful style than that of the ministers who left their mark on the

---

[1] The confusion or loose use of words appears, for instance, in his remark that fullness of sense and compactness of writing are real excellencies, " very proper and taking, to the wise especially " (but since hearers of sermons are mixt people, " a certain laxness of style is necessary for them "), and in his condemnation of what he calls " being too full, and close ", where fullness and compactness apparently represent one and the same defect. *Essay Concerning Preaching*, pp. 63-64.

[2] R.F. JONES, ' The Attack on Pulpit Eloquence in the Restoration ', *JEGP*, XXX (1931), reprinted in *The Seventeenth Century*, 1951, pp. 138-9. J.I. Cope, however, thinks that Glanvill's use of rhetoric in his own sermons " obviates the necessity of attributing Glanvill's defence of rhetoric to Rapin's *Réflexions* ", *op. cit.*, p. 164, n. 57.

[3] *Reflections upon the Eloquence of these Times*, London, 1672 ; *Reflections upon the Use of Eloquence of these Times*, Oxford, 1672.

[4] See F. MADAN, *Oxford Books*, Oxford, 1895-1931, no. 2941.

succeeding age [1]. It is doubtful whether Rapin exerted any direct
influence on pulpit oratory in England ; his influence on critics
and wits was none the less pervasive [2], and soon hardly to be
distinguished from that of Boileau and other French critics. To
this extent, then, he may be said to have contributed to further
the ideals recommended by the advocates of the ' plain ' style.

The many defects which the reformers denounced were slow
to disappear ; that similar advice had to be given to young divines
in Ireland half a century later, appears from Swift's *Letter to a
Young Gentleman entered into Holy Orders.* This tract, R.F. Jones
remarked, " would hardly have been out of place had it appeared
in 1670 instead of 1721 " [3]. Indeed many of Swift's recommendations echo Eachard's, notably his wish that the young divine
should apply himself to the study of the English language [4], while
most of the abuses he censures recall those of the preceding age [5],
though he is heartily glad that Greek and Latin have been driven
out of the pulpit [6]. More important, because it is characteristic of
the trend in Anglican preaching since the Restoration, Swift prefers
a plain convincing argument to the ' art of wetting the handker-
chief ' ; indeed, he is out of conceit with the moving manner of
speaking and advises the young clergyman to

> beware of letting the pathetick part swallow up the rational :
> for I suppose philosophers have long agreed, that passion
> should never prevail over reason [7].

' Pathetic preaching ' was definitely unsavoury to most Anglican

---

[1] And just as different from South's severe and manly wit. Indeed, one
imagines that Rapin would have been even more shocked by South's sallies
and vigour of speech than were some of his contemporaries in England.

[2] See, for instance, Dryden's references to him and Rymer's translation
of his *Reflections on Aristotle's Treatise of Poesie* (1674).

[3] *Op. cit.,* p. 142.

[4] *A Letter to a Young Gentleman entered into Holy Orders,* by a person
of quality (dated January 9, 1719/20), in SWIFT : *Prose Works,* ed. Herbert
Davis, IX : *Irish Tracts 1720-1723 And Sermons,* Oxford, 1948, p. 65. See
also Gilbert BURNET : *A Discourse of Pastoral Care* (1692) and *Directions for
the Conversation of the Clergy, Collected from the Visitation Charges of the
Rt Rev. Father in God, Edward Stillingfleet, Late Ld Bp of Worcester* (1710).

[5] See the 1709 ms. version of Pope's *Essay on Criticism,* ll. 488/9 :

> Ev'n Pulpits pleas'd with merry Puns of yore ;
> Now All are banish'd to th' Hibernian Shore !

Pope's Essay on Criticism 1709, ed. R.M. Schmitz, St. Louis, 1962, p. 62. The
lines were omitted in the 1711 edition.

[6] p. 75.   [7] p. 70.

divines after the Restoration, associated as it was with enthusiasm and ' preaching by the Spirit '; as Swift observed, this

> was in esteem and practice among some Church divines, as well as among all the preachers and hearers of the Fanatick or Enthusiastic Strain [1].

In spite of these few exceptions, strong arguments rather than moving of the passions characterized Anglican sermons after the Restoration, while many Dissenters continued to appeal to the ' affections '. This became the distinguishing mark of the two parties, or at least, it became the habit for members of the Established Church to brand all the fanatics' preaching as an enthusiastic strain. Henceforth Puritans were associated with canting, while Anglicans appeared as the upholders of the plain style. The link between ' rationalism ' and the plain style appears nowhere better than in pulpit oratory, since the new style of sermons, i.e. both the manner and the style proper, was grounded on arguments which in the main distinguished Conformists from Nonconformists [2]: the strong stand on reason and free inquiry, and the rejection of enthusiasm; the belief that the main truths of Christianity are expressed plainly in Scripture and can be conveyed in plain language [3]; the ban on doctrinal controversies which might perplex the hearers needlessly and shake their faith; the stress on edifying doctrine rather than speculation and on practical rather than notional Christianity. Not all Anglicans put the same emphasis on each of these points, but they all agreed in the main, while the general rules laid down in the 1662 *Directions for Preaching* furthered the same ends. These beliefs determined the scope, design, and style of sermons. If the fantastic jargon of the Puritans comes so often under the Anglicans' fire, it is because it is part and parcel of the fanatics' religious doctrine, and highlights the dangerous tendency of their teachings. Butler's knight " could not ope His mouth, but out there flew a Trope ", and this could have been taken

---

[1] p. 78. Yet Swift said: " I have been better entertained, and more informed by a chapter in the Pilgrim's Progress, than by a long discourse upon the will and the intellect, and simple or complex ideas " (p. 77).

[2] At this stage all kinds of Nonconformists are included in the Anglicans' references to them.

[3] Cf. Swift: " a divine hath nothing to say to the wisest congregations of any parish in this Kingdom, which he may not express in a manner to be understood by the meanest among them. And this assertion must be true, or else God requires from us more than we are able to perform ", *op. cit.*, p. 66.

as a text by all those who wrote upon the Puritans' preaching after the Restoration.

Apart from South's sermon on the imposture of words [1], in which the corruption of language is shown to be both the inevitable effect and the cause of loose thinking, the best tract linking doctrinal differences with the use of language is *A Friendly Debate between a Conformist and a Non-Conformist* (1669) by 'a lover of the City and of pure religion', i.e. Simon Patrick, who was to become a Bishop under William. The tract was clearly intended to encourage Dissenters to attend Conformist services rather than have ministers break the law of the land by residing in London [2]. To achieve this purpose Patrick set out to meet the Nonconformists' objections to Anglican services and sermons. The first and main objection is that divines of the Church of England preach " only rational discourses " ; this Patrick counters by showing that rational and spiritual are not opposed : only carnal reason, i.e. reason guided by fleshly lusts, is opposed to spiritual reason, i.e. guided by the gospel of Christ. For the Conformist, direct inspiration by the Holy Ghost was only vouchsafed to the Apostles ; now men can only interpret Scripture by the light of reason ; the private illumination claimed by some to guide their interpretation cannot be distinguished from mere fancy and therefore cannot be trusted. Next, the Nonconformist maintains that his minister moves the affections better ; but, Patrick answers, there are two ways of moving the affections, through the senses and the imagination or through reason and judgement " to engage the affections to its side " :

> If you can be moved by such strength of reason as can conquer the judgment, and so pass to demand submission to the affections, you may find power enough in our pulpits.

If, on the other hand, you expect to be moved

> by melting tones, pretty similitudes, riming sentences, kind and loving smiles, and sometimes dismally sad looks [3],

---

[1] Printed below.

[2] (Simon PATRICK): *A Friendly Debate betwixt two neighbours. The One a Conformist, the other a Non-Conformist. About several weighty matters. Published for the benefit of this City. By a lover of it and of pure religion.* London, 1669. The Conventicle Act had been passed in 1664, and the Five-Mile Act in 1665.

[3] *Ibid.*, p. 16, 15.

then you will seldom find such kind of preaching in the Church, where all kinds of enthusiasm are discouraged. On the other hand, he accuses the Nonconformist ministers of using " new minted words which people take to conceal great mysteries ".

The distinction is therefore clear between a method and style that aims at edification through enlightenment, and emotional appeal by means of mysterious terms and obscure notions. Enlightenment *vs* mystery, rationalism *vs.* obscurantist emotionalism, clear thinking *vs* effusions of the Spirit, such are the distinguishing marks of the two groups. As one reads the religious literature of the Restoration one realizes all the better how powerful was the need for light and order, a need born of the prevailing chaos in the previous age but rendered all the more acute by the continued exploitation, in some quarters, of confusion in thought and language. The triumph of neo-classical standards in literature was, one feels, the expression of the new rationalism on which the Church took its stand in its fight against enthusiasm, as much as of the changed sensibility or of the taste fostered by French models.

Patrick's insistence on reason against inspiration is the more significant as his adversary is not a member of an extreme Sect [1] ; and he is no less outspoken on the need for order and decency, whether in prayers or in ceremonies. To the Nonconformist's plea for praying by the Spirit, that is, effusions in extempore prayers under the motion of the Spirit, he replies that there is no such thing as prayer immediately inspired by the Holy Ghost :

> The Spirit of God does not suggest to any of us, when we pray, the very matter and words, which we utter. If you pretend to this, then those prayers are as much the Word of God as any of David's Psalms, or as any part of the Bible ; and being written from your mouths, may become canonical Scripture [2].

Forms in prayers and ceremonies are lawful, not because they are commanded by God, but because laws are necessary " for the convenient, orderly, and decent worship of God " [3]. Nor does this take away Christian liberty, unless Christians are to be restrained

---

[1] Patrick reminds the Nonconformist of the time when their ministry would not hear of liberty of conscience and refers to the letter of the five members, i.e. the plea for accommodation of the non-separating Congregationalists presented to Parliament in 1643 in *An Apologetical Narration.* The Nonconformist answers that he is not ready to tolerate all Sects.
[2] p. 88.   [3] p. 104.

in nothing, even for public order's sake. By thus using Hooker's argument for ceremonies—over against those who in mid-century had claimed divine authority for them—Patrick and all the Restoration Anglicans emphasized the agreement of the laws of God and of natural law, while the stress on orderly and decent worship is characteristic of their sense of form and preference for clear structures.

Finally, the Nonconformist objects that Anglican sermons only give moral teaching, whereas he expects to hear doctrine expounded in the pulpit. For Patrick, as for his fellow-Anglicans, the two cannot be separated, even less opposed, and doctrinal points that have no bearing on the Christian life are of no interest. This is a tenet which the Church emphasized strongly after the Restoration, in order particularly to oppose Antinomianism, which the Nonconformists' stress on doctrine, the power of godliness, or regeneration, was felt to encourage. Hence, though many Dissenters were by no means Antinomians this was a charge repeatedly levelled against them. Patrick did not say that preaching should be restricted to practice, but like other moderate divines of the Church of England, he certainly favoured moral or practical preaching. This was a characteristic of the men who came to be known as Latitudinarians, and whose principles and practice were defended by Edward Fowler. It is worth noting that both these defenders of the Latitudinarians were to become bishops under William [1].

Like Patrick's *Friendly Debate* the year before, Fowler's tract is intended to promote peace and understanding among Protestants for, he says, " it is high time to be reconciled to moderation and sobriety, to lay aside our uncharitable and (therefore) unchristian heats against each other " [2]. Though the main burden of the argument is a refutation of the Puritans' accusations, Fowler also refers to witticisms directed against these moderate divines from the " Stately Oxonian Theatre ", that is by some High-Churchman, probably South. The main accusation is that Latitudinarians preach reason as the basis of religion, and Fowler shows at great length

---

[1] Many Latitudinarians, notably Tillotson and Burnet, became bishops after the Revolution.

[2] *The Principles and Practices of Certain Moderate Divines of the Church of England*, op. cit. To the Reader. For a similar account of the Latitudinarians, see *Burnet's History of His Own Time*, London, 1724, 1734, Book II.

that reason can be no better employed than here since it is through reason that men know Scripture to be the Word of God. For him, " reason is that power, whereby men are enabled to draw clear inferences from evident principles " [1], and these evident principles are implanted in man : the law of nature is the law of God, though it needs to be perfected by the revealed law, or Word of God. To assert the reasonableness of Christianity is not to equate it with natural religion since reason alone cannot prompt to us most of the duties enjoined by the Gospel [2] ; though faith is consistent with reason, some things exceed our apprehension : the moderate divines preach the reasonableness of faith but they do not demonstrate the consistency of mysteries with our reason as the schoolmen tried to do, thereby rendering many of these mysteries doubtful [3]. It was a central tenet of the Church of England, of the High-Churchmen no less than of the Latitudinarians, that the truths of religion are consistent with reason, though sometimes above the reach of human reason, or, as Tillotson and Stillingfleet never tired of saying, some things in religion are beyond reason, but never against reason.

Attacks on the moderates as mere rational preachers are aimed at their doctrine and at their style in preaching ; this, Fowler shows, is inevitable since the one follows from the other : they endeavour to make the doctrine of the gospel easy and intelligible in order to teach men what to believe and how to live accordingly. All doctrine essential to salvation is expressed perspicuously in Scripture, and so are all necessary duties. The moderate divines are therefore

> far from those mens untoward genius, that delight to exercise their wits in finding out mystical and cabbalistic senses in the plainest parts of Scripture, and in turning everything almost into allegories [4].

They are called by their adversaries ' men of dry reason ' because in preaching they endeavour to conquer their hearers' judgement and to convince them of duty by solid reasons ; they may, indeed, be opposed ' to spiritual preachers ', i.e. to irrational ones [5]. They are further accused of being moral preachers, that is, of preaching

---

[1] p. 70. This, incidentally, reveals the shift from Hooker's right reason to the Restoration concept of reason as discursive reason.
[2] p. 86.   [3] pp. 93-97.   [4] p. 105.   [5] p. 112.

mere morality. This is because in handling the doctrine of justifying faith they make obedience to follow it ; in handling the doctrine
of imputed righteousness, they show the absolute necessity of an
inherent right in the creature ; and in handling the doctrine of
God's grace, they show the indispensableness of men's endeavours [1].
In other words, their preaching is grounded in the belief that
" faith justifies as it implies obedience " [2], an altogether different
doctrine from the Papists' justification by works, and quite consistent with the belief in the freeness of God's grace [3]. In refuting
these accusations Fowler is led to give a detailed exposition of
the Anglican doctrine of justifying faith, imputed righteousness
and God's grace [4]. These were points at issue between the Church
of England [5] and the Puritans, and differences on such doctrinal
matters would necessarily issue in a different method, style, and
purpose in teaching, no less than did the distinction between rational
inquiry and interpretation by the inner light. Hence the stress
laid by many Puritans on the ' moving part ' of oratory : Swift's
dislike of " pathetic preaching " reveals more than the classicist's
repugnance for emotional appeal ; it expresses the High-Churchman's opposition to enthusiastic doctrines and modes of teaching.
The Latitudinarian Tillotson is no less opposed to such notions of
sudden conversions by the Spirit, unless the working of the Spirit
is shown to effect lasting moral regeneration, for, as he repeatedly
emphasizes, true faith issues in works, and to entertain the doctrine
of Christ does not mean to entertain our minds with bare speculations, but to better our lives.

The 1662 *Directions for Preaching* had enjoined that ministers
refrain from discussing " the deep points of election and reprobation
together with the incomprehensible manner of the concurrence of
God's free grace and man's free will, and such other controversies
as depend thereupon " [6]. These points of doctrine could not,
however, be altogether ignored, especially in sermons addressed to
congregations aware of the controversies about them. And many
must have been familiar with the points at issue so that it was
all the more necessary to define the Church's doctrine. Barrow,

---

[1] pp. 114-17.   [2] p. 159.   [3] p. 176.   [4] From. p. 117 tot p. 189.
    [5] Which was still nominally Calvinistic. See Article XVII of the Thirty-
Nine Articles.
    [6] *Directions, op. cit.*, point 2.

South, and Tillotson did preach on justifying faith. None of them, however, peered into the secret manner of the concurrence of God's free grace and man's free will; they only showed that the two were perfectly consistent with each other, and were indispensable for salvation.

Part Two of Fowler's *Principles and Practices* is devoted to the moderate divines' opinions in matters of doctrine, that is, to the doctrines of justifying faith, election, reprobation, and free will, which distinguished the Church of England from the Puritan Calvinists. Towards the end, however, he returns to the fundamental concept of free inquiry based on reason and to the moderate divines' rejection of any pretence at infallibility, whether by direct inspiration from the Spirit or by an infallible judge such as the Roman Church claims to have. For him, as indeed for all Restoration Anglicans, it is clear that God " intended no infallible judge but our own reason, assisted with his blessing " [1]. Fowler thereby defines the so-called *via media* of the Church of England, between the two extremes of enthusiasm and of the infallible Pope or Councils.

While all this may be said to define the Anglican position rather than the Latitudinarians as such, the latter were characterized by their moderation towards men of other persuasions, provided of course these did not openly contradict Scripture [2]. In matters of discipline too, with which Fowler deals in Part III, the Latitudinarians were moderate, and here they parted company with many of their Anglican brethren, for, as Fowler says, " they did not unchurch other churches " [3]. Others, notably South, ' the scourge of the fanatics ', used all their power to oppose any measure tending to accommodation with the Dissenters; some indeed could never be reconciled to the Act of Toleration [4] and did their best to foil any scheme of comprehension [5].

---

[1] p. 306.

[2] Their belief that the Roman Church did contradict Scripture accounts for the violence of a notably temperate man like Tillotson. See his sermons on *The Protestant Religion Vindicated* and his *Discourse on Transubstantiation*, printed below.

[3] p. 323.

[4] See South's sermon on *Galat.*, II, 5, in *op. cit.*, vol. V (sermon 12).

[5] See Beveridge's sermon to Convocation in 1689, when the King's scheme for Comprehension was presented to the clergy: *Concio ad Synodum*, London, 1689.

It may be noted that an early eighteenth-century *Defence of the Doctrine and Discipline of the Church of England* [1] rehearses almost the same accusations of the Nonconformists against " our dry, moral sermons ", but also remarks that they too have given up their fantastic style. Perhaps the Puritans' temper had changed; perhaps the repeated attacks on their jargon had put a curb on their fancy; perhaps ridicule had at long last effected a reformation while Butler's rough knocks had only amused the limited circles of the polite world. If ridicule was an effective weapon, the tract that has the highest claim is doubtless the anonymous *The Scotch Presbyterian Eloquence* (1692), which pretends to offer sayings of the most elegant kind collected from sermons. Section I, ' The true character of the Presbyterian Pastors and people in Scotland ', covers the well-known points: their contempt for mere morality; their fondness for the most mysterious chapters of *Ezekiel*, *Daniel* or *Revelation*; their Antinomianism; their ' desperate doctrines ' of election and reprobation, which " make their fellows distracted "; and above all their way of preaching:

> The most of their sermons are nonsensick raptures, the abuse of mystic divinity, in canting and confounded vocables, oft-times stuffed with impertinent and base similes and always with homely, course, and ridiculous expressions, very unsuitable to the gravity and solemnity that becomes divinity. They are for the most part upon *Believe, believe*; and mistaking faith for a meer recumbency, they value no works but such as tend to propagate presbytery. When they speak of Christ, they represent him as a gallant, courting and kissing, by their fulsome, amorous discourses on the mysterious parables of the Canticles... Some of them have an odd way of acting in the pulpit, personating discourses often by way of dialogue betwixt them and the devil [2].

While Section II, ' Containing some expressions of their printed books ', mostly illustrates the kinds of arguments the Presbyterians conduct, Section III, ' Containing Notes of the Presbyterian Sermons taken in writing from their mouths ', and Section IV, ' Containing some few expressions in the Presbyterian Prayers ', amply illustrate

---

[1] William NICHOLS: *A Defence of the Doctrine and Discipline of the Church of England*, London, 1715.

[2] *The Scotch Presbyterian Eloquence, or, The Foolishness of their Teaching discovered from their books, sermons, and prayers* (by Jacob Curate), London, 1692, pp. 22-23.

the kind of foolish language and ridiculous similes current among
them.   No doubt, the writer is having great fun and may have
added a few touches of his own to the actual expressions taken
from the Presbyterians' mouths ; but unless there was some basis
for this the book would have been ignored, and it was promptly
answered.   This long list of illustrations (from page 97 to page
126) brings home to us not only the extent to which fancy could
be let loose in such sermons, but the kind of religious edification
these may have brought to the hearers.   For all the author's possible
exaggeration, the pamphlet makes us realize what lay behind the
Anglicans' relentless denunciation of the fanatics' jargon and of
their doctrine of the indwelling spirit.   Compared to this the
dryest of rational sermons must have been welcome, and one can
easily understand Tillotson's revulsion from the ' bold sallies of
enthusiasm ' he heard at Whitehall on the fast-day after Cromwell's death, when John Owen, Thomas Goodwin and Peter Sterry
were gathered round the new Protector :

> God was in a manner reproached with the deceased Protec-
> tor's services, and challenged for taking him away so soon.
> Dr. Goodwin, who had pretended to assure him in a prayer,
> a very few minutes before he expired, that he was not to
> die, had now the assurance to say to God, " Thou hast
> deceived us, and we were deceived ".   And Mr. Sterry,
> praying for Richard, used these indecent words, next to
> blasphemy—" Make him the brightness of the father's glory,
> and the express image of his person " [1].

Since both Tillotson and Burnet, who reported the story, were ever
friendly to the Dissenters and actively promoted schemes for comprehension, we may trust their testimony that the best among the
Puritans could be bold with their Maker and ' impertinent ' in their
sallies.   In the circumstances, the great improvement in pulpit
oratory which Birch would have us ascribe wholly to Tillotson,
was bound to be in the direction of reasonableness, decorum and
plainness.

---

[1] BIRCH, op. cit., p. xii, quoting Burnet's History of His Own Time (Bk. I,
in finem).

CHAPTER TWO

ANGLICAN RATIONALISM
IN THE SEVENTEENTH CENTURY

After the Restoration most Anglican divines preached by Explication, Confirmation, and Application. Their sermons began with a brief introduction in which the meaning of the text was made clear from its context ; sometimes a few words might need further explication, by reference to the original or to the Greek translation or by the analogy of faith, i.e. by comparison with catechetical doctrines. This first part might vary according to the circumstances, to the audience addressed or to the text chosen for explication, but in no case would this lead to over-subtle exegesis or crumbling of the text, for the emphasis was always on the general drift of the passage, its plain sense, and its direct bearing on some central points of doctrine and use (or on the occasion). Next, they resolved the text into a few propositions stated clearly and numbered at the outset of the development. Such a method, which Taine called " un squelette avec toutes ses attaches grossièrement visibles " [1], resulted from their wish to show that the doctrine was clearly implied in the text, not a ' cunning observation ' for which the Scripture words were merely a pretext (which, they said, the Puritans were fond of doing). In thus laying their plan bare before their hearers they made sure that the people would grasp the general drift of the argument and follow the development stage by stage ; however irritating this may be to the modern reader, it was a necessary reaction against the inevitable obfuscation of the central truths of Christianity which, they believed, resulted from much Puritan preaching. It should be noted also that in some sermons, addressed to a more refined audience, the skeleton was not made so visible, though the structure was no less clear [2]. The method is most tedious when the same text was developed in

---

[1] *Op. cit.*, III, 267.
[2] See, for instance, the 30 January sermon by South, printed below.

successive sermons, and the argument set out in previous parts was rehearsed before the preacher proceeded to the next point, particularly if each sermon was fairly short [1]. Such was the price to be paid if the congregation was to be edified by clear exposition of doctrine. The same method was usually applied in setting forth the *quod sit* and *cur sit* in the confirmation, which would be based on human as well as on divine testimony. Some preachers might depend more on the one than on the other; some might use testimony for illustration more than for demonstration, but amplification came to be used more sparingly and the stress was laid more on demonstration. This would mostly take into account ' the reason of the thing ', the testimony of Scripture, and the agreement with natural reason. By using such proofs the preachers emphasized the consistency of reason and faith, for it was a central point in their teaching that religion is reasonable, particularly that the Protestant religion can stand the test of reason [2] and that free inquiry is the basis of true faith. They might not all have agreed with Milton that a man may be a heretic in the truth though his belief be true, if he holds it only upon authority; but they did assert that implicit faith is not true faith and they encouraged rational examination of the basic principles of religion.

' Reason ' might mean different things to different men. For some, like Edward Fowler [3], it might be little more than discursive reason, which draws inferences from first principles. For others, like South, it is the principle whereby we discover both truth and goodness, at once an intellectual and a moral faculty, a guide to truth and conduct, since it shows us the real nature of things and thereby determines the choices of the will. South, like the Christian humanists, believed that truth and goodness are inherent in the things themselves, and he strongly opposed the relativist conception of morality which Hobbes had propounded [4]; for him reason conforms to the nature of things, and distinguishes between right and wrong as well as between true and false. He does not, like the Cambridge Platonists, insist that reason needs to be exercised by

---

[1] See, for instance, Tillotson's sermons on Regeneration, printed below.
[2] See, for instance, Tillotson's *The Religion of Protestants Vindicated*, in *The Works of the Most Reverend Dr. John Tillotson*, 8th ed., London, 1720, I, 564, ser. 27.
[3] See quotation 1, p. 69.
[4] See his sermons on *Isa*, V. 20, *The Fatal Imposture, and Force of Words*, printed below.

virtue before it can attain to truth ; but he does stress that depravity obscures reason and makes it unable to grasp truth and goodness. With him, then, ' reason ' comes nearest to the Renaissance
concept of right reason [1].

The shades of the Cambridge Platonists [2] sometimes seem to
hover in the background of Tillotson's thought—as Burnet reminds
us, " there was a Set of as extraordinary Persons, in the University
where he was formed, as perhaps any Age has produced " [3]—and
he sometimes refers to the Candle of the Lord in terms that suggest
their teachings ; but one need only put beside his sermons those
of the Platonist John Smith to realize how far the concept has been
emasculated. Though Tillotson emphasized that a Protestant does
not receive his faith upon authority but assents to the reasonableness of the truths of Christianity, he would not have approved
Milton's plea that we use that light which was given us in order
to " discover onward things more remote from our knowledge ".
Tillotson's reason, in fact, has neither the vigour of Milton's
intellectual ray, nor the effulgence of the Platonists' divine sun-
beam. It is hardly more, indeed, than the rational faculty that
discovers the agreement between truths and tests the evidence.
If it cannot altogether be equated with mere discursive reason, it
is because for him, as for most Anglicans, reason is also the faculty
in which are lodged the prime truths implanted in man by God,
the ' connate ' notions on which they ground their argument for
religion.

For Barrow, the mathematician, the axioms are no less rational
than the corollaries inferred from them ; he too defends Christianity as a rational system resting on prime truths and deduced by
the evidence of reason. His arguments are not unlike those of
Descartes, but to these he adds the proofs from the visible world,
whose order and beauty argue the existence of God and His
perfections [4] ; his defence of Christianity most clearly anticipates

[1] See Robert HOOPES : *Right Reason in the English Renaissance*, Cambridge
(Mass.), 1962.
[2] On the Cambridge Platonists, see F.J. POWICKE : *The Cambridge Platonists*,
London, 1926, and Ernst CASSIRER : *The Platonist Renaissance in England*,
Edinburgh, 1953.
[3] See the funeral Oration, quoted above.
[4] See his Sermons on the Creed, especially on *God the Father, Maker of
Heaven and Earth*, in *The Works of the Learned Dr. Barrow, D.D.*, London,
1683-1687, II, ser. 12.

Newton's physico-theology [1]. Similar arguments were used not only by scientists like Robert Boyle but by many Anglicans who were not members of the Royal Society. This contributed to the development of the liberal theology that was to prevail in the next age, but at this stage all divines would emphasize that Christianity is both reasonable and ' mysterious ', i.e. both agreeable to reason and in some of its revealed truths, beyond reason. One of the clearest statements of this position appears in South's sermon on the Trinity [2], in which he argues with his usual cogency that assent to the mysteries of religion is an act of reason, based on certain and sufficient grounds. Tillotson and Stillingfleet, too, repeatedly assert that the truths of religion are never against reason, though some are beyond the reach of human reason. For all his incipient physico-theology Barrow would have agreed, as had also the Cambridge Platonists, whose rational theology certainly influenced later divines [3].

Agreement with inborn truths, or natural reason, and the test of reason in inquiring into revealed truths are the twin aspects of rationalism which Anglican divines after the Restoration repeatedly emphasized. Though there was ample precedent for this in the tradition of the Church since Hooker, the particular circumstances in which preachers came to assert the truth of their religion would inevitably lead them to stress these points : first, the rise of infidelity and scepticism ; second, the necessity to oppose both the rampant forces of enthusiasm and the no less insidious arguments of the Roman Catholics. That some of these enemies sometimes joined forces appears not only from Charles's Declaration of Indulgence and earlier projects of the same kind, and from the outcries these provoked, but also from the Church of Rome's exploitation of radical scepticism in her apologetics, and from the slur cast on rational theology by both Puritans and Romanists. By stressing the corruption of man's reason and will since the Fall

---

[1] Barrow taught mathematics at Cambridge but later relinquished his chair to his more brilliant pupil Newton. He is said to have encouraged Newton's researches.

[2] Printed below. The distinction was to be emphasized at the time of the Trinitarian controversy.

[3] Both Tillotson and Stillingfleet were at Cambridge when Cudworth and Whichcote taught and preached there ; though Barrow was also a student of Trinity College at that time no trace of the Platonists' doctrine appears in his sermons unless we count as such the agreement of faith and reason, which could have been derived from many other sources.

the Augustinian doctrine of grace emphasized the inability of
' carnal reason ' to reach truth.   On the other hand, the nescience
in which the prevalent Pyrrhonism issued could be used either to
support libertinism or as an argument for acquiescence in truths
received upon authority ;   the fideists emphasized the divorce
between reason and faith in order to recommend *docta ignorantia*,
since, they said, it was only too clear that by exercising reason
men far from reaching truth were led to an *impasse* in which
contradictory propositions could be supported by equal arguments
from reason.   Though Donne was familiar with the modes of
thought of the sceptics, it was only after the Restoration that the
full impact of Pyrrhonism was felt in England [1].   Indeed, from
the sixties we find divines like Tillotson and South propounding
to the infidels something like Pascal's *pari* [2].   It will be remembered
that Pascal himself exploited the scepticism of Montaigñe and of
the libertines to recommend the wise passivity of the soul void
of all human knowledge, and to ground faith in the radically
unknowable, *Deus absconditus*.   His attacks on Descartes for
demonstrating the truths of religion on rational principles suggest
the later attacks on the rational theology of the Church of England,
though he does not seem to have had any direct influence on these.
The wise nescience had found an earlier exponent in Sir Thomas
Browne, who both exercised and distrusted his own reason ;   but
it came to play a prominent part in Roman Catholic apologetics,
which emphasized the difference between discourse of reason and
assent.

Anglican rationalism had been defined in Hooker's answer to
the Puritans, and the tradition was continued by Restoration theologians.   But since Hooker's time the Church had been exposed
to another danger, the appeal of the Roman Church with her
doctrine of infallibility.   It was to combat this that in the late
thirties the defence of reason received a new impetus in the works
of Lucius Cary, Lord Falkland [3], and particularly of Chillingworth,

---

[1] See L.I. BREDVOLD : *The Intellectual Milieu of John Dryden*, Ann Arbor,
1934, ch. II.   Bredvold discusses the relation between scepticism and fideism,
and in ch. IV the prevalence of fideistic arguments in R.C. apologetics in
England after the Restoration.

[2] See Tillotson's *The Wisdom of Being Religious* (1664), op. cit., I, ser. 1,
and South's *The Practice of Religion Enforced by Reason* (1667), op. cit., II,
ser. 1.

[3] Lucius CARY : *Of the Infallibility of the Church of Rome*, London, 1651.

whom Tillotson acknowledged as his master [1]. Falkland and his
friends were concerned about the controversies which threatened
to disrupt the unity of the Church and were soon to throw the
country into anarchy, and they advocated moderation and concord
on the ground that the truths necessary for salvation, on which
both Puritans and Anglicans largely agreed, are expressed plainly
in Scripture and, as Milton was to say, can be found by any man
who searches the Word of God diligently.   Through his mother,
who had been converted to Roman Catholicism [2], Falkland was,
however, led to consider the position of the Roman Church and
her claim to infallibility ; with the result that he rejected the claim
and took his stand on reason.   Even if we grant the Church to
be infallible, he argued, the truth of the proposition must be
grounded on rational arguments ; to accept one's religion because
it is the religion of the country is no safeguard against error.   For
him, then, reason is the ultimate guide to truth ; it leads us to see
that the Scriptures are the Word of God, but not that Christ has
instituted an infallible guide to direct us in reading it, except the
Grace of God as the light by which we see the truth.

Falkland's friend, Chillingworth—who was the godchild of
Laud—was bent, like Donne, on inquiring which is the true
Church and for a time he fell under the spell of Rome.   Yet after
spending a short time at the English College of Douay he came
back dissatisfied, no less sobered indeed than his friend Hales
had been by the Synod of Dordt.   What had attracted him to Rome
was the promise of an infallible guide to satisfy his inquiring
mind [3], but to this spirit unappeased and peregrine Rome did not
provide the right answer.   He was soon to enter the lists with his
Religion of Protestants (1637), which has been compared for the
breadth of its thought to Hooker's *Laws of Ecclesiastical Polity* [4].
For Chillingworth the infallible guide and rule of faith is not the
Pope or some other authority divinely appointed, but the Bible.
The Bible contains all truths necessary for salvation, in plain enough

---

[1] See Tillotson's Preface to *The Rule of Faith*.

[2] There were many Catholics at Court ; Queen Henrietta Maria greatly
favoured them and encouraged priests to convert Protestants.   See Bossuet's
tribute to her zeal in his funeral oration.

[3] Cp. with Dryden's search for an unerring guide in *Religio Laici*, and his
ultimate conversion to Rome.

[4] See TULLOCH, *op. cit.*, I, ch. V, p. 314.   The style, however, is often
cumbrous.

terms for every man to grasp ; those that are too knotty, even for
learned men, are not fundamentals of faith. All that is needed
to read Scripture aright is a free open mind : by following right
reason man can grasp the essential truths of religion. The Romanists argued that but for an infallible guide each man would follow
his own wit and draw his own conclusions; Chillingworth answered :

> You say again confidently, that if this Infallibility be once
> impeached, every Man is given over to his own Wit and
> Discourse : which, if you mean *Discourse* not guiding it
> self by Scripture, but only by Principles of Nature, or
> perhaps by Prejudices and popular Errors, and drawing
> Consequences not by Rule, but Chance, is by no means
> true. If you mean by *Discourse*, right Reason grounded on
> divine Revelation and common Notions written by God in
> the Hearts of all Men, and deducing, according to the never-
> failing Rules of Logick, consequent Deductions from them ;
> if this be it which you mean by Discourse, it is very meet
> and reasonable and necessary, that men, as in all their
> Actions, so especially in that of the greatest importance,
> the Choice of their Way to Happiness should be left unto
> it ; and he that follows this in all his Opinions and Actions,
> and does not only seem to do so, follows always God [1].

The Romanist apologist had distinguished between *discourse*
(of reason) and *assent*, and Chillingworth's vindication of discourse

---

[1] *The Religion of Protestants, A Safe Way to Salvation*, in *The Works*
of William Chillingworth, 10th ed., London, 1742, ' The Preface to the Author
of *Charity Maintained* : with An Answer to his Pamphlet, entituled, A Direction
to N.N. ', p. 15. This was Edward Knott, author of several works affirming
that " Protestancy unrepented destroys Salvation " ; the first of these, *Charity
Mistaken* (1630), was answered by Christopher Potter in *Want of Charitie
justly charged on all such Romanists...* (1633); in reply to which Knott wrote
Mercy and Truth, or Charity Maintained... (1634). In *A Direction to be
observed by N.N....* (1636) Knott accused Chillingworth of being a Socinian.
Chillingworth's *Religion of Protestants*, like most works of controversy of the
time, follows the adversary's work point by point ; most editions print : The
Preface to the author of *Ch. M.* ; then Knott's Preface, followed by Ch's Answer
to the Preface ; Knott's first chapter, then Ch's refutation ; etc. The Life of
the Author, by Tomas Birch, prefixed to the 10th, 1742, edition relates the
circumstances of the controversy, thereby throwing light on the activities of
Roman priests and Jesuits who had been allowed to return to England at the
end of the reign of James I and under Charles I " upon the account of his
marriage with Henrietta " and were busy " in making converts ". This should
be taken into account if we are to assess rightly the importance attached to the
controversy. Charles II's leanings to Rome and the presence of priests in the
entourage of his queen created a similar situation after the Restoration, and
Henrietta Maria continued to protect and advance Roman Catholics. See David
OGG : *England in the Reign of Charles II*, Oxford, (1934) 1962, I, 202-4. For
the Jesuits' influence on James II, see the same author's *England in the Reigns
of James II and William III*, Oxford, (1955) 1963, pp. 165-6.

already implies the shift from right reason to discursive reason ; still, for him as for Restoration Anglicans, the first principles from which reason argues are divine revelation and " the common notions written by God in the hearts of all men ". South will later distinguish between assent of faith and of knowledge, along the same lines as Locke does in the *Essay Concerning Human Understanding*, and he will insist that assent of faith is rational because it is based on certain and sufficient grounds [1]. Tillotson and Stillingfleet will demonstrate that faith is no less an act of reason than acceptance of geometrical truths though it is grounded on moral evidence, not on mathematical demonstration. There was, then, substantial agreement as to what constitutes faith, i.e. not nescience, nor assent to authority, but assent on rational grounds.

In his answer to the second chapter of his adversary's book, Chillingworth distinguishes between reason and private spirit, thus further answering the charge that for lack of an infallible guide men are free to follow their own wits :

> If by a private *Spirit*, you mean a particular Persuasion, that a Doctrine is true, which some men pretend, but cannot prove to come from the Spirit of God : I say, to refer Controversies to Scripture, is not to refer them to this kind of private Spirit. For there is a manifest Difference between saying, *The Spirit of God tells me, that this is the Meaning of such a Text* (which no Man can possibly know to be true, it being a secret Thing) and between saying, *These and these Reasons I have to shew, that this or that Doctrine, or that this or that is the Meaning of such a Scripture ?* Reason being a publick and certain Thing, and exposed to all Mens Trial and Examination. But now, if by *private Spirit* you understand every Man's particular Reason, then your first and second Inconvenience will presently be reduced to one, and shortly to none at all [2].

Reason, then, is a public and certain thing, and cannot in any way be confused with the ' motions of the Spirit ' ; it is open to trial and examination, and, it is implied, it is common to all men.

---

[1] In his sermon on the Resurrection, in vol. V, pp. 185-201. He speaks, however, of the *certainties* of assent, while Locke distinguishes between *certainty* and *certitude*.

[2] *Op. cit.*, p. 111. This is remark nr. 110 Ad § 20, where Knott had said : " by this Principle, all is finally in very deed and truth reduced to the *internal private Spirit*, because there is really no middle way betwixt a *publick external*, and a *private internal* voice ", *ibid.*, p. 73.

This is no other than the *sensus communis* to which the theologians of the next age will appeal constantly, and which they will bring in evidence of the truths of Christianity. Chillingworth thus takes his stand as firmly against private inspiration as against authority. The Restoration Anglicans too were unanimously to reject both, whether they were High-Churchmen like South or Latitudinarians like Tillotson, whose sermon on the *Trial of Spirits*[1] is an outspoken condemnation of the pretence to guidance by the Spirit.

Chillingworth's argument, it must be noted, is not directed against the fideists—after all, his opponent had *argued* at considerable length—but only against the Romanists' inconsistency in now invoking reason, now denying it the power to discern what is true. Chillingworth pleads for rational inquiry into the fundamentals of religion, as Tillotson will do in his vindication of the Church of England from the attacks of later Romanists. Hence, Chillingworth's assertion that :

> For my part, I am certain, that God hath given us our Reason, to discern between Truth and Falshood, and he that makes not this use of it, but believes things he knows not why ; I say, it is by Chance that he believes the Truth, and not by Choice ; and that I cannot but fear, that God will not accept of this *Sacrifice of Fools*[2].

Though Chillingworth is by no means ready to conclude, the Scriptural phrase neatly turns the argument against the Romanist[3].

Chillingworth's friend, John Hales, was another member of the group at Great Tew who preached moderation and wisdom. At the time of the Romanist controversy he helped Chillingworth resist what he called the " Romish corner-creepers ", and he too emphasized the necessity to test one's acquiescence to Christian truths at the bar of reason. His clearest plea for rational inquiry is his sermon *Of Inquiry and Private Judgment in Religion*, on *Gal.* VI. 7 *Be not deceived, God is not mocked ; for whatsoever a man soweth, that shall he also reap.* From this text he argues the great duty laid on each man not to be deceived in matters of belief ; it is all one whether a man deceives himself or allows himself to be deceived, for God has enjoined on all men the duty to be vigilant in seeking truth. " An infallibility therefore there

---

[1] Printed below.   [2] *Op. cit.*, p. 112.
[3] It may be noted also that he does not defend episcopacy as divinely instituted, but like Hooker argues the need for law and decency in the Church.

must be ", for it is unreasonable to suppose that God has enjoined such a duty without appointing a judge to clear doubts and settle scruples. Men have " marvellously wearied themselves in seeking to find out " where this infallibility is, and

> every man finds it, or thinks he finds it, accordingly as that faction or part of the church upon which he is fallen, doth direct him [1].

Infallibility, however, cannot be found in others ; it is, or ought to be, in each of us,

> For, Beloved, infallibility is not a favour impropriated to any one man, it is a duty alike expected at the hands of all, all must have it [2].

To obey the Apostle each man must seek to know *what* it is that is commanded him, and *wherefore* it is commanded, " that is, upon what authority, upon what reason ". For if Christ came to cure the world, he intended to cure us like men, not like beasts :

> Deceit and error are the diseases of the mind ; he that strives to cure it upon bare command, brings you indeed a potion, or rather a drench, which, for ought you know, may as well set on and increase, as remove the error ; but when he opens his authorities, when he makes you conceive his grounds and reasons, then, and not before, he cures your error. They that come and tell you what you are to believe, what you are to do, and tell you not why, they are not physicians but leaches : and if you so take things at their hands, you do not like men, but like beasts [3].

Men should not simply acquiesce in what their teachers tell them, for these too, says Hales, may be deceived, and it will be no excuse in the eyes of God if each man has not sought diligently for himself, and has not inquired what it is that makes his pastor right. Quoting Gerson, as Restoration Anglicans occasionally do, he enters a plea for reason on the ground that the light God has lodged in us must not be hidden under a bushel :

> It is a question made by John Gerson, some time chancellor of Paris, ' Wherefore hath God given me the light of reason and conscience, if I must suffer myself to be led and governed by the reason and conscience of another man ? ' Will any

[1] John HALES, *op. cit.*, III, 149.
[2] *Ibid.*   [3] p. 150.

of you befriend me so far as to assoil this question ? for I must confess I cannot. It was the speech of a good husbandman, 'It is but a folly to possess a piece of ground, except you till it'. And how then can it stand to reason, that a man should be possessor of so goodly a piece of the Lord's pasture, as is this light of understanding and reason, which he hath endued us with in the way of our creation, if he suffer it to lie untilled, or sow not in it the Lord's seed [1] ?

He then distinguishes between due esteem of one's reason and pride, and shows that men's pretence of modesty in this respect is no more than an excuse for their sloth. As to the causes of the current disesteem of reason, they may be found in " the dregs of the Church of Rome not yet sufficiently washed from the hearts of many men", and the Romanists, it is well-known, " suffer nothing to be inquired into which is once concluded by them " ; on the other hand, this distrust of reason also results from the disputatious- ness which " our own ministry " has fostered, thus causing trouble and disquiet and making us long to banish all contentions. Hales, the champion of moderation and of concord [2] in no way confuses concord and " that peace which ariseth out of ignorance ", for this is sloth and not charity. To neglect our own reason, then, is to slight the greatest gift of God :

Hath God given you eyes to see, and legs to support you, that so yourself might lie still, or sleep, and require the use of other men's eyes and legs ? *That* faculty of reason which is in every one of you, even in the meanest that hears me this day, next to the help of God, is your eyes to direct you, and your legs to support you in your course of integrity and sanctity ; you may no more refuse or neglect the use of it ; and rest yourselves upon the use of other men's reason, than neglect your own, and call for the use of other men's eyes and legs [3].

True, Hales was not preaching to unlettered hinds, nor were any of the Restoration divines we are considering here. Swift noted in his *Letter to a Young Clergyman* that Tillotson himself may have preached differently to different audiences. Indeed, it is clear that preachers should have enough common sense not to expound

---

[1] p. 153.
[2] See his *Tract on Schism and Schismatics*, which Laud found too tolerant of the Puritans' claims.
[3] *Op. cit.*, p. 157.

doctrine above their hearers' reach. Affectation of subtlety and of learning was the vice most commonly denounced by the reformers of pulpit oratory, and no doubt there were many bad pastors then as in all ages. The point is that Hales is telling his audience [1] that each Christian must seek to know what he believes, and wherefore. The men who came to listen to Tillotson at St. Lawrence Jewry were no doubt a mixed group of tradespeople and members of the professions; though we need not adopt Taine's superior tone in referring to those people's thirst for edification, we must agree with him that they came to hear a sermon in order to be taught the what and the wherefore of their religion, not to be entertained by the eloquence of the preacher. The very principle of private judgement clearly determined the mode of preaching, and Hales's own sermon—though more ingenious at the beginning, and using illustrations more remote from the text than later divines were to favour—is a good example of the clear exposition that came to be the rule after the Restoration.

Another defence of Scripture as the rule of faith came from Stillingfleet in 1662, *Origines Sacrae, or A Rational Account of the Grounds of Christian Faith*. As he explained in the Preface to the Reader, this work was directed against atheists, who raised three kinds of objection against Scripture:

> The most popular pretences of the Atheists of our Age, have been the irreconcilableness of the account of Times in Scripture, with that of the learned and ancient Heathen Nations; the inconsistency of the belief of the Scripture with the principles of reason: and the account which may be given of the Origin of things from the principles of Philosophy without the Scriptures [2].

In the Epistle Dedicatory he referred to both philosophical and moral libertinism as the origin of the disesteem for the Bible he had set himself against:

> Some accounting the life and practice of it [i.e. true religion],

---

[1] Hales says they might plead in excuse that they have their trades and callings, that they are unlearned, unread, of weak and shallow understandings (p. 151).

[2] Edward STILLINGFLEET: *Origines Sacrae, or A Rational Account of the Grounds of Christian Faith, As to the Truth and Divine Authority of the Scriptures, And the matters therein contained.* The Third Edition Corrected and Amended. London, 1666, sig. B 2 v. (first published 1662).

as it speaks subduing our *wills* to the *will* of *God* (which is the substance of all Religion) a thing too low and mean for their rank and condition in the world, while others pretend a quarrel against the principles of it as unsatisfactory to *Humane reason* [1].

For him, not only is religion consonant with reason, but

the disesteem of the Scriptures upon any pretence what-soever, is the *decay* of *Religion*, and through many wind-ings and turnings leads men at last into the very depth of Atheism [2].

Though Stillingfleet's main target is ostensibly libertinism, and the burden of his treatise to demonstrate the veracity of Scripture, the above remark indicates the link that was to be established by many Anglicans between atheism and ' the disesteem of Scriptures ', which was the main argument of the Romanists for grounding the rule of faith in oral tradition and in the infallibility of their Church. The kinship between Tridentine theology and atheism was to be harped upon by Stillingfleet in his later works and by Tillotson in his sermons ; both stressed the harm done to religion by the Romanists' slight on the evidence of the senses and on the authority of Scripture [3]. Tillotson's zeal against the Romanists may have been all the stronger for his having received " his first education and impressions among those who were then called Puritans ", but Burnet's further remark cannot be dismissed as the expression of his, or Tillotson's, partisan feelings :

He saw, with deep Regret, the fatal Corruption of his Age, while the Hypocrisies and Extravagancies of former times, and the Liberties and Loosness of the present, disposed many to Atheism and Impiety... When he saw that Popery was at the root of this, and that the Design seemed to be laid, to make us first Atheists, that we might be the more easily made Papists, and that many did not stick to own, that we could have no Certainty for the Christian Faith, unless we believed the Infallibility of the Church. This gave him a deep and just Indignation [4].

The High-Churchman South, though less often moved to denounce Romanism, impugned it for much the same reasons, since he too

---

[1] *Ibid.*, sig. a-a v.   [2] *Ibid.*, sig. a v.
[3] See, for instance, Tillotson's *Discourse on Transubstantiation*, printed below.
[4] *Sermon Preached at the Funeral...*, op. cit., p. 15.

grounded assent in the certain evidence of the witnesses of Christ.

In *Origines Sacrae*, Stillingfleet argued first that enquiries after truth gratify ' the most noble faculty of our souls ', reason, since

> all our most laudable endeavours after knowledge now, are only the *gathering up* some *scattered fragments* of what was once an *entire Fabrick*, and the *recovery* of *some precious Jewels* which were *lost* out of sight, and *sunk* in the *ship-wrack* of *humane nature* [1].

The words at once recall Milton's plea in the *Areopagitica* for the recovery of truth, like the disjected members of Osiris scattered to the four winds by the Egyptian Typhoon. Like the Great Rebel, Stillingfleet believed that reason has been obscured by the Fall, but like him he also insisted that

> *God* created the *soul* of *man* not only *capable* of finding the truth of things, but *furnished* him with a sufficient χριτήριον or *touchstone* to discover truth from falsehood, by a *light* set up in his *understanding*, which if he had attended to, he might have *secured* himself from all *impostures* and *deceits*.
>
> ...
>
> There is an *intermediate state* between the former *acquaintance* [i.e. with truth], and the *renewal* of it, wherein all those remaining *characters* of mutual knowledge are *sunk* so deep, and lie so *hid*, that there needs a new fire to be kindled to bring forth those latent *figures*, and make them again appear *legible* [2].

Stillingfleet had earlier recalled " the saying of Plato, that all knowledge is remembrance ", and the influence of his Cambridge masters is perceptible in this passage. Yet for him the main difference between prelapsarian state and our present ' intermediate state ' is that man's knowledge then

> had been more *intellectual* then *discursive* : not so much *imploying* his *faculties* in the *operose deductions* of reason... but had *immediately imployed* them about the *sublimest objects*, not about *quiddities* and *formalities*, but about *him* who was the *fountain* of his *being*, and the *center* of his happiness [3].

---

[1] *Op. cit.*, pp. 1-2.   [2] *Ibid.*, pp. 2, 6.
[3] *Ibid.*, p. 3. Cp. with South's sermon : *So God created man in his own image, op. cit.*, I, ser. 2.

Postlapsarian reason is apt to err, through want of impartial diligence in the search of truth, or because of the near resemblance of truth and error, which " seldom *walks* abroad the world in her own *raiments* " [1].   Stillingfleet then proceeds to show that there is no " certain credibility in any of these " [2] ancient histories which seem to contradict the Scriptures, whether Phoenician and Aegyptian (ch. II), Chaldean (ch. III), or Graecian (ch. IV) history or chronology (ch. V and VI).   Yet, he argues, since it is of the greatest concernment for man to know that he has his original from God, and that

> all things are managed by Divine providence, *it stands to reason that an account of things so concerning and remarkable, should not be always left to the uncertainty of oral tradition* [3].

The matter to be believed cannot be conveyed to man through uncertain oral tradition, neither can it be trusted to be discovered in every age by a spirit of prophecy.   Hence, considering the undoubted nature of Divine Goodness, such an account had to be given to man

> by a publick *recording* of the matters of *Divine revelation* by such a *person* who is enabled to give the world all *reasonable satisfaction*, that what he did was not of any private design of his own head, but that he was *deputed* to it by no less then *Divine authority* [4].

Only thus can men be assured that the matter to be believed is not liable to imposture.   Now, such matters of fact cannot be brought into mathematical demonstrations ;   but matters of fact require no more than moral certainty to produce assent to them [5]. All the conditions of moral certainty are met by the writings of Moses (Book II, ch. I to VII), and the teachings of Christ can stand the same test (ch. VIII to X).   While moral certainty is sufficient to establish the truth of the Old Testament, Stillingfleet is concerned to ground assent to Christ's docrine on rational principles from which the testimony of Christ will appear to be

---

[1] p. 7.   [2] p. 15.   [3] p. 107 (Book II, ch. I).   [4] pp. 108-9.
[5] p. 111.   The examples given by Stillingfleet are those Tillotson later uses in his sermons, e.g. " Who would undertake to prove that *Archimedes* was kild at *Syracuse* by any of the *demonstrations* he was then about ? "

infallible.   Hence, the several ' hypotheses ' he lays down at the
outset, first :

> *Where the truth of a doctrine depends not on the evidence
> of the things themselves, but on the authority of him that
> reveals it, there the only way to prove the doctrine to be
> true, is to prove the Testimony of him that reveals it to be
> infallible* [1].

In developing this point Stillingfleet distinguishes between the
evidence of the thing itself, i.e.

> so *clear* and *distinct* a *perception* of it, that every *one* who
> hath the *use* of his *rational faculties*, cannot but upon the
> *first apprehension* of the *terms* yield a *certain assent* to it [2]

and the kind of evidence necessary to establish the *existence* of
things.   The ' common notices of human nature ', though evident
propositions in themselves, do not argue the existence of the thing
proposed ;   all that discourse of reason can prove is the " non
repugnancy of the thing to our natural faculties ".   While the
certainty and evidence of mathematical demonstrations depend
upon such propositions, the existence of things must be grounded
on other arguments, i.e. on the testimony of the senses.   True, the
senses may deceive us, and the ideas (i.e. images) of things conveyed to the understanding may be fallacious ;   true, the understanding may also draw faulty inferences from the ideas conveyed
to it.   Still, Stillingfleet argues,

> *Supposing* then I should *question* the *truth* of every *thing*
> which is *conveyed* in an *uncertain* way to my mind, I may
> soon *out-go* even *Pyrrho* himself in real *Scepticism* [3].

Since Stillingfleet is in no way prepared to out-go Pyrrho, he must
ground the certainty of knowledge ultimately in the goodness of
God, that is, in the agreement of reason with the nature of things.
Thus, half-way in his argument, there reappears the concept of
right reason as Hooker—and Hooker's masters Aristotle and Aquinas—understood it, a concept based on the principle of cosmic
order reflecting the rationality of God and reflected in the rational
nature of man [4].

---

[1] p. 228 (Book II, ch. 8).   [2] p. 228.   [3] p. 229.
[4] " That law eternal which God himself hath made to himself, and thereby
worketh all things whereof he is the cause and author ;   that law in the admirable

Stillingfleet had posited the goodness of God to show that man must have been given a reliable account of his divine origin ; he also grounded in it our assent to the infallible witness, Christ. He first lays down as the foundation of all physical certainty, i.e. certainty as to the *existence* of things,

> that there is a God, who being infinitely good, will not suffer the minds of men to be deceived in those things, which they have a clear and distinct perception of (without which supposition we cannot be assured of the certainty of any operations of the mind, because we cannot know but we were so made, that we might be then deceived, when we thought ourselves most sure)[1].

Now, since the existence of things cannot be proved from the evidence of the things themselves, the fullest demonstration of them is by infallible testimony. And there are certain ways " whereby to know that a Testimony delivered is infallible " [2]. The question therefore resolves itself into : first, why we believe a divine testimony, and the answer is based on the notion of a perfect and infinitely good God, i.e. a common notion ; second, upon what grounds do we believe this to be a divine testimony ? Natural reason, Stillingfleet says, must assure us that it is of God, and the evidence whereby it may be known to be such

---

frame whereof shineth with most perfect beauty the countenance of that wisdom which has testified concerning herself, ' The Lord possessed me in the beginning of his way, even before his works of old I was set up ; ' (*Prov.* viii.22) that law, which hath been the pattern to make, and is the card to guide the world by ; that law which hath been of God and with God everlastingly ; that law, the author and observer whereof is one only God to be blessed for ever ; how should either men or angels be able perfectly to behold ? The book of this law we are neither able nor worthy to open and look into. That little thereof which we darkly apprehend we admire, the rest with religious ignorance we humbly and meekly adore ". Richard HOOKER : *Of the Laws of Ecclesiastical Polity*, I, i, 5 ; " Man in perfection of nature being made according to the likeness of his Maker resembleth him also in the manner of working ; so that whatsoever we work as men, the same we do wittingly work and freely ; neither are we according to the manner of natural agents any way so tied, but that it is in our power to leave the things we do undone. The good which either is gotten by doing, or which consisteth in the very doing itself, causeth not action, unless apprehending it as good we so like and desire it : that we do unto any such end, the same we choose and prefer before the leaving it undone. Choice there is not, unless the thing which we take be so in our power that we might have refused and left it... To choose is to will one thing before another. And to will is to bend our souls to the having or doing of that which they see to be good. Goodness is seen with the eye of understanding. And the light of that eye, is reason ", *ibid.*, I, vii, 2.

[1] *Op. cit.*, p. 230 (Book II, ch. 8).
[2] *Ibid.*, p. 239.

must be convincing proofs of it, though they need not, and indeed do not, *enforce* assent for there could be no obligation to believe if belief was irresistible [1] : convincing proofs are not to be confused with demonstrative arguments. Stillingfleet develops these convincing proofs, or moral evidence, in the next two chapters : i.e. they are the miracles of Christ, which argue His divine power. Moral evidence, then, is necessary to establish the truth of Christianity. As Stillingfleet himself will say later [2], and as Tillotson also will argue [3], this evidence is evidence from the senses reported by reliable witnesses ; to deny the validity of sense perception is therefore to impugn the foundations of religion : that is why the Anglican divines rejected the doctrine of transubstantiation as defined by Tridentine theology [4]. If the senses cheat us, then there is no basis for certainty at all either in science or in religion. True, the reports of the senses must be checked, or appearances may be confused with reality : just as the natural philosophers were using telescopes and microscopes to correct direct sense perceptions, so the Anglican theologians insisted that true miracles should be distinguished from false ones, and reliable from unreliable witnesses. All this led them to expound more or less explicitly an epistemology that warranted the objectivity of know-

---

[1] This is again Hooker's notion of man as a free agent acting, like God, by rational choice not by compulsion as in the realm of nature. Barrow, South and Tillotson will stress the same point when discussing the force of the arguments propounded for belief in Christ. Assent of faith is therefore to be distinguished from assent to mathematical demonstrations, which have compelling force. Stillingfleet, like other Anglican divines, further argues that Christ was rejected by the Jews not for want of sufficient evidence, but because of their obstinacy.

[2] For instance, in *The Doctrine of the Trinity and Transubstantiation Compared*, London, 1687.

[3] See his *Discourse Against Transubstantiation*, printed below.

[4] From the first the argument about transubstantiation seems to have been vitiated by a misunderstanding about the meaning of the term. Stillingfleet and other Anglican divines took it to mean that the natural flesh and blood of Christ are really present in the Eucharist. The Council of Trent, however, had been careful to distinguish between *substance* and *accidents* (which alone can be perceived by the senses). See Sessio XIII, Caput i : " Principio docet sancta Synodus [...] in almo sanctae Eucharistiae Sacramento, post panis, et vini consecrationem, Dominum nostrum, Jesum Christum, verum Deum, atque hominem, vere, realiter, ac substantialiter sub specie illarum rerum sensibilium contineri. Nec enim haec inter se pugnant, ut ipse Salvator noster semper ad dexteram Patris in coelis assideat, juxta modum existendi naturalem ; et ut multis nihilominus aliis in locis sacramentaliter praesens sua substantia nobis adsit, ea existendi ratione... ", *Sacrosanti et Oecumenici Concilii Tridentini ... Canones et Decreta, Antverpiae*, 1604, p. 72. For present-day Anglican belief, see for instance : J.L.C. DART : *The Old Religion. An Examination into the Facts of the English Reformation*, London, 1956, Ch. 12.

ledge by grounding it in the reliability of sense perceptions as well
as of the 'connate notions'. Both the innate notions and the senses
as reliable organs of information play their part in establishing the
rational evidence of religion ; and both are ultimately grounded
in the goodness of a God who cannot suffer his creatures to be
necessarily deceived by the very means given them to discover
truth. Ultimately, then, the objectivity of knowledge is based on
the concept of right reason. It is no wonder, then, that in *The
Dunciad* Pope described 'the gloomy clerk' as one

> Whose pious Hope aspires to see the day
> When Moral Evidence shall quite decay[1].

Barrow was to demonstrate the existence of God both from
the first principles implanted in man and from the order of the
universe ; Tillotson also was to use both kinds of arguments. If
the physico-theology of the next age may be traced to them, it is
clear, however, that they were a long way from the deists' mechan-
istic view of the universe. True, the common notions too were
to be exploited later in the century as evidence of the sufficiency
of natural religion without a direct revelation from God ; but when
Barrow, Tillotson, and other Anglican divines appeal to these it is
to show that God gave all men a first revelation of His law, which
was to be confirmed by the direct revelation of His Word in the
law of Moses, and perfected by Christ's doctrine, which bare
reason alone could not have discovered : they appeal to the
consensus omnium as evidence of these common notions, not, like
the Deists, in order to bypass revelation. South does not seem
to have preached specifically on the evidence for Christianity, but
in several of his sermons he gives in compressed form the argument
for it based on the rational principles inborn in man[2]. The fact
that he does not argue from the laws of the universe may be an
expression of his conservatism and of his critical attitude towards
natural philosophy[3]. To him the beauty of God's creation and
the admirable contrivance of the universe amply manifest the

---

[1] Book IV, ll. 461-2. Pope, however, also condemns the 'high Priori
Road'. See Alexander POPE : *The Dunciad*, ed. J.R. Sutherland, London, 1962,
and the notes to ll. 462-72.

[2] For instance in the Sermon on the Trinity, 1667, printed below.

[3] See his Latin Oration at the opening of the Sheldonian theatre, which
shocked Evelyn and offended Wallis. See EVELYN's *Diary*, ed. *cit.*, III, 531-2
(9 July, 1669); for John Wallis's letter to Robert Boyle, 17 July, 1669, see
Robert BOYLE : *Works*, ed. Thomas Birch, London, 1744, V, 514.

goodness and bounty of the Creator and prompt man to awe and
wonder, much as it had prompted Hooker to " humbly and meekly
adore ".   It is characteristic of this dialectician and artist that when
demonstrating *Christianity mysterious and the wisdom of God
in making it so*[1] he should justify the wisdom of a mysterious
religion by the fact that it breeds in man awe and wonder and
engages him on the diligent search after truth, and on the ground
that it promises perfect intuitive knowledge to be attained hereafter.
Like Hooker he asserts the fundamental rationality of man *qua*
intellectual being, and stresses that the will only chooses what the
understanding presents to it as good ; hence his insistence on the
danger of misinforming the understanding.   South also emphasizes
that reason may be deflected from its true end by the ' pravity of
the will ', that is, by the affections preventing it from study of,
and application to, its own good[2] ; but he denies that the will as
such can do other than choose what it deems good[3].   All wrong
choices originate in corruption of the understanding,

> which represents to the will things really evil, under the
> notion and character of good[4]

and it is the preacher's task to free the understanding from false
notions : there is no sinful action, he says, " but there is a lie
wrapt up in the bowels of it "[5].   Just as the Devil is the Father
of lies, so

> Christ saves the world by undeceiving it ; and sanctifies
> the will, by first enlightening the understanding[6].

Right thinking is therefore the basis of right action, and South
could have said with Milton that reason is but choosing.   Just as
Hooker had opposed the Calvinistic notion of God as arbitrary

---

[1] *Op. cit.*, III, ser. 6.   The sermon was preached in 1694, i.e. at the time
of the Trinitarian controversy, which fostered the growth of deism.

[2] See his sermon on *John* VII, 7, *op. cit.*, I, ser. 6.

[3] " As for the will, though its liberty be such, that a suitable, or proper
good being proposed to it, it has a power to refuse, or not to choose it ; yet
it has no power to choose evil, considered absolutely as evil ; this being directly
against the nature, and natural method of its working ".   Sermon on *The Fatal
Imposture and Force of Words*, *op. cit.*, II, ser. 9, p. 317 (printed below).

[4] *Ibid.*

[5] Sermon on *Lying Lips are an Abomination to the Lord*, *op. cit.*, I, ser. 12,
p. 471.

[6] *Ibid.*, p. 472.

will [1], so South reaffirms that right reason is the faculty to see truth and to choose right ; man's resemblance to God consists in

> that universal rectitude of all the faculties of the soul, by which they stand apt and disposed to their respective offices and operations [2].

The common notions, then, manifest the goodness of God in creating man rational, they enable man to assent to His Word and lead him to Christ. As South shows in *Christianity Mysterious* our assent to the mysteries of religion is a rational act, based on the infallibility of Christ. And the testimony of Christ is accepted on the no less rational ground of moral certainty.

Hume was to 'outgo Pyrrho' in a way that Stillingfleet could not have foreseen, and many critics have asserted that " the nescience of the *Treatise [of Human Nature]* and the *Inquiry [concerning Human Understanding]* is a legitimate *reductio ad absurdum* of the account of human knowledge in [Locke's] *Essay* " [3]. In the famous controversy that opposed Stillingfleet and Locke, the Bishop obviously misunderstood Locke's theory of knowledge—much as Hume was to do—and took him to task for robbing mysteries of certainty [4]. Now, Locke had distinguished between knowledge and judgement, i.e. between " the perception of the agreement or disagreement of our own ideas " [5] and " the faculty which God has given man to supply the want of clear and certain knowledge, in cases where that cannot certainly be had... ; whereby the mind takes its ideas to agree or disagree... without perceiving a demonstrative evidence in the proofs " [6]. But he had gone on to prove that probability, i.e. " the appearance of such an agreement or disagreement, by the intervention of proofs, whose connection is not constant and immutable, or at least is not perceived to be so, but is, or appears for the most part to be so ", is enough " to induce the mind to judge the proposition to be true or false, rather than the contrary " [7]. Though probability is not knowledge, but " like-

---

[1] " They err therefore who think that of the will of God to do this or that there is no reason besides his will ", *Laws*, I, i, 5.
[2] Sermon on *Gen.* I, 27, *op. cit.*, I, ser. 2, p. 50.
[3] John LOCKE : *An Essay Concerning Human Understanding*, ed. Alexander Campbell Fraser, New York, (1894), 1959, Prolegomena, p. cxxxv. Fraser, however, denies the legitimacy of this *reductio ad absurdum*.
[4] See his *Vindication of the Trinity*, London, 1696.
[5] *An Essay Concerning Human Understanding* (1690), Book IV, ch. IV, § 1.
[6] Book IV, ch. XIX, § 3.   [7] Book IV, ch. XV, § 1.

liness to be true ", it is sufficient " to supply the defect of our knowledge and to guide us where that fails " [1]. The grounds of probability Locke lists are exactly the same as those the theologians had used to demonstrate the veracity of the Gospel, i.e. conformity with our own knowledge, observation, and experience ; and the testimony of reliable witnesses, according to their number, integrity, skill, design, consistency, and tested against contrary testimonies [2].

In *Origines Sacrae* Stillingfleet had concentrated on the testimony of miracles recorded by reliable witnesses ; elsewhere [3] he also used the other grounds of assent, as did Tillotson and Barrow [4]. The divine whose argument comes closest to Locke's, however, is South ; his theory of assent, stated briefly but cogently in several of his sermons, particularly in his sermon on the Trinity (preached between 1663 and 1670) [5] makes one wonder, indeed, if he was one of the five or six men meeting at Christ Church whose discussions led Locke to write the *Essay* [6]. At any rate, one is not surprised to find South later siding with Locke in the controversy with Stillingfleet [7]. Locke had also been attacked by William Sherlock, Dean of St. Paul's, who had denounced his rejection of innate ideas as conducive to atheism, and South had bitterly opposed Sherlock in the Trinitarian controversy [8]. But there is more to the kinship

---

[1] *Ibid.*, §§ 3, 4.

[2] *Ibid.*, § 4. The theologians hardly ever consider "contrary testimonies".

[3] For instance, in *The Doctrine of the Trinity and Transubstantiation Compared*, London, 1687.

[4] See, for instance, Barrow's *Sermons on the Creed*, especially sermon 2, *op. cit.*, II, and Tillotson's *Rule of Faith*.

[5] Printed below.

[6] See *An Essay Concerning Human Understanding*, Epistle to the Reader. South and Locke both came from Westminster School, the former was elected to Christ Church in 1651, the latter in 1652. Locke was a fellow of Christ Church—where South was a canon from 1670—until he was 'expelled' by order of the King in 1684.

[7] See his letters to Locke (25 March, 1697 ; 22 November, 1697 ; 18 June, 1699) now in the Bodleian Library (MS. Locke c. 18).

[8] For the background of this controversy, see W.M.T. Dodds (Mrs. Nowottny): 'Robert South and William Sherlock: Some Unpublished Letters', *MLR*, XXXIX (1944), 215-24. In his Dedication to the Archbishop of Dublin of the third volume of his sermons (1698) South alludes to the support Stillingfleet gave to Sherlock in the Preface to *Vindication of the Trinity* (1696), in which Stillingfleet first attacked Locke. In a MS letter dated 18 July, 1704, now in the Bodleian Library (Ms. Locke c. 18) he expatiates on the insolence of Sherlock in daring to attack Locke's philosophy and person in *A Discourse Concerning the Happiness of Good Men and the Punishment of the Wicked in the Next World*. Locke had no high opinion of Sherlock as a controversialist and regarded him as a time-server. See his letter to Molyneux, 22 February, 1697, quoted by FRASER, *op. cit.*, p. xliii : "A man of no small name, as you know Dr. Sherlock is, has been pleased to declare against my doctrine of no

between Locke and South than opposition to a common adversary [1].

It is usually thought that the problem that started Locke on his epistemological inquiry [2] was the nature of assent, which he expounded in Book IV. The object of this part of the *Essay* is to set down " strict boundaries between faith and reason ", or to distinguish between knowledge and assent. There Locke shows that assent is founded on the highest reason, i.e. on the testimony of God ; but it is for reason to judge whether a particular book be a revelation of God. Faith can never convince us of anything that contradicts our knowledge, since

> we cannot tell how to conceive that to come from God, the bountiful Author of our being, which, if received for true, must overturn all the principles and foundations of know-ledge he has given us ; render all our faculties useless ; wholly destroy the most excellent part of his workmanship, our understandings ; and put a man in a condition wherein he will have less light, less conduct than the beast that perisheth [3].

Implicitly, then, Locke too grounds the certainty of knowledge in the rationality and goodness of God ; this may account for the ease with which he takes for granted the conformity of ideas to reality, thereby ignoring or at least bypassing the problem posed, for instance by Stillingfleet, of the *existence* of things for which there is evidence " in the thing itself ". Further, it appears from Book IV of the *Essay* that one of the chief concerns of Locke was to establish the rationality of faith in contradistinction to enthusiasm,

---

innate ideas, from the pulpit in the Temple ; and as I have been told charged it with little less than atheism... it is possible he may be firm here, because it is also said, he never quits his aversion to any tenet he has once declared against, till change of times, bringing change of interest, and fashionable opinions, open his eyes and his heart, and then he kindly embraces what before deserved his aversion and censure ". This probably refers to Sherlock's face-about in the question of the oath to William, which, Mrs. Nowottny has shown, accounted for South's bitterness in the quarrel. Locke's informant about Sherlock (' it is said... ') may have been South himself ; but see also Edmund CALAMY : *An Abridgement of Mr. Baxter's History of his Life and Times*, London, 1713, I, 485.

[1] South constantly refers to connate or innate ideas whereas Locke demonstrates that there are no such things. But the ambiguity of Locke's term, though he equates it with κοιναί ἔννοιαι, was early pointed out by John Norris of Bemerton in *Cursory Reflections on the* Essay (1700). South would not have contended (any more than Plato or others) that such ideas, if innate, should be most evident to children and idiots ! (Cf. *Essay*, Bk. I, ch. II, §§ 5, 27.)

[2] See FRASER, *op. cit.*, p. lvii.

[3] *Essay*, Bk. IV, ch. XVIII, § 5.

just as he had shown that knowledge resulting from the perception of agreement or disagreement of things is no castle in the air, when there is " a conformity between our ideas and the reality of things " [1]. Moreover, the one example he gives of the kind of truth we cannot receive as revealed by God because it contradicts our clear and distinct knowledge [2], would have been recognized by all his readers since the staple objection of Anglican theology to transubstantiation was, like Locke's, that it contradicts the evidence of our senses and as such " must overturn all the principles and foundations of knowledge (God) has given us and render all our faculties useless ". Locke's epistemological inquiry, then, clearly echoes the issues discussed by Anglican theologians. Without detracting from the originality or interest of the *Essay*, we may well remember that long before it was written Chillingworth, Stillingfleet and others had elaborated a doctrine of rational assent that has much in common with Locke's and to which he was certainly indebted. Anglican divines would have subscribed to his conclusion to chapter XVII (and it is important to remember that Locke next proceeds to repudiate enthusiasm):

> If the provinces of faith and reason are not kept distinct by these boundaries, there will, in matters of religion, be no room for reason at all ; and those extravagant opinions and ceremonies that are to be found in the several religions of the world will not deserve to be blamed [3].

Anglican rationalism after the Restoration was, in fact, defined under the necessity of steering a course between ' extravagant opinions ' and ' extravagant ceremonies ', between enthusiasm and Romanism. This may account for the Anglicans' failure to see that faith involves more than assent of the will and reason issuing in practice. The Puritans, who emphasized the overpowering force of Grace in conversion, were aware of the difference between assent and a living faith [4]. By encouraging the practice of self-examin-

---

[1] *Essay*, Bk. IV, ch. IV, § 3.

[2] " We can never assent to a proposition that affirms the same body to be in two distant places at once ", Bk. IV, ch. XVIII, § 5. Cp. with Tillotson's *Discourse against Transubstantiation*, printed below.

[3] *Essay*, Bk. IV, ch. XVIII, § 11.

[4] The Puritans distinguished between assent, or ' historical faith ', and saving faith, i.e. actual experience of ' a work of grace '. As E.S. Morgan says, " Saving faith must be preceded by historical faith, but historical faith was not necessarily followed by saving faith. " *Visible Saints. The History of a Puritan Idea*, Ithaca, 1965, p. 43.

ation in order to discover if one has received the call of the Spirit, they were led to sound greater depths in the human heart. Many of their spiritual autobiographies reveal the aridity of all belief that is not a real experience felt in the blood and felt along the heart. The sense of dereliction which many of them experienced at times may have driven them to despair, but it also shows that adherence to Christ meant more to them than assent of the mind to His truths and practice consonant with these truths. Their ' indwelling in Christ ' may have sounded no better than madmen's talk to the rationalist Anglicans, but it expressed, however confusedly, something of the nature of mystical experience. Of this only the Cambridge Platonists had a deeper sense, but it was not the aspect of their teaching that was to influence Anglican theology after the Restoration. Barrow said that there was too much Platonizing in his time ; in fact, neither he nor his fellow-Anglicans were prepared to encourage mysticism of any kind, for this was hardly distinguishable from enthusiasm[1]. It would take an 'eccentric' Churchman like William Law in the next century to respond fully to the teachings of Jacob Boehme. Meanwhile, Anglican theology was committed to reason and would not agree that " le cœur a ses raisons que la raison ne connaît pas ".

Stillingfleet's *Origines Sacrae* was intended to combat infidelity and to assert the ' Excellency of Scriptures ' on the ground that these are both suitable to our natural notions of a deity and attested by reliable witnesses, and therefore constitute the true rule of life. His refutation of other accounts of ancient history, however, testifies to the growth of historical criticism in the seventeenth century, which eventually might have some bearing on Biblical criticism. Not all of historical research was prompted by ' infidelity ', and one recalls Wilkins's praise of the Jesuits for their collections of ancient authors. Judging from Stillingfleet's work and from the sermons of other Anglican divines, who sometimes explained their text by referring to the historical circumstances alluded to in the context, it seems that they took ancient writers into account when these confirmed Scripture, but ignored them when they were at odds with the Biblical record. In other quarters, however, historical research was being used for other purposes, i.e. as evidencing the unreliability of the Scripture text. Anglicans, it seems, remained blissfully

[1] On enthusiasm in general, see R.A. KNOX : *Enthusiasm*, Oxford, 1950.

unaware of the implications of the new findings, committed as they
were to the text of the Bible, plain and intelligible to all who search
it diligently ; that such diligence might involve considerable learning, as South repeatedly stressed, cast no reflection on the text,
since they were out to discover what the text meant, not whether
it was trustworthy in all its details [1]. The Church of England's
resistance to historical and philological scholarship may, in fact,
account for the tremendous impact of the Higher Criticism in the
nineteenth century, when it seemed to many that the very foundations of their belief had been destroyed by the new approach to
the text of the Bible, to its transmission, etc. It will be remembered
that Dryden was prompted to examine his own beliefs by the
publication of the translation of Father Simon's *Histoire Critique
du Vieux Testament* (1680)[2] ; while in *Religio Laici* he could be
satisfied with the guidance of the Church of England in points
too dark for his dim reason to comprehend, he was soon moved
to seek an unerring guide in Rome. As L.I. Bredvold has argued [3],
this was quite consistent with the philosophical scepticism which
appears even in the Anglican poem.

Such scholarly work as Father Simon's brought to light errors
and gaps in the Scripture text as transmitted through the ages,
but the unreliableness of the Bible as the rule of faith had been
emphasized many years before the *Histoire Critique* appeared by
the most doughty champion of Romanism in England, ' John Sergeant '. His *Sure-Footing in Christianity* (1665) is a closely argued
—though some might say sophistical—set of discourses showing
that the Scripture text is not trustworthy, which argues the need
for oral tradition as the rule of faith. Lest any should misconstrue
him, that is, probably, suspect him of denying Scripture any value
whatsoever, he declares that

> I argue *ad hominem* ; that is, I manifest what must follow
> out of the principles of those who hold Scripture's letter
> the Rule of Faith, not out of my own or Catholic ones [4].

---

[1] Bossuet himself recognized that " les Anglais sont trop instruits dans
l'Antiquité pour ignorer ... les pratiques de l'ancienne Eglise ". *Histoire des
variations du protestantisme*, Book XIV, § 122.

[2] The edition printed in Paris in 1678 was destroyed by order, a faulty
edition was published in Amsterdam in 1680, and a new, corrected, edition
in 1685. An English translation appeared in 1682 ; Dryden's poem was " written
for " the translator.

[3] *Op. cit.*

[4] J. S(ERGEANT): *Sure-Footing in Christianity, or Rational Discourses on*

Driving the Protestants' reliance on the letter of Scripture *ad absurdum*—for the Anglicans, like Tyndale insisted on the literal interpretation of the Bible—Sergeant shows that the divine authority of Scripture is not self-evident ; even granting it were, he says, which of the books are canonical ? even granting this known, is a true copy preserved, is everything translated correctly, can the printers be trusted not to have altered a single letter ? If it is answered that some of these questions can be solved by skill in history, then it follows that only those skilled in history can have a rule of faith. If it is argued that the fundamentals are clear in Scripture, then who is to decide which are the fundamentals ? From this he goes on to argue that Scripture is neither able to ' settle' unlearned persons, nor of its nature to satisfy rational doubters, nor " convictive of the most obstinate and acute adversaries " [1]. Finally, he argues that Scripture has neither certainty in itself nor ' ascertainableness' to us, thus directly opposing the claim of the Anglicans that assent to Scripture is a rational act. Having thus cleared the ground, Sergeant proceeds to show that tradition, i.e. oral tradition, has all the properties he has denied to Scripture, and concludes with a set of forty-one corollaries showing that oral tradition alone has a real claim to be the rule of faith and is infallible.

The answer to Stillingfleet in the third appendix runs along similar lines, and is intended to counter the argument of his *Rational Account of the Grounds of the Protestant Religion* (1664) [2], in which once again Stillingfleet had vindicated Scripture against oral tradition. Though Sergeant's *reductio ad absurdum* shows the weakness of the Anglicans' position with regard to the authority of Scripture, its chief interest lies in his denigration of the Bible in order to establish the authority of oral tradition and the infalli-

---

the Rule of Faith. *With short Animadversions on Dr. Pierce's Sermon : also on some passages in Mr. Whitby and Mr. Stillingfleet, which concern that Rule,* London, 1665, pp. 39-40. Dr. Pierce's sermon *The Primitive Rule of Reformation,* " in vindication of our Church against the novelties at Rome " was preached before the King at Whitehall on 1 Feb., 1661/2. Obviously such staunch Laudians as Pierce found it necessary to warn their congregations against the danger of Rome, particularly at Court, since the Defender of the Faith was known to have leanings towards Catholicism.

[1] *Ibid.*, p. 28.

[2] *A Rational Account of the Grounds of the Protestant Religion ; Being a Vindication of the Lord Archbishop of Canterbury's* [i.e. Laud's] ' *Relation of a Conference between him and John Fisher the Jesuit* ' *from the Pretended Answer of T.C.,* London, 1664.

bility of Rome. From then on the controversy was to rage between Sergeant as the main champion of Rome, and Stillingfleet and Tillotson as the main defenders of the Church of England[1]. Tillotson, whose *Rule of Faith* in answer to Sergeant came out in 1666, was to continue the fight to the end of his life, rehearsing the arguments against Rome in many sermons, and indeed preaching for Princess Anne a whole series of them on the necessity of holding fast by the Protestant religion at the time when the Church was in sorest need and could only pin her hopes of escaping total destruction on the daughters of James by Anne Hyde.

The issue, then, was between implicit faith, i.e. faith received upon the authority of an infallible Church, and rational inquiry into the grounds of religion. The most thorough-going refutation of the claims of Rome to infallibility was Barrow's *A Treatise of the Pope's Supremacy* (1680), which Tillotson published after his friend's death. If Sergeant had argued closely, so closely indeed that his compact discourses leave no time for the reader to consider the matter from a different viewpoint, Barrow's bulky treatise considers the problem from all possible angles, and he brings all the weight of his learning to bear on the argument. Tirelessly, he examines point after point of his adversaries' claims, and by the end one may well think that the matter is closed. Yet it is characteristic of Barrow's exhaustive treatment that even in the form in which we have it his treatise is unfinished : some arguments, or sentences, are clearly jotted down, awaiting development, and there is no conclusion though the reader has drawn his own conclusions long before the author gives over. Tillotson's *Rule of Faith* (1666) manifests even more clearly the firm stand taken by the Church of England on free inquiry, and his sermons on the same subject, though often marred by his partisan spirit [2], may be regarded as the clearest exposition of the principles of *libre examen*.

---

[1] See, for instance, Stillingfleet's letter to Tillotson in reply to Sergeant's attack, which was printed in Tillotson's *Rule of Faith* (1666). Sergeant answered Tillotson in *A Letter of Thanks* (1666), and in *Faith Vindicated from Possibility of Falsehood* (1667 ; though the title-page says 'Printed at Lovain' it was actually published at London). In the latter Sergeant attacked a passage in Tillotson's sermon *On the Wisdom of Being Religious* (1664), to which Tillotson replied in the preface to his first volume of Collected Sermons (1671). In 1672, i.e. after the Declaration of Indulgence as appears clearly from the Advertisement, Sergeant published *Reason against Raillery, or A Full Answer to Dr. Tillotson's Preface against J.S.*

[2] South is no less partisan in his treatment of the Puritans ; the difference will be discussed below.

It is not surprising that Tillotson's works should have been appreciated by such men as Voltaire who were out to " écraser l'infâme " [1], and his popularity on the Continent in the eighteenth century is easily accounted for by the encouragement he gave to the spirit of free inquiry.

As Tillotson tells us in his advertisement to the reader, Barrow's *Treatise of the Pope's Supremacy* [2] is intended to prove from Scripture, reason, and antiquity that the Pope's claim is indefensible, and we may well agree with him that though others had handled the subject before, Barrow has exhausted it. Indeed, in 290 folio pages he examines the various reasons the Romanists advance to support this claim, and he marshals an impressive number of arguments, from Scripture and from ecclesiastical history, to show first that the Pope's supremacy cannot be proved by the arguments the Romanists use, second that it can be disproved by arguments from the same sources ; moreover, in many cases he shows that the claim can also be impugned " from the nature and reason of things abstractedly considered ". The treatise has all the logic and clarity of a mathematical demonstration, and each ' supposition ' [3] is refuted systematically by positive and negative proof, the cumulative evidence being sufficient to silence any adversary. Yet, Barrow's tone is cool, he is content to list facts and to expound texts of Church history. True, he occasionally breaks into sarcasm or becomes pert, but these incidental flashes hardly alter the general tone of the treatise. Apart from the careful method of the learned controversialist, some points are of special interest to us because they help to define the nature of Anglican rationalism.

---

[1] His *Discourse Against Transubstantiation*, first published in 1684, was translated into French and published at London in 1685. His 5 November Sermon, preached before the House of Commons in 1678, i.e. at the time of the Popish Plot, was also published in French at London in 1679.

[2] Isaac BARROW : *A Treatise of the Pope's Supremacy. To which is added A Discourse Concerning the Unity of the Church* (edited by John Tillotson), 2nd ed., London, 1683.

[3] That is, an argument used to support the Pope's supremacy. Barrow examines seven of them, and probably intended more since he is far from concluding when he breaks off. Supposition I, for instance, i.e. ' That Saint Peter had a primacy over the Apostles ', covers pp. 30 to 76, and discusses the four kinds of primacy that may belong to persons (of worth, of reputation, of order, of power) and shows that the first and second kind belonged to Saint Peter, that the third may have, and the fourth never did. The last point he supports with no less than 20 reasons, the last (testimonies) being subdivided into 6 several heads.

Having shown that the *Professio Fidei Tridentinae* was the
first to make the Pope's supremacy an article of faith, Barrow
contends that it is against Christian liberty, which is enjoined by
Scripture :

> 5. This pretence doth thwart the Scripture, by robbing all
> Christian People of the Liberties, and Rights, with which
> by that Divine Charter they are endowed ; and which they
> are obliged to preserve inviolate.
> Saint *Paul* enjoyneth the *Galatians* to *stand fast in the
> liberty, wherewith Christ hath made us free ; and not to
> be entangled again with the yoke of bondage* ; there is
> therefore a liberty, which we must maintain, and a power
> to which we must not submit ; and against whom can we
> have more ground to doe this, than against him, who pre-
> tendeth to dogmatize, to define Points of Faith, to impose
> Doctrines (new and strange enough) on our Consciences,
> under a peremptory obligation of yielding assent to them ?
> to prescribe Laws, as Divine and necessary to be observed,
> without warrant, as those Dogmatists did, against whom
> Saint *Paul* biddeth us to maintain our Liberty : (so that if
> he should declare *vertue to be vice, and white to be black,
> we must believe him*, some of his Adherents have said,
> consistently enough with his pretences)[1].

Lest this last remark should suggest that Barrow's partisan feelings
have got out of control, it should be noted that he can quote chapter
and verse for this, in fact, the authority for this which Anglicans
never fail to quote, Bellarmine's statement : " Si autem Papa erraret
praecipiendo vitia, vel prohibendo virtutes, teneretur Ecclesia credere
vitia esse bona, et virtutes malas, nisi vellet contra conscientiam
peccare "[2]. Barrow thus takes his stand on Christian liberty, a
concept which in the preceding period had been diversely interpreted and had occasioned endless strife[3]. For him as for his
fellow-Anglicans after the Restoration, this means primarily that
Christ has enjoined to us to examine our faith. To accept such
an authority as the Pope claims to have is highly offensive to a
rational creature, whose service to God should be a free and

---

[1] *Ibid.*, p. 126.   [2] Quoted *ibid.*, p. 137.

[3] On the doctrine of Christian Liberty, see, for instance, A.E. BARKER :
Milton and the Puritan Dilemma, Toronto-London, 1942 ; W. HALLER : *Liberty
and Reformation in the Puritan Revolution*, New York, 1955 ; Godfrey DAVIES :
The Early Stuarts, 1603-1660, Oxford, 1945 ; Christopher HILL : *Society and
Puritanism in Pre-Revolutionary England*, London, 1964.

rational choice, not the effect of compulsion, for therein lies the difference between the Covenant of Law and the Covenant of Grace. To deny this is therefore to return to the bondage of the Jews and to distort Christianity from its true end, to transform it

> from a divine Philosophy designed to improve the reason, to moderate the passions, to correct the manners of men, to prepare men for conversation with God and Angels (by modelling it) to a systeme of politick devices (of notions, of precepts, of rites)[1].

Such an authority will make men renounce their reason and senses, and force them to accept such ' monstrous ' doctrines as transubstantiation ; it will also enforce discipline as divinely ordained, whereas it is clear that ecclesiastical ordinances " were established by law and custom, upon prudential accounts " [2].

Barrow's stress on free choice and on the dignity of reason, as well as his denial that Church discipline was divinely established, recalls Hooker and explains why Barrow and others were so firm in their rejection of any claim to dominion over men's minds :

> Truth cannot be supported merely by humane Authority ; especially that authority is to be suspected, which pretendeth dominion over our minds [3].

Barrow's conception of Christian liberty should not be confused with the liberty of tender consciences which the Puritans had claimed and the Dissenters continued to claim after the Restoration : for him it is the liberty to examine the articles of faith, not the liberty to separate for matters of discipline. The Romanists asserted that acceptance of the Pope's supremacy was the only way to insure the unity of the Church, which, they maintained, the Church of

---

[1] *Op. cit.*, p. 138.   [2] *Ibid.*, p. 162.

[3] p. 148. It is only fair to add that in his seventh Supposition, i.e. ' That the Papal Supremacy is indefectible, and unalterable ', Barrow accords to civil government more power than he does to the Pope, on the ground that " No power can have a higher source, or firmer ground, than that of the Civil Government hath, for *all such power is from heaven*, and in relation to that it is said, *There is no power but from God, the powers that are*, are ordained by God " (p. 271). The texts he quotes were used after the Restoration to expound the doctrine of passive obedience ; here Barrow only argues from them that " It hath ever been deemed reasonable, and accordingly been practised, that the Church in its exteriour form and political administrations should be suted to the state of the world, and Constitution of worldly Governments ; that there might be no clashing or disturbance from each to other " (p. 272). He shows that civil governments are mutable, not ' indefectible and unalterable ', hence though they may sometimes encourage errors, such errors may be redressed later.

Rome had preserved in doctrine and in discipline through the ages. They argued from the many differences among Protestants that far from having restored Christanity to its pristine purity the Reformation had only led to its splitting up into many sects which could not agree on the fundamentals of religion although they all insisted that these were revealed clearly in Scripture. The most famous work in which the disagreements among Protestants are used for this purpose is probably Bossuet's *Histoire des variations du protestantisme* (1688) [1]. Barrow's *Treatise* may be said to illustrate the ' variations de l'Eglise de Rome ', and in his *Discourse Concerning the Unity of the Church* he demonstrates, as Tillotson says in his preface, that there is no need to recognize a visible head over the whole Church for its unity to be preserved. According to Barrow the unity of the visible Church consists in the " consent in faith and opinion concerning all principal matters of doctrine ", though there are " points of less moment, more obscurely delivered " about which Christians may dissent, dispute or err without breach of unity. It also consists in the " bands of mutual charity " uniting all Christians, in their " spiritual cognation and alliance ", in their " incorporation into the mystical body of Christ ", in their peaceable concord, in their pastors' agreement in doctrine, and finally in the " specific unity of discipline ", though here again Churches may differ " in lesser matters of ceremony of discipline " [2]. Barrow stresses that matters of discipline are instituted by human prudence, hence may vary according to time and place ; but he adds :

> VIII. It is expedient that all Churches should conform to each other in great matters of prudential Discipline, although not instituted or prescribed by God : for this is a means of preserving Peace, and is a Beauty or Harmony. For difference of Practice doth alienate Affections, especially in common People [3].

The question is, however, whether the Church must be " under one singular Government or Jurisdiction ". He grants that such a union is possible, but he firmly denies that it is " necessary or that it was ever instituted by Christ " [4]. This view he supports with the same kind of arguments as he uses to refute the claims of the Pope in

---

[1] Bossuet does not seem to have known Barrow's treatise ; in his account of the Reformation in England, he refers only to Burnet's *History of the Reformation in England* (the first two volumes had appeared in 1679 and 1681), which he sharply criticizes.
[2] *Op. cit.*, pp. 297-305.   [3] p. 306.   [4] p. 307.

the *Treatise*. Moreover, he shows that his doctrine of the Church cannot be used to ground the claims of the Separatists, and he asserts that the Recusants in England are schismatics like any other Separatists.

The *Discourse*, like the *Treatise*, was left unfinished, but the last two paragraphs clearly define the position of Restoration Anglicans towards the Church of Rome : Churches which by their voluntary consent adhere in confederation to the Roman Church should not be rejected from communion of charity and peace, says Barrow, " for in that they do but use their Liberty " ; *unless* they maintain impious errors or prescribe ' naughty practices '. For all his antipopish zeal, Tillotson says no less : he never stops denouncing the ' impious doctrines ' and the ' naughty practices ' of the Romanists but he refuses to exclude them from the bonds of Christian charity. The temper of these two stalwart champions of the Church of England against Rome was very different indeed from that of the Jesuit Knott, whose *Charity Mistaken* showed that Protestants being beyond the pale of salvation had no claim on charity, thereby provoking Chillingworth to write his *Religion of Protestants*[1].

Tillotson's *Rule of Faith* (1666) does not adduce as many arguments from ecclesiastical history or from Scripture as does Barrow's *Treatise* ; it depends less for its effect on the force of the cumulative proof than on demonstration of the adversary's faulty logic and of the damaging implications of his statements. While Barrow considered the problem with the detachment of the scholar, Tillotson wrote his book in answer to a specific attack against the Protestant rule of faith, John Sergeant's *Sure-Footing*, and his sarcasms sometimes degenerate into abuse. Nevertheless, he reasons lucidly, and though his developments are sometimes lengthy, the plan of his book and the drift of the argument are clear and unencumbered by the exposition of texts from Scripture

---

[1] Anglicans held, and still hold, that the Roman Church is a branch of Christ's universal church (see HOOKER : *Laws*, III, i, 10). While Nonconformist ministers have to be ordained episcopally before they can hold any ecclesiastical office in the Church of England, Roman Catholic priests who join the Church of England are not re-ordained. Pope Leo XIII's Bull *Apostolicae Curae*, on the other hand, declared Anglican orders null and void. On this, see Stephen NEILL : *Anglicanism*, Harmondsworth, 1958 ; J.L.C. DART : *op. cit.* ; Norman SYKES : *Old Priest and New Presbyter, The Anglican Attitude to episcopacy, presbyterianism and papacy since the Reformation*, Cambridge, 1956.

or from the Councils which often make Barrow's demonstration
heavy-going.   Having shown at the outset that Sergeant's definitions of a rule and of faith are mere tautologies, Tillotson proceeds
to explain the meaning of ' a rule of faith ' :

> A *Rule* (when we speak of a *Rule of Faith*) is a Meta-
> phorical Word, which in its first and proper Sense, being
> applied to *material* and *sensible* Things, is the *Measure*
> according to which we judge of the Straightness and Crook-
> edness of things ;   and from hence it is transferr'd by
> Analogy to Things *Moral* or *Intellectual*.   A *Moral Rule*
> is the *Measure* according to which we judge whether a
> Thing be *Good* or *Evil* ;   and this kind of Rule is that which
> is commonly called a *Law*, and the Agreement or Disagree-
> ment of our Actions to this Rule, is suitably to the Metaphor,
> called *Rectitude* or *Obliquity*.   An *Intellectual Rule* is the
> Measure according to which we judge whether a thing be
> *True* or *False* ;   and that is either *General* or more *Particular*.
> Common Notions, and the acknowledged Principles of
> Reason, are that *General Rule*, according to which we judge
> whether a thing be *True* or *False*.   The particular Prin-
> ciples of every Science are the more *particular Rules*, accord-
> ing to which we judge whether things in that Science be
> *True* or *False*.   So that the *General Notion* of a *Rule* is,
> That it is a *Measure, by the Agreement or Disagreement
> to which, we judge of all Things of that kind to which it
> belongs* [1].

It is essential to define the 'kind of things' to which faith belongs,
for this entails the kind of evidence necessary to ground it, since
this kind of assent differs from assent to mathematical demonstrations, and Tillotson distinguishes between demonstrative and moral
evidence, as Stillingfleet had done and as Locke was to do.   He
is not, at this stage, concerned to show what justifies us in accepting Scripture as the testimony of God, since this was not denied
by Sergeant.   The word faith, he says, may be used generally
" for a Persuasion or Assent of the Mind to any Thing wrought
in us by any kind of Argument ",

> Yet, as it is a Term of Art used by *Divines*, it signifies
> that *particular* kind of Assent which is wrought in us by
> *Testimony* or *Authority*.   So that *Divine Faith*, which we
> are now speaking of, is an Assent to a Thing upon the

---

[1] *The Rule of Faith, or an Answer to the Treatise of Mr. J.S. Entitled
Sure-Footing, etc.* (1666), 11th edition, in *The Works*, ed. *cit.*, I, 564.

> Testimony or Authority of God ; or, which is all one, an *Assent to a Truth upon Divine Revelation* [1].

It follows then that the matter to be settled is

> the Measure according to which we judge what Matters we are to assent to, as revealed to us by God, and what not. And more particularly, *The Rule of Christian Faith* is the Measure, according to which we are to judge what we ought to assent to, as the Doctrine revealed by *Christ* to the World, and what not [1].

For him this cannot be oral or practical tradition as opposed to written tradition, but only Scripture, which is the means whereby the Christian doctrine has been brought down to us. Not that he denies value to *all* oral tradition, which may be a sufficient way of conveying a doctrine in *some* circumstances, as in the case of direct witnesses of Christ ; but the circumstances of Apostolical times no longer obtain, hence recourse can only be had to Scripture. He also recognizes that

> Tradition *Oral* and *Written*, do give us sufficient Assurance that the books of Scripture which we now have, are the very Books which were written by the Apostles and Evangelists ; Nay, farther, that *Oral* Tradition alone is a competent Evidence in this Case ; but withal we deny, That Oral Tradition is therefore to be accounted the *Rule of Faith* [2].

What Tillotson means by such dependence on oral tradition appears from what he says in Part III about the assurance we have that Scripture is a divine revelation. There, and only by the way, he answers the first question to be settled by all Christians, that Scripture is a divine testimony. Of this we can only be assured, he says, by the report of trustworthy witnesses of Christ who were persuaded by His miracles that His power was of God. Acceptance of this tradition ultimately depends on the certain evidence of the senses, for if the Apostles' senses could be deceived, their report of Christ's miracles, resurrection and ascension cannot be trusted. Hence, all doctrine that impugns the validity of sense perception when duly tested saps the very foundations of belief in Christ. This is the ground of Tillotson's and his fellow-Anglicans' repudiation of the doctrine of transubstantiation, since

---

[1] *Ibid.*   [2] *Ibid.*, p. 573.

the proper and necessary *consequence* of this Doctrine is to take away all certainty, and especially the certainty of Sense [1].

Tillotson does not here distinguish between such ' monstrous doctrine ' and the mysteries of religion which he and all Anglicans accepted ; but in his sermons he explained the difference between a doctrine that runs *counter* to reason and the evidence of the senses and is not warranted by Scripture, and a point of belief *beyond* reason but plainly taught by Christ. South was as much concerned to distinguish between the two ; he maintained that there was as clear reason for belief in the *credenda* of religion, though sometimes mysterious, as for practice of the *agenda* [2] ; but he also insisted that " nothing can be an article of faith, that is not true ", and that nothing can be true that is irrational. He could not believe, he said, that God gave men reason for them to ignore it and become brutes, nor eyes for them to pluck them out ; hence, it is as much against the purpose of a perfect, i.e. rational and good, Creator for men to follow ' inbeamings ', ' lights ', and inspirations which contradict reason, as for them to deny the report of their senses, which were created capable of judging of their proper objects. The Trinity is not an object of sense, nor does it contradict reason ; it is above the reach of human reason, not against it, since it is reasonable to believe that the divine nature has a way of subsisting different from that of created beings [3]. South is no less firm than Tillotson in denouncing those that traduce reason as the irreconcilable enemy of religion, though his target is both the enthusiasts and the Romanists.

Tillotson's main objection to reliance on oral tradition is that it undermines the foundations of faith in Christ : in order to establish the infallibility of their Church the Romanists " run to the extremities of scepticism ", though they contradict themselves in asserting both that reason is too dim-sighted to choose its own way, and clear-sighted enough to choose an infallible guide to doctrine. Tillotson, in fact, feared the growth of philosophical scepticism quite as much as he feared the fallacious appeal of Rome. Given the danger of renouncing reason by accepting faith upon

[1] *Ibid.*, p. 635.
[2] See his sermon on *Christianity Mysterious and the Wisdom of God in making it so*, in *Twelve Sermons, op. cit.*, III, ser. 6.
[3] See his sermon on the Trinity, printed below.

authority or by following the inner light, it is easy to understand why in their crusade against infidelity the Anglicans should not have 'traduced' reason, but rather emphasized that reason and faith are agreeable, indeed that faith is the perfection of reason. It is not surprising, either, that both the Puritans' and the Romanists' main objection against Anglican theology was that it assigned such a part to reason in faith. In doing this Anglican divines were continuing a tradition to which Hooker had given magnificent expression, and which had been re-defined by Falkland, Chillingworth and Stillingfleet [1].

In their sermons, Barrow, South, and Tillotson like all Anglican divines opposed the spread of infidelity and met the arguments levelled at Christianity by the modern sceptics. Religious teachers in all ages have no doubt found it necessary to counter the attacks of doubters and scoffers, but after the Restoration there were many reasons why divines should be specially concerned with the growth of scepticism. The term infidelity as used by them refers to both philosophical and practical atheists, i.e. to the modish scoffers and libertines who jibed at religion because it imposes a curb on men's appetites, as well as to those who following bare reason rejected the evidence of the Christian religion ; it also refers to Socinianism and to the materialism of the new Epicurus, or Hobbism, and in the nineties to the natural religion of the Deists. The most thorough-going answer to these various kinds of infidels is probably Tillotson's first published sermon, *The Wisdom of Being Religious* [2]; the care with which he revised his text from edition to edition—now altering a word for greater precision, now transposing a passage to give it greater force, or adding new developments—testifies to the importance of the issues. What he sets out to prove is, in fact, the unreasonableness of infidelity as a rule

---

[1] In his Preface to the first collection of his sermons (1671), which was reprinted in all editions of the *Fifty Four Sermons and The Rule of Faith*, Tillotson answers further charges of Sergeant against a passage from his first published sermon, *The Wisdom of Being Religious*, and says that Sergeant has " honoured (him) with excellent Company, my Lord Faulkland, Mr. Chillingworth, and Dr. Stillingfleet ". *Ibid.*, sig. B v. Hooker's work had been prompted by his opposition to Puritans, Falkland's and Chillingworth's by the need to resist the claims of Rome, Stillingfleet's by the attacks of the libertines. These were also the forces against which Restoration theologians came to define their own position.

[2] Printed below.

of life and as a philosophy. He first states that, though a perfect knowledge of nature requires a wisdom and understanding equal to the Creator's, yet a sufficient knowledge of God and of our duty to him is attainable by man if he uses his reason rightly. He then proceeds to demonstrate that speculative atheism—whether ' Aristotelian ' or Epicurean—is unreasonable

> 1. because it gives no tolerable account of the existence of the world ; 2. Nor does it give any reasonable account of the universal consent of mankind in this apprehension, That there is a God. 3. It requires more evidence for things than they are capable of. 4. The Atheist pretends to know that which no man can know. 5. Atheism contradicts it self [1].

On the first count he argues that the several hypotheses of the atheists—whether the belief that the matter and frame of the world are eternal, or Epicurean or modern materialism—have against them both the universal consent of mankind and the probabilities of reason, and in fact raise more difficulties than they solve. Tillotson then considers the causes to which atheists ascribe the universal belief in God : fear, tradition, and policy of State, i.e. the explanation given by Hobbes in the *Leviathan*. In developing his third objection he makes the usual [2] distinction between the strict demonstrations which mathematical things are capable of, the proof by ' induction of experiments ' in natural philosophy, and the moral arguments which establish things of a moral nature. On the fourth count Tillotson merely shows that to be certain of ' a pure negative ' is more than man can know ; nor does he enlarge on the inner contradictions of atheism. Instead, he goes on to show that speculative atheism works directly against the present interest of men as well as against their future happiness ; at which point he says that even supposing the arguments for and against a God were equal, men should out of mere prudence choose to live by the safer hypothesis [3]. Tillotson next addresses himself to practical

---

[1] *Op. cit.*, p. 6.

[2] His second kind, induction by experiments, was not used by either Stillingfleet or Barrow. But Tillotson was a close friend of Wilkins who, if not the ' onely begetter ' of the Royal Society, was one of the promoters of the new science.

[3] The sermon was first published in 1664, and the earlier version of this passage is even closer to Pascal's wager, e.g. " the hazard and danger is so infinitely unequal, that in point of prudence every man were obliged to incline to the affirmative ; and... to make that the principle to live by " (*op. cit.*, p. 23); the 1664 ed. has " ... to make that the hypothesis to live by ". Though the

atheism, which, he says, argues folly while speculative atheism may be no more than ignorance ; he does not develop the point here, but it is the theme of his sermon on *The Folly of Scoffing at Religion* [1], on 2 *Pet*. III. 3. There he considers the three hypotheses : suppose there were no God, suppose the matter doubtful, suppose it certain that there is a God [2]. Tillotson's answer to the scoffers, if it be granted that there is no God, is characteristic of his tolerant and peaceable temper : since they have no obligation of conscience to dispute against the principles of religion, the atheists should forbear to offend the generality of mankind ; it is a breach of the laws of civil conversation to deride or attack other people's belief unless it is to vindicate truth. Clearly, Tillotson— and indeed most of his contemporaries—cannot envisage any truth other than that of religion, nor allow for obligation of conscience except in the context of religion, and this is an important qualification of their rationalism.

Barrow too preached on ' The Evil and Unreasonableness of Infidelity ' and on ' The Virtue and Reasonableness of Faith ' [3]. He considers infidelity as affected blindness and ignorance of the noblest and most useful truths, resulting from the wrong use of reason, since God has proposed a doctrine intelligible to man's reason, with clear attestations of its divine origin and plain arguments to recommend it. Rather than show that the atheists' views are unreasonable, he examines the causes of such distorted use of reason, i.e. negligence, sloth, dullness of apprehension, perverseness of will, etc., and in conclusion he shows that the evil spirit from which infidelity proceeds best appears from the principles usually espoused with it. The principles he then lists can all be related to Hobbes's philosophy as interpreted by his contemporaries, and indeed Hobbes looms large in all attacks against infidelity. Again applying the pragmatic test, rather than arguing against atheism, Barrow shows how evil infidelity is from its effects upon men's lives. If it be objected that Christians need not be warned against such impious doctrines, Barrow answers that many infidels wear the mask of Christians. Thus he too, though only *in fine*, directs

---

revision clearly shows T.'s fear of misunderstanding, the earlier *hypothesis* reveals the parallel with Pascal's count of probabilities in gambling.

[1] *Op. cit.*, sermon 2.

[2] South considers the same hypotheses in *op. cit.*, II, ser. 1.

[3] Sermons on the Creed, 1 (printed below), 2, 3, The titles, however, are not Barrow's but his editor's, i.e. Tillotson's.

his attack against 'practical atheists', i.e. men of dissolute life. Here, more clearly than in Tillotson, appears the link between doctrine and practice which all Anglicans stressed, that by their fruits ye shall know them. The point will be emphasized in sermon after sermon by all divines, not only in their crusade against 'infidels' but against the Antinomians, or at least against the encouragement given to Antinomianism by some Puritan tenets. Hence, in spite of the King's *Directions for Preachers* enjoining to preachers to avoid controversial matters, the many expositions of the doctrine of Grace, and the stress on the necessity of practice as well as of faith. Hence, also, the Puritans' charge that the Anglicans were mere 'practical preachers'.

In his two sermons on the reasonableness of faith Barrow discusses the nature of faith : if the doctrine is propounded with evident and cogent reason, he asks, what virtue is there in believing ? if no such arguments can be advanced, what fault is there in withholding assent ? Now, for Barrow faith means the knowledge of the most worthy and important truths, not attainable otherwise, but it is knowledge 'in way of great evidence and assurance'. It can be brought to trial at the bar of reason, for our religion, he says, only admits man if he understands and is persuaded of its truth. If the moral evidence establishing the divine origin of our rule of faith does not satisfy a man 'too wise', then reason itself well followed will lead him thither. God not only allows but enjoins us to use our best reason ; to require faith without reason is an impossibility, and to accept a doctrine on bare authority is not faith at all. Faith takes us beyond the sphere of natural light ; whereas pagan philosophers could only seek truth, but had no assurance of it, Christians have such knowledge on the infallible testimony of God, conveyed to them by powerful evidence : for want of this, says Barrow, human wisdom is but blind and lame. It is a foul aspersion on religion to say that it challenges assent without proof. Faith is indeed a gift of God, it cannot grow on bad soil, but many men wilfully obstruct the light of faith for lack of diligence or of sincerity of judgment, or because their appetites influence their judgements. Hence all faith " may be deemed voluntary, no less than intellectual " [1]; it requires both the bare assent of the understanding and the free consent of the will. God has

---

[1] Sermons on the Creed, in *op. cit.*, II, 35.

not made the truths of religion conspicuous to sense, nor demon-
strable by reason like theorems in geometry, which could *compel*
man to believe. God requires a free choice upon rational grounds.
Even greater motives would not work upon those whom these
sufficient reasons do not convince, for they would devise shifts,
forge exceptions and oppose an obstinate will against the truth ;

> Wherefore it was for the common good, and to divine
> wisdom it appeared sufficient, that upon the balance truth
> should much outweigh falshood [1], if the scales were held in
> an even hand, and no prejudices were thrown in against it ;
> that it should be conspicuous enough to eyes, which do not
> avert themselves from it, *or wink* on purpose, or be clouded
> with lust and passion ; it was enough that infidelity is justly
> chargeable on mens wilfull pravity ; and that πρόφασιν οὐκ
> ἔχουσιν, *they have not* (as our Saviour saith) *any reasonable
> excuse for it* [2].

Faith is not, however, a mere " notion swimming in the head ", as
he says in the next sermon [3], it is a tree that bears fruit, and must
issue in practice.

So firmly were Barrow and his fellow-Anglicans convinced that
reason if rightly directed could arrive at the truths of Christianity
that they were unable to envisage that unbelief might result from
other causes than the wrong use of reason through the weakness
or depravity of the will. They would not have said with Pascal :
" Tu ne me chercherais pas si tu ne m'avais déjà trouvé ", but
rather : " seek, and ye shall find ". South argued from the same
premiss in his sermon on *John* VII. 7 [4] : the Christian religion was
recommended to the reason of men with the same authority and
evidence as the law of Moses ; if the Jews, like the later infidels,
rejected it, it was not for want of evidence but because their understanding was obscured by their appetites. Assent to the truths
of religion requires a careful examination of these truths, and this
entails labour. Though it is not in the power of the will to cause
or hinder the assent of the understanding to a thing proposed to it,
yet it is in its power *antecedently* to apply the understanding faculty
to it. After briefly defining assent, and concluding that " incurable
blindness is caused by a resolution not to see ", South moves on to

---

[1] That is, the arguments for religion should outweigh those against it.
[2] *Ibid.*, p. 38.   [3] *Ibid.*, p. 50.   [4] Printed below.

discuss the other point Barrow raises : that faith is a gift of God. Barrow says : " Faith is a fruit of God's Spirit ; but such as will not grow in a bad soil " ; South expresses this much more strongly : faith, he says, is " a ray of such light, as never darts itself upon a dunghill ". This violence is the counterpart of his contempt for all pretences at inspiration as well as of the intellectual vigour he requires in the search after truth : truth, he says, is " a great stronghold, barred and fortified by God and nature " to which the understanding must lay siege. Thus, while insisting that the truths of religion are evident to reason, he is far from suggesting that they are no more than what mere common sense can see plainly and easily. South, indeed, required discipline in all works of the mind, and could have nothing but contempt for loose thinking or loose speaking, for the confused and confusing use of words which issues in intellectual and moral chaos. This intellectual energy is coupled in him with a deeper sense than either Barrow or Tillotson seem to have of the purification of the will necessary before the understanding can see clearly. He often recalls the Cambridge Platonists, particularly in this sermon when he explains that growth in knowledge of religion is required, but that it is a knowledge " men are not so much to study, as to live themselves into " ; purge the heart, he says, and knowledge will break in upon the soul like the sun. Clearly, the life of truth is a long and hard training. If South stressed, as much as did Barrow and Tillotson, that faith must issue in works, he could never have been called a mere practical preacher. For one thing, the *agenda* he recommended were based on what he considered as the main matter of practice enjoined by Christ, self-denial ; and the *credenda* could only be grasped by a mind striving for truth.

As one might expect the fight against infidelity also involved denunciation of the vices of the age, particularly of the profligacy of those whom Tillotson called the practical atheists. Though this again is the theme of many sermons in all ages, it had a particular cogency after the Restoration. It is well known that Burnet lost his chaplaincy to Charles II for remonstrating against the vices of the Court. Restoration sermons abound in pictures of the manners of the age ; Anglican divines cannot be accused of an unfavourable bias since they were committed to preach respect to people in authority, and the vices they censured were most notorious in the polite world and at Court. If anything they were very temperate and often managed to express themselves in covert terms. Only one aspect of this need concern us here, South's denunciation of the imposture of words [1], because it is linked with his censure of the moral relativism associated with Hobbes. Here again, the concept of right reason, as both knowledge of truth and choice of good, is central, and South animadverts on those who abuse men's minds with false notions by using language loosely, on purpose or following the fashion of the times. This calling of evil good and good evil leads to moral anarchy by blurring all differences between good and evil : when a debauchee is called a good-natured man the true nature of things is obscured, and when this becomes the general way of converse ' plausible words ', i.e. words of praise, are used to refer to the most shameful objects. Thus South links the inversion of values so characteristic of Restoration society with the inversion of language, which as the instrument of a rational being should serve to convey the true images of things to the minds of others. It is not surprising, he says, that unbecoming liberties should be more and more common, and be generally approved, if they are usually called " the genteel freedom of the town " : if such terms are now the common coin for vile behaviour, no wonder that vice should stalk the world in full glory. One need only turn to such Restoration comedies as *The Country Wife* to realize that South is not exaggerating the power of words to keep a genteel mask over plain debauchery. It is, however, characteristic of South that he should not confine his censure of the imposture of words to the effect on the manners of the time, but should denounce even more violently the corruption of the mind that follows on such loose use of language. For words are, or should be, instruments of right reason, for communication, not for obfuscation or deception. At this stage in South's argument it is clear from the examples he gives that his target is no longer the ' practical atheists ', but the enthusiasts who lead the blind mob astray : the sheep indeed look up to their pastors, and are fed with empty words which corrupt them from true service to God and from obedience to their prince [2].

---

[1] See the sermon printed below ; there are 3 further sermons on the same text, in *op. cit.*, VI, sermons 1 to 3.

[2] South's denunciation of the abuse of words, and of the exploitation of them for political purposes, may be compared with Orwell's in *Politics and the*

Chillingworth and Hales had been accused of Socinianism for their defence of reason. The charge was to be preferred against many Anglican divines after the Restoration, particularly against Tillotson. True, the word was used as loosely as the word 'atheism' had been in Marlowe's time, and sometimes was little more than a vague term of abuse. Still, by assigning to reason such an important part in faith Anglicanism seemed to many to be barely distinguishable from Socinianism, or later from Deism. In his sermon against unbelief South had referred to Socinus' view that man's assent to Christianity follows from the natural disposition of his mind, in order to show that the Christian doctrine is agreeable to reason [1]. It was only natural that this point should receive particular stress in sermons directed against infidelity, and for this reason, no less than from the natural bent of his mind, Tillotson returned to it again and again. He was also fair enough to give the devil his due, and in one of his sermons [2] he compared favourably the moderation of Socinus with the heat and contentiousness of religious disputants at home. But such fairness was too rare at the time, and Tillotson was at once attacked for daring to praise such an impious man.

However much Anglican divines agreed with Socinus in stating that natural or bare reason is the basis of all faith and directs man to accept Scripture as the Word of God, they also stressed that, as South put it [3], by following reason man will meet another light, or that faith is the perfection of reason, because God has revealed truths which bare reason could not have found out. If Anglican divines use the testimony of heathen philosophers, it is to show both that Christ's teachings agree with what natural reason could teach man and also that something has been superadded which the best philosophers could not have discovered. Natural religion even without revelation, South argues [4], is sufficient to make a

---

English Language and in the Appendix to *1984* on 'The Principles of Newspeak'. South's treatment of the fanatics' jargon suggests that, *mutatis mutandis*, he would have agreed with Orwell that "from time to time one can even, if one jeers loudly enough, send some worn-out and useless phrase—some *jackboot, Achilles' heel, hotbed, melting pot, acid test, veritable inferno*, or other lump of verbal refuse—into the dustbin where it belongs". Though he was the scourge of the Puritans, South might be called a Puritan in regard to language, which he wished to preserve undefiled from such corruption.

[1] See the Sermon printed below, on *John* VII. 7.
[2] On *John* I. 14, in *op. cit.*, I, ser. 44.
[3] *Op. cit.*, II, ser. 11, p. 415.   [4] *Op. cit.*, II, ser. 7.

sinner inexcusable ; but though bare reason is sufficient to tell us
what not to do, it cannot always tell us what to do [1]. The same
is true of the speculative part of doctrine : it agrees with bare
reason, but transcends it since no creature could have discovered
by his mere natural light such truths as Christ's Incarnation and
Atonement. Nor can bare reason fathom such mysteries once they
are revealed ; all it can do is to see that given the immeasurable
distance between finite creatures and an infinite Creator it must
posit a different mode of existence for God, and not limit Him to
what is possible for created beings : to apply to God arguments
from created nature is, South says, to argue *a genere ad genus* [2].
Reason is a ray of divinity, the Candle of the Lord, and " it ought
to be no disparagement to a star, that it is not a sun " [3] ; but it is
often defective and must be guided by the mind of God uttered
in His revealed Word, for " nothing that contradicts the Revealed
Word of God is the voice of Right Reason " [4]. This may seem
to reverse Locke's statement that " no proposition can be received
for divine revelation, ... if it be contrary to our clear and intuitive
knowledge " [5], unless we remember that according to Locke too
we can have no clear and intuitive knowledge of the ' intellectual
world ', and that the narrow inlets by which we receive simple ideas
" are disproportionate to the vast whole extent of all beings " [6].
Similarly, the Anglican divines now stress the sufficiency of reason,
now its limitations according as they demonstrate the foundations
of assent to Christian truths, or the nature of these truths. These
are the two sides of their main argument, which in no way contradict each other.

South's most violent denunciation of Socinianism appears in his
sermon on the mysteriousness of Christianity, preached in 1694,
that is, at the time of the Trinitarian controversy, when the principles and methods of Socinus were used to support the ' liberal
rationalism ' of the Unitarians, and were soon to be used by ' a
certain Mahommetan Christian ', as South calls John Toland, in
Christianity Not Mysterious (1696). This work, though it did
not initiate Deism, gave it a new impetus by exploiting some of

[1] *Op. cit.*, II, ser. 11.
[2] See his sermon on the Trinity, printed below.
[3] See his sermon on *1 John* III. 21, printed below.
[4] *Ibid.*   [5] *Essay*, Bk. IV, ch. XVIII, § 5.
[6] *Ibid.*, ch. III, § 23.

the principles inherent in rational theology and notably in Locke's *The Reasonableness of Christianity* (1695), and by drawing facile conclusions from them which altogether banished mystery from religion.   South animadverted on the harm done to Christianity by these new Socinians (and also by the 'Tritheists' who opposed them [1]) in the dedication to the Archbishop of Dublin prefixed to the third volume of his sermons (1698), in which *Christianity Mysterious and the Wisdom of God in making it so* first appeared, and he may well have chosen to publish this sermon in order to answer the Deists.   In the sermon itself he equates Socinianism with these 'later blasphemies':

> The Socinians indeed, who would obtrude upon the World, (and of late more daringly than ever) a new Christianity of their own inventing, will admit of nothing *mysterious* in this Religion, nothing, which the natural Reason of Man cannot have a clear and comprehensive Perception of : And this not only in Defiance of the express Words of Scripture so frequently and fully affirming the contrary, but also of the constant, universal Sense of all Antiquity unanimously confessing an Incomprehensibility in many of the Articles of the Christian Faith [2].

South, who had never stopped denouncing the danger to religion of the Puritans' mistaken notions, finds such innovations more scandalous than any propounded before even in " those times of confusion both in Church and State betwixt Forty One and Sixty ". But he charges with equal blasphemy those who pretend to resolve the difficulties of the mysteries of religion, for the consequence of this is that these mysteries come to be ridiculed.   This had been the burden of his repeated attacks against Sherlock, the self-appointed champion of the Trinity ;   for, as South says in this sermon,

> he who thinks and says he can understand all *Mysteries*, and resolve all *Controversies*, undeniably shews, that he really understands none [3].

---

[1] South charged William Sherlock, author of *A Vindication of the Holy and Ever-Blessed Trinity* (1690), with Tritheism in his *Animadversions Upon Dr. Sherlock's Book Entituled A Vindication of the Holy ... Trinity*, London, 1693, and in *Tritheism Charged upon Dr. Sherlock's New Notion of the Trinity*, London, 1695.

[2] *Op. cit.*, III, ser. 6, p. 216.   [3] *Ibid.*, p. 252.

In other sermons, for instance on the Incarnation [1], South emphasizes the paradox to human reason of Christ's coming to man ; in another, on the General Resurrection [2], he asserts the incomprehensibility of the doctrine, yet says that reason assents to it because it is revealed plainly by God ; in yet another, on the creation of Adam, he counters the objection that

> the producing *Something* out of *Nothing* is impossible and incomprehensible : Incomprehensible indeed I grant, but not therefore impossible ... (since) it is not always rational to measure the truth of an Assertion by the Standard of our Apprehension [3].

It is also significant that when South published his sermon on *Rom.* I. 20 *So that they are without excuse,* in which he shows that the Gentiles had no excuse for rejecting Christ's teachings since their bare reason should have been satisfied of the truths of the Gospel, he gave it the title : *Natural Religion, without Revelation, shewn only sufficient to render a sinner inexcusable,* a title which does not adequatly sum up the main theme of the sermon [4]. For South, then, there are limits to what reason can do, and rational inquiry must not be pursued beyond a certain point. To apply reason to objects not proper to it is to sin against right reason.

The Anglican position in regard to the use of reason and to its limitations is best exemplified by South, because of the cogency of his statements and the acuteness of his thinking, but also because he was confronted in the nineties with the rise of Deism. Yet Barrow too had set bounds to rational inquiry, on much the same grounds as South. Indeed, in a sermon on the Trinity he develops the same argument against reducing all truths to what human reason can comprehend [5]. Like South, Barrow emphasizes the incomprehensible nature of this mystery :

That there is one Divine Nature or Essence, common unto

---

[1] *Op. cit.,* III, ser. 8.   [2] *Op. cit.,* IV, ser. 6.
[3] *Op. cit.,* I, ser. 2, p. 45.
[4] *Op. cit.,* II, ser. 7. The sermon was preached in 1690 ; vol. II of the Sermons was published in 1694.
[5] This sermon, *A Defence of the Blessed Trinity,* was not included in the *Works* of Barrow published by Tillotson. It first appeared in 1697. The printer, Brabazon Aylmer, tells the readers that the MS. was overlooked by Dr. Tillotson. It is likely that the ' discovery ' was prompted by the growth of Deism.

three Persons incomprehensibly united, and ineffably distinguished... These are notions which may well puzzle our
reason in conceiving how they agree, but should not stagger
our faith in assenting that they are true [1].

Like South too, he condemns both those who flatly deny the
Trinity because they cannot understand it, and those who attempt
to demonstrate these mysteries :

There be those, who, because they cannot untie, dare to
cut asunder these sacred knots ; who, because they cannot
fully conceive, dare flatly to deny them ; who, instead of
confessing their own infirmity, do charge the plain doctrines
and assertions of Holy Scripture with impossibility. Others
seem to think they can demonstrate these mysteries by arguments grounded upon principles of natural light; and express
them by similitudes derived from common experience. To
repress the presumption of the former, and to restrain the
curiosity of the latter, the following considerations... may
perhaps somewhat conduce [2].

He proceeds to submit the following considerations : our reason is
no capable judge of such propositions ; the manner of using our
reason incapacitates us to judge of these matters, because we have
no principles pertinent to discourse on this subject ; even about
things most familiar our reason is weak and short ; we daily see
and observe things, which, did not manifest experience convince
us of their being, we should be apt to disbelieve ; the propositions
delivered by God are more unquestionably true than the experiments
of sense or the principles of any science. Since all divine attributes
baffle our reason, he says, we should meditate upon the incomprehensibility of God in all things belonging to him, not meddle
with his essence, since even seraphim are unable to sustain the
' fulgor ' of His immediate presence. The proper employment of
our mind about these mysteries is not to speculate about them, but
to embrace them with pious credulity. As always with Barrow
the list of considerations is impressive ; compared with South he
may well seem to have viewed the nature and use of reason in all
their aspects, and to have closed the question by exhausting all
the topics. He too states that

---

[1] Isaac BARROW : *Theological Works*, ed. Alexander Napier, Cambridge,
1859, IV, 494.
[2] *Ibid.*, p. 495.

no light in any manner imparted by God can obscure the doctrine declared by him, no doctrine can thwart principles instilled by him [1]

since the various means of knowing truth God has given us cannot clash with each other. Though he elsewhere insists that it is our duty to exercise our reason in religion, he emphasizes the infirmity of man in front of the universe as well as in front of God, and his words look forward to the *Essay on Man* :

> Shall we then, who cannot pierce into the nature of a pebble, that cannot apprehend how a mush-room doth grow, that are baffled in our philosophy about a gnat, or a worm, debate and decide (beyond what is taught us from above) concerning the precise manner of divine essence, subsistence, or generation [2] ?

Barrow, the friend of Newton, knew indeed that sense no less than faith presents us with objects which appear improbable or even inconceivable ; he knew, too, that the observations of sense often prove fallacious. But, like South, he believed in the fundamental unity of all truth, and of knowledge, as deriving ultimately from God, the fountain of all truth, who conveys His light to us either directly or refracted through divers mediums. Reason and faith, then, are not opposed, but only several ways of arriving at different aspects of truth.

From the manuscript of another sermon [3] on *Col. III. 2*, it appears that Barrow had planned two sermons on the same text. They are indeed complementary, for he there argues that man can attain to an adequate knowledge of God, and that God has enjoined on us to apply our understanding to contemplate His admirable perfections, set forth in the works of nature and even more clearly in Scripture. There he defends the proposition that God is the most proper and 'connatural' object of our understanding, that he is intelligible since he is infinitely simple, consistent, and immutable whereas things in nature are in perpetual flux. Whereas we per-

---

[1] *Ibid.*, p. 498.   [2] *Ibid.*, p. 501.
[3] In Trinity College, Cambridge (T.C. MS. 0.10. a. 32). On the last page is the opening of another sermon on the same text, which begins like the preceding. Since it is written on the verso of the last page, however, it is more likely to have been a continuation rather than a rewriting of the other, and probably represents the beginning of the sermon on the Trinity. The sermon was first published by Alexander Napier, in *op. cit.*, IV : *An Adequate Knowledge of God attainable by Man.*

ceive very little of other objects we can perceive the essential attributes of God : His magnificence, infinite goodness, wisdom and power.   God is light and by His light all things are illuminated. Barrow checks himself in this speculation which may seem " too Platonical ", but he argues that though estranged from God since the Fall man still has in him a tendency to know and seek Him, and that it is the most proper operation of our understanding, which was designed to know and converse about God.   The knowledge of God to which we are directed is adequate knowledge such as Barrow has defined, i.e. something that Locke would not have called knowledge at all since Barrow stresses that we can have no clear and distinct ideas about God, that God's being and attributes are incomprehensible to human reason, that indeed divine incomprehensibility is one of these attributes.   It is striking indeed that Barrow, who achieved international fame in his time for his work in mathematics, should base his argument on the intelligibility of God, and conclude that incomprehensibility is one of God's attributes.   South, the stern logician, would never have been guilty of such a faulty reasoning.   However that may be, it is clear that Barrow intended to demonstrate that man's reason is naturally bent towards God, since it is an image of the mind of God.   That he was thereby led to platonize is only natural, since he was expounding the concept of right reason.   But he was not prepared to follow Plato all the way ; indeed, he says, Plato's conceptions are perhaps too much admired at present.   What he wished to teach was reverence for a Creator whose wisdom, goodness, and power are manifested in the universe.   Here, then, we see the two trends of thought merging, if not quite happily, in the one sermon, and both indirectly upholding the rationality of faith.   Elsewhere too Barrow had said that religion does not quench natural light, but confirms and improves it [1] ; that we must exercise our reason upon the acts of Providence if we would understand God's design [2] ; that in interpreting Scripture we should beware of making a text clash with reason and experience [3]; that we should wisely consider God's doing because no good action can follow unless we understand His purpose rightly [4].   For him, then, as for South, faith is

---

[1] See, for instance, the sermon *Against Foolish Talking and Jesting*, printed below.

[2] See *Works*, I, ser. 11.

[3] *Against Foolish Talking and Jesting*.

[4] *Op. cit.*, I, ser. 11.

agreeable to reason but transcends it, and the mysteries we receive upon rational grounds should not be pried into.

The main burden of Tillotson's sermons is the reasonableness of religion ; again and again he shows that Christianity enforces the great duties of natural religion, that natural and revealed religion agree, and that only malicious opposition resulting from the depraved will can prevent us from accepting the evidence of Christ ; he even defines the sin against the Holy Ghost as this wilful resistance to the evidence of the truths of religion. He grounds the excellency of the Christian religion in the fact that it reveals the nature of God more clearly than did the law of Moses, whose moral precepts he elsewhere equates with natural law ; that it gives a more certain and perfect law for the government of our lives, propounds more powerful arguments for us to obey that law, and furnishes better motives to patience and contentedness [1]. In another sermon he shows that the precepts of Christianity are not grievous since the laws of God are reasonable, that is, " suitable to our nature and advantageous to our interest ", that we are not destitute of the power and ability to perform the duties laid on us, and that we have the greatest encouragements for doing so, i.e. the promise of rewards [2]. As one reads his sermon on *The Precepts of Christianity not Grievous* one may well wonder what difference there is, except for the promise of rewards, between Christianity and mere natural religion. And the question forces itself upon us in sermon after sermon, as Tillotson insists that the main duties enjoined by Christ are consonant with natural law, or emphasizes the wisdom of Christianity. In fact, he equates faith with wisdom, as a rule of life that directs us to our own good, and he also shows that religion is not only suitable to our nature, but profitable to us. The stress he lays on the advantage of religion indeed makes many of his sermons most unpalatable to modern readers. When he argues the reasonableness of Christianity we may feel that such a temper and moderation were highly commendable in an age when so much heat was brought to religious disputes ; he could argue with the infidels that they could have no reasonable objection to Christianity, as well as suit the temper of his more pragmatic hearers by showing them what moral good was to be

---

[1] *The Excellency of the Christian Religion*, in op. cit., I, ser. 5.
[2] *The Precepts of Christianity not Grievous*, in op. cit., I, ser. 6.

derived from Christianity. That such moral good was often presented as a practical advantage may be ascribed to the kind of
people he was out to persuade ; but one feels that this also resulted
from the turn of Tillotson's own mind. Indeed, one often wonders
if he had any inkling of the utter incomprehensibility of the Godhead, of the unfathomable wisdom of God's purposes, or even of
the complexities of the human heart. His view of the world is
decidedly untragic and unmysterious, and though he exercised his
reason on the admirable contrivance of the universe he could easily
ignore the more baffling problems with which it confronts man.
He was not, it seems, able to realize the sheer inconceivableness
of the Incarnation, nor to feel the profound awe which the sacrifice
of the divine victim had inspired in earlier ages [1]. In this Tillotson
was not unlike his contemporaries, but his equable temper no less
than the need he felt to reform men's lives by teaching right practice
made him overstress the 'reasonable' side of Christianity. As one
reads him one is constantly reminded that the age of enlightenment
is not far off, and he may well have contributed to popularize a
cool, dispassionate, but also unardent form of religion, which would
soon be hardly distinguishable from Deism [2].

Yet, some aspects of his teachings make the charge of Deism
untenable, such as the part he assigns to Grace or his belief in the
Providence of God at work in the universe and in the lives of men.
Characteristically, these ideas are not developed in the sermons he
first collected for publication, as though he had chosen to present
to the public what seemed to him most urgently needed : the
defence of Christianity on rational grounds, the objections to
implicit faith in an infallible Church, and the enforcement of duties.
In the 1694 volume, however, he collected six sermons, some of
which had been preached in 1679-80. This, he tells his readers
in the advertisement [3], he was prompted to do in answer to the
calumnies of his detractors [4]. Thus at the time when the mysteries

---

[1] The *Six Sermons* published in 1694 deal with : the Divinity of Christ
(I, 43 and 44), the Incarnation of Christ (I, 45 and 46), the Sacrifice and
Satisfaction of Christ (I, 47), and the Unity of the Divine Nature and the
Trinity (I, 48).
[2] On this, see G.R. CRAGG : *The Church and the Age of Reason (1648-
1789)*, Harmondsworth, 1960, ch. 5.
[3] Reprinted in the first folio volume containing *Fifty Four Sermons and
the Rule of Faith*.
[4] See Burnet's funeral sermon : " His endeavouring to make out every thing
in Religion from clear and plain Principles, and with a Fulness of demonstrative

of religion were impugned he published a series of sermons in which he had asserted the mysteriousness of Christianity. There he clearly takes his stand against Socinus and his subtlety of wit in interpreting Scripture, and he refutes the doctrines of the Arians and of the Socinians, who pretended that Christ was a mere creature [1]. The next sermon is wholly devoted to disproving the Socinians' thesis by establishing from the text that the Word had existence before the Incarnation [2]; he there shows that the liberty of interpretation does not entail proposing any interpretation as possible, and he even says that it would be fairer altogether to reject the divine authority of Scripture than to put such disingenuous construction upon it. Since, however, the Socinians claim to have reason on their side when they deny the divinity of Christ and the Trinity, Tillotson is prepared to bring his doctrine to the bar of reason as well as of Scripture. The Socinians say such a doctrine is not only above but contrary to reason; to which Tillotson answers that reason is not able to comprehend such mysteries fully, and that trying to explain them will only entangle the matter : he is content to show that though the doctrine plainly taught by Christ is beyond the reach of our finite understanding it involves no contradiction, and that the Socinians' opinion has greater difficulties and is really absurd.

Tillotson thus comes out as firmly as do Barrow and South for the acceptance of incomprehensible truths provided they are clearly revealed by God. It is, however, characteristic of him that he should remark :

> And thus much may suffice to have said upon this Argument, which I am sensible is mere Controversy : a Thing which I seldom meddle with, and do not delight to dwell upon [3].

It is equally characteristic that in his reflections at the end he should stress the harm done to the Protestant religion by such doubtful

---

Proof, was laid hold on to make him pass for one that could believe nothing that lay beyond the Compass of human Reason ", *op. cit.*, p. 17. For the charge of Socinianism against Tillotson, and the many pamphlets related to it, see Birch's *Life* and L.G. LOCKE : *Tillotson, A Study in Seventeenth Century Literature*, Copenhagen, 1954. Tillotson, whose sympathies were as wide as those of his father-in-law Wilkins, was the friend of Thomas Firmin, a well-known Socinian and patron of the Unitarians.

[1] *Op. cit.*, I, ser. 43.
[2] But he praises Socinus for conducting his argument coolly.
[3] *Ibid.*, p. 459.

interpretations, which serve to give force to the exception of the
Church of Rome against Scripture as the certain rule of faith. He
ends this sermon with a no less significant reminder of Erasmus'
condemnation of subtle arguments, and with a restatement of his
belief that the truths necessary to be believed are delivered plainly
in Scripture :

> God surely hath not dealt so hardly with Mankind as to
> make any thing necessary to be believ'd or practis'd by us
> which he hath not made sufficiently plain to the capacity
> of the unlearned as well as the learned. God forbid that
> it should be impossible for any man to be saved and to get
> to Heaven without a great deal of Learning to direct and
> carry him thither, when the far greatest part of Mankind
> have no learning at all [1].

The difference with South is, however, striking : whereas South
argues that the mysteries of religion exercise our reason—though
it is foolish to try and explain them—Tillotson takes his stand
on the plainness of the truths necessary for salvation. He is not
only genuinely averse to useless controversies, he is also, one feels,
not inclined to search very deeply. Tillotson's conclusion suggests
that, remembering the earlier Puritans' objection to Anglo-Catholic
preachers because they did not preach to the capacity of all hearers,
he was determined to get the message across to the average
Christian ; but it also looks forward to the wastes of the eighteenth
century, when all points beyond the reach of mere common sense
being ignored, Anglican theology will settle in a complacent acceptance of mere practical truths. However much Tillotson may have
combated the obscurantism encouraged by the Church of Rome,
he was likely to encourage another kind of obscurantism in spite
of his stress on free inquiry. His conclusion indirectly answers
the objection Sergeant had raised in *Sure-Footing*, that if Scripture
is to be the rule of faith only learned men will be able to interpret
it. Tillotson himself commanded sufficient learning to carry out
the necessary exegesis, but he did not, like South, emphasize the
need of learning for the pastors ; nor did he, like South, envisage
that the unlearned might need guidance in searching the text of
Scripture. His more ' democratic ' attitude thus brought him near
to emasculating some aspects of the Christian doctrine, and he is

---

[1] *Ibid.*, p. 459.

the ancestor of the liberal theology of the next age through his repeated insistence that it is not safe for our shallow understandings to wade further than Scripture goes before us [1].

Tillotson had no patience with the theologians who use hard words ; in one of his sermons he said :

> And this may suffice to have been spoken in general con-
> cerning that great *Mystery* of the *Hypostatical*, as they
> that love hard words love to call it, or *Personal* Union of
> the *Divine* and *human Natures* in the Person of our *Blessed
> Saviour* [2].

The echo from the attacks against the schoolmen is unmistakable (he had invoked Erasmus in the preceding sermon): not only are knotty points not to be discussed, but obscure ones had better be ignored, since they are too hard to grasp for the common man [3]. Nor did Tillotson consider that hard words might be necessary to distinguish and define ideas. His was the current view about the use of common speech ; when transferred to the realm of thinking one can imagine the oversimplifications this might entail. It is worth noting, however, that starting from the same assumption, that the Bible is the rule of faith, and emphasizing the same point, that men should not try to explain mysteries, South and Tillotson could yet encourage two entirely different attitudes: the one urging disciplined thinking and further inquiry as well as reverential awe, the other content to remain on this middle isthmus, untroubled and unawed by the great mysteries of Christianity. Tillotson could never have written the *Animadversions Upon Dr. Sherlock's Book*, not only because he was a more charitable man than South, but because he never commanded enough dialectical skill to distinguish between *existence* and *essence*, and such like ' scholastic subtleties ', to answer Sherlock's defence of the Trinity. With Tillotson, in fact,

---

[1] *Op. cit.*, I, 463, ser. 45.   [2] *Ibid.*, p. 463.

[3] The sermons published in 1694 were preached ' several years ago ' at St. Lawrence Jewry, and enlarged for publication. The audience he addressed there was far from unlearned, as Burnet tells us in his funeral sermon : " The numerous Assembly that this Lecture brought together, even from the remotest Parts of this wide City ; the great Concourse of Clergy-men who came hither to form their Minds, the happy Union that thereby the Clergy of this great Body grew into, and the blessed Effects this had, are things which it is to be hoped an Age will not wear out of Men's Minds ", *op. cit.*, pp. 19-20. Many of Tillotson's sermons were preached at Lincoln's Inn, where earlier in the century Donne had given the Masters and students quite different fare. On the development of liberal theology in the early eighteenth century, see R.N. STROMBERG : *Religious Liberalism in Eighteenth-Century England*, London, 1954.

reason has been levelled down to the common denominator which
is found in all men ; similarly, the consent of mankind, which he
so often invokes in support of religion, is the experienced fact rather
than the universal nature of the connate notions implanted by God.
For all his belief in the mysteriousness of Christianity, the main
themes of his sermons might not unfairly be reduced to the five
fundamental points of all religions as expounded in Herbert of
Cherbury's *De Veritate* (1623). It is no wonder, then, that he
was accused of Socinianism by his detractors, or that his sermons
contributed to the growth of Deism [1].

In order to refute the atheists Anglicans demonstrated the
rational grounds on which their faith was based, and in their
controversy with Rome they emphasized the necessity of rational
inquiry. Their rationalism was further defined in their arguments
against the Puritans. Not only did they assert that faith is a
form of rational assent, not a private illumination, but in defining
the part played by Grace in this assent they insisted that Grace
cannot work on barren ground, in other words, they insisted on
the cooperation between Grace and reason, not on the fundamental
difference—or opposition—between the two. Though they were
prepared to admit that the Grace of God works by ways unsearchable to man, and may sometimes effect a conversion suddenly, as
it had in the case of St. Paul, they taught that only by due preparation could man make himself fit to receive such a gift. They
also taught that the gift was no less free for requiring such preparation. Similarly, in their doctrine of works, they emphasized
that faith without works is a mere notion " swimming in the head ",
as Barrow said, whereas Christ has enjoined a living faith, and
they opposed Antinomianism—and all doctrines tending thereto—
as well as the doctrine of the power of works to effect salvation
which, they said, the Tridentine profession of faith upheld. To
recommend Christian practice was all the more necessary given the

---

[1] " Thus the ablest of the deists, Matthew Tindal (1657-1733), in his
Christianity as Old as Creation (1730), could quote extensively from such a
man as Tillotson in favour of the use and authority of reason, though with a
view to establishing conclusions that Tillotson would have eschewed. It was
all too easy to overlook the profound difference between the Platonic ' reason ',
with its large admixture of imagination and adoration, and the cool, secular,
logical reason of the ' Age of Reason ', which could lead in the end only to
the scepticism of Voltaire and Hume. " Stephen NEILL, *op. cit.*, p. 182.

general laxity or even profligacy after the Restoration, and given also the repudiation of ' mere morality ' by the enthusiasts. Hence, though the *Directions for Preachers* forbode divines to discuss the knotty points of election and reprobation, it was imperative to correct errors that would nullify Christ's teaching. Such were the problems of justifying faith and of Grace ; in expounding these Anglicans took their stand on the fundamental concept of a perfect, that is, of a rational and good God, against the Puritans' notion of God's arbitrary decrees, as firmly as Hooker had done at the end of the sixteenth century. In fact, like Hales in the preceding age, they bade John Calvin good night.

The Anglicans' reliance on the light of nature was highly offensive to the Puritans, who believed in the radical difference between natural law and the Gospel, and the Anglicans' conception of faith as rational assent ran counter to the Puritans' doctrine about the segregation of the realms of nature and of grace. This had already brought Whichcote into conflict with his Presbyterian master Tuckney in 1651, because he allowed too much to reason [1]. Whichcote, though appointed vice-chancellor of Cambridge University by the Puritan authorities, repeatedly asserted that reason is the Candle of the Lord and therefore must not be put under a bushel. He stated this most emphatically in his twenty-third discourse [2] :

> They are not to be blamed, or looked upon as neglecters of God's grace, and undervaluers of it, or to abate it in the least, who vigorously and with all imaginable zeal call upon men to use, employ and improve the principles of God's creation, that charge it upon men as a point of religion and conscience, to use, employ, and improve the principles of God's creation. I find that some men take offence to hear reason spoken out of pulpit, or to hear those great words of natural light, of principles of reason, and conscience. They are doubtless in a mighty mistake ; for these two things are very consistent, as I shall show by and by ; and there is no inconsistence between the grace of God and the calling upon men carefully to use, improve, and imploy the principles of God's creation, and the telling men they shall meet with no discouragement from God, for as much as

---

[1] See TULLOCH, *op. cit.*, II, 59-74.

[2] Whichcote's *Select Discourses*, in 3 vols., were published in 1698 by the Third Earl of Shaftesbury (who in his preface praised the Cambridge Platonist for his belief in the goodness of man).

He will not leave them, till they first leave Him. And indeed this is a very profitable work to call upon men, to answer the principles of their creation, to fulfil natural light, to answer natural conscience, to be throughout rational in what they do ; for these things have a Divine foundation. *The spirit in man is the Candle of the Lord, lighted by God, and lighting men to God.* It is from God by way of efficiency, and to God finally [1].

Culverwell, another Cambridge Platonist, asserted the same view in his *Discourse of the Light of Nature* (1652). Having stated that it is desirable to give unto reason the things that are reason's, and unto faith the things that are faith's, he proceeds :

There is a twin-light springing from both, and they both spring from the same Fountain of light, and they both sweetly conspire in the same end, the glory of that being, from which they shine... So that to blaspheme *Reason*, 'tis to reproach Heaven it self, and to dishonour the God of *Reason*, to question the beauty of his *Image*, and by a strange ingratitude to slight this great and Royal gift of our Creatour [2].

These quotations amply show what the Cambridge Platonists had to contend against in Puritan circles when they spoke " those great words of natural light ".

After the Restoration the Church's arguments against the infidels and against the Romanists were an implicit repudiation of the Puritan doctrine. Besides, the Anglicans openly disowned the private illuminations the enthusiasts claimed ; all of them warned their congregations to heed the words of the Apostle and try the spirits to see whether they were of God, and for them the only way to try spirits was to measure their revelations against the express Word of God and against the law of God written in men's hearts. Zeal without knowledge, Tillotson argued in a sermon on the 5th of November [3], is not acceptable to God, though it is

---

[1] Quoted in P.E. More and Fr.L. Cross : *Anglicanism, The Thought and Practice of the Church of England, Illustrated from the religious literature of the seventeenth century,* London, 1935, p. 213. Whichcote's discourses were printed from notes ; hence, probably, the repetitions. Though Whichcote was removed from the Provostship of King's College, Cambridge, in 1660, he conformed to the Church and became vicar of St. Lawrence Jewry when Wilkins was elevated to the see of Chester. Tillotson preached his funeral sermon. See vol. I, ser. 24.

[2] Nathanael Culverwell : *An Elegant and Learned Discourse of the Light of Nature,* 1652. Quoted in E.T. Campagnac : *The Cambridge Platonists,* Oxford, 1901, pp. 213-14.

[3] *Op. cit.,* II, ser. 28.

significant enough that he turned the argument against the Roman
Catholics. South, ' the scourge of the fanatics ', never tired of ridiculing the enthusiasts' pretences to inspiration, to preaching by the
Spirit, or to the Spirit ' indwelling ' in some men. His most em-
phatic repudiation of these doctrines appears in two sermons on
Rom. VIII. 14 *For as many as are led by the Spirit of God, are the
sons of God* [1], in which he discusses how the Spirit of God works
in man. He refutes the notion of the personal indwelling of the
Spirit in believers by arguments from reason and from Scripture,
showing that this mistaken belief is based on expressions in Scripture which are clearly metaphorical. The Spirit leads men, he says,
not by giving them transports and visions, but by prescribing laws
to them, by enlightening their understanding and bending their
will and affections ; that is, outwardly by the written Word and
inwardly by the illumination of men's judgement and rectifying of
their will. As to the assertion of some that the Spirit speaks
inwardly to them, this is a " vile and pestilent thing ", since these
men acknowledge no rule or governor of their actions but themselves. He therefore proceeds to demonstrate the folly and mischief of such pretence ; this, he says, is usually alleged to justify
actions that cannot be otherwise warranted, by men who merely
follow the dictates of their own minds and fancies. As South says,
such pretences to guidance by the inner light are generally founded
on the ruins of reason. The other pretence, that a man may
certainly know he has the Spirit in him though he cannot prove it,
can also be disproved : Scripture bids us examine whether the
Spirit of Christ be in us, and try the spirit ; hence, it cannot be
self-evident. Besides, the Spirit of God shows itself now only
by its operations and effects ; to claim a direct revelation of it is
to pretend to have achieved the beatific vision. Hence, whatever
promptings a man may feel in himself, he can never be sure that
the inward voice is the voice of God, nor can he assure others of it [2].
Nor can any argument be drawn from the example of ' eminent
saints ' in the Old Testament, for God has since then given men a
perfect revelation of His will for them to live by. Those alone
who do the works of God are the sons of God, for by their fruits
shall ye know them. Those who pretend to private inspirations

---

[1] *Op. cit.,* V, sermons 7 and 8.   [2] Sermon 7.

are a scandal and reproach to religion, and not to be tolerated by
the State since they destroy the basis of all compact and law by
rejecting reason, which is the principle of all Law [1].

The drift of the second sermon is that those pretenders to the
Spirit should be made to conform to the laws of the land, or be
outlawed [2]; it is, in fact, a plea against toleration of the Dissenters.
Whatever the turn he gives to his argument, South makes clear
the difference between the private judgement that can be tested,
and the individual judgement or inner light that cannot be distinguished from fancy. The Spirit of God does not speak inwardly
to *some* men, it enlightens the understanding of *all* men and leads
them to truth provided they do not resist it. South's view is rooted
in the belief of the rationality of man as reflecting the rationality
of his Maker; the private judgement claimed by the enthusiasts
is as arbitrary as the arbitrary will the Calvinists ascribe to God.
Such doctrine impugns the notion of a perfect, that is, perfectly
rational and good, God in making Him elect to speak to some men
rather than grant all men equal opportunities of salvation. It is,
at bottom, related to the doctrine of eternal election and reprobation,
which the Anglicans opposed most firmly. South's contention that
private revelations cannot be proved to be true reminds us of
Chillingworth's distinction between following one's wit and conceit,
and following reason, which is a public thing common to all men.
Universality, public trial at the bar of reason, conformity with the
written Word, these are tests which the enthusiast cannot stand;
they are the tests which Anglican rationalism deemed necessary
to emphasize in order to resist the fantasies of the illuminati.

This rationalism is further defined in their doctrine of grace
and of justifying faith, in which they also opposed the Puritans
and the encouragement given by their doctrines to Antinomianism.
In a 1661 sermon [3] South explained that what is required to achieve
salvation is not naked but operative faith, and he never departed
from the doctrine that faith must issue in works. The emphasis
on works was apt, however, to be mistaken for undue reliance on
man's ability to work his salvation. With the growth of Deism

---

[1] Sermon 8.
[2] It had been Hooker's plea that to disobey ecclesiastical laws, though not
instituted by God, was to undermine the basis of society, since men are members
of the body politic, whose very existence depends on laws.
[3] *Op. cit.*, III, ser. 4.

this became particularly dangerous, and in 1697 South preached
a sermon on the doctrine of merit and the impossibility of man's
meriting God, in which he stressed that salvation is a free gift of
God since man can never merit salvation [1].   He there impugns
the doctrine of the Pelagians : it is not true, as they—and the
Deists—assert, that man only receives from God the power to
will and to do, and that he can achieve salvation by the right use
of that power and the free determination of his will.   Against this
South stresses the impotency of man, an inconsiderable thing, who
is required to live well in order to be saved but will not be saved
on the merit of his good life.   In yet another sermon [2] South showed
that not only does man owe his salvation to the sacrifice of Christ,
but needs the grace of God to conquer sin : man stands justified
by Christ, not by his own works.   Nor can he repent and purify
himself without the help of grace.   Grace infuses a habit of purity
into the soul, at which stage the soul is merely a passive recipient
of it ; but it must exercise that habit to free itself of the power of
sin, and in this man is a co-worker with God.   Only by applying
the virtue of the blood of Christ to the soul by renewed acts of
faith can man conquer sin and fit his soul for salvation.   Yet, as
the sermon on merit had shown, salvation is not a due, but a free
gift : all that man can do is fulfil the conditions required by God
before He bestows this gift.

In two sermons on *Tit*. I. 1, South grounded the doctrine of
faith and works on the unity of truth and goodness, and on reason
as " the great rule of man's nature " and as itself regulated by
truth [3] ; from this he interprets *the truth after godliness* to mean :
a truth operative to the best of effects.   Hence, this truth involves
a right notion of God and a right notion of the duties of man ;
the two are inseparable, but the two must be defined accurately,

> both in their just latitude and within their due limits, that
> one may not entrench upon or evacuate the other [4],

that is, so as neither to infringe the prerogative of God nor to leave
the creature no scope for duty.   This means repudiating both the
notion of irresistible grace and pre-determination of the will and

---

[1] *Ibid.*, ser. 1.   [2] *Op. cit.*, IV, ser. 12.
[3] *Additional Volumes of Sermons Preached upon Several Occasions*, London,
1744, VII, 89, ser. 5.
[4] *Ibid.*, p. 93.

action, and the notion of the will's ability to make God's work of
salvation effectual [1]. From this South proceeds to show that what
undermines the motives of good life is as such destructive of
religion, for

> faith without works expires, and becomes a dead thing, a
> carcase, and consequently noysome to God [2].

A good life is the condition, though not the cause, of imputation
of Christ's righteousness, and an error in any of the doctrines
concerning the good life is like poison in a fountain. Such is the
notion that nothing of performance is required, that faith alone
justifies ; such also is the doctrine according to which a man may
be acceptable to God for the righteousness and merits of other
saints ; such again is the doctrine exempting believers from the
obligation of the moral law [3], or that which places it in the power
of a man to dispense with the laws of Christ (i.e. the Pope), or
the doctrines of venial sin and supererogation [4]. South thus defines
his position in contradistinction both to the Puritan doctrine of
justification by faith and to Antinomianism, and to the Tridentine
doctrine of merit. As appears from his argument, this view, which
all Anglicans shared, is grounded on the concept of right reason.

In another sermon [5], on *2 Cor.* I. 24 *For by faith ye stand*,
i.e. on the very text invoked by the defenders of justification by
faith, South explains again that by *faith* the Apostle means a living
active principle, not a bare assent, nor temporary conviction however powerful. In words reminiscent of Donne's sonnet *Batter my
heart...* he shows that by faith alone can man resist the enemy that
assaults him from within, his natural corruption ; from Christ alone
issues the power to subdue our natural depravity, but we must put
on the armour of Christ and live according to His doctrine before
we can have a title to God's promises.

South's conception of grace may have undergone some change,
for in a sermon preached shortly before the Restoration, his
emphasis on the free gift of grace brings him dangerously near
to the Calvinistic doctrine of election, though there too he says

---

[1] In developing this point (pp. 94-95) South seems closer to the Calvinists than
he usually is ; but the sermon is not dated, nor was it revised for publication.
Volumes VII-XI were published after his death and in many places the text
is obviously corrupt. See below, *Note on the text.*

[2] *Ibid.,* p. 98.   [3] *Ibid.,* pp. 102-6.   [4] *Ibid.,* pp. 108-20.
[5] *Additional ... Sermons,* VIII, ser. 2.

that God's denial of a perceiving heart infers, but does not cause, the unsuccessfulness of all the means of grace [1]. He also stresses the contrariety of ' carnal wisdom ' to spiritual truths " in as much as there is more hope of the conversion of a sensualist, than of a resolved atheist " [2]. Indeed, he there denies that bare reason can assent to the truths of religion and condemns those who hold

> that the mind of God clearly revealed, and urged with due persuasions, is a suitable object to a rational understanding, which has power enough to close with every object agreeable to it [3],

those, in fact, who hold the very doctrine he was to assert later ; it is no wonder that he did not choose to publish this early sermon. Whatever light this may throw on South's early years as a preacher [4], this sermon is interesting on two counts : first it shows clearly that emphasis on free grace alone goes together with a slight on reason ; second, it suggests that South's later stand on right reason could hardly have led to the more superficial rationalism of the liberal theology of the next age. His emphasis on imputed righteousness in the 1697 sermon reveals his opposition to the mere natural duties, which for the Deists made the sum of religion, and to which the Latitudinarians had given undue prominence in their sermons.

Though Tillotson may be held responsible for these developments, he did not ignore the part played by grace in faith or regeneration ; nor did he deny imputed righteousness. In his sermons on *The Nature of Regeneration, and its Necessity, in order to Justification and Salvation* [5] he explained that the faith meant by the Apostle was not a bare assent, but effectual belief, that is, faith made perfect by charity : only a new creature availeth. This new creation is wrought " by a divine power, of the same kind with that, which created the world ; and raised up Christ Jesus from the dead ". Such creation, however, does not mean that it is the effect of an irresistible act, nor that the creature is merely passive, nor that it is effected in an instant. Though conversion may be effected by such violent means as to be irresistible, as in the case of St. Paul, yet such force is neither necessary nor to be

---

[1] *Ibid.*, ser. 13, p. 370.   [2] *Ibid.*, p. 384.   [3] *Ibid.*, p. 393.
[4] The influence of the Cambridge Platonists is also noticeable in this sermon.
[5] *Op. cit.*, II, sermons 52-56, printed below.

expected, since Scripture says that men often resist the grace of
God. One need only remember the spiritual autobiographies of
such men as Bunyan to grasp what Tillotson is here combating.
According to Tillotson, such conception of the passivity of the
creature in the work of conversion makes void the exhortations
to repent which abound in Scripture. This is not to say that we
can repent of ourselves, which is no better than Pelagianism, but
to hold both that without the power of God no man can repent
and that God will not assist us in this work if we do nothing
ourselves. Tillotson's doctrine is thus substantially the same as
South's : God and man are co-workers, and God, though giving
His grace freely, requires that the soul should be fit to receive it.
Ultimately, Tillotson shows, the Puritan doctrine casts a slur on
God, who offers pardon if men repent, yet is supposed to withhold
from some men the power to repent. Tillotson then refutes the
objections of the Puritans to such concurrence of men in their
conversion, by showing that this does not extenuate the power
of God nor restrict His freedom. In fact, he says, the Puritans
do just this since they confine the Grace of God to themselves.
Moreover, by making God do all in the conversion of sinners, they
implicitly charge God with men's impotency to repent and make
Him the cause of unregeneracy. To this, he opposes the doctrine
of a sufficiency of grace offered to all men. Men are free to
comply with grace or to resist it ; though the grace offered to all
is sufficient, it is effectual to some, but rejected by others. This,
Tillotson argues, both agrees with Scripture and clears God of
injustice [1]. Even though he grants that conversion may sometimes
be sudden, he will not allow that regeneration and sanctification
can ever be. For more is involved here than a sudden entrance
into a new state ; both admit of degrees, and the process is one of
purification, with the help of grace assisting man on the way.
Thus, renovation of our hearts is the real condition of our justification and salvation. The other doctrine, which claims to ascribe
all good to God and none to man, in fact ascribes to God evil.
Though Tillotson does not say this, his doctrine is consistent with
a perfectly rational and good God, while the other posits God
as arbitrary will. This had already been Hooker's contention.

---

[1] Laud ' abominated ' the doctrine of reprobation because " it makes God,
the God of all mercies, to be the most fierce and unreasonable tyrant in the
world ". Quoted in P.E. MORE, op. cit., p. lii.

At the beginning of the last sermon on regeneration, Tillotson apologizes for treating these doctrines " in a more contentious way than is usual " with him, though not out of love of controversy. Indeed few of his sermons deal with this problem, no doubt because he did not love controversy, and this could hardly be treated without considering the other party's objections ; nor does he often refer to it as South so often does, if only by the way. Tillotson was careful to keep clear of all controversial matter ; the consequence was that, whatever his real belief, he gave encouragement to the view that moral virtues made up the sum of religion. His detractors were not altogether wrong in calling him a mere moral preacher. Such a sermon as *The Fruits of the Spirit, the same with Moral Virtues* [1], preached in 1690, may have sounded not unlike Arthur Bury's *The Naked Gospel*, published in the same year. True, Tillotson says at one point that the moral duties are not all religion, but the necessary corrective only comes in the sermon printed next to this one (whether because they were preached in succession, or because the editor, Tillotson's chaplain, thought they should be read together, does not appear from the text). The title of this speaks for itself : *The Necessity of Supernatural Grace, in order to a Christian Life* [2]. There Tillotson shows that without supernatural grace man is incapable of the proper acts of the Christian life, that he needs preventing grace to stir him to what is good, assisting grace to strengthen him, and persevering grace to keep him constant. He shows that this help is necessary because of the impotency of human nature, of the power of evil habits, of the fickleness of human resolution, and of the malice of the devil. Yet he adds that this supposes the concurrence of our endeavours. One might suppose that, as in the case of South, the two sermons represent two different stages in Tillotson's development [3], were it not that it is Tillotson's habit to simplify problems and treat different aspects of them separately rather than in conjunction ; the paradoxes of his religion never exercised his mind as they had exercised the mind of another Anglican divine who, like him, had preached regularly at Lincoln's Inn, John Donne.

For Barrow, too, faith implies both a good use of reason and

---

[1] *Op. cit.*, III, ser. 148, printed below.
[2] *Ibid.*, ser. 149, printed below.   [3] The second is undated.

compliance with the Grace of God : to require faith without reason
is an impossibility, and no man is without the means to produce
faith, but some reject these means by opposing a wilful obstruction
to the light of faith.   As he says in *A Brief Exposition on the
Creed*, which his sermons on the Creed amplify,

> Faith itself is not an arbitrary act, nor an effect of blind
> necessity ; (we cannot believe what we please ; nor can
> be compelled to believe any thing), 'tis a result of judgment
> and choice, grounded upon reason of some kind, after
> deliberation and debate concerning the matter [1] ;

it is a voluntary act, involving the free consent of the will [2].   In
the two sermons on *Rom.* V. 1, he explains in what sense we are
justified by faith : no other faith than persuasion of evangelical
truths was required by the Apostles, he says, and this faith is said
to be the effect of Grace.   But such faith connotes the acts of the
will consequent upon those persuasions : conversion and repentance, as they are a returning to Christ, imply obedience to Christ.
Barrow states clearly that such faith only relates to propositions
revealed by God, or at least deduced from His Word ; it does
not relate to propositions concerning matters of fact, such as that
God loves *me* or has pardoned *my* sins.   Thus he takes his stand
against all pretenders to personal justification, which " many in
these latter ages have deemed and taught " [3].   And he firmly rejects
the doctrine of eternal election : such belief in God's eternal good-
will to *some*, he says, inverts the order of things as declared in
Scripture, where faith is said to be required for man to obtain God's
goodwill ; moreover, it implies the doctrine that no man once in
God's favour can ever quite lose it, and this leads straight to
Antinomianism.   Barrow also repudiates a " more new notion of
faith ", not so plainly false but more obscure and intricate, he says,

---

[1] Isaac BARROW : *A Brief Exposition on the Creed, the Lord's Prayer and
Ten Commandments.*   To which is added the Doctrine of the Sacraments.   *This
on the Creed never published before.*   London, 1697, p. 10.   Tillotson had
published the Explication of the Lord's Prayer, the Decalogue, and the Doctrine
of the Sacraments " in a small manual by itself " ; after the Archbishop's death
the bookseller Brabazon Aylmer, who had published Barrow's sermons (as well
as Tillotson's), brought out in 1697 both the sermon on the Trinity and the
Exposition, which, he says in his Advertisement to the reader, was overlooked
by His Grace.   B. Aylmer, who specialized in theological works, clearly intended
these works to be used as arguments against Deism.
[2] *Op. cit.*, II, ser. 2.   [3] *Ibid.*, ser. 4, printed below.

which makes faith to consist in a recumbency or adherency to Christ himself, not to any proposition taught by him. This, he shows, is at once unintelligible and meaningless, and dangerous because it begets presumptions and perplexities. These false notions of faith, Barrow contends, are clearly unacceptable if one believes in a just and good God, who cannot of all eternity have favoured some of his creatures and doomed others to eternal damnation. The doctrine of recumbency, as distinct from consent or assent, equally nullifies the doctrine of Christ since it implies a passive adherence, whereas Christ has enjoined effectual obedience to his will.

Barrow knew that he had to be specially careful in defining justification since it had been the cause of so much dissension and strife from the time of the Reformation [1]; yet, he says, this only results from men's proneness to wrangle, since the doctrine can be plainly inferred from Scripture, which defines the conditions for a man to be received into the favour of God through baptism or for the sinner through repentance. In what is perhaps one of the finest examples of *explication de texte*, Barrow proceeds to elucidate the meaning of the term in various passages of Scripture, particularly in St. Paul's epistles since the term *justifying faith* may be said to be peculiar to him. Justification can in no way mean making a man intrinsically righteous by infusing habits of grace, since this is not consistent with the drift of St. Paul's reasoning. From the Apostle's use of the term, he says, it appears that justification is dispensed when a man embraces Christianity and avows it in Baptism. This justifying act continues to have effect so long as we live according to Christ's rule. Further, every dispensation of pardon upon repentance is properly speaking a justification, or reinstatement of the covenant made at baptism. Hence, all good Christians may be said to have been justified in baptism, and to continue justified if they persist in faith and obedience. Barrow opposes the notion of special justifications as firmly as that of eternal election : justification is open to all, and the virtues and effects of grace do not continue unless the Christian perform God's will. It was all the more necessary to define such doctrine since justified sinners were apt to claim that as such they were above

---

[1] It is one of Bossuet's main examples of points of doctrine on which Protestants disagree with each other.

the law. To what lengths Antinomianism could go may be gathered
from the autobiographies of justified sinners as well as from attacks
against them ; they are probably best known to the modern reader
through James Hogg's *Confession of a Justified Sinner*, which so
much fascinated Gide.

For Barrow, as for South and Tillotson, faith results from the
right use of reason, which presupposes man's acceptance of the
means of Grace God vouchsafes to everyone. Men are thus co-
workers with God in effecting their salvation, since faith itself is
the joint work of God and of man, and since faith in Christ implies
obedience to Him. Reason and grace can no more be separated
than can faith and works. Though God alone can bend the will
of man and enlighten carnal reason, man must yet strive to understand God's will and to act accordingly. But he must be first
persuaded of the truths of his religion ; it is therefore the preacher's
task to clear men's understandings so that, with the help of grace,
they may bend their wills to assent to them and to do God's work.
It is no use, and it is dangerous, to appeal to men's affections
unless they are first shown the proper objects to which to apply
them. It follows from this that in their sermons the Anglican
divines will be more concerned to show their congregations the
whys and wherefores of Christ's doctrine, and to propound to them
the motives to right action. All moving of the passions, which
does not rest on demonstrations of truths, is to be condemned.
Pathetic preaching was left to the Puritans, whose irrational doctrines accorded with these irrational means of instruction. How
dry much Anglican preaching came to be can be seen from Swift's
sermons, which, as Johnson said, never try to *persuade*. Nor did
Tillotson, though he wished to enforce practice, ever depart from
his cool manner of arguing. That the method of edifying by enlightening the understanding need not have been so arid appears from
Barrow's and even better from South's sermons : as we read the
one we simply marvel at the sheer amplitude of his mind, at the
range of matter he can bring to bear on his subject and at the
wealth of words he has at his command, while the vigour and
cogency of the other's thought and style yield the kind of delight
that only a well-trained artist can give.

Hooker had been moved to write his *Laws of Ecclesiastical
Polity* in answer to those who sought " The Reformation of the

Laws and Orders ecclesiastical in the Church of England "[1]. This
had led him to define the hierarchy of laws, which all ultimately
aspire to the perfect law of God. He had not claimed that the
laws instituted by men are perfect, since all things natural are
imperfect, or immutable, since circumstances might require that
they be altered ; but he had asserted that the light of reason, given
by God to man to distinguish between true and false and between
good and evil, could direct men to discover natural law, which is
but one expression of God's law, and to devise laws for societies
of men. Hooker thought that laws sanctioned by tradition are
likely to be the expression of the voice of nature, though he did
not suggest that they should therefore be followed uncritically.
Since reason derives from God, it should be used not only to interpret the revealed law of God but also to discover its working in
the universe, and to supplement revelation in those domains which
God has not regulated by His express Word. Such, to Hooker,
are the laws regulating societies, and such in particular are the
laws governing the society of Christians, the Church. He denied
that any specific form of Church-government was enjoined in
Scripture, and he argued that, as a thing indifferent, it was to be
regulated by reason in accordance with tradition and custom, or
' the perpetual voice of men '. He did not claim that episcopacy
was divinely instituted, or indeed that it was necessarily the best
discipline. Yet he could find nothing in it that was not consistent
with either the express word of God or the natural law. Hence,
he argued, Puritans should accept this form of Church-government
even though it might not seem to them the purest discipline, because
these ecclesiastical laws had received the consent of the Church
as a whole. These laws are no less binding than those on which
the life of any society is based, for unless all members of a community submit to the laws agreed upon by general consent, the
whole fabric of society will be undermined.

The Puritans, of course, thought otherwise ; they found the
orders and ceremonies of the Church too reminiscent of Rome,
and not only ungrounded in Scripture, but contrary to it. Even
those amongst them who granted matters of discipline to be things
indifferent argued that *since* they were indifferent they could not
be made binding. To Hooker's contention that it was expedient

[1] See the title of his Preface.

to govern the Church by means of laws binding to all, they retorted that Christ had freed men from the bondage of the law, and they pleaded the right of tender consciences not to submit.

During the forties some of the defenders of episcopacy departed from the position held by Hooker and claimed, in answer to their Scripture adversaries, that bishops were divinely instituted. After 1660, however, no such claim was made for episcopacy ; Anglicans of all kinds, as well as the Presbyterians who then conformed, recognized that ecclesiastical laws were grounded on prudence, not on the express word of God. The discipline of the Church was found to agree with reason, to ensure order and decency in divine worship, and to be necessary to preserve unity. To enforce conformity with ecclesiastical laws inevitably meant excluding large numbers of Christians from the Church, and all attempts at accommodation were frustrated by the resistance of the Laudian clergy and by the endless arguments of the Presbyterians at the Savoy Conference, as well as later by the uncompromising stand taken by the High-Churchmen whose influence led to the rejection of various comprehension schemes [1]. In such a climate of intolerance [2], for Anglicans to stress the right and duty of every Christian to inquire into the truths of his religion must have sounded to many outsiders as sheer hypocrisy. Yet, as appears clearly from Barrow's *Unity of the Church*, Christian liberty meant for them that faith is a free and voluntary act, not that individual Christians have a right to separate from the main body of the Church. Ecclesiastical laws, as they are laws regulating particular societies, are grounded in reason ; it is therefore the duty of all members of the community to comply with them.

Defences of the Church ordinances thus reveal another aspect of Anglican rationalism after the Restoration in so far as they are, like Hooker's, based on the concept of law as an expression of reason. How far this kind of rationalism is from the narrow secular rationalism of a later age appears best from South's praise of the Church's services and prayers in opposition to the mangled services

---

[1] For instance in 1667, 1674 and 1680, and again in 1689 when William's scheme for comprehension was rejected by the Lower House of Convocation (largely composed of High-Churchmen) while the bishops (many of whom were Latitudinarians appointed by William after the defection of the Non-jurors) were ready to sponsor it.

[2] And even of persecution. See G.R. CRAGG : *Puritanism in the Period of the Great Persecution*, Cambridge, 1957.

of the Puritans and to the wild outbursts of extempore prayers.
Not only did this High-Churchman require premeditation and discipline in the worship of God, he insisted on the due ordering of
God's temple.   He also knew that as God speaks to the capacity
of men and often expresses profound truths in simple parables, so
the senses may be enlisted in the service of God since they are
the servants and under-officers of the soul[1].   He knew that

> the mind of man, even in spirituals, acts with a corporeal
> dependence, and so is helped or hindered in its operations,
> according to the different quality of external objects that
> incur into the senses[2].

Far from objecting to church music as Baxter did, or from wishing
to strip the churches of all ornaments, like the Parliamentarians
who wrecked several chapels in Cambridge, South praised the
beauty of Church ornaments, the order, dignity, and harmony of
the services, and wished to make all the faculties of man serve to
praise the Creator.   For, he said,

> the grace of God is pleased to move us by ways suitable
> to our nature, and to sanctify these sensible inferior helps
> to greater and higher purposes[3].

His love of the magnificent liturgy of the Church of England,
which the Puritans would have robbed of all power to move the
minds because it appeals to the senses and imagination, finds its
best expression in the sermon he preached at the consecration of a
chapel[4].   He could not envisage an ' abstracted ' kind of worship
within the bare walls of a meeting-house :   this was to him
' indecent ', that is, unworthy of the bountiful Creator to whom
honour is due ; it was also a highly mistaken way of bringing men
to God since the senses are channels through which God may speak
to them.   Above all, one feels, South loved beauty.   He could not,
he said, persuade himself that " God ever designed his Church for
a rude, naked, unbeautiful lump "[5].   To him the beauty of the
world is the expression of God's bounty and of the infinite variety
of His gifts.   Such a variety of gifts should adorn God's Church,
His pastors serving Him according to their diverse abilities and

[1] *Op. cit.*, III, ser. 11, printed below.
[2] *Op. cit.*, I, ser. 7, p. 283.
[3] *Ibid.*, p. 284.   [4] *Op. cit.*, I, ser. 7.
[5] *Op. cit.*, III, ser. 11, printed below.

His temples proclaiming His infinite mercies. South's love for the ceremonies of the Church of England, his admiration for the collects and prayers, his care for the due ordering of the temple, reveal the artist in him. His refusal to see the collects and prayers altered to suit the taste of the precisians expresses more than his conservatism or intolerance ; it is the resistance of the artistic temperament to the mangling of a form of service whose beauty is itself a tribute to God. South had an ear for good prose, and he could see what harm might be done by altering ' mere words ' in Cranmer's fine prayers [1] ; he could not tolerate anything careless in the expression any more than in the manner of praying. In the liturgy, he said, the Church of England has an " excellent Body of Prayers",

> the whole Sett of them being like a String of Pearls, exceeding rich in Conjunction ; and therefore of no small Price and value even single, and by themselves [2].

How could he have tolerated the vague and rude effusions of men transported by the Spirit ? The spouse of God must adorn herself to honour her bridegroom, whose greatness the beauty of the heavens declares. The worship of God, South could have said with Hooker, must be regulated by the same kind of law that governs the universe,

> correspondently unto that end for which it worketh, even ' all things χρηστῶς, in most decent and comely sort ' [3].

As his sermons on extempore prayers show [4], South found in a set form of prayers the best means to intensify the feelings of the faithful, which is the main object of devotion. Christ himself taught His disciples how to pray ; like the Lord's prayer the collects and prayers of the Church concentrate on the essentials and thereby direct the feelings of the faithful towards their proper object : only by application of the heart and mind and by due discipline of the words and feelings can one properly pray by the Spirit. William Beveridge, another staunch High-Churchman, who opposed com-

---

[1] " In the petition ' In all time of our tribulation, in all time of our wealth, in the hour of death and in the day of judgement', the American Prayer Book, on the ground that the word ' wealth ' in the sense of ' well-being ' is somewhat archaic, reads ' in all time of our prosperity '. The rhythm has been irretrievably destroyed ", Stephen NEILL, op. cit., p. 60. There were about six hundred changes in the Revised Prayer Book of 1662.

[2] Op. cit., II, ser. 5, printed below.

[3] Laws, Bk. I, ii, 3.   [4] See chapter I.

prehension with the Dissenters as firmly as South did [1], defended the use of set prayers on the same grounds:

> having the form continually in my mind, being thoroughly acquainted with it, fully approving of every thing in it, and always knowing beforehand what will come next, I have nothing else to do, whilst the words are sounding in mine ears, but to move my heart and affections suitably to them, to raise up my desires of those good things which are prayed for, to fix my mind wholly upon God, whilst I am praising of Him, and so to employ, quicken, and lift up my whole soul in performing my devotions to Him [2].

Far from being empty forms, set prayers help to quicken devotion and raise the soul to God. Such was the classical temper of these Churchmen, who resisted effusions of words and feelings as strongly as they did effusions of the Spirit, and who sometimes censured belief in the inner light and in the promptings of the Spirit as mere romantic notions.

Such, in its main outlines, was the nature of Anglican rationalism after the Restoration. To many to-day it may well seem to be a mixed kind of rationalism; but as people in England then found mixed government the best, many also found the *via media* of the Church of England the best. As Paul Elmer More said,

> It may have looked at the outset like a shift to avoid difficulties, a *modus vivendi*, at the best a 'middle way' as commended by Donne because 'more convenient and advantageous than that of any other Kingdom'. But behind it all the while lay a profounder impulse, pointing in a positive direction, and aiming to introduce into religion, and to base upon the 'light of reason', that love of balance, restraint, moderation, measure, which from sources beyond our reckoning appears to be innate to the English temper [3].

It is idle to speculate how innate this temper was, but Anglican theology after the Restoration no doubt reflects the same blend between abstract principles and the data of experience, each at

---

[1] See his *Concio ad Synodum*, London, 1689. The sermon was preached to Convocation.

[2] William BEVERIDGE: *A Sermon on the Excellency and Usefulness of the Common Prayer* (1681). Quoted in P.E. MORE and Fr.L. CROSS, *op. cit.*, pp. 626-7.

[3] P.E. MORE and Fr.L. CROSS, *op. cit.*, I. The spirit of Anglicanism, p. xxii.

once supporting and qualifying the other, which characterizes the literary criticism of the period, or for that matter of any period in England. It defines a mean not only between the extremes of Romanism and of radical Protestantism, but between the abstract reason and experience.

CHAPTER THREE

CHURCH AND STATE
AFTER THE RESTORATION

James I had had too bitter an experience of Presbyterian Church-government in Scotland to be ready to agree to the English Puritans' demands for reformation of the Church discipline. Though the Hampton Court Conference examined their grievances, it was soon clear that no progress would be made towards satisfying them, especially after the King had expounded to the assembled divines his doctrine of 'No Bishop, no King'. The alliance of Church and Crown was thus sealed, which was to prove fatal to both in mid-century, and James's words came true when the execution of Laud was followed by the 'legal murder' of Charles I. When the Presbyterians of the restored Parliament called upon Charles's son in 1659 to end the anarchy that had followed upon the death of Cromwell, they thought they could ensure 'liberty for tender consciences' by having Charles sign the Declaration of Breda. How such liberty was to be achieved was left for Parliament to decide once the King was restored; meanwhile the Presbyterians were promised mildness and moderation. Since they were committed to the idea of a national Church no less than the Anglicans were—they had had recourse to Parliament to enforce their own discipline, and the 1644 *Directory for Worship* forbidding the use of the Prayer Book had been issued by Parliamentary ordinance—the Presbyterians must have contemplated far-reaching modifications of Anglican discipline since they could hardly have hoped to impose their own. True, another way of solving these problems was open to them, toleration; but this was no more countenanced by the former 'new-forcers of conscience' than by the Laudian clergy, who now began to raise their heads. Indeed, few men had ever contemplated such a solution even in the years of controversy about Christian liberty, when many had suffered under the Presbyterian rule [1]. The five members did not advocate toleration when in 1644 they appealed to Parliament to have the Presbyterian discipline made more flexible so as to provide for gathered churches ; the non-separating Congregationalists in fact demanded no more than accommodation within the national Church. Only when the Accommodation Order proved abortive did the Assembly Congregationalists join forces with the Sects to advocate toleration outside the Church. Some of the Sects rejected the power of civil government altogether, on the ground that the Saints must be free to obey God's commands as revealed to the individual conscience : this put them beyond the jurisdiction of any human law, and the Antinomians even claimed that the elect were above all law. Some Independents as well as the Erastians advocated toleration on secular grounds, as the only means to achieve civil peace, and some came near to urging separation of Church and State. The one who did this most clearly was Roger Williams, who argued from the segregation between the realms of grace and of nature that it was not for the magistrate to devise or enforce any form of Church discipline. Williams was prepared to tolerate every form of belief or even unbelief provided the mere natural state was not endangered ; in fact he was pleading that the civil power need have no concern for the souls of men [2]. The Puritans of New England disagreed with this as much as did their Presbyterian brethren in England, and Williams's experiment in religious toleration could only be carried out in his new-planted colony of Rhode Island. But Hooker, who thought it a gross error to believe that the magistrate need only concern himself with the good of the body, not of the soul, would have disagreed too ; indeed, his conception of the relation between Church and State is decidedly Erastian [3].

[1] See Godfrey DAVIES, op. cit. ; William HALLER, op. cit. ; A.E. BARKER, op. cit. ; A.S.P. WOODHOUSE : Puritanism and Liberty. Being the Army Debates (1647-9) from the Clarke Manuscripts, with Supplementary Documents, London, 1938 ; Don M. WOLFE : Milton in the Puritan Revolution, London, 1941.

[2] For the debates on religious toleration or accommodation in 1643-1645, see Ernest SIRLUCK's Introduction to vol. II of The Complete Prose Works of John Milton, (1643-1648), ed. cit., 1959. The Heads of the Proposals submitted to Charles I by the Council of Officers in 1647 included religious toleration ; but the Presbyterians were no more ready to support the claims of their bitter enemies in 1659 than they had been at the time of the New Model Army's victories. On toleration in England, see W.K. JORDAN : The Development of Religious Toleration in England, London, 1932-1940 (vol. III). On toleration in the sixteenth century, see Joseph LECLER, S. J. : Histoire de la Tolérance au Siècle de la Réforme, Paris, 1955 (vol. II).

[3] On Erastus, see Ruth WESEL-ROTH : Thomas Erastus, Lahr (Baden),

Clarendon's decision to refer the details of the Settlement to Parliament was therefore acceptable both to Presbyterians, who had themselves accepted the decisions of Parliament in Church-government, and to the Laudian Clergy, since observance of the Prayer Book had been enforced under Charles by the notorious Court of High Commission.

As Bosher has shown [1] the Presbyterians made several mistakes. First, by trying to force a religious settlement as soon as possible, when it should have been clear to them that the first Parliament to be returned after the Restoration would comprise a large majority of old Loyalists since many of their own persuasion had been disqualified [2]. Second, by insisting that the King be brought back on terms, an attitude which could only confirm Royalist prejudices against them as no true lovers of monarchy. Third, they too often combined with Roman Catholics against the Anglicans for their loyalty to the national Church not to be suspected. The Anglicans, on the other hand, were not prepared to settle their differences with the Puritans : disagreement on ' things indifferent ' had led to a wholesale onslaught on the Church, now that the Church was restored her faithful members were to guard against such danger. The only thing the Anglicans could have expected of conferences with the Presbyterians was to bring them back into

1954. The Elizabethan Act of Supremacy made the Queen "the only supreme governor of this realm, as well in all spiritual and ecclesiastical things or causes as temporal ". Elizabeth had been loth to accept her father's title of ' supreme head in earth of the Church of England '. Selden remarked : " There's a great deal of difference between Head of the Church and Supreme Governor, as our canons call the King. Conceive it thus : there is in this kingdom of England a College of Physicians. The King is supreme governor of those but not head of them, nor President of the College, nor the best physician. " (quoted in H.R. Trevor-Roper : *Archbishop Laud*, London, 1962, p. 101). As Stephen Neill says, the difference was more than one of words : " In fact, the greater precision of the Elizabethan definition was very important indeed. Late medieval theory distinguished very clearly between *potestas ordinis*, the spiritual or sacramental authority mediated to the bishop or priest in his ordination but derived directly from Christ, and the *potestas jurisdictionis*, the administrative authority by which the Church was ordered. Critics of the English Church had maintained, and sometimes still imagine, that the secular rulers of England have claimed priestly powers within the Church. Elizabeth was rightly concerned to make it plain that this was not so ; though it has to be admitted that she allowed to herself a characteristically Tudor liberty in the interpretation of the limits of the *potestas jurisdictionis* ". *Op. cit.*, p. 102. The position is not unlike that of the Gallicans in the seventeenth century. For attempts at union between the Gallican and the Anglican churches in the early eighteenth century, see N. Sykes, *op. cit.*, pp. 196-207.

[1] *Op. cit.*, pp. 139-42.

[2] A Bill brought in to implement the Declaration of Breda was thrown out by the Commons in October 1660.

the fold, perhaps by conceding some minor points in the Liturgy.

Meanwhile Charles appointed some Puritans as chaplains in ordinary, and offered bishoprics to three Puritans : Edward Reynolds [1] accepted the see of Norwich in September 1660, but both Baxter and Calamy refused to be made bishops. In October 1660, Charles promised to call a national synod to determine differences. The Liturgy was not enforced, and a conference of divines was convened in April 1661, with men like Sanderson, Cosin, Morley, Gauden and Sheldon on the Anglican side, and such Puritans as Reynolds, Baxter, Calamy, Bates and Wallis (the mathematician). It has been said that

> the Puritans were not the rigid Covenanters of the past : as a party they were moderate men like Baxter, who wanted only some ceremonies abolished, and some made optional, freedom for extempore prayers, and the power of the bishops limited by a council of presbyters. They had brought back the King, and thought they could get as much as this [2].

Still, after lengthy debates lasting for more than three months the Conference failed to agree. Convocation then appointed a Committee of bishops to revise the Liturgy (November 1661); though many changes were introduced nothing of importance was conceded to the Puritans. The Revised Prayer Book was accepted by Convocation in December 1661, and by Parliament in April 1662. Parliament had met in May 1661, and was passing legislation against the Puritans [3], with the result that the 1662 Act of Uniformity compelled all ministers to receive episcopal ordination [4] and to declare their unfeigned " assent and consent " to everything " contained and prescribed " not only in the doctrinal articles but

[1] As Bosher remarks, Reynolds should be considered as an Anglican Conformist rather than as a moderate Presbyterian. *Op. cit.*, p. 118. Reynolds had been restored as Dean of Christ Church, to replace the Independent John Owen, when the Presbyterians ejected by Pride's Purge in 1648 were restored to Parliament by Monck in 1659.

[2] H.M. GWATKIN : *Church and State in England to the Death of Queen Anne*, London, 1917, p. 350.

[3] Venner's rising in January 1661, to set up the Fifth Monarchy in London, partly accounts for the extreme violence of these measures.

[4] In the sixteenth and early seventeenth century foreign (and occasionally Scottish) Presbyterian ministers were sometimes licensed to administer the sacraments in the Church of England. After the 1662 Act of Uniformity, however, episcopal ordination was ' indispensable for all present and future holders of any ecclesiastical office whatsoever in the Church of England '. N. SYKES, *op. cit.*, p. 116. Re-ordination of Presbyterian ministers was the stumbling-block in all discussions about comprehension after the Restoration. See Richard BAXTER : *Reliquiae Baxterianae*, ed. M. Sylvester, London, 1696, pt. III.

in the revised Liturgy; they also had to repudiate the Solemn League and Covenant and to subscribe to the doctrine of non-resistance to the prince. As H.M. Gwatkin remarks, the date, St Bartholomew's day, August 24, 1662, had been " maliciously chosen to deprive non-conformists of the half-year's tithes, which fell due a few days later "[1]. Though many Presbyterians conformed, including some who had sat at the Savoy Conference, a large number had to relinquish their ministry. Thus a strong group of Presbyterians—among them such eminent men as Baxter, Calamy, Bates and John Wesley—were driven into dissent, together with the Independents, the Quakers and the more extreme Sects, who in any case would have been excluded from the national Church. The Great Persecution[2] had begun, and the further legislation known as the Clarendon Code only confirmed the rift between the Establishment and Dissent.

Though some Churchmen did not approve of these measures, and Tillotson was notable among them, many felt, not unnaturally, that the men who had all but wrecked the Church in the preceding age should be kept under control. Since Crown and Church had suffered at the hands of the same enemy, the alliance between the two was cemented more firmly than it had been even in the days of Laud, and ' No Bishop, no King ' now seemed truer than ever. This no doubt accounts for the violence and unfairness of many High-Churchmen, notably South, in their treatment of the 'fanatics'. This was no time for them to distinguish between the moderates like Baxter and the mad Fifth-Monarchy men[3]. All were loaded with the same opprobrium : their hands were red with the blood of the Royal Martyr ; they had attempted to reform the Churches to the ground and to new-model the Church[4] ; they had broken the bonds of society and therefore were not to be trusted as citizens ; they were all republicans at heart and would sooner or later attempt on the son what they had achieved by the legal murder of the father ; they were disorderly and unruly, and thirsted after the revenues of the Church ; they encouraged the unlettered hinds to leave their shops and preach by the Spirit ; they stirred rebellion by bewitching the mob with words ; in short, they were out to subvert the order of Church and State, to further anarchy in men's

[1] *Op. cit.*, p. 354.   [2] See G.R. GRAGG, *op. cit.*
[3] On these, see P.G. ROGERS: *The Fifth Monarchy Men*, London, 1966.
[4] Robert SOUTH, *op. cit.*, I, ser. 7.

minds as well as in religion and in the body politic. South argued that they should be regarded as traitors to the State and outlawed since they not only refused to recognize the laws of the land, but were busy destroying them by all sorts of underhand means. Even more deadly was the ridicule that he poured upon them in sermon after sermon, even to mimicking their gestures and tone, as many contemporaries reported. His Mr. Holderforth, with his sneaking manner, nasal tone, and ridiculous jargon, drawing out fantastic similes for hours on end to a bewitched audience of cobblers and tinkers, is as contemptuous a portrait of the fanatic preacher as any drawn by Jonson or by the comic dramatists of the Restoration period.

South was no doubt blinded by his prejudices, and in many of his sermons he preached politics rather than religion. But he would not have agreed that this was meddling with things outside his province; indeed, he most emphatically denied the charge, arguing that it is the pastor's task to enlighten the minds of his hearers and to prevent them from being corrupted by false doctrines and from being drawn into evil practices [1]. In 1685 he prepared a sermon for Westminster School, where he had been a scholar, on the *Virtuous Education of Youth*, but was prevented from delivering it by the death of Charles II. There he argued that after the late confusions had extinguished the morality of the English nation, an *Instauratio Magna* was needed to remedy the effects of these lawless times. The strict and virtuous education of youth is, he says, the only way to prevent such calamities befalling England again; this is incumbent upon parents, schoolmasters and clergy alike. From their early years children should be taught hatred of the twin plagues of Christendom, fanaticism and rebellion, together with their duty to God and to their King. It is the clergy's duty, he says, to make the King's government easy to him; they must undeceive the people about persecution and oppression of tender consciences. But it is also the schoolmasters' duty to instil these principles into children, so that they may lead a virtuous life. Thus South equates virtue with obedience to God and to the King, and the only aspect of it he develops in this sermon is the right behaviour of man as a citizen, i.e. obedience to the King. Whatever modern readers may feel, this was a legitimate claim

[1] See his sermons on *The Fatal Imposture and Force of Words*, op. cit., II, ser. 9; VI, sermons 1 and 2.

in an age that regarded it as the duty of the prince to look after the souls as well as the bodies of his subjects. South was more conservative than most, but his fear of mob rule was shared by such men as Dryden, or, in the next age, Swift. It is no mere accident that in the *Dunciad* the kingdom of dullness spreads from Smithfields and finally overwhelms the whole country. South dreaded the uncreating word as much as did Pope, and his violent attacks against the political corrupters appear in his sermons on the imposture of words. Nor was his defence of order mere subservience to the powers that be; in fact, he was the last person to flatter those in power, and his sharp tongue spared neither high nor low. True, the fanatics were fair game, and South never missed an opportunity of raising the laugh against them. Though this was often a facile way of enlivening a sermon, his bitter opposition to them had deeper sources. He loved order, not just established order, and the ravings of the tub-preachers or the frenzies of the illuminati were distasteful to him. He did not, like his fellow-churchman Swift, ascribe these to the 'mechanical operations of the spirit', but he saw in them a clear example of the topsyturvydom that results from the usurpation of reason by the affections. If the Presbyterians were included in his diatribes it is because, in his view, they were responsible for letting loose this flood of muddy waters: however much they might 'antedate their loyalty' to the upholder of order in the Commonwealth, it was they who had first struck at the root of all order, and had tried to destroy the Church root and branch. As he said in a thirty-January sermon [1], the murder of Charles I had really been committed in forty-one, and his death in forty-nine was no more than the last act of the plot against him. The specialty of rule had been neglected, and degree being vizarded the unworthiest showed as fairly under the mask, South could have said like Ulysses, for he too believed in a hierarchy of laws. If he sneeringly remarked that the cobbler would be better employed at his last than raving about the Spirit, it is because he believed that each man should serve his Maker in the calling to which God has appointed him by giving him the abilities appropriate thereunto. The admirable contrivance of the universe results from its order and variety; in the varieties of gifts God has bestowed upon His creatures there is room for each man to do

---

[1] *Op. cit.*, V, ser. 2, printed below.

his best. To set up as an interpreter of the Word of God without
first being learned in the use of words is mere presumption ; take
but degree away, and discord follows. South, who loved music
and the due order of Church ceremonies, could feel nothing but
horror at the threat of chaos returning upon the world. He was
an aristocrat of the mind ; for him nothing could be achieved
without discipline : the office of the minister required a long and
hard training, and faith was the reward of sustained efforts, to be
crowned by the light suffusing the soul ; it was not to be got by
mere effusions or fitful illuminations. By temperament as well as
by conviction South would be the defender of law and order ; but,
though this does not appear from his sermons, this aristocrat also
took care to have poorer children educated [1].

For all this, South had his blind spots, and the least attractive
side of him is certainly his failure, or refusal, to see the other's
point of view. If this made for trenchancy in the expression of
his thought, it also led him to oversimplify some problems and
through sheer prejudice to dismiss them too highhandedly. Such
was the vexed question of tender consciences. On this, South was
adamant : no accommodation, no relaxation of the penal laws, no
toleration of Dissent. Thus, in a sermon [2] preached at Christ Church
before the University during the Michaelmas Term of 1672 [3],
he rejected the plea of tender conscience most emphatically by
showing that the text of St. Paul which the Puritans had always

---

[1] For his bequests to Christ Church College and other legacies to support
poor students, see his Will, first published by E. Curll in the *Posthumous Works*,
London, 1717. The author of the 'Memoirs of the Life of Dr. Robert South'
relates that as rector of Islip South received " 200 l. *per Annum*, 100 of which,
out of his Generous Temper he allow'd to the Reverend Mr. *Penny*, (Student of
Christ Church) his Curate, and the other, he expended in Educating and
Apprenticing the Poorer Children of that Place ". *Memoirs of the Life of the
Late Rereverend Dr. South*, London, 1721, p. 106.

[2] *Op. cit.*, III, ser. 5.

[3] Charles issued his Declaration of Indulgence on March 15, 1672, and
declared war on the States General on March 17. Parliament was to meet in
the autumn, and eventually met in February 1673. " The Commons concerned
themselves at first ... with a violation of their privileges ", including the King's
Declaration. " They presented an address (Feb. 14, 1673) declaring that penal
laws in matters ecclesiastical could be suspended only by parliament ; this they
coupled with a resolution to bring in a Bill of Relief for Protestant dissenters,
a proposal which was narrowed in committee to ' ease for Protestant subjects
that will subscribe to the doctrines of the Church of England and take the
oaths of allegiance and supremacy ' ". David OGG : *England in the Reign of
Charles II*, I, 365. The drift of South's argument shows that he was equally
opposed to the Bill of Relief since, unlike the Commons, he was not pleading
infringement of Parliamentary prerogatives.

invoked when demanding accommodation (or now, toleration)—
*1 Cor. VIII.12 But when ye sin against the Brethren, and wound
their weak conscience, ye sin against Christ*—had been misinter-
preted by them. The Apostle's command, South contended, was
meant to protect *weak* consciences, i.e. those not yet proficient in
knowledge of Christ's doctrine, who were unable to distinguish
between unlawful and indifferent matters such as the eating of
meat offered in sacrifice to idols as a form of worship or as mere
meat sold on the market. The characteristic of these weak brethren
was to suppose unlawful what was merely indifferent ; hence the
Apostle's command not to offend them by doing in their presence
what they might mistake for a false act of worship, since this might
encourage them to revert to idolatry. Now, says South, such weakness can only be pleaded in case of excusable, not willing or wilful,
ignorance. To wound such a conscience means to rob it of its
peace and embolden it to act against its present persuasion or
judgement. A weak conscience may be wounded by example

> from a kind of implicit Faith in the Goodness and Lawful-
> ness of another's Acting grounded upon a supposal of his
> Piety and Judgment [1]

or by command of a person in power. If the command be from a
private person, as in the Apostle's text, the promise of reward or
threat of punishment may sway the will, and thus lead to a breach
of purity. If it be from the magistrate upon persons under his
jurisdiction, then this cannot be helped, and the command must
be complied with. South does not say this explicitly, but at this
point instead of showing that the weak conscience cannot be
wounded, he proceeds to explain why the supreme magistrate in
devising laws can—and must—only be concerned with the good
of the majority. If a law becomes an occasion of sin to particular
persons, this is extrinsic to the design of the law. As his comparison with God's government of the world shows, this is exactly
Hooker's conception of law as regulating societies for the good
of all or at least of the greatest number. Rather than not devise
a law which he in his best judgement deems necessary to prevent
the majority from being hurt in important matters, the magistrate
must run the risk of weak persons turning this into an occasion of

---

[1] *Op. cit.*, III, p. 186.

sin. And he is " not to answer for the inconveniences which may attend such persons either in their civil or spiritual concerns ". Every law of man, South says elsewhere [1], when the matter is a thing not evil, is the law of God also.

South gives in a nutshell the main burden of Hooker's argument against the Puritans. It is only too clear that the ' weak brethren ' could not have agreed, any more than they did with Hooker ; for their argument still had been that there should be no compulsion to comply *in things indifferent*, observance or non-observance of which could not have hurt the majority *in important matters*. Here, then, South comes very near to affirming that Church ordinances aim at more than ' decency ' in public worship, that in fact they are meant to prevent real harm being done to men's souls. The reason for this appears from one of the conclusions he draws from his explanation of the text : that there is no bound to this plea of weak conscience. Clearly, the ghosts of forty-one were not yet laid, and South feared that such pleas about things indifferent would once again develop into arguments about fundamentals. The reference to the Presbyterians becomes quite clear when he says that those who make this plea for themselves do not endure it in others, and that they scruple neither at sacrilege nor at rebellion nor at the murder of a king. Once again, then, the attack on laws ecclesiastical is linked with breach of peace in the body politic, not simply because of the experience of the Civil War, but because respect or disrespect for laws in one domain argues the same in another domain, since laws, at whatever level, are expressions of the fundamental law to which they all aspire.

South also shows that if the plea is granted the weak conscience will usurp the place of the magistrate, God's vicegerent, to whom is delegated the power to ensure the welfare, both spiritual and corporal, of the community. Such a plea, he implies, posits the superiority of the individual conscience over the rational judgement that directs the framing of laws for the community ; it is a form of self-assertion that impugns the sovereignty of reason, and thereby the sovereignty of God. At this point, however, he is more concerned to draw the practical conclusion that all such pleas of causeless separation should be rejected.

However closely South argues, one of the main weapons he

[1] *Op. cit.*, II, ser. 12.

uses in this sermon is the power of words, or as he elsewhere calls it when speaking of his adversaries, the magic of words. True, his interpretation of the text is wholly warranted by the context ; but once he has established this point, his use of the term ' weak conscience ' clearly ranks the Dissenters among those weak, igno- rant, and wilfully ignorant at that, Christians who fail to distinguish between truth and appearances. Sometimes he does this openly, but he does it insidiously all along : those weak brethren to whom scandal might be brought are merely men who take occasion of the best laws to sin ; they may be driven thereto by implicit faith in the example of others—which suggests that they are no better than the Roman Catholics who had benefited by the Declaration of Indulgence, and with whom they had secretly plotted to obtain relief. Towards the end South's prejudices break into the open, but this matters far less than the lesson he has been driving home all along, that a tender conscience is no other than a weak conscience, that the Dissenters are using fraud to prepossess the minds of men by representing a bad thing under a good name. If that is true, South could beat them at their own game by representing a good thing under a bad name. This is not to say that he was juggling with words, for he had explicated his text carefully ; but as a good orator he did not rely on bare arguments alone to do the full work of persuasion.

This is one of his most characteristic sermons, both for the vigour of his thought and for the pregnancy of the expression ; to the detached observer it is a delight to see how the tender/weak equation insinuates itself into an argument that can stand on its own merit but gains force by this subtle play on words. South was a truly witty preacher, though not in this instance after the fashion of Andrewes. That he should have used his best powers in the cause of intolerance need not detract from our pleasure in reading him. Controversy could bring out the best and the worst in him, and his treatment of Sherlock, for instance, though always lively even in its most scholastic passages, is often scurrilous. In arguments of great moment, such as the defence of order or of right thinking, of the prayers of the Church or of the right use of words, his thought seems to shine the more brightly for the heat he brings to bear on the matter ; the closely reasoned discussion sweeps us along, and his words, at once precise and vivid, give the thought a clear outline. The exposition of the hierarchy of laws in this sermon is only one of many examples of his felicity in compressing an argument to give it driving force as well as to concentrate on essentials. This is the very virtue he praised in the prayers and collects of the Church of England, and he may well have learnt it from these. No wonder he was such a staunch defender of the Liturgy.

South, whose letters to his 'worthy friend Mr. John Locke' express his high regard for the philosopher, could not countenance toleration even after the law of the land made it possible for Dissenters to worship freely. In a sermon on the plea of tender conscience preached in 1691 he said he would not " speak so much as one syllable against the *Indulgence and Toleration* " [1] granted to the opposers of the Constitutions of the Church ; but he added :

> the *Law which tolerates* them in their way of worship (and it does no more) does not *forbid* us to defend ours [2],

and he urged all lovers of the Church to teach young people the right principles for fear they might be induced ' by trimming and time-serving ' to betray the Church of England. Yet he did speak against the Act of Toleration on another occasion, in a sermon that was given wide currency by pirated editions before he himself published it. Though we do not know when the sermon was preached [3], it is clear that South is here resisting attempts at com-

---

[1] Again by implicitly equating the Act of Toleration and the Declaration of Indulgence he suggests that the two are intended to relieve both Roman Catholics and Dissenters rather than to further peace among all Protestants. This was certainly good strategy, but it expressed more than South's partisan zeal : Pope Innocent XI is said to have set greater hopes for relief of the Roman Catholics on William's policy of toleration than on the determination of James II to give all key-posts to Romanists : " So it came about, that William's expedition for the deliverance of Protestantism in England had not only the Pope's approval but his active help, for it was he who brought the Emperor Leopold to full concurrence in it ". GWATKIN, *op. cit.*, p. 370. It should be added, however, that the Pope was then at loggerheads with James's ' paymaster', Louis XIV. See D. OGG : *England in the Reign of James II and William III*, pp. 206-7.

[2] *Op. cit.*, II, ser. 12, p. 447.

[3] *Op. cit.*, V, ser. 12. A manuscript copy of this sermon (not in South's own hand) now in the Bodleian Library (MS. Carte 206) bears the date 4 Aug., 1710. The 1716 pirated edition says that it was " preached in the last century ". Curll mentions no date in his edition of it in the *Posthumous Works* (1717). The date 1710 suggests that the sermon is related to the wave of High-Church feeling aroused by the Whigs' impeachment of Dr. Sacheverell, which brought the Tories back into power ; on the other hand, South writing to Dr. Sloane on 31 May, 1712, mentions the " paralytick blow " he had suffered " two years since " which had deprived him " of the plainnesse and freedome of (his) speech ". (British Museum Additional MS. 4043). It is hard to determine

prehension or at ' easing ' the Dissenters, and trying to put pressure on Convocation or on Parliament by raising the cry of ' the Church in danger ' [1]. Toleration, he says, has had " a law (or something like a law) made in its behalf " but since the laws enjoining conformity have not been repealed, obedience to them remains a duty, and nonconformity a sin. This may seem a very lame argument indeed, but South further shows that the Act of Toleration can have no effect at all on " the nature and quality of the actions commanded or prohibited by the preceding positive laws of the Church " ; the Act indeed takes away the penalties and thus gives temporal impunity, but it cannot warrant the transgression itself or take away the guilt of the action. In a passage characteristic of his conception of law he adds :

> Nor is it able to take off all sorts of Penalties neither ; for as much as those enacted by the Divine Law can never be remitted or *abrogated* by any human Law, or temporal Authority whatsoever. And therefore our Separatists will

the date from internal evidence since South revised his sermons for publication and occasionally added topical references which are sometimes anachronistic (see ' Note on the Text ', below). Besides, before 1711 Occasional Conformity Bills had been " repeatedly passed by Tories in the House of Commons and regularly defeated in the Lords by the Whig bishops ". G.R. CRAGG : *The Church and the Age of Reason*, Harmonsworth, 1960, p. 62.

[1] If the sermon was indeed preached in 1710 it must have contributed to the passing of the Occasional Conformity Bill (1711) " which punished with ruinous fines any man who, having qualified for State or municipal office by taking the Sacrament in an Anglican Church, afterwards attended a place of Nonconformist worship " (G.M. TREVELYAN : *History of England*, London, 1948 [3], p. 500). In the sermon on *The Virtuous Education of Youth*, which South had prepared to preach at Westminster School in 1685 and which he published in the same volume (sermon 1, possibly revised for publication), he had urged his hearers to employ the utmost of their power and interest, " both with King and Parliament, to suppress, utterly to suppress and extinguish, those private, blind, conventicling Schools or Academies of Grammar and Philosophy, set up and taught secretly by Fanaticks, here and there all the Kingdom over " (vol. V, p. 41). This was the purpose of the Schism Act, passed by the Tories in 1714, which " took away from Dissenters the education of their own children, which was to be handed over to persons licensed by Bishops of the Established Church. The many excellent schools that the Non-conformists had established at their own cost were to be suppressed and their teachers turned adrift " (G.M. TREVELYAN, *op. cit.*, p. 500). Only the fall of the Tories on the death of Queen Anne prevented " this peculiarly odious and unnatural form of religious persecution " (*ibid.*). No wonder that on the death of Queen Anne South told a friend " That it was Time for him to prepare for his Journey to a blessed Immortality ; since all that was Good, and Gracious, and the very Breath of his Nostrils had made its Departure to the Regions of Bliss, and Eternal Happiness " (*Memoirs of the Life of the Late Reverend Dr. South*, ed. by E. Curll, London, 1721 [2], p. 138). South was the friend of Francis Atterbury, " the principal high church firebrand " in Convocation (NEILL, *op. cit.*, p. 179), and requested him to perform the last office at his burial (see *Memoirs*, p. 138).

do well to consider, that the Laws of our Church (admitting them to be but human Laws) yet so long as they neither require anything *false in Belief*, nor *immoral in Practice*, stand ratified by that general Law of God, commanding Obedience to all *Lawful*, though but Civil and Temporal Authorities ; and consequently oblige the Conscience, in the Strength of that Divine Law, to an Obedience to all that shall be enacted and enjoined by the said Authorities. So that when God shall come to pass Sentence upon Men for their Disobedience to the same, whether in this World or the next, I fear that no plea of *Toleration* will be able to ward off the *Execution* [1].

This is the same plea as he made in 1672 for obedience to human laws as ultimately deriving from the law of God, but at this later date he was prepared to grant that human laws sometimes allow, though they cannot require, things contrary to the good of men's souls. Hooker had granted the hypothesis that kings might sometimes be wrong and thwart, rather than further, the good of their subjects, in which case he hoped such kings would come to see that this worked against their own good ; such tyranny on the part of kings did not, however, warrant resistance to them. The Church's doctrine of passive obedience after the Restoration was substantially the same as Hooker's, and obedience to the magistrate was enjoined with equal force by all divines, whether High-Churchmen like South or Latitudinarians like Tillotson.

South's thought, however, may have undergone some change ; at least he may have had to clarify his position under the pressure of events which forced him, as they did many Churchmen and loyal Anglicans, to reexamine the notion of Christian obedience to the magistrate. Hooker could ignore this, for he wrote in an age when the Prince's laws agreed with those of the Church. So could South when preaching in the days of the close alliance between Church and State. This was no longer possible under James II, whose open assaults on the Church set many divines thinking. Not that they relinquished the doctrine of passive obedience, for even under such a ' bad ruler ' they still maintained the duty of non-resistance however much they might fear that the light of the Church would soon be put under a bushel. Only when in April 1688 James ordered the clergy to read his Declaration of Indulgence in all

[1] *Op. cit.*, V, ser. 12, p. 473.

churches did seven bishops, with the Archbishop of Canterbury at their head, draw up a petition to the King, in which they declared that they could not in conscience read an illegal Declaration in the House of God [1]. The seven bishops were sent to the Tower and brought to trial. In spite of James's recent appointments to the Bench they were found not guilty by the jury, and on the night of their acquittal an invitation was sent to William of Orange, signed by " leaders of the great interests and parties in England " [2], among them Compton, Bishop of London.

What South thought at the time may be gathered from a brief reference in a sermon he preached in October 1688, in which he warns against the deceit practised by both fanatics and Romanists. Having reminded his hearers how Queen Mary abused her people and performed her promises to them at the stake, he added :

> And I know no Security we had from seeing the same again in our Days, but one or two Proclamations forbidding Bonfires [3].

On 5 November next, i.e. on the anniversary of the Gunpowder Plot and the very day of William's landing at Torbay (of which South could not have known), he preached at Westminster Abbey. His sermon is not inflammatory as were many of those delivered on 5 November, and it is characteristic of him that he should have stressed the kinship between the wicked arts of the Jesuits and

---

[1] David Ogg maintains that " Almost at the first suspicion of this danger, the doctrine [of non-resistance] was thrown over and that too, not by obscure clerics, but by seven bishops. Their protest against being required to order their subordinates to read the Declaration of Indulgence made nonsense of the doctrine of Non Resistance " ; yet Ogg defines this doctrine as follows : " Resistance to the lawful King is both wicked and sacrilegious ; obedience is due to his lawful commands, and submission to those that are otherwise. " *England in the Reigns of James II and William III*, p. 167. It is clear that by enjoining the bishops to order their clergy to read the Declaration, James was requiring more than *passive* obedience to an unlawful command, and the petition of the seven bishops made this clear. The distinction is not unlike the distinction South draws between human laws which allow, but do not require, things contrary to the law of God : for all his opposition to the Act of Toleration he would comply with the laws of the land *and* exhort Christians not to take occasion of this law to commit sin, i.e. to separate from the body of the Church. Ogg's remark only applies to such men as Compton, who both taught passive obedience and signed the invitation to William.

[2] *Ibid.*, p. 202.

[3] *Op. cit.*, I, ser. 12, p. 474. I do not know what proclamations he is referring to. When the seven Bishops were acquitted on 30 June, 1688, bonfires were lit in all parts of London and bonfires were (and are) still lit on the anniversary of the Gunpowder Plot ; the latter would have been discountenanced by James II.

those of the men who acted "under the splendid names of the *Power of Godliness, Christian Liberty*, and *the Scepter and Kingdom of Jesus Christ*"[1]. Yet, he goes on to say, one should not wonder

> that I ascribe these Reformers *Practices* to *Jesuitish Principles*; it being so well known, that the *Jesuit* never acts himself more than under another *Person, Name*, and *Profession*[2].

South stresses, however, that these Sons of Darkness at least have the prudence to manage things better than to fear a change in their Church-government every six months

> or amongst all their *Indulgences* to afford any to their implacable Enemies[3].

The implacable enemies of the Church are of two kinds, but however much Protestants may have surpassed the Jesuits in wickedness, there is no doubt as to who are their real masters. South thus restates his earlier opposition to Declarations of Indulgence, but adroitly directs it against the Romanists. This is only natural since, whatever doubts Protestants may have had about Charles's Declaration, they had no doubt whatever about James's motives, and South had seen Magdalen College, Oxford, turned by the King into a Roman Catholic college in 1687. Yet, the text he had chosen (*Isa.* V. 4) is the complaint of God against the Jewish nation for their ingratitude in spite of the many favours they had received from God. This inevitably leads him to rehearse the many mercies of God to the Church of England : in permitting it to be refined from the superstitious dross of Romish practices, in pouring upon it His choicest blessings, in delivering it from the Armada and in "blowing up the Gunpowder treason itself", but also in breaking the neck of the accursed rebellion. In return for these mercies, he says, we, like the Jews, have encouraged injustice and oppression[4], rapacity and covetousness, luxury and sensuality. The main burden of the sermon is thus the sinfulness and ingrati-

---

[1] After the 1687 Declaration of Indulgence some of the Dissenters sent addresses of thanks to James II, among them William Penn. See GWATKIN, *op. cit.*, p. 372.

[2] *Op. cit.*, V, ser. 9, p. 340.   [3] *Ibid.*, p. 341.

[4] By this South does not, of course, mean the persecution of Dissenters but the stripping of the Loyalists who had lost their estates during the Interregnum. (After the Restoration goods and estates *sold* by the Loyalists to pay the fines imposed upon them were not restored.) The whole passage develops

tude of the nation. It is only to be expected that these sins will
be visited upon the English nation as they were upon the Jews :
by God bereaving them of their best defences, i.e. their laws and
their military force. Now, these were the two instances in which
James's attempt to restore Roman Catholicism appeared most clearly : in subverting the laws of the land, particularly in taking away
the charters of towns and in issuing a Declaration of Indulgence,
and in dismissing many officers in the army to place Roman Catholics in key-positions. The drift of South's sermon must therefore
have been clear to all his hearers, however covertly he expressed
his criticism of James's policy. But at no point did he suggest that
the King should be resisted.

South's later contention that the Act of Toleration only abolishes
penalties against Separatists but does not take away the guilt of
the action shows that he could envisage some distinction between
the realms of secular and of ecclesiastical laws, even though both
were devised for the whole of the community. He was saying no
more, in fact, than that some sins, such as lying, not punished, and
not punishable, by the civil power still remain sins [1]. This was
the thin edge of the wedge through which separation of the two
provinces could be effected, and others had posited such separation
in their defences of religious liberty. While Locke's *Letters on
Toleration* (1689, 1690) and *Two Treatises of Government* (1690)
look forward to the *Déclaration des Droits de l'Homme* and the
American *Declaration of Independence*, South's argument looks
back to *The Laws of Ecclesiastical Polity*. According to Locke
the laws of civil society are meant to remedy the inconveniences
of the state of nature which arise from disregard of the rule of
reason, and to safeguard individual liberty by ensuring that no man
will encroach upon the others' rights ; by the social contract the
natural right of enforcing the rule of reason is transferred to the
community as a whole, but the legislative power thus conferred
on it is to be exerted in accordance with the law of reason. South,
like Hooker, argues that the laws devised by the magistrate for
the good of his subjects are, or should be, an instance of human

the criticism of the Act of Indemnity and Oblivion so often voiced by the
old Loyalists, that the Act meant indemnity for the enemies, and oblivion for
the friends, of the King.

[1] Cp. *Apologie de l'édit du roy sur la pacification de son royaume* (i.e. of
the edict of Amboise), 1563 : " [L'édit] permet deux religions. Quand ainsi
serait, permission n'est pas approbation. " Quoted in J. LECLER, *op. cit.*, II, 69.

law reflecting the law of reason or of God ; if some subjects are thereby inconvenienced it is because *they* fail to conform to reason. The comparison brings into relief the difference between the concept of right reason and the concept of the individual conscience. The latter, which was maintained in the Nonconformist tradition and came to merge with the reason of the eighteenth-century *philosophes*, had been vindicated most eloquently in the years of the ' accursed rebellion ' by Milton. Starting from the same premiss as Hooker and South, that " when God gave man reason, He gave him freedom to choose, for reason is but choosing ", he had pleaded : " Give me the liberty to know, to utter, and to argue freely according to conscience, above all liberties ". Neither Hooker nor South would have granted that the individual's reason may at times conflict with the reason embodied in the laws : to them this was only a form of self-assertion which threatened the rule of reason or of God. The Act of Toleration no less than the arbitrary measures of James II led South to re-examine his position ; if his views remained substantially unchanged he yet felt the need to state clearly that some laws of the magistrate may not be devised for the good of his subjects' souls, and may even constitute an encouragement to sin. Only the laws devised by the Church could then be expected to reflect right reason ; with the High-Churchmen in the Lower House of Convocation [1] he then bitterly resisted all attempts at comprehension. If his position seems to have hardened, it is not only because he was growing old, but because in his view ecclesiastical laws alone could prevent the collapse of order.

Barrow did not share South's anti-fanatic zeal and indeed censured such harsh reviling of others even in the name of the true religion. In a sermon on evil-speaking he exhorts ministers to recommend mildness and moderation by their own example :

> Well indeed it were, if by their example of using mild and moderate discourse, of abstaining from virulent invectives, tauntings and scoffings, good for little but to enflame anger, and infuse ill-will, they would lead men to good practice of this sort : for no examples can be so wholsome, or so mischievous to this purpose, as those which come down from the Pulpit, the place of edification, backed with special authority and advantage [2].

[1] Like his friend Francis Atterbury.
[2] *Op. cit.*, I, ser. 16, p. 226.

The Apostle, says Barrow, enjoins us to speak evil of no man, not even of wicked men ; there are, however, occasions when it is allowable and even necessary to speak ' reproachful words ' ; for instance, in the administration of justice or when ministers inveigh against sin and vice.   Vehemency may sometimes be used in defence of truth, and on particular occasions it is excusable to express dislike of notorious wickedness with some heat of language ; yet even in these cases great caution is required, he says, and moderation is preferable to eruptions of passions, for

> A modest and friendly style doth sute truth ; it, like its authour, doth usually reside (not in the rumbling *wind*, nor in the shaking earthquake, nor in the raging *fire*, but) in the *small still voice* [1].

Barrow goes on to reprove the preposterous method of teaching and of deciding controversies which consists in vexing and angering others with ill language.   According to this quiet and peace-loving scholar, no prejudice or passion should cloud the ' apprehensive faculties ' of the hearers, and to assert a doctrine with heat is to obscure it.   Many of his remarks apply to South, and he is usually thought to have glanced at the Oxford Orator in this sermon, especially when he said that

> Satyrical virulency may vex men sorely ; but it hardly ever soundly converts them [2].

If Barrow's temper inclined him to meekness and charitableness towards others, and if he never had a sharp tongue to use against enemies of the Church, he yet believed in order, discipline, and obedience to temporal and spiritual governors.   Indeed one may even say that his respect for established order is greater than South's, and he never censured people in high places ; compared with the Oxford Orator he may sometimes seem mealy-mouthed, except occasionally in his *Treatise of the Pope's Supremacy*.   In his sermon on *1 Thess.* IV. 11 *And that ye study to be quiet, and to doe your own business*, he grants that in some cases it is allowable to meddle with the affairs of others, but

> We should not (without Cause or Allowance) meddle with our Superiors, so as to advise them, to reprehend them, to blame and inveigh against their Proceedings ; for this

[1] *Ibid.*, p. 233.   [2] *Ibid.*, p. 232.

is to confound the right order of things, to trespass beyond
the bounds of our calling and station ; to doe wrong, not
onely to them, but to the Publick, which is concerned in
the upholding their Power and Respect : It is indeed a
worse Fault than assuming the Ensigns of their Dignity,
or counterfeiting their Stamps ; for that is but to borrow
the Semblance, this is to enjoy the Substance of their
Authority [1].

This is passive obedience driven to its last conclusion ; what
Barrow enjoins, in fact, is uncritical acceptance of whatever decisions are made by authority. With him, one feels, the established
order is sacred and immutable, and each man is to remain for ever
in his station like the stars in their courses. This is more than
Hooker or South would have contended, and not unlike the dessi-
cated concept of rigid order that came to prevail in the eighteenth
century until it was revivified by Burke's notion of the organic
growth of constitutions.

The age was indeed a censorious age, and Barrow's strictures
on the criticisms and murmurings at the legislator, on people's dissatisfaction with the Constitution or with the statesmen's policy,
on clamours of all kinds against the actions of the government,
reflect the ferment of the years after the Restoration. What he
advocates, however, is little short of an implicit faith in governors
which hardly tallies with his insistence that the truths of religion
cannot be accepted upon authority :

> Every one acteth a Prince and a Bishop, or indeed is rather
> a Censour and Controller of both orders ; not considering
> the wrong he committeth, nor the arrogance he practiseth,
> nor the mischiefs which naturally ensue upon such demean-
> our : for to direct, or to check Governours, is in effect to
> exauctorate or depose them, subsituting our selves in their
> room ; and what greater injury can we doe them, or the
> Publick ? to fix or reverse Laws, belongeth to the highest
> Authority and deepest Wisedom, which 'tis enormous pre-
> sumption for us to arrogate to our selves ; by attempting
> such things, we confound the ranks of men, and course of
> things ; we ruffle the World, we supplant publick Tran-
> quillity ; and what greater mischief than this can we doe
> among men [2] ?

[1] *Op. cit.*, I, ser. 21, p. 293.   [2] *Ibid.*, p. 294.

Clarendon, who made South his Chaplain, would have been horrified ; not only the Clarendon who in the Long Parliament was
ready to support measures limiting the prerogatives of the King,
but the Clarendon who referred the Restoration Settlement to
Parliament. Barrow's theory meant conferring on 'the highest
Authority' a power which Elizabeth would not have claimed, at
least in theory. Perhaps Barrow was not aware of the real nature
of 'the Constitution' of his country. What he feared above all,
one feels, is that the world should be ruffled. The truth is that
Barrow lived in a scholar's world, and though he had been tossed
in the storms of the Mediterranean and had grappled with pirates,
what he prized above all was the peaceful life of Trinity College,
from which he viewed the bustle of men in the great world outside.
The manner and style of his sermons suggest the quiet deliberation
of a mind with all time at its disposal, indeed quite unaware of
time passing. As his sentences grow by addition and come to
embrace the vast compass of his thought, so the argument builds
up with consideration being added to consideration until the subject
is exhausted. Whatever the force of each argument the victory
is finally won by the weight of their number more than by the
cogency of the reasoning. Barrow's unconcern with time—and
with his personal appearance—is vouched for by the testimony of
various contemporaries [1], but it could easily be inferred from the
form of his sermons, or of the *Treatise of the Pope's Supremacy*.

Hooker at least had considered the possibility of kings being
bad, though in the circumstances this was only a remote possibility ;
and he had argued that human law, though reflecting the law of
God, was inevitably less perfect than God's. Barrow seems to
have believed that such Divinity doth hedge a King that

> There is a Kind of sacredness in the Mysteries of State ;
> as the Mysteries of Faith do surpass natural reason, so do
> those of State transcend vulgar capacity : as Priests by
> special Grace are qualified best to understand the one ; so
> are Princes by like peculiar assistance enabled to penetrate
> the former [2].

It is almost as though ordination and coronation conferred special

[1] See for instance : Walter POPE : *The Life of Seth, Lord Bishop of Salisbury*, 1697, ed. J.B. Bamborough, Luttrell Reprint Society, no. 21, Oxford, 1961, ch. XX.
[2] *Op. cit.*, p. 294.

powers which make both priests and kings able to peer into the
secret counsels of God. This, of course, Barrow denied when
contending against the Romanists ; but in claiming for kings judgement more than human so that their words " may with us pass for
oracular ", he extends the *potestas ordinis* to both kinds of rulers.
As a consequence he recommends passive obedience as submission
to a divine ordinance, and thus asserts the divine right of kings.
Yet, he also grounds the authority of kings on ' the reason of the
thing ' :

> According to the ordinary reason of things they are best
> able to judge of such things, being, by reason of their
> eminent station, able to discern more, and farther than
> others ... whereas we being placed in a valley, can have
> no good prospect upon the grounds and causes of their
> resolutions and proceedings ; we, for want of sufficient use
> and exercise, cannot skill to balance the contrary weights
> and reasons of things [1].

Hooker and South would simply have said that it is the magistrate's
duty to make laws for the good of all, and therefore to view the
whole of society from a higher prospect. Barrow indeed looks back
to James I rather than to Hooker, and supports the belief in the
King's sacred power, still kept alive in his time, and after, by
Charles II's touching for the King's Evil, and defended by many
staunch Churchmen. For all South's high Toryism one can hardly
imagine him taking the King's touching for the Evil quite seriously ;
it is characteristic that he states the doctrine of passive obedience
in terms that suggest not the divine rights of the King, but rather
the lawyers' maxim that the King can do no wrong.

Barrow devoted a series of sermons [2] to the text usually invoked
to urge obedience to the magistrate, *Heb*. XIII. 17 *Obey them
that have the rule over you* ; he used it to develop the theme of
obedience to spiritual governors, and justify episcopacy, but this
also led him to face the question of the relation between spiritual
and temporal power. Obedience is due to all spiritual guides or
governors of the Church, he says, because

> they are by God's appointment enabled to exercise acts of
> power ; to command, to judge, to check, controll and chastise

---

[1] *Ibid.*, p. 294.
[2] The manuscript text is continuous but was divided by Tillotson into
4 separate sermons, vol. III, sermons 24 to 27 ; printed below.

in a spiritual way, in order to spiritual ends ; (the regulation of God's worship and service, the preservation of order and peace, the promoting of edification in divine knowledge and holiness of life)[1].

Governors must guide the people in the way of truth and duty by giving instruction and by their exemplary practice. But there is distinction of ' degrees and subordinations ' in this guidance, and the Church is an " *acies ordinata*, a well marshalled army " under the " Captain General of our faith and salvation ". This distinction was never questioned in ancient times, Barrow says, except by Arius,

> and no wonder, seeing it standeth upon so very firm and clear grounds ; upon the reason of the case, upon the testimony of Holy Scripture, upon general tradition and unquestionable monuments of antiquity [2].

For him, thus, Church-government is both grounded in Scripture and in reason, and it has the backing of tradition. Hooker had gone no further than to say that episcopacy was consistent with the models found in Scripture ; Barrow seems to treat it as divinely ordained, though also instituted for prudential reasons [3]. This is like his contention that God gives Kings special powers but that they also have greater human skill to decide what is good for the community. This may explain why Barrow was found unacceptable to the authorities under the Commonwealth and refused to conform even to the extent that many loyal Anglicans did at the time [4]. Yet far from marshalling texts in support of this *acies ordinata*

---

[1] *Op. cit.*, III, ser. 24, p. 270.

[2] *Ibid.*, p. 272.

[3] " Thus under the pressure of a century of acute controversy, the Anglican divines had developed a positive, constructive, and consistent apologetic for episcopacy as retained in the Church of England. It was held to be not of dominical but of apostolical appointment, and as *divino jure* only in that sense ; as necessary where it could be had, but its absence where historical necessity compelled did not deprive a church of valid ministry and sacraments. It was necessary to the perfection or integrity of a church, though not to its essence ; and on the ground of its historic continuance in the church, its restoration in the foreign non-episcopal churches was much to be desired. " Norman SYKES, *op. cit.*, p. 81.

[4] In 1655 the Regius professor of Greek at Cambridge, Dr. Duport, resigned in the hope that Barrow would succeed him, but a mandate from Whitehall made the electors appoint somebody else because Barrow was known as a loyalist. Barrow was granted leave of absence by his College and travelled to France, Italy and Constantinople. See P.H. OSMOND : *Isaac Barrow. His Life and Times*, London, 1944, p. 45.

he develops the other two points : the reason of the thing backed by tradition, or, as Hooker would have said, natural reason as expressed in customs generally agreed upon. Reason requires such subordination in order to preserve concord, to establish a decent harmony in worship and service of God, to prevent factions, to guard against heresies, and

> to keep the Church from being shattered into numberless Sects, and thence from being crumbled into nothing [1].

Christianity needs " societies to uphold it ", and no society can abide without " a single undivided authority ". This, Barrow says, " even the chief impugners of Episcopal presidency do by their practice confess ", i.e. the Presbyterians, with their classes, provinces, nations, and moderators of the assemblies. He then briefly refers to Scriptural testimony supporting episcopacy, and to the primitive use of Christians, ending with a vehement repudiation of all such as are so overweeningly presumptuous and so perversely contentious as to oppose the custom and current practice of the Churches through all ages down to the last age.

Barrow proceeds to explain who the governors of the Church are that Christians are to obey, and to distinguish between true and counterfeit guides. The true guides are those who profess the doctrine delivered by Christ and his Apostles in word and writing and confirmed by tradition ; who celebrate the true worship of God

> in a serious, grave, decent manner, purely and without any notorious corruption either by hurtfull errour, or superstitious foppery, or irreverent rudeness [2];

who are fitted to receive ordination by competent endowments of mind and good learning, and are found fit after examination of their abilities and of testimonies concerning their manners and conversation ; who are admitted to their office by due ordination, and thus derive their authority by a continued succession from the Apostles. Barrow leaves out none of the qualifications required of the priest of the Church of England, from authority by episcopal succession to testimony of good principles in practice and doctrine [3].

---

[1] *Op. cit.*, III, p. 272.   [2] *Ibid.*, p. 275.
[3] Owing to Barrow's characteristic way of piling up paragraphs rather than developing them organically, an unfair critic might say that these qualifications

He thereby distinguishes the Anglican clergy both from the priests of the Roman Church, who by superstitious additions have corrupted the true worship of God, and from the Puritans, who fail on practically every other count. To sum up, the true guides are those

> who are acknowledged by the Laws of the Country, an obligation to obey whom is part of that *humane constitution*, unto which we are in all things (not evidently repugnant to God's Law) indispensably bound to submit; whom our Sovereign, God's Vicegerent and nursing Father of his Church among us ... doth command and encourage us to obey [1].

Thus having listed all the distinguishing marks of the true governors of the Church—some of which, such as Apostolic succession, many of his hearers might find hard to discover—he adds an unfailing mark by which to recognize them: they are the pastors of the Church established by the law of the country. His uncompromising Erastianism may sound particularly uncongenial to most modern readers, but he will explain the relation between temporal and ecclesiastical authority at a later stage.

Though it is easy enough to infer from the foregoing description who are the counterfeit guides, Barrow proceeds to list the characters of these seducers: they affect novelties, uncouth notions, big words, and dark phrases; they dote on curious empty speculations, and idle questions, which engender strife and yield no good fruit; they do not ground their opinions on the Word of God, sound reason, and the authority of good men, but warrant them by their own fancy, the impulses of their passions, and pretences to inspiration; they abuse weak and heedless people by shews of mighty zeal,

> by affected forms of speech, by pleasing notions, by prophesying *smooth things, daubing* and *glozing* [2];

are required singly but not together; and this might be particularly damaging for the last requirement, which in fact is no more than a summary of all the foregoing, but is given equal rank with the others. The passage, which is too long to be quoted here, develops as follows: The true guides must be distinguished from the counterfeits. They are: " Those who constantly profess... Those who celebrate... Those who derive their authority... Those whose practice... Those who... appear sober... Those also, who are acknowledged by the Laws of the Country..." (pp. 275-6). Each sentence constitutes a separate paragraph, the word *also* in the last paragraph being particularly infelicitous.

[1] *Ibid.*, p. 276.   [2] *Ibid.*

they intrude themselves into the office of guides without any clear
commission from God, or allowable call from men ; they are not
fitly prepared for the ministry ; they are void of charity, turbulent,
disorderly, violent, and deceitful ; they create dissensions and abet
disturbances ; their doctrine is an empty form of godliness, and
" they fill the minds of men with ill-passions, ill-surmises, ill-will " ;
they are unruly, presumptuous murmurers, who produce nothing
but combustions and seditions in Church and State ; in short
they are

> the Ministers of Satan, the Pests of Christendom, the
> Enemies and Murtherers of Souls [1].

Barrow may have censured South for using invective against the
enemies of truth ; but he could outdo him in passion and zeal for
the House of God.   Though he might not regard his description
of Dissenters as a form of evil-speaking forbidden by the Apostle,
yet he must have realized that he had loaded them with such
opprobrium that they could hardly expect to get a fair hearing.
Indeed, Barrow is using the power of his wit against them no
less than does South ; only it is a different kind of wit, more like
Dryden's lively spaniel that ranges after thoughts and words.
    Barrow next addresses himself to the nature of the duty,
which implies both obedience to the governors' laws and embracing
the doctrine they recommend.   In developing the first point, he
rehearses and expounds the arguments already put forward for
government of the Church, and in showing that obedience was
enforced by the primitive Church he stresses that

> There were not then of old any such cavils and clamours
> against every thing prescribed by Governours ; there were
> no such unconscionable scruples, no such hardhearted pre-
> tences to tender conscience devised to baffle the authority
> of superiours ; had there been such, had men then commonly
> been so froward and factious as now, the Church had been
> soon shivered into pieces, our Religion had been swallowed
> up in confusion, and licentiousness [2].

Clearly, Barrow was not prepared to allow for any scruples of
conscience.   It is significant that in a discourse on obedience to
spiritual guides, where as usual he takes time to amplify and
examine every aspect of the question, he should here dismiss the

---

[1] *Ibid.*, p. 278.   [2] *Ibid.*, ser. 25, p. 285.

problem of conscience as not even worth a minute's consideration. This high-handed treatment suggests an even firmer refusal than South's to hear the other point of view. For all his meekness Barrow sometimes strikes one as an overbearing authoritarian, who is only too ready to consider the matter closed. South, on the contrary, argues it out and thereby at least pays his opponent the tribute of granting his view some consideration.

Barrow does consider the objections to the lawfulness of the Church-government at a later stage, only to refute them by an impressive series of rhetorical questions which reveal the rationale of his doctrine. The basis of his argument is, like Hooker's, that the laws governing men are devised for the good of all; they cannot be expected to be perfect, but then, men live in a real society, not in " the Platonic idea of a Commonwealth "; these laws are based on reason and cannot take into account particular men's fancies, and the purpose of government is thwarted if laws may be suspended at will. Besides, are the objections against obedience as clear and cogent as are the reasons that enforce it? have the scruples such strength as to outweigh the judgement of those whom God has authorized and enabled to devise laws? is it not the purpose of the governors' office to resolve our doubts? are these men in earnest when they ground their nonconformity upon dark subtleties? are not the danger and guilt of bringing about disorder enough to silence scruples? did the Apostles and the primitive Church regard such pretences? Whatever he may have suggested at the beginning, Barrow argues not from Scripture but from the reason of the thing in itself and as evidenced by tradition, which, like Hooker, he believes to embody human reason; it is on this ground that he rejects the plea of conscience. This is consistent with his belief in order and due subordination. But he will also have to explain the grounds and due limits of such subordination in doctrine, since the burden of all his teaching is that implicit faith is not acceptable to God.

Meanwhile, he has shown all the evils that ensue from disregard of the spiritual guides' authority, and he adds that in the present state of things the guilt is aggravated by the ' supervenient guilt ' of disobedience to the laws of the prince and of the country. This raises the question of the relation between secular and spiritual powers, and Barrow deals with it briefly. To secular powers, he says, God has committed

the dispensation of justice, with the maintenance of peace
and order in reference to worldly affairs [1].

Before temporal rulers recognized Christ as their sovereign, ecclesiastical matters were wholly in the hands of spiritual guides, and
to them Christians were obliged to yield obedience.   Now that
political authority backs and fortifies the laws of spiritual governors
by civil sanctions, disobedience incurs a double guilt.   Some pretend that by rejecting episcopal government they transgress no
more than ' a political sanction ', but that alone is a great offence,
since God enjoins us to obey temporal governors in all things not
evidently repugnant to His law ; moreover, the civil law does not
derogate from the ecclesiastical, it only corroborates it, so that each
gains strength from the other.   Barrow's explanation clearly begs
the question ; he does not even seem to realize what the question is.
Hence, he fails to meet the objection that things enjoined by the
magistrate may be repugnant to God's law, and he further fails to
show whence springs this admirable concord between secular and
spiritual powers.   Yet he himself had had experience of a secular
power enjoining things he found repugnant to God's law : he had
refused to take the Covenant, and had left the country until a better
Church-government was restored.   Perhaps he is stating no more,
in this sermon, than that *in fact* the civil and ecclesiastical powers
of the country happened to be working hand in hand.   None the
less it is significant that he should not have made clear the principles
on which such union was based.   After the Revolution the constitution of the country and the Coronation oath imposed on William
were to ensure that the sovereign pledged himself to uphold the
' Reformed Protestant Religion ' ; whether this would have satisfied
Barrow any better than it did South remains an open question ;
but this would at least have given him some ground on which to
base his confidence in the amicable working together of both powers.
But only if his main fear had been, as it was to the men of 1689,
that ' the Reformed Church '—of which even before that date the
King was supreme Governor—might be taken to mean the Church
as reformed by the Council of Trent.   In the present sermon, however, Barrow was arguing against the Dissenters, not against the
Romanists.

Barrow then proceeds to explain what constitutes obedience in

[1] *Ibid.*, p. 288.

doctrine. Here he must consider " one point which perhaps will more hardly be admitted ", i.e. that in some cases " it behoveth to rely barely upon [the governors'] judgment and advice ". Barrow needs to be careful in defining this point since it is all important to distinguish obedience of this kind from implicit faith, which he rejected as firmly as did other Anglicans. Yet, in this sermon he is first concerned to oppose the private judgement invoked by the Puritans. Hence his remark that persons " most contemptuous of authority " are in some cases constrained to rely upon the judgement of others, if only to know what is the literal sense of Scripture according to translations. Hence also his use of arguments which were generally used by the Romanists to refute the Protestants' claim that all truths necessary for salvation are expressed plainly in Scripture and can be understood by any man who diligently searches after truth. Barrow's argument, in fact, is no different from South's in *The Scribe Instructed*, that most men are unable for want of learning to discern the truth ; yet, because of the general drift of his discourse Barrow at first sounds much nearer to the party he opposed so resolutely in his *Treatise of the Pope's Supremacy*. It is only half-way in this development that he states his view unambiguously :

> it is plainly reasonable to follow our Guides in all matters, wherein we have no other very clear and certain light of reason, or revelation to conduct us [1].

He expounds the qualification in order to distinguish this from implicit faith : it is not against conscience but according to it to submit to direction if we do so on the best of reasons, not blindly or upon compulsion ; nor does such submission confer on these guides an infallible authority, for they are men and therefore subject to error. At which point Barrow is led to emphasize the other side of his doctrine, which so far had been kept so much in the background as to be almost ignored, that is, the duty laid on each man to use his own reason, judgement and discretion, so far as he is capable. If this sounds like a face-about, it is because Barrow and the Church of England as a whole stood midway between the two extremes, of the private judgement unaccountable to universal reason and of blind obedience. They could never stress the one to the

---

[1] *Ibid.*, ser. 27, p. 303.

point of nullifying the other, and they had to negociate their way
between excessive claims for personal judgement or for submission.
Thus, in a sermon on obedience, Barrow comes to stress the need
to use reason, to judge independently of authority, to accept nothing upon bare authority, to prove all and hold fast that which
is good, for

> We are accomptable personally for all our actions as agree-
> able or cross to reason ... the ignorance, or errour of our
> guides will not wholly excuse us from guilt... We are bound
> to study truth, to improve our minds in the knowledge and
> love of it, to be firmly persuaded of it in a rational way [1].

Christ himself and his Apostles did not exact credit upon other
terms than rational considerations.   Hence, though we are bound
to obey our guides we must " scan their dictates, and their orders " :

> We may, and are bound, if they tell us things evidently
> repugnant to God's word, or to sound reason and common
> sense, to dissent from them ; if they impose on us things
> evidently contrary to God's Law, to forbear compliance with
> them ; we may in such cases appeal *ad legem et testimonium* ;
> we must not admit a *non obstante* to God's Law [2].

This indeed was uncompromising language ; it also happens
to be the language that many Puritans, and among them the Great
Rebel, could have used to justify non-obedience to the Church.
But Barrow further defines his position by saying that God commands us to use the eyes He has given us, but that where our own
eyes fail us we should use those of our guides.   And his final
advice is that we should forbear *openly* to dissent from our guides
or to contradict their doctrine, except if it be so plainly false as
to subvert the foundations of faith or the practice of holiness,
because this may encourage inconsiderate people to do the same
on mere slight pretexts.   It is, in fact, as though at bottom Barrow
could see the force of the sincere Dissenters' plea, but was loth to
grant it lest it lead to dissent on what Tillotson called ' little
scruples '.   It is also characteristic that in this part of the discussion
what he advocates is the free use of reason, whereas in rejecting
the plea of tender consciences he only spoke of fancy and passion.
It is a pity he did not distinguish as clearly as Chillingworth had
done between public reason and the private judgement that is no

---

[1] *Ibid.*, p. 305.   [2] *Ibid.*, pp. 306-7.

better than fancy. As it is, Barrow gives the impression that the Church of England has a kind of monopoly of reason. No doubt the Dissenters could have answered him that one man's reason is another man's fancy, and that the argument could cut both ways, since this was exactly the Romanists' charge against all Protestants.

Barrow did not live to see the temporal power directly assaulting the Church it was pledged to support ; nor did he so far meddle with the politics of religion as to express any view on Charles's Declaration of Indulgence. His interest in mathematics may have kept him outside the strifes which his fellow-Anglicans had to face, and his aversion from all causes of discord would make him loth to deal with such contentious matter. What he would have done if asked to obey the unlawful commands of a lawful prince may be matter for speculation, but one feels that in any case the peace of Trinity College would have saved him from having to come into open conflict with authority.

The Anglican clergy, who had preached obedience to the magistrate and non-resistance even if commands were unlawful, were faced with a difficult choice when the crown was conferred on William and Mary. They had sworn allegiance to James and, though the Lords and Commons might say that James had ' deserted ', it could be argued that he had done so under compulsion, so that the oaths were still binding [1]. On the other hand, James had clearly run away, had been brought back to England, and then had fled again [2]. No wonder many of his loyal clergy hesitated. Sancroft, Archbishop of Canterbury, whom James had committed to the Tower a few months before, proposed that the King should be restored upon conditions. But who could trust the promises of a king who had broken his pledge whenever he felt strong enough to pursue his own course ? Sancroft's proposal was rejected by the Convention, and he withdrew to his palace. William and Mary were crowned by Compton, Bishop of London, while Sancroft remained at Lambeth and refused to vacate his see. The clergy had to take the oath of allegiance by 1 September, 1689. A large

---

[1] The same difficulty had arisen in the deliberations of both Houses. On this, and on the various solutions envisaged, see BURNET : *History of His Own Time*, Bk IV, *in fine*, and David OGG, *op. cit.*, pp. 224-7. Ogg notes that the Lords " rejected by 55 to 41 the resolution (of the Commons) that the throne was vacant " (p. 226).

[2] See David OGG, *op. cit.*, pp. 218-20.

number of them—including several bishops, some of whom had been tried for refusing to have the Declaration read—felt they could not take the oath as long as James was alive, and were therefore deprived. Some of these, like Thomas Ken, Bishop of Bath and Wells, simply retired and continued faithful members of the Church; others, notably George Hickes, Dean of Worcester, claimed that they alone were keeping the Church of England pure and undefiled, thus initiating the Non-juring schism.

To say, as David Ogg does, that the clergy "were asked to do no more than to admit that an absurd doctrine had been discredited by events"[1] is to apply to the problem a pragmatic test which no one who, like South, believed in the hierarchy of laws could have found acceptable. Taking the oaths to William and Mary involved making a decision which no sincere Churchman could arrive at without re-examining the doctrine of obedience to the magistrate. No doubt there were many time-servers and vicars of Bray then as always. No doubt many, among them Tillotson, were accused of being time-servers though they may have been quite sincere. That the problem was a real one appears from the discussions between Sherlock and South before they decided to take the oaths[2]. Though South was finally satisfied that this was lawful[3], it is clear from his sermon on comprehension with the Dissenters that he did now regard the magistrate as not concerned with the good of his subjects' souls in *all* the laws he devises. That the matter continued to rankle appears from a side-remark in his 1691 sermon on the nature and measures of conscience, in which he rehearses the several duties and virtues of a Christian, such as

> *Temperance, Meekness, Charity, Purity of Heart, Pardoning of Enemies, Patience*; (I had almost said, *Passive Obedience* too, but that such old-fashioned Christianity seems as much

---

[1] *Op. cit.*, p. 234.

[2] See the letters published by W. Dodds (Mrs. Nowottny), *op. cit.*; Miss Dodds shows that South's animus against Sherlock in the Trinitarian controversy had its source in Sherlock's face-about after he had advocated not taking the oaths.

[3] It is unlikely that he was convinced of the legitimacy of William's title to the Crown; he recognized him as *de facto* King, to whom obedience is due even as, according to Hooker and other defenders of passive obedience, it is due to a bad ruler. This is not unlike Fuller's justification for complying in the Interregnum, quoted above. Wood accuses South of having been a time-server under Cromwell, but this malicious gossip's repeated accusations need mean no more than that South was among those whom Bosher calls "conforming Anglicans".

out of Date with some, *as Christ's Divinity and Satisfaction*)[1].

Tillotson himself dissuaded William from pressing the Comprehension Bill lest this should be felt to infringe the rights of Convocation[2] : he too, then, distinguished between a mere secular law, the Toleration Act, and one that involved directions for worship and hence the care for souls. He would not have argued that the sin remained ; but his attitude shows that South's distinction about laws secular and ecclesiastical in the Comprehension sermon was not prompted by mere partisan zeal.

Tillotson not only took the oaths to William and Mary, but he was the trusted adviser of the King, and was to be elevated to the Archbishopric in 1691, when Sancroft had been at last persuaded to leave. Yet, he too had taught obedience to the magistrate and non-resistance, even in the days of James. In an early sermon, on *The Advantages of Religion to Societies*, he had shown that religion tends to the good order and more easy government of human society both because it teaches the magistrate " to rule over men in the fear of God " and because it makes the people " obedient to Government, and conformable to laws " since

> He that hath entertain'd the true principles of Christianity is not to be tempted from his obedience and subjection by any worldly considerations, because he believes that *whosoever resisteth authority resisteth the ordinance of God, and that they who resist shall receive to themselves damnation*[3].

True, he only mentions worldly considerations as a possible motive for disobedience and indeed he never dealt at length with the problem of tender conscience. This should not, however, be taken to mean that he granted the plea of conscience to be legitimate, or he could hardly have remained within the Church. Indeed, he made it clear that the differences among Protestants were not about fundamentals, but about things indifferent, which were made occasions for schism and faction though they were neither necessary nor evil in themselves. He advocated unity among Protestants, especially in view of the common enemy, but he clearly envisaged this as unity within the national Church. To break the unity of

---

[1] *Op. cit.*, II, ser. 11, pp. 424-5.
[2] See BIRCH : *Life, op. cit.*, p. CXVIII.
[3] *Op. cit.*, I, ser. 3, p. 41.

the Church on no weightier ground than 'little scruples' was the
best way to let in the hated enemy :

> And shall little Scruples weigh so far with us, as, by break-
> ing the Peace of the Church about them, to endanger our
> whole Religion ?   Shall we take one another by *the throat
> for a hundred pence*, when our common Adversary stands
> ready to clap upon us an Action of *ten thousand Talents* ?
> Can we in good earnest be contented that rather than the
> *Surplice* should not be thrown out, *Popery* should come in ;
> rather than receive the sacrament in the humble, but indif-
> ferent, Posture of *kneeling*, to swallow the Camel of *Tran-
> substantiation*, and *adore* the Elements of Bread and Wine
> for our God and Saviour ? and rather than submit to a *Set
> Form* of Prayer, to have the Service of God performed in
> an *unknown Tongue* [1] ?

The sermon in which he thus sums up the points at issue between
the Church and the Dissenters—at least, those amongst them with
whom reunion was ever contemplated—was preached at the Yorkshire Feast, i.e. " at the General Meeting of the Gentlemen, and
others, in and near London, Born within the County of York ",
on 3 December, 1678.   Among the audience there might be some
who remembered that Tillotson, a Yorkshire man himself, had first
been bred among Puritans and they would find in this passage a
clear statement of the reason why he had later conformed.   His
appeal to unity is the more significant in view of the circumstances,
since the Popish Plot was soon to be exploited by men who were
no friends of the Church, and had probably been engineered by
them.   As appears from this sermon, Tillotson believed that the
Plot was the work of the Papists, as he seems to have believed
that the Great Fire was also their work [2] ; this may not argue great
critical acumen on his part, but it does show that he was not prepared to join in the outcries against Anglican intolerance : rather

---

[1] *Op. cit.*, I, ser. 20, p. 193.

[2] *Op. cit.*, I, ser. 32, ' A Thanksgiving Sermon for our Deliverance by the
Prince of Orange, Preached at Lincoln's Inn Chapel, January 31, 1688 ' (i.e.
1689).   Having rehearsed the many judgements of God on the English nation,
he comes to the Great Fire : " God sent a terrible and devouring *Fire*, which
in less than *three* Days Time laid the greatest Part of this great *City* in Ashes.
And there is too much reason to believe that the *Enemy* did this ; *that* perpetual
and implacable Enemy of the Peace and Happiness of this Nation " (p. 324).
Tillotson may have been fanning the fire of anti-Roman prejudices by disin-
genuously repeating this ludicrous assertion ; yet one feels that he was himself
as gullible as many of his hearers whenever a Popish Plot was ' discovered '.
He would not have repeated such unproven charges against Dissenters.

he put the blame for the lack of unity on the other party's ' little scruples '.   True, he did not approve of the persecuting zeal of many of his brethren nor of the severe laws against the Dissenters, and he tried several times to find some means of accommodating them.   But this does not mean that he was prepared to support the plea of conscience, even though he could hardly have treated it with the same harshness as South did.   The difference between the two appears clearly in Tillotson's advice not to confine the Church of Christ within too narrow a compass, but rather to " err a little on the favourable and charitable part " [1].   These particular words were meant primarily to oppose the Romanists' claim that none can be saved outside their own Church ; but Tillotson also granted that sincere Catholics might be saved : for all his prejudices and for all his staunch opposition to the doctrines of Rome, he did extend his charity to Christians on both sides, and High-Churchmen felt that he erred more than a little on the favourable part in his treatment of dissenting brethren ; but such was Tillotson's temper.

He again refers to conscience in a sermon preached at White-hall in 1680, *The Protestant Religion Vindicated from the Charge of Singularity*, and says he cannot think that the plea of conscience warrants any man to affront the established religion of the country. The reservations and qualifications in his statement are, however, significant :

> I cannot think (till I be better inform'd, which I am always ready to be) that any pretence of Conscience warrants any Man, that is not extraordinarily commission'd, as the Apostles and first Publishers of the Gospel were, and cannot justify that Commission by Miracles as they did, to affront the establish'd Religion of a Nation (though it be false) and openly to draw Men off from the profession of it in contempt of the Magistrate and the Law : All that Persons of a different Religion can in such a case reasonably pretend to, is to enjoy the private liberty and exercise of their own Conscience and Religion ; for which they ought to be very thankful, and to forbear the open making of Proselytes to their own Religion, (though they be never to sure that they are in the right) till they have either an extraordinary Commission from God to that purpose, or the Providence of

---

[1] *Op. cit.*, I, ser. 31, p. 321.   The sermon, on the Parable of the Ten Virgins, was preached before Princess Anne in 1688, as were others (e.g. vol. II, sermons 2 and 3) to encourage her in holding fast by the Protestant religion.

God make way for it by the permission of connivance of
the Magistrate[1].

The beginning of this passage might seem to refer to the Puritans'
plea of tender consciences ; his answer does meet their argument
and is not unlike his answer to the scoffers, that even on the supposition that religion be false, it is uncivil to affront other men's
belief. It could hardly be contended, however, that Puritans should
have been thankful to enjoy the private liberty and exercise of their
own conscience and religion. The remark, in fact, could only apply
to those members of the King's household and Court who were
allowed to have Roman Catholic chaplains and hear mass in private
chapels. It is they and their priests who could not forbear " the
open making of proselytes ", and it is at them that the whole sermon
is directed since Tillotson is vindicating the Protestant religion from
the Catholics' accusation of novelty ; the point he grants—though
the religion of the country be *false*—is one that the Puritans did
not make ; significantly too, he does not use the specific term *plea*
of *tender* conscience. None the less, Tillotson refuses to countenance the pretence of conscience, though he seems to contemplate
the possibility that the magistrate might permit the open profession
of a different religion ; perhaps he had in mind the period when
the Declaration of Indulgence indeed permitted it or connived at it.

Tillotson's crabbed way of reasoning, or his incapacity to
grapple with a knotty problem, appears from the end of the
paragraph, which was added in a later edition. There he says
that every man has the *right* to publish and propagate the true
religion and to declare it against a false one, which clearly makes
nonsense of his previous assertion ; but, he continues, no man is
under the *obligation* to do so, unless he has as clear a command
from God as the Apostles had, in which case he is to abide all

---

[1] *Op. cit.*, I, ser. 27, p. 283. Printed below. This passage gave offence both
to Anglicans and to Nonconformists. The former accused Tillotson of Hobbism
and of serving the turn of popery ; the latter of pleading the Popish cause
against all the reformers. Tillotson was really grieved at this and explained
to his friends that he had had to prepare this sermon at short notice and was
ordered to print it immediately after delivery. He acknowledged that he had
expressed himself badly, and in all subsequent editions he added a paragraph
to mitigate the effect of this one. Another passage in the same sermon was
thought to be ' pure Hobbism ', and Tillotson altered it as best he could in the
second issue of the first edition, and again when the sermon appeared in *Sermons
and Discourses* (1686). See BIRCH : *Life*, pp. xli-xlviii. For the subsequent
revision see D.D. BROWN : ' The Text of John Tillotson's Sermons ', *The Library*,
XIII (1958), 18-36, and ' The Dean's Dilemna ', *ibid.*, XIV (1959), 282-7.

hazards, including martyrdom. It is not clear whether Tillotson distinguishes between ' publishing the true religion ' and ' constantly professing it ', for which, he had just argued, the subject is bound ' patiently to suffer ' if a false religion be established by law.

Since many of Tillotson's sermons are intended to show the superiority or advantages of the Christian religion, he often stresses that belief in, and fear of, God are the basis of society, because without these all obligations of conscience cease. He repeats this argument in *The Protestant Religion Vindicated*, and he further explains that it properly belongs to the civil magistrate to support the true religion and to take care " that none be permitted to debauch and seduce men from it ". This should have reminded the King—if he had not been asleep [1]—that it was his duty to prevent the Romish priests from making proselytes. Tillotson then goes on to explain what power the civil magistrate in England has in matters of religion, in answer to the Romanists' objection that it has power to decide in matters of religion. According to him the magistrate has the right neither to reject God's true religion, nor to declare what he pleases to be so, since

> he who acknowledgeth himself to derive all his Authority from God, can pretend to none against Him [2].

But he does not say how the magistrate is to know which is the true religion he is to support. Instead he proceeds to define the duties of the subjects if a false religion be established by law :

> the case here is the same as in all other laws that are sinful in the matter of them, but yet made by a lawful Authority ; in this case the Subject is not bound to profess a false Religion, but patiently to suffer for the constant profession of the true [3].

The whole passage thus raises more questions than it purports to answer, and it is doubtful whether any Romanist could have been convinced by such an argument. What Tillotson is out to show

---

[1] " Dr. Calamy's account is, that King Charles II having slept most part of the time while the sermon was delivered, a certain nobleman stepped up to him, as soon as it was over ; and said, ' Tis pity your Majesty slept ; for we had the rarest piece of Hobbism that ever you heard in your life '. ' 'Ods fish, he shall print it then ', answered the King and immediately called the Lord Chamberlain and gave him his command to the Dean to print his sermon ", BIRCH : *Life*, p. xliii.

[2] *Op. cit.*, p. 283.   [3] *Ibid.*

is that the King should enforce the true Protestant religion ; only one part of the passage is at all convincing, the demonstration that it is proper for the magistrate to take care that people are instructed in the true religion.   Obviously Tillotson was loth to say that the true religion should be defined by the Church, not by the civil government, which was exactly the Romanists' contention, for this would have made the King subservient to the spiritual power. Indeed, one of his strongest objections to Roman Catholicism was that it absolved subjects from obedience to kings and even claimed the right to depose them [1].   This, in fact, accounts for the decidedly Erastian position of the Church of England, which was acceptable neither to Roman Catholics nor to the Saints : Pope Pius V's bull of excommunication against Elizabeth, by making all Roman Catholics in England potential traitors to their sovereign, may well have contributed to shaping the Church's Erastianism.   In *The Protestant Religion Vindicated* Tillotson in fact makes the same distinction between *potestas jurisdictionis* and *potestas ordinis* which Elizabeth had insisted on making by altering her title.   But in the context his argument is lame, and ultimately begs the question.

What matters to us, however, is that no less than Hooker— though more confusedly—Tillotson posited that it is the magistrate's duty to take care of his subjects' souls, and that it is the subjects' duty to obey, or suffer patiently under a bad prince. Whether his statement of the subjects' duty to suffer patiently *in the constant profession* of his faith may be called passive obedience is doubtful ; but he certainly advocated non-resistance to a bad ruler.

Tillotson's exposition of the theoretical basis of the doctrine of obedience to governors may be unsatisfactory, but he is no less positive than South on the binding nature of the duty itself.   One of his main accusations against the Roman Church is that by striking at the civil power it dissolves the bonds of human society and subverts peace and order in the world.   He developed this theme not only in his sermon of 5 November, 1678, when the occasion would naturally lend itself to it, but in other sermons as well.   It is significant, however, that he should stress the duty of obedience to the magistrate not in opposition to the Dissenters— though he occasionally says that they should submit to the civil

[1] *Op. cit.*, I, ser. 19 (on 5 Nov., 1678), p. 181.

power—but when urging Protestants to remain steadfast in their
religion. Indeed, it is under James that he was led to emphasize
it as he again and again exhorted men not to depart from their
religion. His two sermons on *The Support of Good Men under
their Sufferings for Religion* [1] were clearly meant to encourage
Protestants against coming persecutions ; there he shows what
support they may expect from God, and why they must resist the
temptation of apostasy. What he recommends is for men to commit
their souls to God's care and custody, to do their duty and to trust
in God's help if they should be brought to extreme sufferings for
religion. He lists all the cases in which men may be said to suffer
for religion, i.e. for not renouncing the true religion ; for making
open profession of it by joining in assemblies of Christians when
ordered to conceal it ; for not betraying their faith by indirect
means ; for maintaining any necessary or fundamental articles in
it ; for asserting and maintaining the purity of the Christian doctrine
and worship ; finally for not disclaiming undoubted truths of God
though it be no fundamental article of religion. The example in
this last case is, as one might expect, refusal to agree silently to
the doctrine of transubstantiation, which, for Tillotson and all
Anglicans, undermines the foundation of certainty by disowning
the right of reason and of common sense. Tillotson is equally
clear on what does not constitute suffering for religion, and he
expounds it as carefully as the former point, thereby distinguishing
sharply between persecution for faith and for what he elsewhere
calls ' little scruples '. He does not countenance indiscreet martyrdom, and his view is characteristic of the temper of his age no less
than of his own reasonableness :

> though God may be pleased to excuse the weakness of
> well-meaning zeal : yet he can approve nothing but what
> is reasonable [2].

Men are not to expose themselves unnecessarily to danger ; neither
do they suffer for their faith but only " for their fancy and for the
wilful and affected error of a mistaken conscience " when they
suffer for indifferent things, " which in heat and passion they call

[1] *Op. cit.*, II, sermons 45 and 46. The sermons are undated but it is clear
from the drift of the argument that Protestants were being threatened with
persecution for their faith, and at one point Tillotson refers to the recent repealing
of the Edict of Nantes (1685).
[2] Sermon 45, p. 313.

superstition and idolatry ". This is zeal without knowledge, and Tillotson had shown in a sermon preached on 5 November, 1682, that this is not acceptable to God ; he thus implicitly links the zeal of the Dissenters with that of the Romanists at the time of the Gunpowder plot. His third qualification, that men are not obliged at all times to make open profession of truths not necessary, once more reveals a slight confusion in his thinking for this is the same as the preceding point : the distinction between fundamentals and things indifferent, or between things necessary for salvation and things not necessary, i.e. based on mere prudential grounds. What he is at pains to stress is that men should hold their peace and not run the risk of both hurting themselves and endangering the public peace of the Church. No doubt he felt it the more necessary to urge unity among Protestants in view of the growing danger from the Romanists ; at the same time the peaceful submission he thus advocates, quoting Erasmus for his purpose, shows to what lengths he was prepared to go to avoid disturbance of the peace.

When explaining how far men may rely upon the providence of God to bear them out in such trials Tillotson grants that God sometimes suffers good men to fall " in order to their more glorious recovery ", as he did in the case of Cranmer, and that some men fail in the hour of trial out of weakness. Tillotson's readiness to accommodate other points of view may sometimes result in confused thinking, but his charity and love of peace are surely his signal virtues, virtues which were all too rare at the time. Here he urges his hearers to refrain from passing a severe judgement on those who fail in the hour of trial, not only because God may be pleased to accept even such a degree of suffering for martyrdom, but because those who have escaped such sufferings have no right to censure others.

Such an appeal to peace and amity among men may have sounded like readiness to compromise on most points ; yet Tillotson stresses that men cannot expect support from God unless they are careful of their duty and do what is required on their part,

> that neither to avoid sufferings, nor to rescue ourselves, out of them, we do any thing contrary to our duty, and a good conscience [1].

Men must neglect no lawful means to preserve themselves from

---

[1] *Op. cit.*, II, ser. 46, p. 319.

sufferings, particularly they must not fall out against each other
and when the enemy is at the gates pursue their heats and animosities. This, in fact, is the main burden of the two sermons : unity
among Protestants to prevent the attack against their common faith.
But Tillotson is equally firm in rejecting unlawful means of self-
protection, such as rebellion against the civil power :

> We must not break any law of God, nor disobey the lawful
> commands of lawful authority, to free ourselves from any
> sufferings whatsoever, because the goodness of no end can
> sanctify evil means, and make them lawful [1].

It is not clear whether he means that commands of lawful authority
are as such lawful, or that only such commands of lawful authority
as are lawful are to be obeyed. And, characteristically again, he
blinks the difficulty ; instead, he proceeds to oppose his doctrine
of obedience founded in the law of God to the doctrine of equi-
vocation and mental reservations taught by casuists of the Roman
Church. He therefore ends his discourse by urging men to prayer
and repentance, the only way in which they may hope to avert the
present danger. Thus, even in the days when ' that terrible storm '
was threatening the Protestant religion, Tillotson advocated non-
resistance to the magistrate.

Many must have found it hard to reconcile such a plea for
passive obedience with the *Thanksgiving Sermon for our Delivery
by the Prince of Orange* which Tillotson preached on 31 January,
1689, that is, before Parliament had solved the constitutional
problem [2] ; his enemies were to remember how quick he had been
to change his mind about obedience to the magistrate. This sermon,
delivered at Lincoln's Inn Chapel, is likely to have contributed to
sway the minds of lawyers who may still have been hesitating about
the legality of the whole procedure ; it certainly prepared them
to accept the Declaration of Rights, on which the two Houses
agreed on 12 February. As Tillotson showed, the text he chose
for the occasion, *Ezra* IX. 13,14, was spoken at a time of public
humiliation but referred to a great deliverance, and cautioned the

---

[1] *Ibid.*, p. 320.

[2] " On 22 January, the first day of the session, a declaration of the Lords
enunciated the genesis of the Convention, namely the invitations extended by
separate conclaves of Lords and Commons to William, requesting him to cause
writs to be issued for its summoning. They then concurred with the Commons
in an address of thanks to the prince, with a formal request that he would
continue to direct the administration of affairs. " David OGG, *op. cit.*, p. 225.

people not to abuse God's mercies. Thus he stressed that the
nation's sins were the cause of all their sufferings and that God
had worked a deliverance for men unworthy of it ; but he concentrated on the sentence threatened in case they relapsed into these
sins. The sin denounced by Ezra was " joining in affinity with
the people of these abominations ", and though Tillotson refrained
from emphasizing this, the parallel would have been clear to his
audience. Instead, he dwells on the judgements visited on the nation
for their sins [1], the last of which was the encouragement given to
the cruel designs of the hated enemy by a prince of that religion.
Only the principles of humanity and of our religion, he says,

> restrained us from Violence and Cruelty, and from every
> thing which had the Appearance of Undutifulness to the
> Government which the Providence of God had set over us [2].

Since Protestants were bound not to resist, deliverance could only
come from Heaven :

> if God had not put it into the Hearts of our Kind Neigh-
> bours and of that incomparable *Prince*, who laid and con-
> ducted that Great Design with so much Skill and Secrecy,
> to have appear'd so seasonably to our Rescue, our Patience
> had infallibly, without a Miracle, been our Ruin [3].

Now, God had manifestly been helped by human agents in putting
this into the heart of William, to whom an invitation had been sent
to come to the rescue of these patient people. What is more,
Tillotson must have known it. Though he may have had second
thoughts about the doctrine of obedience under the pressure of
events, he was disingenuous enough both to restate it now and
to ignore the active part taken by some of these patient people
in bringing the deliverer over to England. Indeed, he went so far
as to compare this great deliverance with that effected by God
on another 5 November. Yet he recommended both unity among
all Protestants and moderation towards the enemies that had all
but brought about the Church's downfall. Finally, applying the
words of his text, he also urged his hearers to resolve never to join
in affinity with the people of these abominations. He expounded
this only as referring to private marriages, but in his audience at

---

[1] Among these, the Great Fire, which he says was the work of the Papists.
[2] *Op. cit.*, II, ser. 32, p. 324.   [3] *Ibid.*

Lincoln's Inn there must have been many who knew that the Bill of Rights then being drafted and debated in committee would provide against a Roman Catholic king reigning in England, and against a king marrying a Papist. In fact, the applications Tillotson draws from his text clearly announce the two Acts soon to be passed : the Declaration of Rights and the Toleration Act. It is only fair to add that on 8 March next, in a sermon at Whitehall before the Queen, he advocated forgiveness of injuries, and forbearance from revenge, urging for the purpose the humanity of the Protestant religion. If the question of passive obedience gave Tillotson no more qualms than the Thanksgiving sermon suggests, then we need not wonder that having preached previously on *The Lawfulness and Obligation of Oaths* [1] he had no difficulty in transferring his allegiance to William.

On 29 May, 1693—the anniversary of the Restoration continued to be solemnized under William—he preached on *The Duty and Reason of Praying for Governors* [2]. After the Declaration of Rights, and in a sermon by a Latitudinarian Archbishop, we can hardly expect this duty to be based on the hierarchy of laws and the ensuing concept of the magistrate as Vicegerent of God. Indeed, Tillotson's view of government owes more to Locke's *Treatises* than to Hooker's *Laws*. For him as for Locke, government is necessary to ensure the security of every man's person and property, because otherwise human society would disband and run into confusion. This implies that for him as for Locke men naturally tend to society—though confusion may ensue—and are not, as Hobbes had argued, naturally hostile to each other. The reason why we should pray for governors is, in the Apostle's words, " that we may live a quiet and peaceable life, in all godliness and honesty " . This comprises two things : security " in our civil rights and interests, in the quiet and peaceable possession of what is our own " [3], and protection " in the free practice and exercise of religion and virtue " [4]. The main benefit men derive from government is thus protection of laws. Tillotson does recognize that

---

[1] *Op. cit.*, I, sermon 22, preached at the Assizes held at Kingston upon Thames, 21 July, 1681. The main burden of the sermon is to repudiate the Quakers' objections to oaths.
[2] *Op. cit.*, II, ser. 30.
[3] This stress on property again echoes Locke.
[4] *Op. cit.*, II, ser. 30, p. 215.

the edge and authority of laws may be, and sometimes is
turned upon the true religion, and the sincere professors
of it [1],

and his answer to the objection is, to say the least, startling :

even then tho' good Men may receive great harms and
injuries from persecuting Princes and Governors ; (as the
primitive Christians did from several of the *Roman* Empe-
rors) yet then it so happens, that good men have some
considerable benefit and protection from the civil government
and laws, being for the most part preserved from the fury
and rage of the multitude ; so that tho' particular persons
undergo the tryal of cruel sufferings, yet much great[er]
numbers do escape and are preserved [1].

He goes on to argue that no human law was ever made against
" several of the main and essential parts of religion ", which makes
one wonder if the Archbishop of Canterbury was prepared to consider that external professions of religion are not essential. If so,
no wonder he was accused of Deism. What he meant, however,
was what he had maintained before, that in time of persecution
Christians might hope and believe that God would effect their
delivery, but meanwhile

were patiently to obey and suffer ... and to pray for the
powers that persecuted them, that they also might be brought
to the acknowledgement of the truth [2].

Now, under a King whom he could trust and who was pledged
by his coronation oath to govern according to ' the statutes in parliament agreed upon, and the laws and customs of the same ' and to
maintain ' the Protestant Reformed Religion established by law ' [3],
Tillotson might well consider the case of a bad ruler as a remote
possibility, as remote indeed as it had been to Hooker under Elizabeth. Yet the difference in outlook is significant : governments
are now intended to secure the liberty of the subject and his right
to worship. A revolution had been effected in doctrines about the
power of the magistrate. Yet, some traces of earlier thinking still
appear in Tillotson : though he does not speak of the body politic
as does South, he still envisages king and people as somehow bound
in an organic connexion, so that they are often punished or

[1] *Ibid.*, p. 216.   [2] *Ibid.*, p. 217.
[3] See David OGG, *op. cit.*, p. 235.

rewarded for the sins or good actions of one another. In this, as
in his thinking about natural law, Tillotson is wandering between
two worlds. His thought reflects the confusion characteristic of a
transitional age, whereas South is firmly anchored in the old order
and can drive his argument to its logical though harsh conclusions.
South felt that with the death of Queen Anne all that was good
had left this world ; Tillotson could have said even before the end
of the century : " Tis well an old age is out, And time to begin
a new ".

*
* *

In his defence of the *acies ordinata* and of ecclesiastical laws
Barrow developed exactly the same argument as that on which
Calvin had based the necessity for the Church to have legislative
powers. Barrow was aware of this since he referred to the ' chief
impugners of episcopacy ' as sharing the same view. Indeed, the
first part of his sermon seems to echo this passage from the
Institutes :

> If we see it to be necessary in all companies of men that
> there should be some police to keep peace and concord
> between them, if in all things there must be some orders,
> to preserve a public civility and even humanity among men,
> then these things ought most of all to be observed in the
> Churches, which are maintained primarily by good order,
> and by discord are altogether disintegrated. Wherefore, if
> we would do our best for the preservation of the Church,
> we must diligently work so that all is done decently and in
> good order, even as St Paul commands. But since there
> are such great contrarieties of mind and of judgement
> between men, no police could hold together among them
> if it were not determined by certain laws, and no order could
> well maintain itself without some certain form. So far from
> rejecting laws that tend to this end, we indeed assert that,
> without them, the Churches would incontinently be dissipated
> and deformed [1].

Calvin may never have contended that the temporal power should
be subject to the spiritual power, but only that the ministers of the
Church were to explain to the Magistracy " the requirements of

---

[1] John CALVIN : *Institutes*, IV, 10, quoted in François WENDEL : *Calvin*,
tr. by Philip Mairet, London, 1963 (Fontana Library, 1965, p. 307). Wendel
quotes from the critical edition by J.D. Benoit of the 1559 ed. of *Institution
de la religion chrestienne* ; the English version is by Wendel's translator.

the Word of God, to which the civil legislation had to conform
itself " [1]. None the less, the experience of James I in Scotland
as well as the developments of Calvinistic rule in New England
revealed that Calvin's doctrine might serve to support theocratic
regimes. After the bitter years of the Interregnum, the Church
could have reversed the saying of James I and proclaimed ' No King,
no Bishop '. Rather than run the risk of being reformed out of
existence the Church clung to the one authority that seemed to
offer a safeguard against new schemes of reformation, i.e. to the
supreme governor in spiritual as well as in temporal matters. In
their statements on the relation between spiritual and temporal
powers divines took care not to suggest submission of the Church
to the State—which would have made them disciples of Hobbes—
any more than subjection of the State to the Church. What they
envisaged, in fact, was an amicable collaboration between the two
powers, as it had been envisaged in the Elizabethan Settlement,
and was made possible again by the Restoration Settlement [2]. By
not pressing a definite theory the Church ensured a measure of
flexibility in its relation with the State. This was gained at the
expense of a clear-cut definition of the rights of each, which were
left as vague as the relations between the Crown and Parliament.
The Church taught obedience to kings and magistrates out of
conviction, not by order of the temporal power. Indeed, it may
be said that " the clergy provided even more strenuous advocates
of the prerogative " of the King than did such men as Clarendon
or Danby [3] ; and this was inevitable after their experience of
Parliament's reforms in the forties. The Anglican divines who
accused the Church of Rome of dissolving the bands of society
by striking at the temporal power—though they often added that
the Roman Church only did so when it suited her policy—might
well have been horrified at the blandishments of the King and the
Royal family which such sober Romanists as Bossuet delivered
from the pulpit. They would have revised their view of the Roman
Church if they could have foreseen that the same flood that was

---

[1] François WENDEL, op. cit., pp. 309-10.
[2] The order of events makes this clear. The Revised Prayer Book was
accepted by Convocation in December 1661, and by both Houses of Parliament
in April 1662. The Act of Uniformity imposing its use and enforcing the
Liturgy received the royal assent on May 19, 1662. See David OGG : England
in The Reign of Charles II, I, 200-1.
[3] David OGG, op. cit., p. 451.

to sweep away monarchy in France also struck at the power of
the Catholic clergy, which had been the strongest support of the
Ancien Régime. The Anglican clergy did resist the notion that
civil authority derives from the people ; most of them did sanction
the theory of Divine Right ; all of them taught passive obedience.
But they usually granted that a king may devise bad laws, and in
fact the doctrine of non-resistance was never enforced so deter-
minedly as when they recognized that the King was ordering things
repugnant to God's law.   Even such a staunch High-Churchman
as South openly condemned Charles's Declaration of Indulgence,
while one looks in vain for criticism of Louis XIV in any of the
sermons of the Roman clergy in France. If the Church's doctrine
of her amicable relation to the King is nowhere defined quite clearly
in theory, it is surely possible to infer it both from the way in which
the Church had been restored and from the practice of her divines,
who were loyal supporters of the government as well as of the
Church, but who did on occasion denounce the actions of the
governors or censure the behaviour of people in high places.   True,
if they openly displeased their master, they might be dismissed
from the Court, as was Burnet, but they did not lose their offices,
or suffer any penalty.

*
* *

One of the clergy's tasks was to preach on public solemnities
appointed by the magistrate, when they might be expected to preach
politics.   Religion and politics were not two distinct spheres, and
the events commemorated were bound up with the life of the
Church : the anniversary of the death of the Royal Martyr, on
30 January ; Royal Oak day, the anniversary of the Restoration,
on 29 May ; and of course the anniversary of the discovery of
the Gunpowder Plot, on 5 November. Under William, the victory
over Louis XIV could also be celebrated as a blessing from God
since it marked the defeat of the hated enemy of the Protestant
religion.

Sermons preached on 30 January involved rehearsing all the
evils suffered at the hands of the Puritans and in most cases would
be the occasion for outbursts of anti-fanatic zeal.   South's sermon
preached at Whitehall on 30 January, 1662/3, was close enough to
the dire events for him to give vent to his indignation and worst

prejudices [1]; in it he charges the fanatics with the foulest sins,
voices his contempt of them, pours ridicule on their ministers, and
denounces the post-dated loyalty of the Presbyterians, who now
decry the action of which they had laid the premisses. Far from
sharing Barrow's view that truth, like its master, speaks in a still
small voice, he justifies his harsh words by saying that the guilt
of these men has made the very strictest truths look like satires
or sarcasms, and bare descriptions sharper than invectives; for
him the bitterest gall is not satire, but mere propriety. Though
he ended his ' poor description ' of the Royal Martyr by saying
that " he was the father of such a son ", he had numbered among
the virtues of Charles I his temperance and his virtuous life, whereby he upbraided the Court by his example particularly in keeping
the bonds of conjugal affection inviolate. Charles II could hardly
have slept at this inflammatory sermon [2]; he certainly caught the
drift of this remark and appreciated the wit of Clarendon's chaplain,
who must have known how bitterly the Chancellor had resented
Charles's intrigue with Lady Castlemaine at the time when his
marriage to the Infanta was being arranged. In this sermon South
violently repudiates all suggestion of indulgence towards these late
rebels to the Crown, and thus openly censures Charles's move
a bare month before to secure freedom of worship for non-
Anglicans [3]: this, says South, is the same as for a man to indulge
a dropsy or a malignant fever, and he supports this view by quoting
from the *Defensio pro Populo Anglicano* by Cromwell's Latin
Secretary, " who like a blind Adder, has spit so much poison upon
the King's person and cause ". Indeed, he went so far in his attack
against the rebels as to conclude :

> and therefore [I] have this only to say of the King's Murder,
> that it is a thing, than which nothing can be imagined more
> *Strange, amazing, and astonishing, except its Pardon.*

He went so far indeed that when he published this sermon [4] he

    [1] Printed below.
    [2] There is a story that when he was one day preaching before the King
at Court South banged the pulpit and turning to Lauderdale asked him not to
snore so loud lest he should awake His Majesty. Quoted in Mark NOBLE :
*A Biographical History of England, from the Revolution to the End of George I's
Reign, Being a Continuation of Rev. Granger's Work* (i.e. James GRANGER :
Biographical History of England, 1779), London, 1806, I, 100.
    [3] See OGG, *op. cit.*, p. 200.
    [4] Vol. V came out in 1717, but was prepared for the press by South himself.

added a note to explain that this was no " reflection upon the Act of Indemnity itself, and much less upon the Royal Author of it " ; yet he had preached the very reverse of indemnity and oblivion.

South was probably unrivalled for violence of language and unfairness to the Puritans, except by Sacheverell in the next age ; but thirty-January sermons generally dealt fire and damnation on the late rebels and their successors the Dissenters.   South was all too easily carried away by his zeal for the House of Christ, and all too often forgot the first command of the Master.   Yet on 29 May, 1670, preaching at Westminster Abbey, he chose for his text *Matt.* V. 44 *But I say unto you, Love your enemies.*   There he shows that Christ added no new precept to the moral law and that his commands are therefore of eternal obligation : Christ did not set himself against the law of Moses, he perfected it.   The whole drift of the sermon is thus the binding nature of the duty to love one's enemies, a strange theme, one might think, for South to develop. As he explains the nature of the duty enjoined by Christ, he is, however, careful to point out that this does not annul the right to self-defence, for, as he puts it in his own pregnant way,

> though I am commanded when my Enemy *thirsts* to *give him Drink*, yet it is not when he thirsts for my *Blood* [1].

Hence, he once more reiterates his warning that princes are in duty bound to secure themselves against insurrections.   Though he preaches mercy, he does not recommend oblivion.

In another sermon preached on 30 January [2] and published after his death and possibly preached under James [3], South explains that the curse foretold by the prophet had its source in " the crying crimson sin of bloodshed " committed by the nation.   Though bloodshed is punishable by bloodshed, he says, it is only for God's deputies to use the sword of justice, and it is only for God to punish princes : for private persons to use the sword against princes is sin and merits the curse of God.   To preserve society men put themselves under government, and the governor is made

---

[1] *Op. cit.*, III, ser. 3, p. 119.   [2] Year unknown.
[3] *Additional ... Sermons*, XI, ser. 2.   The Text, *Hab.* ii, 12 *Wo to him that buildeth a town with blood*, foretelling the Babylonian captivity, would have been particularly appropriate under James.   On the other hand, speaking of the dismal end of those who lift the sword against their prince, South says that some have died in their beds, like " our *late* grand regicide ".

trustee by God to secure men in the free possession and enjoyment
of their lives. The governor who wrings away a man's estate is
accountable to God as a thief, but the subjects have no right to
revenge,

> for not all the Calvins, Bezas, Knoxes, Buchanans, or
> Paraeus's in Christendom with all their principles of Anarchy
> and Democracy ... can by any solid reason make out the
> lawfulness of subjects taking up arms against their Prince [1].

Such rebels have always brought the curse of God upon themselves,
as well appears from the shortness of the government they set up
in this country :

> within five years their infant commonwealth expired ; and
> in five years more Cromwell's mushroom monarchy was at
> an end [2].

To speak severe words of these traitors is not to exercise private
revenge on them ; it is charity to posterity to make them dread the
imitation of such villanies. In the circumstances the harshest terms
are the properest.

For all his loyalty to the King as supreme governor, South
could never forbear to criticize measures that he deemed bad. In
the sermon he preached at Westminster Abbey in 1672 on the
Anniversary of the Restoration he developed the theme of the
unsearchable ways of God's judgements and denounced the ways
in which the self-styled prophets of the preceding age had interpreted the course of events. To conclude he stressed the folly of
making the presumed success of an enterprise a rule of acting, and
instanced this in the terrible guilt of Charles I in acquiescing in
the impeachment and death of Strafford in the hope that the effect
would be good, whereas, says South, it was the King's clear duty
to follow his conscience and protect his loyal servant. South
recommended lawful, religious courses as the only ground on which
to hope for God's blessings, for he said, we cannot expect God's
mercy while atheism, profaneness and irreligion flourish, or, which
is worse, when all religions are countenanced [3]. Even on such an
occasion South could not silently acquiesce in the decisions of the
King and clearly repudiated the recent Declaration of Indulgence.
In another sermon preached on 29 May at Westminster Abbey [4],

---

[1] *Ibid.*, p. 60.   [2] *Ibid.*, p. 64.
[3] *Op. cit.*, V, ser. 6, p. 272.   [4] Year unknown.

on *Ps.* CVI. 7 *Our fathers understood not thy wonders in Egypt*,
he extolled the Providence of God in the government of the
world, especially in the affairs of the Church, as instanced in
the miraculous deliverance from the swarms of locusts that had
pestered the land.   Not only was such help undeserved, he says,
but since then our vices have grown to monstrous heights.   Such
miraculous deliverance was not effected so that men should live
in idleness and luxury :

> God neither dried up the sea, to bring the *Israelites into a
> land flowing with milk and honey*, that they might debauch,
> revel, and surfeit upon that mercy : nor did he, by a miracle
> as great, reinstate a company of poor, distressed exiles in
> the possession of their native country, that they should live
> at that rate of vanity and superfluity, that the world now
> a-days cries out upon them for.   God did not work wonders
> to cloath and feed a few worthless parasites with the riches
> of a Kingdom, to fill their cups with the blood of orphans
> and the tears of the widows.   God did not intend that so
> universal a blessing, big enough for us all, should be diverted
> under ground, into the obscure, narrow channel of a few
> private purses ; leaving so many loyal, suffering, undone
> persons, to sigh and mourn over their destitute condition,
> in the day of a publick joy.   God did not restore us to scoff
> at religion, and to malign his church, as if the nation and
> the government might stand well enough without a church,
> but not without plays [1].

Thus did South treat his polite audience at Westminster Abbey.
Charles must have been tolerant indeed not to reprove this loyal
minister for thus glancing at the use of public moneys " to clothe
and feed a few worthless parasites ", or fill a few private purses,
including those of the King's mistresses.   South anticipates Defoe's
excoriating attack in *The Review* against men's readiness to give
money to see *Hamlet* but not to restore a chapel ; but the gilded
youth that surrounded the King patronized plays of quite a different
nature from *Hamlet*, and there were many Buckinghams or
Rochesters among South's audience at Westminster Abbey.

Such sermons preached on official occasions to select members
of the ruling class cast an interesting light on the supposed subjection of the Church to the temporal power ; they help us to
define, better than any theory would, the true relation between

[1] *Additional ... Sermons*, IX, ser. 4, pp. 122-3.

Church and State after the Restoration. Incidentally, they also account for the ease with which Dryden could tell the story of the unruly Israelites under a monarch who

> His vigorous warmth did, variously, impart
> To Wives and Slaves; And, wide as his Command,
> Scattered his Maker's Image through the Land.

Charles's high esteem for South may well have led him to allow this preacher the liberty which kings used to grant their licensed fools, and we may guess that few divines had either the wit or the courage to speak their minds as freely as South did, supposing that they had such forthright views to put forward. We need only turn to the sermon Barrow preached on 29 May, 1676, to see that some divines confined themselves to enforcing the duty of obedience to, and prayer for, kings and all in authority. In listing the many reasons for this duty Barrow shows that it is an act of charity to the public since the safety of the prince is a great part of the common welfare, even if he is a bad prince. Even the worst of princes, he says, are preferable to want of government, which can only lead to anarchy. Moreover, prayer is the only allowable way of redressing our case if we suffer by, or for, princes; they are not accountable to us, or liable to our correction; we may not even rail at them nor tax their actions, nor complain or murmur against them, for all this is impiety towards God, whose representatives they are. All these sins were committed in the late times, as if, Barrow adds,

> God being implored by Prayer, could not, or would not, had it been needfull, without such irregular courses, have redressed those evils in Church or State, which they pretended to feel, or fear [1].

Even under Nero Paul prescribed prayer for the magistrate; all men can and may do in any circumstances is to beseech God for His blessings. Besides, says Barrow, it has been the practice of the Church in all times, except of the Roman Church, which is more sparing in this service

> for that a superlative regard to the *Solar* or *Pontifical* Authority (as Pope *Innocent* III distinguished) did obscure their devotion to the *Lunar* or *Regal Majesty* [2].

---

[1] *Op. cit.*, I, ser. 10, p. 135.   [2] *Ibid.*, p. 137.

He grants that the Church of England may be accused of being too lavish in her prayers for kings, but, he adds, it is a good fault, particularly in the present state of affairs, since times of danger are most seasonable for having recourse to God's help and mercy in prayer. And the danger is only too clear with the growth of atheism, of profaneness and of dissoluteness of manners, when so many violate the laws and dare to create factions and feuds. As usual Barrow avoids all topical references, so that it is hard to say what particular factions and feuds he has in mind, although there had been considerable trouble since Parliament had reassembled in 1675. What is more important is that Barrow confines himself to the duty in general and states most clearly that subjects may not even discuss the actions of the magistrate. In spite of his peaceful temper Barrow could be more rigid in his doctrine of obedience than South proved to be in practice. On the other hand, he preached no thirty-January sermon, though on occasion he could be hard enough on the Puritans.

Of the 250 published sermons of Tillotson[1] only two seem to have been preached on the Anniversary of the Restoration, and none on 30 January. Of the two sermons on 29 May, one was preached on Ascension day towards the end of the reign of Charles II, his editor tells us[2]; here Tillotson merely mentions the occasion at the beginning and at the end of the sermon, as a further cause to bless God, who by restoring the King has given a great security to the true religion. The other[3] was delivered in 1693. The glory of the day commemorating God's mercy " in ending intestine wars ", he says, has been not a little sullied since, but rather than rake up all these troubles he will rejoice in the happiness England now enjoys under Their present Majesties, by whom the country has been delivered of a great danger to religion and to the laws of the country. William and Mary clearly wished the apostolic succession not to be broken and therefore ordered that 29 May should continue to be solemnized[4]. Tillotson's sermon

[1] Tillotson himself published 54 sermons. His chaplain, Ralph Barker, published 200 more after the Archbishop's death ; though he tells us in the advertisement to the first volume that he has published the sermons exactly as he found them (having transcribed them from T's shorthand), he also says at the end of the last volume that he has sometimes divided a continuous text into two sermons, or two into three.

[2] *Op. cit.*, III, ser. 142.   [3] *Op. cit.*, II, ser. 30.

[4] After 1689 the 5th of November was consecrated to the memory of both the discovery of the Gunpowder Plot and the landing of William at Torbay.

develops approximately the same points as Barrow's, though much more briefly, but as we saw, reveals a new orientation in political thinking in his definition of the aims of civil government.

Sermons on the Gunpowder Plot denounced the other kind of traitors, those who, being absolved by Rome of allegiance to their lawful sovereign, had plotted against the government of the country and were thought to be still plotting to subvert its laws. There is the smell of sulphur in most of these sermons, but the emphasis varies according to circumstances as well as according to the particular bent of the preacher. In 1673 Barrow chose for his text *Ps.* LXIV. 9,10, which refers to the designs of Saul upon David's life and to David's rescue by the special providence of God. The main burden of his sermon is the duty to wisely consider God's doing. In developing this theme he stresses the necessity to exercise our reason on all important occasions in which God's providence manifests itself so that we may render Him due glory; but he also warns men against imputing to God what is in fact the work of His free agents. This is clearly directed against the Puritans' habit of seeing God's special hand in all sorts of events and of interpreting them to their own advantage (South also said that they were prompt to see God's hand in the naval victories of 1652 and 1653, but loth to admit it in similar victories after the Restoration). Barrow then lists all the marks by which men may recognize the working of Providence, and he infers the duties incumbent upon men to fear God, to declare His work, to express religious joy in the effects of Providence, etc. Only at the end does he apply these duties to the occasion; he refrains from exploiting it to stir contention or cast opprobrium on the Romanists even though the Declaration of Indulgence had been the cause of such heated discussions in Parliament in the early months of the year, and was generally attributed in the country at large to Charles's leanings towards Rome. Here, then, as in his later Royal-Oak-day sermon, Barrow kept out of politics and of controversy though he must already have been gathering material for his refutation of the claims of Rome. Like Wilkins (who for a while had also been Master of Trinity College), he believed that all contentious matters should be kept out of sermons; above all he wished to further concord. His sermon on the Gunpowder Plot may be all the more edifying, but it has none of the liveliness that such a lusty contender as South could bring to the matter.

The scourge of the fanatics also turned upon the other enemy of the Church, and for him as for Barrow the commemoration of the Gunpowder Plot was the occasion to expound the doctrine of obedience and the principles on which it rests. He did not, however, limit himself to bare statements of the whys and wherefores ; he attacked the opposite theories and showed that the Puritans and the Romanists were at one in contending that the civil power must be subject to the spiritual. South taught non-resistance, but he did not blink the fact that the nature of the prince was all important. The earliest of his sermons on the Gunpowder Plot, preached at Westminster Abbey in 1663, is more anti-Puritan than one might expect on such an occasion. His text is *Rom.* XIII. 5 *Wherefore ye must needs be subjects, not only for wrath, but also for conscience sake*, which he expounds to show that men are subject to princes not only as they are liable to punishment, but as they are bound in conscience to submit to the magistrate. The drift of the whole sermon is therefore to impugn the plea of conscience as much as the plea that princes are subject to the Pope. The whole chapter of St. Paul's epistle, he says, was intended to enjoin the binding precepts of allegiance to Christians who were then the subjects of a monster, Nero. The reason given by the Apostle is that obedience to the magistrate is obedience to God at the second hand : even a vile magistrate is still an officer by God's institution. At this stage, then, he is prepared to say that such divinity doth hedge a king that

> We are therefore to overlook all Impieties, and Defects, which cannot invalidate the Function[1]. Though *Nero* deserves worthily to be abhorred, yet still the *Emperor* is, and ought to be sacred[2].

To allow a man's conscience to decide which command is lawful and which is not, is to place the legislative power in that man's conscience and to make the subject have a prerogative against the laws. Resistance to the civil magistrate is ' absolutely unlawful ', a mortal sin, and this is grounded both in reason and in Scripture.

---

[1] Given seventeenth- and eighteenth-century punctuation, it is difficult to say whether South means " all impieties and defects which... " or " all impieties and defects, which... ".

[2] *Op. cit.*, V, ser. 5, p. 206.

The Apostle says that " The Powers that are, are ordained of God ", and resistance is

> the Violation of Government, which is the very Soul and Support of the Universe, and the Imitation of Providence. Every lawful Ruler holds the Government by a certain Deputation from God ; and the Commission, by which he holds it, is his Word. This is the Voice of Scripture, this is the Voice of Reason [1].

This is the argument we have encountered before, and it is aimed at the private judgement asserting itself against the law of reason, which reflects the law of God. This doctrine, says South, has been impugned by the sons of Rome and by their offspring, the sons of Geneva. To recount the pernicious doctrines of Rome would be " the stirring of a great sink ", yet he does quote a number of texts from bulls and Councils to prove that Rome means to make princes slaves to popes ; and he adds many examples to show that the popes have in fact deposed kings and stirred rebellion against them, from Henry IV of Germany to Queen Elizabeth. This doctrine, he says, has been confirmed by the Council of Trent, and the clearest comment on it is the Gunpowder Plot. Further, the Popish religion exempts the clergy from the jurisdiction of Kings, " be their crimes what they will ", so that a king cannot punish them,

> So that the King, for any thing that he has to do in these Matters, may sit and blow his Nails ; for use them otherwise, he cannot. He may indeed be plotted against, have Barrels of Powder laid, and Poniards prepared for him : But to punish the sacred Actors of these Villanies, that is reserved only to him, who gave the first Command for the doing them [2].

Here in fact, better than in any theoretical treatment of the subject, we grasp the true source of the doctrine of obedience to the prince. A law there must be, and a chief governor to enforce it : on this all that recognize the need for government are agreed. In face of the conflicting claims to supremacy of the spiritual and the temporal ruler, the choice was clear given the experience of history. The whole weight of English history and the memory of the many encroachments of the Papacy on the jurisdiction of kings, whether

---

[1] *Ibid.*, p. 211.   [2] *Ibid.*, p. 218.

under Henry II or under Elizabeth, lay behind the Church of England's doctrine of obedience to the King. History could not be reversed ; the prerogative of the King was justified by as strong arguments from the past as could be found for the rights of Parliament in the development of common law.

But this is no mere anti-popish sermon, and South next addresses himself to the " true seed " of the sons of Rome, those of Geneva. After quoting texts from " the great Mufti of Geneva ", from Beza, Knox, Buchanan, and Paraeus, he finally descends to the dregs, ' the English Genevizers ', who, by the favour of Providence were given full scope to demonstrate what a monster Puritanism is, such a monster indeed that

> if any Christian Prince should hereafter forget the English Rebellion, and himself, so far as to be deceived with those stale, thread-bare baffled Pretences of *Conscience*, and *Reformation*, he would fall in a great measure unpitied, as a Martyr to his sensless Fondness, and a Sacrifice to his own Credulity [1].

Charles could not have been told more plainly that his late attempt (December 1662) to implement his Declaration of Breda was the action of a senseless, credulous fool. Thus much respect did South have for the *person* of the King in a sermon expounding the sacredness of the King's *office*.

He was to give an even clearer warning in 1675, once again from the pulpit of Westminster Abbey. In this sermon South once more stresses that government is

> a thing perfectly Divine, both as to its Original and Continuance in the World [2].

God invests princes with certain marks and rays of His divine image to overawe and control the spirits of men ;

> this is that properly which in Kings we call *Majesty*, and which no doubt is a kind of Shadow or Portraiture of the Divine Authority drawn upon the Looks and Persons of Princes [3].

He could hardly have gone further in defining the divinity that hedges kings ; yet he may have overemphasized it just because he was not so sure that the shadow of divine authority was drawn

---

[1] *Ibid.*, p. 226.   [2] *Op. cit.*, III, ser. 12, p. 472.   [3] *Ibid.*, p. 473.

upon the person of the present prince. At any rate he took care
to say that kings are sent into the world not only to rule but to
obey, that no prerogative can bar piety, nor exempt them from
using discretion in choosing wise counsellors. The theme of this
sermon, in fact, is the duties of kings rather than the duties of
subjects, and South shows from the beginning that the two are
inseparable. Monarchy is best adapted to the ends of government,
he says, but

> the Greatness and Strength of a Monarchy depends chiefly
> upon the personal qualifications of the Prince or Monarch [1].

Even though God does bestow extraordinary qualities on those
who are to rule in His name, yet it is the bounden duty of princes
to use these gifts. Charles could not have missed the drift of the
argument, especially of the last point, that God saves princes by
disposing their hearts to virtuous and pious courses. South here
invokes the example of the Royal Martyr, and almost says like
Hamlet " Look here, upon this picture, and on this ". Monarchy
may be the image of divine supremacy, the kingly office may be
sacred, but

> it is the *Person* that makes the *Place* considerable, and not
> the *Place him* [2].

If South was clear-sighted enough to see, and courageous
enough to suggest, that Charles came short of the divine image,
his love for him was no less deep. One way by which God saves
sovereign princes, he says, is

> by wonderfully *inclining the Hearts and Wills* of Men to
> a benign Affection towards them [3].

God alone can turn the hearts of a nation " suddenly and irresisti-
bly " : thus was David brought back to his throne after he had fled
from Absalom, thus was England's banished David brought back
in the year sixty. At the same time, however, South clearly warns
Charles that God can sway the hearts of the people away from
princes, as He did when the kingdom was rent from the House of
David and transferred to Jeroboam. It is affection that must bind,
for then allegiance is easy. For all his violent denunciation of the
rebels, South here suggests that the troubles grew from disaffection

---

[1] *Ibid.*, p. 480.   [2] *Ibid.*, p. 483.   [3] *Ibid.*, p. 467.

to the King, and the advice to Charles is clear, not to alienate his subjects' hearts. What he has in mind appears from the inferences he draws from his theme : the duty and behaviour both of princes towards God, and of subjects towards their prince, which he applies to the present King. Charles was rescued from danger in the day of battle and followed by Providence into banishment, where

> neither the barbarous Injuries of his Rebel Subjects at home, nor the Temptations of Foreign Princes abroad, nor all the Arts of *Rome* besides, could in his great Extremity bring [him] over to the *Romish Profession* [1] ;

since his return out to Egypt he

> still continues in the same Communion, which he was in when he went from us, *Carolus a Carolo*, firm and immoveable like the Son of a Father, who could rather part with his Crowns, Kingdoms, and his very Life, than quit his Honour or give up his Religion [2].

If Charles was hoping soon to declare himself openly a Roman Catholic, then he was told kindly but firmly that this was the surest way to alienate his subjects' hearts and to be driven on his foreign travels once more. To South non-resistance was one thing, compliance quite another, and he thought it his business to tell his sovereign what was repugnant to God's law or to the Church's, whose governor he was.

South's third Gunpowder sermon was preached on the day William landed at Torbay ; this is not really an anti-popery sermon, though the main theme, God's complaint for the remissness of his people, is developed to the accompaniment of the storm threatening to overwhelm these ungrateful Israelites : unless they amend, God will take away their laws and their military force, i.e. favour the projects of James tending to destroy English laws and to restore Roman Catholicism in England.

If Tillotson delivered only two sermons on the anniversary of the Restoration, he preached several on the Gunpowder Plot. These mark him as the sturdy advocate of the Protestant cause, as do many of his sermons, e.g. his vindication of the Protestant religion from the charge of novelty, his discourse on Transubstantiation, his sermons on Stedfastness in religion [3] or constancy in

---

[1] *Ibid.*, p. 491.   [2] *Ibid.*
[3] *Op. cit.*, II, sermons 2 and 3.

the profession of the true religion [1], on the danger of apostasy from
the true religion [2] or from Christianity [3], on honesty as the best
preservative against dangerous mistakes in religion [4], or on the
support of good men under their sufferings for religion [5] (several
of these were preached before Princess Anne to encourage her in
resisting the influence of her father's entourage). Though he once
said that stirring up men's passions was like muddying of waters [6],
he seems to have had no objection to stirring anti-popish zeal.
Indeed, the reader soon wearies of his repeated attacks on the
slightest opportunity, especially as they usually develop along the
self-same lines. Tillotson might well have been called the scourge
of the Romanists. If in this he is no worse than South, the effect
is altogether different, for Tillotson everywhere champions sweet
reasonableness and speaks in a sober tone, so that his prejudices
against the Romanists appear to issue not from the heat of his
passion, but from his narrow-mindedness. His attacks are not
flashes of wit, but rather of bad temper. South could be sharp
when scourging any vice or error; Tillotson, it seems, was prepared to overlook many errors for the sake of peace except those
of Rome, and he could then resort to language no doubt less
pungent than South's but often more injurious. However serious
his objections to Roman Catholic doctrines as impugning and forbidding freedom of inquiry, his reiterated criticism of such points
as the—supposed—worship of saints and images suggests that he
was probably unable to see beyond his own limited horizon [7], an
impression which, for all his unfairness, South never gives. It is
only fair to add that Tillotson only published one of his Gunpowder
sermons; in giving to the public all that his master had left behind
Ralph Barker really did the Archbishop a disservice, for Tillotson
when seeing his sermons through the press occasionally left out
passages which he had used elsewhere, and which to the reader
would have been mere repetitions. It would therefore be tedious
to rehearse all his attacks against Rome, and we need only consider

[1] *Op. cit.*, II, sermons 4 to 9.
[2] *Op. cit.*, II, ser. 12.
[3] *Op. cit.*, II, ser. 67.
[4] *Op. cit.*, II, sermons 33, 34 and 35.
[5] *Op. cit.*, II, sermons 45 and 46.
[6] *Op. cit.*, II, ser. 72, p. 532.
[7] Cp. with his credulousness about the Popish Plot and the Great Fire.

the main themes he developed in his sermons on the Gunpowder Plot [1].

The one sermon on this occasion which he published was preached in 1678 to the House of Commons, and develops the theme of love and goodwill among men. Christ came to bring peace, he says, and all revengeful feelings are contrary to the Gospel; nor can they be excused upon any pretence of zeal for God and religion. The Church of Rome cannot plead for her cruelty to men any reason stronger than that which the disciples might have pleaded when Christ rebuked them saying " Ye know not what manner of spirit ye are of ". In applying the doctrine he warns his hearers to beware of a Church which countenances such unchristian spirit, which extirpates heretics with sword and fire, and which deposes kings and absolves subjects from obedience to them. The ' bloody design ' commemorated on 5 November was consonant with these doctrines, and could not have been baffled without a miracle from God, as he hopes the present design will be [2]. In the circumstances it is understandable that Tillotson should have been carried away by his indignation, so far indeed that he had to check himself to remember his text

> and take heed to imitate that *Spirit* which is there con-
> demned, whilst I am inveighing against it [3].

He granted that there were among Papists several persons of great piety and charity—and this was granting far more than many people would have done in these troubled months—but he insisted that the principles of that religion could only abet such hellish designs :

> I doubt not but Papists are made like other Men. Nature
> hath not generally given them such savage and cruel Dis-
> positions, but their Religion hath made them so ... 'tis very
> true, That many Papists would have been excellent persons

---

[1] *Op. cit.*, I, ser. 19 (1678); II, ser. 28 (1682); II, ser. 29 (1686); II, 49 (1688); III, ser. 192 (1684).

[2] The parallel was particularly apt in view of what was feared in those days. " Parliament reassembled on October 21, (1678), when the King announced that he would forbear opinion on the subject of the design attributed to the Jesuits. Therefore both Houses set to work and appointed committees for the examination of witnesses; one was deputed to search the vaults under the Houses... The first of these committees ordered a search under all rooms for gunpowder; and, as the fifth of November approached, the underground inspections became more rigorous. " David OGG, *op. cit.*, II, 570.

[3] *Op. cit.*, I, ser. 19, p. 182.

and very good Men, if their Religion had not hindered them [1].

Though his main theme was peace and goodwill towards men, though he said :

> I speak not this to exasperate *You, worthy Patriots and the great Bulwark of our Religion*, to any *unreasonable* or *unnecessary*, much less *unchristian* Severity against them [2],

it is doubtful whether his sermon did further fairness of judgement ; it did not discourage his hearers from proceeding to the judicial murder of several supposed traitors. Tillotson did acknowledge at the end of his sermon that he had been " transported upon this argument somewhat beyond his usual temper ", but he thought the occasion of the day and the present circumstances would bear him out.

Comparison between South's Gunpowder sermon in 1663 and Tillotson's in 1682 at once reveals both the difference between the two men and the changed circumstances : while the one condemned the doctrines of both Puritans and Romanists, the other exemplifies zeal without knowledge almost exclusively from the practice of the Romanists and only briefly censures zeal about things indifferent ; while South preaches obedience to the magistrate Tillotson enforces the duty of inquiry so that our zeal may be according to knowledge, and his conclusion is :

> God hath given us understandings to try and examine things, and the light of his word to direct us in this tryal ; and if we will judge rashly, and suffer ourselves to be hurried by prejudice or passion, *the errors of our judgement become faults of our lives* [3].

Free inquiry after truth *versus* ignorance and inquisition is again the theme of Tillotson's 1684 sermon. The great vindication of the Protestant religion, he says, is that it is ready to submit to an impartial examination ; the reason why some are so concerned to suppress truth is because their doctrines and deeds might be

---

[1] *Ibid.*, p. 182.

[2] *Ibid.* On October 31, 1678, " the Commons resolved ' that there has been and still is a damnable and hellish plot, contrived and carried on by popish recusants for the assassination and murdering the King, and for subverting the government and rooting out and destroying the Protestant religion ' ". David OGG, *op. cit.*, p. 573.

[3] *Op. cit.*, II, ser. 28, p. 206.

discovered ; he links this secrecy with the black and hellish design of the Gunpowder Plot, and also reminds his hearers of another dark design, the Popish Plot.

In 1686, on the other hand, he chose for his text Christ's words of comfort to the Apostles against coming persecutions (*John* XVI. 2). The burden of his sermon is therefore clear from the outset and his oblique references to the Church of Rome suffice to persuade his hearers that they need not fear the sentence of excommunication pronounced against them since they are in the right while their enemies are swayed by self-conceit. The attack on the Romanists is no less clear for being indirect, but Tillotson's main purpose is obviously to encourage Protestants to remain steadfast in their religion because the Church of Rome plainly ignores the central truths of the Christian religion.

His 1688 sermon is based on the parallel between the Romanists and the Pharisees, whom Christ reproved by saying " I will have mercy, and not sacrifice ". There he demonstrates that Christ did not intend to undermine natural religion, but to perfect it, and in doing so he comes dangerously near to Deism when he asserts that the Christian religion in its prescriptive part is " almost wholly made up of moral duties " and has very little in it

> that is merely *positive* and *instituted*, besides *the two Sacraments*, and praying to God in the name and mediation of *Jesus Christ* [1].

Only in the application does he turn to the occasion of the day, to show that the Romanists release men from their natural duties, by killing men or inciting others to kill men to do God's service. No zeal for positive religion, Tillotson says, can justify the violation of the natural law : the corrupted doctrine of the Church of Rome was manifested this day fourscore years ago, when indeed there was a prodigious sacrifice ; but where was mercy ? He thus turns the argument for natural as above ceremonial laws to the purpose of the day, but the main theme he develops is in no way warped by the occasion for which it was selected. In fact, as one reads this sermon one is struck by Tillotson's detachment from the events ; it is almost as though he no longer felt the danger that had prompted him to offer comfort to his Protestant hearers two

[1] *Op. cit.*, II, ser. 49, p. 350.

years before.   And one cannot help wondering if he knew that
relief was coming, that in fact it had all but arrived.

As ministers of a Church established by law and governed
by the King, Anglican divines were committed to preaching politics,
but their amicable relations with the temporal power were not
unruffled.   They were in no way Statists, even if they stressed,
as Tillotson did, that religion is the best safeguard of government.
From the safe retreat of Trinity College Barrow could look upon the
contentions of the time as utterly to be abhorred.   Neither South
nor Tillotson could ignore the pressure of events or the threats
to the Church.   South could speak his mind freely against the
governor's ill-advised measures, while Tillotson was all too keenly
aware of the danger of Romanism and of the support given to it
at Court.   When the assault on the established Church became
the unmistakable object of the King's policy, both did, in their
several ways, denounce the danger though they still regarded it
as unlawful for subjects to take up arms against the magistrate.
They did not teach civil disobedience, but their obedience then
might well be called passive loyalty.   So far had the folly of James
altered their temper that even High-Churchmen like South could,
though after deep heart-searchings, transfer their allegiance to
another sovereign.

CHAPTER FOUR

BARROW, SOUTH, AND TILLOTSON

ISAAC BARROW (1630-1677)

When Charles II appointed Isaac Barrow Master of Trinity College, Cambridge, in 1672, he remarked that he had bestowed this dignity on the best scholar in England [1]. Barrow had by then achieved eminence in mathematics and in classical scholarship; he was one of the King's chaplains in ordinary, he had preached at Court and manifested his ready wit in encounters with the Earl of Rochester [2] and the Duke of Buckingham, and he was soon to engage in the most thorough-going refutation of the Pope's claim to supremacy. Not his least merit was to have recognized the superior qualifications of his pupil Isaac Newton, whose help in revising his lectures on optics he gratefully acknowledged and to whom he had resigned his chair of mathematics at Cambridge. The King may have been slow to promote this brilliant scholar; and Barrow may have shared the feeling that Charles had passed an Act of Oblivion on his old friends when he wrote the often quoted epigram:

> Te magis optavit rediturum, Carole, nemo,
> Et nemo sensit te rediisse minus.

But the King obviously knew what best suited this learned man, for at Trinity Barrow could pursue his studies in a congenial atmosphere and labour to make his College a renowned centre of learning by laying the foundation of its magnificent library.

His first years at school, however, had been unpromising for he seemed to take more pleasure in fighting than in accidence and syntax. Not until his father had removed him from the Charter-

---

[1] Abraham HILL: 'Some Account of the Life of Dr. Barrow, a letter to the Reverend Dr. Tillotson', prefixed to the folio edition of Barrow's *Works*, London, 1683, I, sig. c. (the letter is dated 10 April, 1683).

[2] See ALLIBONE: *A Critical Dictionary of English Literature*, London, 1859, p. 130.

house and placed him under the care of Martin Holbeach at Fel-
stead school in Essex, did young Isaac apply himself seriously to
study.   His father, who was linen-draper to Charles I and followed
the King to Oxford, was soon unable to provide for him so that
Isaac's master made the boy a ' little tutor ' to one of his school-
fellows, Viscount Fairfax.   In 1643 Barrow was admitted to Peter-
house, where his uncle was a fellow ; when he came to Cambridge
in 1645, however, his uncle had been ejected from his fellowship
and Isaac entered Trinity College.   He was able to complete his
course of studies there thanks to the kindness of Dr. Henry
Hammond.   In 1647, he was chosen scholar of the House ; the
next year he proceeded B.A. and in 1649 he was elected Fellow.
Although he was a protégé of Dr. Hammond, and although he
refused to take the Covenant, Barrow " gained the good will of
the chief governors of the University " [1], notably of the Master
of Trinity, Thomas Hill, who had been intruded by the Parliamentary Visitors, but stood by Barrow [2] when some fellows urged
his expulsion in 1651 because he had extolled James I in a Latin
Oration on the anniversary of the Gunpowder Plot.   Nor does
Barrow seem to have suffered for having failed to take the Engagement [3].   He took his M.A. degree in 1652 and the next year was
incorporated M.A. at Oxford.

Barrow seems to have first intended to become a physician,
" finding the times not favourable to men of his opinion in the
affairs of Church and State " [4], and to this purpose he applied
himself to anatomy, botany and chemistry ; not satisfied with the
science then taught at Cambridge, he studied Bacon and Descartes,
and in one of his theses for his M.A. degree demonstrated that
" Cartesiana hypothesis de materia et motu haud satisfecit praeci-
puis Naturae Phaenomenis " [5].   On being elected fellow, however,
he had taken an oath to make divinity the end of his studies.
According to his first biographer, Abraham Hill [6], it was the study

        [1] Abr. HILL, op. cit., sig. a 2.
        [2] " But the Master silenced them with this ; Barrow is a better man than
any of us ", Abr. HILL, op. cit., sig a 2 v.
        [3] " When the Ingagement was imposed, he subscribed it, but upon second
thoughts, repenting of what he had done, he went back to the Commissioners
and declared his dissatisfaction, and got his name rased out of the list ".
Abr. HILL, op. cit., sig. a 2 v.   For the text of the Engagement, see ch. I,
p. 30, n. 1.
        [4] Ibid.
        [5] Mainly a refutation on Baconian principles.
        [6] Besides Hill's Account, further biographical information may be found in

of chronology, i.e. the chronology of events related in the Bible, which led him to take an interest in astronomy and in geometry, and so, says Hill, " he made his first entry into the mathematics " [1]. He had also proved an excellent Greek scholar for when his tutor, Dr. Duport, himself a reputed philologist, resigned his chair in 1654, he recommended Barrow for his successor. Whether it was felt that Barrow had better concentrate on mathematics, or whether his royalist sympathies were held against him, in any case he was not appointed. Though he still enjoyed the favour of men like Which-cote, the war waged by Barebone's Parliament of nominated Saints against places of learning may have induced him to leave Cam-bridge for a time : he was granted by his college a patent for travelling for three years (with a small allowance), he sold all his books and in June 1655 sailed for France, where his father was staying with the English Court. From Paris he proceeded to Italy, spent some time in Florence and in 1657 took ship for the East, visiting Smyrna and finally Constantinople, where he applied him-self to study of his favourite Father, Chrysostom. On his return the ship was attacked by Barbary pirates and Barrow grappled with them on the deck. After journeying through Germany and Holland he reached England in 1659, and at once sought ordination from Bishop Brownrigg, who had been extruded from his see and had become preacher to the Temple. Barrow returned to Trinity College in September 1659, i.e. after the fall of Richard Cromwell, and found a new master there who was to prove a staunch friend, John Wilkins (soon to be deprived in favour of a nominee of Charles II).

Upon the Restoration Ralph Widdrington, who had succeeded Dr. Duport, resigned his chair, and Barrow was appointed Regius professor of Greek. In 1661 he was given a B.D. degree *honoris causa*, and in 1670 he was created D.D. by royal mandate. Mean-

---

John AUBREY's *Brief Lives*, ed. cit. ; Walter POPE's *The Life of the Right Reverend Father in God Seth* (Ward), *Lord Bishop of Salisbury*, 1697, ed. cit. ; John WARD : *Lives of the Professors of Gresham College*, London, 1740 ; S.P. RIGAUD, ed. : *Correspondence of Scientific Men of the Seventeenth Century*, London, 1841 ; W. WHEWELL : Barrow and his Academical Times, in Barrow's *Theological Works*, ed. Alexander Napier, Cambridge, 1859, vol. IX ; the notice in ALLIBONE's *Critical Dictionary of English Literature*, 1859 ; Canon Overton's biography in *DNB* ; and the Davy MSS. in the British Museum. Not until the twentieth century did a full-length biography of Barrow appear : P.H. OSMOND : *Isaac Barrow. His Life and Times*, London, 1944.

[1] *Op. cit.*, sig. b.

while he gave lectures on Aristotle, which, from his own account in *Oratio Sarcasmica in Schola Graeca*, were not very successful. On the death of Laurance Rooke John Wilkins had him elected professor of geometry at Gresham College (1662) and Barrow resumed his mathematical studies, taking also astronomy into his province since he had to officiate for Walter Pope, then journeying abroad. For two years he lectured regularly at Gresham College, but resigned his post in 1664 when he was appointed to the first chair of mathematics at Cambridge, endowed by Henry Lucas. In 1663 he had been elected Fellow of the Royal Society ; he does not seem to have attended the meetings but he had many friends among the Fellows and kept up an active correspondence with John Collins, F.R.S., to whom he expounded his theorems and whom he asked to send the latest books on mathematical problems [1]. At Cambridge he lectured on optics and on geometry ; his researches " led him towards the discovery of the calculus, and he applied his mathematical method to optical problems in particular " [2]. It was Barrow who " set Newton's genius on fire " [2] and stimulated him to further research. His duties as Lucasian professor left him little time to compose the theological discourses which the statutes of the College required him to write before he could become a College preacher. In 1669 " out of term " [3], he set himself to writing the *Expositions on the Creed, the Lord's Prayer, Decalogue and Sacraments* ; perhaps he was the more inclined to turn to divinity because he had discovered among his pupils one that was likely to excel him in mathematics. At any rate in 1670 he relinquished his professorship in favour of Newton ; henceforth, though he kept up his interest in mathematical problems, Barrow devoted all his time to the study of divinity. In the same year he appeared on the list of the Chaplains at Court, and in 1671 he was appointed College preacher. His uncle Isaac, who had been consecrated Bishop of Man in 1663 and was now Bishop of Asaph, gave him a sinecure in Wales, and Seth Ward, Bishop of Salisbury, offered him a prebend in his Cathedral. On the death of John Wilkins in 1672 the Master of Trinity College, Pearson, succeeded him in the see of Rochester, and Barrow was promoted

---

[1] See S.P. RIGAUD, ed., *op. cit.*, II, 32-76.
[2] J.C. CROWTHER, *op. cit.*, p. 239 (Isaac Newton).
[3] See his letter to John Collins, Easter Eve, 1669, *Correspondence, op. cit.*, II, 71.

to the mastership, to the delight of the fellows and particularly of Newton [1].

Among the tasks Barrow set himself then were the refutation of the Romanist claims and the building of a new library. Though he failed to convince other heads of Houses that the University needed a library, he was tireless in raising funds for the erection of a new library at Trinity and applied in writing to all the friends of the College for subscriptions. He was appointed Vice-Chancellor for the year 1675-1676, and in February 1676 he laid the foundation stone of the new building, to be erected from the designs of Sir Christopher Wren. Unfortunately, Barrow did not live to see this great work completed : while on a visit to London in the Spring of 1677 he caught a fever and died there on the fourth of May. No funeral sermon was preached when this great scholar, the friend of Ray and Newton, of Tillotson and Wilkins, was laid to rest in Westminster Abbey. " The estate he left ", says Abraham Hill, " was books ". His father, Thomas Barrow, entrusted his papers to Tillotson and Hill " with a power to print such of them as they thought proper " [2]. Barrow's memory could not have been served better than by Tillotson's edition of his works, which perpetuated his fame as one of the great Anglican divines.

Though Barrow is regarded as " one of the immediate precursors of Newton and Leibnitz in the invention of differential calculus " [3]—both Newton and Wallis thought highly of him [4]—his fame rests chiefly on his theological works. Not only was he, as Whewell said, a geometer-theologian—he inscribed on the flyleaf of one of his books an invocation to God as Ὁ θεὸς γεωμετρεῖ [5]—, he was at home in Greek and in Hebrew and he was versed in ecclesiastical history. In fact as a scholar he had taken all knowledge into his province. He is said to have remarked " that general scholars did more please themselves, but they who prosecuted particular subjects did more service to others " [6]; he might have achieved greater eminence in mathematics if he had devoted all

---

[1] See Newton's letter to Collins, 10 Dec., 1672 : " We are here very glad that we shall enjoy Dr. Barrow again, especially in the circumstances of Master, nor doth any rejoice at it more than, Sir, your obliged humble servant ". *Correspondence, op. cit.*, II, 347.

[2] John WARD, *op. cit.*, I, 164.   [3] W. WHEWELL, *op. cit.*, p. xxxv.

[4] See *Correspondence, op. cit.*, passim.

[5] See PLUTARCH : *Symposiaca problemata* (VIII, 2, 718 B) : Πῶς Πλάτων ἔλεγε τὸν θεὸν ἀεὶ γεωμετρεῖν ;

[6] Abr. HILL, *op. cit.*, sig. d.

his energy to it, but his particular excellence as a divine lay in his masterful grasp of such a variety of subjects, in the extraordinary fertility of his mind and in the copiousness of his verbal imagination. Whatever theme he handled he always seemed to extend the boundaries of it, and to bring in more arguments from his varied learning to bear on the point at issue. As an experienced philologist he knew the value of words and, as his revisions show, he was not satisfied until he had rendered the full compass of his thought with the utmost precision ; he had a vast store of words at his command to express all the shades of meaning and thus enrich his theme. But his training in mathematics as well as in rhetoric ensured a firm control on the matter in hand, and whatever his amplifications he never allowed them to stray from the theme proposed at the outset. True, in his sermons as in his *Treatise of The Pope's Supremacy* he may be said to break off rather than to conclude, and he always leaves his readers with the impression that he has more to say on the subject. But by the time he comes to an end his readers have travelled with him over a wide expanse, for his trains of thought open up endless vistas. Such fecundity was the product of his many-sided interests, and of the diligence with which he pursued whatever study he was engaged in. Charles II called him an unfair preacher because he exhausted whatever subject he handled and left others nothing to say after him : this may not have been unqualified praise, for one can hardly imagine the Merry Monarch keeping awake through one of Barrow's sermons ; all the same Charles had clearly seen that this preacher's powerful flow of words issued from a richly stored mind.

In his brief account, Abraham Hill stressed " the harmonious, regular, constant tenour " of Barrow's life, and regretted that he could not make his narrative more vivid since there were no shadows to set off his piece. Indeed Barrow seems to have had no enemy nor even to have suffered for his allegiance to the King during the Interregnum. He was of a peaceable temper, wholly engrossed in his studies, and averse from controversies. This temper is reflected in his sermons : the steady march of his mind, moving from consideration to consideration until he seems to have exhausted his theme, suggests the quiet as well as the relentless labours [1] of the scholar's life. Hill also tells us that Barrow was

---

[1] Walter Pope relates that " He was unmercifully cruel to a lean Carcass, not allowing it sufficient Meat or Sleep : during the Winter Months, and some

negligent in his dress ; as Aubrey put it, he " was by no meanes
a spruce man " [1]. Such indifference to his outward appearance has
its counterpart in his lack of concern for the patience, or ease, of
his auditory : not only were his sermons unduly long, even for
an age that loved sermons, but if we are to believe Walter Pope,
he seems to have paid no heed to the reactions of his public, and
to have made little effort to catch their attention.

Coleridge thought that Barrow closed " the first great period in
the English language " [2]. His luxuriousness as well as his Latinisms
often recall the prose-writers of the earlier seventeenth century,
but the structure of his sentences clearly belongs to a later age.
His language is unadorned, he eschews florid imagery as well as
scheme and point—unless one counts as schemes his numerous
reiterations of similar syntactical structures and his endless strings
of " appositions ". He can use vivid images, but on the whole
his style is plain, and the syntax fairly simple. He has moved a
long way from the Ciceronian period, though he does not often
attain the simpler sentence structure of Dryden at his best. At
times he can be brief, but his is not the brevity characteristic of
the pregnant " strong lines ", and since he often repeats the same
movement in successive sentences he always enlarges the meaning.
What he favours is the open structure, which gives him scope to
expand his thought ; his sentences grow by addition and reiteration,
sweeping along in a uniform movement. Though he was a Fellow
of the Royal Society he did not aim at mathematical plainness ;
after all his favourite father was Chrysostom, and like him he had
a rich store of words at his disposal to illustrate his thoughts.
He usually accumulates subordinates or adjuncts, or independent
clauses, built on the same pattern, thereby gradually defining the
meaning, which he then gathers up in a final synthesis. For
instance :

> The gain of money, or of somewhat equivalent thereto, is
> therefore specially termed Profit, because it readily supplieth
> necessity, furnisheth convenience, feedeth pleasure, satisfieth

part of the rest, he rose always before it was light, being never without a Tinder-
Box and other proper utensils for that purpose ; I have frequently known him,
after his first sleep, rise, light, and after burning out his Candle, return to Bed
before Day ". *Op. cit.*, p. 154.

   [1] John AUBREY : *Brief Lives*, ed. cit., I, 91. See also Walter POPE, *op. cit.*,
pp. 148, 155.

   [2] S.T. COLERIDGE : *Table Talk*, ed. H.N. Coleridge, London, 1884, p. 294
(July 5, 1834).

fancy and curiosity, promoteth ease and liberty, supporteth honour and dignity, procureth power, dependencies and friendships, rendreth a man some-body, considerable in the world ; in fine, enableth to doe good, or to perform works of beneficence and charity [1].

Whole passages consist of parallel sentences, in which some of the parts too are expanded : thus an initial statement is elaborated and all the facets of it are revealed progressively as the sentence carries along his varied observations [2].   These enlargements are not dictated by Barrow's care for rhythm, but by his wish to cover the whole of the subject under consideration [3].   In fact he seems to be unmindful of the rhythm of his sentences, as well as of the repetitiveness this method of composition entails.   At times such accumulation makes for a majestic movement entirely in keeping with the thought, and gives weight to it [4] ; at times it merely issues

[1] *Works*, 1683, I, 14 (Sermon II, on *The Profitableness of Godliness*).

[2] For instance :
"First then we may consider, that Piety is exceeding usefull for all sorts of men, in all capacities, all states, all relations ; fitting and disposing them to manage all their respective concernments, to discharge all their peculiar duties, in a proper, just and decent manner.
It rendreth all Superiours equal and moderate in their administrations ; mild, courteous and affable in their converse ; benign and condescensive in all their demeanour toward their Inferiours.
Correspondently it disposeth Inferiours to be sincere and faithfull, modest, loving, respectfull, diligent, apt willingly to yield due subjection and service.
It inclineth Princes to be just, gentle, benign, carefull for their Subjects good, apt to administer Justice uprightly, to protect Right, to encourage Vertue, to check Wickedness.
Answerably it rendreth Subjects loyal, submissive, obedient, quiet and peaceable, ready to yield due Honour, to pay the Tributes and bear the Burthens imposed, to discharge all Duties, and observe all Laws prescribed by their Governours conscionably, patiently, chearfully, without reluctancy, grudging or murmuring.
It maketh Parents loving, gentle, provident for their Childrens good education, and comfortable subsistence ; Children again, dutifull, respectfull, gratefull, apt to requite their Parents.
Husbands from it become affectionate and compliant to their Wives ; Wives submissive and obedient to their Husbands.
It disposeth Friends to be Friends indeed, full of cordial affection and goodwill, entirely faithfull, firmly constant, industriously carefull and active in performing all good offices mutually.
It engageth men to be diligent in their Calling, faithfull to their Trusts, contented and peaceable in their Station, and thereby serviceable to Publick good." *Works*, ed. *cit.*, I, 16 (Sermon 2).

[3] As J.E. KEMPE remarked : "Every sermon ... is exhaustive in the sense of being a comprehensive discussion of all the component parts of his subject. He goes through them all, one by one, step by step, and places each in its right position. The process, it must be owned, is sometimes tedious, but it must also be allowed that the result in the hands of a strong and laborious workman like Barrow is vastly impressive." *The Classic Preachers of the English Church*, London, 1877, pp. 38-39.

[4] See, for instance, the opening of the sermon of the Passion, printed below.

in monotony, even though the cumulative effect may contribute to win assent to the initial proposition. Perhaps it is difficult to judge of the effectiveness of such a manner apart from the inflexions of the speaking voice ; but only a very skilful orator could have modulated such long passages so as to move gradually to a climax in the synthesis, for all the parts are of equal weight and value. It is on this account that Barrow has sometimes been accused of prolixity and of excessive fondness for " appositions ". Though he may become tiresome when his subject does not particularly interest the modern reader—for instance, when he is dealing with the profitableness of piety—it must be granted that his many " appositions " are not mere tautologies. It is no wonder that Coleridge admired Barrow's verbal imagination when, on such un- promising themes as that mentioned above, he could use images like these :

> If from bare worldly wealth ... a man seeketh Honour, he is deluded, for he is not thereby truly honourable ; he is but a shining Earth-worm, a well-trapped Ass, a gaudy Statue, a theatrical Grandee [1],

or distinguish between states of mind or feelings closely akin to each other as in :

> If he propoundeth to himself thence the enjoyment of Plea- sure, he will also much fail therein : for in lieu thereof he shall find care and trouble, surfeiting and disease, weari- some satiety and bitter regret ; being void of all true delight in his mind, and satisfaction in his Conscience ; nothing here being able to furnish solid and stable pleasure [1].

The structure of Barrow's sentences is the same as that of the discourse as a whole, in which he usually offers an impressive number of considerations to support the theme he has explained at the beginning. Though the plan of his sermon is clear and firm enough, he develops each point by means of amplification, often repeating the same syntactical structures in paragraph after para- graph [2]. In fact he often seems to proceed in the manner taught by the rhetoricians, i.e. considering in succession the various *loci* of his theme. The impression is one of abundance and even pro-

---

[1] *Works, ed. cit.,* I, 22 (sermon 2).
[2] For instance, points 1 to 8 under head IV of the Sermon on *Quietness* are built on the same pattern : " 1. Quietness is just and equal, Pragmaticalness is injurious ... 2. Quietness signifieth Humility ..., but pragmaticalness argueth much over-weening and arrogance ... 3. Quietness is beneficial to the World ... ; but pragmaticalness disturbeth the World ... 4. Quietness preserveth Concord

digality, of a comprehensive mind marshalling a variety of arguments drawn from his wide studies as well as from his observation of men and manners. The cumulative effect is impressive, though apt to become wearisome in the long run. His is not the copiousness that Bacon censured, for it is the counterpart of his fertile thought ; none the less he is often closer to the age that held " copy " for the supreme quality of the orator than to the age in which moderation, order in variety, easy and graceful movement, were most prized. While the gentleman of the Restoration affected negligence, Barrow the scholar ploughed his field relentlessly. He had little or no regard for the varied rhythm of prose ; rather he tended to carry on for whole stretches at a time now in one mode, now in another. For instance he will heap up when-subordinates for a whole folio page, all of them built on the same pattern ; or he will have an equally long list of rhetorical questions ; or again he will write a long passage in shorter, simple expository style. What he rarely does is to alternate from the one to the other in the course of a paragraph. Dugald Stewart aptly characterized Barrow's eloquence when he called it vigorous though unpolished [1]. The cumulative force of his amplifications, the power which sustains his long aggregate sentences, the precision with which he distinguishes and defines, and above all his verbal fertility, reveal a bold and vigorous mind moving to its proposed end [2]. Such singleness of purpose made him unmindful of the ease of his movements. Though he showed Newton the way and kept abreast of scientific research in his age, in language and style Barrow was still close to such amphibious creatures as Sir Thomas Browne or even Robert Burton. He never learnt from the conversation of gentlemen the unemphatic, graceful style which was developing in his time. Only occasionally did he use that slightly stylized form of the common speech which Dryden was learning to master in his

and Amity ... ; but pragmaticalness breedeth Dissentions and Feuds ... 5. Quietness ... begetteth tranquillity and peace ... ; but the Busy-Body createth vexation and trouble to himself ... 6. Quietness is a decent and lovely thing ... ; but Pragmaticalness is ugly and odious ... 7. Quietness adorneth any Profession ... ; but Pragmaticalness is scandalous ... 8. Quietness is a safe practice ... ; but Pragmaticalness is dangerous ... " *Works*, ed. cit., III, 304-6.

[1] Preliminary Dissertation to the *Encyclopaedia Britannica*, quoted by ALLIBONE, *op. cit.*

[2] " On every subject, [Barrow] multiplies words with an overflowing copiousness ; but it is always a torrent of strong ideas and significant expressions which he pours forth." Hugh BLAIR : *Lectures on Rhetoric and Belles Lettres*, London, 1783, I, 376.

essays. and which made his friend Tillotson such a successful
preacher. What his style lacks, above all, is the ease and simple
elegance that distinguish Restoration prose at its best.

Though Barrow could be racy at times and use a colloquial
phrase [1], particularly when censuring vice or deprecating vanities,
he used many uncommon, latinate terms which must have baffled
some of his hearers less familiar than he was himself with the
vocabulary of the schoolmen. Sometimes these words were needed
for precision, but most often one feels that they simply were part
of the common speech of the scholars with whom he was conversant. Such a habit was certainly not mere pedantry on his
part, as Abraham Hill already remarked [2]; in fact Barrow himself
objected to the use of " new definitions and uncouth terms " in
mathematics when the new notions could have been expressed " in
the usual manner of speaking " [3]. The Latinisms and obsolete
words seem to have come as naturally to him as did the slang
phrase to L'Estrange or Tom Brown. But the vivid colloquial
expressions often strike a strange note in the midst of a pre-
dominantly learned vocabulary, and are therefore noticed all the
more readily. Moreover, Barrow occasionally used a slightly old-
fashioned word-order, as in :

> this consideration [...] will [...] justify that advice and verify
> that assertion of the *Wise-man* : [...] it well applyed will
> pluck down the high places reared to that great Idol of
> clay in mens hearts [4]

---

[1] Coleridge also noted that he " sometimes adopted the slang of L'Estrange
and Town Brown ", *op. cit.*, p. 294.

[2] " It happened that sometimes he let slip a word not commonly used, which
upon reflexion he would doubtless have altered, for it was not out of affectation ",
op. cit., sig. d. Tillotson altered some of these words (about 70 in all) but he
did not do this consistently. The extent of T's revision of Barrow's vocabulary
has been exaggerated since Napier's edition in 1859 ; as a consequence the
opinion has prevailed that B's original text had far more antiquated or hard
terms than is really the case. On this, see my ' Tillotson's Barrow ', in *English
Studies*, XLV (1964), 193-211, 274-88.

[3] See his letter to Collins, 12 Nov., 1664, in which he censures Mengolus
for using " abundance of new definitions and uncouth terms, so that one must,
as it were, learn new languages to attain to his meaning, though it may be
only somewhat ordinary is couched under them. I esteem this a great fault in
any writer, for much time is spent, and labour employed, to less purpose than
needed, since there is little in any science but may be sufficiently explained
in the usual manner of speaking ; as particularly M. Des Cartes his geometry
doth plainly shew, where so many useful rules are delivered without any new
words or definitions at all ". *Correspondence, op. cit.*, pp. 40-41.

[4] *Works, ed. cit.*, III, 161 (Sermon 14, *The Consideration of our Latter
End*).

which strikes the modern reader as the more quaint because of the
vividness of the image that follows ; or again in :

> I shall onely farther remark, that the word here used is by
> the *Greek* rendred ἐπαινεθήσονται, *they shall be praised* ... [1]

or again in :

> You farther considering this signal testimony of Divine
> Goodness, will thereby be moved to hope and confide in
> God ...[1]

Barrow's abundant quotations from Scripture or from the Fathers, even more than his vocabulary and syntax, make him akin
to the preachers of the preceding age. Besides, he was fond of
indicating in the margin more references even than those from
which he had actually quoted in the sermon ; as a consequence
his works appear slightly forbidding to the modern reader, who,
from a mere look at his pages, might infer that his demonstrations
are all from authority. This would be a gross mistake, for Barrow
always grounds his arguments on the reason of the thing as much
as on the word of Scripture or of any of its commentators. But
he makes plentiful use of illustrations from such sources to support
his argument or to enlarge upon his theme. This distinguishes
him decidedly from most of his Anglican contemporaries, and
notably from South and Tillotson, who make only sparing use of
authority and rarely give references to their sources. Barrow therefore seems to owe more to the method of the schoolmen, though
his thought is probably more alien to theirs than was South's, for
instance ; in this as in so much else he appears as the scholar-
preacher. Such display of learning was beginning to be less and
less relished by his contemporaries, as the gentleman or *honnête
homme* came to take precedence over the scholar, who was too
often mistaken for a mere pedant. But Barrow was an experienced
philologist and he often explained the exact meaning of his text
by reference to the Greek or even the Hebrew words, or by comparing the various passages in which a particular term is used in
Scripture. Several of his sermons open with such exegesis, from
which modern critics might profitably learn how to proceed in their
explication de texte. He does not labour the point, or " crumble "
his text after the manner of Andrewes, but he makes clear what

[1] *Ibid.*, I, 158, 159 (Sermon 11, *On the Gunpowder-Treason*).

is the precise value of the terms used in his text. A good example of this may be found in his sermons on justifying faith and justification by faith [1]. His care for words, here as in his amplifications, merely reflects his care for right thinking, since to him as to his brother Anglicans the false notions regarding faith resulted from the abuse of words. Barrow may be more concerned than were most of his contemporaries with the niceties of his text, but this never leads him into far-fetched observations from the text. Perhaps it should be remembered that most of his sermons were preached to university audiences [2], though the Orator of Oxford University, Robert South, preached to similar audiences in a quite different manner. To such hearers, Barrow's style would have sounded less old-fashioned than it would to a City congregation or at Court. The few sermons which we know to have been delivered elsewhere are not, however, noticeably different in method or style. Barrow's friend, Tillotson, or the former Master of Trinity, Wilkins, even when preaching to distinguished audiences eschewed such appeal to authority, and unlike Barrow relied on demonstration rather than amplification to carry their point.

Barrow's manner may seem slightly antiquated in the context of Restoration sermon literature, but the advantage of his style of preaching appears best when he is dealing with the commonplaces of morality. There, though the theme be trite, the wealth of his observations, supported by confirmations from his sources, often gives new vigour to the old truths. The best instance of this is probably his Spital sermon on *Bounty to the Poor*, which, Walter Pope tells us, lasted for three hours and a half, and which he published " with what farther he had prepared to say ". The sermon is too long [3] to be included in the present selection, and a brief outline of it can hardly suggest the amazing wealth of considerations and the wide variety of observations with which he enriches this worn-out theme. The sermon in fact images the

---

[1] Printed below.

[2] Caroline F. Richardson said that " the majority of Barrow's sermons ... were written to be read, not to be preached ". *English Preachers and Preaching*, 1640-1670, New York, 1928, p. 86. I do not know where she found such information, unless she thus interpreted the following words of Hill: " and he took a course very convenient for his publick person as a Preacher, and his private as a Christian ; for those Subjects which he thought most important to be considered for his own use he cast into the method of Sermons for the benefit of others ". *Op. cit.*, sig. c.

[3] See *Works, ed. cit.*, I, 421-63.

liberal bounty which it recommends through the rich outpourings
from Barrow's own store. Having explained the meaning of his
text, *Ps*. CXII.9, he proceeds to demonstrate it by propounding considerations under five several heads : the advantages with which
Scripture represents this duty to us and presses it upon us (pp. 425-
33); the reasonableness and equity of the laws of charity in
regard to God (pp. 433-42), in regard to our neighbour (pp. 442-
47), in regard to ourselves (pp. 447-51), and in regard to our
wealth itself (pp. 451-9). He concludes by giving instances of
the felicity proper to a bountiful person (pp. 459-63). As such
these topics have nothing uncommon or new, nor have the several
considerations under each head ; thus under the fourth he develops
the following points : 1. What is he whose need craves our
bounty ? 2. Whence comes the distinction between our poor neighbour and ourselves ? 3. One main end of this difference among
us is that some men's industry and patience might be exercised
by their poverty while other men should by their wealth have
ability of practising justice and charity. 4. Poverty itself is no
such contemptible thing. 5. Every poor man is our near kinsman.
6. He is nearly allied to us by society of common nature and more
strictly joined to us by the bands of spiritual consanguinity. Each
point, however, is developed with such strength of argument and
such wealth of detailed observation that Barrow seems to have
pictured the vast scene of human actions, at least in respect to
wealth or the want of it. Barrow may have been no spellbinder,
but he obviously knew what to say to a City congregation and
dwelt on such considerations as were likely to impress the rich
merchants and tradesmen who were only too apt to consider their
commercial success as a mark of God's favour. His appeal for
support to the City hospitals must have made them take the doctrine
of stewardship to heart. But Barrow could use the same wealth of
description to define " so versatile and multiform " a thing as wit [1],
which again images his own kind of wit, i.e. his inventiveness and
verbal fertility.

Canon Overton remarked that Barrow formed a link between
two generations of Churchmen, since he was supported in his youth
by the defender of the Laudian Church, Dr. Hammond, and later

---

[1] See his sermon *Against Foolish Talking and Jesting*, printed below.

became the friend of Tillotson [1]. If Barrow was old-fashioned in his language and style of preaching, as a theologian he was very much of his age and he has often been classed with the Latitude-men. Like his Anglican brethren he believed that faith is the perfection of reason and that a living faith must issue in practice. Like them he demonstrated the absurdity of infidelity, and he grounded his belief in Scripture on reason and the testimony of the senses. He proved the being of God from the frame of the world, from human nature, from universal consent and from supernatural effects ; but like them too he insisted that bare reason alone is not sufficient, that Christianity is both reasonable and mysterious. He censured both the implicit faith of the Romanists and the doctrine of eternal election or reprobation of the Puritans [2]. In matters of discipline he opposed the claims of the separatists and upheld the order and decency of the established Church ; above all he opposed the claims of the Roman Church to be the sole heir of Christ, and of the Pope to infallibility in matters of doctrine and discipline. He recommended obedience to the pastors and governors of the Church ; he preached passive obedience to the civil magistrate [3] and as a faithful member of the national Church he duly solemnized such anniversaries as the fifth of November and Royal Oak day. Yet in his sermons he did not allow himself to be drawn into controversy beyond the necessary refutation of what were to him dangerous views ; indeed he was markedly moderate in his censure of enemies of the Church and never slandered or ridiculed them as did some of his brethren, notably South. He believed that rebuke should be mild and affectionate rather than harsh, and that pastors should speak in the still voice of their Master. Yet he could be firm in demonstrating the folly of unbelief or of slander, or the heinousness of sin. He was averse from all excesses, an equable and peace-loving man, and such was the temper he tried to instil into his hearers. He was too much the geometer-theologian ever to express the ardour of faith or to convey the sense of the unfathomable mystery of the Godhead and the poignancy of the mystery of the divine sacrifice. Though his sermon on the Passion [4] is more " pathetic "

---

[1] J.H. OVERTON : *Life in the English Church, 1660-1714*, London, 1885, p. 39.

[2] See Chapter II : Anglican Rationalism, above.

[3] See Chapter III : Church and State after the Restoration, above.

[4] Printed below.

than his expositions of the Creed, yet one cannot help feeling that
he hardly realized the full significance of the Atonement. If in
many ways he recalls the Norwich Doctor, yet unlike him he was
not ready to be teased out of thought by an O ! Altitudo. Rather
he envisaged the beatific vision as the full revelation of the many
theorems which his geometer-God could grasp at one glance [1]. His
was a deep and earnest, but not an ardent faith ; nor was he
perturbed by the immense distance between the Creator and His
creatures. Though he emphasized the necessity to do the will of
God before the full light of truth might be granted us, he hardly
seems to have been aware that more was needed than a rational
conviction to enable man to walk upright. Too often indeed the
choice seems to be as simple and as easy as between two propositions in mathematics, one of which is plainly false. That is why,
perhaps, his moral sermons and even his sermons on the love of
God seem so dry to us.

Like many of his Anglican brethren Barrow was a " moral
preacher " and recommended such virtues as patience, industry,
love of our neighbour, etc. These sermons are not likely to appeal
much to the modern reader, any more than are the majority of
those on the Creed. The sermons printed below have been chosen
because they deal with matters which were of central concern to
the Anglican divines and which may be deemed to reflect important
aspects of the thought of the day. Such were the rise of infidelity
and the danger of scoffing at religion, the problem of justifying
faith, and the question of obedience to spiritual guides. The sermon on the Passion has been included because in it Barrow achieves
greater intensity than is usual with him, and at times recalls the
great Anglican divine who in his sermons as well as in his poems
could make his hearers or readers realize the baffling nature of
the central event in Christianity. Such a choice inevitably reflects
the editor's taste and interests, but it is hoped that it will present
to the modern reader a fair sample of the oratory of Isaac Barrow.

ROBERT SOUTH (1634-1716)

Robert South, ' the scourge of the fanatics ', outlived most of his
contemporaries, yet in March 1709 Narcissus Luttrell thought him

[1] See his prayer to 'Ο θεὸς γεωμετρεῖ, quoted by HILL, op. cit., sig. b 2 v.

dead [1] and in June of the same year Swift wrote to Lord Halifax :

> Pray, My Lord, desire Dr South to dy about the Fall of
> the Leaf, for he has a Prebend of Westminster which will
> make me your neighbor, and a Sinecure in the Country,
> both in the Queen's Gift ; which my Friends have often
> told me would fitt me extreamly [2].

In October, however, Halifax remarked : " Dr South holds out
still, but He can not be immortal " [3], nor would " the gentle winter
[of 1709/10] carry off the old man " [4]. Swift was to be dis-
appointed of his hopes, for the Queen had been dead almost two
years and Swift consigned to his Dublin deanery when on Tuesday, 10th July, 1716, " Christ Church bell rung for the death of
Dr South " [5]. The last rites at his burial were performed, as he
had desired, by his friend Atterbury, former Dean of Christ
Church, and now Bishop of Rochester, who was later to be involved in attempts to restore the Pretender and sentenced to banishment. A funeral oration was spoken by the Captain of the Westminster scholars, of whom South had been one, but it was left to
the ' unspeakable Curll ' to publish the—anonymous—Memoirs of
the Life of Dr South (1716). His collected Works, reissued first
by his bookseller Jonah Bowyer and then by Jacob Tonson, included
no biography ; nor did the additional volumes published by Charles
Bathurst in 1744. While the works of Tillotson, Chillingworth,
and Stillingfleet, among others, appeared in folio editions, South's
sermons were only available in octavo collections. They delighted
such men as Johnson [6] and Fielding [7] but were probably too much

---

[1] Narcissus LUTTRELL : A Brief Historical Relation of State Affairs from
September 1678 to April 1714, Oxford, 1857, VI, 417. 12 March, 1708/9.
[2] Jonathan SWIFT : Correspondence, ed. Harold Williams, Oxford, 1963,
I, 143. Postscript to a letter to Lord Halifax, dated : Leicester, Jun. 13th, 1709.
[3] Ibid., p. 150.   [4] Ibid., p. 159.
[5] Reliquiae Hearnianae : The Remains of Thomas Hearne, Extracts from
his Diaries, collected by Philip BLISS, Oxford, 1857, I, 365. South died on
8 July.
[6] See Boswell's Life of Johnson, ed. cit., III, 248. "South is one of the
best, if you except his peculiarities, and his violence, and sometimes coarseness
of language." (7 April, 1778). Johnson's familiarity with South's sermons
appears from his many quotations in the Dictionary. According to Lewis Freed,
South is cited 1,092 times in Vol. I (' The Sources of Johnson's Dictionary ',
Unpublished Dissertation, Cornell, 1939 ; quoted in P.K. ALKON : ' Robert South,
William Law, and Samuel Johnson ', Studies in English Literature, VI, 1966,
3, 500, n. 4).
See Allan WENDT : ' Fielding and South's " Luscious Morsel " : A Last
Word ', N. & Q., ccii (N.S. IV), 256-7.

out of tune with the prevailing temper to be thought worthy of
further editions. When in 1795 a well-intentioned man proposed
to publish extracts from South's sermons he found that his proposals had shocked one of the readers of the *Evangelical Magazine,*
who reminded him that the sermons had been inspired by the Devil
himself. The editor thought it necessary to explain that " whatever other acrimonious parts were ", the passages he had selected
could not have been so written ; he further explained that he
had searched his heart before proceeding with his work and was
satisfied that he had not been " headstrong and self-willed in the
matter ", that in any case " truth is certainly the same in itself,
whoever may be the speaker or writer ". Such was, in some circles
at least, the inability of sermon readers to respond to wit and their
ignorance of the events to which the sermons referred that this
editor himself was unable to understand the sentence of South
censured by his Evangelical critic :

> Having sent my proposals, respecting an abridgement of
> South, to the printer of the *Evangelical Magazine,* (a bene-
> volent and useful publication) when, upon a visit at Not-
> tingham, I took up the *Magazine* for *May,* and dropping
> upon page 205, I read the following lines :
> " The saying of a celebrated divine, more remarkable for
> " the brilliancy of his *wit,* than the fervor of his *piety,* has
> " been often quoted and too often credited, viz. *That the*
> " *study of the book of Revelation either found persons mad*
> " *or made them so* †. We shall be in little danger of feeling
> " an improper bias from *his* decision, if we pay any defer-
> " ence to the judgment of the amiable and candid Doddridge,
> " who thought his (i.e. South's) discourses dictated by so
> " bad a spirit, that he said, if ever any sermons were written
> " by the inspiration of the devil, it was Dr South's. "

> † No pious, sensible man can agree to this witty but weak
> observation of the doctor's, because it contradicts Rev. I.3 [1].

The tide had long turned against South's bracing and pungent
expositions of High-Church doctrine and Tory loyalty. Readers
of a ' benevolent and useful ' magazine could certainly not counten-

---

[1] *The Beauties of South,* Extracts from the Works of Robert South, London,
1795. Preface, p. v. The sentence quoted is from Sermon 11 in Volume II,
on *1 John* III. 21, *An Account of the Nature and Measures of Conscience.* The
editor of *The Beauties of South* obviously knew nothing of the Puritans' use,
and abuse, of the Book of *Revelation,* to which South refers in his sermon.

ance such a witty and violent preacher, and for many years his
reputation was to suffer from this emphasis on benevolence and
usefulness, while the practical preachers were relished for their
moderation, and the best exponent of Latitudinarianism, Tillotson,
was proposed as a model for style by essayists and grammarians
alike. South's manner was no more congenial to the Victorians,
and the Whig historians taking their cue from Macaulay could
hardly be expected to redress the balance. Canon Overton is one
of the few to have done South justice in the nineteenth century,
and he pointed out the chief cause of the decline in the reputation
of this great Anglican divine when he remarked that " so far from
avoiding controversy, (South) sniffed the battle from afar " and
" hardly ever preached without dealing some shrewd blows to his
adversaries on the right hand and on the left ". He hits hard,
said Overton, but he hits fair :

> If some of his utterances startle us, we must remember that
> our forefathers were not so mealy-mouthed as we are, and
> that congregations were used to hear a spade called a spade,
> even in the pulpit [1].

South was probably the best preacher of his age, and he had a
mind of the highest order ; if his sermons had been more widely
read in the eighteenth century they might have infused some
intellectual vigour into the life of the Church. Instead, the mealy-
mouthed triumphed ; even though three collected editions of his
sermons appeared in the nineteenth century [2] he is hardly known
to the modern reader. Yet as writer and thinker he may stand
beside his fellow High-Churchman Swift, who like him dealt so
many shrewd blows that he, too, failed to get preferment. South's
letter to Harley refusing the deanery of Westminster might well
have been written by the Dean of St. Patrick :

> My Most Honoured Lord,
>   Could my present circumstances, and condition, in any
> Degree come up to the Gracious, and surpriseing offer lately
> brought me from her Majesty, I should with the utmost
> Gratitude, and Deepest Humility Cast my self at Her Royall
> Feet, and with Both Armes Embrace it.
>   But alas, my Lord, That Answer which Alexander the

---

[1] J.H. OVERTON, op. cit., p. 239.   [2] In 1823, 1843 and 1865.

Great once gave a Souldier petitioning Him for an Office in his Army may no lesse properly become her majesty to my Poor Self, (though not *Petitioning for*, but *prevented by* her Princely Favour,) *Freind*, said He, *I own that I can give thee this Place, but I cannot make thee Fitt for it.* And this, my Lord, is my unhappy case.

For haveing, for now above these *Fourty years*, the Best, the Ablest, and most usefull part of my Age, not bin thought fitt by my Superiors, to serve the Crown or Church in any other way, or Station, than what I have held hitherto, I cannot, but in modesty (and, even, in *Respect to them*) judge myself unworthy, and unfitt to serve them in any higher, or greater Post now ; being grown Equally super-annuated to the *Active*, as well as *Enjoying* Part of Life.

For Age, my Lord, is not to be *Defyed*, nor forced by All, that Art, or Nature can doe, to retreat one step backward : And even the Richest Spread Table, with the Kindest Invitations to it, Come but too late to one, who has lost both his Stomack, and his Appetite too.

In fine, my good Lord, after the Utmost Acknowledgement, Duty and Devotion paid to the Sacred *Fountain-Head* from which all this Goodnesse flowes, the same Gratitude, in the *very next place*, commands me, with the Profoundest Deference to Own, and Blesse that Noble *Channell*, by which it has so liberally passed upon,
> (Great Sir)
>> Your Honours most obliged, Humble, and obedient Servant
>>> Robert South.

Westminster Abbey,
8 June, 1713,
Nothing, my Lord, afflicts me more than that I am disabled from bringing your Honour, these my Acknowledgements (and many more with them) in Person my Self [1].

If South suffered neglect from the mealy-mouthed, he was no better served by the malicious gossip to whom we owe most of our knowledge of life at Oxford in the second half of the seventeenth century. Anthony Wood's pique against South has often been attributed to the heartless joke the Doctor made when Wood complained of a painful disorder ; but as the editor of *The Life and Times of Anthony Wood* has shown, the antiquary had long dis-

---

[1] British Museum MS. Loan (Portland Papers) 29/200. The letter was published by the Historical Manuscripts Commission in the *Reports on the MSS. of the Duke of Portland*, London, 1901, V, 295.

liked the preacher whose wit spared no man [1]. Though Wood's
Athenae Oxonienses remains the most reliable source for information on South as on other Oxford men, his relation must be checked
against other contemporary evidence, for the view he gives of his
fellow-Oxonians is often coloured by his gall. Nor should it be
forgotten that he was expelled from the University after the second
earl of Clarendon had sued him for libel of his father on the
publication of his biographical dictionary in 1691-2. Since South
was Chaplain to Clarendon, Wood's severe judgement on him may
be the more untrustworthy. The *Memoirs* published by Curll is
not wholly reliable either, and it ignores the aspersions of Wood.
It is the more unfortunate that no scholarly biography of South
has yet appeared [2] and that for biographical material we must rely
on the scattered references which served as a basis for the life of
South in the *Dictonary of National Biography* (by Alexander Gordon), supplemented by a few letters which have come to light since,
for these still leave unsolved the question of South's attitude in the
years preceding the Restoration.

South was the son of a London merchant who suffered some
loss during the Civil War [3]. In 1647 he was entered a King's
scholar at Westminster School under Dr. Busby, where, says
Wood, " he obtained a considerable stock of grammar and philological learning, but more of impudence and sauciness " [4]. According to the author of the *Memoirs*, " he made himself remarkable...
by Reading the Latin Prayers in the School, on the Day of King

---

[1] " William Huddesforth relates : ' A. Wood complained to Dr. South of
a disorder with which he was much afflicted, and which terminated in his death :
viz. a painful suppression of urine ; upon which South, in his jocose manner,
told him, that if he could not make water he must make earth. Anthony went
home, and wrote South's Life '. And he then goes on to say that this heartless
joke of South's on Wood's disorder called forth ' the severe and in some respects,
unjust, character of South in the *Athenae* ', adding ' it was South's custom, if
not foible, to suffer neither sacredness of place, nor solemnity of subject, to
restrain his vein of humour '. But it will be seen from the Diaries etc. that
Robert South had been disliked by Wood for many years. " *The Life and
Times of Anthony Wood, Antiquary of Oxford, 1632-1695, Described by himself*.
Collected from his Diaries and other Papers by Andrew Clark, Oxford, 1900,
III, 492.

[2] Dr. Donald E. Fitch, of the University of California at Santa Barbara,
is working on a biography of South.

[3] See his ' Petition to His Highness the Lord Protector of the Commonwealth ', dated 2 December, 1656, for money owing to him for goods seized
in the *Discovery* in 1645 off the coast of Ireland. British Museum MS. Addit.
5716, f. 13.

[4] *Athenae Oxonienses*, ed. Philip Bliss, Oxford, 1813-1820, IV, 632.

Charles the 1st's Martyrdom, and praying for his Majesty by Name " [1]. In 1651 he was elected to Christ Church (where Locke followed him the next year). In 1654 he contributed a poem to *Musarum Oxoniensium* ᾿ΕΛΑΙΟΦΟΡΙΑ, i.e. verses to the Protector celebrating the Peace with Holland [2], and the next year he proceeded B.A. In or about that time, according to Wood, " he was appointed to do some exercise in the public and spacious refectory " of the College, the whole scope of which was " little other than a most blasphemous invective against godliness, and the most serious and conscientious professors of it " [3]. It was during this public exercise that he was first seized with a qualm ; henceforward, says Wood,

> he seemed to be much more serious than before, and by degrees insinuated himself into the good opinion of the then present dean of his house, Dr Owen, as also with those of the presbyterian and independent party thereof [4].

The anonymous author of the *Memoirs* gives a very different account of South's attitude at the time. According to him John Owen, Vice-Chancellor of the University, opposed South's proceeding M.A. in 1657, because he had been found in episcopal meetings making use of the Book of Common Prayer, after the example of John Fell [5]. In 1658 South received ordination from a deprived bishop [6] and the next year he was incorporated M.A.

---

[1] *Memoirs of the Life of the Late Reverend Dr. South*, Second edition, London, 1721, p. 4.

[2] The poem was reprinted by Curll in *Opera Latina Posthuma*, London, 1717, p. XIII.

[3] *Athenae Oxonienses, op. cit.*, p. 632. Wood's source is *Mirabilis Annus Secundus*, London, 1662, a collection of prodigies and of judgements visited upon men who blasphemed against godliness or railed at the Dissenters. South's fit in the pulpit at Whitehall was interpreted by this ' fanatic ' as such a judgement, a view also shared by Richard Baxter. See *Reliquiae Baxterianae, or Mr Richard Baxter's Narrative of the most memorable Passages in his Life and Times Faithfully published from his own original Manuscripts* by Matthew Sylvester, London, 1696, II, 380.

[4] *Ibid.*

[5] *Op. cit.*, pp. 6-8. It should be remembered, however, that Owen did not try to hunt down loyal Churchmen ; the College historian says : " without his tacit connivance it would not have been possible for John Fell, Dolben, and Allestree to maintain the Church of England services throughout the time of the Commonwealth, at Beam Hall, opposite Merton Chapel ; and when Pocock, the famous Orientalist, after losing his Canonry at Christ Church for refusing to take the engagement, was in danger of being deprived of his living of Childrey, Owen interposed promptly and effectually on his behalf ". H.L. THOMPSON : *Oxford University, College Histories*, Oxford, 1900, p. 70 (Christ Church).

[6] See *Memoirs*, p. 10. Wood says nothing of this and may even suggest

at Cambridge. Wood says that in his sermons at St. Mary's, South " still appeared the great champion for Calvinism against Socinianism and Arminianism " and ingratiated himself with the Independents, but changed sides when the Presbyterians began to lift their heads, and again when the success of Monck foreshadowed the restoration of Charles II. Not only does Wood brand South as a time-server, he further accuses him of turning informer to the royalists [1]. Wood reiterated these charges in other notes which were published in the *Life and Times* [2]; needless to say, the anonymous *Memoirs* does not mention any such changes of allegiance.

For lack of further evidence it is hard for us to decide which of the two versions is to be credited. The earliest sermon South himself published, preached at the Assizes in July 1659, is directed against the Independents, and does not particularly glance at the Presbyterians ; in later sermons he often attacked the Presbyterians and accused them of hypocrisy for pleading not-guilty of the murder of the King though they had been the first to rebel ; but this does not confute Wood's view, since he implies that South was the more violent against the Presbyterians because he had earlier sided with them. Among the sermons published from South's notes after his death only one suggests that in the fifties his conception of grace may have been closer to that of the strict Calvinists [3]. What makes it hard to accept Wood's version is not so much the discrepancy with the account given in the *Memoirs*—which was clearly intended as a panegyric—but the difficulty of reconciling such an attitude on the part of South with the credit he enjoyed among men who either had been ejected or were known for their loyalty to the Church, many of whom had been at Oxford in the years preceding the Restoration [4]. John Owen was ousted from the Deanery of

that this is not true : " In 1657 he proceeded in arts, became a chief and eminent member of that society, and preached frequently (*I think without any orders*)". *Op. cit.*, pp. 632-3 ; my italics. According to the *DNB*, South was ordained by Thomas Sydserf, the only one of the Scottish bishops deposed to be alive at the time of the Restoration.

[1] *Op. cit.*, pp. 633-4.

[2] See : Notes on the affairs of the University under the Puritan domination, 1648-1660, *Life and Times*, I, pp. 368-9. F. Madan still repeats the charge : " he had submitted under the Commonwealth, and was regarded as a time-server ". *Oxford Books*, Oxford, 1931, III, 143.

[3] See Chapter II, p. 136.

[4] John Fell, Dolben and Allestree, who had served in the royalist forces, were deprived of their studentships by the Parliamentary Visitors, but remained

Christ Church in 1659 and Edward Reynolds, who had been ' thrust in ' by Parliament in 1648 but forced to leave in 1651 when he refused to take the Engagement, was restored as Dean when the secluded Members were re-admitted to Parliament ; after the Restoration Reynolds was replaced by George Morley, who had been ejected in 1641 and who became Bishop of Worcester in 1660 ; John Fell, son of the former Dean, then succeeded him and remained Dean of Christ Church even after he was elevated to the see of Oxford in 1676 [1]. Now, John Fell had stayed in Oxford all through the Interregnum and was among those who were " suffered to meet quietly ... every Lord's Day ... (to celebrate) divine service according to the worship of the Church of England " [2]; he was closely associated with the Laudians who remained aloof from the Establishment and he kept in touch with the exiled leaders of the Church party [3] ; he can hardly have been ignorant of the sympathies of a Christ-Church man who, from Wood's own account, so actively canvassed his views. If South did succeed in ingratiating himself with the new masters, Fell must have demurred when, in August 1660, such a time-server was elected Public Orator of the University. Moreover, Clarendon who, as appears from recent research [4], had actively prepared the Restoration settlement and kept in touch with loyal Churchmen during the Protectorate, and who was elected Chancellor of Oxford University in October 1660, could hardly have failed to hear something of the intrigues of the man whom he appointed his Chaplain in 1661. True, one of South's friends, the learned orientalist Edward Pocock, had submitted when the Parliamentary visitors ejected Samuel Fell from Christ Church ; but another disaffected Churchman who had no wish to conform and even made his parish a centre of propaganda for the Anglican cause [5], Jasper Mayne, must have been a friend of South's or he would hardly have made him one of his executors [6].

at Oxford during the Commonwealth. See note 5 to p. 234 above. When Dolben was consecrated Bishop of Rochester in 1666 South preached the sermon at Lambeth Chapel.

[1] See Anthony Wood : *The History and Antiquities of the Colleges and Halls in the University of Oxford*, ed. John Gutch, Oxford, 1786, I.

[2] *Visitors' Register*, p. 358, quoted in V.H.H. Green, *op. cit.*, p. 147.

[3] See Bosher, *op. cit.*, p. 30.

[4] See Bosher, *op. cit.*, passim.

[5] *Ibid.*, p. 29. As Bosher says, such " disaffected conformists ... constituted, from the Protector's viewpoint, a dangerous fifth column within the Establishment ".

[6] See Anthony Wood : *Fasti*, ed. Philip Bliss, Oxford, 1813-1820, II, 373.

Unless South was a consummate actor—though we know that
he could mimic his enemies in the pulpit, Wood's account rather
suggests that he blazoned his views at St. Mary's—he could hardly
have succeeded in hoodwinking so many men whose chief concern
was to make possible the restoration of Anglican discipline. If
Wood alone was able to see through the mask, he must have been
gifted with uncommon insight. Rather, one feels, he was such a
Paul Pry [1] that he was kept out of the secret counsels of the
Churchmen who were busy preparing the future. On the other
hand, though the anonymous author of the *Memoirs* is sometimes
inaccurate, he may have been a Christ-Church man and have
reported the opinion current in the College; for whatever were
Curll's methods, his claim to have obtained from Dr. Aldrich, late
Dean of Christ Church, the three sermons he printed together
with the life of South, and the letter which South sent from
Poland to his friend Edward Pocock, seems to have been justified :
the sermons are close enough to represent an earlier version of
the texts South himself prepared for the press, and Curll does not
seem to have got into trouble with South's executors; neither
Atterbury, who had succeeded Aldrich as Dean of Christ Church
before being elevated to the see of Rochester, and who was still
in a position to defend his friend's memory, nor any other Christ-
Church man seems to have given Curll the lie. If the printer had
good authority for his texts, his anonymous biographer may also
have had reliable information for the Life. For all these reasons,
and in the absence of further evidence, it is safer at least to suspend judgement, especially since more recent experience of troubled
times and conflicts of loyalties may incline the twentieth-century
reader to take a less clear-cut view of the men who in the Interregnum had to decide how best to serve their Church. As Bosher
has shown in *The Making of the Restoration Settlement*, sincere
Churchmen could argue with equal honesty and pertinency both
for and against accepting modifications in the ritual so as to preserve the essentials of true worship; while some eminent Churchmen encouraged men to take the Engagement [2] others dissuaded

---

[1] See *Life and Times, op. cit.*, II, 259 : " Mar. 10 (1673). Dr (Ralph)
Bath(urst) told me that he was told that I used to listen at the Com(mon)
chamber and else(where) and that I never spoke well of any man. This I
suppose came from Dr (Robert) South's chamber for he was there that day
at din(ner) or after and Dr Bath(urst) told me this at night Q(aere)."

[2] For instance, Dr. Sanderson.

them from it [1]. Opinion among the Anglican clergy was divided
as to which was the best way to preserve the Church from utter
destruction, and many were accused of being time-servers simply
because, like Fuller, " they felt able to join in the life of the
Establishment when denied their first desire ", that is, " to live
under that Church government they best affected " [2].

Whatever South's feelings may have been during the last years
of the Protectorate, in the sermon he preached at St. Mary's,
Oxford, on 24 July, 1659 [3], he took as his theme the denial of Christ
before men. In this discourse—to which he gave the title *Interest
Deposed*—he considered the many ways in which men deny Christ
and His truths, and the causes of such denial, but he also discussed
how far a man may consult his safety in time of persecution. This
must have been a dangerous theme for him to pitch upon if he had
been a time-server, particularly in a place where he was well-
known. He did make clear that " he does not deny Christ by
flying, who therefore flies that he may not deny him ", and that
it is wiser for a man to conceal his judgement rather than make
rash professions of faith, for " he ... that thus throws himself upon
the sword, runs to heaven before he is called for ; where though
perhaps Christ may in mercy receive the man, yet he will be sure
to disown the martyr ". But he went on to state that a man is
sometimes bound to confess Christ openly though he thereby court
persecution, and specifically that " Ministers of God are not to
evade, or take refuge " by flying or by concealing their judgement.
He had reminded his audience at the outset that on sending out
His ministers Christ had enjoined them to be both wise as serpents
and harmless as doves. He had also availed himself of the occasion
of his text to insist that Christ needed a *learned* and faithful
ministry [4], which may indeed have pleased the Presbyterians no
less than the Anglicans among his hearers, but this is a theme to
which South was to revert again and again, particularly in *The
Scribe Instructed*, a sermon he preached at St. Mary's, Oxford,
on 29th July, 1660, which constitutes one of the best defences of
the use of learning for pastors. South, who under Dr. Busby had

---

[1] For instance, Dr. Hammond.
[2] BOSHER, *op. cit.*, p. 27.
[3] *Op. cit.*, I, ser. 3, printed below.
[4] When he published this sermon in the first volume of the collected edition
(1692) South added a footnote referring readers to the 1653 decision of Parliament to encourage a godly and *faithful* rather a godly and *learned* ministry.

already acquired " a considerable stock of grammar and philological learning ", distrusted all ' promptings of the Spirit ' and felt nothing but contempt for the premium set by the Triers on the godly deport- ment of those who interpreted God's Word without rightly under- standing the words of Scripture. Not all the supporters of a godly and faithful ministry were ignorant men, and South must have been aware that the Independent Dean of Christ Church, John Owen, was himself a learned man. None the less by casting a slur on human learning they sapped the basis of sound scholarship on which all explication of texts must be built. The Assize sermon may therefore be considered as a tract for the times.

So was the sermon South preached shortly after at Lincoln's Inn [1], in which he demonstrated that ecclesiastical policy is the best policy, that is, that the best way to strengthen the civil power is to establish the worship of God in the right exercise of religion, and that the surest means to destroy religion is to 'embase' the teachers of it by divesting them of all temporal privileges and by admitting ignorant persons to the ministry. The drift of this sermon is that the Temple must be rebuilt ; though the usurper Jeroboam in the text is clearly to be equated with Cromwell, there is little doubt as to how the Temple is to be rebuilt, i.e. so as to restore episcopal discipline. Here again, however, South directs his main attacks against those who claimed that human learning is not a necessary requisite for the ministry, i.e. against men connected with the Inde- pendents, not with the Presbyterians. Since, however, he con- siders the civil power as the mainstay of true religion—he states emphatically that the civil power cannot be subjected to the eccle- siastical power—; since he also blames the late confusions on the frequent innovations and changes which ultimately cast suspicion on religion, it is easy to guess that the Presbyterians too are responsible for the destruction of the Temple. At this stage, how- ever, South does not accuse them openly, and Anthony Wood may have thought that he was waiting to see which way the cat would jump before committing himself. Perhaps, one should remember that South, who had been admitted to Christ Church in the year that the Independent Owen succeeded Edward Reynolds as Dean, and was a student at the time when " the hotheads in Parliament

---

[1] The two sermons were published together in 1661 as *Interest Deposed and Truth Restored* ; the dedication is dated 25 May, 1660.

and elsewhere were anxious ... to suppress all Universities " (1653
and 1654) and when the Quakers arrived in Oxford (1654)[1], had
had direct experience of the rule of the Saints but had no particular
reason to resent the measures of the Presbyterians who, by the
time he came to Oxford, had ceased to play any part in the direction of affairs.   True, South contributed a poem in praise of Cromwell, who had become Chancellor of Oxford University in 1651 ;
but even the bitterest enemies of the Protector must have recognized
that the Peace he had concluded with the Dutch was advantageous
to England, and the collection of poems by Oxford graduates was
fitly called ἘΛΑΙΟΦΟΡΙΑ.

South's attacks against the Presbyterians were to be voiced
soon after the Act of Uniformity was passed, notably in a sermon
preached on 30 January, 1663 [2], in which he laid the disturbances
in Church and State at the door of those who had initiated the
further reformation of religious discipline.   Such innovations had
led to the utter destruction of the Church and to the ' execrable
murder' of the King ; henceforth South was to include the Presbyterians in his opprobrium, all the more as they formed the most
important group among the Dissenters and therefore represented
the main danger to the restored discipline of the Church at a time
when efforts were made towards obtaining either comprehension
of the Dissenters or indulgence for Dissenters and Romanists alike.
Though the sermon preached at Lincoln's Inn is not directed against
the Presbyterians one can foresee the stand South will take in the
matter of the Church's treatment of Dissenters, for he stresses the
danger to religion of attempts to purify it, as well as the need
for a close alliance between the civil and the ecclesiastical power.

In spite of Wood's assertions it is therefore tempting to believe
that when South was chosen Public Orator of the University in
August 1660, the emissaries of Clarendon who had been active in
Oxford during the Protectorate must have concurred in, if not
suggested, the choice.   Clarendon himself was to become Chancellor of the University in October, and the next year he appointed
South his chaplain.   According to Wood it was Clarendon who

being much delighted with a sermon [South] had preach'd

---

[1] F. MADAN, op. cit., III, 33.
[2] Op. cit., V, ser. 2, printed below.

before him, ... made way for him to preach the same sermon
again before his majesty [1].

This was probably the first time South preached at Whitehall,
but his reputation as an orator had preceded him there, for, as
Wood relates,

> happy was he or she amongst the greatest wits in the town,
> that could accommodate their humour in getting convenient
> room in the Chappel at Whitehall, to hang upon the lips
> of this so great an oracle [2].

Perhaps Wood overdoes this, for his account is so shaped as to
show that pride must have a fall : in the midst of this sermon
South swooned and could not proceed, and Wood relates this with
evident gusto, quoting the ' fanatic's ' comment on this in *Mirabilis
Annus Secundus*, which interprets the fit as a rebuke from the Lord
for South's contemptuous references to the Puritans [3].

---

[1] *Athenae Oxonienses, ed. cit.*, IV, 635.

[2] *Ibid.*

[3] This is Richard Baxter's account of the event: "this man [i.e. South]
being Houshold Chaplain to the Lord Chancellor, was appointed to preach
before the King ; where the crowd had high expectations of some vehement
satyr. But when he had preached a quarter of an hour, he was utterly at a
loss, and so unable to recollect himself, that he could go no further ; but cryed
(*The Lord be merciful to our infirmities*) and so came down. But about a
month after, they were resolved yet that Mr. S. should preach the same sermon
before the King, and not lose their expected applause. And preach it he did
(little more than half an hour, with no admiration at all of the hearers). And
for his encouragement the sermon was printed. And when it was printed many
desired to see what words they were that he was stopped at the first time.
And they found in the printed copy all that he had said first, and one of the
next passages which he was to have delivered, was against me for my Holy
Commonwealth". *Op. cit.*, II, 380. Baxter's account is clearly inaccurate
on one point : it was not a month later but the next Sunday, 20 April, 1662,
that South was asked to deliver his sermon again (see WOOD, *op. cit.*, p. 636);
on this second occasion Pepys intended to go and "hear South, my Lord
Chancellor's Chaplain, the famous preacher and oratour of Oxford, who the
last Lord's day did sink down in the pulpit before the King, and could not
proceed" (Samuel PEPYS : *Diary*, ed. H.B. Wheatley, 1962, I, 208). Another
point in Baxter's narrative is also puzzling, for the sermon (on *Eccles.* VII.10)
does not seem to have appeared in print in South's lifetime : it was first
published in 1744 in the Additional Volumes (Sermon 14 in vol. VII); yet it
is true that South does refer to those who "raise *Models of State*, and *Holy
Common Wealths*, in their little *discontented* closets ; (or) arraign a Council
before a Conventicle" (VII, 304). There may have been a surreptitious edition,
though it has not been traced by bibliographers ; but Baxter's words seem to
imply that South was asked to print this sermon, hence, presumably, had a
license for printing. No such item appears among the books licensed by
L'Estrange. Like the author of *Mirabilis Annus Secundus* Baxter tends to interpret the diseases of his enemies as rebukes from God ; for a similar comment
on Dr. Creighton "who was used to preach Calvin to Hell, and the Calvinists

With no less a patron than the Lord High Chancellor of England and with such fame as a preacher, South was, as his anonymous biographer says, " in the Road to Church Preferments "[1]. In March 1663 he was installed prebendary of St. Peter's, Westminster, and in October he was created B.D. and D.D. on letters from Clarendon,

> though strenuous opposition was made against the Grant of that Favour by the Batchelors of Divinity, and Masters of Arts, who were against such a Concession, by reason that he was a Master of Arts but of six years standing [2].

It is one of fate's little ironies that South was finally admitted B.D. and D.D. " by the double presentations " of John Wallis, Savilian Professor of Geometry, who was also accused by Wood (and Aubrey) of being elected Custos Archivorum through the perjury of the senior proctor on account of services rendered to the Protector [3]. In 1664 South was incorporated D.D. at Cambridge and given a sinecure in Wales by Clarendon.

On the fall of the Chancellor [4] in 1667 South became chaplain to the Duke of York. By then he had preached several times at Whitehall and at Westminster Abbey and was highly valued by Charles II, who made him one of his chaplains in ordinary. As Public Orator of the University he had delivered a Latin speech to the King when he visited Oxford in 1663, and again when the Court came to Oxford during the plague in 1665, and he had also preached to the Queen on that occasion ; he had delivered the funeral oration (in Latin) on the death of Archbishop Juxon in 1663. In May 1669 he had to congratulate Cosmo de Medici on

---

to the Gallows ; and by his scornful revilings and jests, to set the Court on a laughter, [and] was suddenly, in the pulpit, (without any sickness) surprized with astonishment, worse than Dr South, the Oxford Orator, had been before him ", see *ibid.*, III, 36.

[1] *Memoirs*, p. 16.

[2] *Ibid.* Wood gives a more colourful account of this, reiterating the charge that S. had preached against the King's cause when he " closed with the independents ", and adding that *all* the B.D's and M.A's opposed the passing of Clarendon's letters, but that the proctor " according to his usual perfidy " declared him passed by the majority of the house. *Op. cit.*, p. 637.

[3] See *The Royal Society : Its Origins and Founders*, ed. cit., ' The Rev. John Wallis ', by J.F. Scott, p. 61.

[4] Clarendon resigned his Chancellorship of Oxford University in December 1667 ; Archbishop Sheldon was elected in his place, but never actually and formally took up the Chancellorship (see F. MADAN, *op. cit.*, III, 212). In August 1669 James Butler, Duke of Ormonde, was elected Chancellor of the University (*ibid.*, p. 229).

behalf of the University, and in July he spoke at the dedication
of the Sheldonian Theatre. In this speech he lavished praise on
Archbishop Sheldon and on Wren, but his attack on the Royal
Society as underminers of the Universities [1] (i.e. because the Society
proposed to grant University degrees) offended not only Evelyn
but John Wallis [2]. The year after he was installed canon of Christ
Church.

South must have remained on good terms with his former
patron's family for when Laurence Hyde, second son of Clarendon,
was sent as ambassador extraordinary to congratulate Sobieski on
his election to the throne of Poland, he took South with him as
his chaplain. South resigned from the office of Public Orator
in October 1677 [3] and on December 16, 1677, he sent an account
of his travels to his friend and fellow-canon at Christ Church,
Edward Pocock, then Regius professor of Hebrew. This letter,
published by Curll as part of the *Memoirs*, shows that South took
an interest in the history and geography of the country he visited,
in its religious and economic affairs, in the state of learning, in the
laws, language and customs of the people, in the privileges and
in the administration of the cities, etc. Though not a systematic
report, South's letter is full of interesting details and of keen
observations on things and people. Shortly after his return he
became rector of Islip in Oxfordshire (1678). There he rebuilt
the Chancel of the Church (1680), built a new parsonage, and,
as Wood himself remarks, " exercised much his charity there ".
Indeed Thomas Hearne noted in his diary on 28 November, 1705 :

> Dr South told Dr Hudson that he was resolved never to
> pocket a farthing of the income of the parsonage of Islip,
> and that he had already new built and beautified the chancel
> of the church, built a noble parsonage house, with outhouses
> and all other conveniences, both for the parson and tennant :
> and that besides he had all along sent several boys to schole,

---

[1] John EVELYN : *Diary, ed. cit.*, III, 531-2 (9 July, 1669).

[2] See the letter from John Wallis to Robert Boyle, dated 17 July, 1669 :
" After the voting of this letter, Dr South, as university orator, made a long
oration. The first part of which consisted of satyrical invectives against
Cromwell, fanaticks, the Royal Society, and new philosophy ; the next of
encomiasticks in praise of the Archbishop, the Theatre, the Vice-Chancellor,
the architect, and the painter ; the last, of execrations against fanaticks, con-
venticles, comprehension, and new philosophy ; damning them *ad inferos, ad
gehennam* ". Robert BOYLE : *Works*, ed. Thomas Birch, London, 1744, V, 514.

[3] Autograph in the Bodleian Library, MS. Rawlinson, C. 936 f. 57. South's
successor as Public Orator was Thomas Cradock.

and bound them out to apprentiships, and has lately purchased some land to be settled upon the parish for ever,
for these uses.   And that moreover he intended to lay out
what he had received from his canonry of Christ Church,
upon small vicarages, and as Dr Hudson inferred from something in his discourse, upon such vicarages as belonged to
Christ Church [1].

According to the author of the *Memoirs* the living was worth 200*l*
per *annum* ; " out of his generous temper " South allowed his
curate 100*l* and expended the rest " in educating and apprenticing
the poorer children of that place " [2].   Wood's account of South's
life in *Athenae Oxonienses* closes at this point ; he merely adds that
" to this day, (Apr. I an. 1694)" South kept his rectory, sinecure
and two prebendships, but lived upon his temporal estate at Caversham near Reading

> in a discontented and clamorous condition for want of more
> preferment (as many people in Oxon think) or else respect
> and adoration which he gapes after [3].

Perhaps Wood thought that since South no longer lived at Oxford
he could not faithfully report his doings.   He might, however,
have mentioned that South was recommended for the see of Oxford
in 1686 on the death of John Fell, since this was at least matter
connected with the place whose history he was writing.   Whatever
Wood's gall his last sentences sum up adequately the main charac-
teristics of the divine he disliked so much : his charity and his
bitterness.

South was probably justified in feeling discontent, for when
he was once preaching before the King at Westminster Abbey,
Charles is said to have remarked to Lord Rochester :

> *Ods fish,* Lory, *Your Chaplain must be a Bishop, therefore
> put me in mind of him at the next Death* [4].

But Charles must have forgotten this promise, as he did so many

---

[1] *Reliquiae Hearnianae, op. cit.,* I, 68.
[2] *Op. cit.,* p. 106.
[3] *Op. cit.,* p. 637.
[4] *Memoirs,* p. 108.   This remark is usually said to have been made when
South was preaching on *Prov.* XVI.33, in which sermon he gave an account of
" such a bankrupt, beggarly fellow as Cromwell, first entering the Parliament
House with a threadbare, torn Cloak and a greasy Hat " ; but this sermon as
published by South (*op. cit.,* I, ser. 8) is dated 22 February, 1685, at which
time Charles II was dead.

others. When South was offered an Archbishopric in Ireland after
the accession of James II [1], he declined the offer. According to
the author of the *Memoirs*, James also found South unacceptable when the Earl of Rochester proposed him as a champion
of the cause of the Church against two Romanists nominated by
the King, because then as always South denounced all attempts
at toleration which were canvassed with equal zeal by both Papists
and Dissenters. On the death of John Fell, Evelyn noted in his
diary that South was among the candidates for the bishopric of
Oxford and the Deanery of Christ Church, but he added :

> Dr Walker (now apostatizing) came to Court, and was
> doubtlesse very buisy [2].

Though he was recommended for this office by no less a man
than Archbishop Sancroft [3], South was not preferred. It is easy
to guess why such a staunch opponent of all indulgences was not
acceptable to James II, but South seems to have been accused of
having, in a letter shown to the King, reflected upon Obadiah
Walker, Master of University College, who was celebrating mass
in his College, for on 26 August he wrote to Sancroft to clear
himself of the charge [4]. Samuel Parker was elevated to the see
of Oxford, while John Massey was made Dean of Christ Church.
This was clearly part of James's " policy of infiltration " [5], since
both were known for their leanings to Rome.

At the Revolution, South, who had been loyal to his King even
though he could not countenance his religious policy [6], was faced
with a difficult choice. Bishop Kennett noted in his biographical
memoranda that South

---

[1] *Ibid.*, p. 110. The offer was made through the recommendation of
Laurence Hyde, then Earl of Rochester and Lord High Treasurer of England,
and of his brother, the Earl of Clarendon, then Lord Lieutenant of Ireland.

[2] *Op. cit.*, IV, 519 (11 July, 1686).

[3] See Sancroft's letter to the King in : George D'OYLY : *The Life of
William Sancroft, Archbishop of Canterbury*, London, 1821, I, 234. The letter,
dated 29 July, 1686, is in the Bodleian Library (Tanner MS. 30 f. 91). South
was more than willing to accept this office : see his letter of thanks to Sancroft
in the Bodleian Library, Tanner MS. 30, f. 91 (dated 27 July, 1686).

[4] The letter, dated 26 August, 1686, is in the Bodleian Library (Tanner
MS. 30, ff. 109-10).

[5] David OGG, *op. cit.*, p. 167.

[6] Wood records that on the reception of James II at Oxford, in September
1687, the King " talked to Dr (Robert) South and commended his preaching,
whereupon he answered that he alwaies did and would shew himself loyall in
his preaching, or to that effect ". *Life and Times, op. cit.*, III, 238.

made a demurr upon submitting to the Revolution, and thought himself deceived by Dr Sherlock, which was the true foundation of the bitter difference in writing about the Trinity [1].

Both Sherlock and South hesitated about taking the oaths of allegiance to William and Mary. As appears from letters exchanged between them and from an account of their discussions written by South, Sherlock changed his mind at least twice : he first declared himself ready to take the oaths ; then he argued against the lawfulness of them and wished " to suppress all report of his previous discourse in favour of them " [2], even accusing South of spreading the report ; finally—after the battle of the Boyne—he decided to comply. By July 1689, however, South had satisfied himself that it was lawful to take the oaths [3], but Sherlock's change of front, together with his accusations, must have rankled, for the books South wrote against Sherlock in the Trinitarian controversy " are spiced with allusions to breaking of oaths and turning of coats " [4]. The same view of Sherlock is reflected in a letter from Locke to Molyneux, dated 22 February, 1697 ; since Locke and South were exchanging friendly letters at the time South may have been the informant who told the author of the *Essay* what to think of his adversary [5]. South must have felt the more bitter when Sherlock was made Dean of St. Paul's under the new sovereigns [6]. He himself refused the offer of one of the sees vacated by the Non-Jurors in 1691, declaring

that notwithstanding he himself saw nothing that was contrary to the Laws of God, and the common practice of all

[1] British Museum MS. Lansdowne 987, f. 242 v.

[2] The letters and an extract from this account were first published by W.M.T. DODDS in ' Robert South and William Sherlock : Some Unpublished Letters ', in *MLR*, XXXIX (1944), 215-24.

[3] *Ibid.*, p. 216. In his answer to Sherlock's ' base letter ' South reminds him of this : " Sir, I do again affirm that Sovereign Power actually possess'd (especially without consent and call of the people) answers all or most of the ends of Government and that bare Right or Title void of such power answers no end or use of Government at all, and I leave it to you to prove the contrary position if you can. ". *Ibid.*, p. 217. For a different view, see SWIFT : *Sentiments of a Church-of-England Man*, sect. II, in *Prose Works*, ed. cit., II, 13-16.

[4] W.M.T. DODDS, *loc. cit.*, p. 215.

[5] For quotation see Ch. II, p. 96, n. 8. On 18 July, 1704, South drew Locke's attention to the base accusations against him in Sherlock's *Discourse Concerning the Happiness of Good Men and the Punishment of the Wicked in the Next World* (1704). See Bodleian MS. Locke, C. 18, f. 174.

[6] When Tillotson became Archbishop of Canterbury.

Nations to submit to Princes in Possession of the Throne, yet others might have their Reasons for contrary Opinion ; and he bless'd God, that he was neither so Ambitious, nor in want of Preferment, as for the sake of it, to build his Rise upon the Ruines of any one Father of the Church, who for Piety, good Morals, and strictness of Life which every one of the Deprived Bishops were famed for might be said not to have left their Equal[1].

Though South had taken the oaths he could not be reconciled to the Act of Toleration and he actively opposed all schemes for comprehension with the Dissenters. In his sermons he repeatedly warned against the danger to the Church of altering the ritual so as to please the Nonconformists. Such innovations smacked too much of those proposed in the forties, which resulted in " reforming the Churches to the ground " ; all attempts to restore the pristine purity of the divine service would only leave the Church naked and all the more exposed to the danger of Socinianism. Tirelessly South denounced this danger and the fallacy of the plea of tender consciences. To him this was a repetition of the war waged earlier in the century against his beloved Church, and, not unnaturally, he fought with as much violence as he had in the sixties in order to preserve the Restoration settlement. In fact he was fighting a rearguard action[2] which his former patron, Clarendon,

---

[1] *Memoirs*, p. 115.

[2] See, for instance, the Epistle Dedicatory to the University of Oxford in his second volume of sermons, dated 17 November, 1693 :

"Amongst which, the chief Design of some of them (i.e. sermons) is to assert the Rights and Constitutions of our excellently Reformed Church, which of late we so often hear reproached (in the modish Dialect of the present Times) by the name of *Little Things* ; and that in order to their being laid aside, not only as *Little*, but *Superfluous*. But for my own part, I can account nothing *Little* in any Church, which has the Stamp of undoubted Authority, and the Practice of primitive Antiquity, as well as the Reason and Decency of the Thing itself, to warrant and support it. Though, if the supposed Littleness of these matters should be a sufficient Reason for the laying them aside, I fear, our Church will be found to have more *Little Men* to spare, than *Little Things*.

But I have observed all along, that while this *Innovating* Spirit has been striking at the *Constitutions* of our Church, the same has been giving several bold and scurvy strokes at some of her *Articles* too : An evident Demonstration to me, that whensoever her *Discipline* shall be destroy'd, her Doctrine will not long survive it. " (*Op. cit.*, II, sig. A 2 v - A 3.)

See also his letter to Dr. Finch, Warden of All Souls, dated 19 November, 1695, relating that a number of divines having waited upon the Court near Althrop had been summarily dismissed, while the Dissenters were entertained sumptuously. (Bodleian Library MS. Ballard, vol. 34, p. 16.) See also his letter to Dr. Charlett, Master of University College, dated 11 May, 1695, urging him to accept the Vice-Chancellorship when Dr. Aldrich would leave, because

would certainly have approved, and he was as much out of step
with the then leaders of the hierarchy as the Lord Chancellor had
been with the merry gang of Charles II. No wonder he was bitter
and discontented.

Meanwhile he began to prepare his sermons for the press, and
the first collected volume appeared in 1692. But other matters
also engaged his energy. In 1690 Arthur Bury had published *The
Naked Gospel* ; a spate of Socinian tracts followed, expounding
views similar to those put forward in Stephen Nye's *A Briefe
History of the Unitarians, called also Socinians* (1687), which had
been published at the suggestion of Thomas Firmin, a friend of
Tillotson's. William Sherlock promptly entered the lists and in
1690 published *A Vindication of the Doctrine of the Holy and
Ever Blessed Trinity, and the Incarnation of the Son of God.*
(Imprimatur, June 9, 1690). Unfortunately Sherlock was no trained
controversialist, and his book did more harm than good to the cause
he had espoused. South was quick to seize this opportunity to turn
the tables on the man who had accused him of treachery. In
*Animadversions upon Dr Sherlock's Book Entituled A Vindication
of...*, published anonymously in 1693, he demonstrated that far
from having proved three distinct persons in the Godhead, Sherlock,
now Dean of St. Paul's, had proved three distinct gods, and
shown by his very explanations that he did not know the true
nature of the mysteries of faith, which is to be above reason.
South reiterated his attacks in *Tritheism Charged upon Dr Sherlock's New Notion of the Trinity* (1695)[1] and in other works which
recent research has conclusively attributed to him [2]. The Trinitarian controversy raged for several years until the King interposed (February 1693) and directed the archbishops and bishops
to allow no preacher to express any doctrine other than that contained in the three Creeds and in the Thirty-Nine Articles [3]. South

as a true Church-of-England man he would be able to defend the Church, now
" browbeaten and runn down by Whiggs and Latitudinarians " (Bodleian Library
MS. Ballard, vol. 34, f. 17).

[1] In answer to Sherlock's *Defence* of his *Vindication*, published in 1695.

[2] W.M.T. DODDS, *loc. cit.*, attributes to him *A Short History of Valentinus
Gentilis the Tritheist ... Wrote in Latin, by Benedictus Aretius ... and now
Translated into English for the use of Dr Sherlock ...* (1696) and *Decreti Oxo-
niensis Vindicatio* (1696). The latter is a vindication of the Decree of Convocation censuring the Fellow of University College, Oxford, who in a sermon
had asserted the same principles as Dr. Sherlock.

[3] Unitarianism was officially condemned when, on 3 January, 1694, the
Lords spiritual and temporal ordered Their Majesties' Attorney-General to pro-

obeyed, but he resented the liberty taken by his opponent's friend Edward Stillingfleet, then Bishop of Worcester, in referring to the controversy in the preface to his *Vindication of the Trinity* (1696, written in answer to Toland's *Christianity Not Mysterious*). When South published the third volume of his collected sermons in 1698, he referred, in the Epistle Dedicatory to Narcissus Boyle, Archbishop of Dublin, to the royal injunctions for composing disputes about the Trinity, and he glanced at the bishop who had debased his style and character so low as to defend the Tritheist. Included in this volume was a sermon South had preached at Westminster Abbey in 1694 on *Christianity Mysterious, and the Wisdom of God in Making it so*, in which he not only refers to the many innovations and blasphemies against the Christian doctrine, as well as to the naked truths and naked gospels published in recent years, but clearly glances at Sherlock when he says :

> he who thinks and says he can understand all *Mysteries,* and resolve all *Controversies,* undeniably shews, that he really understands none [1].

What with preaching, collecting his sermons, and writing against Sherlock, South must have been very busy during the nineties. One cannot help wondering if he had time to spare on that other controversy in which several Christ-Church men engaged at the time, and if so, whether he shared their views. It was Henry Aldrich, Dean of the College, who requested Charles Boyle to edit the *Epistles of Phalaris* (published 1695) after Temple's *Essays on Ancient and Modern Learning* had appeared. When, in the Appendix to the second edition of Wotton's *Reflections on Ancient and Modern Learning* (1697), Bentley proved that the *Letters* were spurious, Boyle set out to defend their genuineness (1698) and was helped in this task by other Christ-Church men : Atterbury, Smallridge and Alsop. South could hardly have remained ignorant of this ; our complete lack of information on the view he took of this quarrel is the more irritating since the controversy was to prompt a young satirist whose wit is akin to South's to write *The Battle of the Books*.

South was now more and more estranged from the hierarchy,

---

secute the author and the printer of *A Brief but Clear Confutation of the Doctrine of the Trinity.*

[1] *Op. cit.,* III, ser. 6, pp. 251-2.

but he was probably active among his brethren in the Lower House
of Convocation, whose opposition to the Latitudinarian bishops he
may have abetted.   He was keeping abreast of the latest developments in philosophy and of other works published at the time : he
read Locke's replies to Stillingfleet, and approved of them, as he
did of Locke's confutation of Malebranche (not yet published);
he thought so highly of the *Essay* that he suggested that Locke
should have it translated into Latin so as to reach a wider public ;
and he also drew Locke's attention to Sherlock's aspersions on his
philosophy and character[1].   His spirits must have revived on the
accession of Queen Anne.   If William had protected the Dissenters, the High-Church Queen might be counted upon to reverse
his policy.   The Tories were quick to launch an attack against the
Act of Toleration, though some years went by before they could
take the most decisive step against the Dissenters.   South must
have approved of the Schism Act (1714), which aimed at destroying the Dissenting academies, for he chose to publish, as the first
sermon in his fifth volume[2], a discourse on the virtuous education
of youth which he had prepared to deliver at Westminster School
in 1685 and in which he advocated the suppression of such academies[3].   He must also have welcomed the Occasional Conformity
Bill (1711), for in several sermons he had derided the men of
tender conscience who did not scruple to conform occasionally in
order to be allowed to hold office.   The death of the Queen and
the final triumph of the Whigs must have shattered his hopes for
ever, and we can well believe his biographer, who reports that on
the death of Queen Anne, South told a friend

That it was time for him to prepare for his Journey to a

---

[1] See the five letters from South to Locke preserved in the Bodleian Library
(MS. Locke C. 18) and dated : 25 March, 1697 ; 22 September, 1697 ; 18 June,
1699 ; 6 December, 1699 ; and 18 July, 1704.   In the essay on South in
J.E. KEMPE, *op. cit.*, W.C. Lake said that South may have had a part in the
expulsion of Locke from Christ Church. Lake does not cite his source. Nothing
of this appears in the various accounts of Locke's ' expulsion ' (see, for instance :
Lord GRENVILLE : *Oxford and Locke*, 1829 ; Peter KING : *Life of John Locke*,
London, 1830 ; Ch.J. FOX : *A History of the Early Part of the Reign of James
the Second*, London, 1857 ; Lord MACAULAY : *History of England from the
Accession of James II*, London, 1861, vol. I ; H.R. FOX BOURNE : *Life of John
Locke*, London, 1876, vol. I).   Nor was South present when the King's mandate
for the removal of Locke from his studentship was " read in chapter and ordered
to be put in execution " (see the Chapter Book of Christ Church, from 20 March,
1648 to 24 December, 1688, f. 249, 15 November, 1684).

[2] Published after his death, but prepared for the press by himself.

[3] Since South revised his sermons for publication this may be a later addition.

blessed Immortality ; since all that was Good, and Gracious, the very Breath of his Nostrils had made its Departure to the Regions of Bliss, and Eternal Happiness [1].

His health was failing—according to the *Memoirs* he had a " bloody flux " followed by " the Strangury " about the time he published his third volume of sermons (1698)—and

> During the greatest part of the Reign of Queen *Anne*, he was in a State of Inactivity, and the Infirmities of Old Age growing upon him, he performed very little of the Duties of his Ministerial Function, otherwise than when his health would allow of his going to the Abbey Church at *West-minster*, to be present at Divine Service [2].

Now as ever spiteful tongues were ready to blame him for excessive or foolish criticism, and he did his best to protect himself against such slanderers [3]. He could still be active in behalf of his friends [4] or of High-Churchmen : we are told that he interceded in favour of Dr. Sacheverell when this high-flying Tory was brought to trial, and that when almost on his deathbed he had himself carried to Westminster in order to cast his vote in favour of the late Duke of Ormonde's brother as Chancellor of Oxford University [5]. But when, on the death of Sprat in 1713, he was offered the deanery

---

[1] *Memoirs*, p. 138.

[2] *Ibid.*, p. 136.

[3] See his letter to Robert Freind, Second Master of Westminster School, dated 27 April, 1706, in which he complains of having his name traduced through the folly of an indiscreet person at Oxford, who had preached an inflammatory sermon, and asks Freind to lay the matter plainly before the Bishop of Exeter, John Trelawney (a Christ-Church man and one of the seven Bishops imprisoned by James II), British Museum MS. Loan 29/193 (Portland Papers) f. 115. The canons of Christ Church were eager to clear both South and their College of such malicious imputations, for William Stratford wrote to a friend on 22 April, 1706, asking him to warn South, and again on 27 April, to Robert Harley, on the same subject. See *Harley Papers*, ed. by the Historical Manuscripts Commission, London, 1891, vol. IV, pp. 295, 297.

[4] See his letter of 18 Nov. 1703, to Dr. Hudson, Headkeeper of the Bodleian Library, asking him to assist a London physician in finding the books he needs (British Museum MS. Sloane 4276, f. 86).

[5] *Memoirs*, pp. 137, 139. The Duke of Ormonde, who was Chancellor of Oxford University, died in 1688. Convocation was hastily summoned to prevent the King appointing one of his nominees, and elected as Chancellor the late Duke's Grandson James Butler, now second Duke of Ormonde (who married the daughter of South's patron, Laurence Hyde, then Earl of Rochester). In 1715 the Duke of Ormonde was impeached for communicating with the Pretender, fled to France, and was attainted. His brother Charles, Earl of Arran, thus had a double claim on South's loyalty (it was he who, in his capacity as Chancellor, conferred the M.A. degree on Johnson after the completion of his *Dictionary* in 1755).

of Westminster, South declined the honour [1], and his friend Francis
Atterbury, then Dean of Christ Church, became Dean of Westminster as well as Bishop of Rochester.

South seems to have resided most of the time at Caversham [2],
corresponding with his friends at Oxford and preparing his sermons
for the press. He probably preached very little, if at all, in his
last years, for he suffered a " paralytic blow " in 1710 and in 1712
complained of dizziness in the head [3]. William Stratford, who
visited him several times at Caversham, thought in August 1713
that South was beginning " to fail in his understanding " [4]; if so
the change must have come pretty quickly, for in his letter to the
Earl of Oxford, dated 8 June, 1713, declining the deanery of
Westminster, South appears at his best, spicing his gratitude with
irony, but expressing it with a flourish worthy of such a rhetorician.
Besides, he was then preparing his fourth volume of sermons for
the press, and was to prepare two more before his death. Perhaps
Stratford's impression came from the fact that, as South complained
to Dr. Sloane, the paralytic blow had bereft him of the plainness
of his speech.

If South ever failed in his understanding, he had certainly
recovered by the time he made his will on 30 March, 1714, and
when he added codicils to it on 2 June of the same year. Thomas
Hearne found that South " made but a foolish will " because he
left all he had (apart from many bequests!) " to a widow that
lived with him " [5]. Bishop Kennett, on the other hand, was content
to note in his memoranda that South " left her the greatest part
of his Estate, which got her an able husband " [6]. That ' arrant

---

[1] See his letter to Harley, quoted pp. 231-2.
[2] See his Last Will and Testament, Memoirs, p. 80: " Also to the poor
of the Parish of Cavesham, alias Caversham, in Oxfordshire, where I have dwelt
for many years last past, I give Ten Pounds, ... "
[3] See his letters to Dr. Sloane in the British Museum, Addit. MS. 4043,
f. 47 (31 May, 1712), f. 118 (Christmas Day, 1712), f. 247 (24 April, 1714).
[4] See his letter to Edward Harley, in the Harley Papers, ed. cit., VII, 261.
[5] Op. cit., I, 365.
[6] British Museum MS. Lansdowne 987, f. 242. South left all his lands
" in or bordering upon the parish of Cavesham, alias Caversham, in the County
of Oxon ", as well as those in Kentish Town, to Mrs. Margaret Hammond and
her assigns " during her natural life, without impeachment of, or for any manner
of Waste whatsoever, done or committed during her time of Widowhood or
single Life only, which from my heart I desire she would continue to her Lives
end, and that for her own sake and interest, as well as my satisfaction, for that
otherwise neither she nor I can tell what havock an Husband will make upon
the Premises ". See South's Last Will and Testament, in Memoirs, p. 70.

knave' Curll, who specialized in this kind of publications, included South's Last Will and Testament in the *Memoirs*, so that all could read the long list of benefactions South had designed : to Christ Church, to the Bodleian Library (for buying books), to the incumbents of several vicarages, to poor ministers' widows, etc. If South was bitter and could lash out against his own or his Church's enemies, he could also, as Wood himself noted, exercise his charity on a large scale.

★
★ ★

In his memoranda Bishop Kennett wrote that South " had a great deal of ill nature with a good deal of good humour, and good manners in him "[1]. Evelyn, as well as Burnet, found him an ill-natured man ; Wood thought him an insolent fellow embittered by his failure to get preferment ; Humphrey Prideaux wrote to a friend that South was perpetually discontented[2]. From his heartless joke to the ailing Wood it is easy to imagine that South's sharp tongue must have made him many enemies. It is equally clear from his sermons that he could never suffer fools gladly, and from his treatment of Sherlock that he could be merciless when striking at his adversaries. Far from compounding disputes, he went out of his way to join issue with his enemies, whether dead or alive[3]. Yet, if he could not restrain his tongue nor forget an injury, if he was always ready to wound or rail, those he attacked appear to have been guilty in his eyes of more than personal offence. He had the temper of a crusader and dealt his blows without respect of persons, charging at any that seemed to him to insult at the honour due to the Church. He was not the man to compromise ; as his biographer says,

> Lukewarmness in Devotion was what his Soul abhor'd, and
> he look'd upon *Sectarists* of all sorts, as Enemies, who tho'

---

[1] *Loc. cit.*, f. 242v.

[2] " A Mr Wal (i.e. George Walls) is of a restless disposition... and will never enjoy tranquillity of mind, but envy and discontent will perpetually be knawering there. Dr South and he are almost of the same disposition as to this point, perpetually discontented. " Humphrey PRIDEAUX, Dean of Norwich : *Letters to John Ellis 1674-1722*, ed. E.M. Thompson, London, 1875, p. 56 (2 February, 1677).

[3] See his footnote to sermon 12, in vol. III (1698) ridiculing a sentence in one of Tillotson's sermons (T. had died in 1694).

different in Persuasion, join'd together in Attempts for the
Destruction of the Holy Catholick Church [1].

He heaped ridicule and contempt upon the enemies of the Church,
and in his zeal for God's House he did not stop to distinguish or
to inquire into motives : all were branded as dangerous fanatics
who did not wholeheartedly espouse the cause of the Church as
established by law.   As a consequence his world, no less than
Bunyan's, seems to be the battleground of angels of light and
angels of darkness ; with no less violence than Bunyan he denounces all those who, in one way or another, truckle to the powers
of darkness.   His outright rejection of any plea for accommodation
or toleration, his relentless opposition to any form of relief for
men of a different persuasion, suggest the singleness of purpose of
the Christian soldiers of an earlier generation.   A staunch champion of unity in doctrine and discipline, he resisted the tide that
was gathering momentum in this sceptical age, an age that was
ultimately to learn the benefits of toleration.   No wonder South
felt stranded on a strange shore after the Whig revolution had
triumphed ;   no wonder his bitterness increased and he felt discontented.   Yet this was the man who, in the late nineties, was
writing to his " worthy esteemed " friend Locke, taking delight in
his work and commending his philosophy.   Whatever his prejudices, he must have had a mind of a high order to value the apostle
of tolerance, and to have been thought worthy by him of perusing
the new chapters of the *Essay* as they were written : far from
joining in the outcry against the *Essay*, South ascribed the opposition to it to spite and envy, probably sensing rightly that Locke
was being attacked, not for the philosophy he was expounding,
but for being the author of *The Reasonableness of Christianity*.
If South was adamant on the subject of the Dissenters, if he refused
to acknowledge the sincerity of their plea, it is probably because
he formed his views at a time when the mere idea of toleration
could not even be entertained, and he never changed his position.
He championed an order that was fast disappearing, and in this
as in so much else he resembles the Tory satirists of the next age,
Swift and Pope ;   like them he thought that the accession of the
Hanovrians ushered in the reign of Dullness, like them too he used

---

[1] *Memoirs*, p. 113.

the power of his wit to defend right thinking against all encroachments of ' dullness '.

As Allibone quaintly puts it, South was " equally distinguished
for learning, wit, loyalty, pecuniary generosity, personal disinter-
estedness, and theological and political intolerance " [1]. His wit was
probably resented more deeply than his intolerance ; among his
fellow-Anglicans many were as ready as he was to have the Dissenters persecuted, but to him alone was paid the honour of being
called the scourge of fanaticism. He was Charles II's favourite
preacher and highly valued by the wits, but his reputation as a
witty preacher has done him more harm than good. Johnson's
robust sense made him prefer South to the tamer Tillotson [2] ; but
many turned away, shocked if not disgusted by South's sallies,
or were unable to stomach his strong arguments and strong language. South was to be accused again and again of debasing the
pulpit by his unseemly wit, even by reverend gentlemen who should
have recognized that many of his ' indecent ' metaphors had their
source in Scripture ; but by then the Bible too needed to be bowd-
lerized, and such strong meat was no longer acceptable from a
preacher. Like Swift South has suffered for calling a spade a
spade ; even those who could appreciate his qualities often warned
their readers that he was to be admired but not imitated [3].

Barrow knew how multiform a thing is wit, and South certainly
exemplified various kinds of it in his sermons, from buffoonery in
the pulpit, or at least something like it [4], to what Pope would have

---

[1] *Op. cit.*

[2] *Boswell's Life of Johnson*, ed. cit., III, 247-8.

[3] Characteristic of this attitude is the view expressed by G.G. PERRY in
his *History of the Church of England from the death of Elizabeth to the Present
Time*, London, 1864, II, 660 : " For popularity in sermons, South stands preeminent, no man being so much followed and so much valued by the wits. But
the popularity of South was a vicious one, and though possessed of great genius
and skill, he owed the favour with which he was regarded to his constant and
somewhat scurrilous attacks on the fanatics and the rebels. A man who was
admired because he ventured upon a nearer approach to buffoonery in the pulpit
than others dared to do, can scarcely have a high reputation as a divine, whatever may belong to him as a clever, caustic and witty writer. "

[4] Bishop Kennett notes in his memoranda that South " laboured very much
to compose his sermons, and in the pulpit workt up his body when he came to a
piece or any notable saying ", *loc. cit.*, p. 242v. Mark Noble defends South's
use of wit as follows : " It has been objected that he preached wit : he thought,
perhaps, that in Charles II's reign, as wit was the instrument of profligacy,
it was lawful to make it the vehicle to teach religion and to deter from vice ",
and in a footnote he relates the following story : " Preaching before Charles II
and his equally profligate courtiers, he perceived in the middle of his sermon
that sleep had taken possession of his hearers. Stopping and changing the

called true wit (Addison might not have concurred, but then he was somewhat mealy-mouthed himself and preferred the more moderate, and duller, Tillotson [1]). South's characteristic kind of wit is first and foremost an acuteness and subtlety of thought given a clear outline and a sharp edge by the accurate phrasing, which is often though not always pointed. It is a gift for thinking clearly and for expressing his thought with precision, in a nervous sentence, eschewing all decoration but often rendering it more concrete by a vivid metaphor; a gift for terse and pregnant statements in a closely argued demonstration as well as for lively images illuminating the meaning; a gift for the telling phrase that etches out the thought and drives it home with the swiftness and ease of an arrow. For the movement is easy and natural, the syntax is that of speech so that the colloquial phrase comes as naturally as the exact definition; the proverb is as much at home in such discourse as the Scriptural or the homely metaphor, and the concrete image demonstrates as much as does the abstract reasoning. Though South had ample store of learning and had been trained in the subtle methods of the Schools, his sermons are unencumbered by pedantic references to authorities; these he merely mentions without giving chapter and verse for them, so that his demonstration moves along lightly. He leaves out all superfluities, compressing instead of expanding, arguing instead of considering. Whereas Barrow develops all the places in his theme, South demonstrates the whys and wherefores, states the objections and refutes them: he is the dialectician setting forth the logical basis of his propositions, and rounding off his argument when he can write Q.E.D.

---

tone of his voice, he called thrice to Lord Lauderdale, who, awakened, stood up: "My Lord" says South very composedly "I am sorry to interrupt your repose, but I must beg that you will not snore quite so loud, lest you should awaken his majesty", and then as calmly continued his discourse." Mark NOBLE, op. cit., I, 100.

[1] The Tatler praised South's "admirable discourse" on The Ways of Pleasantness (sermon 1 in vol. I) saying that "this charming discourse has in it whatever wit and wisdom can put together" and quoted an extract from it, The Tatler, no. 205 (Saturday July 29 to Tuesday Aug. 1, 1710). This must be the only time a sermon by South was said to be charming. It is characteristic of the aim pursued by The Tatler, as well as of the public the periodical was intended for, that this particular sermon was recommended to the readers. These must have been surprised on turning to the full text, for the passage quoted in no way suggests the main drift of the sermon, i.e. not only that the pleasures of the mind are the only true ones, but that "it is only a pious life, led exactly by the rules of a severe religion, that can authorize a man's conscience to speak comfortably to him". Op. cit., I, 23 (my italics).

Whereas Barrow forever amplifies, his sentences no less than his theme, South condenses even to epigrammatic brevity. Hence the impression of pungency and directness. Sometimes he demonstrates by means of narrative, as he does in the sermon of 30 January ; but here again his relation must be followed step by step for each point tells in the total effect. While one is often tempted to skip some of Barrow's developments, to miss one stage in South's argument is fatal, so strict is the logic of his development. Of course he sometimes offers various reasons to establish one point, but in general they move gradually nearer to the centre or to a climax.

Though both Barrow and South build their sermons on the same pattern, i.e. explication, confirmation and application, the total effect is quite different. While Barrow's impress the reader through the cumulative weight of his considerations, South's exercise the mind through the quick movement of his arguments. Not only does South rely on demonstration rather than authorities, but he eschews all unnecessary explications. He can apply his learning to the elucidation of a text and compare various versions of it, or define the exact meaning [1] of a term on which he grounds his argument : most often, however, he grounds his explication on the plain meaning of the text as it appears from the context. The sermon recommended to the readers of *The Tatler* [2], on the pleasantness of religion (1665), is as good an example as any of South's usual manner. His text is *Prov.* III. 7 *Her ways are ways of pleasantness* [3]. He first distinguishes between pleasure and sensuality, and refutes the notion that religion designs to make the world a great monastery since the aim of religion is not to thwart but to perfect nature. He then states the objection that self-denial and the discipline of the Cross are required of men for them to become disciples of Christ ; to which he answers first that pleasure is a relative thing, second that the state of man by nature differs from the state of man by grace, since in the former the sensitive appetites rule while in the latter " reason sways the sceptre ". He next faces

---

[1] For instance in the sermon on the Trinity, printed below ; or in the sermon on the Resurrection (III, 10), where he compares the version of the Septuagint with the Hebrew text in order to explain the meaning of the text from the Acts ; or again, in a sermon on *Luke* XI. 35 (III, 2), he distinguishes between the two meanings of *recta ratio* before expounding his text ; or in a sermon on *Isa.* LIII. 8 (III, 9) he examines the various interpretations given to the text in order to prove that it refers to Christ.

[2] See note 1, p. 256.   [3] *Op. cit.*, I, ser. 1.

the further objection that to pass from one state to the other is a laborious and irksome task. He therefore defines the nature of repentance, which implies both sorrow for sin and a change of life ; but the sorrow is sweetened by the prospect of deliverance and the difficulty of changing lies in the first entrance into the new life. Having refuted the opposite view, he can now expound the properties that enhance the pleasure of religion : first, it is the proper pleasure of man's mind, whether considered as pleasure of speculation (i.e. of the understanding) or of practice (i.e. of conscience) ; second, it is a pleasure that never satiates ; third, this pleasure is in nobody's power but in his that has it. From all which he concludes : ways that are not of pleasantness are not truly ways of religion, no bodily exercise can touch the soul, for " it is not the back, but the heart that must bleed for sin ".

Barrow also preached on the same text (1661), and the difference in method appears at once if we compare the two sermons [1]. While South simply refers to the context to make clear that by wisdom is meant religion, Barrow begins by explaining the words of his text, and he defines wisdom as " an habitual skill or faculty of judging aright about matters of practice, and chusing according to that right judgment, and conforming the actions to such good choice ". Important differences follow from this, for Barrow's definition of wisdom makes the text almost a tautology ; indeed, a malicious reader might suggest that all he sets out to show is that wisdom is wise. After the explication he proceeds to develop the reasons to confirm the text, and he lists no less than sixteen of them : 1. wisdom is delectable because it is a revelation of truth and a detection of error ; 2. it is pleasant in its consequences ; 3. it assures us that we take the best course ; 4. it begets in us a hope of success in our actions ; 5. it prevents discouragement ; 6. it makes all the troubles incident to life bearable ; 7. it has always a good conscience attending it ; 8. it confers a facility in action ; 9. it begets a sound complexion of the soul ; 10. it acquaints us with ourselves ; 11. it procures and preserves a constant favour and fair respect of men ; 12. it instructs us to examine, compare and rightly value the objects of our affections ; 13. it distinguishes the circumstances and appoints the fit seasons of action ; 14. it discovers our relations and duties in respect of men ; 15. it acquaints

---

[1] Barrow's is Sermon 1 in vol. I (*op. cit.*).

us with the nature and reason of true religion ; lastly, it attracts the favour of God. Each of these points is amplified by means of further statements of the same kind or of examples. Characteristic of such a treatment is that the order in which the various considerations are listed hardly matters, and that many more could be added, though no present-day reader would wish Barrow had expanded further on this trite theme. Not only is his conception of wisdom much more commonplace and his conception of religion more practical than South's, but his developments soon become tiresome.

When reading South's sermon, on the other hand, the interest never flags [1] because all through is felt the vigorous mind and the active thought moving to its proposed end. The sermon gives the kind of rational pleasure it recommends as superior to mere sensuality : the argument is bracing, the outline clear ; the thought moves forward, the style is direct and easy, whether in the compressed definitions of basic points [2] or in the telling comparisons which bring the truths home to the reader [3]. Some of these images may jolt the reader who is used to more ' refined ' language from the pulpit. Yet it is obvious that the often quoted example of the stillness of the sow at her wash is meant to produce the shock of recognition ; not only is it proper in its context, but South was keeping due decorum in thus branding the pleasures

---

[1] The two sermons are of about the same length. The consecration sermon preached by South (I, 5 ; 25 November, 1666) is also more argumentative than that preached by Barrow (I, 12 ; 4 July, 1663).

[2] For instance : " That Pleasure is Man's chiefest Good, (because indeed it is the perception of Good that is properly Pleasure) is an Assertion most certainly true, though under the common Acceptance of it, not only false, but odious : For according to this, Pleasure and Sensuality pass for Terms equivalent ; and therefore, he that takes it in this Sense, alters the Subject of the Discourse. Sensuality is indeed a Part, or rather one kind of Pleasure, such an one as it is : For Pleasure in general, is the consequent Apprehension of a suitable Object, suitably apply'd to a rightly disposed Faculty ; and so must be conversant both about the Faculties of the Body, and of the Soul respectively ; as being the Result of the Fruitions belonging to both. " *Op. cit.*, I, 2.

[3] For instance : " For there is no doubt, but a Man, while he resigns himself up to brutish Guidance of Sense and Appetite, has no relish at all for the spiritual, refined Delights of a Soul clarified by Grace and Virtue. The Pleasures of an Angel can never be the Pleasures of a Hog. " *Ibid.*, p. 7. Or " The Mind of Man is an image, not only of God's Spirituality, but of his Infinity. It is not like any of the Senses, limited to this or that Kind of Object ... It is (as I may so say) an Ocean, into which all the little Rivulets of Sensation, both external and internal, discharge themselves. " *Ibid.*, p. 7. Or : " How vastly disproportionate are the Pleasures of the Eating, and of the Thinking Man ? Indeed as different as the Silence of an *Archimedes* in the Study of a Problem, and the Stilness of a Sow at her Wash. " *Ibid.*, p. 18.

of the epicure. This, at least, was due decorum as understood by
the true classicists, though it may have offended against the canons
of propriety set up by an effete generation more concerned with
airs and graces or with respectability. South has the same vigour
as Latimer, though none of his roughness ; like him he believed
that congregations should be waked out of their torpor, both
spiritual and physical. That a preacher of God's Word should
use none but gentle or genteel words would have seemed to him
as absurd as to cleanse the Bible of all expressions that might shock
the tender sensibilities of a respectable middle-class reader. He
can be scurrilous or ' indecent ' and has no objection to mudslinging.
In a sermon on the Gunpowder Plot he refers to the Romanists'
doctrine that kings may be lawfully resisted, cast off and deposed,
and says :

> It would be like the stirring of a great Sink, which would
> be likelier to annoy, than to instruct the Auditory, to draw
> out from thence all the Pestilential Doctrines and Practices
> against the Royalty and Supremacy of Princes [1],

after which he proceeds to quote chapter and verse for this, from
Gratian and from papal bulls. Such strong expressions were
required by his theme for, as he said in a sermon on the Execution
of Charles I :

> This is the black Subject and Occasion of this Day's
> Solemnity. In my Reflexions upon which, if a just Indigna-
> tion, or indeed even a due Apprehension of the blackest
> Fact, which the Sun ever saw, since he hid his Face upon
> the Crucifixion of our Saviour, chance to give an Edge to
> some of my Expressions, let all such know, the Guilt of
> whose Actions has made the very strictest Truths look like
> Satyrs, or Sarcasms, and bare Descriptions sharper than
> Invectives : I say, let such Censurers (whose Innocence lies
> only in their Indemnity) know, that to drop the blackest Ink,
> and the bitterest Gall upon this Fact, is not Satyr, but
> Propriety [2].

No doubt, he can be ' indecent ' ; for instance when, explaining
that lust darkens the mind, he concludes :

> The *Light within him* [i.e. the man who surrenders to lust]
> shall grow every Day less and less, and at length totally

---

[1] *Op. cit.*, V, ser. 5, p. 511.   [2] *Op. cit.*, V, ser. 2, p. 57.

and finally go out, and that in a *stink* too.   So hard, or
rather utterly unfeasible is it for Men to be zealous Votaries
of the *blind God*, without losing *their Eyes* in his Service,
and it is well if their Noses do not follow [1].

It is characteristic, however, that some of his telling images come
from Scripture or are slight variations of Scriptural phrases ; for
instance, speaking of repentance he says : " let him hang his head
as a bulrush " [2], and elsewhere : " if a man carries a luxurious soul
in a pining body, or the aspiring mind of a Lucifer in the hanging
head of a bulrush, he fasts only to upbraid his Maker " [3] (cp.
Isa. LVIII. 5); in a consecration sermon he argues that it is also
the bishop's task to preach, for " where God gives a talent, the
episcopal Robe can be no napkin to hide it in " [4] (cp. *Luke* XIX. 20
and *Matth.* XXV. 24).   Some of these phrases are hardly distinguishable from homely similes or proverbial expressions, which
he uses with equal ease.   For instance in the consecration sermon
he says that if scorn and rebuke are the only rewards of loyalty,
then " many will chuse rather to neglect their duty safely and
creditably, than to get a broken pate in the Church's service " [5] ;
in the sermon preached on 30 January, 1663, speaking of the Presbyterians who deny all responsibility for the murder of Charles I,
he accuses them of covering " their prevarications with fig-leaves " [6].
This is an image he often uses to brand hypocrites of one kind or
another [7] ;   though the phrase may sound humorous to-day it was
still in current use at the time in its transferred sense and may have
had no such effect ;   similarly, the Episcopal robe used as a napkin may sound jocular to men less familiar with *Luke* than with
Matthew.

It is not always easy for the modern reader to say if an image
struck South's hearers as jocular, but from contemporary evidence
it is clear that he often drew a laugh from his audience, no doubt
from his words as much as from the emphasis he put upon them.

---

[1] *Op. cit.*, III, ser. 2, p. 74.   [2] *Op. cit.*, IX, ser. 6, p. 181.
[3] *Op. cit.*, IX, ser. 5, p. 148.   [4] *Op. cit.*, I, ser. 5, p. 187.
[5] *Ibid.*, p. 193.   [6] *Op. cit.*, V, ser. 2, printed below.
[7] For instance : " It was indeed the way of many in the late times to
bolster up their crazy, doating Consciences, with ... odd Confidences ...   All
of them (as they understood them) mere Delusions, Trifles, and Fig-leaves ".
Op. cit., II, ser. 1, p. 41. " What pitiful Fig-leaves, What senseless and ridiculous Shifts are these, not able to *silence*, and much less to *satisfy* an accusing
Conscience ". *Op. cit.*, II, ser. 8, p. 298.

One can easily imagine that he gave his telling phrases the necessary relief, especially when they came in an upsurge of passion, as they so often did. What is clear even to the modern reader is that his language has its roots in the common speech, not only of the gentlemen but of the people. He did use the precise abstract vocabulary of philosophy, but he could also draw on the fund of racy expressions which a later generation was to consider as vulgar. His style has the ease of the best prose of the age, and the natural rhythm of the spoken word, but it also has the strength and vividness which only the bolder minds like Dryden could achieve in an age that set such store on polish and grace. Though Evelyn admired South's sermons, one cannot help feeling that he must occasionally have found them too strong meat for his refined palate.

Like Dryden South had a gift for ridicule, and his portraits of the fanatic preacher or of the beggarly fellow in his threadbare cloak and greasy hat smack of Doeg or Og. More often, however, he darts a poisoned arrow in the form of an aphorism or an epigram, of an antithesis or a pun. His quibbles are seldom mere *jeux de mots* for they usually occur when he is stating pungent truths, and they are often half submerged, as they are in Pope. Thus in the sermon on the pleasantness of religion, in which he opposes the pleasures of the mind to those of the body, and true self-denial to mere bodily exercises, he concludes :

> The Truth is, if Mens Religion lies no deeper than their skin, it is possible that they may scourge themselves into very great Improvements [1].

Or, in the sermon on *So God created Man in his own Image*, he compares the insight Adam had into the nature of things with the knowledge which philosophers have achieved through hard labour :

> Study was not then a Duty, Night-watchings were needless ; The Light of Reason wanted not the Assistance of a Candle [2].

In the sermon on *Ecclesiastical Policy the best Policy* he refers to the new lights, sudden impulses of the Spirit and extraordinary calls which have been alleged to subvert the order of the Church, and adds :

---

[1] *Op. cit.*, I, ser. 1, p. 36.   [2] *Op. cit.*, I, ser. 2, p. 54.

the Church must needs wither, being blasted with such Inspirations [1].

Speaking of the privileges formerly enjoyed by the Church through the favour of the civil power, he says :

> We envy not the Greatness and Lustre of the *Romish* Clergy, neither their scarlet Gowns, nor their scarlet Sins [2].

The literal application of the figurative expression, or the deliberate collocation of the literal and the figurative sense, does indeed surprise or even startle, and as such may provoke laughter ; South is certainly being witty, whether he is being jocular is open to question. Sometimes he quibbles to contrast the ways of the world with the ways of God, and the grim joke is then given its full force, as in the sermon on *Shamelessness in Sin*, in which he refers to the habit of paying visits to worthless people :

> But now all possible Courtship and Attendance is thought too little to be used towards People infamous and odious, and fit to be *visited* by none but by *God himself*, who visits after a very different Manner from the Courtiers of the World [3].

It is but a step from such puns or quibbles to the pregnant phrasing on the one hand, and to the 'unseemly' similes on the other. For instance, comparing prelapsarian man to the best philosophers, he says :

> An *Aristotle* was but the Rubbish of an *Adam*, and Athens but the Rudiments of Paradise [4].

Or, in the same sermon, explaining that man was created free to stand :

> We were not born crooked ; we learnt these Windings and Turnings of the Serpent [5].

As appears from this quotation, the pungency of his statements often results from the collision of the concrete and the abstract. When explaining that the service of Christ demands self-denial and may be attended with persecution, he reminds his hearers that

---

[1] *Op. cit.*, I, ser. 4, p. 151.   [2] *Op. cit.*, I, ser. 5, p. 205.
[3] *Op. cit.*, IV, ser. 3, p. 122.   [4] *Op. cit.*, I, ser. 2, p. 55.
                              [5] *Ibid.*, p. 60.

The Church is a Place of Graves, as well as of Worship
and Profession [1].

His concrete examples often serve to clinch the argument and
drive it home more vividly, thus :

> Ignorance indeed, so far as it may be resolved into natural
> Inability, is, as to Men, at least, inculpable ; and conse-
> quently, not the Object of Scorn, but Pity ; But in a
> Governour, it cannot be without the Conjunction of the
> highest Impudence : For who bid such an one aspire to
> teach, and to govern ? A Blind Man sitting in the Chimney
> Corner is pardonable enough, but sitting at the Helm, he
> is intolerable. If men will be ignorant and illiterate, let
> them be so in private, and to themselves, and not set their
> Defects in an high Place, to make them visible and con-
> spicuous. If Owls will not be hooted at, let them keep close
> within the Tree, and not perch upon the upper Boughs [2].

Some of his conceits remind one of the preachers of an earlier
age ; for instance in a sermon on Good Friday he says :

> He who would recount every Part of Christ that suffered
> must read a Lecture of *Anatomy* [3].

Like them too he sometimes elaborates the conceit, without however
resorting to mere ingenuity. Thus he begins a sermon on the
Resurrection with the favourite conceit of the Jacobean divines :

> Christ, the great *Sun of Righteousness*, and Saviour of the
> World, having by a glorious Rising, after a *Red*, and a
> *Bloody* Setting, proclaim'd his Deity to Men, and Angels ;
> and by a complete Triumph over the two grand Enemies of
> Mankind, *Sin* and *Death*, set up the everlasting Gospel in the
> room of all false Religions, has now (as it were) changed
> the *Persian* Superstition into the Christian Devotion ; and
> without the least Approach to the Idolatry of the former,
> made it henceforth the Duty of all Nations, *Jews*, and
> *Gentiles*, to worship the *Rising Sun* [4].

South often uses something like a parable and he introduces with
equal ease matter from the Bible or from the popular fables, sometimes even in conjunction, without any discrepancy being felt or
lack of 'propriety', so that one is sometimes reminded of the

---

[1] *Op. cit.*, I, ser. 3, p. 105.   [2] *Op. cit.*, I, ser. 5, p. 208.
[3] *Op. cit.*, III, ser. 9, p. 349.   [4] *Op. cit.*, V, ser. 4, pp. 157-8.

allegories of life in mediaeval cathedrals. The allegory is usually
compressed, but he sometimes develops it as when he relates the
story of Jeroboam, who is viewed as the type of the late usurper,
or when he applies the text of *Matt.* XXII.12 to the need for sacramental preparation, a text which he calls " a parabolical Description
of God's vouchsafing to the World the invaluable Blessing of the
Gospel " [1] and which he himself uses parabolically, the whole sermon being an extended metaphor. The same turn of mind is found
in such passages as this, from *Interest Deposed* :

> The Subject I have here pitched upon, may seem improper
> in these Times, and in this Place, where the Number of
> Professors, and of Men, is the same ; where the Cause
> and Interest of Christ has been so cried up ; and Christ's
> personal Reign and Kingdom so call'd for, and expected.
> But since it has been still preached up, but acted down ;
> and dealt with, as the Eagle in the Fable did with the Oister,
> carrying it up on high, that by letting it fall he might dash
> it in Pieces : I say, since Christ must reign, but his Truths
> be made to serve ; I suppose it is but Reason to distinguish
> between Profession and Pretence, and to conclude that Men's
> present crying, *Hail King*, and *Bending the Knee* to Christ,
> are only in order to his future Crucifixion [2].

South did not deal in grand generalities ; here the particular
occasion of the betrayal of Christ as well as the late rule of the
Saints are recalled vividly, and the false promise aptly related to
the story of the eagle and the oyster. In his instructions to preachers South reminded them that God spoke to the capacity of men
and that Christ often uttered His truths in parables because the
senses are the channels through which to reach the understanding.
For a preacher to insist only upon universals, he said, is " but a
cold, faint, languid way of persuading or dissuading ". He himself
used the concrete as an " underofficer " of the truth propounded,
as in

> Christ demands the Homage of your understanding : He
> will have your *Reason* bend to him, you must put your
> Heads under his Feet [3].

Conviction, he told young preachers, is from particulars. With

---

[1] *Op. cit.*, II, ser. 8, p. 273.   [2] *Op. cit.*, I, ser. 3, p. 84.
          [3] *Op. cit.*, I, ser. 3, p. 93.

him, the concrete is, as often as not, a homely simile, which some
may feel debases the truth propounded but which usually gives it
new vigour. In the consecration sermon he argues that the spiritual
order must be fortified with some power that is temporal, for

> If the Bishop has no other defensatives but Excommunica-
> tion, no other Power but that of the Keys, he may, for any
> notable Effect that he is like to do upon the Factious and
> Contumacious, surrender up his Pastoral Staff, shut up his
> Church, and put those Keys under the Door[1].

Speaking of pride and of the difference between a man when he
is poor and when he has been given preferment, he says :

> His mind, like a Mushroom, has shot up in a Night[2] ;

or about the persecutions of the early Christians :

> They came so fast upon the Christians, that all the inter-
> mission they had from one Persecution, was but a kind of
> pause or breathing time (a short *Parenthesis* of ease) to
> enable them for another[3].

South's frequent use of metaphors and similes results from his
conception of rhetoric, which, like Bacon's, is based on faculty
psychology : for him the senses are the underofficers of the understanding, and the imagination has the power to sway the will by
presenting to the mind objects to be desired or shunned. Images
therefore function as arguments, not as decoration ; they persuade
through their clearness and vividness as much as do the conceptual
statements. South often refers to the use of figurative language
in Scripture as a means to utter truths in a form suitable to the
apprehension of men. Like his fellow-Anglicans, he insisted that
the true meaning of Scripture is the literal, but he did not altogether
ignore the typological. True, he mostly touched upon this in order
to show that the Jewish religion presented types and shadows of
truths which were to be revealed later in their full light[4] ; all the

---

[1] *Op. cit.*, I, ser. 5, p. 196.   [2] *Op. cit.*, IV, ser. 2, pp. 83-84.
                    [3] *Op. cit.*, V, ser. 11, p. 425.
  [4] " The *Jews* indeed drew their Religion from a purer Fountain than the
Gentiles ; God himself being the Author of it ; and so both ennobling and
warranting it with the Stamp of Divine Authority. Yet God was pleased to
limit his Operations in this Particular to the Narrowness and small Capacities
of the Subject which he had to deal with ; and therefore the *Jews* being
naturally of a gross and sensual Apprehension of Things, had the Oeconomy
of their Religion, in many Parts of it, brought down to their Temper, and were
trained to *Spirituals* by the Ministry of Carnal Ordinances. Which yet God

same, his own use of imagery suggests that he was closer to the
men that saw correspondences everywhere than to the natural
philosophers of his own age. He was too strict a thinker ever to
let his mind dwell on fancied analogies, and he had been too often
shocked by the extravagant interpretations of the Saints to hunt
for types and shadows in the remotest corners; but the world
around him was full of concrete particulars imaging the truths he
wished to expound to his hearers. In his use of language no less
than in his thought South is therefore closer to writers of an earlier
generation; and yet he sounds far more modern than Barrow,
who shared all the interests of the new age. By temper he was a
conservative, yet a conservative that could infuse new vigour in
the old traditions or modes of thought, and through his nimble
wit give life and force to the language by wielding the old and
the new, the abstract and the concrete, the conceptual and the
figurative.

All of South's sermons are tracts for the times; not only does
he deal with urgent problems, but he expounds his themes with
particular reference to the specific circumstances, always calling
up to his hearers' minds the concrete background to which the truths
contained in his text are applicable. Topical references abound in
his sermons, to men, events, or doctrines of the day or of the recent
past, and many of his examples or even incidental comparisons are
drawn from the scene around him [1]. This may account for the
inability of later sermon readers to get the full gist of what he was
saying, and for such misunderstandings as that exemplified in the

---

was pleased to advance in their Signification, by making them Types and
Shadows of that glorious Archetype that was to come into the World, his own
Son ... He therefore being the Person to whom all the Prophets bore witness,
to whom all Ceremonies pointed, and whom all the various Types prefigured... "
op. cit., III, ser. 7, p. 288. " (the Mosaick Law) stood in the World for the
Space of two thousand Years; till at length in the Fullness of Time, the Reason
of Men ripening to such a Pitch, as to be above the Pedagogy of Moses's Rod,
and the Discipline of Types, God thought fit to display the Substance without
the Shadow, and to read the World a Lecture of an higher and more sublime
Religion in Christianity ", op. cit., I, ser. 6, p. 215.

[1] Thus, when explaining that the Dissenters' plea for moderation, which
they ground on the text of St. Paul Let your moderation be known unto all
men, is an abuse of words, he says: " And possibly some Bibles, of a later
and more correct Edition, may by this time have improved the Text, by putting
Trimming into the Margin". Op. cit., VI, ser. 1, p. 32. In a sermon on
Temptation he concludes one of his points like this: " And in the very worst
Circumstances which he can be in, it will be hard to prove that our Allegiance
to the King of Kings (according to the new, modish, Whig-Doctrine relating to
our temporal King) is only Conditional ", op. cit., VI, ser. 9, pp. 317-8.

preface to the 1795 *Beauties of South* ; but it certainly enhances
the vividness of his discourses and gives the modern reader a keen
sense of their relevancy to the problems confronting men after the
Restoration.   Like the similes these allusions keep the argument
firmly anchored in the concrete reality, and through their immediacy
add force and substance to the principles South defines.

If South's metaphors contribute to the vividness of his style,
and earned him a reputation for wit, he is no less a master of the
terse and pregnant statement.   True wit, he said, is a severe and
manly thing, and in this kind of wit he was himself supreme.   His
thought is etched out with precision and vigour.   Just as his paragraphs hinge on *for, therefore, since, though,* and the like, so he
compresses his sentences to the essentials, for instance :

> Others held a fortuitous Concourse of Atoms ; but all seem
> jointly to explode a Creation ; still beating upon this Ground,
> that the *producing Something out of Nothing* is impossible
> and incomprehensible : Incomprehensible indeed I grant, but
> not therefore impossible [1] ;

or again :

> Reputation is Power, and consequently to despise is to
> weaken [2].
> Disobedience, if complyed with, is infinitely encroaching,
> and having gain'd one Degree of Liberty upon Indulgence,
> will demand another upon Claim.   Every vice interprets a
> Connivance an Approbation [3].

In a sermon on " love your enemies " he says :

> And though I am commanded when my enemy *thirsts* to
> *give him Drink*, yet it is not when he thirsts for my *Blood* [4].

When demonstrating that faith must issue in works, and that
neither assurance of salvation nor profession of faith nor delight
in sermons will save a man's soul, he has a lover of sermons ask
if this will not set him right for heaven, and answers :

> Yes, no doubt, if a man were to be *pulled up to Heaven*
> *by the Ears* ; or the Gospel would but reverse its Rule, and

[1] *Op. cit.,* I, ser. 2, p. 45.   [2] *Op. cit.,* I, ser. 5, p. 200.
[3] *Ibid.,* p. 210.   [4] *Op. cit.,* III, ser. 3, p. 119.

declare, *That not the Doers of the Word, but the Hearers only should be justified* [1].

In a sermon on temptation he insists that the wary Christian must fill every minute with business because

> *Grace* abhors a *Vacuum* in Time, as much as *Nature* does in Place [2].

In such examples the vigour of the thought is all in the compact, vivid statement. It may be noted that several of these examples either begin or conclude a paragraph, thus serving as syntheses, much as do the vivid comparisons, clinching the argument or defining a truth to be demonstrated.

South's style is often Senecan in its brevity, but his arguments are not developed in equally terse statements, for the strain on his hearers—or even readers—would be too hard, and the movement would become as jerky as Andrewes's. On the contrary, the sentences are linked closely, and form a train of argument moving swiftly to the point he wants to make. The parts are usually short, or fairly short, independent clauses, so that the stages in the process can be grasped clearly, and the argument followed easily thanks to the strict logic. Having established his point South often applies the abstract to the concrete, thus wielding together the ' reason of the thing ' and the truth of experience, on both of which he grounds his propositions. The following paragraph may serve to illustrate this method and style, yet it is not particularly striking in its context :

> Reputation is Power, and consequently to despise is to weaken. For where there is Contempt, there can be no Awe ; and where there is no Awe, there will be no Subjection ; and if there is no Subjection, it is impossible, without the Help of the former Distinction of a Politick Capacity, to imagine how a Prince can be a Governour. He that makes his Prince despised and undervalued, blows a Trumpet against him in Mens Breasts, beats him out of his Subjects Hearts, and fights him out of their Affections ; and after this, he may easily strip him of his other Garrisons, having already dispossessed him of his strongest, by dismantling him of his Honour, and seizing his Reputation [3].

---

[1] *Op. cit.*, III, ser. 4, p. 166.   [2] *Op. cit.*, VI, ser. 10, p. 345.
[3] *Op. cit.*, I, ser. 5, p. 200.

If South could both argue with the subtlety of a trained logician at home in scholastic arguments and strike home with a colloquial phrase or racy idiom, it is because he could move so easily from principles to facts, from the abstract to the concrete. Because he does this all along, his homely similes hardly ever seem out of place even though they may sometimes offend the nicer critics. When similar idioms appear in Barrow's slightly pedantic prose the reader is apt to be jarred [1], while South's rhythm and sentence structure make them sound right. His style may owe something to the Senecans, but the main influence is certainly that of the Bible, both in the pattern of his sentences and in the inclusiveness of his idiom. He can hardly, one feels, have approved of the attempts to pare down the language and to restrict it to ' correct usage ' for he moves through the whole range of the language with complete freedom. Indeed he seems to be above such concerns as propriety and correctness as if he was " to the manner born ".

For South as for the great neo-classicists decorum did not mean starched formality or mere politeness. When he wishes to diminish, as the old rhetoricians said, and he often does so wish, he uses diminishing figures. He does not feel bound to the level tone of the more moderate or more lukewarm preachers, but lashes out when occasion offers, and he often has good precedent for such violence of language, as when he says :

> And this may suffice concerning the second Way of embasing God's Ministers ; namely, by intrusting the Ministry with raw, unlearned, ill-bred Persons ; so that what *Solomon* speaks of a Proverb in the Mouth of a Fool, the same may be said of the Ministry vested in them, that it is like a *Pearl in a Swine's Snout* [2].

Such ' unseemly ' similes are indeed frequent in his sermons. As he said in *The Scribe Instructed*, " Piety engages no man to be dull ", and he saw no reason why he should restrain the power of his wit in serving his Church. Nor did he believe that gentle admonitions could reclaim the wicked or discourage the enemies of order in Church and State. He was too much the aristocrat

---

[1] Coleridge noted that Barrow is below South in dignity. *Anima Poetae*, ed. E.H. Coleridge, London, 1895, p. 47 (Nov. 13, 1803).

[2] *Op. cit.*, I, ser. 4, p. 162.

not to speak out boldly and state what he considered as vital truths with all the means at his disposal.   He was a powerful preacher just because through the vigour of his intellect and the liveliness of his imagination he could infuse new life into the old truths and make them shine with all the brightness of his sprightly wit.   Again and again the brilliant phrase is sparked off this hard flint, " what oft was thought but ne'er so well expressed ".   Such gems abound in his sermons, for instance :

> I confess, God has no need of any Man's Parts, or Learning ; but certainly then, he has much less need of his Ignorance, and ill Behaviour [1].

> The Doctrine that teaches Alms, and the Persons that need them, are by such equally sent packing [2].

> No man is esteemed any ways considerable for Policy, who wears Religion otherwise than as a Cloak ; that is, as such a Garment as may both *cover* and *keep him warm*, and yet hang *loose* upon him too [3].

> For the sensual Epicure, he also will find ... that there is no *Drinking*, or *Swearing*, or *Ranting*, or *Fluxing* a Soul out of its *Immortality* [4].

> Such are their [i.e. the Romish Casuists'] *Pardons* and *Indulgences*, and giving Men a share in the *Saints Merits*, out of the Common Bank and Treasury of the Church, which the *Pope* has the sole custody and disposal of, and is never kept *shut* to such as come with an *open hand* [5].

> Conscience, if truly tender, never complains without a Cause, though I confess, there is a new fashioned sort of *Tenderness of Conscience*, which always does so.   But that is like the *Tenderness* of a Bog or Quagmire, and it is very dangerous coming near it, for fear of being swallowed up by it. For when Conscience has once acquired this *artificial Tenderness*, it will strangely enlarge, or contract its Swallow as it pleases ; so that sometimes a Camel shall slide down with Ease, where at other times, even a Gnat may chance to stick by the way.   It is, indeed, such a kind of *Tenderness*, as makes the Person, who has it, generally very *tender of obeying the Laws*, but never of *breaking them*.   And there-

[1] *Op. cit.*, I, ser. 4, p. 159.   [2] *Op. cit.*, I, ser. 6, p. 234.
[3] *Op. cit.*, I, ser. 9, p. 346.   [4] *Op. cit.*, II, ser. 1, p. 40.
[5] *Op. cit.*, II, ser. 11, p. 399.

fore, since it is commonly at such variance with the *Law*, I think the *Law* is the fittest Thing to deal with it [1].

When quoted out of context the memorable phrases are apt to suggest the happy turns which grace the talk of so many wits in Restoration comedy ; yet, while these are often mere airy nothings, delightful but soon forgotten, South's wit is usually sparked off by the urgency of the thought or the passion of his indictement. Though he would have been offended by the comparison, his telling phrases are not unlike those of another intensely serious writer when he branded the " hireling wolves, whose Gospel is their maw ", or echoed the cries of the stall-reader when he " did but prompt the age to quit their clogs " and found that he had cast pearls to hogs [2] ; the difference is that South could use homely images for purposes other than denunciation, but with equal force, for instance :

> But the severe Notions of Christianity turned all this upside down, filling all with Surprize and Amazement ; they came upon the World, like Light darting full upon the Face of a Man asleep, who had a Mind to sleep on, and not to be disturbed [3].

Far from " drawing away the attention from the subject to the epigrammatic diction ", as some critics have said [4], South's lucky resultances of thought and words must have exercised his hearers' wits and compelled them to think. Right thinking was the aim of all his teaching, but it was the kind of thinking that involves both the intellect and the imagination. His defence of fancy in *The Scribe Instructed* shows that for him the imagination must contribute to make a lively impression on the hearers' minds and thereby make them realize more powerfully the exact bearing of the ideas propounded to them. For South, as for Pope, wit (as imagination) and judgement were to act as close partners in setting forth the truths of religion. In this, as in so much else, he was resisting the tide that was ultimately to effect the severance of judgement from fancy ; he was, in fact, true to an earlier conception of reason. If for Donne truth stood on a huge hill, cragged and steep, for South it was " a great strong-hold, barred and forti-

---

[1] *Op. cit.*, II, ser. 12, p. 466.
[2] For South's bitter reference to Milton, see his 30 January sermon, printed below.
[3] *Op. cit.*, I, ser. 6, p. 222.
[4] Lord Brougham, in the *Edinburgh Review*, quoted by Allibone, *op. cit.*

fied by God and Nature ", to be laid siege to in a kind of warfare, and only to be reached by men perpetually on the watch,
" observing all the avenues and passes to it ", and making their
approaches accordingly [1]. The avenues he chose to pursue in his
sermons may not always have conformed with the nicer judges'
sense of propriety, but there is no doubt that he laid siege to his
hearers' indifference or slumbering consciences and that his nimble
wit taught them the discipline necessary to reach what he considered as all-important truths.

Like other Anglican divines South preached on the duties of
religion ; like them he believed and taught that faith must issue
in works, but in no way can he be called a practical preacher. His
main purpose in teaching was to enlighten the understanding and to
correct errors of judgement rather than to fortify the will. Among
the truths he was out to enforce were the fundamental articles of
belief, particularly those that were impugned in his day, such as
the Trinity and the mysteriousness of Christianity ; like his contemporaries, he also demonstrated the absurdity of unbelief. The
main evil against which he fought in sermon after sermon, however,
was the corruption of doctrine and discipline deriving from what
he believed to be a false conception of faith and of worship. With
the utmost violence he denounced new schemes of Church government, extempore prayers or preaching by the Spirit. However
partisan he may appear in his unremitting opposition to all pleas
of tender conscience, the stand he took against such ' impostures '
is the logical outcome of his conception of religion, which requires
discipline in thought and emotion as well as decency and order in
the service of God. He condemned all looseness in thinking as in
worshipping, and disorder in the State as in the Church. Believing
as he did that the civil power is the necessary prop of the spiritual
power, he attacked the enemies of both with equal fire, and in
many of his sermons he preached politics as well as religion. These
are probably the sermons which modern readers will enjoy most,
because of South's intense concern for the issues at stake in his
time. Such are his sermons on *Interest Deposed*, on *Ecclesiastical
Policy*, on the *Nature and Measures of Conscience*, on the *Fatal
Imposture and Force of Words*, or the sermon on the anniversary

---

[1] *Op. cit.*, I, ser. 6, printed below.

of the execution of Charles I. Those on *Extempore Prayers*, or
The Scribe Instructed as well as the doctrinal sermons, on the
Pentecost or the Trinity or against unbelief, define with particular
cogency the beliefs and temper of this particular divine, which
determined the stand he took on political and ecclesiastical issues.
All of South's sermons evince the same qualities of thought and
style, even those few which deal with more commonplace themes
such as ingratitude or lying. As a consequence an editor is hard put
to it to select from such an *embarras de richesses*. Sermons which
appealed to earlier anthologists, such as that on *So God Created
Man in his own Image*, or particularly delighted his contemporaries,
such as that on *The Lot is cast into the Lap*, do not appear in the
present selection though they too are likely to interest the modern
reader. Much that is good had to be left out of the selection, but
it is hoped that from this handful of sermons the reader will be
able to gather that South was indeed " a writer of rare distinction "
and that we cannot afford to ignore " a man who thinks so clearly
and precisely and powerfully as South invariably does "[1].

John Tillotson (1630-1694)

Such was the popularity of Tillotson as a preacher that, when
his last remains were taken to the church where he had preached
so often, the streets were lined by mourning crowds and

> there was a numerous train of coaches filled with persons
> of rank and condition, who came voluntarily to assist at
> that solemnity from Lambeth to the church of St Lawrence
> Jewry [2].

His publisher did not hesitate to pay his widow two thousand five
hundred pounds for the copyright of his posthumous sermons [3],
which proved to be a good investment since in the next fifty years
the sermons went through edition after edition. Tillotson's fame
had by no means waned when, in 1752, J. and R. Tonson issued a
new folio edition, for which Thomas Birch wrote a life of the

---

[1] James SUTHERLAND : ' Robert South ', in *A Review of English Literature*,
I, (1960), 6-7.
[2] Thomas BIRCH, *op. cit.*, p. ccxxii.
[3] See *The Tatler*, no. 101 (1709). Birch, and Macaulay after him, says
2,500 guineas. Cp. with this the sum paid to Dryden for his *Aeneis*, i.e.
1,300 pounds.

author. Birch, who also edited the works of Chillingworth, Bacon,
and Boyle among others, may have been no writer, as Johnson said [1],
but he collected plenty of material and gave such a detailed account
of Tillotson's life that later biographers have found little to add
to his account [2]. Since the main facts are readily available to the
twentieth-century reader [3], only a brief outline of Tillotson's life
need be given here.

John Tillotson, the son of a Yorkshire clothier of strict Puritan
persuasion, was entered a pensioner at Clare Hall, Cambridge, in
1647 and proceeded B.A. in 1650. Some time after he was elected
Fellow of the College, and he took his M.A. degree in 1654. At
the time he was himself a Puritan, but according to one of his
pupils he heard many sermons and, being eclectic, refused to bind
himself to opinions [4]. Soon after leaving Cambridge in 1656 he
became tutor to the son of Edmund Prideaux, Cromwell's Attorney
General; he was in London when the Protector died on 3 September, 1658, and happening to be present at Whitehall when
some Puritan divines were keeping a fast-day, he was shocked by
the bold sallies of enthusiasm offered as prayers by such men as
John Owen and Peter Sterry. This may have contributed to sway
his sympathies, though he was still to remain among the Puritans
for some time. He was ordained, probably in 1661, by Thomas
Sydserf, the one Scottish bishop still living [5], but was deprived of
his fellowship at Clare Hall when Peter Gunning was readmitted
after the Restoration [6]. From 1661 to 1662 he was curate at

---

[1] " 'Tom is a lively rogue; he remembers a great deal, and can tell many
pleasant stories; but a pen is to Tom a torpedo, the touch of it benumbs his
hand and brain: Tom can talk; but he is no writer' ". Sir John HAWKINS:
The Life of Samuel Johnson, ed. B.H. Davis, London, 1961, p. 93.

[2] Some few mistakes have been corrected, such as the date of Tillotson's
christening, i.e. 10 October, 1630, not 3 September (see L.G. LOCKE, *op. cit.*,
p. 16) or the date of his election as lecturer to St. Lawrence Jewry, i.e. 1661
not 1663 (see D.D. BROWN: *An Edition of Selected Sermons of John Tillotson*,
Unpublished M.A. thesis, London, 1956; the correction is from John Mackay's
unpublished dissertation on Tillotson).

[3] Besides Birch's Life and the notice by Alexander Gordon in the *DNB*,
see James MOFFAT's Introduction to *The Golden Book of Tillotson*, 1926, and
Louis G. LOCKE, *op. cit.*, Ch. I.

[4] See Beardmore's account, appended to BIRCH's *Life*, *op. cit.*, p. cclxv.

[5] According to *Alumni Cantabrigienses*, ed. John Venn and J.A. Venn,
Cambridge, 1927, this was circa 1661. Though Sydserf had been intimate with
Laud and deposed by the General Assembly and though he had joined Charles I
at Newcastle in 1645, Tillotson's ordination by him does not mean that he was
then ready to conform, since Sydserf was accused of ordaining all those who
came to him " promiscuously ".

[6] See Beardmore's account, *op. cit.*, p. cclxvii.

Cheshunt, Hertfortshire, and in December 1661 he was appointed Tuesday lecturer at St. Lawrence Jewry. He had sat with the Presbyterians at the Savoy Conference, but when the Act of Uniformity was passed he conformed to the discipline of the Church of England. In 1663 he became rector of Keddington, Suffolk, where the minister had been ejected, but where the congregation clearly favoured Gospel preachers, since Tillotson's parishioners complained that he did not preach Jesus Christ. He resigned this living when he was elected Preacher to Lincoln's Inn in November 1663. From then on he was to preach regularly to the lawyers on the Sunday and to the City congregation on the Tuesday, often delivering the same discourse in both places and attracting to St. Lawrence Jewry many people who had heard him on the Sunday.

His acquaintance with John Wilkins, then vicar of St. Lawrence, probably dates from these years ; in 1664 Tillotson married Wilkins's stepdaughter, i.e. the daughter of Robina Cromwell, sister to the Protector, and in the following years he worked with Wilkins on his *Essay towards a Real Character and Philosophical Language* (published in 1668). His close association with Wilkins and his work on a philosophical language probably strengthened his taste for perspicuity and simplicity in his style of preaching ; it may also have contributed to make him less careful of the exact meaning of words and of the distinctions between near synonyms, since the ' real character ' aimed at devising signs to represent words, but had by its very nature to restrict the number of such signs, which inevitably entailed ignoring differences of meaning. It was probably in recogniton of his work with Wilkins, and at the latter's suggestion, that he was elected a Fellow of the Royal Society in 1671. Of his contribution to the transactions of the Society nothing is known beyond the fact that he communicated to the Fellows Halley's report on the comet. When Wilkins was elevated to the see of Chester in 1668 Tillotson was chosen to preach the consecration sermon, and Whichcote, whom Tillotson had known at Cambridge, became vicar of St. Lawrence Jewry, so that the City church continued to foster the peaceable temper and the moderation which distinguished these three men in an age when partisan feelings ran so high. After Wilkins's death in 1672 Tillotson brought out his *Principles and Duties of Natural Religion* (1675) and his *Sermons* (1677), thus further contributing to popularize both the reasonable view of Christianity and the plain style

of preaching of the man who had done so much to promote concord
among Christians.

Meanwhile Tillotson himself had become known to the reading
public [1] : in 1663 he preached before the Lord Mayor and Aldermen of the City a sermon on *The Wisdom of Being Religious*
and, as was usual on such occasions, he was asked to print it
" with what farther he had prepared to deliver ". The sermon,
first published in 1664, develops the main themes on which he was
to preach all through his life : the reasonableness of Christianity,
the absurdity of irreligion, the nature of operative faith, and the
necessity of the good life. The emphasis on the agreeableness of
faith and reason and on the need for faith to issue in practice
marked him out at once as the rational, moral preacher, more
concerned with practice than with nice points of doctrine, but
determined to oppose the growth of infidelity and of any doctrine
tending thereunto. Soon after this he was to enter the lists and
challenge the main champion of Romanism, which he considered
as destructive of all religion because it sapped the very foundation
of true faith, the evidence of reason and of the senses. *The Rule
of Faith*, in answer to John Sergeant's *Sure-Footing*, appeared in
1666 and from then on Tillotson never missed an opportunity of
attacking the Romanists' doctrine or practices. In the same year
he was created D.D. and in 1668 he took part, with Wilkins and
Stillingfleet, in negociations with the Dissenters Manton, Bates
and Baxter. This attempt to promote a Bill of Comprehension,
which had been first proposed by Sir Orlando Bridgeman, Keeper
of the Great Seal, and by Lord Chief Baron Hales, was frustrated
by the opposition it met in the House of Commons. Yet Tillotson
never gave up the hope of bringing about the Union of Protestants,
who, as he saw, would be stronger if they could oppose a united
front to the Romanists ; he once more worked for agreement
with the Dissenters in 1674, and again after the Revolution when
a Comprehension Bill was before the House of Commons. Though
a sincere member of the Church of England, Tillotson never shared
the persecuting zeal of many of his Anglican brethren : not only
were such partisan feelings alien to his moderate and equable
temper, but he did not believe that the discipline of the Church

[1] In 1662 had appeared the sermon he preached, before he had conformed,
at the Morning Exercise in Cripplegate ; but this was first printed anonymously
together with the other sermons delivered on that occasion.

as laid down in the Restoration Settlement was necessarily the best, and he was prepared to give way to the Dissenters on some points of ceremony in order to further peace and union among Protestants. He thereby antagonized many Churchmen, who were prompt to brand him as no true son of the Church, particularly after he had become primate of that Church.

In 1668 Charles II made Tillotson—some say, reluctantly—one of his Chaplains. At Court no less than in the City Tillotson denounced the danger of Popery and on one occasion at least provoked the Duke of York, who forbade him to print his sermon [1]. In 1670 he was made a Prebendary, and in 1672 became Dean, of Canterbury; he was also made a Prebendary, then a Canon, of St. Paul's (1675). His friend Isaac Barrow having died in 1677, Tillotson was entrusted by Barrow's father with the manuscript works left by that divine, with a power to print as much as he thought fit. The task of sorting out the manuscripts must have taken up a great deal of Tillotson's time in the next few years, for he edited his friend's works with great care and brought out not only *A Treatise of the Pope's Supremacy* (1680) but three folio volumes of sermons (1683-7)[2]. This was by no means his only occupation in these years, for besides preaching regularly at Lincoln's Inn and St. Lawrence Jewry, and occasionally at Court or to the House of Commons, he also helped to further the scheme for the diffusion of the Bible in Welsh, together with Stillingfleet, Whichcote and some Nonconformist ministers [3], and he helped his friend, the Unitarian Thomas Firmin, in his work for prison reform and other charitable organisations.

In 1683 the Rye House Plot led to the arrest of his friend Lord Russell, who was sentenced to death. Tillotson visited him in the Tower and, though he never doubted the integrity of Russell, he tried to persuade him that he was deluded in thinking resistance to the King lawful when the basic rights of the people were threatened. He failed to convince his friend, and attended him faithfully to the scaffold; but his letter urging on Russell the duty of passive obedience, which somehow was circulated at the time,

[1] *The Hazard of Being Saved in the Church of Rome*, which was printed surreptitiously in 1673.
[2] See 'Note on the Text of Barrow's Sermons', below.
[3] Among them Thomas Gouge, whose funeral sermon Tillotson was to preach on 4 November, 1681 (Vol. I, ser. 23).

was to be remembered by his enemies after he had taken the oaths to the new Sovereigns in 1689.

In 1683 Tillotson also preached the sermon at the funeral of Whichcote. The year after appeared his *Discourse against Transubstantiation*, which was promptly translated into French. With the accession of James the threat to the Protestant religion became more and more precise ; though Tillotson went on preaching passive obedience to the civil magistrate, he pressed more urgently than ever the duty to remain steadfast to the Protestant religion, particularly in a number of sermons delivered before Princess Anne. He was grieved to find that some of the Nonconformists were ready to support the King's scheme of Indulgence, and he remonstrated with his friend William Penn for thus playing into the hands of the Romanists. He, on his side, was doing all in his power to help the French Protestant ministers who had sought refuge in England after the Revocation of the Edict of Nantes in 1685, and who with their little flocks of exiles were a standing reproach to those English Protestants who pretended to ignore James's real purpose in promulgating an Indulgence. Tillotson's health was impaired and he had been struck in his deepest affections : in 1687 he lost his only remaining child and suffered an apoplectic fit. Though still sick he at once responded to the call of Archbishop Sancroft and attended the meeting of the London clergy when, in 1688, James ordered his Declaration of Indulgence to be read in churches. What Tillotson's feelings were at the time, and the stand he took in this emergency, can easily be guessed ; yet there is no evidence that he had anything to do with the invitation sent to William and signed by no less a man than Compton, Bishop of London. Tillotson may, however, have known of it and of the preparations on foot in Holland. In any case he promptly took the oaths to William and Mary, unlike many Churchmen who, having taught non-resistance, did hesitate before transferring their allegiance to the new Sovereigns. As early as 31 January, 1689, Tillotson preached at Lincoln's Inn a sermon on the happy deliverance of the Church, which left no doubt as to his own choice of allegiance and which may even have been intended to sway the lawyers' opinion [1].

Tillotson, who had known William of Orange since 1677, was

---

[1] See Chapter III, above.

asked to preach before the King and Queen at Hampton Court on 14 April, 1689, i.e. only three days after they had been crowned. On 27 April he was made Clerk of the King's Closet, and in November he succeeded Stillingfleet, now Bishop of Worcester, as Dean of St. Paul's.   Though he had been offered one of the bishoprics left vacant by the Non-Jurors, he begged rather to be made Dean and, as appears from his correspondence with Lady Russell, he only reluctantly accepted the Primacy, which William had designed for him from the first.   After Sancroft had at last vacated his see, Tillotson was elected, and consecrated at Bow Church on 31 May, 1691.   As he had foreseen he was attacked more bitterly than ever, particularly by Non-Jurors, chief among whom was George Hickes, who was to be appointed ' bishop ' by the exiled James.   Tillotson was accused of being a Socinian, an Anabaptist, no true friend of the Church, and not even a son of the Church since it was claimed that he had never been baptized at all (though his baptism had been duly entered in the parish register of Halifax [1]).   Tillotson wisely forbore to answer these charges, but the *Sermons Concerning the Divinity and Incarnation of Our Blessed Saviour*, which he published in 1693, were probably intended to counteract the effect of such attacks and to show that his doctrine was sound.   These attacks must have abated for a while, for in the preface to his next collection, *Six Sermons* (1694), he expressed his relief at being released from the " irksome and unpleasant work of controversy and wrangling about religion ". Yet, after his death High-Churchmen (among them South) and Non-Jurors alike returned to the attack, and his friend Gilbert Burnet had to vindicate his memory.   In November 1694 Tillotson was seized with a sudden illness while at Chapel ; he died a few days after in the arms of his friend, ' the pious Mr Nelson '.

Tillotson was no doubt a man of catholic sympathies.   Brought up as a child in a strict Puritan family, he was attended in his last illness by a Non-Juror ; among his friends he numbered such different men as Isaac Barrow, John Sharp, Gilbert Burnet, Robert Nelson—who had been educated in the family of Nicholas Ferrars at Little Gidding—Thomas Firmin the Socinian and promotor of charitable organisations, Dr. Bates the Presbyterian vicar, Richard Baxter, William Penn the Quaker, and William Prince of Orange.

[1] See L.G. LOCKE, *op. cit.*, p. 16.

In the age of the great persecution he worked for agreement with
the Dissenters and union among Protestants.   True, he was as
violent in his denunciation of the Romanists as he was mild in his
treatment of dissenting Protestants.   This may seem surprising in
such an eminently charitable man ; but even though he was ready
to compromise on most points of discipline for the sake of peace,
there were some points of doctrine which he thought could not be
assailed without the very foundations of religion being wrecked.
To him Romanism was evil because it both destroyed the basis of
all faith and made a mock of moral principles ; for this reason he
could give the Papists no quarter.   His relentless opposition to the
claims of Rome was based on his belief that the Romanists' religion
was destructive of the good life and endangered the peace of
society, which to him were the primary if not the ultimate ends of
religion, and it was precisely because of the paramount importance
of practice to him that he was ready to relax discipline and seek
agreement with the Dissenters so as to further concord among
Christians and peace in society.   How much weight he put on
living well appears not only from his sermons, but also from his
stern expostulations with men of dissolute life, such as the Earl
of Shrewsbury [1].   Nor did he merely preach charity and mildness
to men of good will, or promote schemes for charitable institutions ;
he could also exert himself on behalf of men who suffered for
conscience sake, such as the French ministers [2] or friends who had
been ejected [3].   His former pupil at Cambridge, John Beardmore,
tells us that

> He was one of a very sweet nature, friendly and obliging,
> and ready to serve his friends any way that he could by
> his interest and authority, when they applied to him ; and

[1] See his letter to the Earl, in BIRCH, op. cit., p. XXXVIII.   See also the
letter to Sir Thomas Colepepper, 15 July, 1681, and the letter to Lady Henrietta,
daughter of the Earl of Berkeley, 1682, ibid., pp. lxi, lxvi.
[2] See, for instance, his letter of 11 August, 1686, recommending a French
minister, in Bodleian Library MS. Tanner, vol. 30, f. 99.
[3] See Baxter's account of one Francis Holdcraft, Fellow of Clare Hall,
bedfellow of Tillotson, who was ejected from his living but went on preaching
privately at Cambridge until he was arrested in 1663.   On being released in
1672 he returned to his preaching and was again imprisoned.   " A like indictement with the former being intended, a certiorari was procured for him on the
account of a debt, which brought him up to the Fleet.   There he lay for a
while ; but discharging his debt, he was at length released.   But in this and
his former troubles, he had great experience of the kindness of his old friend
Dr Tillotson. "   Edmund CALAMY, op. cit., II, 86.

this he did freely and generously, without any oblique designs to serve himself. He was very affable and conversible, not sour or sullen, not proud or haughty, not addicted to any thing of moroseness, affected gravity, or to keep at a great distance from those that were much his inferiors ; but open and free, gentle and easy, pleasant and amiable, to those especially that he was acquainted with, or that he looked upon as honest and good [1].

Such an account of Tillotson's character will be readily accepted by anyone who has read his sermons, for these reflect the sweet reasonableness and kindness of the man ; the temper of the speaker which shines through the words on the page and must have been even more perceptible from the tone of his voice, must have greatly contributed to win the favour of his hearers. What is harder to imagine is that Tillotson's " common and familiar discourse was witty and facetious " [2], not only because there is no evidence of wit in his sermons—he would have thought it ' indecent '—but because his very style seems to preclude a capacity for wit [3]. His natural gentleness, his lack of formality in his intercourse with men must have inclined him to develop the easy and natural style which was so much admired by his contemporaries. The smooth flow of his sentences, the relaxed syntax, the preference for unemphatic rhythms, the varied sentence structure no less than the simplicity of his diction suggest the informality of speech. The thought is never compressed or involved ; rather he prefers to enlarge, often by means of doublets which tend to blur outlines. As a consequence the thought seems to be less precise, and to match that of the average hearer. Since he eschews not only learned references but also technical terms, since he uses the natural words in their natural order, he must have given his congregation the impression that they were hearing from the pulpit the same kind of language as they were using in everyday life ; and the truths he taught them must have sounded all the more familiar as he never drove the argument beyond the point where the average hearer might be expected to feel on familiar ground. If he made

---

[1] BIRCH, *op. cit.*, p. cclxxiv.   [2] *Ibid.*
[3] The one example of his wit that is usually quoted is his remark about South, that he wrote like a man but bit like a dog, and when South replied that he had rather bite than fawn, Tillotson's rejoinder that he would choose to be a spaniel rather than a cur. See BIRCH, *op. cit.*, p. ccxxv.

the language of everyday life the instrument of religion, it was in order to make his religious teaching an integral part of everyday life. In this he was eminently the practical preacher, and his lucid exposition of the basic truths and duties of Christianity must have been the more readily accepted as his great design was, to use Beardmore's words, to make men wisely religious, that is, to require neither too strenuous an exercise of their intellects nor to press too hard duties upon them. Not only did he usually select for confirmation the kind of arguments that would be easily grasped by his hearers, and dwell in the application on the immediate duties of the Christian life—on those of the second rather than of the first table—but he often demonstrated that the practice of religion was the most profitable and sensible way of life. Thus both in matter and manner he kept a level course, never soaring too high nor probing too deep, rather relaxing than tautening the tension. His slack rhythms and fairly loose syntax image the lack of rigour of his thought and teaching.

If the redundancies suggest the diffuseness of his thought, the simplicity and perspicuity of his diction as well as the varied movement of his sentences make it easy for both hearer and reader to follow his developments. For his method is clear, indeed, excessively so to the modern reader; each of his discourses is short [1] and in each he considers or discusses no more than a few points, stressing each stage in the development. Moreover, his sentences, though loose if compared with more highly patterned prose, are clear and orderly, compound rather than complex, and it appears from his revisions that he was concerned to make the relations between the parts as clear to the reader as they had been to the hearer from the modulation of the speaking voice [2]. Burnet said in his funeral oration that Tillotson found pulpit oratory deficient and therefore set to himself a pattern that would make the essential truths of Christianity easily accessible to the average man. This was probably deliberate, and Tillotson may have had to train himself in this easy, perspicuous manner, for though many reformers had earlier emphasized the necessity for preachers to

---

[1] Tillotson (and the editor of the posthumous sermons) often printed two or more sermons as one, but some were published as they were preached, i.e. as successive parts of a series of sermons on the same text.

[2] See D.D. BROWN : " John Tillotson's Revisions and Dryden's ' Talent for English Prose ' ", *RES*, NS, XII (1961), 24-39.

speak to the capacity of their hearers, it appears from the first two sermons of Tillotson to be published that at that early stage he used to include more considerations and longer developments under each head than he was to do later. Perhaps *The Wisdom of Being Religious* is no conclusive proof of this since it was enlarged for publication (and further revised for later editions) and since Tillotson may well have considered this as an opportunity to compose a fully argued refutation of atheism. The sermon he preached at the Morning Exercise at Cripplegate before he conformed to the Church of England [1], on the other hand, already develops themes to which he will return again and again in later sermons [2] and its drift is similar to that of his later teaching ; but the method of it is different from that of his other discourses. The plan is clear enough—explication of the rule expressed in the text ; grounds of this rule ; instances in which we ought chiefly to practise it ; uses—but each part is subdivided and the third has further subdivisions. Thus he first explains that the rule is reasonable, certain, and practicable, and under this last head he not only refutes two objections but develops four means to make the practice of this duty easy. He then proceeds to the grounds of this rule, of which he lists five. The next part, instances, constitutes the main body of the sermon ; he considers nine such instances, i.e. in matters of civil respect and conversation, of kindness and courtesy, of charity and compassion, of forbearance and forgiveness, of report and representation of other men and their actions, of trust and fidelity, of duty and obedience, of freedom and liberty, and finally in matters of commerce and contracts which arise from thence. Given the kind of audience he is addressing he naturally develops the last point at greater length, giving it in fact more space than to all the others taken together. He is careful not to specify " what is the exact righteousness in matter of contracts " because he is unacquainted with affairs of the world, but he gives a general rule for the conduct of such affairs, explicates it by considering

[1] He never published it, nor was it included in the posthumous collections of his sermons until 1752, i.e. in Birch's edition. It appeared anonymously in a collection of sermons preached on the same occasion.

[2] For instance, the general proposition, " whatsoever you would that men should do unto you, do ye even so to them " ; the bonds of human society ; tolerance of other people's opinions, particularly in religious matters ; equitable dealing with others ; charity towards all men ; and especially the stress on morality as the chief part of religion, that is, an outspoken defence of works, since loving one's neighbours is the only way to love God.

particular kinds of contracts, and finally lays down special rules
for directing commerce, on occasion of which he answers several
possible objections.   The sum of all this is the duty to use plainness in all commercial dealings.   Under the last head, uses, he
develops only two points : the heinousness of revenge and the
need to respect the second table of the Law.   The drift of the
whole sermon is thus to teach these righteous men, whose respect
for the first table of the Law is so deep, that unless they love the
brother whom they have seen they merely pretend to love the God
they have not seen.   The last part of the sermon in fact emphasizes
that to despise such exhortations as mere morality is to nullify
Christ's teaching.

Not only is the overall structure of the sermon less simple than
in the later discourses, but parts of it are more argumentative.   This
may suggest that the audience as well as the preacher were used to
the dialectical method of the Calvinists, but it is worth noting that
the general tone as well as the arguments themselves is secular rather
than religious, that Tillotson's quotations are from Descartes and
Cicero as well as from the Bible.   Though the argument may sound
dry at the beginning, Tillotson meets his hearers on their own ground
so that the particular problems with which they are faced in their
everyday life as shopkeepers or merchants are treated specifically.
Tillotson is clearly able to speak their own language and to discuss
particular cases to which the duty applies ; and he also knows the
casuistry and subterfuges that many of them are apt to use in their
business dealings.   As a consequence he sounds much closer to
the concrete reality than he does in most of his later sermons, in
which the teaching is usually of a general nature.   True, he was
never to forget that as a moral teacher he had to consider cases
in which men might not see clearly which was the right choice,
and several of his later sermons indeed examine such particular
cases [1] ; but these often sound like mere casuistry, whereas in the
Morning Exercise the pressure of the business world, of the actual
situations in which his hearers would have to do unto others the
things they would that others should do unto them, makes the
sermon more cogent and more lively.   To the modern reader the
topicality enhances, rather than detracts from, the interest because

---

[1] For instance, the two sermons on *The Nature and Necessity of Restitution*,
op. cit., III, ser. 116 and 117.

the aptness of the duty enforced, and the way in which it is related
to the particular men to whom the sermon is addressed, vividly
define the ethos of that class of citizens, their virtues as well as
their shortcomings. Before he achieved the correctness which was
to earn him such high fame in the eighteenth century Tillotson
would have to become a little more remote from this earthy reality
and to deal more in the grand generalities which delighted those
readers. The modern reader, on the other hand, is more likely
to be attracted by the sermons in which Tillotson was moved to
take his stand on some problem that had a specific bearing on the
life and thought of his age. His success as a preacher no doubt
came from his ability to use the common speech of the day, but
by the time he chose to appear before the reading public his speech
was keyed to that of a public which prized ' decency ' in subject
matter as well as in language, a kind of decency which excluded
flashes of wit as well as flights of fancy, vigorous thinking as well
as strong language, the severe discipline of thoughts and words as
well as the harsh touch of reality. If Tillotson was such a master
of the middle style it is probably because as a truly temperate man
and an apostle of moderation in all things he felt perfectly at home
in this middle zone and feared all extremes.

The style that was praised so often in the next generation or
two was a style of thinking as much as of speaking, and if the
Morning Exercise strikes a different note it is because Tillotson
treats his theme in a more direct manner rather than because he
uses language more vividly. Here already one notices his tendency
to blur outlines and to slacken his rhythms by means of doublets[1] ;
but one also recognizes his ability to state a point clearly and
simply, though in no way strikingly. For instance, to show that
the rule laid down in his text ought to be practised in matters of
freedom and liberty he says :

> In matters of *freedom* and *liberty*; which are not deter-
> mined by any natural or positive Law, we must permit as
> much to others, as we assume to ourselves ; and this is a
> sign of an equall, and temperate person, and one that justly
> values his understanding and power. But there is nothing
> wherein men usually deal more unequally with one another,

---

[1] See for instance the headings of the various instances of the duty,
mentioned above.

than in indifferent opinions and practices of Religion : I account that an indifferent opinion which good men differ about, not that such an opinion is indifferent as to truth or error, but as to salvation or damnation, it is not of necessary belief. By an indifferent practice in Religion, I mean that which is in its own nature, neither a duty, nor a sin to do or omit. Where I am left free, I would not have any man to rob me of my liberty ; or intrench upon my freedome, and because he is satisfied, such a thing is lawfull, and fit to be done, expect I should do it, who think it otherwise ; or because he is confident such an opinion is true, be angry with me, because I cannot believe as fast as he. ... And do not say that thou art in the right, and he that differs from thee in the wrong, and therefore thou mayst impose upon him, though he may not upon thee. Hath not every man this confidence of his own opinion and practice [1] ?

This is as good an example as any of Tillotson's lucid expository prose, in which the simple statement leads easily to the advice or unemphatic rhetorical question. Here already appears his ability to manage pauses in the development while linking the stages, as well as to join dissimilar members having a similar syntactic function. Though several sentences have approximately the same length, the structure and rhythm vary from one to the other : the link between the sentences is of the same kind as the link between the parts, that is, taking up a point and developing it through contrast or through definition or through qualification, and using the turn that is natural to speech (e.g. " not that such an opinion is indifferent ... "). The level tone is kept all through, yet the variety of movement ensures the smooth flow through the paragraph. Nothing, however, is arresting here ; nor is anything emphasized, though the shift from the general to the personal gives relief to the thought. It is characteristic, however, that the language is not concrete, that the statements are general even when applied to I or thou ; Tillotson is dealing with men's attitude to each other, but what he expresses appears as a truth of experience rather than as an experienced fact, it is midway between the abstract and the concrete. This is certainly an apt way of expressing such commonplaces, one that is particularly apposite for the essay, with its mixture of general and particular. Compared with the

[1] *The Morning-Exercise at Cripplegate, or, Several Cases of Conscience Practically Resolved*, by Sundry Ministers, London, 1664, p. 228.

essay style of an earlier age or with that of Halifax, for instance, Tillotson's is looser and more ' natural ' ; its sentence structure and varied rhythm are not unlike those which Dryden was gradually to achieve, but the relaxed tension in thought and movement suggests a less vigorous temper, one indeed which is more akin to Addison's.

Tillotson can be concise at times, but he has few memorable phrases, and even when his sentence bites more sharply—usually when he brands the Romanists' doctrines or practices—it is never as pregnant as South's, for instance.   Thus when stressing the need for rational enquiry in religious matters he says :

> Is it credible, that God should give a Man judgment in the most fundamental and important Matter of all, viz.   *To discern the true Religion*, and *the true Church, from the false* ; for no other end, but to enable him to choose once for all to whom he should resign and enslave his Judgment for ever ?   Which is just as reasonable as if one should say, that God hath given a Man Eyes for no other end, but to look out once for all, and to pitch upon a discreet Person to lead him about blindfold all the days of his life [1].

Yet, he tends to repeat the same idea, and often the same key-words, making his point through iteration rather than through the vigour of the expression.   Thus the above quotation concludes a paragraph in which the same idea has been rehearsed in several sentences, which may indeed have contributed to drive the point home to his hearers, but which to the reader is merely repetitive since the thought does not progress or become more precise :

> Now, as the *Apostle* reasons in another Case, if Men be fit to judge for themselves in so great and important a Matter as the choice of their Religion, why should they be thought *unworthy to judge in lesser Matters* ?   They tell us indeed that a Man may use his judgment in the choice of his Religion ; but when he hath once chosen, he is then

---

[1] *Op. cit.*, I, ser. 21, p. 202.   See also in the same sermon, p. 201 : "This liberty *St Paul* allowed ; and tho' he was inspired by God, yet he treated those whom he taught like Men ".   In *Objections against the True Religion Answer'd*, speaking of vicious habits, he says : " he that is deeply engaged in Vice is like a Man laid fast in a Bogg, who by a faint and lazy struggling to get out, does but spend his strength to no purpose, and sinks himself the deeper into it : The only way is, by a resolute and vigorous effort to spring out, if possible, at once ".   *Ibid.*, ser. 28, p. 293.

for ever to resign up his Judgment to their Church. But what tolerable Reason can any Man give, why a Man should be fit to judge upon the *whole*, and yet unfit to judge upon *particular* Points ? especially if it be considered, that no Man can make a discreet Judgment of any Religion, before he hath examined the particular Doctrines of it, and made a judgment concerning *them* [1].

The effect of the more telling sentences that follow [2] is partly destroyed by the repetition. It is as though Tillotson intended to tone down rather than to give life and force to the ideas he is expounding. What his style and thought lack is sinewy strength, and the slackness of his rhythms in fact images this lack of energy. This was no doubt Tillotson's natural bent, but his revisions show that he deliberately tended to expand or dilute, thereby destroying whatever terseness his sentences may have had originally ; which suggests that the voice in the pulpit probably toned down rather than gave relief to the more telling phrase or comparison. For instance, the following sentence from the quarto version of *The Wisdom of Being Religious* :

> And tho' we have sufficient assurance of another state, yet not so great evidence as if we ourselves had been in the other world, and seen how all things are there

was revised in the folio edition to :

> And tho' we have sufficient assurance of another state, yet no man can think we have so great evidence ... [3].

This stylistic characteristic strikes us all the more when he translates some apophthegm, for instance in :

---

[1] *Ibid.*, ser. 21, p. 202.

[2] See preceding quotation. See also another passage on vicious habits : " But vicious habits have a greater advantage, and are of a quicker growth. For the corrupt nature of man is a rank soil to which vice takes easily, and wherein it thrives apace. The mind of man hath need to be prepared for piety and virtue ; it must be cultivated to that end, and ordered with great care and pains : But vices are weeds that grow wild and spring up of themselves. They are in some sort natural to the Soil, and therefore they need not to be planted and watered, 'tis sufficient if they be neglected and let alone. So that vice having this advantage from our nature, it is no wonder if occasion and temptation easily draw it forth. " *Ibid.*, ser. 10, p. 97 (*Of the Deceitfulness and Danger of Sin*).

[3] *Op. cit.*, ser. 1, p. 26 (1664 ed. p. 50). See also in the same sermon : " such a thing as a future state *after this life* ", or " that he is a spirit, and consequently, *that he is* invisible " ; the words italicized were added in the later version (1664, p. 46 ; folio p. 24).

I will now conclude this whole Discourse with a *Saying* which I heard from a great and judicious Man, *Non amo nimis argutam Theologiam ; I love no Doctrines in Divinity which stand so very much upon quirk and subtilty* [1].

The evidence from the revisions seems to be contradicted by Tillotson's preface to the *Six Sermons*, in which he says :

> The *style* of them is more loose and full of words, than is agreeable to just and exact *Discourses* : But so I think the *Style* of *Popular Sermons* ought to be. And therefore I have not been very careful to mend this matter ; chusing rather that they should appear in that native simplicity in which, many years ago, they were first fram'd, than dress'd up with too much Care and Art [2] ;

but the style of these sermons is not markedly different from his usual manner, which is indeed " loose and full of words ".

Tillotson's style was defined by Felton in terms which recall Denham's description of the Thames in *Cooper's Hill* [3], a description which itself suggests the stylistic ideals of the age :

> The famous Tillotson is all over natural and easy in the most unconstrained, and freest elegancy of thoughts and words : his course, both in his reasoning and his style, like a gentle and even current, is clear and deep, and calm and strong. His language is so pure, no water can be more ; it floweth with so free, uninterrupted a stream, that it never stoppeth the reader or itself. Every word possesseth its proper place [4].

The smooth surface is seldom ruffled, for even when Tillotson allows himself to be carried away by his anti-popish zeal, he soon breaks off and returns to his level tone. Nor do images appear to enliven the exposition or to strike a more vivid note. As Burnet said, he retrenched all embellishments ; like other members of the Royal Society he seems to have regarded metaphorical language with distrust and to have eschewed it as much as possible. He thereby achieved the unaffected plain style which many reformers of pulpit oratory had called for. Given his hearers' interest in the

---

[1] *Op. cit.*, I, ser. 44, p. 459.   [2] *Op. cit.*, I, p. 504.

[3] " Though deep, yet clear, though gentle yet not dull, Strong without rage, without o'er-flowing full. "

[4] Henry FELTON : *A Dissertation on Reading the Classicks, and Forming a Just Style*, London, 1713, pp. 154-5.

kind of thought he was expounding one can understand that, as Beardmore tells us,

> The audience generally stood or sat, with the greatest attention, and even waited upon his discourses, hanging upon his lips [1],

for he never taxed their attention or powers and he always gave them something profitable to consider. It is doubtful, however, whether such a style could have riveted the attention of less eager listeners. While Barrow's verbal imagination or South's manly wit arouse our interest in the themes they treat, the reader who does not come to Tillotson's sermons for edification is likely to appreciate the clear and easy style only when the matter treated is of particular interest, that is, defines the preacher's position and belief as a Church-of-England man of the time, for the prosaic quality of his thought and mind is made all the more obvious by the plainness and simplicity of his style.

Tillotson's limitations are most obvious when he deals with themes which would require bolder and more imaginative thinking as well as greater powers of expression. Such, for instance, is his sermon on *The Happiness of a Heavenly Conversation* [2]. Though it may be readily granted that such happiness cannot be fully represented or even apprehended, yet Tillotson's failure to suggest the transcendent nature of the heavenly state is surely characteristic of his own prosaic mind. From his explication of the text, that the phrase is " an allusion to a City or Corporation, and to the privileges and manners of those who are free of it ", it may be guessed that he will bring the heavenly Jerusalem down to the City of London ; whatever he may say, the bliss he attempts to define does not sound altogether different from the peace and contentment to be found in the worldly state, except that it is unmixed with evil, " very great in itself ", and will have no end. True, he also adds that it is " far above any thing that we can now conceive or imagine ", but his words and thoughts are so commonplace that they hardly convey the inexpressible quality he takes for granted. Rather he applies himself to the way in which men may come to be made partakers of this blessed state, and to the—obvious—effects which such considerations should have on their lives. How pedes-

---

[1] *Op. cit.*, p. cclxxxiii.   [2] *Op. cit.*, I, ser. 8 (on *Phil.* III. 20).

trian his thought and style is appears most clearly when he weaves
biblical phrases into his sentences, for instance :

> How should we welcome the thoughts of that happy hour,
> when we shall make our escape out of these prisons, when
> we shall pass out *of this howling wilderness into the pro-*
> *mised Land* ; when we shall be removed from all the troubles
> and temptations of a wicked and ill-natured world ; when
> we shall be past all storms, and secured from all further
> danger of shipwreck, and shall be safely landed in the
> regions of bliss and immortality [1] ?

The amplification merely tones down, so that everything sounds
flat and stale.   Yet this sermon was remembered by Addison, who
refers to it in No. 600 of *The Spectator*, from which it may be
inferred that for all the insipid style and prosaic thought Tillotson's
considerations struck a chord in some of his readers as well as
hearers [2].   These must have been satisfied with such a tame prospect and with the sweet reasonableness of the heavenly state ;
they must have been reassured that no violent disruption was to
be feared [3].

The one quality that a twentieth-century reader is likely to
prize as much as did Tillotson's contemporaries, is his urbanity,
which is the key to his simplicity and ease.   Compared with Barrow
he sounds much more modern, but he has none of South's raciness ;

---

[1] *Op. cit.*, I, 87-88.

[2] The kind of thought and expression that was apt to please eighteenth-
century readers may be gathered from a manuscript note " a beautiful peri-
phrasis " in my own copy of the sermons, where the following passage is
marked : " When we consider that we have but a little while to be here, that
we are upon our journey travelling towards our heavenly Country where we
shall meet with all the delights we can desire, it ought not to trouble us much
to endure storms and foul ways, and to want many of those accommodations
we might expect at home.   This is the common fate of Travellers, and we must
take things as we find them and not look to have everything just to our mind.
These difficulties and inconveniences will shortly be over, and after a few days
will be quite forgotten, and be to us as if they had never been.   And when we
are safely landed in our own Country, with what pleasure shall we look back
upon those rough and boisterous Seas which we have escaped ? "   *Op. cit.*, I,
86.   It should be remembered that the sermon was published by Tillotson, hence
that he had the opportunity to revise it.

[3] Though it is clear that Tillotson's purpose is to persuade his hearers to
lead the good life here so as to be fit to partake of the blessed state, and though
he urges them to become perfect in their lives here on earth, yet the smooth
continuity rather than the strenuous ascent is conveyed by such statements as
these : " Our souls will continue for ever what we make them in this world.
Such a temper and disposition of mind as a man carries with him out of this
life he shall retain in the next " (p. 85).   Contrast with this Keats's valley of
soul-making.

his is the common speech of gentlemen, without any attempt at the grace or at the strength that better stylists could achieve. He seems to talk to his congregation, to be one of them, and to share their interests and troubles. If his listeners did hang upon his lips it is not because he was a spellbinder, which he would have despised, but probably because his manner in the pulpit and particularly the modulations of his voice brought him close to his public, as well as because " he brought down Divinity to the level of his congregation " [1]. From his earnest manner they could feel that the truths he was expounding or the duties he was enforcing mattered as greatly to him as to them, but his amiable tone and easy style must have banished all stiffness from religion as well as from the intercourse between speaker and listeners. If South's manly wit often suggests the aristocrat, if the discipline of his thought and language urges on his hearers the necessity to exert their minds, Tillotson's more relaxed manner made his teaching more accessible to a larger section of churchgoers. It gave him the kind of popularity that the essayists of the next century were hoping to achieve ; like Tillotson they were concerned to bring if not divinity at least edification down to the level of their public. While South's incisiveness looks forward to Swift and Pope, Tillotson's smoothness and correctness look forward to Addison. In the treatment of his themes, in his temper, and in his style, Tillotson anticipates the periodical essayists ; no wonder that he was recommended so often to their readers.

Besides his unconstraint, the eighteenth century praised the purity of Tillotson's diction, the propriety of his language, or his correctness. To an age that felt the lack of any certain standards of correctness he appeared to have used none but proper words, and to have used every word in its proper place. Such unanimous tribute intimates that, whatever his shortcomings as a stylist, he had a sense of language from which even men like Dryden could learn [2]. Pope numbered Tillotson among the prose writers whose

---

[1] John STOUGHTON : *Ecclesiastical History of England, The Church of the Revolution*, London, 1874, p. 193.

[2] The remark attributed to Dryden by Congreve in his Dedication of the *Dramatic Works* (1717) has puzzled many critics : " I have frequently heard him own with Pleasure, that if he had any Talent for English Prose, it was owing to his having often read the Writings of the great Archbishop Tillotson ". For a discussion of Dryden's possible debt to T., see D.D. BROWN : ' John Tillotson's Revisions and Dryden's " Talent for English Prose " ', *RES*, NS, XII (1961), 24-39. Locke also recommended T. for perspicuity and propriety

works might serve as a basis for a dictionary, and he is reported
to have said :

> There is hardly any laying down particular rules for writing
> our language, or whether such a particular use of it is
> proper : one has nothing but authority for it. Is it in Sir
> William Temple, or Locke, or Tillotson ? If it be, we may
> conclude that it is right, or at least won't be looked upon
> as wrong [1].

If usage could be defined from Tillotson's sermons it is surely
because even in the next age his style was felt to be idiomatic both
in vocabulary and in syntax ; besides, one cannot help feeling that
his sense of propriety and his preference for the abstract or general
must have appealed to those who prized correctness above all.
His reputation must still have been high in the last quarter of the
century since Johnson hesitated to go against the current in not
recommending him for imitation in the pulpit [2] ; Johnson's own
objection, however, may have derived from the style rather than
from the language Tillotson used, for he " could but just endure
the smooth verbosity " of this divine [3]. Earlier in the century,
Steele among others [4] had praised Tillotson for reprehending vice

> in words and thoughts so natural, that any man who reads
> them would imagine he himself could have been the Author
> of them [5].

By thus applying to him Boileau's definition of true wit, formulated

---

(see : *Thoughts Concerning Reading and Study for a Gentleman*, in *Works*,
1801, III, 271).

[1] Joseph SPENCE : *Observations, Anecdotes and Characters of Books and
Men*, ed. E. Malone, London, 1820, I, 58-59.

[2] " ' I should not advise a preacher at this day to imitate Tillotson's style ;
though I don't know, I should be cautious of objecting to what has been
applauded by so many suffrages. " *Boswell's Life of Johnson*, ed. cit., III,
247-8 (7 April, 1778). Hugh BLAIR praised the purity and perspicuity of T.'s
language, but found him feeble and languid (Lecture XIX) or loose and diffuse
(Lecture X). *Op. cit.*, I, 192, 393.

[3] John HAWKINS, *op. cit.*, p. 116.

[4] In *Of Style* (1698) John HUGHES recommended ' the Incomparable Tillotson' for his 'Easiness and beautiful Simplicity'. *Poems on Several Occasions.
With some Select Essays in Prose*, London, 1735, I, 254.

[5] *The Spectator*, No. 103. The essay includes a long quotation from Tillotson's sermon on Sincerity (II, 1), which was quoted again in *The Spectator*,
No. 352. Many later references to Tillotson in eighteenth-century periodical
essays are to this very sermon, which suggests that *The Spectator* may have
been influential in creating a taste for his style. It may be worth noting that
Steele's praise in introducing the sermon is based on Burnet's in the funeral
oration ; hence also, perhaps, the view prevalent in the 18th century that the
reform of pulpit oratory was largely the work of Tillotson.

more pregnantly in the *Essay on Criticism*, Steele clearly ranked
Tillotson among the writers from whom eighteenth-century readers
could form a true taste.   Yet, if Steele's words anticipate Johnson's
more famous dictum, his use of them in reference to Tillotson
suggests that for him ' what oft was thought ' meant just what to
Johnson seemed to depress wit below its natural dignity ;   for
Tillotson lacked that strength of thought which Johnson considered
as essential to true wit :   the verbosity which the great critic disliked is bound up with the diffuseness of the thought, and one is
not surprised to learn from Boswell that he preferred stronger meat,
even though occasionally coarse [1].   To Addison, on the other hand,
Tillotson was ' the great British Preacher ', and this must have
been a widely accepted view at the time since it was not necessary
to mention his name when quoting from one of his sermons [2].
Tillotson, one feels, was the very model to propound to those who
aspired to education or who had to be reformed by gentle means,
for he was himself both gentle and genteel, eminently kind and
sober, but, one must conclude, unexciting.

The history of Tillotson's reputation in the two centuries after
his death throws light not only on standards of taste in style but
on changing modes in religious thought [3].   His popularity in the
years after the Restoration was largely due, as Canon Overton
said, to the fact that he hit the popular taste [4], i.e. gave his public
the kind of teaching it was ready for after the storms and passions
of the Interregnum.   His moderate views and sober temper were
equally suited to an age in which liberal theology made such
progress as to be at times hardly distinguishable from Deism ;   he
himself had been called a Deist for reducing, or seeming to reduce,
religion to the practice of virtue.   He was, indeed, a forerunner
of the enlightenment, and his moral discourses must have delighted

---

[1] See his remark on South, quoted above.

[2] *The Spectator*, No. 557.   The quotation is again from the sermon on
Sincerity.   See also *The Tatler*, No. 101 : " The most eminent and useful author
of the age we live in ... Everyone will know that I here mean ... the late
Archbishop of Canterbury ".   See also Lord Orrery to Swift in 1740 : " I am
preaching to Tillotson ", *Correspondence*, ed. cit., V, 194.

[3] Louis G. Locke attempts to do this for T's literary reputation, *op. cit.*,
Ch. IV and V, but he fails to relate the various pronouncements he quotes to
the standards of the several critics.   He does not quote Johnson's censure of
T's verbosity, but relates the remark from Boswell's *Life* to the prevalence
of another kind of prose, " balanced, rhetorical, elaborate, and typically John-
sonian " (p. 147).

[4] See OVERTON, *op. cit.*, p. 247.

the same readers as did the moral essays of the period. That he came under fire in some quarters may appear from John Wesley's introduction to a selection from Tillotson's sermons in *A Christian Library*, in which he warns the reader :

> I have the rather inserted the following Extracts for the sake of two sorts of people. Those who are unreasonably prejudiced *for*, and those who are unreasonably prejudiced *against* this great man. By this small specimen it will abundantly appear, to all who will at length give themselves leave to judge impartially, that the Archbishop was as far from being the *worst*, as from being the *best* of the English writers [1].

In nineteenth-century collections of sermons, Tillotson is no longer given pride of place ; in some he does not even appear at all [2], and one imagines that he was hardly popular with divines influenced by the Oxford Movement [3]. Macaulay noted that posterity had reversed the judgement of Tillotson's contemporaries, who thought he surpassed all rivals living or dead ; but he himself found that

> Tillotson still keeps his place as a legitimate English classic. His highest flights were indeed far below those of Taylor, of Barrow, and of South ; but his oratory was more correct and equable than theirs ... His reasoning was just sufficiently profound and sufficiently refined to be followed by a popular audience with that slight degree of intellectual exertion which is a pleasure. His style is not brilliant, but it is pure, transparently clear, and equally free from levity and from the stiffness which disfigure the sermons of some eminent divines of the seventeenth century. He is always serious : yet there is about his manner a certain graceful ease which marks him as a man who knows the world, who has lived in populous cities and in splendid courts, and who has conversed, not only with books, but with lawyers and merchants, wits and beauties, statesmen and princes. The greatest charm of his compositions, however, is derived from

---

[1] John WESLEY : *A Christian Library. Choicest Pieces of Practical Divinity*, in 30 volumes (first published in 1750 in 50 volumes), London, 1826, vol. XXVII.

[2] For instance, in Christopher WORDSWORTH's *Christian Institutes*, London, 1837. Wordsworth, who was Master of Trinity College, Cambridge, naturally gives large extracts from Barrow, but he also includes two sermons by South.

[3] James BROGDEN's *Illustrations of the Liturgy and Ritual. Sermons and Discourses selected from the works of Eminent Divines of the Seventeenth Century*, London, 1842, 3 vols., has five extracts from Barrow and two from South, but none from Tillotson.

the benignity and candour which appear in every line, and which shone forth not less conspicuously in his life than in his writings [1].

Tillotson's benignity and candour, no less than his Latitudinarianism, must indeed have shone forth in his writings for such a rhetorician as Macaulay to endorse the earlier eighteenth-century judgement of a divine whose stylistic qualities are so different from his own. Macaulay rightly assessed the reasons why Tillotson pleased the readers of *The Spectator* : he was sufficiently profound and sufficiently refined, and he required no more than a slight degree of intellectual exertion ! For whatever reason, posterity reversed this judgement and Henry Hallam noted that Tillotson's sermons, which

> were for half a century more read than any in our language ... are now bought almost as waste paper, and hardly read at all [2].

While complete editions of South and of Barrow appeared in the nineteenth century, Tillotson only appeared in a selection [3], which is probably the best way to honour his memory for many of his moral discourses certainly make dull reading to-day [4]. Yet, of the three divines under consideration in this study he is the only one with whom twentieth-century readers are likely to be acquainted, through the selections from his writings edited by James Moffat as *The Golden Book of Tillotson* (1926). Moffat, however, did not print any one sermon in full, he only gave extracts. The procedure is not unlike that of *The Spectator*, and is probably justified in an age that may be interested in style but is no longer addicted to sermons. Though the extracts form an attractive anthology they cannot suggest the specific qualities of Tillotson as a preacher. Only by following the development of one of his themes can the modern reader rightly assess both his qualities and his limitations, as well as the change that had come over pulpit oratory since the days of the great Jacobean divines. His sermons herald

---

[1] *Op. cit.*, III, 468-9.
[2] Henry HALLAM : *Introduction to the Literature of Europe in the Fifteenth, Sixteenth, and Seventeenth Centuries*, Paris, 1839, IV, 103.
[3] TILLOTSON : *Sermons*, Selected, edited and annotated by the Rev. G.W. Weldon, London, 1886.
[4] Particularly those in volumes II and III, i.e. those Tillotson did not publish himself.

a new age, in thought and feeling as well as in style ; they fore-
shadow the supersession of devotional literature by the essay and
look towards the future which the Whig Revolution contributed
to shape, to an age in which the divines had less to say than the
philosophes and in which the values of civilized living were prized
more highly than religious zeal.   His sermons have neither the
ardency of religious fervour nor the energy of disciplined thought ;
instead they let in the light of common day and engage men to
live amicably together, to tolerate each other's opinions and to be
regardful of their duties to each other in order to salvation.

Though Tillotson was indeed a practical preacher, though right
living rather than right thinking was for him the Law and the
Prophets, yet he did believe and teach that religion is the only
certain foundation of the good life, and that Christianity is the
best of all religions, as well as the only true one, because it gives
the highest assurance of rewards and punishments to encourage and
sanction the practice of virtue.   To him religion is the only safe
basis on which societies can subsist, since it lays " the greatest
obligation upon conscience to all civil offices and moral duties " [1],
both upon the magistrate and upon the subjects.   Religion alone
is the basis of mutual trust among men ; religion alone can curb
individual interests and further the good of the community as a
whole ; religion alone can make men obedient to laws not only
out of fear but for conscience sake.   In an age in which scepticism
and atheism were gaining ground Tillotson stressed that no government could subsist without belief in God, because men need to be
restrained by other than human laws ; but he also insisted that the
duties of religion are conformable to those taught by natural law.
He was out to make men wisely religious, by showing them that
it is in their own interest to practise virtue, but also by demonstrating the agreeableness of the Christian religion to natural religion,
and by opposing the notion that virtue and vice are founded upon
custom. He attacked infidelity because to him it was both repugnant to reason and destructive of the common bonds of humanity ;
likewise, in his constant warfare against Romanism he asserted
the need both to inquire rationally into the grounds of faith and
to further concord among men. When he touched upon doctrines
controverted by some Protestants, such as the irresistible power

---

[1] *Op. cit.*, I, ser. 3, p. 41 (*The Advantages of Religion to Societies*).

of Grace, it was again to show that they subvert practice and thereby nullify the very excellence of Christianity, i.e. that it commands all virtues and obliges men to a holy life.

Tillotson's insistence that religion is the highest kind of wisdom, that it is not only true but advantageous to individual men and to societies may at times sound very worldly indeed ; but this is redeemed by his natural kindliness and by his deep concern for concord among men, which led him not only to dwell on the clear notions of religion rather than discuss subtle points that might raise controversies, but also to further reconciliation with Protestant brethren who agreed on fundamental points of belief. If such middle-of-the-road position [1] lacks depth, it is marked by a genuine desire for peace and by tolerance, a virtue not preeminent among Tillotson's contemporaries. His teaching hardly stimulates to heroic action or sublime selflessness [2] ; it is more likely to prompt these nameless unremembered acts of kindness and of love which won him the hearts of men and women of all ranks.

The sermons printed below will, it is hoped, help the reader to form an adequate view of Tillotson the preacher, of his thought and style no less than of his temper. *The Wisdom of Being Religious* and *The Folly of Scoffing at Religion* are probably his fullest refutation of infidelity ; they outline the main themes of his teaching and throw light on the thought and temper of the age. Since he stood out in his time as one of the main champions against Rome and as such appealed to many readers abroad in the eighteenth century, the selection includes several of his anti-popish

---

[1] Coleridge said in *The Christian Observer*, 1845 : "Tillotson, Hoadly, and the whole sect of Syncretists and Coalitionists, I utterly reject." quoted in *Coleridge on the Seventeenth Century*, ed. R.F. Brinkley, Durham (N.C.), 1955, p. 267.

[2] "Tillotson had the ambition of establishing in the weary, worn out, distracted, perplexed mind and heart of England a Christianity of calm reason, of plain, practical English good sense ...   To some, Tillotson—profoundly religious, unimpeachable as to his belief in all the great truths of Christianity, but looking to the fruits rather than the dogmas of the Gospel—guilty of candour, of hearing both sides of a question—and dwelling if not exclusively, at least chiefly, on the Christian life, the sober, unexciting Christian life—was Arian, Socinian, Deist, Atheist ...   The calm, equable, harmonious, idiomatic sentences of Tillotson, his plain practical theology, fell as a grateful relief, upon the English ear and heart. To us the prolix, and at times languid, diffuseness of Tillotson is wearisome ... but Tillotson must be taken with his age ; and if we can throw ourselves back upon his age, we shall comprehend the mastery which he held, for a century at least, over the religion and over the literature of the country." H.H. MILMAN : *Annals of St Paul's Cathedral*, London, 1868, pp. 419-21.

sermons, in which he enforces the duty of rational inquiry into the truths of religion. In *Instituted Religion not Intended to Undermine Natural* he restates the relation between natural religion and Christianity and further defines his objections to Romanism, while in the sermon on *Regeneration* he expounds the Anglican doctrine of grace in contradistinction to the views of other Protestant Churches or Sects at the time. The sermon on *The Fruits of the Spirit the Same with Moral Virtues* shows how close he sometimes comes to Deism, while *The Necessity of Supernatural Grace, in order to a Christian Life,* is sufficient evidence that he did not altogether equate Christianity with the mere practice of moral duties. It has not been thought fit to reprint any of his more practical discourses ; as literature they certainly rank lowest and, whatever Addison and Steele may have thought, they are better classed with the useful manuals of devotion : no doubt they served their purpose in their time, and in the next age, but they are unlikely to appeal to the common reader to-day.

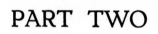

PART TWO

ISAAC BARROW

NOTE ON THE TEXT
OF BARROW'S SERMONS

Only one of Barrow's sermons appeared in his lifetime, *The Duty and Reward of Bounty to the Poor* [1], which was published at the request of the Lord Mayor and Aldermen of the City of London, before whom it had been preached, " with what farther he had prepared to deliver at that time " [2]. The sermon he preached at the Guildhall Chapel on Good Friday, 1677, *Upon the Passion of Our Blessed Saviour* [3], was also published by order of this Court, but was still in the press when Barrow died on May 4, 1677. The next year a collection of his sermons was brought out by Brabazon Aylmer, *Sermons Preached Upon Several Occasions* [4], with a dedication by Barrow's father and an advertisement by the " publisher ". A second collection, *Several Sermons Against Evil-Speaking* [5], appeared in 1678, and a third one, *Of the Love of God and Our Neighbour*, in 1680 [6], with a similar dedication and advertisement. In 1680 too, but shortly before the third volume of sermons, two more of Barrow's English works had been printed for Brabazon Aylmer : *A Treatise of the Pope's Supremacy*, to

---

[1] *The Duty and Reward of Bounty to the Poor* : In a Sermon preached at the Spittal Upon Wednesday in Easter Week, Anno Dom. MDCLXXI, By Isaac Barrow, D.D., Fellow of Trinity College in Cambridge, and Chaplain in Ordinary to His Majesty. London, Printed for Brabazon Aylmer ... MDCLXXI (Advertised in *T.C.*, I, 78, July 1671 ; *Wing* 933). Octavo. A second edition appeared in 1677 (*T.C.*, I, 279, May 1677) and a third in 1680 (Not in *T.C.*).

[2] See the order of the Court, sig. A 1v.

[3] *A Sermon Upon the Passion of Our Blessed Saviour* : Preached at Guildhall Chappel on Good Friday, the 13th day of April, 1677. By Isaac Barrow, D.D., late Chaplain in Ordinary to His Majesty, and Master of Trinity College in Cambridge. London, Printed for Brabazon Aylmer ... MDCLXXVII (Advertised in *T.C.*, I, 271, May 1677 ; *Wing* 954). Quarto. A second edition appeared in 1678 and a third in 1682 (Neither is mentioned in *T.C.*).

[4] London, 1678 (*T.C.*, I, 287, November 1677. Advertised as *Twelve Sermons* ...). Octavo. A second edition appeared in 1679 (*T.C.*, I, 345 ; February 1679), and a third in 1680 (not advertised in *T.C.*).

[5] London, Printed for Brabazon Aylmer, 1678 (*T.C.*, I, 318 ; June 1678. Advertised as " *(Ten) Sermons* ... published by the Reverend J. Tillotson, Dean of Canterbury "). Octavo. A second edition appeared in 1678, a third in 1682 (neither was advertised in *T.C.*).

[6] London, Printed for Brabazon Aylmer, 1680 (*T.C.*, I, 401 ; June 1680). Octavo.

which is added A Discourse Concerning the Unity of the Church [1].
These were " published " by John Tillotson, Dean of Canterbury,
who was also the " publisher " of the collected sermons [2]. The
Gunpowder Plot sermon published in the first collection also
appeared separately in 1679 and in 1679/80 [3], as did the *Discourse
Concerning the Unity of the Church* [4] in 1680. The next work
of Barrow to be published by Tillotson was *A Brief Exposition
of the Lord's Prayer and the Decalogue, To which is added, The
Doctrine of the Sacraments*, which came out in 1682 [5]. In the
same year Brabazon Aylmer circulated Proposals [6] for the first
and second folio volumes of the *Works* of Barrow, the first to
contain all the works in English [7] which had already been published, the second to contain the Sermons on the Creed; the
subscribers were asked to make their first payment by the 1st of
February (1683) since the first volume was then in the press and
" to be finished by the 25th of March ". The second volume was
announced as in the press in the *Term Catalogue* for November
1682 [8], and in June 1683 were advertised *The Works of the
Learned Isaac Barrow ... published by the Reverend Dr. Tillotson,
Dean of Canterbury* [9]. The third volume of the folio *Works*,
containing forty-five sermons upon several occasions, appeared in
1686 [10], but some of these sermons had been published the year
before in an octavo edition printed for Brabazon Aylmer [11]. A

---

[1] London, 1680 (*T.C.*, I, 367; November 1679). Quarto.

[2] See the advertisement in *T.C.*, I, 318, and the " list of books printed for
B. Aylmer " at the end of the 1680 edition of *Bounty to the Poor* and at
the end of the 1682 edition of the sermon *Upon the Passion*: " All the said
books of the Learned Dr. Isaac Barrow (except the Sermon of Bounty to the
Poor) are since the author's death published by Dr. Tillotson, Dean of Canterbury ". The advertisements of the octavo collections were incorporated into the
signed advertisement of the folio edition.

[3] Both printed for Brabazon Aylmer (*T.C.*, I, 340; February 1679. *T.C.*,
I, 377; November 1679). Quartos.

[4] For Brabazon Aylmer (*T.C.*, I, 401; June 1680). Octavo.

[5] For Brabazon Aylmer (*T.C.*, I, 470; February 1682). Octavo.

[6] See the Sheet in the Bodleian Library (no. 804).

[7] Barrow's *Lectiones Opticae* and *Lectiones Geometricae* had been published
separately (in 1670) and together (in 1672) and his *Archimedis Opera*; *Apollo-
nii Pergaei Conicorum lib. 4*; *Theodosii Sphaerica Methodo nova illustrata et
succincte demonstrata* in 1675 (*T.C.*, I, 26, 49, 105, 206).

[8] *T.C.*, I, 517.

[9] *T.C.*, II, 24. The subscribers were desired " to send their last Payment
and Receipts, and to take up their Books; both Volumes being finished ".

[10] *T.C.*, II, 173; May-June 1686. Reprinted in 1693 (*T.C.*, II, 457; May
1693).

[11] *T.C.*, II, 135; June 1685: *Of Contentment, Patience, and Resignation to
the Will of God. Several Sermons ... Never before printed*. The sermons *Of*

fourth volume, containing Barrow's Latin Works, appeared in 1687 ; these were not included in the later editions of the folio *Works*, in 1700, 1716, 1722, 1741 (corrected), nor in the 1751 octavo edition deriving from the last folio *Works*.

The sermons not sent to the press by Barrow himself were thus edited by Tillotson, at the request of or with the consent of Barrow's father, who signed the dedications [1]. In 1697, however, Brabazon Aylmer brought out two works which, he says in The Bookseller's Advertisement, had been overlooked by the Archbishop : a sermon on *Col.* III.2, to which Aylmer gave the title : *A Defence of the B. Trinity* [2], and *A Brief Exposition on the Creed* [3]. We may probably take the bookseller's word that Tillotson had overlooked the sermon on the Trinity, " which might very easily be in so great a number " [4], and there is no reason to doubt that the 1697 edition was set up from Barrow's autograph sermon [5]. Yet, one cannot help speculating on the extraordinary flair of Aylmer, which made him discover among such a number of manuscripts one on the very doctrine that was causing so much controversy at the time. Not only did he publish the sermon, but from this he extracted a few significant passages which he published in 1698 as *A Brief State of the Socinian Controversy concerning Trinity in Unity* [6]. Clearly, Aylmer's discovery was prompted by his wish to publish one more item in vindication of the Trinity [7],

---

Industry were also published separately in 1692, and those on *The Consideration of our Latter End* and on the *Mischief of Delaying Repentance* in 1694.

[1] Volume I (1683) of the folio *Works* is dedicated to the Rt. Hon. Heneage, Earl of Nottingham ; Volume II (1683) to the King ; Volume III (1686) to Princess Anne. "According to John Ward, " the manuscripts of [Barrow's] own composing were intrusted to the care of Dr. John Tillotson (afterwards Archbishop of Canterbury) and Abraham Hill esquire, with a power to print such of them, as they thought proper ". *Lives of the Professors of Gresham College*, *op. cit.*, p. 164. Hill wrote the " Account of the Life of Dr. Barrow " prefixed to Volume I (dated 10 April, 1683). Brabazon Aylmer paid Thomas Barrow £ 470 for the copyright of the first folio volume. See Isaac BARROW : *The Theological Works*, ed. Alexander Napier, 1859, vol. I, Appendix O.

[2] Never before printed. London, 1697 (*T.C.*, III, 11 ; May 1697).

[3] *A Brief Exposition on the Creed, the Lord's Prayer, and Ten Commandments, To which is added the Doctrine of The Sacrament ... This on the Creed never before Published*, London, 1697 (*T.C.*, III, 1 ; February 1697). Octavo.

[4] *Ibid.*, sig. A 3.

[5] *Ibid.*, sig. A 3 v.

[6] *T.C.*, III, 73 ; June 1698. " Twenty-fours ". 2d. These are extracts from the 1697 edition, with page references to it.

[7] Aylmer also published *A Seasonable Vindication of the B. Trinity, Being an Answer to this Question, Why do you believe the Doctrine of the Trinity? Collected from the Works of the Most Reverend, Dr. John Tillotson, Late Lord Archbishop of Canterbury, And the Right Reverend, Dr. Edward Stillingfleet,*

which makes one wonder if Tillotson had not ignored rather than overlooked this manuscript of Barrow's.

Doubt has also been cast on Tillotson's ignorance of the *Exposition on the Creed*. Alexander Napier, who edited Barrow's *Theological Works* in 1859, granted that Tillotson must have been ignorant of its existence " at one period at least of his long editorial labours "; but he argued that it must have fallen " under his notice " while he was preparing the Sermons on the Creed for publication since Napier believed he had found evidence that Tillotson used portions of the *Exposition* " in order to supplement and connect the series of these Expository Discourses "[1]. It should be remembered, however, that Barrow turned long parts of the *Exposition* into sermons (though he revised some passages in the process); moreover, the MS. used by Aylmer for his 1697 edition was not used by Tillotson, who may have drawn from other manuscript *sermons* now lost in order to " supplement and connect " the series[2]. All we can say is that Tillotson *may* have seen a manuscript of the *Exposition on the Creed*, and decided not to publish it since much of this had been incorporated into the Sermons on the Creed[3].

One of Barrow's autograph sermons, however, seems never to have come " under the notice " of either Tillotson or Aylmer. Apparently this manuscript was mislaid and only restored to Trinity College, Cambridge, in the nineteenth century. On this manuscript (Trinity College, MS. O.10.a.32) is a note signed by Dr. W. Whewell, the then Master of Trinity College, to the effect that this sermon of Barrow's was " received from Rev. R. Parkinson, Nov. 1851 ". It is not listed in the manuscript *Catalogue of Dr. Isaac Barrow's MSS in Trinity College* prepared by Lee (Trinity College, MS. R.17.13). Barrow's 1859 editor, Alexander Napier, who first printed this sermon in the *Theological Works*, explained that the manuscript had been " found by the late Dr. Parkinson among the papers of Dr. Byrom, while engaged in pre-

---

now Lord Bishop of Worcester. (*T.C.*, III, 11; May 1697). This book is advertised in the list at the end of *A Defence of the B. Trinity*.

[1] Isaac BARROW: *The Theological Works*, Cambridge, 1859, Preface, I, xxi, xxii.

[2] See my article on ' Tillotson's Barrow ', *English Studies*, XLV (1964), 193-211, 274-88.

[3] Whole passages from the *Exposition* are reproduced *verbatim* in the sermons, not only as published by Tillotson but in Barrow's manuscripts.

paring them for publication in the Chetham Society's Works, and by him restored to Trinity College "[1]. There is no reason to believe that Tillotson ever knew of this sermon, whose text, like that of the sermon on the Trinity, is *Col.* III. 2 ; we can only speculate on the reasons why it was mislaid, though a remark by Ward may give us a clue : Barrow, he says, " was very communicative to all, who desired his assistance, which unhappily proved in some instances a prejudice to the public, by the loss of many of his papers, that were lost and never returned "[2].

Except for the sermons on *Bounty to the Poor* and on the *Passion*, and for the two published after Tillotson's death by Aylmer (1697) and by Napier (1859), all the sermons of Barrow were edited by Tillotson, and in this edition they were read in the eighteenth century, and in the nineteenth until Napier published the *Theological Works*, collated with the extant manuscripts. Tillotson's procedure in preparing his friend's works for the press has, however, been repeatedly criticized, most severely indeed by Napier, on whose views later critics have based their strictures[3]. Napier, in fact, accused Tillotson of tampering with Barrow's sermons, by making verbal revisions, erasing whole sentences, and rearranging some of the sermons, particularly dividing some into smaller units. The impression one derives from Napier's preface is that Tillotson's Barrow was indeed a heavily edited text[4].

Collation of Tillotson's text with the manuscript sermons he used has revealed, however, that Napier had not done justice to Barrow's first editor[5]. Not only did Tillotson select the " best "

[1] *Op. cit.*, Preface, I, xix.
[2] John WARD, *op. cit.*, p. 164.
[3] See W.F. MITCHELL, *op. cit.*, *passim*, and P.H. OSMOND, *op. cit.*, Preliminary Note, stating that "any edition of Barrow's theological writings other writings other than that of Alexander Napier (Cambridge University Press, than that of Alexander Napier (Cambridge University Press, 1859) must be rejected as unauthentic ".
[4] "The MSS. shew, that Tillotson, startled and offended by the strange words so frequently used by Barrow, was *in the habit* of substituting for them more simple expressions ; and that occasionally he erased passages ... The process of erasure has occasionally been so mischievously effective as to defy all attempts at restoration ... But Tillotson permitted himself to take further liberties .... ". *Op. cit.*, pp. xiv, xv. My italics.
[5] See ' Tillotson's Barrow ', *loc. cit.* The manuscripts used by Tillotson bear the printer's marks. All the extant manuscripts of Barrow's sermons, except one, are now in the Library of Trinity College. The manuscript in the British Museum (Lansdowne 356, folios 58-69v.) has the following note on the fly-leaf : "Brabazon Aylmer the Bookseller gave me this Sermon. Febr. 15. 1694. Joh. Strype." The manuscripts in Trinity College were catalogued by the Reverend J. Lee, who indicated for each portion of manuscript the corresponding

texts for his edition, but his revisions of them are by no means as far-reaching as Napier would have us think. True, he did sometimes revise, he did divide some of the longer sermons, and he may occasionally have used a short passage from the *Exposition* ; but the verbal revisions are slight and few in number : far from being in the habit of substituting common words for obsolete or latinate ones, Tillotson altered no more than 70 such words in texts which cover about 1500 folio pages, and he retained many. Moreover, though in two or three cases he had no authority for dividing the text, in several others the division had evidently been intended by Barrow. Napier's excessive strictures are probably to be

volume, number and page in the 1683-1687 folio edition ; the note : " with the printer's marks " refers to the octavo or folio editions by Brabazon Aylmer ; some manuscripts have the note : " with the printer's marks to some other edition ", probably a 19th-century edition. Three more volumes of Barrow's manuscripts were added to the collection after this catalogue was compiled : two, i.e. R.9.33 and R.10.14, have no printer's marks ; the third is O.10.a.32 referred to above.

The manuscripts of some sermons have not come down to us (John Strype's note on the manuscript in the British Museum suggests that Brabazon Aylmer disposed of some of them); for some sermons only drafts survive (e.g. for the sermons against Evil-Speaking); for some there are only imperfect copies (e.g. for sermon 7 in vol. II); for some there is only one manuscript version (e.g. for sermon 1 in vol. I); for some there are two (e.g. for sermon 2 in vol. III), three (e.g. for sermon 4 in vol. I) or even four versions (e.g. for sermon 4 in vol. III): in such cases there is sometimes a fair copy plus drafts, sometimes two fair copies plus a draft, sometimes none but rough drafts ; for several sermons, there are two more or less full versions. From this may be inferred how much work was involved in Tillotson's sorting out his friend's papers. Though I have not collated all the versions, it is obvious from those I have compared that Tillotson always selected what appears to be the final version.

Lee's catalogue describes the contents of the several volumes of manuscripts, each of which contains several sermons or parts of sermons (plus other material). It may therefore be of interest to identify the manuscripts on which Tillotson's texts were based :

Volume I. Sermon 1 : R.10.26. Sermons 2 to 7 : R.10.25. Sermons 8 and 9 : R.10.26. Sermons 10 and 11 : R.10.25. Sermon 12 : R.10.27. The MSS. for Sermons 13 to 22 are not extant. Sermons 23 to 27 : R.10.25. The MSS. for Sermons 28 to 32 are not extant.

Volume II. Sermons 1 to 7 : R.10.17 (the MSS. for Sermons 5 and 7 are imperfect). The MS. for Sermon 8 is not extant. Sermons 9 to 12 : R.10.17 (the MSS. for Sermons 9 and 12 are imperfect). Sermons 13 to 26 : R.10.21 (the MSS. for Sermons 13, 16, 19, 20 are imperfect). The MS. for Sermon 27 is not extant. Sermon 28 : R.10.18. Sermons 29 and 30 : R.10.17. Sermon 31 : R.10.18. Sermon 32 : R.10.17. Sermons 33 and 34 : R.10.18.

Volume III. The MS. for Sermon 1 is not extant. Sermons 2 to 4 : R.10.18. Sermons 5 to 9 : R.10.26. The MS. for Sermon 10 is not extant. Sermons 11 to 23 : R.10.18. Sermons 24 to 27 : R.10.19. Sermons 28 and 29 : R.10.23. Sermons 30 and 31 : R.10.19. The MSS. for Sermons 32 to 35 are not extant. Sermons 36 to 40 : R.10.21. Sermons 41 and 42 : R.10.25. The MS. for Sermon 43 is not extant. Sermon 44 : British Museum MS. Lansdowne 356. The MS. for Sermon 45 is not extant.

ascribed to his own failure to notice that in the manuscripts many
of the words written above other words crossed out are, in fact,
revisions by Barrow himself inked over by Tillotson, and that the
breaks in the longer sermons clearly show that Barrow intended
to deliver the parts on successive occasions (though he did not
end each part with " Amen " nor repeat his text at the beginning
of the next).   After comparing Tillotson's edition with the autograph version of the sermons, one must conclude that he was a
reliable editor, even though he occasionally—very occasionally—
made his friend's vocabulary conform with current usage.   In fact,
his long editorial labours deserve nothing but praise from all except
carping critics.

Napier's editorial policy, on the other hand, is also open to
criticism.   Through excessive respect for the state of the manuscripts, he failed to interpret and to reach beyond the facts to
Barrow's intentions : though he granted that some of the longer
sermons could hardly have been delivered at such length, he printed
them as continuous texts even when blanks in the manuscripts
imply the intended division.   He also failed to note the difference
between on the one hand Barrow's own revisions inked over or
reproduced in the margin by Tillotson to help the printer, and on
the other emendations by the editor [1].   Finally, in many cases he
gave in footnotes additional matter from other manuscript versions
of the same sermons : however interesting such further developments may be to a student of Barrow's thought, it should be made
clear that in some cases at least the sermon had been reshaped
from one version to the next, and that the developments appearing
in one manuscript do not really fit into the other version.   True,
this does not often distort the overall structure of Barrow's sermons
since these grow by accretion rather than from a centre ; none
the less, the impression is misleading.   Since no editor can contemplate publishing all the extant versions of the sermons, the
only thing to do is to decide which version of each sermon to print.
This is clearly what Tillotson did, and after comparing several
versions of several sermons one must conclude that he chose the
best texts, i.e. those that appear to represent the last stage of
composition, even when Barrow had made a fair copy at an earlier

---

[1] In some cases it is impossible to distinguish, for instance when a sentence
is crossed out.

stage [1]. It was not Tillotson's purpose to give the public an insight
into his friend's method of composition ; but in a scholarly edition,
such as Napier seems to have intended [2], it might have been interesting to find the successive versions [3] of one sermon. From these,
indeed, one gathers how Barrow went to work and how his sermons
grew. For one thing one realizes that for him revising usually
meant expanding, adding more " considerations " or developing
some point at greater length. One realizes also that the purely
verbal revisions were few, generally for the purpose of enlarging
rather than in order to obtain greater precision, and that they were
seldom dictated by stylistic considerations : Barrow simply found
he had more to say on the matter, and more of the same kind, so
that one sees him reaching further and further afield and stopping
merely for lack of time, indeed often envisaging further considerations even at that point. Though, as Tillotson said, he seems to
have exhausted the subjects he treated, obviously he never felt he
had reached a final point. Now, Napier told his readers what
was Barrow's method of composition, but he did not illustrate it
from the manuscripts : in fact he gave no more than the texts
Tillotson had selected (restored to what he thought was their
original form), plus additions in footnotes and in one case a second,
imperfect, sermon on the same text [4].

The copy text for the sermons printed below is Tillotson's folio
edition—from which the eighteenth-century editions derived—
collated with the extant manuscripts which bear the printer's marks :
Against Foolish Talking and Jesting (vol. I, ser. XIV); *Upon the
Passion of our Blessed Saviour* (vol. I, ser. XXXII); *Of the Evil
and Unreasonableness of Infidelity* (vol. II, ser. I ; Trinity College,
Cambridge, MS. R.10.17, ff. lv to 11); *Of Justifying Faith* (vol. II,
ser. IV ; T.C. MS. R.10.17, ff. 30 to 44); *Of Justification by Faith*
(vol. II, ser. V ; T.C. MS. R.10.17, ff. 45 to 57)[5]; *Of Obedience*

---

[1] For an example of this, see ' Tillotson's Barrow ', *loc. cit.* Napier did
not question Tillotson's choice but used the same manuscript versions for his
edition.

[2] Though he does not identify the manuscripts on which his texts are based,
nor those from which the additional matter in footnotes is extracted.

[3] It is not always clear in what order the various versions were composed,
but in some cases, where the revisions written above the line or in the margin
are incorporated into the text of another version, the relation is clear.

[4] *Rejoice Evermore*, i.e. sermon 11 in Tillotson's vol. III.

[5] f. 53 is missing, i.e. just over one page in the folio edition (p. 81/2),
from " ... *Teach me to doe thy will* " to " Wherefore the other sense ... " ;
(pp. 444-6 below).

to our Spiritual Guides and Governours (vol. III, ser. XXIV to XXVII ; T.C. MS. R.10.19, ff. 140 to 163 v). The copy used is the 1683-1687 *Works* in the British Museum. A few obvious misprints have been silently emended ; variant readings from the MSS. (*B.*) are given in footnotes, Tillotson's emendations on the manuscript are referred to as *T.*, while readings of the *Works* which have no such authority, but which may also derive from Tillotson, are referred to as *1683* for sermons in vol. II and as *1686* for sermons in vol. III.

Except for *Upon the Passion*, the titles of these sermons are those Tillotson inserted when preparing the MSS. for the press ; these titles have been retained. The sermons on *Obedience to our Spiritual Guides and Governours* form a continuous text in the MS. ; Tillotson divided this into four parts, without altering the text (except for a slight syntactical change in the sentence he divides between ser. XXIV and ser. XXV). Besides altering a few words, he occasionally added a capital or modernized the spelling, but he did not emend the punctuation. This was left to the printer, who kept as close as possible to Barrow's pointings, but normalized the spelling fairly consistently, no doubt in accordance with printing-house usage.

The changes in punctuation from manuscript to printed text are few [1], and most of them are of three kinds :

(a) deletion of the comma before *and* in a sequence of more than two (and sometimes of two) words and phrases, e.g. *B.* ' Christian history, and doctrine ', *1683* ' Christian history and doctrine ' (p. 410, l. 19, below);

(b) insertion of a comma after *that is, in fine*, or before an interpolated adjunct or qualification, e.g. *B.* ' that doctrine, which being supposed true, he cannot ', *1683* ' that doctrine, which, being ... ' (p. 393, l. 23, below);

(c) a semi-colon or a colon instead of a period, or vice-versa, e.g. *B.* ' *in the Lord their God.* whence ', *1683* ' *in the Lord their God* : Whence ' (p. 383, l. 29, below); *B.* ' advantage : it levelleth ', *1683* ' advantage. It levelleth ' (p. 387, ll. 3/4, below); *B.* ' or state : this ', *1683* ' or state : This ' (p. 387, l. 9, below); *B.* ' sullen folks ; so that ', *1683* ' sullen folks : So that ' (p. 387, l. 17,

---

[1] In the sermon *Of the Evil and Unreasonableness of Infidelity*, about 20 ; in *Of Justifying Faith*, about 65 ; in *Justification by Faith*, about 40 ; in *Of Obedience to our Spiritual Guides and Governours*, about 50.

below). Changes of this kind do not, in fact, affect either the meaning or the rhythm of Barrow's text, since the only differ-ence that may sometimes be involved is the length of the pause. Besides Barrow himself does not always use a capital after a period[1], and often uses one after a colon or a semi-colon, so that it is not always clear where he intends to begin a new sentence. The same difficulty arises with parentheses, which Barrow and the printer sometimes use without other marks of punctuation at the end. When Barrow does use a mark of punctuation together with a parenthesis, this mark generally follows the parenthesis, whereas in the printed text it always precedes the parenthesis.

Apart from these details the compositor(s) followed the text very closely ; Dryden's remark that " the printer has enough to answer for in false pointings " obviously does not apply to Bra-bazon Aylmer. Though Barrow's usage may at first perplex the reader, the punctuation of the 1683-1687 *Works* has been retained in the present edition, except in a few cases where the original pointing is apt to be misleading to-day, or where it has seemed necessary to clarify the author's meaning.

The spelling, capitals and italics have also been retained, but not the long *s*. Neither the printer's occasional emendations in punctuation nor the variant spellings have been recorded, but it may be of interest to list here some of Barrow's spellings which the printer normalized fairly consistently.

Then after a comparative is always emended to *than*. Genitives singular and (usually) genitives of plurals not ending on a sibilant are printed with an apostrophe, while Barrow spells : *our Lords discourse, Gods help, mens revolting*, etc. as well as *the Apostles proceeding, the hearers discretion*, etc. While Barrow always writes *do* as *doe*, the *e* has been crossed out systematically at the beginning of several manuscripts, probably by Tillotson ; yet in the printed text the spelling *doe* is retained for the full verb, while the substitute and the auxiliary are spelt *do*. In the *Works*, final -*e* is often deleted ; for instance, Barrow spells : *to complaine, to/a designe, to expresse, to heare, to professe, to speake, to thinke*, etc. ; *eare, mischiefe, soule, fooles, meanes*, etc. ; *baptisme, king-dome, blindnesse*, etc. ; *cleare, firme, vaine*, etc. ; *carelesse, faith-*

[1] Christopher COOPER distinguishes between a period and a semiperiod ; the word following the latter begins with a small letter. See *The English Teacher* (1687), ed. Bertil Sundby, Lund-Copenhagen, 1953, p. 114.

lesse, etc. ; *chiefely, duely, truely*, etc. Conversely, *e* is sometimes inserted ; thus while Barrow usually spells *largly, only, wholsome*, the printer spells *largely, onely, wholesome*. Barrow's spelling *ey* is consistently altered to *eye* (so is *eysore* to *eyesore*), a *ly* to a *lye*, and *themselvs* to *themselves*.

Final *-yes* (*-yeth, -yed, -yer, -yest*) is always altered to *-ies* (*-ieth, -ied, -ier, -iest*). Thus Barrow spells : *curiosityes, facultyes, infirmityes, mysteryes, testimonyes* ; *denyeth, implyeth, justifyeth* ; *buryed, justifyed, tyed* ; *happyer, happyest, wealthyer, wealthyest*, etc. Final *-y* is also altered to *-i* before a suffix, thus in : *faulty-nesse, happynesse, naughtynesse* ; *dutyfull, pityfull* ; *dayly*, etc. Similarly, final *-y* is altered to *-ie* in some verbs, nouns and adjectives, such as : *to ly, to justify, to signify* ; *apostasy, contro-versy* ; *easy*.

Whereas Barrow often has double consonants at the end of a word [1], the printer uses a single letter (though he occasionally keeps the double consonant, e.g. *dugg, patt*); besides all adjectives in *-al* (e.g. *carnall, graduall, naturall, sociall, universall*, etc.), Barrow spells for instance : *to admitt, to cavill, to putt, to shunn* ; *sinn, sonn* ; *farr, allmost, to differr*. Barrow also spells : *to improove, to reproove, to loose*, etc., whereas the printer uses a single letter. Conversely, in the middle of a word the printer some-times uses a double consonant where Barrow has a single letter ; thus the manuscripts have *to bafle* (and occasionally *baffle*), *to medle, to setle, to puzle*, while the printed text has *to baffle* (also *to bafle*), *to meddle*, but also *to setle* and *to puzle*.

Prefix *in-* is sometimes altered to *en-*, thus in *injoin, inquire* ; similarly *de* is emended to *di* in *devest*. Suffix *-or* is emended to

---

[1] In this and in other respects, Barrow's spelling may be compared with Pope's. " To the printer we may safely assign responsibility for normalizing Pope's spelling and mending his indifference to apostrophes. Pope's commonest curiosity in spelling was doubling consonants : eccho, fitt, jewells, levell, moralls, pupills, setts, spurr, triffles, and witt. He tended to use uncalled for e's, as in criticisme, combate, seldome. But his favorite false endings were : practise, sence, and most favorite, nonsence (4 times). " R.M. SCHMITZ : *Pope's Essay on Criticism 1709*. A study of the Bodleian Manuscript Text, St. Louis, 1962, p. 15. It should be noted, however, that these were by no means " curiosities in spelling ", nor peculiar to Pope. On this, see for instance : Christopher COOPER : *English Teacher*, 1687, ed. cit., and *The Writing Scholar's Companion*, 1695, ed. E. Ekwall, Halle, 1911. The ' illogicalities and inconsistencies ' of English spelling were expounded by G.W. in *Magazine, or Animadversions on the English Spelling*, 1703, ed. David Abercrombie, Augustan Reprint Society, Publication no. 70, Los Angeles, 1958.

-our in *author, professor, propagator, transgressor,* etc. While
Barrow spells *encountring, administring,* the printed text has *encountering, administering.* The spelling *ei* is altered to *ie* in *breif,
mischeif, cheif,* and *beleif* ; *join, conjoin, jointly,* etc. are usually
altered to *joyn, conjoyn, joyntly.* Finally the following words are
emended almost all through : *practise* (noun) to *practice, yeeld* to
yield, souldyer to *souldier, counsail* to *counsel, accompt* to *account,
wracked* to *racked, country* to *countrey, assistance* to *assistence,
allege* to *alledge,* (though *allege* also occurs). Barrow's spelling
endewed was emended by Tillotson on the manuscript to *endued,*
and the printer followed this direction, though in the third volume
endewed occasionally appears.

Most of the emendations thus reflect later spelling usage, but
we should not expect absolute consistency in spelling any more
than in punctuation. The copy text has for instance : *system/
systeme, custom/custome, Christendom/Christendome, baffled/
bafled, account/accompt, alledge/allege, joyned/joined,* etc. (Barrow too uses alternate spellings, for instance : *believe/beleive,
meerly/merely, cleare/clear, termes/terms,* etc.). The variant spellings of the *Works* have been retained except in one case : the word
Saint has been abbreviated as *St.,* though the two abbreviated forms
(*S.* and *St.*) appear in the manuscripts as well as in the printed text.

The margins of Barrow's manuscripts are loaded with references
and quotations : the copy text reproduces these faithfully, but such
a procedure was impracticable in the present edition[1]. All references have been transferred to the foot of the page, and superior
figures have been inserted into the text, although Barrow himself
seldom indicates where the references belong[2]. These references
often include the page of the edition he was using ; whenever
possible his quotations have been checked with editions more easily
available to the modern reader : these will be found between square
brackets. Obsolete words have been glossed, and a few notes have
been added : these too will be found between square brackets.

---

[1] In Napier's edition references to Scripture are printed in the margin ;
quotations and other references in footnotes.
[2] He very occasionally does ; his marks (*, †, //) are reproduced in the
footnotes.

Against Foolish Talking and Jesting

Ephes. V. 4—Nor foolish talking, nor jesting, which are not convenient.

Moral and political Aphorisms are seldom couched in such terms, that they should be taken as they sound precisely, or according to the widest extent of signification ; but do commonly need exposition, and admit exception : otherwise frequently they would not onely clash with reason and experience, but interfere, thwart and supplant one another. The best Masters of such wisedom are wont to interdict things, apt by unseasonable or excessive use to be perverted, in general forms of speech, leaving the restrictions, which the case may require or bear, to be made by the hearers or interpreters discretion : whence many seemingly-formal prohibitions are to be received onely as sober cautions. This observation may be particularly supposed applicable to this precept of St. *Paul*, which seemeth universally to forbid a practice commended (in some cases and degrees) by Philosophers as vertuous, not disallowed by Reason, commonly affected by men, often used by wise and good persons ; from which consequently if our Religion did wholly debar us, it would seem chargeable with somewhat too uncouth [1] austerity and sourness [2] : from imputations of which kind as in its temper and frame it is really most free, (it never quenching natural light, or cancelling the dictates of sound Reason, but confirming and improving them ;) so it carefully declineth them, injoyning us, that
* *if there be any things* προσφιλῆ, *(lovely,* or gratefull to men,) *any things* εὔφημα, *(of good report* and repute,) *if there be any vertue and any praise,* (any thing in the common apprehensions of men held worthy and laudable,) we should *mind those things* [3], that is,

---

[1] [strange, uncommon].
[2] οἱ [δὲ] μήτ' [αὐτοὶ ἂν] εἰπόντες μηθὲν γελοῖον τοῖς τε λέγουσι δυσχεραίνοντες ἄγριοι καὶ σκληροὶ δοκοῦσιν εἶναι. Arist. *Ethics*, IV, viii [*Eth. Nic.*, IV, 14, 1128 a, 7-9].
[3] * *Phil.*, IV, 8.

should yield them a regard answerable to the esteem they carry among rational and sober persons.

Whence it may seem requisite so to interpret and determine St. *Paul's* meaning here concerning *Eutrapelia*, (that is, facetious speech, or raillery, by our Translatours rendred *Jesting*,) that he may consist with himself, and be reconciled to *Aristotle*, who placeth this practice in the rank of Vertues ; or that Religion and Reason may well accord in the case ; supposing, that if there be any kind of Facetiousness innocent and reasonable, conformable to good manners, (regulated by common sense, and consistent with the tenour of Christian Duty, that is, not transgressing the bounds of Piety, Charity and Sobriety,) St. *Paul* did not intend to discountenance or prohibit that kind.

For thus expounding and limiting his intent, we have some warrant from himself, some fair intimations in the words here. For first, what sort of facetious speech he aimeth at, he doth imply by the fellow he coupleth therewith ; μωρολογία, (saith he) ἢ εὐτραπελία, *foolish talking, or facetiousness* : such Facetiousness therefore he toucheth as doth include Folly, in the matter or manner thereof. Then he farther determineth it, by adjoyning a peculiar quality thereof, unprofitableness, or impertinency ; τὰ μὴ ἀνήκοντα, *which are not pertinent*, or conducible to any good purpose : whence may be collected, that it is a frivolous and idle sort of Facetiousness which he condemneth.

But, however, manifest it is [a], that some kind thereof he doth earnestly forbid : whence, in order to the guidance of our pratice, it is needfull to distinguish the kinds, severing that which is allowable from that which is unlawfull ; that so we may be satisfied in the case, and not on the one hand ignorantly transgress our duty, nor on the other trouble our selves with scruples, others with censures, upon the use of warrantable liberty therein.

And such a resolution seemeth indeed especially needfull in this our Age, (this pleasant and jocular Age,) which is so infinitely addicted to this sort of speaking, that it scarce doth affect or prize any thing near so much ; all reputation appearing now to vail [1] and stoop to that of being a Wit : to be learned, to be wise, to be good, are nothing in comparison thereto ; even to be noble and rich are inferiour things, and afford no such glory. Many at least, (to

---

[a] But, however, manifest it is,] *1683* But however manifest it is,
[1] [yield].

purchase this glory, to be deemed considerable in this faculty, and enrolled among the Wits,) do not onely *make shipwreck of conscience*, abandon Vertue, and forfeit all pretences to wisedom ; but neglect their estates, and prostitute their honour : so to the private damage of many particular persons, and with no small prejudice to the publick, are our Times possessed and transported with this humour. To repress the excess and extravagance whereof, nothing in way of discourse can serve better, than a plain declaration when and how such a practice is allowable or tolerable ; when it is wicked and vain, unworthy of a man endued with Reason, and pretending to honesty or honour.

This I shall in some measure endeavour to perform.

But first it may be demanded what the thing we speak of is, or what this Facetiousness doth import ? To which question I might reply as *Democritus* did to him that asked the definition of a Man, *'Tis that which we all see and know*[1] : any one better apprehends what it is by acquaintance, than I can inform him by description. It is indeed a thing so versatile and multiform, appearing in so many shapes, so many postures, so many garbs, so variously apprehended by several eyes and judgments, that it seemeth no less hard to settle a clear and certain notion thereof, than to make a pourtraict of *Proteus*, or to define the figure of the fleeting Air. Sometimes it lieth in pat allusion to a known story, or in seasonable application of a trivial saying, or in forging an apposite tale : sometimes it playeth in words and phrases, taking advantage from the ambiguity of their sense, or the affinity of their sound : sometimes it is wrapped in a dress of humorous expression[2] ; sometimes it lurketh under an odd similitude ; sometimes it is lodged in a sly question, in a smart answer, in a quirkish reason, in a shrewd intimation, in cunningly diverting, or cleverly retorting an objection : sometimes it is couched in a bold scheme of speech, in a tart Irony, in a lusty Hyperbole, in a startling Metaphor, in a plausible reconciling of contradictions, or in acute Nonsense : sometimes a scenical representation of persons or things, a counterfeit speech, a mimical look or gesture passeth for it : sometimes an affected simplicity, sometimes a presumptuous bluntness

---

[1] [ἄνθρωπός ἐστιν ὃ πάντες ἴδμεν. *Fragmente der Vorsokratiker*, ed. H. Diels, 1952 ; II, 178, no. 165].

[2] Eadem, quae, si imprudentibus excidant, stulta sunt ; si simulamus, venusta creduntur. QUINT. *Instit. Orat.* VI, iii, [23].

giveth it being : sometimes it riseth onely from a lucky hitting upon what is strange, sometimes from a crafty wresting obvious matter to the purpose : often it consisteth in one knows not what, and spring-eth up one can hardly tell how.   Its ways are unaccountable and inexplicable, being answerable to the numberless rovings of fancy and windings of language.   It is, in short, a manner of speaking out of the simple and plain way [1], (such as Reason teacheth and proveth things by,) which by a pretty surprizing uncouthness [2] in conceit or expression doth affect and amuse [3] the fancy, stirring in it some wonder, and breeding some delight thereto.   It raiseth Admiration, as signifying a nimble sagacity of apprehension, a special felicity of invention, a vivacity of spirit, and reach of wit more than vulgar : it seeming to argue a rare quickness of parts, that one can fetch in remote conceits applicable ; a notable skill, that he can dexter-ously accommodate them to the purpose before him ; together with a lively briskness of humour, not apt to damp those sportfull flashes of imagination.   (Whence in *Aristotle* [4] such persons are termed ἐπιδέξιοι, *dexterous* men ; and εὔτροποι, men of facil or versatile manners, who can *easily turn* themselves to all things, or turn all things to themselves.)   It also procureth Delight, by gratifying curiosity with its rareness, or semblance of difficulty ; (as monsters, not for their beauty, but their rarity ; as jugling tricks, not for their use, but their abstruseness, are beheld with pleasure ;) by diverting the mind from its road of serious thoughts ; by instilling gayety and airiness of spirit ; by provoking to such dispositions of spirit in way of emulation or complaisance ; and by seasoning matters, otherwise distastfull or insipid, with an unusual, and thence gratefull tang.

But saying no more concerning what it is, and leaving it to your imagination and experience to supply the defect of such explication, I shall address my self to shew, first, when and how such a manner of speaking may be allowed ; then, in what matters and ways it should be condemned.

---

[1] Et hercle omnis salse dicendi ratio in eo est, ut aliter, quam est rectum verumque, dicatur.   QUINT. [*Ibid.*, VI, iii, 89].

[2] [strangeness, novelty].   [3] [puzzle].

[4] *Eth.* IV, viii [*Eth. Nic.*, IV, 14, 1128 a, 17]. Εὐτράπελος λέγεται ὁ ποικίλος, ὁ παντοδαπὸς, ὁ ἄστατος, ὁ εὔκολος, ὁ πάντα γινόμενος.   CHRYS. in *Eph. Or.* 17. [*Hom. in Epist. ad Eph.*, XVII, cap. v, MIGNE, *Patrol. gr.*, t. 62, col. 119].

1. Such Facetiousness is not absolutely unreasonable or un-lawfull, which ministreth harmless divertisement, and delight to conversation : (harmless, I say, that is, not intrenching upon Piety, not infringing Charity or Justice, not disturbing Peace.) For Christ-ianity is not so tetrical, so harsh, so envious, as to bar us continually from innocent, much less from wholsome and usefull pleasure, such as humane life doth need or require[1]. And if jocular discourse may serve to good purposes of this kind ; if it may be apt to raise our drooping spirits, to allay our irksome cares, to whet our blunted industry, to recreate our minds being tired and cloyed with graver occupations[2] ; if it may breed alacrity, or maintain good humour among us ; if it may conduce to sweeten conversation and endear society ; then is it not inconvenient, or unprofitable. If for those ends we may use other recreations, employing on them our ears and eyes, our hands and feet, our other instruments of sense and motion ; why may we not as well to them accommodate our organs of speech, and interiour sense ? Why should those games which excite our wits and fancies be less reasonable, than those whereby our grosser parts and faculties are exercised ? Yea, why are not those more reasonable, since they are performed in a manly way, and have in them a smack of Reason ; seeing also they may be so managed, as not onely to divert and please, but to improve and profit the mind, rouzing and quickning it, yea sometimes enlightning and instructing it, by good sense conveyed in jocular expression[3] ?

It would surely be hard, that we should be tied ever to knit the brow, and squeeze the brain, (to be always sadly dumpish ; or seriously pensive,) that all divertisement of mirth and pleasantness should be shut out of conversation : and how can we better relieve our minds, or relax our thoughts, how can we be more ingenuously chearfull, in what more kindly way can we exhilarate our selves and others, than by thus *sacrificing to the Graces*[4], as the Ancients call'd it ? Are not some persons always, and all persons sometimes, uncapable otherwise to divert themselves, than by such discourse ? Shall we, I say, have no recreation ? or must our recreations be

---

[1] Δοκεῖ δὲ ἀνάπαυσις καὶ ἡ παιδιὰ ἐν τῷ βίῳ εἶναι ἀναγκαῖον. Arist. *Eth.* IV, viii, [*Eth. Nic.*, IV, 14, 1128 b, 3-4].

[2] Danda est remissio animis ; meliores acrioresque requieti surgent, etc. Sen. *De Tranq.* 15 [xvii, 5].

[3] — ridentem dicere verum Quid vetat ? [Hor. *Sat.*, I, i, 24-5].

[4] θύε ταῖς χάρισι· ita Plato Xenocratem morosiorem monuit. [Diogenes Laertius, IV, 2, 6].

ever clownish, or childish, consisting merely in rustical efforts, or in petty sleights of bodily strength and activity ? Were we in fine obliged ever to talk like Philosophers, assigning dry reasons for every thing, and dropping grave sentences upon all occasions, would it not much deaden humane life, and make ordinary conversation exceedingly to languish ? Facetiousness therefore in such cases, and to such purposes, may be allowable.

2. Facetiousness is allowable, when it is the most proper instrument of exposing things apparently base and vile to due contempt. It is many times expedient, that things really ridiculous should appear such, that they may be sufficiently loathed and shunned ; and to render them such is the part of a facetious wit, and usually can onely be compassed thereby. When to impugn them with down-right reason, or to check them by serious discourse, would signifie nothing ; then representing them in a shape strangely-ugly to the fancy, and thereby raising derision at them, may effectually discountenance them. Thus did the Prophet *Elias* expose the wicked superstition of those who worshipped *Baal* : *Elias* (saith the Text) *mocked them, and said, Cry aloud ; for he is a God, either he is talking, or he is pursuing, or he is in a journey, or peradventure he sleeps, and must be awaked* [1]. By which one pregnant instance, it appeareth, that reasoning pleasantly-abusive in some cases may be usefull. The Holy Scripture doth not indeed use it frequently ; (it not suting the Divine simplicity and stately gravity thereof to doe so ;) yet its condescension thereto at any time sufficiently doth authorize a cautious use thereof. When sarcastical twitches are needfull to pierce the thick skins of men, to correct their lethargick stupidity, to rouze them out of their drouzy negligence ; then may they well be applied : when plain declarations will not enlighten people, to discern the truth and weight of things, and blunt arguments will not penetrate, to convince or persuade them to their duty ; then doth Reason freely resign its place to Wit, allowing it to undertake its work of instruction and reproof.

3. Facetious discourse particularly may be commodious for reproving some vices, and reclaiming some persons ; (as Salt for cleansing and curing some sores.) It commonly procureth a more easie access to the ears of men, and worketh a stronger impression on their hearts, than other discourse could do. Many who will not

[1] *1 Kings* XVIII, 27.

stand a direct reproof, and cannot abide to be plainly admonished of their fault, will yet endure to be pleasantly rubb'd, and will patiently bear a jocund wipe ; though they abominate all language purely bitter or sour, yet they can relish discourse having in it a pleasant tartness : you must not chide them as their master, but you may gibe with them as their companion : if you doe that, they will take you for pragmatical[1] and haughty ; this they may interpret friendship and freedome. Most men are of that temper ; and particularly the Genius of divers persons, whose opinions and practices we should strive to correct, doth require not a grave and severe, but a free and merry way of treating them. For what can be more unsutable and unpromising, than to seem serious with those who are not so themselves, or demure with the scornfull ? If we design either to please or vex them into better manners, we must be as sportfull in a manner, or as contemptuous as themselves. If we mean to be heard by them, we must talk in their own fashion, with humour and jollity : if we will instruct them, we must withall somewhat divert them : we must seem to play with them, if we think to convey any sober thoughts into them. They scorn to be formally advised or taught ; but they may perhaps be slily laughed and lured into a better mind. If by such complaisance we can inveigle those Dottrels[2] to hearken to us, we may induce them to consider farther, and give Reason some competent scope, some fair play with them. Good Reason may be apparelled in the garb of Wit, and therein will securely pass, whither in its native homeliness it could never arrive : and being come thither, it with especial advantage may impress good advice ; making an offender more clearly to see, and more deeply to feel his miscarriage ; being represented to his fancy in a strain somewhat rare and remarkable, yet not so fierce and frightfull. The severity of reproof is tempered, and the reprover's anger disguised thereby. The guilty person cannot but observe, that he who thus reprehends him is not disturb'd or out of humour, and that he rather pitieth than hateth him ; which breedeth a veneration to him, and imparteth no small efficacy to his wholsome suggestions. Such a Reprehension, while it forceth a smile without, doth work remorse within ; while it seemeth to tickle the ear, doth sting the heart. In fine, many whose foreheads are brazed and hearts steeled against all blame, are yet not of

[1] [conceited].   [2] [silly persons].

proof against derision ; divers, who never will be reasoned, may be raillied into better order : in which cases Raillery, as an instrument of so important good, as a servant of the best Charity, may be allowed.

4. Some Errours likewise in this way may be most properly and most successfully confuted ; such as deserve not, and hardly can bear a serious and solid confutation. He that will contest things apparently [1] decided by sense and experience, or who disavows clear Principles of reason, approved by general consent, and the common sense of men, what other hopefull way is there of proceeding with him, than pleasantly to explode his conceits ? To dispute seriously with him, were trifling ; to trifle with him is the proper course : since he rejecteth the grounds of Reasoning, 'tis vain to be in earnest ; what then remains, but to jest with him ? To deal seriously, were to yield too much respect to such a baffler, and too much weight to his fancies ; to raise the man too high in his courage and conceit ; to make his pretences seem worthy the considering and canvasing. Briefly, perverse obstinacy is more easily quelled, petulant impudence is sooner dashed, Sophistical captiousness is more safely eluded, Sceptical wantonness is more surely confounded in this, than in the simple way of discourse.

5. This way is also commonly the best way of defence against unjust reproach and obloquy. To yield to a slandrous reviler a serious reply, or to make a formal plea against his charge, doth seem to imply, that we much consider, or deeply resent it ; whereas by pleasant reflexion on it we signify, the matter onely deserves contempt, and that we take our selves unconcerned therein. So easily without care or trouble may the brunts of malice be declined or repelled.

6. This way may be allowed in way of counterbalancing, and in compliance to the fashion of others. It would be a disadvantage unto Truth and Vertue, if their defenders were barred from the use of this weapon ; since it is that especially whereby the patrons of Errour and Vice do maintain and propagate them. They being destitute of good reason, do usually recommend their absurd and pestilent notions by a pleasantness of conceit and expression, bewitching the fancies of shallow hearers, and inveagling heedless persons to a liking of them : and if, for reclaiming such people,

---

[1] [clearly, plainly].

the folly of those Seducers may in the like manner be displayed
as ridiculous and odious, why should that advantage be refused ?
It is Wit that wageth the war against Reason, against Vertue,
against Religion ; Wit alone it is that perverteth so many, and so
greatly corrupteth the world : It may therefore be needfull, in our
warfare for those dearest concerns, to sort the manner of our
fighting with that of our adversaries, and with the same kind of
arms to protect Goodness, whereby they do assail it. If Wit may
happily serve under the banner of Truth and Vertue, we may
imprest it for that service ; and good it were to rescue so worthy
a faculty from so vile abuse. It is the right of Reason and Piety,
to command that and all other endowments ; Folly and Impiety
do onely usurp them : just and fit therefore it is, to wrest them
out of so bad hands, to revoke them to their right use and duty.

It doth especially seem requisite to doe it in this Age, wherein
plain Reason is deemed a dull and heavy thing. When the mental
appetite of men is become like the corporeal, and cannot relish any
food without some piquant sawce, so that people will rather starve,
than live on solid fare ; when substantial and sound discourse
findeth small attention, or acceptance ; in such a time, he that can,
may in complaisance, and for fashion's sake, vouchsafe to be facetious; an ingenious vein coupled with an honest mind may be a good
talent ; he shall employ Wit commendably, who by it can further
the interests of Goodness, alluring men first to listen, then inducing
them to consent unto its wholsome dictates and precepts.

Since men are so irreclaimably disposed to mirth and laughter,
it may be well to set them in the right pin, to divert their humour
into the proper chanel, that they may please themselves in deriding
things which deserve it, ceasing to laugh at that which requireth
reverence or horrour [1].

It may also be expedient to put the world out of conceit, that
all sober and good men are a sort of such lumpish or sour people,
that they can utter nothing but flat and drowzy stuff ; by shewing
them, that such persons, when they see cause, in condescension, can
be as brisk and smart as themselves ; when they please, can speak
pleasantly and wittily as well as gravely and judiciously. This
way at least, in respect to the various palates of men, may for
variety sake be sometimes attempted, when other means do fail :

[1] [awe].

when many strict and subtle arguings, many zealous declamations, many wholsome serious discourses have been spent, without effecting the extirpation of bad principles, or conversion of those who abett them ; this course may be tried, and some perhaps may be reclaimed thereby.

7. Furthermore, the warrantableness of this practice in some cases may be inferr'd from a parity of reason, in this manner : If it be lawfull, (as by the best authorities it plainly doth appear to be,) in using Rhetorical schemes, Poetical strains, involutions of sense in Allegories, Fables, Parables and Riddles, to discoast [1] from the plain and simple way of speech ; why may not Facetiousness, issuing from the same principles, directed to the same ends, serving to like purposes, be likewise used blamelesly ? If those exorbitancies of speech may be accommodated to instill good Doctrine into the head, to excite good Passions in the heart, to illustrate and adorn the Truth, in a delightfull and taking way ; and facetious discourse be sometime [2] notoriously conducible to the same ends ; why, they being retained, should it be rejected ? especially considering how difficult often it may be, to distinguish those forms of discourse from this, or exactly to define the limits which sever Rhetorick and Raillery. Some elegant figures and tropes of Rhetorick (biting Sarcasms, sly Ironies, strong Metaphors, lofty Hyperbole's, Paronomasies, Oxymorons, and the like, frequently used by the best speakers, and not seldome even by Sacred Writers) do lie very near upon the confines of Jocularity, and are not easily differenced from those sallies of wit, wherein the lepid [3] way doth consist : so that were this wholly culpable, it would be matter of scruple, whether one hath committed a fault or no, when he meant onely to play the Oratour, or the Poet ; and hard surely it would be to find a judge, who could precisely set out the difference between a Jest and a Flourish.

8. I shall onely adde, that of old even the sagest and gravest persons (persons of most rigid and severe Vertue) did much affect this kind of discourse, and did apply it to noble purposes. The great introducer of moral wisedom among the Pagans did practise it so much, (by it repressing the windy pride and fallacious vanity of Sophisters in his time,) that he thereby got the name of ὁ εἴρων,

---

¹ [to depart from].   ² [sometimes].   ³ [pleasant, jocose, facetious].

the Droll [1] : and the rest of those who pursued his design, do by numberless stories and Apophthegms recorded of them appear well skilled, and much delighted in this way. Many great Princes, (as *Augustus Caesar* [2] for one, many of whose Jests are extant in *Macrobius* [3],) many grave Statesmen, (as *Cicero* particularly, who composed several books of Jests [4],) many famous Captains [5], (as *Fabius M. Cato* the Censor, *Scipio Africanus, Epaminondas, Themistocles, Phocion*, and many others, whose witty Sayings together with their Martial exploits are reported by Historians,) have pleased themselves herein, and made it a condiment of their weighty businesses. * So that practising thus, (within certain rule and compass) we cannot erre without great patterns, and mighty patrons [6].

9. In fine, since it cannot be shewn, that such a sportfulness of wit and fancy doth contain an intrinsick and inseparable turpitude ; since it may be so cleanly, handsomely and innocently used, as not to defile or discompose the mind of the speaker, not to wrong or harm the hearer, not to derogate from any worthy subject of discourse, not to infringe decency, to disturb peace, to violate any of the grand duties incumbent on us, (Piety, Charity, Justice, Sobriety,) but rather sometimes may yield advantage in those respects ; it cannot well absolutely and universally be condemned [7] : and when not used upon improper matter, in an unfit manner, with excessive measure, at undue season, to evil purpose, it may be allowed. It is bad objects, or bad adjuncts, which do spoil its indifference and innocence : it is the abuse thereof [8], to which (as all pleasant things are dangerous, and apt to degenerate into baits of intemperance and excess) it is very liable, that corrupteth it ; and seemeth to be the ground, why in so general terms it is prohibited by the Apostle. Which prohibition to what cases,

---

[1] [Socrates. See CICERO : *De Officiis*, I, 30 ; QUINTILIAN : *Instit. Orat.* IX, ii, 46 ; ARISTOTLE : *Eth. Nic.*, IV, 13, 1127 a, 22 - b, 22].

[2] CIC. *de Orat.* 2 [II, liv, 216].

[3] [*Conviviorum Primi Diei Saturnaliorum*. Lib. II, cap. iv].

[4] [See QUINT. *Instit. Orat.* VI, iii, 5].

[5] [See CIC. *de Orat.* II, liv sqq.].

[6] * The two greatest men and gravest divines of their time (S. GREG. NAZ. and S. BASIL) could entertain one another with facetious Epistles. (GREG. NAZ. Ep. 7 ad Basil. Σὺ σκῶπτε καὶ διάσυρε, etc. Et Ep. 8). [MIGNE, *Patrol. gr.*, t. 37, Ep. 4 & 5].

[7] Τὸ γελᾶν καὶ ἀστεῖα λέγειν οὐ δοκεῖ μὲν ὡμολογημένον ἁμάρτημα εἶναι, ἄγει δὲ etc. CHRYS. 'Ἀνδρ. ιε' [= Ad Populum Antiochenum, Homil. XV ; MIGNE, *Patrol. gr.*, t. 49, col. 158].

[8] Ὁ [γὰρ] εὐτραπελευόμενος κατήγορος ἔσται ταχέως. CHRYS. [*Hom. in Epist. ad Eph.*, XVII, cap. v ; MIGNE, *Patrol. gr.*, t. 62, col. 120].

or what sorts of Jesting it extendeth, we come now to declare.

II.1. All profane Jesting, all speaking loosely and wantonly about Holy things, (things nearly related to God and Religion,) making such things the matters of sport and mockery, playing and trifling with them, is certainly prohibited, as an intolerably-vain and wicked practice. It is an infallible sign of a vain and light spirit, which considereth little, and cannot distinguish things, to talk slightly concerning persons of high dignity, to whom especial respect is due ; or about matters of great importance, which deserve very serious consideration. No man speaketh, or should speak, of his Prince that which he hath not weighed, whether it will consist with that veneration which should be preserved inviolate to him : And is not the same, is not much greater care to be used in regard to the incomparably-great and glorious Majesty of Heaven ? Yes surely : as we should not without great awe think of him ; so we should not presume to mention his Name, his Word, his Institutions, any thing immediately belonging to him, without profoundest reverence and dread. It is the most enormous sauciness that can be imagined, to speak petulantly or pertly concerning Him ; especially considering, that what-ever we do say about him, we do utter it in his presence, and to his very face. *For there is not* (as the Holy Psalmist considered) *a word in my tongue, but lo, O Lord, Thou knowest it altogether* [1]. No man also hath the heart to droll, or thinks raillery convenient in cases nearly touching his life, his health, his estate, or his fame : and are the true life and health of our Soul, are interest in God's favour and mercy, are everlasting glory and bliss affairs of less moment ? are the treasures and joys of Paradise, are the damages and torments in Hell more jesting matters ? No certainly, no : in all reason therefore it becometh us, and it infinitely concerneth us, when-ever we think of these things, to be in best earnest, always to speak of them in most sober sadness [2].

The proper objects of common mirth and sportfull divertisement are mean and petty matters ; any thing at least is by playing therewith made such : great things are thereby diminished and debased ; especially Sacred things do grievously suffer thence, being with extreme indecency and indignity depressed beneath themselves,

---

[1] Ps. CXXXIX, 4.   [2] [seriousness].

when they become the subjects of flashy wit, or the entertainments of frothy merriment : to sacrifice their honour to our vain pleasure, being like the ridiculous fondness of that people, which (as *Ælian* reporteth [1]) worshipping a Fly, did offer up an Oxe thereto. These things were by God instituted, and proposed to us for purposes quite different ; to compose our hearts, and settle our fancies in a most serious frame ; to breed inward satisfaction, and joy purely spiritual ; to exercise our most solemn thoughts, and employ our gravest discourses : All our speech therefore about them should be *wholsome* [2], apt to afford good instruction, or to excite good affections ; *good*, (as St. *Paul* speaketh) *for the use of edifying, that it may minister grace unto the hearers* [3].

If we must be facetious and merry, the field is wide and spacious ; there are matters enough in the world beside these most august and dreadfull things, to try our faculties, and please our humour with ; every-where light and ludicrous things occur : it therefore doth argue a marvellous poverty of wit, and barrenness of invention, (no less than a strange defect of goodness, and want of discretion,) in those who can devise no other subjects to frollick upon beside these, of all most improper and perillous ; who cannot seem ingenious under the charge of so highly trespassing [4] upon decency, disclaiming wisedom, wounding the ears of others, and their own consciences. Seem ingenious, I say ; for seldome those persons really are such, or are capable to discover any wit in a wise and manly way. 'Tis not the excellency of their fancies, which in themselves usually are sorry and insipid enough, but the uncouthness [5] of their presumption ; not their extraordinary wit, but their prodigious rashness, which is to be admired. They are gazed on, as the doers of bold tricks, who dare perform that which no sober man will attempt : they do indeed rather deserve themselves to be laughed at, than their conceits. For what can be more ridiculous, than we do make our selves, when we thus fiddle and fool with our own Souls ; when, to make vain people merry, we incense God's earnest displeasure ; when, to raise a fit of present laughter, we expose our selves to endless wailing and woe ; when, to be reckoned Wits, we prove our selves stark wild : Surely to this case we may accommodate that of a truly-great Wit, King

[1] [*De Animalibus*, XI, 8].
[2] *Tit.* II, 8.
[3] *Eph.* IV, 29.
[4] [unless they trespass].
[5] [strangeness, novelty].

Solomon; I said of laughter, It is mad; and of mirth, What doeth it [1] *?*

2.   All injurious, abusive, scurrilous Jesting, which causelesly or needlesly tendeth to the disgrace, damage, vexation, or prejudice in any kind of our Neighbour, (provoking his displeasure, grating on his modesty, stirring passion in him,) is also prohibited [2].   When men, to raise an admiration of their wit, to please themselves, or gratify the humour of other men, do expose their Neighbour to scorn and contempt, making ignominious reflexions upon his person or his actions, taunting his real imperfections, or fastning imaginary ones upon him, they transgress their duty, and abuse their wits ; 'tis not urbanity, or genuine facetiousness, but uncivil rudeness, or vile malignity [3].   To doe thus, as it is the office of mean and base spirits, (unfit for any worthy or weighty employments,) so it is full of inhumanity, of iniquity, of indecency and folly.   For the weaknesses of men, of what kind soever, (natural, or moral, in quality, or in act,) considering whence they spring, and how much we are all subject to them, and do need excuse for them, do in equity challenge compassion to be had of them ; not complacency to be taken in them, or mirth drawn from them ; they, in respect to common humanity, should rather be studiously connived at and concealed, or mildly excused, than wilfully laid open, and wantonly descanted upon ; they rather are to be deplored secretly, than openly derided.

The Reputation of men is too noble a sacrifice to be offered up to vain-glory, fond pleasure, or ill humour ; it is a good far more dear and pretious, than to be prostituted for idle sport and divertisement.   It becometh us not to trifle with that, which in common estimation is of so great moment ; to play rudely with a thing so very brittle [4], yet of so vast price ; which being once broken or crackt, it is very hard, and scarce possible, to repair. A small transient pleasure, a tickling the ears, wagging the lungs, forming the face into a smile, a giggle, or a humme, are not to be purchased with the grievous distast and smart, perhaps with the real damage and mischief of our Neighbour, which attend upon

---

[1] *Eccles.* II, 2.

[2] — solutos Qui captat risus hominum, famamque dicacis, Hic niger est. HOR. *Sat.* I, 4 [82-4].

[3] ὁ δὲ βωμολόχος ἥττων ἐστὶ τοῦ γελοίου, καὶ οὔτε ἑαυτοῦ οὔτε τῶν ἄλλων ἀπεχόμενος, εἰ γέλωτα ποιήσει. ARIST. *Eth.* IV, viii [*Eth. Nic.,* IV, 14, 1128 a, 33-35].

[4] *Vitrea fama.* HOR. [*Sat.,* II, 3, 222].

contempt[1]. This is not Jesting surely, but bad earnest : 'tis wild mirth, which is the mother of grief to those whom we should tenderly love ; 'tis unnatural sport, which breedeth displeasure in them whose delight it should promote, whose liking it should procure : it crosseth the nature and design of this way of speaking ; which is, to cement and ingratiate society, to render conversation pleasant and sprightly, for mutual satisfaction and comfort.

True Festivity[2] is called *Salt*, and such it should be, giving a smart, but savoury relish to discourse ; exciting an appetite, not irritating disgust ; cleansing sometime, but never creating a sore : and, ἐὰν μωρανθῇ, *if it become thus insipid*, or unsavoury, *it is thenceforth good for nothing, but to be cast out, and to be troden under foot of men*[3]. Such Jesting which doth not season wholsome or harmless discourse, but giveth a haut-goust[4] to putid and poisonous stuff, gratifying distempered palates and corrupt stomachs, is indeed odious and despicable folly[5], *to be cast out* with loathing, *to be troden under foot* with contempt. If a man offends in this sort to please himself, 'tis scurvy malignity ; if to delight others, 'tis base servility and flattery : upon the first score he is a buffoon to himself ; upon the last, a fool to others[6]. And well in common speech are such practisers so termed, the grounds of that practice being so vain, and the effects so unhappy. *The heart of fools* (saith the Wise man) *is in the house of mirth*[7] ; meaning, it seems, especially such hurtfully-wanton mirth : for it is (as he farther telleth us) the property of fools, to delight in doing harm ; (*It is a sport to a fool to doe mischief*[8].) Is it not in earnest most palpable folly, for so mean ends to doe so great harm ; to disoblige men in sport ; to lose friends, and get enemies, for a conceit[9] ;

---

[1] *Prov.* XXVI, 18, 19. As a mad man who casteth firebrands, arrows, and death ; So is the man that deceiveth his neighbour, and saith, Am I not in sport ? — οἱ ἐνεδρεύοντες τοὺς [ἑαυτῶν] φίλους. LXX.

[2] [mirthfulness, cheerful urbanity].

[3] *Matt.* V, 13.

[4] [a high piquant flavour].

[5] Nimium risus pretium est, si probitatis impendio constat. QUINT. [*Instit. Orat.*, VI, iii, 35].

[6] Εἰ καλὸν τὸ πρᾶγμα, τί τοῖς μίμοις ἀφίεται ; μίμος γίνῃ, καὶ οὐκ αἰσχύνῃ ; CHRYS. [*Hom. in Epist Ad Eph.*, XVII, cap. v ; MIGNE, *Patrol. gr.*, t. 62, col. 119].

[7] *Eccles.* VII, 4.

[8] *Prov.* X, 23. Fools make a mock of sin. *Prov.* XIV, 9.

[9] Potius amicum quam dictum perdidi. [QUINT. *Instit. Orat.*, VI, iii, 23]. — dummodo risum / Excutiat sibi, non hic cuiquam parcet amico. HOR. *Sat.* I, iv [34-5]. — dicax idem, et Tiberium acerbis facetiis irridere solitus : quarum apud praepotentes in longum memoria est. TAC. *V. Ann.*, p. 184 [*Annales*, V, ii].

out of a light humour to provoke fierce wrath, and breed tough
hatred ; to engage one's self consequently very far in strife, danger
and trouble ?   No way certainly is more apt to produce such effects
than this ; nothing more speedily enflameth, or more thoroughly
engageth men, or sticketh longer in mens hearts and memories,
than bitter taunts and scoffs : whence this hony soon turns into
gall ; these jolly Comedies do commonly terminate in wofull Tragedies.

Especially this scurrilous and scoffing way is then most detestable, when it not onely exposeth the blemishes and infirmities of
men, but abuseth Piety and Vertue themselves ; flouting persons
for their constancy in Devotion, or their strict adherence to a
conscientious practice of Duty ; aiming to effect that which *Job*
complaineth of, *The just upright man is laughed to scorn* [1] ; resem-
bling those whom the Psalmist thus describeth, *Who whet their
tongue like a sword, and bend their arrows, even bitter words,
That they may shoot in secret at the perfect* [2] ; serving good men
as *Jeremy* was served, *The word of the Lord* (saith he) *was made
a reproach unto me, and a derision daily* [3].

This practice doth evidently in the highest degree tend to the
disparagement and discouragement of Goodness ; (aiming to expose
it, and to render men ashamed thereof;) and it manifestly proceedeth from a desperate corruption of mind, (from a mind hardned
and emboldned, sold and enslaved to wickedness :) whence they
who deal therein are in Holy Scripture represented as egregious
sinners, or persons superlatively wicked, under the name of *Scorners* ; (λοιμοὺς, *Pests*, or pestilent men, the *Greek* Translatours call
them, properly enough in regard to the effects of their practice ;)
concerning whom the Wise man (signifying how God will meet
with them in their own way) saith, *Surely the Lord scorneth the
scorners* [4]. Ἐμπαίκτας, *Scoffers*, (or *Mockers*,) St. *Peter* termeth
them, *who walk according to their own lusts* [5]; who not being willing
to practise, are ready to deride Vertue ; thereby striving to seduce
others into their pernicious courses.

This offence also proportionably groweth more criminal, as it
presumeth to reach persons eminent in dignity or worth, unto whom
special veneration is appropriate. This adjoyneth sauciness to
scurrility, and advanceth the wrong thereof into a kind of sacri-

[1] *Job* XII, 4.   [2] *Ps.* LXIV, 3, 4.   [3] *Jer.* XX, 8.
[4] *Prov.* III, 34.   [5] 2 *Pet.* III, 3.

lege. 'Tis not onely injustice, but profaneness, to *abuse the Gods*[1].
Their station is a sanctuary from all irreverence and reproach ;
they are seated on high, that we may onely look up to them with
respect ; their defects are not to be seen, or not to be touched by
malicious or wanton wits, by spitefull or scornfull tongues : the
diminution of their credit is a publick mischief, and the State it self
doth suffer in their becoming objects of scorn ; not onely themselves are vilified and degraded, but the great affairs they manage
are obstructed, the justice they administer is disparaged thereby.

In fine, no Jesting is allowable, which is not throughly innocent[2] :
it is an unworthy perverting of wit, to employ it in biting and
scratching ; in working prejudice to any man's reputation, or interest ; in needlesly incensing any man's anger, or sorrow ; in raising
animosities, dissensions and feuds among any.

Whence it is somewhat strange, that any men from so mean
and silly a practice should expect commendation, or that any should
afford regard thereto ; the which it is so far from meriting, that
indeed contempt and abhorrence are due to it.   Men do truly
more render themselves despicable than others, when, without just
ground, or reasonable occasion, they do attaque others in this way.
That such a practice doth ever find any encouragement or acceptance, whence can it proceed, but from the bad nature and small
judgment of some persons ?   For to any man who is endued with
any sense of goodness, and hath a competence of true wit, or a
right knowledge of good manners, (who knows—*inurbanum lepido
seponere dicto*[3],) it cannot but be unsavoury and loathsome.   The
repute it obtaineth is in all respects unjust.   So would it appear,
not onely were the cause to be decided in the court of morality,
because it consists not with Vertue and Wisedom ; but even before
any competent judges of wit it self.   For he overthrows his own
pretence, and cannot reasonably claim any interest in wit, who
doth thus behave himself : he prejudgeth himself to want wit,
who cannot descry fit matter to divert himself or others : he
discovereth a great straitness and sterility of good invention, who
cannot in all the wide field of things find better subjects of dis-

---

[1] *Exod.* XXII, 28.
[2] Πόρρω δὲ τοῦτο Χριστιανοῦ, τὸ κωμῳδεῖν. CHRYS. *in Eph. Or.* 17 [*Hom.
in Epist. ad Eph.*, XVII, cap. v, MIGNE, *Patrol. gr.*, t. 62, col. 120].

Γλῶσσαν ἔχεις, οὐχ ἵνα ἕτερον κωμῳδήσῃς, ἀλλ᾽ ἵνα εὐχαριστήσῃς τῷ Θεῷ.
Ibidem.
[3] HOR. [*Ars Poet.*, 273].

course; who knows not how to be ingenious within reasonable compass, but to pick up a sorry conceit is forced to make excursions beyond the bounds of honesty and decency.

Neither is it any argument of considerable ability in him that haps to please this way: a slender faculty will serve the turn. The sharpness of his speech cometh not from wit so much as from choler, which furnisheth the lowest inventions with a kind of pungent expression, and giveth an edge to every spitefull word[1]: so that any dull wretch doth seem to scold eloquently and ingeniously. Commonly also Satyrical taunts do owe their seeming piquancy, not to the speaker, or his words, but to the subject, and the hearers; the matter conspiring with the bad nature, or the vanity of men, who love to laugh at any rate, and to be pleased at the expence of other mens repute; conceiting themselves extolled by the depression of their neighbour, and hoping to gain by his loss. Such customers they are that maintain the bitter Wits, who otherwise would want trade, and might go a begging. For commonly they who seem to excell this way, are miserably flat in other discourse, and most dully serious: they have a particular unaptness to describe any good thing, or commend any worthy person; being destitute of right *Idea's*, and proper terms answerable to such purposes: their representations of that kind are absurd and unhandsome; their Elogies[2] (to use their own way of speaking) are in effect Satyrs, and they can hardly more abuse a man than by attempting to commend him; like those in the Prophet, who were *wise to doe ill, but to doe well had no knowledge*[3].

3. I pass by, that it is very culpable to be facetious in obscene and smutty matters. Such things are not to be discoursed on either in jest, or in earnest; they must not, as St. *Paul* saith, be *so much as named* among Christians[4]: to meddle with them is not to disport, but to defile one's self, and others. There is indeed no more certain sign of a mind utterly debauched from Piety and Vertue, than affecting such talk. But farther,

4. All unseasonable Jesting is blameable. As there are some proper seasons of relaxation, when we may *desipere in loco*[5]; so are there some times, and circumstances of things, wherein it con-

---

[1] Obtrectatio et livor pronis auribus accipiuntur. Quippe adulationi foedum crimen servitutis, malignitati falsa species libertatis inest. TAC. *Hist.* I init. [i].
[2] [eulogies].   [3] *Jer.* IV, 22.
[4] *Eph.* V, 3.   [5] [HOR. *Carm.* IV, xii, 28].

cerneth and becometh men to be serious in mind, grave in demeanour, and plain in discourse ; when to sport in this way is to doe
indecently, or uncivilly, to be impertinent, or troublesome [1].

It comporteth not well with the presence of Superiours, before
whom it becometh us to be composed and modest : much less with
the performance of Sacred offices, which require an earnest attention, and most serious frame of mind.

In deliberations and debates about affairs of great importance,
the simple manner of speaking to the point is the proper, easie,
clear and compendious way : facetious speech there serves onely
to obstruct and entangle business, to lose time, and protract the
result [2]. The Shop and Exchange will scarce endure Jesting in
their lower transactions : the Senate, the Court of justice, the
Church do much more exclude it from their more weighty Con-
sultations. Whenever it justleth out, or hindereth the dispatch of
other serious business, taking up the room, or swallowing the time
due to it, or indisposing the minds of the audience to attend it,
then it is unseasonable and pestilent. Παίζειν, ἵνα σπουδάζῃς. To
play, that we may be seriously busy [3], is the good rule (of Ana-
charsis,) implying the subordination of sport to business, as a
condiment, and furtherance, not an impediment or clog thereto.
He that for his sport neglects his business, deserves indeed to be
reckoned among children ; and childrens fortune will attend him,
to be pleased with toys, and to fail of substantial profit.

'Tis, again, improper (because indeed uncivil, and inhumane)
to jest with persons that are in a sad or afflicted condition [4] ; as
arguing want of due considering, or due commiserating their case :
it appears a kind of insulting upon their misfortune, and is apt to
foment their grief. Even in our own case (upon any disastrous
occurrence to our selves) it would not be seemly to frollick it thus ;
it would signify want of due regard to the frowns of God, and the
strokes of his hand ; it would cross the Wise man's advice, In the
day of prosperity be joyfull, but in the day of adversity consider [5].

---

[1] Vitandum nè petulans, nè superbum, nè loco, nè tempore alienum, nè
praeparatum et domo allatum videatur [quod dicimus]. QUINT. [Instit. Orat.,
VI, iii, 33].

[2] Μή μοι τὰ κόμψ᾽, ἀλλ᾽ ὧν πόλει δεῖ. Eurip. ARIST. Pol. 2. 4 [Fragment 16,
from Aeolus, quoted in Pol., III, 4, 1277 a, 19].

[3] ARIST. Eth. X, vi [Eth. Nic., X, 6, 1176 b, 33. παίζειν δ᾽ ὅπως σπουδάζῃ,
κατ᾽ ᾽Ανάχαρσιν].

[4] Adversus miseros inhumanus est jocus. QUINT. [Instit. Orat. VI, iii, 33].

[5] Eccles. VII, 14.

It is also not seasonable, or civil, to be jocund in this way with those who desire to be serious, and like not the humour. Jocularity should not be forcibly obtruded, but by a kindly conspiracy (or tacit compact) slip into conversation : consent and complaisance give all the life thereto. Its design is to sweeten and ease society : when to the contrary it breedeth offence or encumbrance, it is worse than vain and unprofitable. From these instances we may collect when in other like cases it is unseasonable, and therefore culpable. Farther,

5. To affect, admire, or highly to value this way of speaking, (either absolutely in it self, or in comparison to the serious and plain way of speech,) and thence to be drawn into an immoderate use thereof, is blameable. A man of ripe age, and sound judgment, for refreshment to himself, or in complaisance to others, may sometimes condescend to play in this, or any other harmless way : but to be fond of it, to prosecute it with a carefull or painfull eagerness, to dote and dwell upon it, to reckon it a brave or fine thing, a singular matter of commendation, a transcendent accomplishment, any-wise preferrable to rational endowments, or comparable to the moral excellencies of our mind, (to solid Knowledge, or sound Wisedom, or true Vertue and Goodness,) this is extremely childish, or brutish, and far below a man. What can be more absurd, than to make a business of play, to be studious and laborious in toys, to make a profession or drive a trade of impertinency [1] ? what more plain non-sense can there be, than to be earnest in jest, to be continual in divertisement, or constant in pastime ; to make extravagance all our way, and sauce all our diet ? Is not this plainly the life of a child, that is ever busie, yet never hath any thing to doe ? or the life of that mimical brute, which is always active in playing uncouth [2] and unlucky tricks ; which, could it speak, might surely pass well for a professed Wit ?

The proper work of Man, the grand drift of humane life, is to follow Reason, (that noble spark kindled in us from Heaven ; that Princely and powerfull faculty, which is able to reach so lofty objects, and to achieve so mighty works ;) not to sooth fancy, that brutish, shallow and giddy power, able to perform nothing worthy much regard. *We are not* (even *Cicero* could tell us) *born for play and jesting ; but for severity, and the study of graver and greater*

---

[1] Σπουδάζειν, καὶ πονεῖν παιδιᾶς χάριν, ἠλίθιον φαίνεται, καὶ λίαν παιδικόν. ARIST. *Eth.* X, 6 [*Eth. Nic.*, X, 6, 1176 b, 32-33].   [2] [strange, novel].

affairs [1]. Yes, we were purposely designed, and fitly framed, to understand and contemplate, to affect and delight in, to undertake and pursue most noble and worthy things ; to be employed in business considerably profitable to our selves, and beneficial to others : We do therefore strangely debase our selves, when we do strongly bend our minds to, or set our affections upon such toys.

Especially to doe so is unworthy of a Christian ; that is of a person who is advanced to so high a rank, and so glorious relations ; who hath so excellent objects of his mind and affections presented before him, and so excellent rewards for his care and pains proposed to him ; who is engaged in affairs of so worthy nature, and so immense consequence : for him to be zealous about quibbles, for him to be ravished with puny conceits and expressions, 'tis a wondrous oversight, and an enormous indecency.

He indeed that prefers any faculty to Reason, disclaims the privilege of being a Man, and understands not the worth of his own Nature ; he that prizes any quality beyond Vertue and Goodness, renounces the title of a Christian, and knows not how to value the dignity of his profession. It is these two (Reason and Vertue) in conjunction, which produce all that is considerably good and great in the world. Fancy can doe little ; doeth never any thing well, except as directed and wielded by them. Do pretty conceits or humourous talk carry on any business, or perform any work ? No ; they are ineffectual and fruitless : often they disturb, but they never dispatch any thing with good success. It is simple Reason (as dull and dry as it seemeth) which expediteth all the grand affairs, which accomplisheth all the mighty works that we see done in the world. In truth therefore, as one Diamond is worth numberless bits of Glass ; so one solid Reason is worth innumerable Fancies : one grain of true Science and sound Wisedom in real worth and use doth outweigh loads (if any loads can be) of freakish Wit. To rate things otherwise, doth argue great weakness of judgment, and fondness of mind. So to conceit [2] of this way, signifieth a weak mind ; and much to delight therein, rendreth it so : nothing more debaseth the spirit of a man, or more rendreth it light and trifling [3].

---

[1] Neque enim ita generati a natura sumus, ut ad ludum jocumque facti videamur, sed ad severitatem potius, et ad quaedam studia graviora, atque majora. Cic. *Off.* I [xxix, 103].

[2] [to form such a conception, to think thus].

[3] ὡς μὴ συμβαίνειν κατὰ ταὐτὸν ψυχῆς νῆψιν καὶ εὐτραπελίας διάχυσιν. BAS.

Hence if we must be venting pleasant conceits, we should doe it *as if we did it not*, carelesly and unconcernedly ; not standing upon it, or valuing our selves for it : we should doe it with measure and moderation ; not giving up our selves thereto, so as to mind it, or delight in it more than in any other thing : we should not be so intent upon it, as to become remiss in affairs more proper or needfull for us ; so as to nauseate serious business, or disrelish the more worthy entertainments of our minds. This is the great danger of it, which we daily see men to incurr ; they are so be-witched with a humour of being witty themselves, or of hearkning to the fancies of others, that it is this onely which they can like or savour, which they can endure to think or talk of. 'Tis a great pity, that men who would seem to have so much wit, should so little understand themselves. But farther,

6. Vain-glorious ostentation this way is very blameable. All ambition, all vanity, all conceitedness, upon what-ever ground they are founded, are absolutely unreasonable and silly : but yet those, being grounded on some real ability, or some usefull skill, are wise and manly in comparison to this, which standeth on a foundation so manifestly slight and weak. The old Philosophers by a severe Father were called *animalia gloriae* [1], *animals of glory* ; and by a Satyrical Poet they were termed *bladders of vanity* [2] : but they at least did catch at praise from praiseworthy knowledge ; they were puff'd up with a wind which blowed some good to mankind ; they sought glory from that which deserved glory if they had not sought it ; it was a substantial and solid credit which they did affect, resulting from successfull enterprises of strong reason, and stout industry : but these *animalcula gloriae*, these flies, these insects of glory, these, not bladders, but bubbles of vanity, would

---

Const. Mon. 12 [*Constitutiones Asceticae,* cap. xii ; MIGNE, *Patrol. gr.,* t. 31, col. 1376].

Πολλοὺς [= πολλὰ] συμβαίνει τοὺς περὶ τὰ τοιαῦτα ἀσχολουμένους, τοῦ ὀρθοῦ λόγου διαμαρτάνειν, τῆς ψυχῆς πρὸς γελοιασμὸν διαχεομένης, καὶ τὸ τῆς φρονήσεως σύννουν καὶ πεπυκνωμένον καταλυούσης. *Ibid.*

Jocorum frequens usus omne animis pondus omnemque vim eripiet. SEN. *de Tranq.* c. 15 [xvii, 6].

Ἡ εὐτραπελία μαλακὴν ποιεῖ τὴν ψυχὴν, ῥᾴθυμον, ἀναπεπτωκυῖαν. CHRYS. *in Eph.* 17 [*Hom. in Epist. ad Eph.,* XVII, cap. v ; MIGNE, *Patrol. gr.,* t. 62, col. 119].

[1] TERTULL. [philosophus, animal gloriae. *De Anima,* cap. 1 ; MIGNE, *Patrol. lat.,* t. 2, col. 687].

[2] κενεῆς οἰήσιος ἔμπλεοι ἀσκοί. TIMON. ['Εκ τῶν Σιλλῶν, in *Analecta Vet. Poetarum Graecorum,* ed. Brunck, II, 68].

be admired and praised for that which is no-wise admirable or laudable [1]; for the casual hits and emergencies of roving fancy; for stumbling on an odd conceit or phrase, which signifieth nothing, and is as superficial as the smile, as hollow as the noise it causeth. Nothing certainly in nature is more ridiculous than a self-conceited Wit, who deemeth himself some-body, and greatly pretendeth to commendation from so pitifull and worthless a thing as a knack of trifling.

7. Lastly, it is our duty never so far to engage our selves in this way, as thereby to lose or to impair that habitual seriousness, modesty and sobriety of mind, that steddy composedness, gravity and constancy of demeanour, which become Christians. We should continually keep our minds intent upon our *high calling*, and grand interests; ever well tuned, and ready for the performance of holy Devotions, and the practice of most serious duties with earnest attention and fervent affection: Wherefore we should never suffer them to be dissolved into levity, or disordered into a wanton frame, indisposing us for religious thoughts and actions. We ought always in our behaviour to maintain, not onely τὸ πρέπον, a fitting *decency*, but also τὸ σεμνὸν, a stately *gravity* [2], a kind of venerable majesty, sutable to that high rank which we bear of God's Friends, and Children; adorning our holy profession [3], and guarding us from all impressions of sinfull vanity [4]. Wherefore we should not let our selves be transported into any excessive pitch of lightness, inconsistent with or prejudicial to our Christian state and business. Gravity and Modesty are the fences of Piety, which being once slighted, sin will easily attempt and encroach upon us. So the old *Spanish* Gentleman may be interpreted to have been wise, who, when his Son upon a voyage to the *Indies* took his leave of him, gave him this odd advice, *My Son, in the first place keep thy Gravity, in the next place fear God* [5]: intimating, that a man must first be serious, before he can be pious.

---

[1] Risus — tenuissimus ingenii fructus. Cɪᴄ. *de Orat.* 2 [Risum quaesivit, qui est mea sententia vel tenuissimus ingeni fructus. II, lx, 247].

[2] *Phil.* IV, 8; *1 Tim.* III, 8.

[3] *Tit.* II, 10.

[4] Dictum potius aliquando perdet quam minuet auctoritatem. Qᴜɪɴᴛ. 6. 3. [*Instit. Orat.* VI, iii, 30].

[5] Sᴛʀᴀᴅ. *Infam. Famiani* [*Gasparis Scioppii Infamia Famiani, ... Animadversationes... in Famiani Stradae Decadem Primam de Bello Belgico,* Sorae, 1658, pp. 227-8: " Istic enim parentibus mos esse fertur, ut filios in Italiam, Belgium aut extremas Orbis Indias iter jam ingressuros salutaribus vitae agendae prae-

To conclude, as we need not be demure, so must we not be impudent ; as we should not be sour, so ought we not to be fond ; as we may be free, so we should not be vain ; as we may well stoop to friendly complaisance, so we should take heed of falling into contemptible levity. If without wronging others, or derogating from our selves, we can be facetious ; if we can use our wits in jesting innocently, and conveniently ; we may sometimes doe it : but let us, in compliance with St. *Paul's* direction, beware of *foolish talking and jesting, which are not convenient.*

Now the God of grace and *peace—make us perfect in every good work to doe his will, working in us that which is well pleasing in his sight, through Jesus Christ, to whom be glory for ever and ever* [1]. Amen.

ceptis instruant, cumque eos jam domo pedem extulisse vident, hoc monitorum omnium compendium de fenestra prospicientes abeuntibus succlament : *Hyo, te enconcienda la gravedad, y despues et temor de Dios,* id est, Fili, gravitatem inprimis tibi cordi esse moneo, proxime Dei metum. "].
    [1] *Heb.* xiii, 20, 21.

A Sermon upon the Passion of Our Blessed Saviour
[Preached at the Guildhall Chapel on Good Friday, 1677]

Phil. II. 8. And being found in fashion as a man, he humbled himself, and became obedient unto death, even the death of the Cross.

When, in consequence of the original apostacy from God, which did banish us from Paradise, and by continued rebellions against him, inevitable to our corrupt and impotent nature, mankind had forfeited the amity of God [1], (the chief of all goods, the fountain of all happiness,) and had incurred his displeasure, (the greatest of all evils [2], the foundation of all misery :)

When poor man, having deserted his natural Lord and Protectour, *other Lords had got dominion over him* [3], so that he was captivated by the foul, malicious, cruel Spirits, and enslaved to his own vain mind, to vile lusts, to wild passions [4]:

When, according to an eternal rule of justice, that sin deserveth punishment [5], and by an express Law, wherein death was enacted [6] to the transgressours of God's command [7], the root of our stock, and consequently all its branches stood adjudged to utter destruction [8]:

When, according to St. *Paul's* expressions, *all the World was become guilty before God,* (or * subjected to God's Judgment [9] ;) † *all men (Jews and Gentiles) were under sin* [10], || *under condemnation* [11], * *under the curse* [12]; † *all men were concluded into disobedience* [13], and || *shut up together* (as close Prisoners) *under sin* [14] ; * *all men had sinned, and come short of the glory of God* [15]:

---

[1] Cyril c. *Jul.* 8, p. 278. 9, 303 [*Adversus Julianum*, Migne, *Patrol. gr.*, t. 76, col. 925, 965].

[2] *Joh.* III, 36 ; *Col.* III, 6.   [3] *Isa.* XXVI, 13.

[4] Iren. III, 33, 34 ; III, 8 [*Contra Haereses*, lib. III, cap. xxii, xxiii & viii, Migne, *Patrol.* gr., t. 7].   [5] *Gen.* IV, 7.

[6] [decreed].   [7] *Gen.* II, 17.

[8] Iren V, 16. [*Op. cit.*]   [9] * *Rom.* III, 19 ; ὑπόδικος τῷ Θεῷ.

[10] † *Rom.* III, 9.   [11] || *Rom.* V, 16, 18.

[12] * *Gal.* III, 10.   [13] † *Rom.* XI, 32 ; εἰς ἀπείθειαν.

[14] || *Gal.* III, 22.   [15] * *Rom.* III, 23.

† Death had passed over all, because all had sinned [1] :

When, for us, being plunged into so wretched a condition, no visible remedy did appear, no possible redress could be obtained here below : (For, what means could we have of recovering God's favour, who were apt perpetually to contract new debts and guilts, but not able to discharge any old scores ? What capacity of mind or will had we to entertain mercy, who were no less stubbornly perverse and obdurate in our crimes, than ignorant or infirm ? How could we be reconciled unto Heaven, who had an innate antipathy to God and goodness ? [|| *Sin* (according to our natural state, and secluding Evangelical grace) *reigning in our mortal bodies* [2], * *no good thing dwelling in us* [3] ; there being a predominant *law in our members, warring against the law of our mind, and bringing us into captivity to the law of sin* [4] ; a main ingredient of our † *old man* [5] being a || *carnal mind*, which is *enmity to God*, and *cannot submit to his Law* [6] ; we being * *alienated from the life of God by the blindness of our hearts* [7], and *enemies in our minds by wicked works* [8] ?] How could we revive to any good hope, who were *dead in trespasses and sins* [9], God having withdrawn his quickning Spirit ? How at least could we for one moment stand upright in God's sight, upon the natural terms, excluding all sin, and exacting perfect obedience [10] ?)

When this, I say, was our forlorn and desperate case, then Almighty God, out of his infinite goodness, was pleased to look upon us (as he sometime did upon *Jerusalem, lying polluted in her blood* [11]) with an eye of pity and mercy, so as graciously to design a redemption for us out of all that wofull distress : And no sooner by his incomprehensible wisedom did he foresee we should lose our selves, than by his immense grace he did conclude to restore us.

But how could this happy design [12] well be compassed ? how, in consistence with the glory, with the justice, with the truth of God, could such enemies be reconciled, such offenders be pardoned,

---

[1] † *Rom.* V, 12.   [2] || *Rom.* VI, 12, 14, 20, 22.
[3] * *Rom.* VII, 18, 5.   [4] *Rom.* VII, 23.
[5] † *Rom.* VI, 6 ; *Col.* III, 9 ; *Eph.* IV, 22.
[6] || *Rom.* VIII, 7 ; οὐχ ὑποτάσσεται.
[7] * *Eph.* IV, 18.   [8] *Col.* I, 21 ; *Rom.* V, 10.
[9] *Eph.* II, 5 (*Rom.* VI, 13, 11).
[10] *Ps.* CXLIII, 2 ; *Exod.* XXXIV, 7.   [11] *Ezek.* XVI, 6.
[12] *Eph.* I, 4, 9, 11 & III, 11 ; *2 Tim.* I, 9 ; *1 Pet.* I, 20 ; *Rev.* XIII, 8 ; *Rom.* XVI, 25 ; *Tit.* I, 2.

such wretches be saved ? Would the Omnipotent Majesty, so
affronted, design to treat with his rebels immediately, without an
intercessour or advocate ? Would the Sovereign Governour of
the world suffer thus notoriously his right to be violated, his
authority to be slighted, his honour to be trampled on, without
some notable vindication or satisfaction ? Would the great Patron
of Justice relax the terms of it, or ever permit a gross breach
thereof to pass with impunity ? Would the immutable God of
truth expose his veracity or his constancy to suspicion, by so
reversing that peremptory sentence of death upon sinners, that
it should not in a sort eminently be accomplished [1] ? Would the
most righteous and most holy God let slip an opportunity so
advantageous for demonstrating his perfect love of innocence, and
abhorrence of iniquity ? Could we therefore well be cleared from
our guilt without an expiation, or re-instated in freedom without
a ransome, or exempted from condemnation without some punishment ?

No : God was so pleased to prosecute his designs of goodness
and mercy, as thereby no-wise to impair or obscure, but rather to
advance and illustrate the glories of his sovereign dignity, of his
severe justice, of his immaculate holiness, of his unchangeable
steddiness in word and purpose. He accordingly would be sued
to for peace and mercy : nor would he grant them absolutely,
without due compensations for the wrongs he had sustained ; yet
so, that his goodness did find us a Mediatour, and furnish us with
means to satisfy him. He would not condescend to a simple
remission of our debts ; yet so, that, saving his right and honour,
he did stoop lower for an effectual abolition of them. He would
make good his word, not to let our trespasses go unpunished ;
yet so, that by our punishment we might receive advantage. He
would manifest his detestation of wickedness in a way more
illustrious ; than if he had persecuted it down to Hell, and irre-
versibly doomed it to endless torment.

---

[1] ATHAN. *De Incarn.*
[καὶ γὰρ καὶ ὁ θάνατος, ὡς προεῖπον, νόμῳ λοιπὸν ἴσχυε καθ᾽ ἡμῶν · καὶ οὐχ οἶον
τε ἦν τὸν νόμον ἐκφυγεῖν, διὰ τὸ ὑπὸ Θεοῦ τεθεῖσθαι τοῦτον τῆς παραβάσεως χάριν.
Καὶ ἦν ἄτοπον ὁμοῦ καὶ ἀπρεπὲς τὸ γινόμενον ἀληθῶς. Ἄτοπον μὲν γὰρ ἦν εἰπόντα
τὸν Θεὸν ψεύσασθαι, ὥστε νομοθετήσαντος αὐτοῦ, θανάτῳ ἀποθνήσκειν τὸν ἄνθρωπον,
εἰ παραβαίη τὴν ἐντολήν, μετὰ τὴν παράβασιν μὴ ἀποθνήσκειν, ἀλλὰ λύεσθαι τὸν
τούτου λόγον. Οὐκ ἀληθὴς γὰρ ἦν ὁ Θεός, εἰ, εἰπόντος αὐτοῦ ἀποθνήσκειν ἡμᾶς, μὴ
ἀπέθνησκεν ὁ ἄνθρωπος. MIGNE, *Patrol. gr.*, t. 25, col. 105.]
Gen. II, 17.

But how might these things be effected ? Where was there
a Mediatour proper and worthy to intercede for us ? Who could
presume to solicit and plead in our behalf ? Who should dare to
put himself between God and us, or offer to skreen mankind from
the divine wrath and vengeance ? Who had so great an interest
in the Court of Heaven, as to ingratiate such a brood of apostate
enemies thereto ? Who could assume the confidence to propose
terms of reconciliation, or to agitate a new covenant, wherewith
God might be satisfied, and whereby we might be saved ? Where,
in Heaven or Earth, could there be found a Priest fit to atone for
sins so vastly numerous, so extremely hainous ? And whence should
a sacrifice be taken, of value sufficient to expiate for so manifold
enormities, committed against the infinite Majesty of Heaven ?
Who could *find out the everlasting redemption* [1] of innumerable
souls, or lay down a competent ransome for them all ? not to say,
could also purchase for them eternal life and bliss ?

These are Questions which would puzzle all the wit of man,
yea, would gravel all the wisedom of Angels to resolve : for plain
it is, that no creature on earth, none in Heaven, could well undertake or perform this work.

Where on earth, among the degenerate sons of *Adam*, could be
found *such an High Priest as became us, holy, harmless, undefiled,
separate from sinners* [2] ? And how could a Man, however innocent
and pure as a Seraphim, so perform his duty, as to doe more than
merit or satisfie for himself ? How many lives could the life of
one man serve to ransome ; seeing that it is asserted of the greatest
and richest among men, that *None of them can by any means
redeem his brother, or give to God a ransome for him* [3].

And how could available help in this case be expected from
any of the Angelical hoast ; seeing (beside their being in nature
different from us, and thence improper to merit or satisfy for us ;
beside their comparative meanness, and infinite distance from the
Majesty of God) they are but our fellow-servants, and have obligations to discharge for themselves, and cannot be solvent for more
than for their own debts of gratitude and service to their infinitely-
bountifull Creatour ; they also themselves needing a Saviour, to
preserve them by his grace in their happy state ?

---

[1] αἰωνίαν λύτρωσιν εὑρομενος. *Heb.* IX, 12.
[2] *Heb.* VII, 26.   [3] *Ps.* XLIX, 7.

Indeed, no creature might aspire to so august an honour, none could atchieve so marvellous a work, as to redeem from infinite guilt and misery the noblest part of all the visible creation : none could presume to invade that high prerogative of God, or attempt to infringe the truth of that reiterated Proclamation, *I, even I am the Lord, and beside me there is no Saviour* [1].

Wherefore, seeing that a supereminent dignity of Person was required in our Mediatour, and that an immense value was to be presented for our ransome ; seeing that *God saw there was no man, and wondred* (or took special notice) *that there was no intercessour* : it must be *his arme* alone that could *bring salvation* [2] ; none beside God himself could intermeddle therein.

But how could God undertake the business ? Could he become a suitour or intercessour to his offended self ? could he present a sacrifice, or disburse a satisfaction to his own justice ? could God alone contract and stipulate with God in our behalf ? No ; surely Man also must concur in the transaction : some amends must issue from him, somewhat must be paid out of our stock : humane will and consent must be interposed, to ratify a firm covenant with us, inducing obligation on our part. It was decent and expedient, that as Man, by wilfull transgression and presumptuous self-pleasing, had so highly offended, injured and dishonoured his Maker ; so Man also, by willing obedience, and patient submission to God's pleasure, should greatly content, right and glorify him.

Here then did lie the stress ; this was the knot which onely divine wisedom could loose. And so indeed it did in a most effectual and admirable way : for in correspondence to all the exigencies of the case, (that God and Man both might act their parts in saving us,) the blessed eternal word, the onely Son of God, by the good will of his Father, did vouchsafe to intercede for us, and to undertake our redemption ; in order thereto voluntarily being sent down from Heaven, assuming humane flesh, subjecting himself to all the infirmities of our frail nature, and to the worst inconveniences of our low condition ; therein meriting God's favour to us, by a perfect obedience to the Law, and satisfying God's justice by a most patient endurance of pains in our behalf ; in completion of all willingly laying down his life for the ransome

---

[1] *Isa.* XLIII, 11 ; XLV, 21 ; *Hos.* XIII, 4.
[2] *Isa.* LIX, 16. κατενόησε. LXX.

of our souls, and pouring forth his bloud in sacrifice for our sins [1].

This is that great and wonderfull *mystery of godliness* [2], (or of our holy Religion,) the which St. *Paul* here doth express, in these words concerning our blessed Saviour ; *Who being in the form of God, thought it no robbery to be equal with God, but made himself of no reputation, and took upon him the form of a servant, and was made in the likeness of men : And being found in fashion as a man, he humbled himself, and became obedient unto death, even the death of the Cross.*

In which words are contained divers points very observable. But seeing the time will not allow me to treat on them in any measure as they deserve ; I shall (waving all the rest) insist but upon one particular, couched in the last words, *Even the death of the Cross* [3] ; which by a special emphasis do excite us to consider the manner of that holy Passion, which we now commemorate : the contemplation whereof, as it is most seasonable, so it is ever very profitable.

Now then in this kind of Passion we may consider divers notable adjuncts ; namely these. 1. Its being in appearance criminal. 2. Its being most bitter and painfull. 3. Its being most ignominious and shamefull. 4. Its peculiar advantageousness to the designs of our Lord in suffering. 5. Its practical efficacy.

I. We may consider our Lord's Suffering as Criminal ; or as in semblance being an execution of justice upon him. *He* (as the Prophet foretold of him) *was numbred among the transgressours* [4] ; and God (saith St. *Paul*) *made him sin for us who knew no sin* [5] : that is, God ordered him to be treated as a most sinfull or criminous [6] person, who in himself was perfectly innocent, and void of the least inclination to offend.

So in effect it was, that he was impeached of the highest crimes ; as a violatour of the Divine Laws in divers instances ; as a designer to subvert their Religion and Temple ; as an Impostour, deluding and seducing the people ; as a Blasphemer, assuming to himself

[1] *Eph.* I, 8 ; *Luke* I, 78 ; *Eph.* I, 5 ; *Tit.* III, 4 ; *Rom.* V, 8 ; *Gal.* IV, 4 ; *John* VI, 38 ; *Heb.* X, 7 ; *John* I, 14 ; *Heb.* V, 2 ; IV, 15 ; *Eph.* I, 5.
  Constit. Apost. VIII, xii [MIGNE, *Patrol. gr.,* t. 1, col. 1102].
  1 Tim. II, 6 ; *Tit.* II, 14 ; *Heb.* IX, 15 ; II, 9 ; *Col.* I, 22.
[2] *1 Tim.* III, 16.   [3] Θανάτου δὲ σταυροῦ [*Phil.* II, 8].
[4] *Isa.* LIII, 12.   [5] *2 Cor.* V, 21.
              [6] [guilty of crime].

the properties and prerogatives of God[1]; as a seditious and rebellious person, *perverting the nation*[2], inhibiting payments of tribute to *Caesar*, usurping Royal Authority, and styling himself *Christ a King*[3]: in a word, as a Malefactour, or one guilty of enormous offences; so his persecutours avowed to *Pilate*, *If*, said they, *he were not a malefactour, we would not have delivered him up unto thee*[4]. As such he was represented and arraigned; as such, although by a sentence wrested by malicious importunity, against the will and conscience of the Judge, he was condemned, and accordingly suffered death.

Now whereas any death or passion of our Lord, as being in it self immensely valuable, and most pretious in the sight of God, might have been sufficient toward the accomplishment of his general designs, (the appeasing God's wrath, the satisfaction of Divine Justice, the expiation of our guilt;) it may be inquired, why God should thus expose him, or why he should chuse to suffer under this odious and ugly character[5]? Which inquiry is the more considerable[6], because it is especially this circumstance which crosseth the fleshly sense, and worldly prejudices of men, so as to have rendred the Gospel offensive to the superstitious *Jews*, and despicable to conceited Gentiles. For so *Tryphon* in *Justin Martyr*[7], although, from conviction by testimonies of Scripture, he did admit the *Messias* was to suffer *hardly*, yet that it should be in this *accursed* manner, he could not digest. So the great adversaries of Christianity (*Celsus*[8], *Porphyrie*[9], *Julian*[10],) did with most contempt urge this exception against it. So St. *Paul* did observe, that *Christ crucified was unto the Jews a stumbling-block, and unto the Greeks foolishness*[11]. Wherefore to avoid those scandals, and that we may better admire the Wisedom of

---

[1] *John* V, 18, 10, 30 etc.; VII, 12; *Matt.* XXVI, 61; XXVII, 40.
[2] *Luke* XXIII, 2; *Matt.* XXVII, 63.
[3] *Const. Apost.* V, xiv [MIGNE, *Patrol. gr.*, t. 1, col. 876].
[4] *John* XVIII, 30. κακοποιός.
[5] Cur si Deus fuit, et mori voluit, non saltem honesto aliquo mortis genere affectus est? etc. LACT., IV, 26 [*Divin. Instit.* MIGNE, *Patrol. lat.*, t. 6, p. 529].
[6] [proper to be considered].
[7] JUST. M. *Dial.*, p. 317 [*Dialogus cum Tryphone Judaeo*, MIGNE, *Patrol. gr.*, t. 6, col. 689].
[8] ORIG. *c. Cels.*, II, p. 83; VII, p. 368 [MIGNE, *Patrol. gr.*, t. 11, col. 860, 1498].
[9] AUG. *de Civ. Dei*, X, 28 [MIGNE, *Patrol. lat.*, t. 41, col. 307].
[10] CYRIL. *c. Jul.*, VI, p. 194 [MIGNE, *Patrol. gr.*, t. 76, col. 796-7].
[11] *1 Cor.* I, 23.

God in this dispensation, it may be fit to assign some Reasons intimated in Holy Scripture, or bearing conformity to its Doctrine, why it was thus ordered. Such are these.

1. As our Saviour freely did undertake a life of greatest meanness and hardship, so upon the like accounts he might be pleased to undergo a death most lothsome and uncomfortable. There is nothing to man's nature (especially to the best natures, in which modesty and ingenuity do survive) more abominable than such a death. God for good purposes hath planted in our constitution a quick sense of disgrace ; and of all disgraces that which proceedeth from an imputation of crimes is most pungent ; and being conscious of our innocence doth heighten the smart ; and to reflect upon our selves dying under it, leaving the World with an indeleble stain upon our name and memory, is yet more grievous. Even to languish by degrees, enduring the torments of a long, however sharp disease, would to an honest mind seem more eligible, than in this manner, being reputed and handled as a villain, to find a quick and easie dispatch.

Of which humane resentment may we not observe a touch in that expostulation, *Be ye come out as against a thief with swords and staves*[1] ? If as a man he did not like to be prosecuted as a thief ; yet willingly did he chuse it, as he did other most distastfull things, pertaining to our nature, (*the likeness of man,*) and incident to that low condition, (*the form of a servant,*) into which he did put himself : such as were, to endure penury, and to fare hardly, to be slighted, envied, hated, reproached through all his course of life.

It is well said by a Pagan Philosopher, that *No man doth express such a respect and devotion to Vertue, as doth he who forfeiteth the repute of being a good man, that he may not lose the conscience of being such*[2]. This our Lord willingly made his case, being content not onely to expose his Life, but to prostitute his Fame, for the interests of Goodness.

Had he died otherwise, he might have seemed to purchase our wellfare at a somewhat easie rate ; he had not been so complete a sufferer ; he had not tasted the worst that man is liable to

---

[1] *Luke*, XXII, 52 ; *Matt.* XXVI, 55.
[2] Nemo mihi videtur pluris aestimare virtutem, nemo illi magis esse devotus, quam qui boni viri famam perdidit, ne conscientiam perderet. SEN. *Ep.* LXXXI [20].

endure : there had been a comfort in seeming innocent, detracting from the perfection of his sufferance.

Whereas therefore he often was in hazzard of death, both from the clandestine machinations, and the outrageous violences of those who maligned him[1], he did industriously shun a death so plausible[2], and honourable, if I may so speak ; it being not so disgracefull to fall by private malice, or by sudden rage, as by the solemn deliberate proceeding of men in publick authority and principal credit[3].

Accordingly this kind of death did not fall upon him by surprize, or by chance ; but he did *from the beginning*[4] foresee it ; he plainly with satisfaction did aim at it : He (as it is related in the Gospels) did *shew* his Disciples, that it was incumbent on him by God's appointment and his own choice ; that *he ought* ('tis said) *to suffer many things, to be rejected by the chief Priests, Elders and Scribes, to be vilified by them, to be delivered up to the Gentiles, to be mocked, and scourged, and crucified*[5], as a flagitious slave. Thus would our blessed Saviour, in conformity to the rest of his voluntary afflictions, and for a consummation of them, not onely suffer in his Body by sore wounds and bruises, and in his Soul by dolefull agonies, but in his Name also and Reputation by the foulest scandals ; undergoing as well all the infamy as the infirmity which did belong to us, or might befall us : thus meaning by all means throughly to express his charity, and exercise his compassion towards us ; thus advancing his merit, and discharging the utmost satisfaction in our behalf.

2. Death passing on him as a Malefactour by publick sentence, did best sute to the nature of his undertaking, was most congruous to his intent, did most aptly represent what he was doing, and imply the reason of his performance. For we all are guilty in a most high degree, and in a manner very notorious ; the foulest shame together with the sharpest pain is due to us for affronting our glorious Maker, we deserve an open condemnation and exemplary punishment : wherefore he, undertaking in our stead to bear all, and fully to satisfie for us, was pleased to undergo the like judgment and usage ; being termed, being treated as we should

---

[1] *John* V, 18 ; VIII, 37, 40, 59 ; VII, 1, 19, 25 ; X, 32, 39.
[2] [commendable].   [3] [great reputation].   [4] *John* VI, 64.
[5] *Matt.* XVI, 21 ; *Luke* IX, 22 ; XVIII, 32 ; *Mark* IX, 31.

have been, in quality of an hainous Malefactour, as we in truth are. What we had really acted in dishonouring and usurping upon God, in disordering the world, in perverting others, that was imputed to him ; and the punishment due to that guilt was inflicted on him. *All we like sheep have gone astray, we have turned every one to his own way ; and the Lord hath laid on him the iniquities of us all*[1]. He therefore did not onely sustain an equivalent pain for us, but in a sort did bear an equal blame with us, before God and Man.

3.   Seeing *by the determinate counsel of God*[2] it was appointed that our Lord should die for us, and that not in a natural, but violent way, so as perfectly to satisfie God's justice, to vindicate his honour, to evidence both his indignation against sin, and willingness to be appeased ; it was most fit that affair should be transacted in a way, wherein God's right is most nearly concerned, and his providence most plainly discernible ; wherein it should be most apparent that God did exact and inflict the punishment, that our Lord did freely yield to it, and submissively undergo it, upon those very accounts. All *judgment* (as *Moses* of old did say) *is God's*[3], or is administred by authority derived from him, in his name, for his interest ; all Magistrates being his officers, and instruments, whereby he governeth and ordereth the world, his natural Kingdom : whence that which is acted in way of formal judgment by persons in authority, God himself may be deemed in a more special and immediate manner to execute it, as being done by his commission, in his stead, on his behalf, with his peculiar superintendence. It was therefore in our Lord a signal act of deference to God's Authority and Justice, becoming the person sustained by him of our Mediatour and Proxy[4], to undergo such a judgment, and such a punishment ; whereby he received a doom as it were from God's own mouth, uttered by his Ministers, and bare the stroke of justice from God's hand, represented by his instruments. Whence very seasonably and patiently did he reply to *Pilate, Thou hadst no power over me,* (or *against me,*) *except it were given thee from above*[5] : implying, that it was in regard to the originally Supreme Authority of God his Father, and to his

---

[1] *Isa.* LIII, 6.   [2] *Acts* II, 23.   [3] *Deut.* I, 17.
[4] [becoming him as our mediator and proxy].
[5] *John* XIX, 11. κατ᾽ ἐμοῦ.

particular appointment upon this occasion, that our Saviour did
then frankly subject himself to those inferiour powers, as to the
proper ministers of Divine Justice. Had he suffered in any other
way, by the private malice or passion of men, God's special providence in that case had been less visible, and our Lord's obedience
not so remarkable. And if he must die by publick hands, it must
be as a criminal, under a pretence of guilt and demerit ; there
must be a formal process, how full soever of mockery and outrage ;
there must be testimonies produced, how void soever of truth or
probability ; there must be a sentence pronounced, although most
corrupt and injurious : for no man is in this way persecuted, without colour of desert : otherwise it would cease to be publick
authority, and become lawless violence ; the Persecutour then
would put off the face of a Magistrate, and appear as a Cut-throat,
or a Robber.

4. In fine, our Saviour hardly with such advantage, in any
other way, could have displayed[1] all kinds of Vertue and Goodness,
to the honour of God, to the edification of men, to the furtherance
of our Salvation.

The Judgment-Hall, with all the passages leading him thither,
and thence to execution, attended with guards of souldiers, amidst
the crouds and clamours of people, were as so many theatres, on
which he had opportune convenience, in the full eye of the world,
to act divers parts of sublimest Vertue : to express his insuperable
Constancy, in attesting truth, and maintaining a good conscience[2] ;
his Meekness, in calmly bearing the greatest wrongs ; his Patience,
in contentedly enduring the saddest adversities ; his intire resignation to the will and providence of God ; his peaceable submission
to the law and power of man ; his admirable charity, in pitying,
in excusing, in obliging those by his good wishes, and earnest
prayers for their pardon, who in a manner so injurious, so despite-
full, so cruel, did persecute him, yea, in gladly suffering all this
from their hands for their salvation ; his unshakeable Faith in God,
and unalterable Love toward him, under so fierce a trial, so dreadfull a temptation. All these excellent Vertues and Graces, by the
matter being thus ordered, in a degree most eminent, and in a
manner very conspicuous ,were demonstrated, to the praise of God's

---

[1] [hardly could our Saviour have displayed with such advantage].
[2] *John* XVIII, 37 ; *1 Tim.* VI, 13.

Name, and the commendation of his Truth ; for the settlement of our Faith and Hope, for an instruction and an encouragement to us of good practice in those highest instances of Vertue.

It is a passable notion among the most eminent Pagan Sages, that no very exemplary Vertue can well appear otherwise than in notable misfortune[1]. Whence 'tis said in *Plato*, that to approve a man heartily *righteous, he must be scourged, tortured, bound, have his two eyes burnt out, and in the close, having suffered all evils, must be impaled*[2], or crucified. And, * *It was* (saith *Seneca*) *the cup of poyson which made* Socrates *a great man, and which out of prison did transfer him to Heaven*[3], or did procure to him that lofty esteem ; affording him opportunity, to signalize his constancy, his equanimity, his unconcernedness for this world and life. And, *The vertue* (saith he again) *and the innocence of* Rutilius *would have lain hid, if it had not* (by condemnation and exile) *received injury ; while it was violated, it brightly shone forth*[4]. And he that said this of others, was himself in nothing so illustrious, as in handsomely entertaining that death to which he was by the bloody Tyrant adjudged. And generally, the most honourable persons in the judgment of posterity for gallant worth, to this very end (as such Philosophers teach) were by divine providence delivered up to suffer opprobrious condemnations and punishments, by the ingratefull malignity of their times[5]. So that the *Greeks*, in consistence with their own wisedom and experience, could not reasonably scorn that Cross which our good Lord (did not onely, as did their best Worthies, by forcible accidental constraint undergo, but) advisedly by free choice did undertake, to recommend the most excellent Vertues to imitation, and to promote the most noble designs that could be, by its influence.

So great Reason there was, that our Lord should thus suffer as a Criminal.

[1] Magnum exemplum nisi mala fortuna non invenit. SEN., *De Prov.*, c, iii [4].

[2] Ὁ δίκαιος μαστιγώσεται, στρεβλώσεται, δεδήσεται, ἐκκαυθήσεται τὼ ὀφθαλμώ, τελευτῶν πάντα κακὰ παθὼν ἀνασχινδυλευθήσεται. PLAT. *De Rep.*, II [361 E - 362 A].

[3] * Cicuta magnum Socratem fecit. SEN. *Ep.* XIII [14].

Calix venenatus, qui Socratem transtulit e carcere in coelum. SEN. *Ep.* LXVII [7].

Aequalis fuit in tanta inaequalitate fortunae, etc. SEN. *Ep.* CIV [28].

[4] Rutilii innocentia ac virtus lateret, nisi accepisset injuriam ; dum violatur, effulsit. SEN. *Ep.* LXXIX [14].

[5] SEN. *de Prov.* II, III, etc. ; PLUT. *de Stoic. Contr.*, p. 1931 [*De Stoicorum Repugnantiis*, 37 = *Moralia*, 1051 C].

II. We may consider, that in that kind his Suffering was most bitter and painfull. Easily we may imagine what acerbity of pain must be endured by our Lord, in his tender Limbs being stretched forth, racked, and tentered [1], and continuing for a good time in such a posture ; by the *piercing his hands and his feet* [2], parts very nervous and exquisitely sensible, with sharp nails, (so that, as it is said of *Joseph, the iron entered into his Soul* ;) [3] by abiding exposed to the injuries of the Sun scorching, the wind beating, the weather searching his grievous wounds and sores. Such a pain it was ; and that no stupefying, no transient pain, but one both very acute and lingring : for we see, that he together with his fellow-sufferers had both presence of mind, and time to discourse. Even six long hours did he remain under such torture [4], sustaining in each moment of them beyond the pangs of an ordinary death. But as the case was so hard and sad, so the reason of it was great, and the fruit answerably good. Our Saviour did embrace such a Passion, that in being thus content to endure the most intollerable smarts for us, he might demonstrate the vehemence of his love ; that he might signifie the hainousness of our sins, which deserved that from such a person so heavy punishment should be exacted ; that he might appear to yield a valuable compensation for those pains which we should have suffered ; that he throughly might exemplifie the hardest duties of obedience and patience.

III. This manner of Suffering was (as most sharp and afflictive, so) most vile and shamefull ; being proper to the basest condition of the worst men, and unworthy of a free-man, however nocent [5] and guilty [6]. It was *servile supplicium*, a punishment never by the *Romans*, under whose Law our Lord suffered, legally inflicted upon free-men, but upon slaves onely ; that is, upon people scarcely regarded as men, having in a sort forfeited or lost themselves. And among the *Jews* that execution which most approached thereto, and in part agreed with it, (for their Law did not allow any so inhumane punishment,) hanging up the dead bodies of some that had been put to death, was held most infamous and execrable : for, *Cursed*, said the Law, *is every one that hangeth upon a tree* [7] ;

---

[1] [stretched on tenders].   [2] *Ps.* XXII, 16.   [3] *Ps.* CV, 18.
[4] *Mark* XV, 25, 34.   [5] [guilty, criminal].
[6] Quod etiam homine libero, quamvis nocente, videatur indignum. LACT. [*Divin. Instit.*] IV, 26 [MIGNE, *Patrol. lat.*, t. 6, p. 529].
[7] *Deut.* XXI, 23 ; *Gal.* III, 13.

cursed, that is, devoted to reproach and malediction : *accursed by God* [1], saith the Hebrew, that is, seeming to be rejected by God, and by his special order exposed to affliction.

Indeed, according to the course of things, to be set on high, and for continuance of time to be objected [2] to the view of all that pass by, in that calamitous posture, doth infuse bad suspicion, doth provoke censure, doth invite contempt and scorn, doth naturally draw forth language of derision, despight and detestation ; especially from the inconsiderate, hard-hearted and rude vulgar, which commonly doth think, speak and deal according to event and appearance : (—*Sequitur fortunam semper, & odit damnatos*—[3]) Whence θεατρίζεσθαι, *to be made a gazing-stock*, or an object of reproach to the multitude, is by the Apostle mentioned as an aggravation of the hardships endured by the Primitive Christians. And thus in extremity did it befall our Lord : for we reade [4], that the people did in that condition mock, jear and revile him, drawing up their noses, abusing him by scurrilous gestures, letting out their virulent and wanton tongues against him ; so as to verifie that prediction, *I am a reproach of men, and despised of the people : All they that see me laugh me to scorn ; they shoot out the lip, they shake the head, saying, He trusted in the Lord, let him deliver him, seeing he delighted in him* [5].

The same persons who formerly had admired his glorious works, who had been ravished with his excellent discourses, who had followed and favoured him so earnestly, who had blessed and magnified him [6], (*for he*, saith St. *Luke, taught in the Synagogues, being glorified by all* [7],) even those very persons did then behold him with pitiless contempt and despight. In correspondence to that prophecie, *they look and stare upon me* [8], εἱστήκει ὁ λαὸς θεωρῶν, *the people stood gazing* [9] on him, in a most scornfull manner, venting contemptuous and spitefull reproaches ; as we see reported in the Evangelical Story.

Thus did our blessed Saviour *endure the cross, despising the shame* [10]. *Despising the shame*, that is not only simply disregarding

---

[1] Τοῦτο γὰρ μόνον τῆς τελευτῆς τὸ εἶδος ὑπὸ ἀρὰν ἔκειτο, CHRYS. Tom. 6 Or. 61 [*Contra Judaeos et Gentiles, Quod Christus sit Deus*, MIGNE, *Patrol. gr.*, t. 48, col. 825].   [2] [presented].   [3] [JUVENAL, *Sat.* X, 73-4].
[4] *Luke* XXIII, 35, 36. Ἐξεμυκτήριζον, ἐνέπαιζον.
Matt. XXVII, 39. ἐβλασφήμουν.
[5] *Ps.* XXII, 6, 7, 8.   [6] *Matt.* IX, 33 ; XXI, 9 ; XII, 23.
[7] *Luke* IV, 15.   [8] *Ps.* XXII, 17.
[9] *Luke* XXIII, 35.   [10] *Heb.* XII, 2.

it, or (with a Stoical haughtiness, with a Cynical immodesty, with a stupid carelesness) slighting it as no evil ; but not eschewing it, or not rating it for so great an evil, that to decline it he would neglect the prosecution of his great and glorious designs.

There is innate to man an aversation and abhorrency from disgracefull abuse, no less strong than are the like antipathies to pain : whence *cruel mockings and scourgings* [1] are coupled as ingredients of the sore persecutions sustained by God's faithfull Martyrs. And generally men with more readiness will embrace, with more contentedness will endure the cruelty of the latter, than of the former ; Pain not so smartly affecting the lower sense, as being insolently contemned doth grate upon the fancy, and wound even the mind it self. For, *the wounds* of infamy *do* (as the *Wise-man* telleth us) *go down into the innermost parts of the belly* [2], reaching the very heart, and touching the soul to the quick.

We therefore need not doubt, but that our Saviour as a man, endowed with humane passions, was sensible of this natural evil ; and that such indignities did add somewhat of loathsomness to his cup of affliction ; especially considering, that his great charity disposed him to grieve, observing men to act so indecently, so unworthily, so unjustly toward him : yet in consideration of the glory that would thence accrue to God, of the benefit that would redound to us, of the *joy that was set before him* [3], when *he should see of the travel of his soul, and be satisfied* [4], he most willingly did accept, and most gladly did comport [5] with it. He *became a curse for us* [6], exposed to malediction and reviling : He *endured the contradiction* (or obloquy) *of sinfull men* [7] : He was *despised, rejected and disesteemed of men* [8] : He in common apprehension was deserted by God, according to that of the Prophet, *We did esteem him stricken, smitten of God, and afflicted* [9] ; himself even seeming to concur in that opinion. So was he *made a curse for us*, that *we*, as the Apostle teacheth, might *be redeemed from the curse of the Law* [10] ; that is, that we might be freed from the exemplary punishment due to our transgressions of the Law, with the displeasure of God appearing therein, and the disgrace before

---

[1] *Heb.* XI, 36.
[2] *Prov.* XVIII, 8 ; XII, 18.
[3] *Heb.* XII, 2.
[4] *Isa.* LIII, 11.
[5] [bear, put up].
[6] *Gal.* III, 13.
[7] *Heb.* XII, 3.
[8] *Isa.* LIII, 3.
[9] *Isa.* LIII, 4.
[10] *Gal.* III, 13.

the world attending it. He chose thus to *make himself of no
reputation* [1], vouchsafing to be dealt with as a wretched slave, and
a wicked miscreant, that we might be exempted, not onely from
the torment, but also from the ignominy which we had merited ;
that together with our life, our safety, our liberty, we might even
recover that honour which we had forfeited and imbezzled.

But lest any should be tempted not sufficiently to value these
sufferances of our Lord, as not so rare, but that other men have
tasted the like ; lest any should presume to compare them with
afflictions incident to other persons, as *Celsus* [2] did compare them
with those of *Anaxarchus* and *Epictetus* ; it is requisite to consider
some remarkable particulars about them.

We may then consider, that not onely the infinite dignity of
his Person, and the perfect Innocency of his life did inhance the
price of his Sufferings ; but some Endowments peculiar to him,
and some Circumstances adhering to his design, did much augment
their force.

He was not onely, according to the frame and temper of humane
nature, sensibly touched with the pain, the shame, the whole com-
bination of disasters apparently waiting on his Passion ; as God
(when he did insert sense and passion into our nature, ordering
objects to affect them) did intend we should be, and as other men
in like circumstances would have been ; but in many respects
beyond that ordinary rate : so that no man, we may suppose, could
have felt such grief from them as he did, no man ever hath been
sensible of any thing comparable to what he did endure ; that
passage being truly applicable to him, *Behold and see, if there be
any sorrow like to my sorrow, which is done unto me, wherewith
the Lord hath afflicted me in the day of his fierce anger* [3] ; as that
unparallel'd *sweating out great lumps of bloud* [4] may argue ; and
as the terms expressing his resentments [5] do imitate. For, in respect
of present evils, he said of himself, *My soul is exceeding sorrowfull
to death* ; he is said ἀδημονεῖν, *to be in great anguish* [6] and anxiety,
to be in *an agony* [7] or pang of sorrow. In regard to mischiefs

---

1 *Phil.* II, 7.
2 ORIG. *c. Cels.* VII, p. 368 [MIGNE, *Patrol. gr.*, t. 11, col. 1498].
3 *Lam.* I, 12.   4 *Luke* XXII, 44.
5 [feelings, emotions].   6 *Matt.* XXVI, 37, 38.
                      7 *Luke* XXII, 44.

which he saw coming on, he is said to be *disturb'd in spirit* [1], and to be *sore amazed* [2], or dismayed at them. To such an exceeding height did the sense of incumbent evils, and the prospect of impendent calamities, the apprehension of his case, together with a reflexion on our condition, skrew up his affections.

And no wonder that such a burthen, even the weight of all the sins (the numberless most heinous sins and abominations) that ever were committed by mankind, by appropriation of them to himself, lying on his shoulders, he should feel it heavy, or seem to croutch and groan under it ; that in the mystical Psalm, applied by the Apostle to him, he should cry out, *Innumerable evils have compassed me about, mine iniquities have taken hold upon me, so that I am not able to look up : they are more than the hairs of my head, and my heart faileth me* [3]. The sight of God's indignation so dreadfully flaming out against sin, might well astonish [4] and terrify him : To stand, as it were, before the mouth of Hell belching fire and brimstone in his face ; to lie down in the hottest furnace of Divine vengeance ; to quench with his own heart-bloud the wrath of Heaven, and the infernal fire, (as he did in regard to those who will not rekindle them to themselves,) might well in the heart of a man beget unconceivable and unexpressible pressures of affliction. When such a father (so infinitely good and kind to him, whom he so dearly and perfectly loved) did hide his face from him, did frown on him, how could he otherwise than be mightily troubled ? Is it strange that so hearty a love, so tender a pity, contemplating our sinfulness, and experimenting our wretchedness, should be deeply touched ? To see, I say, so plainly, to feel so throughly the horrible blindness, the folly, the infidelity, the imbecillity, the ingratitude, the incorrigibility, the strange perverseness, perfidiousness, malice and cruelty of mankind in so many instances, (in the treason of *Judas*, in the denial of *Peter*, in the desertion of all the Apostles, in the spite and rage of the Persecutours, in the falshood of the Witnesses, in the abuses of the People, in the compliance of *Pilate*, in a general conspiracy of Friends and Foes to sin,) all these surrounding him, all invading him, all discharging themselves upon him ; would it not astone [5] a mind so pure ? would it not wound a heart so tender and full of charity ?

[1] *John* XIII, 21 ; XII, 27. [2] *Mark* XIV, 33.
[3] *Heb.* X, 5 ; *Ps.* XL, 12. [4] [dismay]. [5] [stun, stupefy].

Surely, any of those persons who fondly do pretend unto, or
vainly do glory in a sullen apathy, or a stubborn contempt of the
evils incident to our nature and state, would in such a case have
been utterly dejected : The most resolved Philosopher would have
been dashed into confusion at the sight, would have been crushed
into desperation under the sense of those evils which did assault him.

With the greatness of the causes, the goodness of his constitution did conspire to encrease his Sufferings. For surely, as his
complexion was most pure and delicate, his spirit most vivid and
apprehensive, his affections most pliant and tractable ; so accordingly would the impressions upon him be most sensible, and consequently the pains which he felt (in body or soul) most afflictive.

That we in like cases are not alike moved ; that we do not
tremble at the apprehensions of God's displeasure, that we are not
affrighted with the sense of our sins, that we do not with sad
horrour resent our danger and our misery, doth arise from that
we have very glimmering and faint conceptions of those matters ;
or that they do not in so clear and lively a manner strike our fancy ;
(not appearing in their true nature and proper shape, so heinous
and so hideous as they really are in themselves and in their consequences;) or because we have but weak persuasions about them ;
or because we do but slightly consider them ; or from that our
hearts are very hard and callous, our affections very cold and dull,
so that nothing of this nature (nothing beside gross material affairs)
can mollifie or melt them ; or for that we have in us small love to
God, and a slender regard to our own welfare ; in fine, for that
in spiritual matters we are neither so wise, so sober, so serious,
nor so good or ingenuous, in any reasonable measure, as we should
be. But our Saviour in all those respects was otherwise disposed.
He most evidently discerned the wrath of God, the grievousness
of sin, the wretchedness of man, most truly, most fully, most
strongly represented to his mind : He most firmly believed, yea
most certainly knew, whatever God's Law had declared about
them : He did exactly consider and weigh them : His heart was
most soft and sensible, his affections were most quick and excitable
by their due objects : He was full of dutifull love to God, and
most ardently desirous of our good, bearing a more than fraternal
good-will towards us. Whence 'tis not so marvellous that as a
Man, as a transcendently-wise and good man, he was so vehe-
mently affected by those occurrences, that his imagination was so

troubled, and his passions so stirred by them ; so that he thence did suffer in a manner, and to a degree unconceivable ; according to that ejaculation in the *Greek* Liturgies, Διὰ τῶν ἀγνώστων σου παθημάτων ἐλέησον ἡμᾶς, Χριστὲ [1], *By thy unknown sufferings, O Christ, have mercy on us.* But farther.

IV. We may consider, that this way of Suffering had in it some particular Advantages, conducing to the accomplishment of our Lord's principal designs.

Its being very notorious, and lasting a competent time, were good Advantages. For if he had been privately made away, or suddenly dispatched, no such great notice would have been taken of it, nor would the matter of fact have been so fully proved, to the confirmation of our faith, and conviction of infidelity ; nor had that his excellent deportment under such bitter affliction (his most Divine Patience, Meekness and Charity) so illustriously shone forth. Wherefore to prevent all exceptions, and excuses of un-belief, (together with other collateral good purposes,) Divine Providence did so manage the business, that as the course of his life, so also the manner of his death, should be most conspicuously remarkable. *I spake freely to the world, and in secret have I done nothing* [2], said he of himself ; and, *These things* (said St. *Paul* to King *Agrippa*) *were not done in a corner* [3]. Such were the proceedings of his life, not close or clancular [4], but frank and open ; not presently hushed up, but leisurely carried on in the face of the world, that men might have the advantage to observe and examine them. And as he lived, so he died most publickly and visibly ; the world being witness of his Death, and so prepared to believe his Resurrection, and thence disposed to embrace his Doctrine ; according to what he did foretell, *I being lifted up from the Earth, shall draw all men to me* [5] : for he drew all men by so obvious a Death to take notice of it, he drew all well-disposed persons from the wondrous consequences of it to believe on him [6]. And, *As* (said he again) *Moses did exalt the Serpent in the Wilderness, so must the Son of man be exalted* [7]. As the elevation of that

---

[1] [Not identified].　　　　[2] *John* XVIII, 20.
[3] *Acts* XXVI, 26.　　　　[4] [secret, underhand].
[5] *John* XII, 32.
[6] IREN. II, 26 [*Adversus Haereses*, MIGNE, *Patrol. gr.*, t. 7, col. 763].
[7] *John* III, 14.

mysterious Serpent did render it visible [1], and did attract the eyes
of people toward it ; whereby, God's power invisibly accompanying that Sacramental performance, they were cured of those mor-
tiferous [2] stings which they had received : so our Lord, being
mounted on the Cross, allured the eyes of men to behold him, and
their hearts to close with him ; whereby, the heavenly virtue of
God's Spirit co-operating, they became saved from those destructive sins, which from the Devil's serpentine instigations they had
incurred.

Another Advantage of this kind of Suffering was, that by it
the nature of that Kingdom which he did intend to erect was
evidently signified : that it was not such as the carnal people did
expect, an external, earthly, temporal Kingdom, consisting in domination over the bodies and estates of men, dignified by outward
wealth and splendour, managed by worldly power and policy,
promoted by forcible compulsion and terrour of arms, affording
the advantages of safety, quiet, and prosperity here ; but a Kingdom purely spiritual, celestial, eternal ; consisting in the gover-
nance of mens hearts and minds ; adorned with endowments of
wisedom and vertue ; administred by the conduct and grace of
God's Holy Spirit ; upheld and propagated by meek instruction,
by vertuous example, by hearty devotion, and humble patience ;
rewarding its loyal Subjects with spiritual joys and consolations
now, with heavenly rest and bliss hereafter. No other Kingdom
could he presume to design, who submitted to this dolorous and
disgracefull way of suffering : No other exploits could he pretend
to atchieve by expiring on a Cross : No other way could he rule,
who gave himself to be managed by the will of his adversaries :
No other benefits would this forlorn case allow him to dispense.
So that well might he then assert, *My Kingdom is not of this
world* [3] ; when he was going in this signal way to demonstrate
that important truth.

It was also a most convenient touch-stone to prove the genuine
disposition and worth of men [4] ; so as to discriminate those wise,
sober, ingenuous, sincere, generous souls, who could discern true
goodness through so dark a cloud, who could love it though so
ill-favouredly disfigured, who could embrace and avow it notwith-

---

[1] Iren. IV, 5 [*op. cit.*, col. 979].   [2] [deadly].
[3] *John* XVIII, 36.   [4] *Luke* II, 35.

standing so terrible disadvantages ; it served, I say to distinguish those *blessed* ones, who *would not be offended in him* [1], or by *the scandal of the cross* [2] be discouraged from adhering to him, from the crew of blind, vain, perverse, haughty people, who, being scandalized at his adversity, would contemn and reject him.

Another considerable Advantage was this, that by it God's special Providence was discovered, and his glory illustrated in the propagation of the Gospel [3]. For how could it be, that a person of so low parentage, of so mean garb, of so poor condition, who underwent so lamentable and despicable a kind of death, falling under the pride, and spite of his enemies, so easily should gain so general an opinion in the world (even among the best, the wisest, the greatest persons) of being *the Lord of life and glory* [4] ? how, I say, could it happen, that such a miracle could be effected without God's aid and special concurrence ? That King *Herod*, who from a long reign in flourishing state, with prosperous success in his enterprises, did attain the name of Great ; or that *Vespasian*, who triumphantly did ascend the imperial Throne, should either of them, by a few admirers of worldly vanity, seriously be held, or in flattery be call'd the *Messias* ; is not so strange : but that one who was trampled on so miserably, and treated as a wretched caitiff, should instantly conquer innumerable hearts, and from such a depth of extreme adversity, should be advanced to the sublimest pitch of glory ; that *the Stone which the builders* with so much scorn *did refuse*, should *become the head-stone of the corner ; this* (with good assurance we may say) *was the Lord's doing, and it is marvellous in our eyes* [5].

Hereby indeed *the excellency of divine power* [6] and wisedom was much glorified ; by so impotent, so improbable, so implausible means accomplishing so great effects [7] ; subduing the world to obedience of God, not by the active valour of an illustrious Hero, but through the patient submission of a poor, abused and oppressed person ; restoring mankind to life and happiness by the sorrowfull death of a crucified Saviour.

---

[1] *Matt.* XI, 6.
[2] *Gal.* V, 11 ; *1 Pet.* II, 7, 8 ; *1 Cor.* I, 23.
[3] CHRYS. Tom. 6 *Orat.* 61 [*Contra Judaeos et Gentiles, Quod Christus sit Deus*, MIGNE, *Patrol. gr.*, t. 48, col. 825].
[4] *1 Cor.* II, 8 ; *Jas.* II, 1.
[5] *Ps.* CXVIII, 22, 23.
[6] *2 Cor.* IV, 7.
[7] *1 Cor.* I, 27.

V. Lastly, The consideration of our Lord's Suffering in this
manner is very usefull in application to our practice : No point is
more fruitfull of wholsome instruction, none is more forcible to
kindle devout affections, none can afford more efficacious inducements and incentives to a pious life. For what vertue will not a
serious meditation on the Cross be apt to breed and to cherish ?
to what duty will it not engage and excite us ?

1. Are we not hence infinitely obliged, with most humble
affection and hearty gratitude to adore each person of the blessed
Trinity ?

That God the Father should design such a Redemption for us ;
not sparing his own Son, (the Son of his love, dear to him as
himself,) but *delivering him up for us* [1], to be thus dealt with for
our sake : That God would endure to see his Son in so pitifull a
condition, to hear him groaning under so grievous pressures, to
let him be so horribly abused ; and that for us, who deserved
nothing from him, who had demerited so much against him ; for
us, who were no friends to him, (for *even when we were enemies,
we were reconciled to God by the death of his Son* ;) [2] who were
not any ways commendable for goodness or righteousness : (for
Christ did suffer for sinners, the just for the unjust [3] ; and * *God
commended his love to us, that while we were sinfull, Christ died
for us* :) [4] That God thus should *love us, sending his Son to be a
propitiation for our sins* [5], in so dismal a way of suffering, how
stupendious is that goodness ? how vast an obligation doth it lay
upon us to reciprocal affection ? If we do owe all to God, as our
Maker, from whose undeserved bounty we did receive all that we
have ; how much farther do we stand indebted to him as the
authour of our Redemption, from whose ill-deserved mercy we
receive a new being, and better state ; and that in a way far more
obliging ? For God created us with a word, without more cost
or trouble : but to redeem us, stood him in huge expences and
pains ; no less than the debasing his onely Son to our frailty, the
exposing him to more than our misery, the withdrawing his face,
and restraining his bowels from his best beloved. If a *Jew* then
were commanded by Law, if a *Gentile* were obliged by Nature,

---

[1] *Rom.* VIII, 32 ; *Col.* I, 13.   [2] *Rom.* V, 10.
[3] *1 Pet.* III, 18 ; *Rom.* V, 6 ; *2 Cor.* V, 19.
[4] * *Rom.* V, 8.   [5] *1 John* IV, 10.

to *love God with all his heart and all his soul*[1]; what affection doth a Christian, under the law and duty of Grace, owe unto him? by what computation can we reckon that debt? what faculties have we sufficient to discharge it? what finite heart can hold an affection commensurate to such an obligation?

And how can it otherwise than inflame our heart with love toward the blessed Son of God, our Saviour, to consider that merely out of charitable pity toward us, he purposely came down from Heaven, and took our flesh upon him, that he might therein undergo those extreme acerbities of pain, and those most ugly indignities of shame for us[2]? *Greater love* (said he) *hath no man than this, that a man lay down his life for his friends*[3]: But that God should lay down his life, should pour forth his bloud, should be aspersed[4] with the worst crimes, and cloathed with foulest shame, should be executed on a Cross as a malefactour and a slave, for his enemies and rebellious traitours, what imagination can devise any expression of charity or friendship comparable to this? Wherefore if love naturally be productive of love, if friendship justly meriteth a correspondence in good-will, what effect should the consideration of so ineffable a love, of so unparallel'd friendship have upon us?

How can any serious reflexion on this event fail to work hearty gratitude in us toward our good Lord? For put case[5] any person for our sake (that he might rescue us from the greatest mischiefs, and purchase for us the highest benefits) willingly should deprive himself of all his estate, (and that a very large one,) of his honour, (and that a very high one,) of his ease and pleasure, (and those the most perfect and assured that could be;) that he should expose himself to the greatest hazzards, should endure the sorest pains, and most disgracefull ignominies; should prostitute his life, and in most hideous manner lose it, merely for our sake: Should we not then apprehend and confess our selves monstrously ingratefull, if we did not most deeply resent such kindness; if upon all occasions we did not express our thankfulness for it; if we did not ever readily yield all the acknowledgment and all the requital

---

[1] [*Mark* XII, 33].
[2] *Eph.* III, 19; V, 2, 25; *Gal.* II, 20; *Apoc.* [*Rev.*] I, 5.
[3] *John* XV, 13, οὐδεὶς ἔχει, ἵνα τις —
[4] [injuriously and falsely charged].   [5] [suppose].

we were able ?   The case in regard to our blessed Saviour is like
in kind ; but in degree, whatever we can suppose doth infinitely
fall below the performances of him for us, who stooped from the
top of Heaven, who laid aside the Majesty and the Felicity of God
for the infamies and the dolours of a Cross, that he might redeem
us from the torments of Hell, and instate us in the joys of Paradise.   So that our obligations of gratitude to him are unexpres-
sibly great ; and we cannot with any face deny our selves to be
most basely unworthy, if the effects in our heart and life be not
answerable.

Nor should we forget, that also upon this account we do owe
great love and thanks to God the Holy Ghost, who, as he did
originally conspire in the wonderfull project of our Redemption,
as he did executively by miraculous operation conduct our Saviour
into his fleshly Tabernacle, as he did by unmeasurable communi-
cations of Divine virtue [1] assist his Humanity through all the course
of his life ; so in this juncture he did inspire him with Charity
more than humane, and did support him to undergo those pressures
with invincible patience ; and so did sanctifie all this Sacerdotal
performance, that our Lord, as the Apostle doth affirm, *did through
the eternal Spirit offer himself without spot to God* [2].

2.   What surer ground can there be of Faith in God, what
stronger encouragement of Hope, than is suggested by this consideration ?   For if God stedfastly did hold his purpose [3], and
faithfully did accomplish his word [4] in an instance so distastfull
to his own heart and bowels ; how can we ever suspect his constancy and fidelity in any case ? how can we distrust the completion
of any Divine promise ?

If God spared not his own Son, but delivered him up for us,
to the suffering of so contumelious [5] affliction, how can we any
ways be diffident of his bounty, or despair of his mercy ; *how*
(as the Apostle doth argue) *shall he not also with him freely give
us all things* [6] *?*

If ever we be tempted to doubt of God's goodness, will not
this experiment thereof convince and satisfy us ?   For what higher
kindness could God express, what lower condescension could he

---

[1] *John* III, 34.
[3] *1 Pet.* I, 20 ; *Eph.* I, 4.
[5] [shameful].

[2] *Heb.* IX, 14.
[4] *Luke* I, 70.
[6] *Rom.* VIII, 32.

vouchsafe, by what pledge could he more clearly or surely testify his willingness and his delight to doe us good, than by thus ordering his dearest Son to undergo such miseries for us ?

If the greatness of our sins discourageth us from entertaining comfortable hopes of mercy, will it not rear our hearts, to consider that such a punishment hath been inflicted to expiate them, which might content the most rigorous severity [1] ; that such a price is laid down to *redeem us from the curse* [2], which richly may suffice to discharge it ; that such a sacrifice [3] hath been offered, which God hath avowed for most available [4], and acceptable to himself ? So that now what can justice exact more from us ? what have we farther to doe, than with a penitent and thankfull heart to embrace the mercy purchased for us ? *Who is he that condemneth*, seeing *Christ hath died* [5], and *hath his own self born our sins in his own body on the tree* [6] ? Whatever the wounds of our Conscience be, is not *the bloud of the Cross* [7], tempered with our hearty repentance, and applied by a lifely faith, a sovereign balsam, of virtue sufficient to cure them ? and may we not *by his stripes be healed* [8] ? Have we not abundant reason, with the Holy Apostle, to *joy in God through our Lord Jesus Christ* ; *by whom we have received the atonement* [9] ? Is it not to depreciate the worth, to disparage the efficacy of our Lord's Passion, any ways to despair of mercy, or to be disconsolate for guilt ; as if the Cross were not enough worthy to compensate for our unworthiness, or our Saviour's patience could not ballance our disobedience ?

3. It indeed may yield great joy and sprightly consolation to us, to contemplate our Lord upon the Cross, exercising his immense Charity toward us, transacting all the work of our Redemption, defeating all the enemies, and evacuating all the obstacles of our Salvation [10].

May we not delectably consider him as there stretching forth his Armes of kindness, with them to embrace the World, and to

---

[1] Quis de se desperet, pro quo tam humilis esse voluit Filius Dei ? Aug. de Ag. Chr. c. 11 [*De Agone Christiano*, XI, Migne, *Patrol. lat.*, t. 40, p. 298].

[2] *Gal.* III, 13. [3] *Eph.* V, 2 ; *1 Pet.* I, 19.

[4] [efficacious]. [5] *Rom.* VIII, 34.

[6] *1 Pet.* II, 24. [7] [*Col.* I, 20].

[8] *1 Pet.* II, 24. [9] *Rom.* V, 11.

[10] Extendit in passione manus suas, etc. Lact. IV, 26 [*Divin. Instit.*, Migne, *Patrol. lat.*, t. 6, p. 530]. *Isa.* LXV, 2.

receive all mankind under the wings of his protection ? as there spreading out his Hands, with them earnestly inviting and in-treating us to accept the overtures of grace, procured by him for us ?

Is it not sweet and satisfactory, to view our great High Priest on that high Altar offering up his own pure Flesh, and pouring out his pretious bloud, as an universal complete Sacrifice, propitiatory for the sins of mankind [1] ?

Is it not a goodly object to behold humility and patience so gloriously rearing themselves above all worldly, all infernal pride and insolence ; by the Cross ascending unto the celestial Throne of Dignity and Majesty superlative ?

Is it not pleasant to contemplate our Lord there standing erect, not onely as a resolute sufferer, but as a noble Conquerour, where *having spoiled principalities and powers, he made a solemn shew triumphing over them* [2] ?   Did ever any Conquerour, loftily seated in his triumphal Chariot, yield a spectacle so gallant and magnificent ? was ever tree adorned with trophees so pompous and splendid ?

To the exteriour view and carnal sense of men, our Lord was then indeed exposed to scorn and shame ; but to spiritual and sincere discerning, all his and our enemies did there hang up as objects of contempt, utterly overthrown and undone.

There the Devil, that *strong* and sturdy *one* [3], did hang up bound in chains, disarmed and rifled, quite baffled and confounded, mankind being rescued from his tyrannick power [4].

There the World, with its vain pomps, its counterfeit beauties, its bewitching pleasures, its fondly-admired excellencies, did hang up all defaced and disparaged ; as it appeared to St. *Paul* : for, *God* (saith he) *forbid that I should glory save in the Cross of Christ, by which the world is crucified to me, and I unto the world* [5].

There, in a most lively representation, and most admirable pattern, was exhibited *the mortification of our flesh, with its affec-*

---

[1] Lev. IX, 22 ; Chrys. Tom. [V] *Orat.* 82 [*De Cruce et Latrone*, Migne, *Patrol. gr.*, t. 49, col. 399].
   P. Leo I [*De Passione Domini*, Migne, *Patrol. lat.*, t. 54, col. 313-384].
[2] *Col.* II, 15.
[3] *Matt.* XII, 29. ὁ ἰσχυρός ; *Luke* XI, 21, 22.
[4] *Heb.* II, 14.   [5] *Gal.* VI, 14.

tions and lusts[1] ; and our *old man was crucified, that the body of sin might be destroyed*[2].

There our sins, being (as St. *Peter* telleth us) *carried up by him unto the gibbet*[3], did hang as marks of his victorious prowess, as malefactours by him *condemned in the flesh*[4], as objects of our horrour and hatred.

There Death it self hung gasping, with its sting pulled out, and all its terrours quelled ; his Death having prevented ours, and induced Immortality[5].

There all wrath, *enmity*, strife, (the banes of comfortable life,) did hang *abolished in his flesh*, and *slain upon the Cross*[6], *by the bloud whereof he made peace, and reconciled all things in heaven and earth*[7].

There manifold yokes of bondage, instruments of vexation, and principles of variance, even all *the hand-writing of ordinances that was against us*, did hang up *cancelled* and *nailed to the Cross*[8].

So much sweet comfort by spiritual consideration may be extracted from this event, which in appearance was most dolefull, but in effect the most happy that ever by Providence was dispensed to the world. Farther,

4. This consideration is most usefull to render us very humble and sensible of our weakness, our vileness, our wretchedness. For how low was that our fall, from which we could not be raised without such a depression of God's onely Son ? how great is that impotency, which did need such a succour to relieve it ? how abominable must be that iniquity, which might not be expiated without so costly a sacrifice ? how deplorable is that misery, which could not be removed without commutation of so strange a suffering ? Would the Son of God have so *emptied*, and abased himself for nothing[9] ? would he have endured such pains and ignominies for a trifle ? No surely ; if our guilt had been slight, if our case had been tolerable, the Divine wisedom would have chosen a more cheap and easie remedy for us.

---

[1] *Gal.* II, 20 ; V, 24 ; *Col.* III, 5 ; *Rom.* VIII, 13.
[2] [*Rom.* VI, 6.]   [3] *1 Pet.* II, 24.
[4] *Rom.* VIII, 3.
[5] *1 Cor.* XV, 54, 55 ; *2 Tim.* I, 10 ; *Heb.* II, 14.
[6] *Eph.* II, 15, 16.   [7] *Col.* I, 20.
[8] *Col.* II, 14.   [9] *Phil.* II, 7. ἑαυτὸν ἐκένωσε.

Is it not madness of us to be conceited [1] for any worth in our selves, to confide in any merit of our works, to glory in any thing belonging to us, to fancy our selves brave, fine, happy persons, worthy of great respect and esteem ; whenas our unworthiness, our demerit, our forlorn estate did extort from the most gracious God a displeasure needing such a reconciliation, did impose upon the most glorious Son of God a necessity to undergo such a punish-ment in our behalf ?

How can we reasonably pretend to any honour, or justly assume any regard to our selves, whenas the First-born of Heaven, *the Lord of glory* [2], partaker of Divine majesty, was fain to *make himself of no reputation*, to put himself into *the garb of a servant* [3], and under the imputation of a malefactour, to bear such disgrace and infamy in our room, in lieu of the confusion due to us ?

What more palpable confutation can there be of humane vanity and arrogance, of all lofty *imaginations* [4], all presumptuous con-fidences, all turgid humours, all fond self-pleasings and self-admirings, than is that tragical cross, wherein, as in a glass, our foul deformity, our pitifull meanness, our helpless infirmity, our sad wofulness are so plainly represented ?

Well surely may we say with St. *Austin, Let man now at length blush to be proud, for whom God is made so humble* [5]. [And since (as he doth add) *this great disease of Soul did bring down the Almighty Physician from Heaven, did humble him to the form of a servant, did subject him to contumelies, did suspend him on a Cross, that this tumour by virtue of so great a medicine might be cured ;*] [6] may not he well be presumed incurable, who is not cured of his pride by this medicine [7] ; in whom neither the reason of the case, nor the force of such an example can work humility ?

5. But farther, while this contemplation doth breed sober humility, it also should preserve us from base abjectness of mind :

---

[1] [possessed with a good opinion].   [2] *1 Cor.* II, 8.
[3] *Phil.* II, 7.   [4] *2 Cor.* X, 5.

[5] Jam tandem erubescat homo esse superbus, propter quem factus est humilis Deus. AUG. *in Ps. 18* [*Ennarationes in Psalmos*, Ps. 18, II, MIGNE, *Patrol. lat.*, t. 36, col. 163].

[6] Iste ingens morbus, omnipotentem Medicum de caelo deduxit, usque ad formam servi humiliavit, contumeliis egit, ligno suspendit ; ut per salutem tantae medicinae curetur hic tumor. *Ibid.*

[7] Quae superbia sanari potest, si humilitate Filii Dei non sanatur ? AUG. *de Agone Chr.* cap. xi [MIGNE, *Patrol. lat.*, t. 40, col. 297].

for it doth evidently demonstrate, that according to God's infallible judgment, we are very considerable [1]; that our Souls are capable of high regard; that it is a great pity we should be lost and abandoned to ruine. For surely, had not God much esteemed and respected us, he would not for our sakes have so debased himself, or deigned to endure so much for our recovery; Divine justice would not have exacted or accepted such a ransome for our Souls, had they been of little worth. We should not therefore slight our selves, nor demean our selves like sorry contemptible wretches, as if we deserved no consideration, no pity from our selves; as if we thought our Souls not worth saving, which yet our Lord thought good to purchase at so dear a rate [2]. By so despising or disregarding our selves, do we not condemn the sentiments, do we not vilifie the sufferings of our Lord; so with a pitifull meanness of spirit joyning the most unworthy injustice and ingratitude [3]? Again,

6. How can we reflect upon this event without extreme displeasure against, and hearty detestation of our sins? those sins which indeed did bring such tortures and such disgraces upon our blessed Redeemer? *Judas*, the wretch who betrayed him, the *Jewish* Priests who did accuse and prosecute him, the wicked rout which did abusively insult over him, those cruel hands that smote him, those pitiless hearts that scorned him, those poisonous tongues that mocked him and reviled him, all those who were the instruments and abettours of his affliction, how do we loath and abhor them? how do we detest their names, and execrate their memories? But how much greater reason have we to abominate our sins, which were the true, the principal actours of all that wofull tragedy? *He was delivered for our offences* [4]: They were indeed the Traitours, which by the hands of *Judas* delivered him up. *He that knew no sin, was made sin for us* [5], that is, was accused, was condemned, was executed as a sinner for us. It was therefore we, who by our sins did impeach him; the spitefull Priests were but our Advocates: We by them did adjudge and sentence him; *Pilate*

---

[1] [worthy of regard].

[2] Aut vero pro minimo habet Deus hominem, propter quem mori voluit Unicum suum? Aug. *in Ps.* 148 [*Ennar.*, Migne, *Patrol. lat.*, t. 37, col. 1942].

Si vobis ex terrena fragilitate viles estis, ex pretio vestro vos æstimate, Aug. [not identified].

[3] *Acts* XIII, 46.   [4] *Rom.* IV, 25.   [5] *2 Cor.* V, 21.

was but drawn in against his will and conscience, to be our spokes-
man in that behalf : We by them did inflict that horrid punishment
on him ; the *Roman* Executioners were but our Representatives
therein. *He became a curse for us* [1] ; that is, all the mockery,
derision and contumely he endured, did proceed from us ; the
silly people were but properties acting our parts. Our sins were
they that cryed out, *Crucifige*, (*Crucify him, crucify him,*) [2] with
clamours more loud and more importunate than did all the *Jewish*
rabble : it was they, which by the borrowed throats of that base
people did so outrageously persecute him. *He was wounded for
our transgressions, and bruised for our iniquities* [3] : It was they
which by the hands of the fierce souldiers, and of the rude popu-
lacy, as by senseless engines, did buffet and scourge him ; they
by the nails and thorns did pierce his flesh, and rend his sacred
body. Upon them therefore it is most just and fit that we should
turn our hatred, that we should discharge our indignation.

7. And what in reason can be more powerfull toward working
penitential sorrow and remorse, than reflexion upon such horrible
effects, proceeding from our sins ? How can we forbear earnestly
to grieve, considering our selves by them to have been the perfidious
betrayers, the unjust slanderers, the cruel persecutours, and barbarous murtherers of a Person so innocent and lovely, so good
and benign, so great and glorious ; of God's own dear Son, of
our best Friend, of our most gracious Redeemer ?

8. If ingenuity will not operate so far, and hereby melt us
into contrition ; yet surely this consideration must needs affect
us with a religious Fear [4]. For can we otherwise than tremble to
think upon the heinous guilt of our sins, upon the dreadfull fierceness of God's wrath against them, upon the impartial severity of
Divine judgment for them, all so manifestly discovered, all so
livelily set forth in this dismal spectacle ? If the view of an ordinary execution is apt to beget in us some terrour, some dread
of the Law, some reverence toward Authority ; what awfull impressions should this singular example of Divine Justice work
upon us ?

How greatly we should be moved thereby, what affections it
should raise in us, we may even learn from the most inanimate

[1] *Gal.* III, 13.   [2] [*Luke* XXIII, 21 ; *John* XIX, 6, 15.]
[3] *Isa.* LIII, 5.   [4] *Ps.* CXIX, CXX.

creatures : for the whole world did seem affected thereat with horrour and confusion ; the frame of things was discomposed and disturbed ; all Nature did feel a kind of compassion and compunction for it. The Sun (as from aversion and shame) did hide his face, leaving the World covered for three hours with mournfull blackness ; the bowels of the Earth did yern [1] and quake ; the Rocks did split ; the Veil of the Temple was rent ; the Graves did open themselves, and the dead Bodies were rouzed up. And can we then (who are the most concerned in the event) be more stupid than the Earth, more obdurate than Rocks, more drowzy than interr'd Carcases, the most insensible and immovable things in nature ? But farther,

9. How can the meditation on this event doe otherwise than hugely deter us from all wilfull disobedience and commission of sin ? For how thereby can we violate such engagements, and thwart such an example of obedience ? how thereby can we abuse so wonderfull goodness, and disoblige so transcendent charity ? how thereby can we reject that gentle dominion over us, which our Redeemer did so dearly purchase, or renounce *the Lord that bought us* [2] at so high a rate ? with what heart can we bring up on the stage, and act over that direfull tragedy, renewing all that pain and all that disgrace to our Saviour ; as the Apostle teacheth that we do by Apostacy, *crucifying to our selves the Son of God afresh, and putting him to an open shame* [3] ? Can we without horrour *tread under foot the Son of God, and count the bloud of the Covenant an unholy thing* [4] ; (as the same divine Apostle saith all wilfull transgressours doe ;) [5] vilifying that most sacred and pretious bloud [6], so freely shed for the demonstration of God's mercy, and ratification of his gracious intentions toward us, as a thing of no special worth or consideration ; despising all his so kind and painfull endeavours for our Salvation ; defeating his most charitable purposes, and earnest desires for our welfare ; rendring all his so bitter and loathsome Sufferings in regard to us utterly vain and fruitless, yea indeed very hurtfull and pernicious ? for if

---

[1] [were deeply moved].
[2] *2 Pet.* II, 1 ; *Tit.* II, 14 ; *1 Pet.* I, 18, 19 ; *Rom.* XIV, 9 ; *2 Cor.* V, 15 ; *1 Cor.* VI, 20.
[3] *Heb.* VI, 6. ἀνασταυροῦντες.   [4] *Heb.* X, 29.
[5] Ἑκουσίως ἁμαρτανόντων ἡμῶν, ver. 26 [*Heb.* X].
[6] Κοινὸν ἡγησάμενος [*Heb.* X, 29].

the Cross do not save us from our sins, it will much aggravate
their guilt, and augment their punishment; bringing a severer
condemnation, and a sadder ruine on us. Again,

10. This consideration affordeth very strong engagements to
the practice of charity towards our Neighbour. For what heart
can be so hard, that the bloud of the Cross cannot mollifie into a
charitable and compassionate sense? Can we forbear to love those,
toward whom our Saviour did bear so tender affection, for whom
he was pleased to sustain so wofull tortures and indignities? Shall
we not, in obedience to his most urgent commands, in conformity
to his most notable example, in gratefull return to him for his
benefits, who thus did gladly suffer for us, discharge this most
sweet and easie duty towards his beloved friends? Shall we not
be willing, by parting with a little superfluous stuff for the relief
of our poor brother, to requite and gratifie him, who, to succour
us in our distress, most bountifully did part with his wealth, with
his glory, with his pleasure, with his life it self[1]? Shall we not
meekly comport[2] with an infirmity, not bear a petty neglect, not
forgive a small injury to our brother, whenas our Lord did for us,
and from us bear a Cross, to procure remission for our innumerable most heinous affronts and offences against Almighty God[3]?
Can a heart void of mercy and pity, with any reason or modesty
pretend to the mercies and compassions of the Cross? Can we
hope, that God for *Christ*'s sake will pardon us, if we for *Christ*'s
sake will not forgive our Neighbour?

Can we hear our Lord saying to us, *This is my command, That
ye love one another, as I have loved you*[4]; and, *Hereby shall all
men know that ye are my disciples, if ye love one another*[5]? Can
we hear St. *Paul* exhorting, *Walk in love, as Christ also hath
loved us, and hath given himself for us, an offering and a sacrifice
to God for a sweet-smelling savour*[6]; and, *We that are strong
ought to bear the infirmities of the weak—For even Christ pleased
not himself, but, as it is written, The reproaches of them that
reproached thee, fell on me*[7]? Can we attend to St. *John*'s arguing,
*Beloved, if God so loved us, then ought we also to love one another.
Hereby we perceive the love of God, because he laid down his life*

---

[1] *2 Cor.* VIII, 9.   [2] [bear with, endure].
[3] *Eph.* IV, 32; *Col.* III, 13.   [4] *John* XV, 12.
[5] *John* XIII, 35.   [6] *Eph.* V, 2.
                        [7] *Rom.* XV, 1, 3.

for us: wherefore we ought to lay down our lives for the brethren[1]*?*

Can we, I say, consider such Precepts, and such Discourses, without effectually being disposed to comply with them for the sake of our crucified Saviour; all whose Life was nothing else but one continual recommendation and enforcement of this duty; but his Death especially was a pattern most obliging, most incentive thereto? This use of the Point is the more to be regarded, because the Apostle doth apply it hereto, our Text coming in upon that occasion; for having pathetically exhorted the *Philippians* to all kinds of charity and humble condescension, he subjoyneth, *Let this mind be in you, which was in Christ Jesus; Who being in the form of God, etc.*[2].

11. But furthermore, what can be more operative than this point toward breeding a disregard of this World with all its deceitfull vanities, and mischievous delights; toward reconciling our minds to the worst condition into which it can bring us; toward supporting our hearts under the heaviest pressures of affliction which it can lay upon us? For can we reasonably expect, can we eagerly affect, can we ardently desire great prosperity, whenas the Son of God, our Lord and Master, did onely taste such adversity? How can we refuse, in submission to God's pleasure, contentedly to bear a slight grievance, whenas our Saviour gladly did bear a Cross, infinitely more distastefull to carnal will and sense than any that can befall us? Who now can admire those splendid trifles, which our Lord never did regard in his life, and which at his death onely did serve to mock and abuse him? Who can relish those sordid pleasures, of which he living did not vouchsafe to taste, and the contraries whereof he dying chose to feel in all extremity? Who can disdain or despise a state of sorrow and disgrace, which he, by voluntary susception[3] of it, hath so dignified and graced; by which we so near resemble and become conformable to him[4]; by which we concur and partake with him; yea, by which in some cases we may promote, and after a sort complete his designs, *filling up*, (as St. *Paul* speaketh) *that which is behind of the afflictions of Christ in our flesh*[5]?

[1] *1 John* IV, 11; III, 16.   [2] *Phil.* II, 5, 6.
[3] [assumption, acceptance].
[4] *Rom.* VIII, 17; *Phil.* III, 10; *Apoc.* [*Rev.*] I, 5; *1 Pet.* IV, 13.
[5] *Col.* I, 24.

Who now can hugely prefer being esteemed, approved, favoured, commended by men, before infamy, reproach, derision, and
persecution from them ; especially when these do follow conscientious adherence to righteousness ?   Who can be very ambitious
of worldly honour and repute, covetous of wealth, or greedy of
pleasure, who doth observe the Son of God chusing rather to hang
upon a Cross [1], than to sit upon a Throne ; inviting the clamours
of scorn and spite, rather than acclamations of blessing and praise ;
devesting himself of all secular power, pomp, plenty, conveniences
and solaces ; embracing the garb of a slave, and the repute of a
malefactour, before the dignity and respect of a Prince, which were
his due, which he most easily could have obtained ?

Can we imagine it a very happy thing, to be high and prosperous in this World, to swim in affluence and pleasure [2] ?   Can we
take it for a misery, to be mean and low, to conflict with some
wants and straits here ; seeing the Fountain of all happiness, did
himself purposely condescend to so forlorn a state, and was pleased
to become so deep a sufferer ?   If with devout eyes of our mind
we do behold our Lord, hanging naked upon a gibbet, besmeared
all over with streams of his own bloud, groaning under smart
anguish of pain, encompassed with all sorts of disgracefull abuses,
yielding (as it was foretold of him) *his back to the smiters, and
his cheeks to them who plucked off the hair, hiding not his face
from shame and spitting* [3] ; will not the imagination of such a
spectacle dim the lustre of all earthly grandeurs and beauties, damp
the sense of all carnal delights and satisfactions, quash all that
extravagant glee which we can find in any wild frolicks, or riotous
merriments ? will it not stain all our pride, and check our wantonness ? will it not dispose our minds to be sober, placing our happiness in things of another nature, seeking our content in matters of
higher importance ; preferring obedience to the will of God before
compliance with the fancies and desires of men ; according to that
precept of St. *Peter, Forasmuch then as Christ hath suffered for
us in the flesh, arm your selves likewise with the same mind—so
as no longer to live the remaining time in the flesh, to the lusts of*

---

[1] Cogitemus crucem ejus, et divitias lutum putabimus. HIER. *Ad Nepot.
Epist.* 2. [Epistola LII, MIGNE, *Patrol. lat.*, t. 22, col. 536].
[2] Quis beatam vitam esse arbitretur in iis, quae contemnenda esse docuit
Filius Dei ? AUG. *de Ag. Chr.* cap. 11 [MIGNE, *Patrol. lat.*, t. 40, col. 297].
[3] *Isa.* L, 6.

men, but to the will of God [1] ?

12. This indeed will instruct and incline us chearfully to submit unto God's will, and gladly to accept from his hand what-ever
he disposeth, however grievous and afflictive to our natural will ;
this point suggesting great commendation of Afflictions, and strong
consolation under them. For if such hardship was to our Lord
himself a school of duty, *he* (as the Apostle saith) *learning
obedience from what he suffered* [2] ; if it was to him a fit mean
of perfection, as the Apostle doth again imply when he saith, *that
it became God to perfect the captain of our salvation by suffering* [3] ;
if it was an attractive of the Divine favour even to him, as those
words import, *Therefore the Father loveth me, because I lay down
my life* [4] ; if it was to him a step toward glory, according to that
saying, *Was not Christ to suffer, and so to enter into his glory* [5] ?
yea, if it was a ground of conferring on him a sublime pitch of
dignity above all Creatures, *God for this obedience having exalted
him, and given him a name above all names* [6] ; *We seeing Jesus—
for the suffering of death, crowned with glory and honour* [7] ; the
heavenly Society in the *Revelations* with one voice crying out,
*Worthy is the Lamb that was slain (who redeemed us to God by
his bloud) to receive power, and riches, and wisedom, and strength,
and honour, and glory, and blessing* [8] : If Affliction did minister
such advantages to him ; and if by our conformity to him in undergoing it, (with like equanimity, humility, and patience) it may
afford the like to us ; what reason is there that we should any-
wise be discomposed at it, or disconsolate under it ? Much greater
reason, surely, there is, that, with St. *Paul*, and all the Holy
Apostles [9], we should * rejoyce, boast, and exult in our tribulations :
far more cause we have, with them, to esteem it a favour, a privilege,
an ornament, a felicity to us, than to be displeased and discontented
therewith.

To doe thus is a duty incumbent on us as Christians. For,
† *He*, saith our Master, *that doth not take up his cross, and follow*

---

[1] *1 Pet.* IV, 1, 2 *Graec.*

[2] *Heb.* V, 8. ἔμαθεν ἀφ᾽ ὧν ἔπαθεν.

[3] *Heb.* II, 10.

[4] *John* X, 17.

[5] *Luke* XXIV, 26.

[6] *Phil.* II, 9.

[7] *Heb.* II, 9.

[8] *Rev.* V, 12, 9.

[9] * *Rom.* V, 3 ; *Col.* I, 24 ; *Matt.* V, 12 ; *Luke* VI, 23 ; *Phil.* I, 29 ;
Acts V, 41 ; *Jas.* I, 2 ; *Heb.* X, 34 ; *1 Pet.* I, 7 ; *Heb.* XII, 2 ; *1 Cor.* I, 4 ;
1 Thes. III, 3 ; *Rom.* VIII, 29 ; *Acts* XIV, 22 ; *2 Tim.* III, 12.

*me, is not worthy of me; He that doth not carry his cross, and
go after me cannot be my disciple* [1]. He that doth not willingly
take the cross when it is presented to him by God's hand, he that
doth not contentedly bear it when it is by providence imposed on
him, is no-wise worthy of the honour to wait on *Christ*; he is
not capable to be reckoned among the Disciples of our heavenly
Master [2]. He is *not worthy of Christ*, as not having the courage,
the constancy, the sincerity of a Christian; or of one pretending
to such great benefits, such high privileges, such excellent rewards,
as *Christ* our Lord and Saviour doth propose. He *cannot be
Christ's disciple*, shewing such an incapacity to learn those needfull lessons of humility and patience dictated by him; declaring
such an indisposition to transcribe those Copies of submission to
the divine will, self-denial, and self-resignation, so fairly set him by
the instruction and example of *Christ*: for *Christ* (saith St. *Peter*)
*suffered for us, leaving us an example, that we should follow his
steps* [3].

13. The willing susception and the chearfull sustenance of the
Cross is indeed the express condition, and the peculiar character
of our Christianity; in signification whereof, it hath been from
most ancient times a constant usage to mark those who enter into
it with the figure of it. The Cross, as the instrument by which
our peace with God was wrought, as the stage whereon our Lord
did act the last part of his marvellous obedience, consummating
our redemption, as the field wherein the Captain of our salvation
did atchieve his noble victories, and erect his glorious trophees over
all the enemies thereof, was well assumed to be the badge of our
profession, the ensign of our spiritual warfare, the pledge of our
constant adherence to our crucified Saviour [4]; in relation to whom
our chief hope is grounded, our great joy and sole glory doth
consist: for *God forbid*, saith St. *Paul, that I should glory save
in the cross of Christ* [5].

14. Let it be *to the Jews a scandal* [6], (or offensive to their
fancy, prepossessed with expectations of a *Messias* flourishing in

[1] † *Matt.* X, 38; XVI, 24; *Luke* XIV, 27; IX, 23.
[2] GREG. NAZ. *Orat.* 38, p. 623 [*In Theophania*, MIGNE, *Patrol. gr.*, t. 36,
col. 327-9].
[3] *1 Pet.* II, 21. ὑπολιμπάνων ὑπογραμμὸν.
[4] τὸ τρόπαιον τοῦ σταυροῦ. *Const. Apost.* VIII, xii [MIGNE, *Patrol. gr.*, t. 1,
col. 1092].
[5] *Gal.* VI, 14.   [6] *Cor.* I, 23.

secular pomp and prosperity,) let it be *folly to the Greeks*, (or seem absurd to men puff'd up and corrupted in mind with fleshly notions and maxims of worldly craft, disposing them to value nothing which is not gratefull to present sense or fancy,) that God should put his own most beloved Son into so very sad and despicable a condition [1]; that salvation from death and misery should be procured by so miserable a death; that eternal joy, glory and happiness should issue from these fountains of sorrow, and shame; that a Person in external semblance devoted to so opprobrious usage, should be the Lord and redeemer of mankind, the king and judge of all the world; Let, I say, this doctrine be scandalous and distastefull to some persons tainted with prejudice; let it be strange and incredible to others blinded with self-conceit; let all the inconsiderate, all the proud, all the profane part of mankind openly with their mouth, or closely in heart, slight and reject it: yet to us it must appear gratefull and joyous; to us it is πιστὸς λόγος, a *faithfull* and most credible *proposition worthy of all acceptation, that Jesus Christ came into the world to save sinners* [2], in this way of suffering for them: To us, who discern by a clearer light, and are endowed with a purer sense, kindled by the divine Spirit; from whence we may with comfortable satisfaction of mind apprehend and taste, that God could not in a higher measure, or fitter manner illustrate his glorious attributes of goodness and justice, his infinite grace and mercy toward his poor creatures, his holy displeasure against wickedness, his impartial severity in punishing iniquity and impiety, or in vindicating his own sacred honour and authority, than by thus ordering his onely Son, cloathed with our nature, to suffer for us; that also true vertue and goodness could not otherwise be taught, be exemplified, be commended and impressed with greater advantage.

Since thereby indeed a charity and humanity so unparallel'd, (far transcending theirs who have been celebrated for devoting their lives out of love to their countrey, or kindness to their friends,) a meekness so incomparable, a resolution so invincible, a patience so heroical, were manifested for the instruction and direction of men; since never were the vices and the vanities of the world (so prejudicial to the welfare of mankind) so remarkably dis-

---

[1] Orig. *in Cels.* II, p. 79 [Migne, *Patrol. gr.*, t. 11, col. 852].
[2] *1 Tim.* I, 15; *2 Tim.* II, 11.

countenanced ; since never any suffering could pretend to so worthy and beneficial effects, the expiation of the whole world's sins [1],
and reconciliation of mankind to God, the which no other performance, no other sacrifice did ever aim to procure ; since, in fine,
no vertue had ever so glorious rewards, as sovereign dignity to
him that exercised it, and eternal happiness to those that imitate it ;
since, I say, there be such excellent uses and fruits of the cross
born by our Saviour : we can have no reason to be offended at it,
or ashamed of it ; but with all reason heartily should approve,
and humbly adore the deep wisedom of God, together with all
other his glorious attributes displayed therein. To whom therefore,
as is most due, let us devoutly render all glory and praise. And,

Unto him that loved us, and washed us from our sins in his
bloud, and hath made us Kings and Priests unto God and his
Father, to him be glory and dominion for ever and ever [2]. *Blessing,*
and honour, and glory, and power, be unto him that sitteth upon
the throne, and unto the Lamb, for ever and ever [3]. *Amen.*

---

[1] *1 John* II, 2 ; *2 Cor.* V, 19.
[2] *Apoc.* [*Rev.*] I, 5, 6.
[3] *Apoc.* [*Rev.*] V, 13.

OF THE EVIL AND UNREASONABLENESS OF INFIDELITY

Heb. III.12. Take heed, Brethren, lest there be in any of you an evil heart of unbelief.

If the causes of all the sin and all the mischief in the world were carefully sought, we should find the chief of all to be Infidelity; either total or gradual. Wherefore to dehort[1] and dissuade from it is a very profitable design; [a] and this, with God's assistence, I shall endeavour from these words; in which two particulars naturally do offer themselves to our observation; an assertion implyed, that Infidelity is a sinfull distemper of heart; and a duty recommended, that we be carefull to void, or correct that distemper; of these to declare the one, and to press the other shall be the scope of my discourse.

That Infidelity is a sinfull distemper of heart, appeareth by divers express testimonies of Scripture, and by many good reasons grounded thereon.

It is by our Saviour in terms called *Sin; when he is come, he will reprove the world of sin,—Of sin, because they believe not in me*[2] : and, *If I had not come, and spoken unto them, they had not had sin; but now they have no cloak for their sin*[3] ; and, *If ye were blind, ye should not have had sin; but now ye say, we see, therefore your sin abideth*[4]. What sin? that of Infidelity, for which they were culpable, having such powerfull means and arguments to believe imparted to them, without due effect.

It hath a Condemnation grounded thereon; *He* (saith our Saviour) *that believeth not, is condemned already, because he hath not believed in the name of the only begotten Son of God*[5] ; but

[a] and this... in which] *T.*

[1] [use exhortation to dissuade]. [2] *John* XVI, 8, 9.
[3] *John* XV, 22; VIII, 24. [4] *John* IX, 41.
[5] *John* III, 18; XII, 48. Οὐ γὰρ μόνον τὸ μὴ εἴκειν ταῖς ἐντολαῖς τοῦ Χριστοῦ, ἀλλὰ καὶ τὸ ἀπιστεῖν αὐταῖς χαλεπωτάτην ἐπάγει τὴν κόλασιν. CHRYS. ad Demet. Tom. 6, p. 40. [*De Compunctione. Ad Demetrium*, MIGNE, *Patrol. gr.*, t. 47, col. 396].

Condemnation ever doth suppose faultiness.

It hath sore punishment denounced [1] thereto ; *God* (saith St. *Paul*) *shall send them strong delusion, that they should believe a lye, that they all might be damned who believed not the truth, but had pleasure in unrighteousness* [2] ; and, Our Lord (saith he) at his coming to judgment, will *take vengeance on them that know not God, and that obey not the Gospel of our Lord Jesus Christ* [3] ; whence among those, who *have their part in the lake burning with fire and brimstone, the fearfull, and unbelievers* [4] (that is they who fear to profess, or refuse to believe the Christian Doctrine) are reckoned in the first place ; which implyeth Infidelity to be a heinous sin.

It is also such, because it is a *transgression of* a principal *Law*, or divine Command ; *this* (saith St. *John*) is ἡ ἐντολὴ αὐτοῦ, *the command of him that we should believe* [5] ; *this* (saith our Lord) *is* τὸ ἔργον τοῦ θεοῦ, *the* signal *work of God* (which God requireth of us) that *ye believe on him, whom he hath sent* [6] ; that was a duty, which our Lord and his Apostles chiefly did teach, injoin and press ; wherefore correspondently Infidelity is a great sin ; according to St. *John*'s notion, that *sin is* ἀνομία, *the transgression of a Law* [7].

But the sinfulness of Infidelity will appear more fully by considering its nature and ingredients ; its causes ; its properties and adjuncts ; its effects and consequences.

I.   In its nature it doth involve an affected blindness and ignorance of the noblest and most usefull truths ; a bad use of reason, and most culpable imprudence ; disregard of God's providence, or despight [8] thereto ; abuse of his grace ; bad opinions of him, and bad affections toward him ; for

God in exceeding goodness and kindness to mankind hath proposed a doctrine [9], in it self *faithfull and worthy of all acceptation* [10], containing most excellent truths instructive of our mind and directive of our practice, toward attainment of Salvation and Eternal felicity : special overtures of mercy and grace most needfull to us in our state of sinfull guilt, of weakness, of wretchedness ; high

---

[1] [promulgated as a threat].
[2] *2 Thess.* II, 11, 12.
[3] *2 Thess.* I, 8.
[4] *Apoc.* [*Rev.*] XXI, 8.
[5] *1 John* III, 23.
[6] *John* VI, 29 ; *Mark* I, 15.
[7] *1 John* III, 4.
[8] [scorn].
[9] *Tit.* II, 11 ; III, 4.
[10] *1 Tim.* I, 15.

encouragements and rich promises of reward for obedience ; such a doctrine with all its benefits, Infidelity doth reject, *defeating the counsel of God*, crossing his earnest *desires* of our welfare, *despising his goodness, and patience* [1].

To this doctrine God hath yielded manifold clear attestations, declaring it to proceed from himself ; ancient presignifications and predictions ; audible voices and visible apparitions from heaven, innumerable miraculous works, providence concurring to the maintenance and propagation of it against most powerfull oppositions and disadvantages [2] ; but all these testimonies Infidelity slighteth, not fearing to give their Author the lye, which wicked boldness St. *John* chargeth on it ; *He* (saith the Apostle) *that believeth not God, hath made him a liar ; because he believeth not the testimony that God gave of his Son* [3].

Many plain arguments, sufficient to convince our minds, and win our belief, God hath furnished ; the dictates of natural conscience, the testimony of experience, the records of history, the consent of the best and wisest Men, do all conspire to prove the truth, to recommend the usefulness of this Doctrine ; but Infidelity will not regard, will not weigh, will not yield to reason.

God by his providence doth offer means and motives, inducing to belief, by the promulgation of his Gospel, and exhortation of his Ministers [4] : but all such methods Infidelity doth void and frustrate ; *thrusting away the word* [5], *turning away the ear from the truth* [6], *letting the seed fall beside us* [7], *casting away the Law of the Lord of hosts* [8] ; in effect (as those in *Job*) *Saying to God, depart from us, for we desire not the knowledge of thy ways* [9].

God by his grace *doth shine upon our hearts* [10], doth attract our wills to compliance with his will, doth excite our affections to relish his truth [11] ; but Infidelity doth *resist his Spirit* [12], doth quench the heavenly light [13], doth smother all the suggestions and motions of divine grace within us.

What God asserteth, Infidelity denieth, questioning his vera-

---

[1] *Luke* VII, 30 ; *Matt.* XXIII, 37 ; *1 Tim.* II, 4 ; *Luke* X, 16 ; *Rom.* II, 4 ; *2 Pet.* III, 9, 15.
[2] *1 Pet.* I, 10 ; *Acts* III, 18 ; *Luke* XXIV, 44 ; *Heb.* II, 4 ; *Acts* IV, 33 ; XIX, 20 ; II, 17 ; VI, 7 ; XII, 24.
[3] *1 John* V, 10. [4] *2 Cor.* V, 20. [5] *Acts* XIII, 46.
[6] *2 Tim.* IV, 4. [7] *Matt.* XIII, 4. [8] *Isa.* V, 24.
[9] *Job* XXI, 14. [10] *Job* XXII, 28.
[11] *John* VI, 44 ; *2 Cor.* IV, 16 ; *Apoc.* [*Rev.*] III, 20.
[12] *Acts* VII, 51. [13] *1 Thes.* V, 19 ; *2 Cor.* IV, 4.

city : what God commandeth, Infidelity doth not approve, contesting his wisedom ; what God promiseth, Infidelity will not confide in, distrusting his fidelity, or his power : Such is its behaviour (so injurious, so rude, so foolish) toward God, and his truth ; this briefly is its nature, manifestly involving great pravity [1], iniquity and impiety.

II.   The causes, and sources from whence it springeth (touched in Scripture, and obvious to experience) are those which follow.

1.   It commonly doth proceed from negligence, or drowsy inobservance and carelesness ; when men being possessed with a *spirit of slumber* [2], or being amused [3] with secular entertainments do not mind the concerns of their Soul, or regard the means by God's mercifull care presented for their conversion ; being in regard to religious matters of *Gallio*'s humour, *caring for none of those things* [4] ; thus, when the King in the Gospel sent to invite persons to his wedding-feast, it is said, οἱ δὲ ἀμελήσαντες ἀπῆλθον, they *being careless or not regarding it, went their ways one to his field, another to his trade* [5].   Of such the Apostle to the *Hebrews* saith, *How shall we escape*, τοιαύτης ἀμελήσαντες σωτηρίας *who regard not so great salvation* [6], exhibited to us ?   Of such Wisedom complaineth ; *I have called, and ye refused ; I have stretched out my hand, and no man regarded* [7].   *No man* ; the greatest part indeed of men are upon this account Infidels, for that being wholly taken up in pursuit of worldly affairs and divertisements, in amassing of wealth, in driving on projects of ambition, in enjoying sensual pleasures, in gratifying their fancy and humour with vain curiosities, or sports, they can hardly lend an ear to instruction ; so they become unacquainted with the notions of Christian doctrine ; the which to them are as *the seed falling by the way side* [8], which those *fowls of the air* do snatch and devour before it sinketh down into the earth, or doth come under consideration.   Hence is unbelief commonly termed not *hearing God's voice*, not hearkning to God's word, the dinn of worldly business rendring men deaf to divine suggestions.

2.   Another source of Infidelity is sloth, which indisposeth men

---

[1] [depravity].   [2] *Rom.* XI, 8.   [3] [absorbed].
[4] *Acts* XVIII, 17.   [5] *Matt.* XXII, 5.   [6] *Heb.* II, 3.
[7] *Prov.* I, 24 ; *Isa.* LXV, 12 ; LXVI, 4 ; *Jer.* VII, 31.
[8] *Matt.* XIII, 4.

to undergo the fatigue of seriously attending to the doctrine propounded, of examining its grounds, of weighing the reasons inducing to believe ; whence at first hearing, if the notions hap not
to hit their fancy, they do slight it before they fully understand it,
or know its grounds ; thence at least they must needs fail of a
firm and steady belief, the which can alone be founded on a clear
apprehension of the matter, and perception of its agreeableness to
reason : So when the *Athenians* did hear St. *Paul* declaring the
grand points of faith, somewhat in his discourse, uncouth [1] to their
conceit, [a] falling from him, some of them did scorn, others did
neglect his doctrine ; *some mocked, others said we will hear thee
again of this matter* [2] : So *Agrippa* was *almost persuaded to be a
Christian* [3], but had not the industry to prosecute his inquiry, till
he arrived to a full satisfaction [4]. A solid faith, (with clear understanding and firm persuasion) doth indeed, no less than any
science, require sedulous, and persevering study ; so that as a man
can never be learned, who will not be studious ; so a sluggard
cannot prove a good believer.

3. Infidelity doth arise from stupidity, or dulness of apprehension (I mean not that which is natural, for any man in his
senses, how low soever otherwise in parts or improvements, is
capable to understand the Christian doctrine, and to perceive reason
sufficient to convince him of its truth, but) contracted by voluntary
indispositions and defects ; a stupidity rising from mists of prejudice, from steams of lust and passion, from rust grown on the
mind by want of exercising [5] it in observing and comparing things ;
whence men cannot apprehend the clearest notions plainly represented to them, nor discern the force of arguments however evident
and cogent ; but are like those wisards in *Job*, who *meet with
darkness in the day time, and grope at noon day, as in the night* [6].

This is that, which is so often charged on the *Jews* as cause
of their infidelity ; who *did hear but not understand, and did see
but not perceive ; because their heart was gross, and their ears
were dull of hearing, and their eyes were closed* [7] ; this is that

---

[a] falling from him] *T.* ; *B.* intercurring

[1] [strange, uncommon].   [2] *Acts* XVII, 32.   [3] *Acts* XXVI, 28.
[4] [long enough to arrive...].   [5] *Heb.* V, 14.
[6] *Job* V, 14 ; *Isa.* LIX, 10 ; *Deut.* XXVIII, 29.
      [7] *Acts* XXVIII, 26, 27 ; *Matt.* XIII, 14, 15 ; *Isa.* VI, 9 ; *John* XII, 40 ;
Rom. XI, 7, 8, 25 ; *Eph.* IV, 18 ; *Isa.* XXIX, 10 ; *Ezek.* XII, 2 ; 2 *Cor.* III,
14 ; *Mark* III, 5 ; VI, 52 ; VIII, 17.

πώρωσις καρδίας, that *numbness of heart*, which is represented as the common obstruction to the perception and admission of our Lord's doctrine ; this our Lord blamed in his own Disciples, when he [a] rebuked them thus ; *O fools, and slow of heart to believe all that the Prophets have spoken* [1] ; Of this the Apostle doth complain, telling the *Hebrews*, that they were uncapable of improvement in knowledge, because they were νωθροὶ ταῖς ἀκοαῖς, *dull of hearing* [2] for want of skill and use, *not having their senses exercised to discern both good and evil* [3] : there is indeed to a sound and robust faith required a good perspicacy of apprehension, a penetrancy of judgment, a vigour and quickness of mind, grounded in the purity of our faculties, and confirmed by exercise of them in consideration of spiritual things.

4. Another cause of Infidelity is a bad judgment ; corrupted with prejudicate [4] notions, and partial inclinations to falshood. Men are apt to entertain prejudices favourable to their natural appetites, and humours ; to their lusts, to their present interests ; dictating to them, that wealth, dignity, fame, pleasure, ease, are things most desirable, and necessary ingredients of happiness ; so that it is a sad thing in any case to want them ; all men have strong inclinations byassing them toward such things, it is a hard thing to shake off such prejudices, and to check such inclinations [5] ; it is therefore not easie to entertain a doctrine representing such things indifferent, obliging us sometimes to reject them, always to be moderate in the pursuit and enjoyment of them ; wherefore Infidelity will naturally spring up in a mind not cleansed from those corruptions of judgment.

5. Another source of Infidelity is perverseness of Will, which hindreth men from entertaining notions disagreeable to their fond, or froward humour : ὦ γενεὰ ἄπιστος καὶ διεστραμμένη, *O faithless and perverse generation* [6], those Epithets are well coupled, for he that is perverse will be faithless ; in proportion to the one the other bad quality will prevail. *The weapons of the Apostolical warfare* (against the Infidel world) *were* as St. *Paul* telleth us, *mighty to the casting down of strong holds* [7] ; so it was ; and the Apostles

---

[a] rebuked them] *T.* ; *B.* did increpate

[1] *Luke* XXIV, 25.   [2] *Heb.* V, 11.
[3] *Heb.* V, 14.   [4] [preconceived, biased].
[5] *Matt.* XVI, 23 ; *John* VI, 60, 66.   [6] *Matt.* XVII, 17.
                         [7] *2 Cor.* X, 4.

by their discourse and demeanour effectually did force many a strong fortress to surrender : but the will of some men is an impregnable bulwark against all batteries of discourse [1] ; they are so invincibly stubborn, as to hold out against the clearest evidence, and mightiest force of reason ; if they do not like what you say, if it cross any humour of theirs, be it clear as day, be it firm as an Adamant, they will not admit it ; you shall not persuade them, though you do persuade them. Such was the temper of the *Jews*, whom St. *Stephen* therefore calleth a *stiff-necked people, uncircumcised in heart and ears* [2] ; who although they did hear the most winning discourse, that ever was uttered, although they saw the most admirable works that ever were performed, yet would they not yield to the doctrine ; the mean garb of the persons teaching it, the Spirituality of its design, the strict goodness of its precepts, and the like considerations not sorting with their fancies, and desires ; they hoping for a *Messias*, arrayed with gay appearances of external grandeur and splendour ; whose chief work it should be to settle their Nation in a state of worldly prosperity and glory.

6. This is that hardness of heart, which is so often represented as an obstruction of belief : this hindred *Pharaoh*, notwithstanding all those mighty works performed before him, from *hearkning* to God's word [3] ; and regarding the mischiefs threatned to come on him for his disobedience ; *I will not* (said he) *let Israel go* [4] ; his will was his reason, which no persuasion, no judgment could subdue : This was the cause of that monstrous Infidelity in the *Israelites* ; which baffled all the methods, which God used to persuade and convert them ; *Notwithstanding* ('tis said) *they would not hear, but hardned their necks, like to the neck of their fathers, that did not believe in the Lord their God* [5] : Whence that exhortation to them ; *To day if you will hear his voice, harden not your hearts* [6]. And to obduration the disbelief of the Gospel upon the Apostles preaching is in like manner ascribed ; St. *Paul* ('tis said in the *Acts*) *went into the Synagogue and spake boldly for the space of three months, disputing and perswading the things con-*

---

[1] [reasoning]. οὐ πάντας δυσωπεῖ τὰ σημεῖα, ἀλλὰ μόνους τοὺς εὐγνώμονας. *Const. Apost.* VIII, 1. [MIGNE, *Patrol. gr.*, t. 1, col. 1064].
[2] *Acts* VII, 51, 54 ; *Jer.* VI, 10 ; IX, 26.
[3] *Exod.* VII, 4, 22 ; VIII, 15, 19 ; IX, 12.
[4] *Exod.* IX, 7.   [5] *2 Kings* XVII, 14.
[6] *Ps.* XCV, 7, 8 ; *Heb.* III, 8.

cerning the Kingdome of God: But divers were hardned and
believed not [1] : and, *Exhort one another daily* (saith the Apostle)
lest any of you be hardned (in unbelief) *through the deceitfulness*
of sin [2].

7. Of kin to that perversness of heart is that squeamish delicacy and niceness of humour, which will not let men entertain or
savour [a] any thing any wise seeming hard or harsh to them, if they
cannot presently comprehend all that is said, if they can frame any
cavil, or little exception against it, if every scruple be not voided, if
any thing be required distastefull to their sense ; they are offended,
and their faith is choaked ; You must to satisfie them, *speak to*
them smooth things [3], which no wise grate on their conceit, or
pleasure : So when our Lord discoursed somewhat mysteriously,
representing himself in the figure of heavenly bread (typified by
the *Manna* of old) given for the World, to sustain men in life ;
Many of his disciples hearing this, said this is a hard saying,
who can hear it ? and—*from that time many of his disciples went*
back, and walked no more with him [4] ; this is that which is called
being—*scandalized at the word* [5] ; and *stumbling at it* [6] ; concerning which our Saviour saith, *Blessed is he, whoever shall not be*
offended in me [7].

In regard to this weakness, the Apostles were fain [8] in their
Instructions to use prudent dispensation, proposing onely to some
persons the most easie points of Doctrine, they not being able to
digest such as were more tough and difficult : *I have* (saith St.
Paul) fed you with milk, and not with meat ; for hitherto ye were
not able to bear it—*for ye are yet carnal* [9] ; and *Ye* (saith the
Apostle to the *Hebrews*) *are such as have need of milk, and not*
of strong meat [10].

Such were even the Apostles themselves in their minority ; *not*
savouring the things of God ; being *offended at* our Lord's discourses [11], when he spake to them of suffering ; and with his condition, when he entred into it.

---

[a] any thing any wise]; *B., 1683* any thing, any wise

[1] *Acts* XIX, 8, 9.
[2] *Heb.* III, 13 ; *Mark* XVI, 14.
[3] *Isa.* XXX, 10 ; *John* VI, 63.
[4] *John* VI, 60, 66.
[5] *John* VI, 61.
[6] *1 Pet.* II, 8.
[7] *Matt.* XI, 6 ; XXIV, 10 ; XIII, 21.
[8] [obliged].
[9] *1 Cor.* III, 2.
[10] *Heb.* V, 12.
[11] *Matt.* XVI, 23 ; XXVI, 31.

8. With these dispositions is connected a want of love to truth ; the which if a man hath not, he cannot well entertain such notions as the Gospel propoundeth, being no wise gratefull to carnal sense and appetite : This cause St. *Paul* doth assign of the *Pagan* Doctors falling into so gross errours and vices, *because they did not like to retain God in their knowledge* [1] ; and of mens revolting from Christian Truth to Antichristian Imposture—*because they received not the love of truth, that they might be saved : for which cause God shall send them strong delusion, that they should believe a lye* [2] : Nothing indeed, but an impartial and ingenuous love of truth (overbalancing all corrupt prejudices and affections) can engage a man heartily to embrace this holy and pure Doctrine, can preserve a man in a firm adherence thereto.

9. A grand cause of Infidelity is pride, the which doth interpose various bars to the admission of Christian truth ; for before a man can believe, πᾶν ὕψωμα, *every height* (every towring imagination and conceit) *that exalteth it self against the knowledge of God, must be cast down* [3].

[a] Pride fills a man with vanity and an affectation of seeming wise in special manner above others, thereby disposing him to maintain Paradoxes and to nauseate common truths receiv'd and believ'd by the generality of mankind.

A proud man is ever averse from renouncing his prejudices, and correcting his errours ; doing which implyeth a confession of weakness, ignorance and folly, consequently depresseth him in his own conceit, and seemeth to impair that credit, which he had with others from his wisedom ; neither of which events he is able to endure.

He that is wise in his own conceit, will hug that conceit, and thence is uncapable to learn ; *there is*, saith *Solomon, more hope of a fool than of him* [4] ; and He that affecteth [5] the praise of Men, will not easily part with it for the sake of truth ; whence, *How* (saith our Lord) *can ye believe, who receive glory one of another* [6]? how can ye, retaining such affections, be disposed to avow your selves to have been ignorants and fools, when as ye were reputed for learned and wise [7] ? how can ye endure to become Novices,

[a] Pride... ...mankind] *T.* ; *B.* Vanity or affectation of seeming wise in speciall manner above others, thence disposing to maintain paradoxes, to nauseate common truths etc.

[1] *Rom.* I, 28. [2] *Thess.* II, 10, 11. [3] *2 Cor.* X, 5.
[4] *Prov.* XXVI, 12. [5] [aspires to]. [6] *John* V, 44 ; XII, 43.
[7] *1 Cor.* III, 18.

who did pass for Doctors ? how can ye allow your selves so blind and weak, as to have been deceived in your former judgment of things ?

He that is conceited [1] of his own wisedom, strength of parts, and improvement in knowledge cannot submit his mind to notions, which he cannot easily comprehend and penetrate ; he will scorn to have his understanding baffled or puzled by sublime mysteries of Faith ; he will not easily yield any thing too high for his wit to reach, or too knotty for him to unloose : *How can these things be* [2] ? what reason can there be for this ? I cannot see how this can be true : this point is not intelligible ; so he treateth the dictates of Faith ; not considering the feebleness and shallowness of his own reason : Hence *not many wise men according to the flesh* [3] (or who were conceited of their own wisedom, relying upon their natural faculties and means of knowledge) not many *Scribes, or disputers of this world* [4] did imbrace the Christian Truth, it appearing absurd and foolish to them [5] ; it being needfull, that a man should *be a fool, that he might* (in this regard) *become wise* [6].

The prime notions of Christianity do also tend to the debasing humane conceit, and to the exclusion of all glorying in our selves ; referring all to the praise and glory of God, ascribing all to his pure mercy, bounty and grace [7] : It representeth all men heinous sinners, void of all worth and merit, lapsed into a wretched state, altogether impotent, forlorn, and destitute of ability to help or relieve themselves ; such notions proud hearts cannot digest ; they cannot like to avow their infirmities, their defects, their wants, their vileness, and unworthiness ; their distresses and miseries ; they cannot endure to be entirely and absolutely beholden to favour and mercy for their happiness ; such was the case of the *Jews* ; who could not believe, because—*going about to establish their own righteousness, they would not submit to the righteousness of God* [8]. *Dextra mihi Deus* [9] ; every proud man would say, with the profane *Mezentius*.

Christianity doth also much disparage and vilify [10] those things,

---

1 [possessed with a good opinion].   2 *John* III, 9.
3 *1 Cor.* I, 26 ; II, 6 ; *John* VII, 26.   4 *1 Cor.* I, 20.
5 *1 Cor.* II, 14.   6 *1 Cor.* III, 18.
7 *Rom.* III, 27 ; IV, 2, 16 ; IX, 11 ; XI, 6 ; *1 Cor.* I, 29 ; III, 21 ; *Eph.* II, 9 ; *Tit.* III, 5.
8 *Rom.* X, 3 ; IX, 31.   9 [*Aeneis* X, 773].
10 [lower or lessen in worth or value].

for which men are apt much to prize and pride themselves ; it
maketh small accompt of wealth, of honour, of power, of wit, of
secular wisedom, of any humane excellency or ᵃworldly advantage.
It levelleth the Rich and the Poor, the Prince and the Peasant, the
Philosopher and Idiot in spiritual regards ; yea far preferreth the
meanest and simplest person, endued with true Piety above the
mightiest and wealthiest, who is devoid thereof : In the eye of it,
The righteous is more excellent than his neighbour [1], whatever he
be in worldly regard or state : This a proud man cannot support ;
to be divested of his imaginary privileges, to be ᵇthrown down
from his perch of eminency, to be set below those, whom he so
much despiseth, is insupportable to his Spirit.

The practice of Christianity doth also expose men to the scorn,
and censure of profane men ; who for their own solace, out of envy,
revenge, diabolical spite, are apt to deride and reproach all conscientious, and resolute practisers of ᶜtheir duty, as silly, credulous,
superstitious, humorous, morose, sullen folks : So that he that will
be good, must resolve to bear that usage from them ; like *David* ;
*I will yet be more vile, than thus, and will be base in my own
sight* [2] : but with these sufferings a proud heart cannot comport ;
it goeth too much against the grain thereof to be contemned.

Christianity doth also indispensably require duties, point-blank
opposite to pride ; it placeth humility among its chief vertues, as a
ᵈ foundation of piety ; it enjoineth us to think meanly of our selves,
to disclaim our own worth and desert, to have no complacency or
confidence in any thing belonging to us; not to aim at high things [3];
to wave the regard and praise of men : it exacteth from us a sense
of our vileness, remorse and contrition for our sins, with humble
confession of them, self-condemnation and abhorrence [4]: it chargeth
us to bear injuries and affronts patiently, without grievous resentment, without seeking or so much as wishing any revenge ; to undergo disgraces, crosses, disasters willingly and gladly : it obligeth
us *to prefer others before our selves* [5], sitting down in the lowest
room, yielding to the meanest persons ; to all which sorts of duty
a proud mind hath an irreconcilable antipathy [6].

ᵃ worldly] *T.* ; *B.* mundane   ᵇ thrown down] *T.* ; *B.* detruded
ᶜ their] *T.*   ᵈ foundation] *T.* ; *B.* base

[1] [*Prov.* XII, 26.]   [2] *2 Sam.* VI, 22.   [3] *Rom.* XII, 3, 16.
[4] *Job* XLII, 3, 6.   [5] *Rom.* XII, 10 ; *Phil.* II, 3.
[6] *1 Pet.* V, 5 ; *Luke* XIV, 10 ; *Rom.* XII, 16.

A proud man, that is big and swollen with haughty conceit and stomach [1] cannot stoop down so low, cannot shrink in himself so much as to *enter into the strait gate, or to walk in the narrow way, which leadeth to life* [2] : He will be apt to contemn wisedom and instruction [3].

Shall I (will he say) such a Gallant as I, so accomplished in worth, so flourishing in dignity, so plump with wealth, so highly regarded, and renowned among men, thus pitifully crouch and sneak ? shall I deign to avow such beggarly notions, or bend to such homely duties ? shall I disown my perfections, or forgo my advantages ? shall I profess my self to have been a despicable worm, a villainous caitiff, a sorry wretch ? shall I suffer my self to be flouted as a timorous Religionist, a scrupulous Precisian, a consciencious Sneaksby [4] ? shall I lie down at the foot of mercy, puling in sorrow, whining in confession, bewailing my guilt, and craving pardon ? shall I allow any man better, or happier than my self ? shall I receive those into consortship, or equality of rank with me, who appear so much my inferiours ? shall I be misused, and trampled on without doing my self right ; and making them smart, who shall presume to wrong or cross me ? shall I be content to be nobody in the world ? So the proud man will say in his heart, contesting the doctrines and duties of our Religion, and so disputing himself into Infidelity.

10. Another spring of Infidelity is pusillanimity, or want of good resolution and courage : δειλοὶ καὶ ἄπιστοι, *Cowards and Infidels* [5] are well joyned among those who are devoted to the fiery *Lake* ; for timorous men dare not believe such doctrines, which engage them upon undertaking difficult, laborious, dangerous enterprizes ; upon undergoing hardships, pains, wants, disgraces ; upon encountering those mighty and fierce enemies, with whom every faithfull man continually doth wage war.

They have not the heart to look the World in the face, when it frowneth at them, menacing persecution and disgrace ; but *when affliction ariseth for the word, they are presently scandalized* [6]. It is said in the Gospel, that *no man spake freely of our Lord for fear*

---

[1] [pride, haughtiness].
[2] *Matt.* VII, 13, 14 ; *Prov.* I, 7, 30 ; V, 12 ; XIII, 13.
[3] *Isa.* V, 24 ; *Eze.* XX, 13, 16, 24 ; *Acts* XIII, 41 (καταφρονηταὶ); *Luke* X, 16 ; *Rom.* II, 4.
[4] [a mean-spirited person].   [5] *Apoc.* [*Rev.*] XXI, 8.
[6] *Matt.* XIII, 21.

of the Jews [1] ; as it so did smother the profession and muzle the mouth ; so it doth often stifle Faith it self, and quell the heart, men fearing to harbour in their very thoughts points dangerous, and discountenanced by worldly power.

They have not also courage to adventure a combat with their own flesh, and *those lusts, which war against their Souls* [2] ; to set upon correcting their temper, curbing their appetites, bridling their passions ; keeping flesh and bloud in order ; upon pulling out their right Eyes, and cutting off their right Hands, and crucifying their Members ; it daunteth them to attempt duties so harsh and painfull.

They have not the resolution to withstand and repell temptations and in so doing to *wrestle with Principalities and Powers* ; to resist and baffle the *strong one* [3]. To part with their ease, their wealth, their pleasure, their credit, their accommodations of life [4], is a thing, any thought whereof doth quash all inclination in a faint and fearfull heart of complying with the Christian Doctrine.

Christianity is a Warfare [5], living after its rules is called *fighting the good fight of Faith* [6] ; every true Christian is a *good souldier of Jesus Christ* [7] ; the state of Christians must be sometimes like that of the Apostles ; who were *troubled on every side, without were fightings, within were fears* [8] : great courage therefore, and undaunted resolution are required toward the undertaking this religion, and the persisting in it cordially.

11. Infidelity doth also rise from sturdiness, fierceness, wildness, untamed animosity of spirit ; so that a man will not endure to have his will crossed, to be under any law, to be curb'd from any thing, which he is prone to affect.

12. Blind zeal, grounded upon prejudice, disposing men to stiff adherence unto that, which they have once been addicted and accustomed to, is in the Scripture frequently represented as a cause of Infidelity. So the *Jews* being *filled with zeal, contradicted the things spoken by St. Paul* [9] ; flying at his doctrine, without weighing it ; So *by instinct of zeal* did St. *Paul* himself *persecute the*

---

[1] *John* VII, 13 ; IX, 22 ; XIX, 38.
[2] *Jas.* IV, 1 ; *1 Pet.* II, 11 ; *Rom.* VII, 23.
[3] *Eph.* VI, 12, 11.   [4] *Luke* XIV, 33.
[5] *1 Tim.* I, 18 ; *Heb.* XII.   [6] *1 Tim.* VI, 12.
[7] [*2 Tim.* II, 3.]   [8] *2 Cor.* VII, 5.
[9] *Acts* XIII, 45 ; XVII, 5 ; V, 17 ; *Rom.* X, 2 ; *Gal.* IV, 17.

Church [1] ; being *exceedingly zealous for the traditions delivered by his fathers* [2].

In fine, Infidelity doth issue from corruption of mind by any kind of brutish lust, any irregular passion, any bad inclination or habit [3] : any such evil disposition of soul doth obstruct the admission or entertainment of that doctrine, which doth prohibit and check it ; doth condemn it, and brand it with infamy ; doth denounce [4] punishment and woe to it : whence *men of corrupt minds, and reprobate concerning the faith* [5] ; and *Men of corrupt minds, destitute of the truth* [6], are attributes well conjoyned by St. *Paul*, as commonly jumping together in practice ; And *to them* (saith he) *that are defiled and unbelieving is nothing pure, but even their mind, and conscience is defiled* [7] ; such pollution is not onely consequent to, and connected with, but antecedent to Infidelity, blinding the mind so as not to see the truth, and perverting the will so as not to close with it.

Faith and a good conscience are twins, born together, inseparable from each other, living and dying together ; for the first, *faith* is (as St. *Peter* telleth us) nothing else but *the stipulation of a good conscience* [8], fully persuaded that Christianity is true, and firmly resolving to comply with it : and, *The end* (or drift, and purport) *of the Evangelical doctrine is charity out of a pure heart, and a good conscience, and faith unfeigned* [9] ; whence those Apostolical precepts, *to hold the mystery of faith in a pure conscience* [10] ; and, *to hold faith and a good conscience, which some having put away, concerning the faith have made shipwrack* [11] ; a man void of good conscience will not embarke in Christianity ; and having laid good conscience aside, he soon will make shipwrack of faith, by apostacy from it. Resolute indulgence to any one lust, is apt to produce this effect.

If a man be covetous, he can *hardly enter into the kingdom of heaven* [12], or submit to that heavenly law, which forbiddeth us *to*

---

[1] *Phil.* III, 6, κατὰ ζῆλον διώκων.

[2] *Gal.* I, 14 ; *Acts* XXVI, 11, περισσῶς ἐμμαινόμενος [αὐτοῖς].

[3] Οὐ ῥᾴδιον πονηρίᾳ συντρεφόμενον ἀναβλέψαι ταχέως πρὸς τὸ τῶν παρ' ἡμῖν δογμάτων ὕφος, ἀλλὰ χρὴ πάντων καθαρεύειν τῶν παθῶν τὸν μέλλοντα θηρᾶν τὴν ἀλήθειαν. CHRYS. *in 1 Cor. Or. 8* [In Ep. I ad Cor., Hom. VIII, MIGNE, *Patrol. gr.*, t. 61, col. 70].

[4] [promulgate as a threat].   [5] *2 Tim.* III, 8.   [6] *1 Tim.* VI, 5.

[7] *Tit.* I, 15.   [8] *1 Pet.* III, 21.   [9] *1 Tim.* I, 5.

[10] *1 Tim.* III, 9.   [11] *1 Tim.* I, 19.   [12] *Matt.* XIX, 29.

treasure up treasures upon earth [1]; which chargeth us to be liberal
in communication of our goods [2]; so as to give unto every one that
asketh [3]; which in some cases requireth to sell all our goods, and
to give them to the poor [4]; which declareth, that whosoever doth
not bid farewell to all that he hath, cannot be a disciple of Christ [5];
which ascribeth happiness to the poor [6], and denounceth woe to the
rich, who have their consolation here [7]; Preach such doctrine to
a covetous person, and as the young Gentleman, who had great
possessions, he will go his way sorrowfull [8]; or will doe like the
Pharisees, who were covetous, and having heard our Saviour discourse such things, derided him [9]; for the love of money (saith
St. Paul) is the root of all evil, which while some coveted after,
they have erred from the faith; ἀπεπλανήθησαν, they have wandred
away [10], or apostatized from the faith.

If a man be ambitious, he will not approve that doctrine, which
prohibiteth us to affect, to seek, to admit glory, or to doe any thing
for its sake [11]; but purely to seek God's honour, and in all our
actions to regard it as our principal aim : which greatly disparageth
all worldly glory as vain, transitory, mischievous [12]; which commandeth us in honour to prefer others before our selves [13], and to
sit down in the lowest room [14]; which promiseth the best rewards
to humility, and menaceth, that whoever exalteth himself, shall
be abased [15]; the profession and practice whereof are commonly
attended with disgrace; such doctrines ambitious minds cannot
admit; as it proved among the Jews; who therefore could not
believe, because they received glory from one another [16]; who
therefore would not profess the faith, because they loved the glory
of men rather than the glory of God [17].

If a man be envious, he will not like that doctrine, which
enjoyneth him to desire the good of his neighbour, as his own;

[1] Matt. VI, 19.
[2] 1 Tim. VI, 18; Heb. XIII, 16; Luke XVI, 9.
[3] Luke VI, 30.   [4] Matt. XIX, 21.   [5] Luke XIV, 33.
[6] Luke VI, 20.   [7] Luke VI, 24.   [8] Matt. XIX, 22.
[9] Luke XVI, 14, Ἐξεμυκτήριζον αὐτὸν.
[10] 1 Tim. VI 10.
[11] Phil. II, 3; Gal. V, 26; John XII, 43; V, 44; Matt. VI, 1.
[12] 1 Pet. I, 24; 1 Cor. VII, 31; 1 John II, 16.
[13] Rom. XII, 10.   [14] Luke XIV, 10.
[15] Matt. XXIII, 12; Luke XIV, 11; XVIII, 14.
[16] John V, 44.   [17] John XII, 43.

to have complacence[1] in the prosperity and dignity of his brethren[2];
not to seek his own, but every man anothers wealth[3], or welfare;
to *rejoice with them that rejoice; and mourn with those that
mourn*[4]; which chargeth us *to lay aside all envyings and emulations*[5], under pain of damnation; he therefore who is possessed
with an envious spirit, or *evil eye*[6]; will look ill upon this doctrine;
as the *Jews* did, who being *full of envy*[7] and emulation, did reject
the Gospel; it being a grievous eye-sore to them, that the poor
Gentiles were thereby admitted to favour and mercy.

If a man be revengefull or spitefull, he will be scandalized at
that law, which commandeth us *to love our enemies, to bless those
that curse us, to do good to them that hate us, to pray for them
that despitefully use us*[8]; which forbiddeth us to *resist the evil*[9];
to render evil for evil, or railing for railing[10]; which chargeth us
to bear patiently, and freely to remit all injuries, under penalty of
forfeiting all hopes of mercy from God[11]; which requireth us to
depose all wrath, animosity, and malice[12], as inconsistent with our
salvation; which doctrine how can a heart swelling with rancour-
ous grudge, or boiling with anger embrace? seeing it must be *in
meekness that we must receive the engrafted word, that is able to
save our souls*[13].

If a man be intemperate, he will loath that doctrine, the precepts
of which are, that we be *temperate in all things*, that *we bring
under our bodies*[14], that we *endure hardship as good souldiers of
Christ*[15]; to *avoid all excess*[16]; to *possess our vessels in sanctification and honour*[17]; to *mortifie our members upon earth*[18]; to
crucifie the flesh with its affections and lusts[19]; to *abstain from
fleshly lusts, which war against the soul*[20]; with which precepts
how can a luxurious and filthy heart comport[21]?

---

[1] [delight].
[2] *1 Cor.* XII, 26 συγχαίρειν; *1 Cor.* X, 24.
[3] *Phil.* II, 4.   [4] *Rom.* XII, 15.
[5] *1 Pet.* II, 1; *Gal.* V, 21; *Rom.* XIII, 13; *Jas.* III, 14, 16.
[6] [*Mark* VII, 22.]   [7] *Acts* XIII, 45; V, 17; XVII, 5.
[8] *Matt.* V, 44; *Rom.* XII, 20, 17.   [9] *Matt.* V, 39; *1 Cor.* VI, 7.
[10] *1 Pet.* III, 9; *1 Thess.* V, 15.
[11] *Col.* III, 13; *Eph.* IV, 32; *Matt.* VI, 15; XVIII, 35.
[12] *Col.* III, 8; *1 Pet.* II, 1; *Gal.* V, 20; *Eph.* IV, 31.
[13] *Jas.* I, 21.   [14] *1 Cor.* IX, 25, 27.
[15] *2 Tim.* II, 3; I, 8; IV, 5.   [16] *Eph.* V, 18.
[17] *1 Thess.* IV, 4.   [18] *Col.* III, 5.
[19] *Gal.* V, 24.   [20] *1 Pet.* II, 11.
                    [21] [bear, endure].

In fine, whatever corrupt affection a man be possessed with, it will work in him a distaste, and repugnance to that doctrine, which indispensably, as a condition of salvation, doth prescribe and require universal holiness, purity, innocence, vertue and goodness [1] ; which doth not allow any one sin to be fostered or indulged ; which threatneth wrath, and vengeance upon all impiety, iniquity, impurity, wherein we do obstinately persist [2] ; indifferently [3], without any reserve or remedy ; *wherein the wrath of God is revealed from heaven upon all ungodliness and unrighteousness of men, that detain the truth in unrighteousness* [4].

An impure, a dissolute, a passionate soul cannot affect [5] so holy notions, cannot comply with so strict rules, as the Gospel doth recommend ; as a sore eye cannot like the bright day ; as a sickly palate cannot relish savoury food [6]. *Every one that doth evil, hateth the light* [7], because it discovereth to him his own vileness, and folly ; because it detecteth the sadness and wofulness of his condition ; because it kindleth anguish and remorse within him ; because it checketh him in the free pursuit of his bad designs, it dampeth the brisk enjoyment of his unlawfull pleasures, it robbeth him of satisfaction and glee in any vicious course of practice.

Every man is unwilling to entertain a bad conceit of himself, and to pass on himself a sad doom : he therefore will be apt to reject that doctrine, which, being supposed true, he cannot but confess himself to be an arrant fool, he cannot but grant himself a forlorn wretch.

No man liketh to be galled, to be stung, to be racked with a sense of guilt, to be scared with a dread of punishment ; to live under awe and apprehension of imminent danger ; gladly therefore would he shun that doctrine, which demonstrateth him a grievous sinner, which speaketh dismal terrour, which thundreth ghastly woe upon him.

---

[1] *Col.* II, 11 ; *Eph.* IV, 22 ; *Rom.* VI, 6 ; *1 Thess.* IV, 3.
[2] *Eph.* V, 6 ; *Col.* III, 6.
[3] [upon all equally, without qualification].
[4] *Rom.* I, 18 ; II, 8.   [5] [be drawn to].
[6] ῾Η ἐμπαθὴς ψυχὴ οὐ δύναται μέγα τι καὶ γενναῖον ἰδεῖν, ἀλλ᾽ ὥσπερ ὑπὸ τινὸς λήμης θολουμένη ἀμβλυωπίαν ὑπομένει τὴν χαλεπωτάτην. CHRYS. *in Joh.* Orat. XXV [*In Joannem, Orat. XXIV,* MIGNE, *Patrol. gr.,* t. 59, col. 148].
῎Εστι γαρ, ἔστι καὶ ἀπὸ τρόπων διεφθαρμένων, οὐκ ἀπὸ πολυπραγμοσύνης μόνον ἀκαίρου σκοτωθῆναι τὴν διάνοιαν. *Ibid.* [col. 147].
[7] *John* III, 20.

He cannot love that truth, which is so much his enemy, which so rudely treateth and severely persecuteth him ; which telleth him so bad and unwelcome news. ª *They hated knowledge, and did not chuse the fear of the Lord*[1].

Who would be content to deem omnipotency engaged against him ? to fancy himself standing on the brink of a fiery lake, to hear a roaring Lion, ready to devour him ; to suppose that certain, which is so dreadfull and sad to him ?

Hence it is, that *the carnal mind is enmity to God*[2] ; hence do bad men *rebel against the light*[3] ; hence *Foolish men shall not attain to wisedom, and sinners shall not see her, for she is far from pride, and men that are lyars cannot remember her*[4].

Hence a man resolvedly wicked cannot but be willing to be an Infidel, in his own defence, for his own quiet and ease ; faith being a companion very incommodious, intollerably troublesome to a bad conscience[5].

Being resolved not to forsake his lusts, he must quit those opinions, which cross them ; seeing it expedient that the Gospel should be false, he will be inclinable to think it so ; thus he sinketh down, thus he tumbleth himself headlong into the gulf of Infidelity.

The custome of sinning doth also by degrees so abate, and at length so destroy the loathsomness, the ugliness, the horrour thereof, doth so reconcile it to our minds, yea conciliateth such a friendship to it, that we cannot easily believe it so horrid and base a thing ᵇ as by the Gospel it is represented to us.

Vitious practice doth also weaken the judgment, and stupify the faculties[6]. So that we cannot clearly apprehend, or judge soundly about spiritual matters.

ª *They hated... Lord*] B. ; *1683* [in margin].
ᵇ as by the... to us.] *T.* ; *B.* as it is by the Gospel represented to us.

[1] *Prov.* I, 29 ; V, 12.   [2] *Rom.* VIII, 7.
[3] *Job* XXIV, 13.   [4] *Ecclus* XV, 7.
[5] τὸ ἀπιστεῖν ταῖς ἐντολαῖς ἐκ τοῦ πρὸς τὴν ἐκπλήρωσιν ἐκλελύσθαι τῶν ἐντολῶν γίνεται, etc. CHRYS. *Tom. VI. Orat. XII* (p. 140). [*De Compunctione. Ad Demetrium*, MIGNE, *Patrol. gr.*, t. 47, col. 396.]

ὥστε εἰ μέλλομεν ἐρριζωμένην ἔχειν τὴν πίστιν, πολιτείας ἡμῖν δεῖ καθαρᾶς τῆς τὸ πνεῦμα πειθούσης μένειν, καὶ συνέχειν ἐκείνης τὴν δύναμιν. Οὐ γὰρ ἐστιν, οὐκ ἐστὶ βίον ἀκάθαρτον ἔχοντα, μὴ καὶ περὶ τὴν πίστιν σαλεύεσθαι, etc. CHRYS. *Tom. V, Orat. LV.* [*De Verbis Apostoli* : Habentes autem eumdem spiritum fidei..., MIGNE, *Patrol gr.*, t. 51, col. 280.]

[6] ἡ πονηρία φθαρτικὴ τῶν ἀρχῶν. — Vid. CHRYS. *in Joh. Orat V* (p. 582) [καὶ ἀπλῶς ἅπας ὁ τὴν ἁμαρτίαν ποιῶν, τῶν μεθυόντων οὐδὲν διενήνοχε καὶ μαινομένων, etc. *In Joannem, Hom.* V, MIGNE, *Patrol. gr.*, t. 59, col. 58].

The same also quencheth God's spirit, and driveth away his grace, which is requisite to the production and preservation of faith in us.

14. In fine, from what spirit Infidelity doth proceed we may see by the principles, commonly with it espoused, for its support and countenance, by its great Masters and Patrons ; all which do rankly savour of baseness, and ill nature.

They do libel and revile mankind as void of all true goodness ; from the worst qualities, of which they are conscious themselves or can observe in others, patching up an odious character of it ; thus shrowding themselves under common blame from that which is due to their own wickedness ; and dispensing with that charity and honesty, which is by God's law required from them toward their neighbour : and having so bad an opinion of all men, they consequently must bear ill-will toward them ; it not being possible to love that, which we do not esteem.

They allow nothing in man to be immaterial, or immortal ; so turning him into a beast, or into a puppet, a whirlegig [1] of fate or chance.

They ascribe all actions and events to necessity or external impulse, so rasing the grounds of justice, and all vertue ; that no man may seem responsible for what he doth, commendable or culpable, amiable or detestable.

They explode all natural difference of good and evil ; deriding benignity, mercy, pity, gratitude, ingenuity, that is all instances of good nature, as childish and silly dispositions.

All the reliques of God's image in man, which raise him above a beast, and distinguish him from a fiend, they scorn and expose to contempt.

They extoll power as the most admirable, and disparage goodness as a pityfull thing ; so preferring a Devil before an Angel.

They discard conscience, as a bugbear, to fright children and fools ; allowing men to compass their designs by violence, fraud, slander, any wrongfull ways ; so banishing all the securities (beside selfishness and slavish fear) of government, conversation and commerce ; so that nothing should hinder a man (if he can doe it with advantage to himself and probable safety) to rebell against his

---

[1] [plaything, sport].

Prince, to betray his Country, to abuse his friend, to cheat any man with whom he dealeth.

Such are the principles (not onely avowed in common discourse, but taught and maintained [a] in the writings) of our Infidels; whereby the sources of it do appear to be a deplorable blindness, and desperate corruption of mind; an extinction of natural light, and extirpation of good nature. Farther,

III. The naughtiness [1] of Infidelity will appear by considering its effects and consequences; which are plainly a spawn of all vices and villanies; a deluge of all mischiefs, and outrages upon the earth: for faith being removed, together with it all conscience goeth, no vertue can remain; all sobriety of mind, all justice in dealing, all security in conversation are packed away; nothing resteth to encourage men unto any good, or restrain them from any evil; all hopes of reward from God, all fears of punishment from him being discarded. No principle, or rule of practice is left, beside brutish sensuality, fond self-love, private interest, in their highest pitch, without any bound or curb; which therefore will dispose men to doe nothing but to prey on each other, with all cruel violence, and base treachery. Every man thence will be a God to himself, a Fiend to each other; so that necessarily the world will thence be turned into [b] a *Chaos* and a Hell, full of iniquity and impurity, of spite and rage, of misery and torment. It depriveth each man of all hope from providence, all comfort and support in affliction, of all satisfaction in conscience; of all the good things which faith doth yield.

The consideration of which numberless and unspeakable mischiefs hath engaged Statesmen in every Common-wealth to support some kind of faith, as needfull to the maintenance of publick order, of traffick, of peace among men.

It would suffice to persuade an Infidel, that hath a scrap of wit (for his own interest, safety and pleasure) to cherish faith in others, and wish all men beside himself endued with it.

It in reason obligeth all men to detest Atheistical supplanters of faith, as desperate enemies to mankind, [c] enemies to government,

[a] in the writings) of] *1683*; B. in writings) by
[b] a *chaos* and] probably *T*.
[c] enemies to government] possibly *T*.

[1] [sinfulness, evil].

destructive of common society ; especially considering that of all religions that ever were, or can be, the Christian doth most conduce to the benefit of publick society ; injoyning all vertues usefull to preserve it in a quiet and flourishing state, teaching Loyalty under pain of damnation.

I pass by, that *without faith no man can please God* [1] ; that Infidelity doth expose men to his wrath, and severest vengeance ; that it depriveth of all joy and happiness ; seeing Infidels will not grant such effects to follow their sin, but will reject the supposition of them as precarious, and fictitious.

To conclude therefore the point, it is from what we have said, sufficiently manifest, that Infidelity is a very sinfull distemper, as being in its nature so bad, being the daughter of so bad causes ; the sister of so bad adjuncts, the mother of so bad effects.

But this you will say is an improper subject : for is there any such thing as Infidelity in *Christendome* ; are we not all Christians, all believers, all baptized into the faith, and professours of it ? do we not every day repeat the *Creed*, or at least say *Amen* thereto ? do we not partake of the holy Mysteries, sealing this profession ? what do you take us for ? for *Pagans* ? this is a subject to be treated of in *Turky*, or *in partibus infidelium*. This may be said ; but if we consider better, we shall find ground more than enough for such discourse ; and that Infidelity hath a larger territory than we suppose : for (to pass over the swarms of Atheistical apostates, which so openly abound, denying or questioning our Religion) many Infidels do lurk under the mask of Christian profession. It is not the name of Christian, or the badges of our Religion that make a Christian ; no more than a Cowle doth make a Monk, or the Beard a Philosopher : there may be a Creed in the mouth, where there is no faith in the heart, and a Cross impressed on the forehead of an Infidel ; *with the heart man believeth to righteousness* [2] : *Shew we thy faith by thy works* [3], saith St. *James* : if no works be shewed, no faith is to be granted, as where no fruit, there no root, or a dead root, which in effect and moral esteem is none at all.

Is he not an Infidel, who denieth God ? such a *renegado* is every one that liveth profanely, as St. *Paul* telleth us [4]. And have

[1] *Heb.* XI, 6.
[2] *Rom.* X, 10.
[3] *Jas.* II, 18.
[4] *Tit.* I, 16.

we not many such *renegado's* ? if not, what meaneth that monstrous
dissoluteness of life, that horrid profaneness of discourse, that
strange neglect of God's service, a ᵃ desolation ¹ of God's law ?
where such luxury, such lewdness, such avarice, such uncharitable-
ness, such universal carnality doth reign, can faith be there ? can
a man believe there is a God, and so affront him ? can he believe
that Christ reigneth in heaven, and so despise his laws ? can a man
believe a judgment to come, and so little regard his life, a heaven
and so little seek it, a hell and so little shun it ?—Faith therefore
is not so rife, Infidelity is more common than we may take it to be :
Every sin hath a spice of it, some sins smell rankly of it.

To it are attributed all the rebellions of the *Israelites*, which
are the types of all Christian professours, who seem travellers in
this earthly wilderness toward the heavenly *Canaan* ; and to it
all the enormities of sin, and overflowings of iniquity may be
ascribed.

I should proceed to urge the Precept, that we *take heed thereof* ;
but the time will not allow me to doe it : ᵇ I shall only suggest
to your Meditation the heads of things.

It is Infidelity, that maketh men covetous, uncharitable, discontent, pusillanimous, impatient.

Because men believe not providence, therefore they do so gree-
dily scrape, and hoard.

They do not believe any reward for charity, therefore they will
part with nothing.

They do not hope for succour from God, therefore are they discontent, and impatient.

They have nothing to raise their spirits, therefore ᶜ are they
abject.

Infidelity did cause the Devils Apostasie.

Infidelity did banish Man from Paradise (trusting to the Devil,
and distrusting God's word.)

Infidelity (disregarding the warnings and threats of God) did
bring the deluge on the World.

ᵃ desolation] *1683* ; *B.* violation
ᵇ I shall onely suggest to your Meditation the heads of things] *T.* ; *B.* let it
therefore suffice to have declared its naughtynesse which alone may be a strong
inducement to avoid it.
ᶜ are they] *T.*

¹ [utter devastation].

Infidelity did keep the *Israelites* from entring into *Canaan*, the type of Heaven ; as the Apostle to the *Hebrews* doth insist [1].

Infidelity indeed is the root of all sin, for did men heartily believe the promises to obedience, and the threats to disobedience, they could hardly be so unreasonable as to forfeit the one, or incurr the other : did they believe that the Omnipotent, All-wise, Most just and severe God did command and require such a practice, they could hardly dare to omit or transgress.

[a] Let it therefore suffice to have declared the evil of Infidelity, which alone is sufficient inducement to avoid it.

---

[a] Let it ... avoid it] *T.* (see sentence deleted above, p. 398).

[1] *Heb.* III, 19 ; IV, 6 ; etc.

Of Justifying Faith

Rom. V. 1. *Therefore being justified by faith we have peace with God, through our Lord Jesus Christ.*

Therefore; that word implies the text to be a conclusion (by way of inference, or of recapitulation) resulting from the precedent discourse; it is indeed the principal conclusion, which (as being supposed a peculiar and a grand part of the Christian doctrine, and deserving therefore a strong proof and clear vindication) St. *Paul* designed by several arguments to make good. Upon the words, being of such importance, I should so treat; as first to explain them, or to settle their true sense; then to make some practical application of the truths they contain.

As to the explicatory part, I should consider first, what the faith is, by which we are said to be justified; 2. what being justified doth import; 3. how by such faith we are so justified; 4. what the peace with God is, here adjoined to justification; 5. what relation the whole matter bears to our Lord Jesus Christ; or how through him being justified we have peace with God; in the prosecution of which particulars it would appear, who the persons justified are, and who justifies us; with other circumstances incident [1].

I shall at this time onely insist upon the first particular, concerning the notion of Faith proper to this place, in order to the resolution of which inquiry, I shall lay down some usefull observations: and

1. *First,* I observe, that *Faith,* or belief in the vulgar acception doth signifie (as we have it briefly described in *Aristotle's* Topicks) a σφοδρὰ ὑπόληψις [2], *an earnest opinion* or persuasion of mind concerning the truth of some matter propounded. Such an opinion being produced by, or grounded upon some forcible reason (either

---

[1] [pertinent]. [2] *Top.* IV, v [126 b, 18].

immediate evidence of the matter ; or sense and experience ; or
some strong argument of reason, or some credible testimony ; for
whatever we assent unto, and judge true upon any such grounds
and inducements, we are commonly said to believe)[1] this is the
popular acception of the word ; and according thereto I conceive
it usually signifies[2] in holy Scripture ; which being not penn'd
by Masters of humane art or science ; nor directed to persons of
more than ordinary capacities or improvements, doth not intend to
use words otherwise than in the most plain and ordinary manner.

Belief therefore in general, I suppose, denotes a firm persuasion
of mind concerning the truth of what is propounded ; whether it
be some one single proposition (as when *Abraham* believed, that
God was able to perform what he had promised[3] ; and *Sarah,
that God, who had promised was faithfull*)[4] or some systeme of
propositions, as when we are said to *believe God's word*[5] (that is
all, which by his Prophets was in his name declared) to *believe
the truth*[6] (that is all the propositions taught in the true religion
as so) to *believe God's commandments*[7] (that is the doctrines in
God's Law to be true, and the precepts thereof to be good) to
believe the Gospel[8] (that is to be persuaded of the truth of all
the propositions asserted, or declared in the Gospel.)

2. I observe *Secondly*, that whereas frequently some person,
or single thing is represented (*verbo tenus*) as the object of faith,
this doth not prejudice, or in effect alter the notion I mentioned ;
for it is onely a figurative manner of speaking, whereby is always
meant the being persuaded concerning the truth of some proposition
(or propositions) relating to that person or thing : for otherwise
it is unintelligible how any incomplex thing (as they speak) can
be the complete, or immediate object of belief : beside simple
apprehension (or framing the bare *Idea* of a thing) there is no

---

[1] Aut proba esse quae credis ; aut si non probas, quomodo credis ? TERTUL.
Adv. Marc. V, 1. [MIGNE, *Patrol. lat.*, t. 2, col. 501].

ὅταν γάρ πως πιστεύῃ καὶ γνώριμοι αὐτῷ ὦσιν αἱ ἀρχαί, ἐπίσταται. ARIST.
Eth. VI, iii [4].

'Αριστοτέλης δὲ τὸ ἑπόμενον τῇ ἐπιστήμῃ κρῖμα ὡς ἀληθές, τὸ δέ τι πίστιν
εἶναι φησί. CLEM. *Strom.* II, p. 287. [cap. IV, MIGNE, *Patrol. gr.*, t. 8, col. 945.]

ἔνιοι γάρ πιστεύουσιν οὐδὲν ἧττον οἷς δοξάζουσιν ἢ ἕτεροι οἷς ἐπίστανται.
ARIST. *Eth.* VII, iii [*Eth. Nic.*, VII, 5, 1146 b, 29-30].

[2] [has this meaning].   [3] *Rom.* IV, 21 ; *Heb.* XI, 19.
[4] *Heb.* XI, 11.   [5] *Ps.* CVI, 24 ; LXXVIII, 32.
[6] 2 *Thess.* II, 12.   [7] *Ps.* CXIX, 66.
[8] *Mark* I, 15 ; *Phil.* I, 27.

operation of a man's mind terminated upon one single object; and belief of a thing surely implies more than a simple apprehension thereof: what it is, for instance, to believe this, or that proposition about a man, or a tree (that a man is such a kind of thing, that a tree hath this, or that property) is very easie to conceive; but the phrase believing a man, or a tree (taken properly, or excluding figures) is altogether insignificant, and unintelligible: indeed to believe (πιστεύειν) is the effect τοῦ πεπεῖσθαι (of a persuasive argument,) and the result of ratiocination; whence in Scripture it is commended, or discommended, as implying a good or bad use of reason. The proper object of Faith is therefore some proposition deduced from others by discourse[1]; as it is said, that *many of the Samaritans believed in Christ, because of the woman's word, who testified that He told her all that ever she did*[2]; or as St. *Thomas believed, because he saw*[3]; or as when it is said, that *many believed on our Lord's name, beholding the miracles which he did*[4]; when then, for example, the *Jews* are required to believe *Moses*[5] (or to believe in *Moses*, after the *Hebrew* manner of speaking) it is meant, to be persuaded of the truth of what he delivered, as proceeding from divine revelation; or to believe him to be what he professed himself, a messenger or prophet of God. So *to believe the Prophets*[6] (or in the Prophets, בִּנְבִיאָיו) was to be persuaded concerning the truth of what they uttered in God's name (that the doctrines were true, the commands were to be obeyed, the threats and promises should be performed, the predictions should be accomplished: *to believe all which the Prophets did say*, as our *Saviour* speaks[7], *to believe all things written in the Prophets*, as St. *Paul*.)[8] So to *believe God's works* (a phrase we have in the *Psalms*)[9] signifies, to be persuaded, that those works did proceed from God, or were the effects of his good providence: to *believe in man*[10] (that which is so often prohibited, and dissuaded) denotes the being persuaded, that man in our need is able to relieve and succour us; lastly *to believe in God*[11] (a duty so often injoyned, and inculcated) is to be persuaded, that God is [a]true

---

[a] true] *T.*; *B.* veracious

[1] [reasoning].
[2] John IV, 39.
[3] John XX, 29.
[4] John II, 23.
[5] *Exod.* XIV, 31; XIX, 9; *John* V, 45; etc.
[6] 2 Chron. XX, 20.
[7] *Luke* XXIV, 25.
[8] *Acts* XXIV, 14.
[9] *Ps.* LXXVIII, 32.
[10] *Jer.* XVII, 5; XLVI, 25.
[11] *Ps.* CXVIII, 8, etc.

in whatever he says, faithfull in performance of what he promises ;
perfectly wise, powerfull and good ; able and willing to doe us
good ; the being persuaded, I say, of all these propositions, or such
of them as sute the present circumstances and occasion, is to believe
in God : thus, in fine, to believe on a person, or thing, is onely a
[a] short expression (figuratively) denoting the being persuaded of
the truth of some proposition relating in one way, or other to that
person, or thing (which way is commonly discernible by considering the nature, or state of such a person, or such a thing) the use
of which Observation may afterward appear.

3. I observe *thirdly*, that (as it is ordinary in like cases
concerning the use of words) the word *belief* is by a kind of
synechdoche, (or *metonymie* if you please) so commonly extended
in signification, as together with such a persuasion as we spoke of
to imply whatever by a kind of necessity (natural, or moral) doth
result from it ; so comprehending those acts of will, those affections of soul, and those deeds, which may be presumed consequent
upon such a persuasion : for instance, when God commanded
Abraham to forsake his country, promising him a happy establishment in the land of *Canaan*, with a perpetual blessing upon his
posterity ; *Abraham* was persuaded concerning the power, and
fidelity of God ; and concerning the truth of what was promised
and foretold ; in that persuasion his faith, according to the first,
proper and restrained sense, did consist : but because from such
a persuasion (being sincere, and strong enough)[1] there did naturally, and duly result a satisfaction, or acquiescence in the matter
injoyned as best to be done ; a choice, and resolution to comply
with God's appointment ; an effectual obedience ; a cheerfull
expectation of a good issue thereupon ; therefore all those dispositions of soul, and actions concurring become expressed by the
name of faith (that first persuasion being the principle, and root
of them :) for it is for his faith that he is highly commended ; it is
for it that he obtained so favourable an approbation and acceptance
from God : Yet supposing *Abraham* to have had such a persuasion
concerning God ; and yet to have disliked what God required, or
to have resolved against doing it, or to have indeed disobeyed,
or to have disregarded the happy success ; it is plain that *Abraham*

---

[a] short] *T.* ; *B.* curt.

[1] *Rom.* IV, 20.

as to the whole matter deserved rather much blame, than any commendation ; and would not upon that account have had *righteousness imputed to him*, and have been *called the friend of God* [1] : when therefore his *faith* is so magnified, that *word* comprehends not his bare persuasion onely, but all those concomitants thereof, which if they had not gone along therewith, it had been a proof, that such a persuasion was not sincere (not ἀνυπόκριτος πίστις, *an undissembled faith* ; such as St. *Paul* commends in *Timothy* [2]) or not strong enough (not ἀδιάκριτος πίστις, *an undoubting faith*) [3] but a *weak* [4], a *small* [5], a *dead* [6], an ineffectual faith ; which come under blame, and [a] reproof. But the effect shewed, that he did not (as St. *Paul* says) ἀσθενεῖν τῇ πίστει, had not a weak, or sickly faith [7] ; nor *staggered at the promise of God* ; but *was strong in faith, giving glory to God* [8] ; which he did not onely in believing his word, but in suting his affections, and yielding obedience thereto : (πίστει ὑπήκουσεν ἐξελθεῖν, *by faith he obeyed, so as to forsake his country*, says the *Apostle* to the *Hebrews* [9] ;) And Faith thus taken is not onely a single act of a man's understanding, or will, but a complex of many dispositions and actions, diffused through divers faculties of a man, denoting the whole complication of good dispositions, and actions relating to one matter ; which attend upon a true and earnest persuasion concerning it ; right choice, submission and satisfaction of mind, firm resolution, dutifull obedience, constant and cheerfull hope ; or the like.

4. I observe more nearly to our purpose, *fourthly*, that the Faith here spoken of (being here, and otherwhere put absolutely, or by it self, without any adjunct of limitation or distinction) is often set down with terms annexed thereto, explaining and determining it ; being sometimes styled the *faith of Christ, of Jesus, of God* (τοῦ χριστοῦ, τοῦ ἰησοῦ, τοῦ θεοῦ) sometimes *faith upon Christ* (εἰς χριστὸν, and ἐπὶ χριστὸν) *faith in Christ* (ἐν χριστῷ) *faith to Christ, to the Lord, to God* (πιστεύειν τῷ χριστῷ, τῷ κυρίῳ, τῷ θεῷ) faith *upon the name of Christ* (εἰς ὄνομα) *faith of his name* (πίστις

---

[a] reproof. But] *1683* reproof, but   B. reproofe. but

[1] *Jas.* II, 23.   [2] *1 Tim.* I, 5 ; *2 Tim.* I, 5.
[3] *Jas.* III, 17 ; *Rom.* IV, 20.
[4] *Rom.* XIV, 1 : *1 Cor.* VIII, 10 ; *Rom.* IV, 19.
[5] *Matt.* VI, 30 ; VIII, 26 ; etc.   [6] *Jas.* II, 17, 20 ; *Gal.* V, 6.
[7] *Rom.* IV, 19.   [8] *Rom.* IV, 20.
[9] *Heb.* XI, 8.

τοῦ ὀνόματος) *faith to his name* (τῷ ὀνόματι ;) [1] which phrases,
all questionless denoting the same thing, do imply this faith to
consist in being persuaded concerning the truth of some propositions chiefly relating to our Lord and Saviour *Jesus Christ*, either
as grounded upon his Authority, or appertaining to his Person :
Now what such propositions are we may learn from other expressions, descriptions, or circumlocutions declaring the nature and
quality of this faith : it is sometimes called *the belief of the Gospel*
(that is of the whole systeme of doctrines, and laws, and promises,
and prophecies taught, delivered, or declared by Christ, and his
Apostles. *Repent*, said St. *John the Baptist, and believe the Gospel*)[2] the *belief of the truth* [3], (that body of truth, signally so called,
which was taught by the same Authours) the *acknowledgment of
the* same *truth* (* πιστὸς, and ἐπεγνωκὼς τὴν ἀλήθειαν are in St. *Paul*
the same :)[4] equivalent to those descriptions of this faith are those
expressions, which set it out by yielding assent (generally) to what
our *Lord Christ*, and his *Apostles* taught, or to some chief points
of their doctrine, inferring [5] the rest ; the ª *believing* [6], ᵇ *hearing* [7],
ᶜ *receiving the word of God, of Christ, of the Apostles* [8], ᵈ the
receiving Christ's testimony [9], and (which is the same) * *receiving
Christ himself* [10]; ᶠ *coming unto Christ* [11] (that is as disciples to
their Master, as servants to their Lord, as persons oppressed and
enslaved to their Deliverer) ᵍ *The believing* (and *knowing*) *that
Jesus was sent by God, and came from him* [12]; The believing,

---

[1] *Rom*. III, 3, 22, 26 ; *Gal*. II, 16, 20 ; III, 22 ; *Phil*. III, 9 ; *Apoc*. [*Rev*.]
II, 13 ; XIV, 12.
εἰς. *Acts* XX, 21 ; XXIV, 25 ; XXVI, 18 ; *Col*. II, 5 ; etc.
ἐπί. *Heb*. VI, 1 ; *Acts* IX, 42 ; XXII, 19 ; etc.
ἐν. *Gal*. III, 26 ; *1 Tim*. III, 13 ; *2 Tim*. III, 15 ; *Acts* XIII, 39 ; etc.
τῷ χριστῷ. *Acts* V, 14 ; XVI, 34 ; XVIII, 8 ; XXVII, 25 ; *John* V, 24 ; X, 37,
    38 ; XIV, 11 ; etc.
εἰς ὄνομα. *John* I, 12 ; II, 23 ; *1 John* V, 13 ; etc.
τοῦ. *Acts* III, 16.
τῷ. *1 John* III, 23.
    [2] *Matt*. I, 15 ; *Phil*. I, 27 ; *1 Pet*. IV, 17.
    [3] *2 Thess*. II, 12, 13.
    [4] * *1 Tim*. IV, 3 ; II, 4 ; *Tit*. I, 1 ; *Heb*. X, 26 ; *1 Tim*. II, 4 ; etc.
    [5] [implying].
    [6] ª *John* V, 46, 47.
    [7] ᵇ *John* XII, 47.
    [8] ᶜ *John* XII, 48 ; XVII, 8 ; *Acts* XI, 1.
    [9] ᵈ *John* III, 33.
    [10] * *John* I, 12 ; XIII, 20 ; V, 43.
    [11] ᶠ *John* VI, 37, 44, 65 ; V, 40 ; *Matt*. XI, 28.
    [12] ᵍ *John* XVII, 8 ; V, 24 ; VI, 29 ; XI, 42 ; XVI, 30 ; XVII, 21.

that *Jesus* was, what he professed himself to be [1] ; [k] the *confessing,
that Jesus Christ is come in the flesh ; that Jesus is the Christ,
the Son of God, He which should come into the world ; the King
of Israel ; that God raised him from the dead* [2] ; by the belief of
which one point, as involving the rest, St. *Paul* expresseth this
faith : [1]*If thou* (saith he) *shalt confess with thy mouth the Lord
Jesus, and shalt believe with thy heart, that God raised him from
the dead, thou shalt be saved* [3].

The result upon considering all which expressions declaratory
of the nature of this Faith (for this surely is not different from
that, which is so commonly otherwhere represented in our Saviour,
and his Apostles discourses and writings, as a great duty required
of us ; as a vertue (or act of vertue) highly commendable, as an
especial instrument of our salvation, as a necessary condition prerequisite to our partaking the benefits, and privileges by divine
favour conferred on Christians) the result I say is this, that by this
Faith (as to the first, and primary sense thereof) is understood
the being truely and firmly persuaded in our minds, that *Jesus* was
what he professed himself to be, and what the Apostles testified
him to be ; the *Messias*, by God designed, foretold and promised
to be sent into the world, to redeem, govern, instruct and save
mankind ; our Redeemer and Saviour ; our Lord and Master ;
our King and Judge ; the Great high Priest, and Prophet of God ;
the being assured of these, and all other propositions connexed
with these ; or in short, the being thoroughly persuaded of the
truth of that Gospel ; which was revealed and taught by Jesus
and his Apostles. That this notion is true those descriptions of
this faith, and phrases expressing it, do sufficiently shew ; the
nature and reason of the thing doth confirm the same ; for that
such a faith is, in its kind and order, apt and sufficient to promote
God's design of saving us ; to render us capable of God's favour ;
to purge our hearts, and work that change of mind, which is
necessary in order to the obtaining God's favour, and enjoying
happiness ; to produce that obedience, which God requires of us,
and without which we cannot be saved ; these things are the
natural results of such a persuasion concerning those truths ; as

---

[1] *John* VIII, 24 ; XIII, 29.
[2] [k]*1 John* IV, 2, 15 ; *John* IV, 42 ; *1 John* V, 1, 5 ; *John,* I, 49 ; XX, 31 ;
Acts VIII, 37.
[3] [1]*Rom.* X, 9 ; *John* VI, 45 : ὁ ἀκούσας παρὰ τοῦ πατρὸς καὶ μαθών.

natural, as the desire and pursuit of any good doth arise from the
clear apprehension thereof, or as the shunning of any mischief
ᵃ doth follow from the like apprehension ; as a persuasion that
wealth is to be got thereby, makes the merchant to undergo the
dangers and pains of a long voyage ; (verifying that, *Impiger
extremos currit mercator ad Indos, Per mare pauperiem fugiens,
per saxa, per ignes*)[1] as the persuasion that health may thereby
be recovered, engages a man not onely to take down the most
unsavoury potions, but to endure cuttings and burnings *ut valeas
ferrum patieris, et ignes*)[2] as a persuasion, that refreshment is to be
found in a place, doth effectually carry the hungry person thither :
So a strong persuasion that Christian Religion is true, and the way
of obtaining happiness, and of escaping misery doth naturally produce a subjection of heart, and an obedience thereto ; and accordingly we see the highest of those effects which the Gospel offers,
or requires, are assigned to this faith, as results from it, or adjuncts
thereof : Regeneration ; *Whosoever*, saith St. *John, believeth that
Jesus is the Christ, is born of God*[3] ; Spiritual union with God ;
*Whosoever shall confess, that Jesus is the Son of God, God
abideth in him, and he in God*[4] : *if what ye have heard from the
beginning, abide in you, ye shall also abide in the Father and the
Son*[5]. The obtaining God's love ; *The father loves you, because
you have loved me, and have believed, that I came from God*[6] ;
Victory over the world : *Who is he, that overcometh the world,
but he who believeth that Jesus is the Son of God*[7] ? Freedom
from spiritual slavery ; and becoming true disciples of Christ ;
*If ye abide in my word, ye are truly my disciples ; and ye shall
know the truth, and the truth shall set you free*[8]. Obtaining everlasting life ; *He that heareth my word, and believeth him that sent
me* (that is, who believeth my word, which is indeed the word of
God, who sent me, and in whose name I speak) *hath everlasting
life*[9]. And, *These things were written, that you may believe that
Jesus is the Christ, the Son of God, and that believing it, you may
have life in his name*[10]. Interest in God and Christ, *He that

ᵃ doth follow] *T.*

[1] [*Hor.,* Ep. I, i, 45-6.]
[2] [unidentified, but cf. OVID : *Rem. Amoris,* 229 : ut corpus redimas, ferrum
patieris et ignes].
[3] *1 John* V, 1, 12.   [4] *1 John* IV, 15.   [5] *1 John* II, 23, 24.
[6] *John* XVI, 27 ; *2 Thess.* II, 13 ; *Eph.* I, 13 ; *Acts* XV, 7, 9.
[7] *1 John* V, 5.   [8] *John* VIII, 31, 32.
[9] *John* V, 24.   [10] *John* XX, 31.

abideth in the doctrine of Christ, He (οὗτος) hath the Father and
the Son[1]. Verily verily I say unto you, he that believeth upon me,
hath eternal life[2]. Rising with Christ (that is as to capacity and
right :) Buried with him in baptism, wherein you are risen with
him through faith of the operation of God; who raised him from
the dead[3]. Being saved : Whoever confesses with his mouth the
Lord Jesus to be the Son of God; and in his heart believes that
God raised him from the dead, shall be saved[4]. Lastly being
justified ; for (St. Paul adjoins) a man believeth (in the manner
before [a] mentioned) to righteousness; and with the mouth confession is made to salvation[5]. So we see, that the chief of those
excellent benefits, to the procuring of which faith (however understood) is any-wise conducible, or requisite, do belong to the persuasion concerning Evangelical truths. We may also observe in
the history concerning our Lord, and his Apostles proceedings
toward persons, whom they had converted to Christianity, and did
admit to [b] a participation of the privileges thereof, that no other
faith was by them required in order thereto ; upon such a persuasion appearing they received them into the Church, baptized
them, pronounced unto them an absolution from their sins, and a
reception into God's favour : This was the faith of Martha, which
gave her interest in the promise of eternal life : Every one (said our
Saviour to her) living, and believing in me, shall never die : dost
thou believe this? she saith unto him : Yes Lord, I have believed,
that thou art the Christ, the Son of God, which should come into
the world[6] : this was the faith, for which our Saviour commends
St. Peter, and pronounces him happy[7] : Upon appearance of this
faith St. Peter baptized and admitted into the Church the three
thousand persons whom he had converted (Then, says the Text,
they who gladly (or willingly) received his word (that is, were
persuaded of the truth of that doctrine, which is before set down
concerning our Lord) were baptized ; and the same day were added
(to the Church) about three thousand souls)[8] Upon the like faith
the Samaritans were baptized (ὅταν ἐπίστευσαν τῷ Φιλίππῳ, when

---

[a] mentioned] probably T.; B. touched
[b] a] T.

[1] 2 John 9.   [2] John VI, 47 ; III, 36, 15, 16.
[3] Col. II, 12.   [4] Rom. X, 9.   [5] Rom. X, 10
[6] John XI, 26, 27.   [7] Matt. XVI, 16 ; John VI, 69.
[8] Acts II, 41. οἱ [μὲν οὖν] ἀσμένως ἀποδεξάμενοι τὸν λόγον.

they gave credence to Philip's doctrine :) [1] and upon the same account did the same *Evangelist* say it was lawfull to baptize the *Eunuch*, and accordingly did perform it : *If*, saith *Philip*, *thou believest with thy whole heart, it is lawfull* (or thou mayst be baptized) *He answering said, I believe that Jesus Christ is the Son of God : so he baptized him* [2] : This was the faith, upon which St. *Paul* baptized *Lydia*, *when she had yielded assent unto* (so προσέχειν doth import in the *Acts* ; not onely προσέχειν νοῦν to yield attention, but προσέχειν πίστιν to give assent unto) *the things spoken by St. Paul* [3] ; thus also of those *Jews* in another place of the *Acts*, when St. *Paul* had *opened, and alledged, out of the Scriptures, that Christ was to suffer, and to rise again from the dead, and that Jesus was the Christ*, it is said, τινὲς αὐτῶν ἐπείσθησαν, καὶ προσεκληρώθησαν, *were persuaded*, and *consorted with Paul, and Silas* [4] (that is, were received into Christian communion with them.) The same is intimated in other passages of the Apostolical history ; by all which it appears, that the Apostles method was to declare, and inculcate the main points of the Christian history and doctrine, attesting to the one, and proving the other by testimonies and arguments proper to that purpose ; and whoever of their hearers declared himself persuaded of the truth of what they taught, that he did heartily assent thereto, and resolved to profess and practice accordingly, him without more to doe, they presently baptized, and instated him in the privileges appertaining to Christianity ; or (in St. *Paul*'s language) did justify them, according to their subordinate manner, as the ministers of God. And thus did the Primitive Church practise after the Apostles ; as *Justin* the *Martyr* fully relates of it : — ὅσοι ἂν πεισθῶσι, καὶ πιστεύωσιν ἀληθῆ ταῦτα τὰ ὑφ' ἡμῶν διδασκόμενα, καὶ λεγόμενα εἶναι, καὶ ποιεῖν οὕτως δύνασθαι ὑπισχνῶνται, etc. — ἄγονται ὑφ' ἡμῶν ἔνθα ὕδωρ ἐστὶ, καὶ τρόπον ἀναγεννήσεως, ὃν καὶ ἡμεῖς αὐτοὶ ἀνεγεννήθημεν, ἀναγεννῶνται [5]. *Whoever* (saith he) *are persuaded, and do believe these things by us taught, and said to be true, and undertake that they can live so according to them ;—are brought thither, where water is, and are regenerated after the same manner as we have been regenerated.* I farther add, that even this faith

---

[1] *Acts* VIII, 12.   [2] *Acts* VIII, 37, 38.   [3] *Acts* XVI, 14, 15.
[4] *Acts* XVII, 3, 4 ; IX, 20 ; XVI, 32 ; XVII, 11, 12.
[5] *Apol.* [*Apologia Prima Pro Christianis*, cap. 61. MIGNE, *Patrol. gr.*, t. 6, col. 419].

is expressed to be the effect of divine grace, and inspiration ; for, when St. *Peter* had confessed that *Jesus was the Christ, the Son of the living God*, our *Saviour* tells him, *That flesh and blood had not revealed that unto him, but his Father in heaven* [1] ; and, *No man* (St. *Paul* tells us) *can call Jesus Lord, but by the holy Ghost* [2] ; And, *Every Spirit, which confesseth Jesus Christ to have been come in the flesh, is of God* (saith St. *John*) [3]. So that even, this is a faith, in respect to which the holy Ghost is called *the spirit of faith* [4], which is the *fruit of the spirit* [5] ; and *the gift of God* [6] ; that which *no man can* have without *God's drawing him* ; and teaching him ; *No man can come unto me except the Father that hath sent me shall draw him* (ἐχλύσῃ αὐτὸν.) *Every one that hath heard from the Father, and hath learned, cometh unto me* [7] : to which it is ordinarily required, that God should *open the heart*, as he did *Lydia*'s heart, *to attend, and assent unto what St. Paul taught* [8] : Neither doth the Scripture (as I conceive) attribute any thing unto faith, which doth not agree to this notion.

We might lastly adjoin, that this was the common, and current notion of Faith among the ancient Christians ; neither do we, I suppose, meet with any other in their Writings ; all which things do abundantly confirm the truth thereof.

5. But I must farther observe particularly (in correspondence to what was before more generally observed,) that this Faith doth not onely denote precisely, and abstractedly such acts of mind, such opinions and persuasions concerning the truth of matters specified, but doth also connote, and imply [9] (indeed comprehend according to the meaning of those, who use the word) such acts of will, as, supposing those persuasions to be real and complete, are naturally consequent upon them, and are in a manner necessarily coherent with them ; a firm resolution constantly to profess, and adhere unto the doctrine, of which a man is so persuaded ; to obey all the laws and precepts, which it contains ; forsaking in

---

[1] *Matt.* XVI, 17.
[2] *1 Cor.* XII, 3 ; *1 Cor.* II, 10 ; *2 Cor.* IV, 6 ; *2 Pet.* I, 19.
[3] *1 John* IV, 2 ; *Eph.* I, 17, 18.　　　[4] *2 Cor.* IV, 13.
[5] *Gal.* V, 22.　　　　　　　　　[6] *Eph.* II, 8 ; *Phil.* I, 29.
[7] *John* VI, 44, 45.　　　　　　[8] *Acts* XVI, 14.
[9] Cum [ut diximus] hoc sit hominis Christiani fides, fideliter [Christum credere, et hoc sit Christum fideliter credere], Christi mandata servare, sit absque dubio, ut nec fidem habeat qui infidelis est, nec Christum credat, qui Christi mandata conculcat. SALV. *de Provid* IV, i [De Gubernatione Dei, MIGNE, *Patrol, lat.*, t. 53, col. 69].

open profession, and in real practices all principles, rules, customes, inconsistent with those doctrines and laws ; that which is called *conversion*, or *returning to the Lord* (that is, leaving a course of rebellion, and disobedience to those laws, which the Lord in the Gospel commands, and resolvedly betaking themselves to the observance of them) πολύς τε ὄχλος πιστεύσας ἐπέστρεψεν ἐπὶ τὸν Κύριον, *a great multitude* (it is said) *believing, did return unto the Lord* [1] ; their faith did carry with it such a conversion. Hence this faith is styled πειθαρχεῖν θεῷ (*to obey God's command,*) ὑπακούειν τῷ εὐαγγελίῳ, *to obey the Gospel,* ὑπακούειν τῇ πίστει, *to obey the faith* [2] ; ὑποταγὴ τῆς ὁμολογίας εἰς τὸ εὐαγγέλιον (*subjection of professing the gospel of Christ*) [3] *with purpose of heart to adhere unto God* [4] ; *stipulation of a good conscience toward God* [5] (that which St. *Peter* intimates, as a necessary concomitant of baptism, it being a sincere undertaking, and engaging ones self to obey God's commandments) in fine, to *repent* ; which is either adequately the same thing with faith, or included therein, according to the Apostolical meaning of the word ; for that remission of sins, which is sometime made the consequent of faith, is otherwise expresly annex'd to repentance : The summe of the Gospel our Saviour himself expresses by the preaching in his name *repentance, and remission of sins in all nations* [6] : and *Repent* (St. *Peter* preached,) *and let every one of you be baptized* [7] : And, *Repent,* (said he again) *and return, that your sins may be blotted out* [8] ; and, *Then to the Gentiles* (say those in the *Acts*) *hath God given repentance unto life* [9] ; which signifies the same with that other expression concerning the same persons, *God's having purified their hearts by faith* [10] ; in which places I take repentance to import the same thing with faith ; being in effect nothing else, but sincere embracing Christian Religion. Now the word *faith* is thus extended (beyond its natural and primary force) to comprehend such a compliance of will, or purpose of obedience, because this doth naturally arise from a persuasion concerning the truth of the Gospel, if it be real and strong enough, in that degree, which Christianity requires, and supposes to the effects mentioned in the Gospel ; if it be ἐν τῇ

---

[1] *Acts* XI, 21 ; IX, 35 ; XIV, 15 ; XXVI, 18.
[2] *Acts* V, 32 ; *1 Thess.* I, 8 ; *Rom.* I, 5 ; VI, 17 ; XVI, 17.
[3] *2 Cor.* IX, 13.   [4] *Acts* XI, 23.   [5] *1 Pet.* III, 21.
[6] *Luke* XXIV, 47.   [7] *Acts* II, 38.   [8] *Acts* III, 19 ; XVII, 30.
[9] *Acts* XI, 18.   [10] *Acts* XV, 9.

καρδία *in the heart* (or a hearty faith) as St. *Paul* speaks [1]; if it
be such, as *Philip* exacts of the *Eunuch*, a belief ἐξ ὅλης τῆς καρδίας,
from the whole heart [2]; if it have that due plerophorie [3], that
stability, that solidity, which the Apostles speak of [4] : for a weak,
faint, slight, ill-grounded, ill-rooted opinion concerning the truth
of the Gospel (such as those in another case had, whom our Saviour
rebuked with a τί δειλοί ἐστε, ὀλιγόπιστοι ; *why are ye fearfull,
O ye small in faith* [5]? such as St. *Peter* had, when our Saviour
said to him, ὀλιγόπιστε τί ἐδίστασας ; *O thou of small faith, why
didst thou doubt* [6]? which faith could not keep them, nor him from
sinking ; not such as those had, who *heard the word, and gladly
received it ; but wanted root, so that, when persecution, or affliction did arise for the word ; they were presently scandalized* [7];
not such a faith, as those many *Rulers* had, who are said to have
*believed in Jesus, but for fear of the Pharisees, did not confess
him* [8]; not such, as *Simon Magus* had, who is said to *have believed
Philip*, but to no good effect, *because his heart was not right before
God* [9]; he having not thoroughly resolved to obey the Gospel;
not such as *Agrippa* had, whom St. *Paul* had *almost persuaded
to be a Christian*)[10] these sorts of faith are in comparison to that
we speak of but equivocally so called ; it includes a firm resolution
to perform carefully all the duties injoyned to Christians, to undergo patiently all the crosses incident to Christianity ; it is the same
with becoming a disciple of Christ, which a man cannot be without
renouncing all other interests and concernments, without *denying
ones self, forsaking all and following him* ; without *taking his yoke
upon him, going after, and bearing his cross* [11] : it supposes (as
our Saviour also teaches us,) that a man hath cast up with himself
the gain and loss he is like to receive by the bargain ; and being
satisfied therein to contract *bonâ fide* with God ; that a man hath
weighed all the pains and dangers he shall be put upon by entering
into this warfare [12]; and so resolvedly to adventure upon it ; it is
productive of *love to the truth*, yea of love to God, and charity to

---

[1] *Rom.* X, 9.　　　[2] *Acts* VIII, 37.　　　[3] [fullness of assurance].
[4] *Heb.* X, 22, 23 ; VI, 11, 12 ; *1 Thess.* I, 5 ; *Col.* I, 23 ; II, 5, 7 ; IV, 12 ;
2 Cor. VIII, 7.
[5] *Matt.* VIII, 26.　　　[6] *Matt.* XIV, 31.　　　[7] *Matt.* XIII, 20, 21.
[8] *John* XII, 42.　　　[9] *Acts* VIII, 12, 21.　　　[10] *Acts* XXVI, 28.
[11] *Matt.* X, 38 ; XI, 29 ; *Luke* IX, 23 ; XIV, 26, 27 ; XVI, 24.
[12] *Matt.* XIII, 44, 45 ; *Luke* XIV, 28, 31.

men ; without which all faith is unprofitable, and ineffectual, [a] as St. *Paul* teaches us[1]. In short, this Faith is nothing else but a true, serious, resolute embracing Christianity ; not onely being persuaded that all the doctrines of Christ are true, but submitting to his will and command in all things[2].

But to prevent mistakes, and remove objections, I shall yet further observe,

6. That this Faith hath, although not an adequate, yet a peculiar respect unto that part of Christian truth, which concerns the mercifull intentions of God toward mankind, and the gracious performances of our Saviour in order to the accomplishing them ; the promises of pardon to our sins, and restoral[3] into God's favour upon the terms propounded in the Gospel, of sincere faith and repentance ; whence, the Gospel is called λόγος καταλλαγῆς (*the word of reconciliation*) and this is expressed as a summary of the Apostolick ministery or message ; that *God was in Christ reconciling the world, not imputing their sins*[4] ; And, this our Saviour did order, in especial manner to be preached in his name[5] ; this accordingly they did mainly propound and inculcate ; that God had exalted *Jesus to his right hand as a Prince and a Saviour, to give repentance unto Israel, and remission of sins*[6] ; *that he should receive remission of sins, whoever did believe in his name*[7] ; *Let it be known unto you, brethren, that by this man remission of sins is* * *denounced unto you*[8], (so did they preach.) Whence this faith is (*signanter*) called *belief in the blood of Christ*[9] : Indeed of all Christian doctrines this is most proper first to be propounded and persuaded ; as the most attractive[10] to the belief of the rest ; most encouraging and comfortable to men ; most apt to procure glory to God by the illustration of his principal attributes, his justice and his goodness[11] ; most sutable to the state of things between God, and man ; for men being in a state of rebellion and enmity toward God, in order to their reducement[12] and recovery thence it was

---

[a] as St. *Paul* teaches us] possibly *T*.

[1] *2 Thess.* II, 10 ; *1 Cor.* XIII, 2 ; *Gal.* V, 6.
[2] Credere se in Christum quomodo dicit, qui non facit quod Christus facere praecipit ? CYPR. *De Unit. Eccl.* [MIGNE, *Patrol. lat.*, t. 4, col. 511].
[3] [restoration].   [4] *2 Cor.* V, 18, 19.
[5] *Luke* XXIV, 47.   [6] *Acts* V, 31.
[7] *Acts* X, 43.   [8] *Acts* XIII, 38, * καταγγέλλεται.
[9] *Rom.* III, 25.   [10] [tending to draw towards].
[11] *Rom.* III, 26 ; XV, 9 ; *Eph.* I, 6.
[12] [being brought back to their previous state].

most proper that in the first place an overture of mercy and pardon should be made ; an act of oblivion should be passed and propounded to them : Yet are not these propositions and promises the adequate or entire object of this faith ; for other Articles of faith are often propounded in a collateral order with those, yea sometimes (as in the case of the *Eunuch*) others are expressed, when that is not mentioned ; but onely understood [1] : neither if any one should believe all the doctrines of that kind ; if he did not withall believe that *Jesus* is his Lord, and shall be his Judge ; that there shall be a resurrection of the dead, and a judgment to come, with the like fundamental verities of our Religion, would he be a believer in this sense.

7. I observe farther, that this Faith doth relate onely to propositions revealed by God [2] (or at least, deduced from principles of reason, such as are, that there is a God ; that God is good, veracious [3] and faithfull ; that our religion is true in the gross ; that the holy Scriptures were written by divine inspiration ; which propositions we believe upon rational grounds and motives) not unto other propositions concerning particular matter of fact, subject to private conscience or experience ; nor to any conclusions depending upon such propositions : For instance, it is a part of this faith to believe that God is mercifull and gracious ; that he bears good will unto, and is disposed to pardon every penitent sinner ; or (which is all one) that supposing a man doth believe, and hath repented, God doth actually love him, and doth forgive his sins ; this is, I [a] say, indeed a part of the faith we speak of, its object being part of the Gospel revealed unto us : but the being persuaded that God doth love me, or hath pardoned my sins, or that I am in a state of favour with God, may, as my circumstances may be, not be my duty ; however it is no part of this faith, but a matter of opinion, dependent upon private experience : For such a persuasion must be grounded upon my being conscious to my self of having truly and thoroughly repented (this being required by God,

---

[a] say,] ; *B, 1683* say

[1] *Acts* VIII, 37 ; *Rom.* X, 9.
[2] Fides dicit, parata sunt magna et incomprehensibilia dona a Deo fidelibus suis ; dicit spes mihi illa bona servantur ; charitas dicit curro ego ad illa. BERN. [Dicit ergo fides : parata sunt magna et inexcogitabilia bona a Deo fidelibus suis. Dicit spes : mihi illa servantur. Nam tertia quidem charitas : curro mihi ait ad illa. *Serm. X, in Ps. XC.* MIGNE, *Patrol. lat.*, t. 183, col. 221].
[3] [truthful].

as a necessary condition toward my obtaining pardon and his
favour) of having performed which duty I may presume, when it
is false (and therefore cannot then be obliged to believe it) and
may doubt, when it is true, and that not without good reason ;
considering the blindness and fallibility of man's mind, and that
man's *heart is deceitfull above all things* [1], as the Prophet tells us ;
upon which account, then a man may not be obliged to have such
a persuasion : it is indeed a great fault to doubt, or distrust on
that hand, which concerns God ; about his goodness, his truth,
his wisedom, or power ; but it is not always (perhaps not commonly) blameable to question a man's own qualifications, or his
own performances, whether in kind, or degree they be answerable
to what God requires [2] ; *that* is inconsistent with true faith, but
this not : We cannot have any good religious affections toward
God, if we do not take him to be our gracious father ; but we may
have in us such affections toward him, and he may be favourably
disposed toward us, when we suspect our selves to be untoward
children, *unworthy* (as the *prodigal Son* in the Gospel confessed
himself) *to be called the sons of God* [3] ; the *Centurion*, in the
Gospel did confess himself *unworthy that Christ should enter under
his roof* ; but he declared his persuasion, that *if Christ should
onely speak a word, his child should be healed* ; and our *Saviour*
thereupon professes, *that he had not found so much faith in Israel* [4] :
to the *blind men* imploring his relief our Saviour puts the question,
Do ye believe that I can doe this ? they answered, *Yes Lord* ; he
required no more of them ; but said thereupon, *according to your
faith, let it be done unto you* [5]. And that for which *Abraham* the
Father of believers his faith is represented so acceptable, is, his
firm persuasion concerning God's power [6] ; *because* (saith St. *Paul*)
he had a plerophory [7], *that what was promised, God was able to
perform* ; by doing thus, he was a believer, and thereby *gave glory
to God* (as the *Apostle* there adds ;) [8] if we do not then distrust
God, we may have faith, although we distrust our selves. It is

---

[1] *Jer.* XVII, 9.
[2] Qui perseveraverit usque ad finem, hic salvus erit ; quicquid ante finem
fuerit, gradus est, quo ad fastigium salutis ascenditur, non terminus, quo jam
culminis summa teneatur, etc. CYPR. *De Unit. Eccl.*, p. 259. [MIGNE, *Patrol.
lat.*, t. 4, col. 532.]
[3] *Luke* XV, 19.   [4] *Matt.* VIII, 8, 10.
[5] *Matt.* IX, 28, 29 ; XV, 27, 28.   [6] *Rom.* IV, 21, 11 ; *Heb.* XI, 19.
[7] [fullness of assurance].   [8] *Rom.* IV, 20 πληροφορηθείς, 21.

true (generally, and absolutely speaking) we should endeavour so fully and clearly to repent, and to perform whatever God requires of us[1]; that we may thence acquire a good hope concerning our state; we should labour, that *our hearts may not condemn us*[2] of any presumptuous transgressing our duty; and consequently that we may become in a manner confident of God's favour toward us; but when we have done the best we can, even when we are not conscious of any enormous fault or defect, yet we may consider with St. *Paul, that we are not thereby justified*[3]; but abide liable to the more certain cognisance and judgment of God, *who seeth not as man seeth*[4]; that we are not capable, or competent judges of our selves; nor are ever the better for thinking well of our selves; since (as St. *Paul* tells us again) *he is not approved that commends himself, but whom the Lord commendeth*[5]: for that, *delicta sua quis intelligit? who can thoroughly understand and scann his own errours*[6]? *who can say I have made my heart clean, I am purged of my sin*[7]? who can know (if the *Psalmist* implieth that he could not) untill God hath searched him and discovers it, *whether there be any secret way of wickedness in him*[8]; whether he be sufficiently grieved for having offended God, fully humbled under the sense of his sins, thoroughly resolved to amend his life? however it often happens that true faith and sincere repentance are in degree very defective; in which case we may, without prejudicing the truth of our faith, suspect the worst, yea I conceive it is more safe, and commendable so to doe[9]: if in any, then chiefly, I suppose, in this most important and critical affair, the Wise-man's sentence doth hold, *Blessed is he that feareth always*[10]; so feareth, as thereby to become more solicitous and watchfull over his heart, and ways[11]; more carefull and studious of securing his salvation finally; to render his calling and election in the event more firm[12], and in his apprehension more hopefull. I dare say of two persons otherwise alike qualified, he that upon this ground (fearing his own unworthiness, or defect of his performances) is

---

[1] *Col.* I, 23; *Heb.* III, 6.   [2] *1 John* III, 21.   [3] *Cor.* IV, 4.
[4] *1 Sam.* XVI, 7.   [5] *2 Cor.* X, 18.   [6] *Ps.* XIX, 12.
[7] *Prov.* XX, 9.   [8] *Ps.* CXXXIX, 24.
[9] μὴ ὑφηλοφρόνει, ἀλλὰ φοβοῦ. *Rom.* XI, 20.
[10] *Prov.* XXVIII, 14.
[11] Nunquam est de salute propriâ mens secura sapientis. Salv. *ad Eccl. Cath.* II [*Adv. Avaritiam*, Migne, *Patrol. lat.*, t. 53, col. 191].
[12] *2 Pet.* I, 10.

most doubtfull of his state, doth stand really upon better terms
with God [1] ; as the *Pharisee*, who *justified himself*, and took himself to be in a very good condition, was indeed *less justified* (somewhat the less for that conceit of his) than the poor *Publican*, who
was sensible of his own unworthiness, and condemned himself in
his own opinion [2] : the great danger lies on that hand of being
presumptuous, arrogant and self-conceited, which God hates ; and
on this hand there usually lies humility, modesty and poverty of
Spirit, which God loves. *As every high thing* (every elevation
of mind) *is abominable in God's sight* [3] ; and he *depresseth him
that exalteth himself* [4] ; so lowly thoughts are gracious in God's
regard ; *he raiseth him, that humbleth himself, and is lowly in his
own eyes* [5] : he hath an especial respect to him, *that is of a poor
and contrite heart, and trembleth at his word* [6]. It is a property
of good men (being such as often reflect upon their own hearts
and ways, and thence discern the defects in them) with *Jacob*,
to think themselves *less than the least of God's mercies* [7] ; with
David to be *afraid of God's judgments* [8] ; it is their duty to pass
the time of *their sojourning here in fear, to work out their salvation
with fear and trembling* [9]. I may add, that sometime [10] a person
much loving God, and much beloved of him, may be like a *Pelican
in the wilderness, and an Owle of the desert* [11] ; from an apprehension of God's anger may have *no soundness in his flesh, nor
rest in his bones by reason of his sin* [12] ; may have his *spirit over-
whelmed, and his heart within him desolate* [13] : may fear that his
sins have *separated between him and his God* [14] ; and that he is
forsaken of God [15] ; God *hiding his face, and withdrawing his
light of his countenance*, he may be *troubled* ; may have *his soul
cast down and disquieted within him* [16] ; may be ready to say,
I am cut off from before thine eyes [1] ; even such a man in such a

---

[1] Quem censeas digniorem, nisi emendatiorem ? Quem emendatiorem, nisi
timidiorem ? TERTULL. *de Poenit.* VI [MIGNE, *Patrol. lat.*, t. 1, col. 1350].
   [2] *Luke* XVIII, 14 ; X, 29.   [3] *Luke* XVI, 15.
   [4] *Luke* XVIII, 14 ; *2 Sam.* XXII, 28 ; *Ps.* XXXIV, 18.
   [5] [*Matt.* XXIII, 12.]   [6] *Isa.* LXVI, 2 ; LVII, 15.
   [7] *Gen.* XXXII, 10.   [8] *Ps.* CXIX, 120.
   [9] *1 Pet.* I, 17 ; *Phil.* II, 12 ; *2 Pet.* I, 10.
   [10] [sometimes].   [11] *Ps.* CII, 6.
   [12] *Ps.* XXXVIII, 3.   [13] *Ps.* CXLIII, 4.
   [14] *Jer.* V, 25.   [15] *Matt.* XXVII, 46 ; *Ps.* XXII, 1.
   [16] *Ps.* XXX, 7 ; LXXXIX, 46 ; XLII, 5 ; LXIX, 16.

state of distress and doubt, may continue a believer; he retaining honourable thoughts of God (in which the worth and vertue of true faith consisteth) although dejected by the conscience of his own infirmities, by suspicion of his own indispositions, and consequently by the fear of God's displeasure.

Farther, that this faith doth not essentially include a respect to such particular propositions, or does not (as many in these two latter ages have deemed and taught) consist in our being persuaded that our sins are pardon'd, or our persons just in God's esteem[2]; that we are acceptable to God, and stand possessed of his favour, it appears from hence, that faith is in holy Scripture represented in nature precedaneous[3] to God's benevolence (especial I mean, not general benevolence, for that prevents[4] all acts and dispositions of us, or in us) to his conferring remission of sins, accepting and justifying our persons; it is a previous condition, without which (as the *Apostle* teaches us) *it is impossible to please God*[5]; it is a reason of God's love (*The Father*, saith our Lord, *loves you, because ye have loved me, and believed that I came from God*)[6] it is a ground of divine acceptation and good-will (*Abraham believed God*, saith St. *James, and it was accounted unto him for righteousness, and he was called the friend of God*)[7] it is a mean[8], or instrument (so it is constantly represented) by which we are justified, obtain God's favour, and the remission of our sins; and therefore is in order of nature previous and prerequisite thereto; it is therefore required before baptism, in which remission of sins is consigned: God justifies, accepts and pardons him, that hath been impious, but not him that is an infidel: This is the method plainly declared in Scripture; wherefore if faith implyes a persuasion that God hath remitted our sins, it must imply an antecedent faith (even a justifying faith, antecedent to it self,) or that we believe before we believe, and are justified before we are justified. I add, that by this notion many, or most (I will not after the

---

[1] *Ps.* XXXI, 22.

[2] Sed fide hoc beneficium accipiendum est, qua credere nos oportet, quod propter Christum nobis donentur remissio peccatorum et justificatio. AUG. *Conf.*
Quare cum dicit Justificamur fide: vult te intueri filium Dei, sedentem ad dextram Patris, mediatorem, interpellantem pro nobis: et statuere, quod tibi remittantur peccata, quod justus, id est acceptus reputeris. MELANCT. *Loc. com.*, p. 418 [De vocabulo fidei; 1552 ed., Basil., p. 215 (1561, p. 223)].

[3] [antecedent].   [4] [precedes].   [5] *Heb.* XI, 6.
[6] *John* XVI, 27.   [7] *Jas.* II, 23.   [8] [means, intercessor, mediator].

Council of *Trent* say all) humble and modest Christians are excluded from being believers ; even all those who are not confident
of their own sincerity and sanctity, and consequently cannot be
assured of their standing in God's favour : and on the other side,
the most presumptuous, and fanatical sort of people are most certainly the truest and strongest believers, as most partaking of the
most essential property thereof, according to that notion ; for of
all men living such are wont to be most assured of God's especial
love unto them, and confident that their sins are pardoned ; Experience sufficiently shews this to be true, and consequently that
such a notion of Faith cannot be good.

Much less is that notion of faith right, which defines faith to
be a firm and certain knowledge of God's eternal good-will toward
us particularly, and that we shall be saved ; which notion (taught
in the beginning of the Reformation by a man of greatest name
and authority) [1] was thus lately expressed by the *Professours* of
Leyden in their *Synopsis purioris Theologiae : Faith* (they say, in
their definition thereof) *is a firm assent—by which every believer
with a certain trust resting in God, is persuaded not onely that
remission of sins is in general promised to them who believe, but
is granted to himself particularly, and eternal righteousness, and
from it life, by the mercy of God,* etc. [2] which notion seems to be
very uncomfortable, as rejecting every man from the company of
believers, who is either ignorant or doubtfull, not onely concerning
his present, but his final state ; who hath not, not onely a good
opinion, but a certain knowledge of his present sincerity and
sanctity ; yea not onely of this, but of his future constant perseverance therein ; so that if a man be not sure he hath repented, he is
(according to this notion) sure that he hath not repented, and is
no believer : how many good people must this doctrine discourage

---

[1] Nunc justa fidei definitio nobis constabit, si dicamus esse divinae erga nos
benevolentiae firman certamque cognitionem, etc. — Jam in divina benevolentia,
quam respicere dicitur fides, intelligimus salutis ac vitae aeternae possessionem
obtineri, etc.   CALV. *Inst.* III, [ii], 7 & 28 compar., [Lugd. Batav., 1654,
pp. 188(b), 197(a)].

[2] ... firmus assensus ... quo certa fiducia in Deo acquiescens, firmiter unusquisque fidelis statuit, non solum promissam esse credentibus in genere remissionem peccatorum, sed sibi in particulari concessam, aeternamque justitiam, et ex
ea vitam, etc. [*Synopsis Purioris Theologiae, Disputationibus quinquaginta dua-
bus comprehensa, Ac conscripta* per Johannem Polyandrum, Andream Rivetum,
Antonium Walaeum, Antonium Thysium, SS. Theologiae Doctores et Professores
in Academia Leidensi, Lugd. Batav., 1658. Disputatio XXXI, De Fide et Perse-
verantia Sanctorum, Thesis VI, p. 373].

and perplex ? to remove it, we may consider, 1. that it altogether inverts and confounds the order of things declared in Scripture, wherein Faith (as we observed before) is set before obtaining God's good-will, as a prerequisite condition thereto ; and is made a means of salvation (*without faith it is impossible to please God* [1] ; *By grace we are saved, through faith* [2].) And if we must believe before God loves us, (with such a love as we speak of) and before we can be saved ; then must we know that we believe before we can know that God loves us, or that we shall be saved ; and consequently we must indeed believe before we can know that God loves us, or that we shall be saved. But this doctrine makes the knowledge of God's love and of salvation in nature antecedent to faith, as being an essential ingredient into it ; which is preposterous : Consider this circle of discourse [3] : A man cannot know that he believes, without he does believe (this is certain) a man cannot know that he shall be saved, without knowing he doth believe (this is also certain, for upon what ground, from what evidence can he know his salvation, but by knowing his faith.) But again backward, A man (say they) cannot believe (and consequently not know that he believes) without being assured of his salvation : What an inextricable maze and confusion is here ? this doctrine indeed doth make the knowledge of a future event to be the cause of its being future [4] ; it supposes God to become our friend (as *Abraham* was by his faith) [5] by our knowing that he is our friend ; it makes us to obtain a reward by knowing that we shall obtain it ; it supposes the assurance of our coming to a journeys end to be the way of getting thither ; which who can conceive intelligible, or true ? Our *Saviour* doth indeed tell us, that it is *the way to life* everlasting (or conducible to the attaining it) *to know* (that is, to believe, as it is interpreted in the 8th verse of that chapter ; for what upon good grounds we are persuaded of, or judge true, we may be said to know) *the true God, and Jesus Christ, whom he hath sent* [6] ; but he doth not say it is life everlasting (or conducible to the obtaining it) to know, that we shall have life everlasting : that were somewhat strange to say. St. *Peter* exhorts us to *use diligence to make our calling and election sure* [7] (or firm, and

---

[1] *Heb.* XI, 6.
[2] *Eph.* II, 8 ; *Rom.* X, 9.
[3] [circular argument].
[4] [the cause of its taking place].
[5] *Jas.* II, 23.
[6] *John* XVII, 3, 8.
[7] *2 Pet.* I, 10.

stable) but he doth not bid us know it to be sure ; if we did know it to be so, what need should we have to make it so ; yea how could we make it so ? he doth not injoyn us to be sure of it in our opinion, but to secure it in the event by sincere obedience, and a holy life ; by so impressing this persuasion upon our minds, so rooting the love of God and his truth in our hearts, that no temptation may be able to subvert our faith, or to pluck out our charity. 2. This notion plainly supposes the truth of that doctrine, that no man being once in God's favour can ever quite lose it ; the truth of which I shall not contest now (nor alledge the many clear passages of Scripture, nor the whole tenour of the Gospel, nor the unanimous consent of all Christendom for fifteen hundred years against it) but shall onely take notice, that their notion of faith necessarily presupposing the truth of this doctrine is yet thereby everted [1] : for it follows thence, that no man, who doth not assent to that doctrine, is, or can be a believer : for he that is not assured of the truth of that opinion (although we suppose him assured of his present sincerity, and being in a state of grace) cannot know that he shall be saved : So that onely such as agree with them in that opinion can be believers, which is somewhat hard, or rather very absurd ; and to aggravate this inconvenience I adjoyn ; 3. that according to their notion scarce any man (except some have had an especial revelation concerning their salvation) before the late alterations in Christendom, was a believer ; for before that time it hardly appears, that any man did believe, as they do, that a man cannot fall from grace ; and therefore scarce any man could be assured, that he should be saved ; and therefore scarce any man could be a believer in their sense.

St. *Augustine* himself (whose supposed patronage stands them in so much stead upon other occasions) hath often affirmed [2], that divers have had given them that faith, that charity, that justification, wherein if they had dyed, they should have been saved ; who yet were not saved : which persons surely, when they were in that good state, (admitting them according to St. *Augustine*'s supposal [3] to have been in it) were as capable of knowing their salvation, as any other man can be, yea St. *Augustine* himself (considering

---

[1] [overthrown].
[2] *De Corr. et Gr.*, cap. ix, xiii ; [MIGNE, *Patrol. lat.*, t. 44]; *De Dono Persev.*, cap. viii, xiii [*ibid.*, t. 45].
[3] [assumption].

that *Accidere cuiquam quod potest, cuivis potest*[1], what was another man's case might be his, there being no ground of difference)
could not be more sure of his [a]own salvation at any time, than
such persons were at that time : According to St. *Augustine's*
judgment therefore no man could know that he should be saved
(his salvation depending upon perseverance, which in his opinion
not being given to all, must as to our knowledge (whatever it might
be in respect to God's decree) be contingent and uncertain) it
follows I say upon his suppositions, yea he expresly affirms it ;
(*lib. 2. de dono pers.*) *Itaq* ; (says he) *utrum quisq ; hoc (perse-
verantiae) munus acceperit, quamdiu hanc vitam ducit, incertum
est : Whether any have received this gift of perseverance while
he leads this life is uncertain*[2]. Wherefore St. *Augustine* could
not be assured of his own salvation ; and therefore (according
to these mens sense) he was no believer, no Christian ; which I
suppose yet they will not assert, though it be so plainly consequent
on their own position. I might, 4. ask of them, if a man should
confess ingenuously, that although he did hope for mercy from
God in that day, yet that he was not assured of his salvation,
whether such a person should be rejected from Christian communion, as no believer : it seems, according to their notion of faith,
he should ; since by his own (in this particular infallible) judgment
it is notorious that he (as being no believer) hath no title unto,
or interest in the privileges of Christianity ; but this proceeding
would very much depopulate the Church, and banish from it, I
fear, the best (the most humble and modest, yea the wisest and
soberest) members thereof.

But so much I think suffices for the removal of that new harsh
notion, to say no worse of it.

There is another more new than that, devised by some[3] (who

[a] own] probably *T.*

[1] [not identified].
[2] [cap. i ; MIGNE, *Patrol. lat.*, t. 45, col. 993].
  ... nec sibi quisque ita notus est, ut sit de sua crastina conversatione securus.
AUG. *Ep.* cxxi, ad Probam [*Epist.* CXXX (alias 121), cap. ii, MIGNE, *Patrol.
lat.*, t. 33, col. 495].
  In hoc mundo et in hac vita nulla anima possit esse secura. *Ibid.* [col. 494].
  Quamdiu vivimus in certamine sumus, et quamdiu in certamine nulla est certa
victoria. HIER. *adv. Pelag.* II, 2 [MIGNE, *Patrol. lat.*, t. 23, col. 565].
[3] AMES *Med.* I, xxvii. Christus adaequatum objectum [GUILIEL. AMESII :
Medulla Theologica, Amstelod,, 1628. § 17, p. 119 : Fides igitur illa proprie
dicitur justificans, qua incumbimus in Christum ad remissionem peccatorum et
salutem. Christus enim est adequatum objectum fidei, quatenus fides justificat.

perceived the inconveniences of the former notions, yet it seems did affect to substitute some new fine one in their room) which if it be not so plainly false, yet is (it seems) more obscure and intricate : it is this ; that Faith is not an assent to propositions of any kind, but a recumbency [1], leaning, resting, rolling upon, adherency [2] to (for they express themselves in these several terms, and others like them) the person of Christ ; or, an apprehending and applying to our selves the righteousness of Christ ; his person it self, and his righteousness, as simple incomplex things ; not any proposition (that they expresly caution against) are the objects, say they, of our faith : they compare our faith to a hand that lays hold upon Christ, and applyes his righteousness ; and to an eye that looks upon him, and makes him present to us ; and by looking on him (as on the brazen Serpent) cures us : but this notion is so intricate, these phrases are so unintelligible, that I scarce believe the devisers of them did themselves know what they meant by them ; I do not, I am sure : for what it is for one body to lean upon, or to be rolled on another ; what for one body to reach at, and lay hold upon another ; what it is to apply a garment to one's body, or a salve to one's wounds, I can easily understand ; but what it is for a man's mind to lean upon a person (otherwise than by assenting unto some proposition he speaks, or relying upon some promise he makes) to apply a thing, otherwise than by consenting to some proposition concerning that thing, I cannot apprehend, or [a] reach. There is not (as we noted before) any faculty or operation of a man's mind, which answers the intent of such notions or phrases. Let me put this case : suppose a great Province had generally revolted from its Sovereign, whereby the People thereof had all deserved extreme punishment sutable to such an offence ; but that the King moved with pity, and upon the intercession of his onely beloved Son (together with a satisfaction offered and performed by him) should resolve to grant a general pardon to them, upon just, and fit, and withall, very easie terms ; And that

[a] reach. There]; 1683 reach, there B. reach. there

Fides etiam non alia ratione justificat, nisi quatenus apprehendit illam justitiam, propter quam justificamur : illa autem justitia non est in veritate alicujus axiomatis, cui assendum praebemus, sed in Christo solo, qui factus est pro nobis peccatum, ut nos essemus in ipso justitia. 2 Cor., V, 21].

[1] [reclining on, reliance upon ; as Barrow intimates the exact meaning is far from clear].

[2] [attachment (see recumbency)].

for the execution of this gracious purpose toward them, he should
depute and send his Son himself among them to treat with them,
by him declaring his mercifull intentions toward them, with the
conditions, upon complyance wherewith all, or any of them should
be pardon'd their offence, and received into favour; those conditions being, suppose it, that first they should receive and acknowledge his Son for such as he professed himself to be (the King's
Son indeed, who truly brought such a message unto them from
his Majesty) then that they should seriously resolve with themselves, and solemnly engage to return unto their due allegiance;
undertaking faithfully for ever after to observe those laws, which
the said Prince in his Father's name should propound unto them.
Suppose farther, that the Prince in pursuance of this commission
and design, being come into the Country, should there send all
about Officers of his, injoyning them to discover the intent of his
coming, what he offered, and upon what terms; withall, impower-
ing them in his name to receive those, who complyed, into favour,
declaring them pardoned of all their offences, and restored to the
benefit of the King's protection, and all the privileges of loyal
subjects; suppose now, that these Officers should go to the people,
and speak to them in this manner: The King makes an overture
of pardon and favour unto you upon condition, that any one of
you will recumbe [1], rest, lean upon, or roll himself upon the person
of his Son (rest upon his person, not onely rely upon his word,
that you are to understand) or in case you will lay hold upon, and
apply to your selves his Son's righteousness, by which he hath
procured of the King his Father, this mercy and favour for you
(not onely being persuaded that he hath performed thus much for
you, this is not [a] enough;) do you think these messengers should
thus well express themselves, or perform their message handsomely
and with advantage? should not they do much better, laying aside
such words of metaphor and mystery, to speak in plain language;
telling them, that their King his Son (by plain characters discernible to be truely such) was come among them upon such an
intention; that if they would acknowledge him, and undertake
thereafter to obey him, they should receive a full pardon, with
divers other great favours and advantages thereby? the case is

[a] enough;)] ; *B. 1683* enough)

[1] [recline on; see *recumbency* above].

apparently so like to that which stands between God and man, and doth so fully resemble the nature of the Evangelical dispensation, that I need not make any application, or use any more argument to refute that notion ; I shall onely say that I conceive these new phrases (for such they are, not known to ancient Christians, nor delivered, either in terms, or sense in Scripture, for the places alledged in favour or proof of them by *Ames* [1], one of the first broachers of them, (all we may presume that they could find anywise seeming to favour their notion) doe not, as if time would permit might easily be shewed, import any such thing, but are strangely misapplied) [a]that, I say, these phrases do much obscure the nature of this great duty, and make the state of things in the Gospel, more difficult and dark than it truly is ; and thereby seem to be of bad consequence, being apt to beget in people both dangerous presumptions and sad perplexities : for they hearing that they are onely, or mainly bound to have such a recumbency upon Christ, or to make such an application of his righteousness, they begin (accordingly as they take themselves to be directed) to work their minds to it ; and when they have hit upon that posture of fancy, which they guess to sute their Teachers meaning, then they become satisfied, and conceit [2] they believe well, although perhaps they be ignorant of the principles of the Christian faith, and indisposed to obey the precepts of our Lord : sometimes, on the other side, although they well understand, and are persuaded concerning the truth of all necessary Christian doctrines, and are well disposed to observe God's commandments, yet because they cannot tell whether they apprehend Christ's person dexterously, or apply to themselves his righteousness in the right manner, as is prescribed to them (of which it is no wonder that they should doubt, since it is so hard to know what the doing so means) they become disturbed and perplexed in their minds ; questioning whether they do believe or no : Thus by these notions (or phrases rather) are some men tempted fondly to presume, and other good people are wofully discouraged by them ; both being thence diverted, or withdrawn from their duty : whereas what it is to believe, as Christians anciently did understand it, and as we have assayed to explain it, is very easy to conceive ; and the taking it so, can have no other

---

[a] that, I say,] ; *B. 1683* that I say

[1] [*op. cit.* § 18, p. 119].   [2] [imagine].

than very good influence upon practice, as both reason (as we have insinuated) shews, and the Scripture largely and plainly affirms. But let thus much suffice for the enquiry concerning the genuine nature and notion of Faith proper to this place (that faith by which in this Text we are said to be Justified) the other particulars I cannot so much as touch upon at this time.

I end with those good prayers of our Church :

O Lord, from whom all good things do come, Grant to us thy humble servants, that by thy holy inspiration we may think those things that be good ; and by thy mercifull guiding may perform the same, through our Lord Jesus Christ [1]. Amen.

Almighty and Everlasting Lord, give unto us the encrease of faith, hope and charity, and that we may obtain that which thou dost promise, make us to love that which thou dost command, through Jesus Christ our Lord [2]. Amen.

---

[1] Fifth Sunday after Easter.   [2] 14th Sunday after Trinity.

Of Justification by Faith

Rom. V. 1. *Therefore being justified by faith we have peace with God, through our Lord Jesus Christ.*

In order to the understanding of these words I did formerly propound divers particulars to be considered and discussed : the *first* was, What that Faith is, by which Christians are said to be justified ? This I have dispatched : The *next* is, What Justification doth import ? the which I shall now endeavour to explain ; and I am concerned to perform it with the more care and diligence, because the right notion of this term hath in latter times been canvased with so much vehemence of dissension and strife.

In former times, among the *Fathers* and the *School-men*, there doth not appear to have been any difference or debate about it ; because (as it seems) men commonly having the same apprehensions about the matters, to which the word is applicable, did not so much examine or regard the strict propriety of expression concerning them : consenting in *things*, they did not fall to cavil and contend about the exact meaning of *words*[1]. They did indeed consider distinctly no such point of doctrine as that of *justification*, looking upon that *word* as used incidentally in some places of Scripture, for expression of points more clearly expressed in other terms ; wherefore they do not make much of the *word*, as some *Divines* now do.

But in the beginning of the Reformation, when the discovery of some great errours (from the corruption and ignorance of former times) crept into vogue, rendred all things the subjects of contention, and multiplyed controversies, there did arise hot disputes about this Point ; and the right stating thereof seemed a matter of great importance[2] ; nor scarce was any controversie prosecuted

---

[1] περὶ λεξειδίων μικρολογεῖν. GREG. NAZ. [? Cf.: αἴσχιον δὲ ἡμῖν ὃ ἐγκαλοῦμεν παθεῖν, καὶ μικρολογίαν καταγινώσκοντας, αὐτοὺς μικρολοεῖσθαι περὶ τὰ γράμματα. *Oratio* XL, MIGNE, *Patr. gr.*, t. 36, col. 440].

[2] Articulus stantis, et cadentis Ecclesiae. LUTH. [*Comment. in Epist. ad*

with greater zeal and earnestness: whereas yet (so far as I can discern) about the real Points of doctrine, whereto this *word* (according to any sense pretended) may relate, there hardly doth appear any material difference; and all the Questions depending, chiefly seem to consist about the manner of expressing things, which all agree in; or about the extent of the signification of words capable of larger, or stricter acception: whence the debates about this Point among all sober and intelligent persons might (as I conceive) easily be resolved, or appeased, if men had a mind to agree, and did not love to wrangle; if at least a consent in believing the same things, although under some difference of expression, would content them, so as to forbear strife.

To make good which observation, tending as well to the illustration of the whole matter, as to the stating and decision of the controversies about it, let us consider the several divine acts, to which the term Justification is, according to any sense pretended, applicable: I say divine acts; for that the justification we treat of is an act of God simple or compound (in some manner) respecting, or terminated upon man, is evident, and will not I suppose be contested; the words of St. *Paul* in several places so clearly declaring it; as in that, *Who shall lay any thing to the charge of God's elect? it is God that justifieth*, and in that, *To him that worketh not, but believeth on him that justifieth the ungodly, his faith is counted for righteousness* [1]: Now according to the tenour of Christian doctrine such acts are these.

1. God (in regard to the obedience performed to his will by his beloved Son, and to his intercession) is so reconciled to mankind, that unto every person, who doth sincerely believe the Gospel, and (repenting of his former bad life) doth seriously resolve thereafter to live according to it, he doth (upon the solemn obsignation [2] of that faith, and profession of that resolution in Baptism) entirely remit all past offences, accepting his person, receiving him into favour; assuming him into the state of a loyal subject, a faithfull

---

Galat., Pref., in *Opera* (1611) IV, 5. See also: *Antithesis verae et falsae Ecclesiae*, 1541, sig. Bv, C 4 and 4 v; *Catechismus Major*, 1544, p. 78; *Deutsche Antwort Luthers auf König Heinrichs von England Buch* (1522), *Sämmtliche Werke*, Erlangen, 1826-53, XXVIII, 365; *Eine andre Predigt am Sonntage nach Christi Himmelfahrt*, *ibid.*, L, 10-11, 26-31; *Tischreden, Von dem Herrn Christo*, no. 667, 691, *ibid.*, LVIII, 133, 146, etc.].

[1] *Rom.* VIII, 83; IV, 5; III, 26.
[2] [formal ratification].

servant, a dutifull Son ; and bestowing on him all the benefits and privileges sutable to such a state ; according to those passages : *It behoved Christ to suffer—and that repentance, and remission of sins should be preached in his name among all nations*[1] : *Then Peter said unto them, Repent, and be baptized every one of you in the name of Jesus Christ, for the remission of sins*[2] ; and, *To him give all the Prophets witness, that through his name, whosoever believeth in him shall receive remission of sins*[3] ; and, *God was in Christ reconciling the world unto himself, not imputing their sins*[4] ; and in other places innumerable.

2.   As any person persisting in that sincere faith, and serious purpose of obedience, doth assuredly continue in that state of grace and exemption from the guilt of sin, so in case that out of humane frailty such a person doth fall into the commission of sin, God (in regard to the same performances and intercessions of his Son) doth upon the confession and repentance of such a person remit his sin, and retain him in or restore him to favour ; according to those sayings of St. *John : If we confess our sins, he is faithfull, and just to forgive us our sins, and to cleanse us from all unrighteousness ;* and, *If any man sin, we have an advocate with the Father Jesus Christ, the righteous*[5].

3.   To each person sincerely embracing the Gospel, and continuing in stedfast adherence thereto, God doth afford his holy Spirit, as a principle productive of all inward sanctity and vertuous dispositions in his heart, enabling also and quickning him to discharge the conditions of faith, and obedience required from him, and undertaken by him ; that which is by some termed making a person just, infusion into his Soul of righteousness, of grace, of vertuous habits ; in the Scripture style it is called *acting by the Spirit*[6], *bestowing the gift of the holy Ghost*[7], *renovation of the holy Ghost*[8], *creation to good works*[9], *sanctification by the Spirit*[10], etc. which phrases denote partly the collation[11] of a principle enabling to perform good works, partly the design of religion tending to that performance.

---

[1] *Luke* XXIV, 46, 47.   [2] *Acts* II, 38 ; III, 19 ; V, 31.
[3] *Acts* X, 43.   [4] *2 Cor.* V, 19 ; *Rom.* III, 24, 25.
[5] *1 John* I, 9 ; II, 1.
[6] *Rom.* VIII, 14 ; *Gal.* IV, 6 ; *1 Cor.* II, 12 ; *2 Tim.* II, 7 ; *Rom.* VIII, 9.
[7] *Acts* II, 38.   [8] *Tit.* III, 5 ; *Eph.* II, 22.
[9] *Eph.* II, 10 ; IV, 23.   [10] [*2 Thess.* II, 3 ; *1 Pet.* I, 2.]
[11] [bestowal].

Now all these acts (as by the general consent of Christians, and according to the sense of the ancient Catholick Church, so) by all considerable Parties seeming to dissent, and so earnestly disputing about the Point of Justification, are acknowledged and ascribed unto God ; but with which of them the act of Justification is solely or chiefly coincident ; whether it signifieth barely some one of them, or extendeth to more of them, or comprehendeth them all (according to the constant meaning of the word in Scripture) are questions coming under debate, and so eagerly prosecuted : Of which questions whatever the true resolution be, it cannot methinks be of so great consequence, as to cause any great anger or animosity in dissenters one toward another, seeing they all conspire in avowing the acts, whatever they be, meant by the word *Justification*, although in other terms ; seeing all the dispute is about the precise and adequate notion of the word *Justification* : whence those questions might well be waved as unnecessary grounds of contention ; and it might suffice to understand the points of doctrine which it relateth to in other terms, laying that aside as ambiguous and litigious. Yet because the understanding the rightest, or most probable notion of the word may somewhat conduce to the interpretation of the Scriptures, and to clearing the matters couched in it, somewhat also to the satisfaction of persons considerate and peaceable, I shall employ some care faithfully (without partiality to any side) to search it out, and declare it : in order whereto I shall propound some Observations, seeming material.

I.   Whereas it were not hard to speak much, and criticise about the primitive sense of the word, and about its various acceptions both in holy Scripture and other Writings, I do question whether doing that would be pertinent, or conducible to our purpose of understanding its right notion here : for knowing the primitive sense of words can seldom or never determine their meaning any where, they often in common use declining from it [1] ; and the knowing variety of acceptions doth at most yield onely the advantage of chusing one sutable to the subjacent [2] matter and occasion. We are not therefore to learn the sense of this word from mere *Grammarians*.

---

[1] Verba valent ut nummi. [unidentified].
[2] [serving as basis, under examination].

II. The sense of this word is not to be searched in extraneous [1] Writers ; both because no matter like to that we treat upon did ever come into their use or consideration, and because they do seldom or never use the word in a sense any-wise congruous to this matter : in them most commonly the word διxαιόω doth signifie (as the like word ἀξιόω) to deem a thing just [2], equal, or fit (or simply to deem about [3] a thing.) Sometimes also (yet not often, as I take it) being applyed to an action, or cause, it importeth to make it appear lawfull, or just, as when we ordinarily say to justify what one saith or doeth ; (whence διxαίωμα in *Aristotle* is an argument proving the justice of a cause, *firmamentum causae*) but in them [4] very seldom or never it is applyed to persons ; and an example, I conceive, can hardly be produced, wherein it is so used.

III. In the Sacred Writings at large it is commonly applyed to persons, and that according to various senses, some more wide and general, some more restrained and particular. It there sometime denoteth generally to exercise any judicial act upon, in regard unto, or in behalf of a person ; to doe him right, or justice, in declaring the merit of his cause, or pronouncing sentence about him ; in acquitting, or condemning him for any cause, in obliging him to, or exempting him from any burthen, in dispensing to him any reward or punishment, indifferently : thus *Absalom* said, *O that I were made a judge in the land, that every man, which hath any sute or cause might come unto me*, והצדקתיו, xαὶ διxαιώσω αὐτὸν, *and I would justify him*, that is, *I would doe him right* [5] : and, in the 82. *Psalm* this charge is given to the Princes, or Judges ; *Defend the poor, and fatherless*, הצדיקו, διxαιώσατε, *justify the poor and needy* [6] ; that is, doe right, and justice to them.

But more particularly the word signifieth (and that according to the most usual and current acception) so to doe a man right, as to pronounce sentence in his favour, as to acquit him from guilt, to excuse him from burthen, to free him from punishment ; whence we most often meet with the word placed in direct opposition to that of condemnation : as in that law, *If there be a controversie*

---

[1] [outside Scripture].
[2] Ἐδιxαίωσαν [οἱ πατέρες], ἀντὶ τοῦ δίxαιον [εἶναι] ἔxριναν. BALS. *in Syn. Chalced.* Can. 1 [Theodorus Balsamon : *In Canones Synodi Chalcedonensis*, Canon 1, MIGNE, *Patrol. gr.*, t. 137, col. 384].
[3] [to judge].   [4] [in these extraneous writers].
[5] 2 Sam. XV, 4.   [6] Ps. LXXXII, 3.

between men, and they come unto judgment, that the Judges may judge them, then they shall justifie the righteous, and condemn the wicked [1]: And in Solomon's prayer, Then hear thou in heaven, and doe, and judge thy servants, condemning the wicked, to bring his way upon his head, and justifying the righteous, to give him according to his righteousness [2]: and in the Proverbs, He that justifieth the wicked, and he that condemneth the just, even both are an abomination unto the Lord [3]: And, in the Gospel our Saviour saith; By thy words thou shalt be justified, and by thy words thou shalt be condemned [4].

In consequence upon this sense, and with a little deflection from it, to justifie a person sometime [5] denoteth to approve him, or esteem him just, a mental judgment, as it were, being passed upon him; so wisedom is said to be justified, that is, approved by her children [6]: So in the Gospel some persons are said to justifie themselves [7], that is, to conceit themselves righteous: and the Publican went home justified rather than the Pharisee [8], that is, more approved and accepted by God: So also it is said, that All the people, and the Publicans justified God, being baptized with John's baptism [9]; they justified God, that is, they declared their approbation of God's proceeding, in the mission of John.

In like manner, Justification is taken for exemption from burthens; as where in the Acts St. Paul saith, And from all things, from which by the Law of Moses ye could not be justified, in this is every one that believeth justified [10].

It may also sometimes be taken for deliverance from punishment; as where in the Law God saith: The innocent and righteous slay thou not; for I will not justifie the wicked [11]; that is, not let him escape with impunity; according to that in the Proverbs; Though hand joyn in hand the wicked shall not go unpunished [12].

IV. We may observe, that (as every man hath some phrases and particular forms of speech in which he delighteth, so) this term is somewhat peculiar to St. Paul, and hardly by the other

[1] Deut. XXV, 1.
[2] 1 Kings VIII, 32; 2 Chr. VI, 23.
[3] Prov. XVII, 15.
[4] Matt. XII, 37; Isa. V, 23; XLIII, 9.
[5] [sometimes].
[6] Matt. XI, 19.   [7] Luke X, 29; XVI, 15.
[8] Luke XVIII, 14.
[9] Luke VII, 29.   [10] Acts XIII, 39.
[11] Exod. XXIII, 7.
[12] [Prov. XI, 21.]

Apostles applyed to that matter, which he expresseth thereby:
they usually in their Sermons, and Epistles, do speak the same
thing (whatever it be) in other terms, more immediately expressive
of the matter [1].   St. *James* indeed doth use it, but not so much,
it seemeth, according to his usual manner of speech, as occasionally;
to refute the false and pestilent conceits of some persons [2], who
mistaking St. *Paul's* expressions and doctrine, did pervert them to
the maintenance of *Solifidian* [3], *Eunomian* [4] and *Antinomian* positions, greatly prejudicial to good practice.   And seeing the term
is so proper to St. *Paul* in relation to this matter, the right sense
and notion thereof seemeth best derivable from considering the
nature of the subject he treateth on, observing the drift of his discourse and manner of his reasoning, comparing the other phrases
he useth equivalent to this, and interpretative of his meaning.

V.   Following this method of enquiry, I do observe and affirm
that the last notion of the Word, as it is evidently most usual in
the Scripture, so it best suteth to the meaning of St. *Paul* here,
and otherwhere commonly, where he treateth upon the same matters;   that God's justifying solely, or chiefly, doth import his
acquitting us from guilt, condemnation and punishment, by free
pardon and remission of our sins, accounting us, and dealing with
us as just persons, upright and innocent in his sight and esteem:
the truth of which notion I shall by divers arguments and considerations make good.

1.   This sense doth best agree to the nature of the subject
matter, and to the design of St. *Paul's* discourse;   which I take
to be this, the asserting the necessity, reasonableness, sufficiency
and excellency of the Christian dispensation in order to that, which
is the end of all Religion, the bringing men to happiness, and

---

[1] *Acts* XIII, 39;   II, 38;   III, 19;   V, 31;   X, 43;   XXII, 16;   *Luke*
XXIV, 47.

[2] [*Jas.* II, 21.]

[3] ['One who holds that faith alone, without works, is sufficient for justification.   The doctrine is based on *Rom.* iii.28, where Luther rendered πιστει by
"allein durch den Glauben"' (OED).   The term was mostly used to refer
(often pejoratively) to Luther's *articulus stantis aut cadentis Ecclesiae*, to which
Barrow alludes above (p. 428).   See in OED the quotation from Coleridge:
'The heroic Solifidian Martin Luther himself'.   St. James's Epistle is usually
believed to have glanced at the Simonians and Nicolatians, to whom Barrow
seems to attribute beliefs held by later churches or sects.   See Eunomians below.]

[4] [followers of Eunomius, extreme Arians, condemned by the Council of
Constantinople in 381].

consequently to the rendring men acceptable to God Almighty, who is the sole Authour and donour of happiness ; this is that, which in general he aimeth to assert and maintain.

This, I say, is that which he chiefly driveth at, to maintain, that it is not unreasonable that God should so proceed with men (whose good and felicity, as their gracious Maker, he greatly tendreth,) as the Christian Gospel declareth him to doe, but that rather such proceeding was necessary and fit in order to our salvation ; and withall conformable to the ordinary method of God's proceedings toward the same purpose.

Now God's proceeding with man according to the Gospel, the general tenour thereof doth set out to be this ; that, God, out of his infinite goodness and mercy, in consideration of what his beloved Son, our blessed Lord hath performed and suffered, in obedience to his will, and for the redemption of mankind (which by transgression of his laws and defailance [1] in duty toward him had grievously offended him and fallen from his favour, was involved in guilt, and stood obnoxious [2] to punishment) is become reconciled to them (passing by, and fully pardoning all offences by them committed against him) so as generally to proffer mercy upon certain reasonable and gentle terms, to all that shall sincerely embrace such overtures of mercy, and heartily resolve to comply with those terms, required by him ; namely, the returning and adhering to him, forsaking all impiety and iniquity, constantly persisting in faithfull obedience to his holy commandments : this, I say, is the proceeding of God, which the Christian Gospel doth especially hold forth, and which according to our Lord's commission and command the Apostles did first preach to men [3] ; as whosoever will consider the drift and tenour of their preaching, will easily discern ; which therefore St. *Paul* may reasonably be supposed here to assert and vindicate against the *Jews*, and other Adversaries of the Gospel ; consequently the terms he useth should be so interpreted as to express that matter ; whence being justified, will imply that which a person embracing the Gospel doth immediately receive from God, in that way of grace and mercy ; *viz.* an absolution from his former crimes, an acquittance from his debts, a state of innocence and guiltlesness in God's sight, an exemption from vengeance and punishment ; all that which by him sometimes, and

---

[1] [failing].   [2] [liable].   [3] *Luke* XXIV, 47.

by the other Apostles is couched under the phrases of *remission of sins* [1], having sins *blotted out* [2] and *washed away* [3], being *cleansed from sin* [4]; and the like: Thus considering the nature of the matter, and design of his discourse, would incline us to understand this word.

2. Again, the manner of his prosecuting his discourse, and the arguments by which he inferreth his conclusions concerning the Gospel, do confirm this notion. He discourseth, and proveth at large, that all mankind, both *Jews* and *Gentiles*, were *shut up under sin* [5], that *all had sinned and did fall short of the glory of God* [6] (that is, of rendring him his due glory by dutifull obedience) that *every mouth was stopped*, having nothing to say in defence of their transgressions, and *that all the world stood obnoxious to the severity of God's judgments* [7]; that not onely the light of nature was insufficient to preserve men from offending inexcusably, even according to the verdict of their own consciences, but that the written Law of God had (to manifold experience) proved ineffectual to that purpose [8], serving rather *to work wrath* [9], to bring men under a curse, to aggravate their guilt, to convince them of their sinfulness, to discourage and perplex them; upon which general state of men (so implicated in guilt, so lyable to wrath) is consequent a necessity either of condemnation and punishment, or of mercy and pardon.

He doth also imply (that which in the *Epistle* to the *Galatians*, where he prosecuteth the same argument, is more expresly delivered) that no precedent dispensation had exhibited any manifest overture, or promise of pardon; for the light of nature doth only direct unto duty, condemning every man in his own judgment and conscience [10], who transgresseth it, but as to pardon in case of transgression it is blind and silent; and the law of *Moses* rigorously exacteth punctual obedience, denouncing [11] in express terms a condemnation and curse to the transgressours thereof in any part [12]; from whence he collecteth, that *no man can be justified by the works of the Law* [13], (*natural*, or *Mosaical*; or that no precedent

---

[1] *Acts* XIII, 38; II, 38; V, 31.   [2] *Acts* III, 19.
[3] *Acts* XXII, 16.   [4] *1 John* I, 7.
[5] *Rom.* III, 9; XI, 32; *Gal.* III, 22.   [6] *Rom.* III, 23.
[7] *Rom.* III, 19 ὑπόδικος, ὑπόχρεως.   [8] *Rom.* VIII, 3; *Gal.* III, 21.
[9] *Rom.* IV, 15; III, 20; VII, 7; *Gal.* II, 16, 19; *Rom.* V, 20; VII, 8.
[10] *Rom.* I, 20; II, 15.   [11] [proclaiming].
[12] *Gal.* III, 10, 22.   [13] *Rom.* III, 20.

dispensation can justify any man) and that *a man is justified by faith*, or hath absolute need of such a justification as that, which the Gospel declareth and tendreth ; λογιζόμεθα οὖν, *we hence* (saith he) *collect*, or argue, *that a man is justified by faith, without the works of the Law* [1] : which justification must therefore import the receiving that free pardon, which the criminal and guilty world did stand in need of, which the forlorn and deplorable state of mankind did groan for, without which no man could have any comfort in his mind, any hope, or any capacity of salvation. If the state of Man was a state of rebellion, and consequently of heinous guilt, of having forfeited God's favour, of obnoxiousness [2] to God's wrath ; then that justification, which was needfull, was a dispensation of mercy, remitting that guilt, and removing those penalties.

Again, St. *Paul* commendeth the excellency of the Evangelical dispensation from hence, that it entirely doth ascribe the justification of men to God's mercy and favour, excluding any merit of man, any right or title thereto grounded upon what Man hath performed ; consequently advancing the glory of God, and depressing the vanity of Man : *If* (saith he) *Abraham were justified by works, he had whereof to boast, for that to him, who worketh, wages are not reckoned as bestowed in favour, but are paid as debt* [3] ; so it would be, if men were justified by works, they might claim to themselves the due consequences thereof, impunity and reward ; they would be apt to please themselves, and boast of the effects arising from their own performances ; but if, as the Gospel teacheth, *men are justified freely (gratis) by God's mercy and grace* [4], without any regard to what they formerly have done, either good, or bad, those who have lived wickedly and impiously (upon their complyance with the terms proposed to them) being no less capable thereof, than the most righteous and pious persons [5] ; then *where is boasting ? it is excluded* [6] ; then surely no man can assume any thing to himself, then all the glory and praise are due to God's frank goodness : the purport of which reasoning (so often used) doth imply, that a man's justification signifieth his being accepted or approved as just, standing *rectus in curia*, being in God's esteem,

---

[1] *Rom.* III, 28.   [2] [liability to injury].
[3] *Rom.* IV, 2, 4 ; III, 27 ; *Tit.* III, 5 ; *Eph.* II, 9 ; *Rom.* XI, 6.
[4] *Rom.* III, 24.   [5] *Rom.* IV, 5.
[6] *Rom.* III, 27 ; *Eph.* II, 9.

and by his sentence absolved from guilt and punishment, the which cannot otherwise be obtained, than from divine favour declared and exhibited in the Gospel; according as St. *Paul* otherwhere fully speaketh: *To the praise of the glory of his grace, wherein he hath made us accepted in the beloved; in whom we have redemption through his bloud, the forgiveness of sins, according to the riches of his grace* [1].

Again, St. *Paul* expresseth Justification as an act of judgment, performed by God, whereby he declareth his own righteousness, or justice; that justice consisting in acceptance of a competent satisfaction offered to him in amends for the debt due to him, and in reparation of the injury done unto him, in consequence thereof acquitting the debtour, and remitting the offence; so those words declare: *Being justified freely by his grace, through the redemption that is in Christ Jesus; whom God hath set forth to be a propitiation, through faith in his bloud, to declare his righteousness for the remission of sins that are past, through the forbearance of God; to declare at this time his righteousness, that he might be just, and the justifier of him, which believeth in Jesus* [2]: Justification there we see is expressed [3] a result of Christ's redemption, and the act of God consequent thereon; so is remission of sins; God by them joyntly demonstrating his justice, and goodness, so that they may be well conceived the same thing diversly expressed, or having several names according to some divers formalities of respect [4]. So in other places, sometimes justification, sometimes remission of sins are reckoned the proper and immediate effects of our Saviour's passion: *Being* (saith St. *Paul* in the 5th to the *Romans*) *justified by his bloud, we shall be saved by him from wrath* [5]: and *In whom* (saith he again in the first of the Epistle to the *Ephesians*) *we have redemption through his bloud, the forgiveness of sins* [6]; which argueth the equivalency of these terms.

So likewise a main point of the Evangelical Covenant on God's part is made [7] justifying of a man by his faith, or upon it [8]; and remission of sins upon the same condition, is also made [9] the like principal point, which sometime is put alone as implying all the benefits of that covenant.

[1] *Eph.* I, 6, 7.   [2] *Rom.* III, 24, 25, 26.   [3] [said to be].
[4] [formal aspects under which it is considered].
[5] *Rom.* V, 9.   [6] *Eph.* I, 7; *Col.* I, 14.   [7] [is said to consist in].
[8] *Gal.* III *per tot.*; *Rom.* XI, 27.   [9] [is said to be].

Again, justification is by St. *Paul* made the immediate conse-quent, or special adjunct of Baptism ; therein he saith we *die to sin* [1] (by resolution and engagement to lead a new life in obedience to God's commandment) and so dying we are said to be justified from sin (that which otherwise is expressed, or expounded by being freed from sin ;) [2] now the freedom from sin obtained in Baptism is frequently declared to be the remission of sin then conferred, and solemnly confirmed by a visible seal.

Whereas [3] also so frequently we are said to be *justified by faith*, and according to the general tenour of Scripture the imme-diate consequent of faith is Baptism ; therefore dispensing the benefits consigned in Baptism is coincident with justification ; and that dispensation is frequently signified to be the cleansing us from sin by entire remission thereof [4].

3. Farther, The same notion may be confirmed by comparing this term with other terms and phrases equivalent, or opposite to this of justification.

One equivalent phrase is imputation of righteousness: *As* (saith St. *Paul*) *David speaketh of that man's blessedness, unto whom God imputeth righteousness without works ; Blessed are they, whose iniquities are forgiven, and whose sins are covered ; Blessed is the man, to whom the Lord will not impute sin* [5] ; whence to him that considers the drift and force of St. *Paul*'s discourse it will clearly appear, that justification, imputing righteousness, not imputing sin, and remission of sin are the same thing ; otherwise the Apostle's discourse would not signifie or conclude any thing.

For confirmation of his discourse (arguing free justification by God's mercy, not for our works) St. *Paul* also doth alledge that place in the Psalm, *For in thy sight shall no man living be justified* [6] ; the sense of which place is evidently this, that no man living, his actions being strictly tried and weighed, shall appear guiltless, or deserve to be acquitted ; but shall stand in need of mercy, or can no otherwise be justified than by a special act of grace.

Again, imputing faith for righteousness is the same with justi-fying by faith (*Abraham believed God, and it was counted unto*

---

[1] *Rom.* VI, 2.   [2] *Rom.* VI, 6, 7, 18, 22.   [3] [considering].
[4] *Eph.* V, 26 ; *Tit.* III, 5 ; *Acts* XIII, 38 ; XXII, 16.
[5] *Rom.* IV, 6, 7, 8.
[6] *Rom.* III, 19 ; *Gal.* II, 16 ; *Ps.* CXLIII, 2.

him for righteousness)[1] but that imputation is plainly nothing else, but the approving him, and taking him for a righteous person in regard to his faith.

Again, justification is the same with being righteous before God, as appeareth by those words : *Not the hearers of the Law are just before God, but the doers of the Law shall be justified*[2] ; but being just before God, plainly signifieth nothing else but being accepted by God, or approved to his esteem and judgment.

Being reconciled to God seemeth also to be the same with being justified by him ; as appeareth by those words, *Much more then being now justified by his bloud, we shall be saved from wrath through him ; for if when we were enemies, we were reconciled to God by the death of his Son, much more being reconciled, we shall be saved by his life*[3] : where πολλῷ μᾶλλον δικαιωθέντες, and πολλῷ μᾶλλον καταλλαγέντες, seem to signifie the same ; but that reconciliation is interpreted by remission of sins : *God was in Christ, reconciling the World unto himself, not imputing their trespasses unto them*[4].

To obtain mercy[5] is another term signifying justification, and what doth that import but having the remission of sins in mercy bestowed on us ?

Again, Justification is opposed directly to condemnation : *As* (saith he) *by the offence of one man* (judgment came) *upon all men to condemnation, so by the righteousness of one man* (the free gift came) *upon all men to justification of life*[6] (*justification of life*, that is, a justification so relating to life, or bestowing a promise thereof, as the condemnation opposite thereto respected death, which it threatned) In which place St. *Paul* comparing the first *Adam* with his actions, and their consequences, to the second *Adam* with his performances, and what resulted from them, teacheth us, that as the transgression of the *first* did involve mankind in guilt, and brought consequently upon men a general sentence of death, [a](forasmuch as all men did follow him in commission of sin ;) so the obedience of the *second* did absolve all men from guilt, and restored them consequently into a state of immortality (all men,

---

[a] forasmuch as] *T.* ; *B.* taking in that

[1] *Rom.* IV, 3, 22 ; *Gal.* III, 6.
[3] *Rom.* V, 9, 10.
[5] *Rom.* XI, 30, 31, 32 ; *1 Pet.* II, 10.

[2] *Rom.* II, 13.
[4] *2 Cor.* V, 19.
[6] *Rom.* V, 16, 18.

under the condition prescribed, who (as it is said) should *receive
the abundance of grace, and of the gift of righteousness* [1] tendered
to them ;) the justification therefore he speaketh of doth so import
an absolution from guilt and punishment, as the condemnation
signifieth a being declared guilty, and adjudged to punishment.

Bellarmine indeed (who in answering to this place objected
against his doctrine, blunders extremely, and is put to his trumps [2]
of Sophistry) telleth us, that in this place to maintain the parallel
or *antithesis* between *Adam* and *Christ*, justification must signifie
infusion of grace, or putting into a man's soul an inherent righteousness ; because *Adam*'s sin did constitute [3] us unjust with an
inherent unrighteousness [4] : but (with his favour) justification and
condemnation being both of them the acts of God, and it being
plain, that God condemning doth not infuse any inherent unrighteousness into man, neither doth he justifying (formally) (if the
antithesis must be patt,) put any inherent righteousness into him :
inherent unrighteousness in the former case may be a consequent
of that condemnation, and inherent righteousness may be connected
with this justification ; but neither *that*, nor *this* may formally
signifie those qualities respectively: as the inherent unrighteousness
consequent upon *Adam*'s sin is not included in God's condemning,
so neither is the inherent righteousness proceeding from our Saviour's
obedience contained in God's justifying men.

[a] But, however, most plainly (and beyond all evasions) justification and condemnation are opposed otherwhere in this *Epistle* :
Who (saith St. *Paul*) *shall lay any thing to the charge of God's
elect ?* (or criminate against them) *'tis God who justifieth, who
is he that condemneth ?* [5] what can be more clear, than that there
justification signifieth absolution from all guilt and blame ?

4. Farther, this notion may be confirmed, by excluding that
sense, which in opposition thereto is assigned, according to which
justification is said to import not onely remission of sin, and
acceptance with God, but the making a man intrinsecally righteous,
by infusing into him (as they speak) [6] a habit of grace, or charity ;
the putting into a man a *righteousness, by which* (as the Council

---

[a] But, however,] ; *B. 1683* But however

[1] *Rom.* V, 17.   [2] [his last expedients].   [3] [render].
[4] BELLARM. *de Justific.* II, iii ; I, i. [*Opera*, 1619, IV, 897 ; 814-5.]
[5] *Rom.* VIII, 33, 34. τίς ἐγκαλέσει κατὰ [ἐκλεκτῶν Θεοῦ ;].
[6] BELLARM. [*ibid.*] II, iii [ut supra].

of *Trent* expresseth it) *We are renewed in the spirit of our mind, and are not onely reputed, but are called, and become truly righteous, receiving righteousness in our selves* [1].

Now admitting this to be true, as in a sense it surely is, that whoever (according to St. *Paul's* meaning in this *Epistle*) is justified, is also really at the same time endewed with some measure of that intrinsick righteousness, which those men speak of (for as much as that faith, which is required to justification, (being a gift of God, managed by his providence, and wrought by his preventing [2] grace,) doth include a sincere and stedfast purpose of forsaking all impiety, of amendment of life, of obedience to God, which purpose *cleanseth the heart*, and is apt to produce as well inward righteousness of heart, as outward righteousness of practice; for that also to every sound believer upon his faith is bestowed the spirit of God, as a principle of righteousness, dwelling in him, directing, admonishing, exciting him to doe well [3]; assisting and enabling him sufficiently to the performance of those conditions, or those duties, which Christianity requireth, and the believer thereof undertaketh; which, the man's honest and diligent endeavour concurring, will surely beget the practice of all righteousness, and in continuance of such practice will render it habitual) avowing, I say, willingly, that such a righteousness doth ever accompany the justification St. *Paul* speaketh of, yet that sort of righteousness doth not seem implyed by the word Justification, according to St. *Paul's* intent, in those places, where he discourseth about justification by faith; for that such a sense of the word doth not well consist with the drift and efficacy of his reasoning, nor with divers passages in his discourse. For

1. Whereas St. *Paul* from the general depravation of manners in all men (both *Jews* and *Gentiles*) argueth the necessity of such a justification, as the Christian Gospel declareth and exhibiteth, if we should take Justification for infusing an inherent quality of righteousness into men, by the like discourse we might infer the

---

[1] Justitiam in nobis recipientes. [Hujus justificationis causae sunt... demum unica formalis causa est justitia Dei; non qua ipse justus est, sed qua nos justos facit; qua videlicet ab eo donati, renovamur spiritu mentis nostrae; et non modo reputamur, sed vere justi nominamur, et sumus, justitiam in nobis recipientes unusquisque suam secundum mensuram. *Canones et Decreta*, Sessio VI, De Justificatione, cap. vii; (Antwerpiae, 1604, p. 35)].

[2] [prevenient].

[3] *Rom.* VIII, 9; *1 Cor.* III, 16; *Acts* II, 38; *Eph.* IV, 23, 24; *2 Cor.* V, 17.

imperfection and insufficiency of Christianity it self, and consequently the necessity of another dispensation beside it ; for that
even all Christians (as St. *James* saith) do offend often, and commission of sin doth also much reign among them[1] ; so that St. *Paul's*
discourse (justification being taken in this sense) might strongly
be retorted against himself.

2.   Supposing that sense of Justification, a *Jew* might easily
invalidate St. *Paul's* ratiocination, by saying, that even their Religion did plainly enough declare such a justification, which God
did bestow upon all good men in their way, as by their frequent
acknowledgments and devotions is apparent ; such as those of the
Psalmist : *Create in me a clean heart, O God, renew a right Spirit
within me* [2]. *Teach me to doe thy will, for thou art my God* [3] :
*Make me to go in the path of thy commandments ; incline my
heart unto thy testimonies* [4] ; which sort of prayers God hearing
did infuse righteousness, and justified those persons in this sense ;
so that Christianity herein could not challenge any thing peculiar,
or could upon this score appear so necessary, as St. *Paul* pretendeth.

3.   From the justification St. *Paul* speaketh of, all respect to
any works, and to any qualifications in men (such as might beget
in them any confidence in themselves, or yield occasion of boasting)
is excluded ; it cannot therefore well be understood for [5] a constituting Man intrinsecally righteous, or infusing worthy qualities
into him ; but rather for an act of God terminated upon a man as
altogether unworthy of God's love, as impious, as an enemy, as
a pure object of mercy ; so it is most natural to understand those
expressions, importing the same thing ; *God justifieth the ungodly* [6] ; *we being sinners Christ dyed for us* [7] (purchasing, as the
following words imply, justification for us) *being yet enemies we
by his death were reconciled* [8] (or justified, for reconciliation and
justification, as we before noted, do there signify the same.)

4.   *Abraham* is brought in as an instance of a person justified
in the same manner, as Christians are according to the Gospel :
but his justification was merely the approving and esteeming him
righteous, in regard (not to any other good works, but) to his

---

[1] *Jas.* III, 2.   [2] *Ps.* LI, 10.   [3] *Ps.* CXLIII, 10.
[4] *Ps.* CXIX, 35, 36.   [5] [to mean].   [6] *Rom.* IV, 5.
[7] *Rom.* V, 8.   [8] *Rom.* V, 10.

stedfast faith, and strong persuasion concerning the power and faithfulness of God—because *he was fully persuaded, that what God had promised he was able to perform* [1]; to which faith and justification consequent thereon, St. *Paul* comparing those of Christians subjoyneth ; *Now it was not written for his sake alone, that it was imputed to him, but for us also, to whom it shall be imputed, if we believe on him, that raised up Jesus our Lord from the dead* [2]. As then it were an idle thing to fansie a righteousness, upon the score of that belief, dropt into *Abraham* ; and as his being justified is expresly called, having righteousness, upon the account of his faith, imputed (or ascribed) to him ; So our justification (like and answerable to his) should correspondently be understood, the approving and accounting us, notwithstanding our former transgressions, as righteous persons, in regard to that honest and stedfast faith, wherein we resemble *that Father of the faithfull.*

Even St. *James* himself, when he saith that *Abraham* and *Rahab* were justified by works, 'tis evident that he meaneth not that they had certain righteous qualities infused into them, or were made thence by God intrinsecally more righteous than they were before, but that they were approved and accepted by God, because of the good works they performed (in faith and obedience to God) one of them offering to sacrifice his Son, the other preserving the Spyes sent from God's people.

5.   The so often using the word Imputation of righteousness, instead of Justification, doth imply this act not to be a transient operation upon the soul of Man, but an act immanent to God's mind, respecting Man onely as its object, and translating him into another relative state : With this sense that word excellently well agreeth, otherwise it were obscure, and so apt to perplex the matter, that probably St. *Paul* would not have used it.

6.   Again, When it is said again and again, that *faith is imputed for righteousness*, it is plain enough, that no other thing in Man was required thereto ; to say, that he is thereby sanctified, or hath gracious habits infused, is uncouth [3] and arbitrarious : the obvious meaning is, that therefore he is graciously accepted and approved, as we said before.

7.   We might in fine add, that the word Justification is very seldom, or never used in that sense of making Persons righteous,

---

[1] *Rom.* IV, 21.   [2] *Rom.* IV, 23, 24.   [3] [strange, uncommon].

or infusing righteousness into them. *Bellarmine* and *Grotius* [1], having searched with all possible diligence, do alledge three or four places, wherein (with some plausible appearance) they pretend it must be so understood ; but as they are so few, so are they not any of them thoroughly clear and certain ; but are capable to be otherwise interpreted without much straining ; The clearest place, *Dan.* XII.3 the LXX reade מצדיקים, ἀπὸ δικαίων, which the *Hebrew*, and sense will bear [2]. Wherefore the other sense, which we have maintained, being undeniably common and current in the Scripture, and having so many particular reasons shewing it agreeable to St. *Paul's* intent, seemeth rather to be embraced.

In St. *Paul's* Epistles I can onely find three or four places, wherein the word *Justifying* may with any fair probability be so extended as to signify an internal operation of God upon the Soul of men ; they are these ;

*And such were some of you ; but ye have been washed, but ye have been sanctified, but ye have been justified in the name of Christ Jesus, and * by the Spirit of our God* [3] ; where Justification being performed by the Spirit of God, seemeth to imply, a spiritual operation upon a man's soul, as an ingredient thereof.

According to his mercy he saved us, by the laver of regeneration, and renewing of the holy Ghost ; which he poured on us richly by Jesus Christ our Saviour ; that being justified by his grace, we may be made heirs ; according to the hope of everlasting life [4] ; where God's justifying us by the Grace of Christ seemeth to include the renewing by the holy Ghost.

He that dyeth, is justified from sin [5] ; where St. *Paul* speaking about our obligation to lead a new life in holy obedience, upon account of our being dedicated to Christ, and renouncing sin in

---

[1] [BELLARMINE: *op. cit.*, p. 898; GROTIUS: *Annotationes in Epistolas Pauli*; ad Romanos, *Opera*, Amstelodami, 1679, t. II, vol. II, p. 672 ; yet cp. *Defensio Fidei Catholicae de Satisfactione Christi adv. Faustum Socinum, ibid.*, t. III, p. 304 : "Quanquam enim abluere, mundare, et voces similes significare possint aut efficere ne peccata committantur in posterum, aut commissa ne apparent, posterior tamen interpretatio Scripturae phrasi est convenientior. Sic deleri iniquitates exponitur peccatorum non recordari, *Esaiae*, xliii, 25, et mundare ab iniquitate idem esse ostenditur quod condonare, *Jerem.* xxxiii, 8."].

[2] Barrow is probably referring to the translation of *Daniel* by Theodotion (end of 2nd C.), which appears in all but two of the mss. of the Septuagint, but he leaves out the article (ἀπὸ τῶν δικαίων) in accordance with the Hebrew word he quotes. I owe this to my colleague Professor Ch. Fontinoy.

[3] *1 Cor.* VI, 11. * ἐν [τῷ πνεύματι τοῦ Θεοῦ ἡμῶν].

[4] *Tit.* III, 5, 6, 7.   [5] *Rom.* VI, 7.

Baptism, may be interpreted to mean a being really in our hearts purified and freed from sin.

Whom he predestinated, those he called ; and whom he called, those he justified, and whom he justified, those he glorified[1] ; where the chief acts of God toward those, who finally shall be saved, being in order purposely recited, and Justification being immediately (without interposing Sanctification) coupled to Glorification, the word may seem to comprize Sanctification.

If considering these places (which yet are not clearly prejudicial to the notion we have made good, but may well be interpreted so as to agree thereto) it shall seem to any, that St. *Paul* doth not ever so strictly adhere to that notion, as not sometime to extend the word to a larger sense, I shall not much contend about it ; It is an ordinary thing for all Writers to use their words sometimes in a larger, sometimes in a stricter sense ; and it sufficeth to have shewn, that where St. *Paul* purposely treateth about the matter we discourse upon, the purport of his discourse argueth, that he useth it according to that notion, which we have proposed.

8.   I shall onely add one small observation, or conjecture favouring this notion ; which is the probable occasion of all St. *Paul's* discourse and disputation about this Point, which seemeth to have been this.   That Christianity should (upon so slender a condition or performance, as that of Faith) tender unto all persons indifferently, however culpable, or flagitious their former lives had been, a plenary remission of sins and reception into God's favour, did seem an unreasonable and implausible thing to many[2] ; The *Jews* could not well conceive, or relish that any man so easily should be translated into a state equal, or superiour to that, which they took themselves peculiarly to enjoy ; The *Gentiles* themselves (especially such as conceited well of their own wisdom and vertue) could hardly digest it ; *Celsus* in *Origen* could not imagine or admit that bare faith should work such a miracle[3], as presently to turn a dissolute person into a Saint, beloved of God, and designed to happiness.

Zozimus saith of *Constantine*, that he chose Christianity as the onely Religion, that promised impunity and pardon for his

---

[1] *Rom.* VIII, 30.

[2] Vid. CYRIL. *adv. Julian.*, lib. VII, p. 248, where justification is very well described.   [MIGNE, *Patrol. gr.*, t. 76, col. 880].

[3] φιλὴ πίστις.   [*Contra Celsum*, I, MIGNE, *Patrol. gr.*, t. 11, col. 673].

enormous [1] practices [2] ; intimating his dislike of that Point in our Religion ; This prejudice against the Gospel St. *Paul* removeth ; by shewing that because of all mens guilt and sinfulness such an exhibition of mercy, such an overture of acceptance, such a remission of sin was necessary in order to salvation, so that without it no man could be exempted from wrath and misery ; and that consequently all other Religions (as not exhibiting such a remission,) were to be deemed in a main Point defective : When therefore he useth the word Justification to express this matter, it is reasonable to suppose that he intendeth thereby to signify that remission, or dispensation of mercy.

It may be objected that St. *Austin* and some others of the *Fathers* do use the word commonly according to the sense of the *Tridentine* Council : I answer, that the point having never been discussed, and they never having thoroughly considered the sense of St. *Paul*, might unawares take the word as it sounded in *Latine*, especially the sense they affixed to it, signifying a matter very true and certain in Christianity. The like hath happened to other *Fathers* in other cases ; and might happen to them in this, not to speak accurately in points that never had been sifted by disputation. More I think we need not say in answer to their authority.

VI. So much may suffice for a general explication of the notion ; but for a more full clearing of the Point, it may be requisite to resolve a question concerning the time, when this act is performed, or dispensed ; It may be enquired when God justifieth, whether once, or at several times, or continually ; To which question I answer briefly :

1. That the justification which St. *Paul* discourseth of, seemeth in his meaning, onely or especially to be that act of grace, which is dispensed to persons at their Baptism, or at their entrance into the Church, when they openly professing their faith, and undertaking the practice of Christian duty God most solemnly and formally doth absolve them from all guilt, and accepteth them into a state of favour with him ; that St. *Paul* onely or chiefly respecteth [3] this act, considering his design, I am inclined to think, and many passages in his discourse seem to imply.

---

[1] [monstrous].
[2] [ZOSIMI *Historiae Novae*, ed. Henricus Stephanus, 1581, II, 61].
[3] [takes into account].

If his design were (as I conceive it probable) to vindicate the
proceeding of God, peculiarly declared in the Gospel, in receiving
the most notorious and heinous transgressours to grace in Baptism,
then especially must the justification he speaketh of relate to that ;
to confirm which supposition we may consider, that

i. In several places Justification is coupled with baptismal
regeneration and absolution : *Such were some of you, but ye have
been washed, ye have been sanctified, ye have been justified in the
name of Christ Jesus* [1] : (where by the way being sanctified, and
being justified, seem equivalent terms, as in that place, where Christ
is said to *have given himself for the Church, that he might sanctify it, and cleanse it with the washing of water by the Word* [2],
Sanctification (I conceive) importeth the same thing with Justification.)   Again, *He saved us by the laver of Regeneration, that
having been justified by his grace, we may be made heirs of everlasting life* [3].

ii.   St. *Paul* in expressing this act, as it respecteth the faithfull,
commonly doth use a tense referring to the past time : he saith
not δικαιούμενοι, being justified, but δικαιωθέντες, *having been justified* ; not δικαιοῦσθε, ye are justified, but δικαιώθητε, ye have been
justified [4], namely at some remarkable time, that is at their entrance
into Christianity.   (Our Translatours do render it according to the
present time, but it should be rendred, as I say, in our Text, and
in other places.)

iii.   St. *Paul*, in the 6th to the *Romans*, discourseth thus ; Seeing we in Baptism are cleansed and disentangled from sin, are
dead to it, and so justified from it, God forbid that we should
return to live in the practice thereof, so abusing and evacuating
the grace we have received ; which discourse seemeth plainly to
signifie, that he treateth about the justification conferred in Baptism.

iv.   He expresseth the justification he speaketh of by the words
πάρεσις τῶν προγεγονότων ἁμαρτημάτων, *the passing over foregoing
sins* [5], which seemeth to respect that universal absolution, which is
exhibited in Baptism.   *Being* (saith he) *justified freely by his
grace, through the redemption, that is in Christ Jesus ; whom God
hath set forth to be a propitiation through faith in his bloud, to*

[1] *1 Cor.* VI, 11.   [2] *Eph.* V, 25, 26 ; *Heb.* X, 29.
[3] *Tit.* III, 5, 6, 7 ; *Heb.* X, 22, 23.
[4] *Rom.* V, 1, 9 ; *Tit.* III, 7 ; *1 Cor.* VI, 11.
[5] *Rom.* III, 25.

declare his righteousness, for the remission of sins that are past,
through the forbearance of God.

v. The relation this justification hath to faith, being dispensed
in regard thereto (or upon condition thereof) doth infer the same :
Faith is nothing else, but a hearty embracing Christianity, which
first exerteth it self by open declaration and avowal in Baptism
(when we *believe with our hearts to righteousness, and confess with*
our mouth to salvation ;)[1] to that time therefore the act of Justification may be supposed especially to appertain : (then, when the
Evangelical covenant is solemnly ratified, the grace thereof especially is conferred.) Upon such considerations I conceive that
St. *Paul*'s justification chiefly doth respect that act of grace, which
God consigneth to us at our Baptism. But farther,

2. The vertue and effect of that first justifying act doth continue (we abide in a justified state) so long as we do perform the
conditions imposed by God, and undertaken by us at our first
justification; *holding fast the profession of our hope without waver-*
ing [2] ; *keeping faith, and a good conscience* [3] ; so long as we do
not forfeit the benefit of that grace by *making shipwreck of faith*
and a good conscience [3], relapsing into infidelity, or profaneness
of life. Our case is plainly like to that of a subject, who having
rebelled against his Prince, and thence incurred his displeasure,
but having afterward upon his submission by the clemency of his
Prince obtained an act of pardon, restoring him to favour, and
enjoyment of the protection and privileges sutable to a loyal subject,
doth continue in this state, [a] untill by forsaking his allegiance, and
running again into rebellion, he so loseth the benefit of that pardon,
that his offence is aggravated thereby ; so if we do persevere firm
in faith and obedience, we shall (according to the purport of the
Evangelical covenant) continue in the state of grace and favour
with God, and in effect remain justified ; otherwise the virtue of
our justification ceaseth ; and we in regard thereto are more deeply
involved in guilt.

3. Although Justification chiefly signifieth the first act of grace
toward a Christian at his Baptism, yet (according to analogy of
reason, and affinity in the nature of things) every dispensation

[a] untill] *T.* ; *B.* while.

[1] *Rom.* X, 9, 10.   [2] *Heb.* X, 23.
[3] *1 Tim.* I, 19 ; *2 Pet.* II, 20, etc. ; *Heb.* X, 26, 38 ; VI, 1.

of pardon granted upon repentance, may be styled Justification ;
for as particular acts of repentance, upon the commission of any
particular sins, do not so much differ in nature, as in measure or
degree from that general conversion, practised in embracing the
Gospel ; So the grace vouchsafed upon these penitential acts, is
onely in largeness of extent, and solemnity of administration
diversified from that ; Especially considering that repentance after
Baptism is but a reviving of that first great resolution and engagement we made in Baptism [1] ; that remission of sin upon it is onely
the renovation of the grace then exhibited ; that the whole transaction in this case is but a reinstating the covenant then made (and
afterward by transgression infringed) upon the same terms, which
were then agreed upon ; that consequently (by congruous analogy)
this remission of sins, and restoring to favour granted to a penitent
are onely the former justification reinforced : whence they may
bear its name ; but whether St. *Paul* ever meaneth the word to
signifie thus, I cannot affirm.

Now according to each of these notions all good Christians
may be said to have been justified ; they have been justified by a
general abolition of their sins, and reception into God's favour in
Baptism ; they so far have enjoyed the virtue of that gracious
dispensation, and continued in a justified state, as they have per-
sisted in faith and obedience ; they have upon falling into sin,
and rising thence by repentance, been justified by particular remis-
sions. So that *having been justified by faith, they have peace with
God, through our Lord Jesus Christ* [a].

---

[a] Jesus Christ.] *T.* ; *B.* Jesus Christ, which having peace with God, and how
it comes through our Lord Jesus Christ, what it imports shall be the matter of
another discourse.

[1] Poenitentia imitatur baptismatis gratiam. Hier. *adv. Pelag.* I, 10 [Migne,
Patrol. lat., t. 23, col. 550].

OF OBEDIENCE TO OUR SPIRITUAL GUIDES AND GOVERNOURS

Heb. XIII.17. *Obey them that have the rule over you.*

Obedience unto Spiritual Guides and Governours is a duty of great importance ; the which to declare and press is very seasonable for these times, wherein so little regard is had thereto : I have therefore pitched on this Text, being an Apostolical precept, briefly and clearly enjoining that duty : and in it we shall consider and explain these two particulars : 1. The persons, to whom obedience is to be payed. 2. What that obedience doth import, or wherein it consisteth : and together with explication of the duty, we shall apply it, and urge its practice.

I. As to the persons, unto whom obedience is to be performed, they are generally speaking all Spiritual Guides, or Governours of the Church (those *who speak to us the word of God, and who watch for our souls*[1], as they are described in the context) expressed here by a term very significant and apposite, as implying fully the nature of their charge, the qualification of their persons, their rank, and privileges in the Church, together consequently with the grounds of obligation to the correspondent duties toward them. There are in Holy Scripture divers names and phrases appropriate to them, each of them denoting some eminent part of their office, or some appurtenance thereto ; but this seemeth of all most comprehensive ; so that unto it all the rest are well reducible : the term is ἡγούμενοι, that is *Leaders*, or *Guides*, or *Captains* ; which properly may denote the subsequent particulars in way of duty, or privilege appertaining to them.

1. It may denote eminence of dignity, or superiority to others : that they are (as it is said of *Judas* and *Silas* in the *Acts*)[2] ἄνδρες ἡγούμενοι ἐν ἀδελφοῖς, *principal men among the brethren* : for to *lead* implieth precedence, which is a note of superiority and

---

[1] *Heb.* XIII, 7, 17.   [2] *Acts* XV, 22.

preeminence.   Hence are they styled προεστῶτες [1], *Presidents* or
Prelates ; οἱ πρῶτοι [2], *the first*, or *prime* men ; οἱ μείζους, *the greater*,
Majors, or Grandees among us : *He* (saith our *Lord*) *that will be
the first among you, let him be your servant* [2] ;   and *He that is
greater among you, let him be as the younger ; and he that is chief,
as he that doth serve* [3] ;   where ὁ μείζων, and ὁ ἡγούμενος (the
greater and the *Leader*) are terms equivalent, or interpretative the
one of the other ;   and our *Lord* in those places as he prescribeth
humility of mind and demeanour ;   so he implieth difference of
rank among his Disciples : whence to render especial respect and
honour to them, as to our betters, is a duty often enjoined [4].

2.   It doth imply power, and authority : their superiority is
not barely grounded on personal worth or fortune ;   it serveth not
merely for order, and pomp ;   but it standeth upon the nature of
their office, and tendeth to use : they are by God's appointment
enabled to exercise acts of power ;   to command, to judge, to check,
controll, and chastise in a spiritual way, in order to spiritual ends ;
(the regulation of God's worship and service, the preservation of
order and peace, the promoting of edification in divine knowledge
and holiness of life) so are they ἡγούμενοι, as that word in common
use (as the word ἡγεμὼν of kin to it) doth signify *Captains* and
Princes ;   importing authority to command and rule ;   (whence the
Hebrew word נשיא a *Prince* is usually rendred by it [5] ;   and ὁ
ἡγούμενος, is the title, attributed to our *Lord*, to express his Kingly
function, being the same with ἀρχηγὸς, the *Prince* or *Captain*)
Hence are they otherwise styled κυβερνήσεις [6] (*Governours*) ἐπί-
σκοποι [7] (*Overseers*, or *Superintendents*, as St. *Hierome* rendreth
it) [8] *Pastors* [9] (a word often signifying *rule*, and attributed to civil
Governours) πρεσβύτεροι [10] (*Elders*, or *Senators* ; the word denoteth
not merely age, but office and authority) οἱ ἐπιμελοῦντες [11], *such as
take care for*, the *Curators*, or *Supravisors of the Church* : Hence
also they are signally and specially in relation unto God styled
δοῦλοι (*the Servants*) διάκονοι (*the Ministers*) ὑπηρέται (*the Officers*) λειτουργοὶ (*the publick Agents*) οἰκονόμοι (*the Stewards*)

[1] *1 Tim.* V, 17 ; *Rom.* XII, 8 ; *1 Thess.* V, 12.
[2] *Matt.* XX, 27.   [3] *Luke* XXII, 26.
[4] *Phil.* II, 29 ; *1 Thess.* V, 13 ; *1 Tim.* V, 17.
[5] *Matt.* II, 6 ; *Acts* V, 31.
[6] *1 Cor.* XII, 28.   [7] *Acts* XX, 28.
[8] [*Epistola* CXLVI, Migne, *Patrol. lat.*, t. 22, col. 1193].
[9] *Ps.* LXXVIII, 71.   [10] *1 Pet.* V, 2.
[11] *2 Sam.* V, 2 ; VII, 7 ; *1 Tim.* III, 5.

συνεργοὶ (the Coadjutors, or Assistants) πρέσβεις (the Legates)
ἄγγελοι (the Angels, or Messengers) of God [1]; which titles imply,
that God by them, as his substitutes and instruments, doth administer the affairs of his spiritual Kingdom : that as by secular
Magistrates (his Vice-gerents and Officers) he manageth his Universal temporal Kingdom, or governeth all men in order to their
worldly peace and prosperity ; so by these spiritual Magistrates
he ruleth his Church, toward its spiritual welfare and felicity.

3. The word also doth imply direction, or instruction ; that is
guidance of people in the way of truth and duty, reclaiming them
from errour and sin : this as it is a means hugely conducing to
the design of their office, so it is a principal member thereof :
whence διδάσκαλοι [2], Doctours, or Masters in doctrine, is a common
name of them ; and to be διδακτικοὶ [3], able and apt to teach (ἱκανοὶ
διδάξαι and πρόθυμοι) [4] is a chief qualification of their persons ;
and to attend on teaching, to be instant in preaching, to labour in
the word and doctrine are their most commendable performances [5] :
hence also they are called Shepherds, because they feed the souls
of God's people with the food of wholsome instruction ; Watch-
men, because they observe mens ways, and warn them when they
decline from right, or run into danger ; the Messengers of God,
because they declare God's mind and will unto them for the regulation of their Practice.

4. The word farther may denote exemplary Practice ; for to
lead implieth so to go before, that he who is conducted may follow ;
as a Captain marcheth before his troop ; as a Shepherd walketh
before his flock, as a Guide goeth before the Traveller, whom he
directeth ; hence they are said to be, and enjoined to behave themselves as patterns of the flock ; and the people are charged to
imitate, and follow them [6].

Such in general doth the word here used imply the persons
to be, unto whom obedience is prescribed ; but there is farther
some distinction to be made among them ; there are degrees and
subordinations in these guidances ; some are in regard to different

---

[1] 2 Tim. II, 24 ; Rom. XV, 16 ; 1 Cor. IV, 1, 2 ; III, 9 ; VI, 4 ; XVI, 15 ;
2 Cor. VI, 4 ; Tit. I, 1 ; Gal. IV, 14 ; Apoc. [Rev.] I, 29.
[2] Eph. IV, 11 ; 1 Cor. XII, 28 ; Rom. XII, 7.
[3] 1 Tim. III, 2.   [4] 2 Tim. II, 24 ; II, 2.
[5] 1 Tim. IV, 13, 16 ; V, 17 ; 2 Tim. IV, 2 ; Col. I, 28.
[6] 1 Pet. V, 3 ; 1 Tim. IV, 12 ; Phil. III, 17 ; Tit. II, 7 ; 2 Thess. III, 9, 7 ;
Heb. XIII, 7 ; 1 Thess. I, 6 ; 1 Cor. XI, 1 ; IV, 16.

persons both empowred to guide, and obliged to follow, or obey.

The Church is *acies ordinata*, a well marshalled Army ; where-in under the *Captain General of our faith and salvation*[1] (*the Head of the Body*[2], the Sovereign Prince and Priest, the *Arch-pastor*[3], the chief *Apostle of our profession*[4], and *Bishop of our Souls*)[5] there are divers Captains serving in fit degrees of subordination ; Bishops commanding larger regiments, Presbyters ordering less numerous companies ; all which by the bands of common faith, of mutual charity, of holy communion, and peace being combined together do in their respective stations govern and guide, are governed and guided : The Bishops, each in his precincts guiding more immediately the Priests subject to them ; the Priests, each guiding the people committed to his charge ; all Bishops and Priests being guided by Synods established, or congregated upon emergent occasion ; many of them ordinarily by those principal Bishops, who are regularly setled in a presidency over them ; according to the distinctions constituted by God and his Apostles, or introduced by humane prudence, as the preservation of order and peace (in various times and circumstances of things) hath seemed to require ; to which subordination the two great *Apostles* may seem to have regard, when they bid us ὑποτάσσεσθαι ἀλλήλοις, *to be subject to one another*[6] ; their injunction at least may, according to their general intent (which aimeth at the preservation of order and peace) be well extended so far.

Of this distinction there was never in ancient times made any question[7], nor did it seem disputable in the Church, except to one malecontent (*Aerius*)[8] who did indeed get a name in story[9], but never made much noise, or obtained any vogue in the World : very few followers he found in his heterodoxy ; No great body even of *Hereticks* could find cause to dissent from the Church in this point ; but all *Arians, Macedonians*[10],

---

[1] [*Heb.* II, 10.]   [2] [*Col.* I, 18.]   [3] *1 Pet.* V, 4.
[4] *Heb.* III, 1.   [5] [*1 Pet.* II, 25.]
[6] *1 Pet.* V, 5 ; *Eph.* V, 21 ; *Phil.* II, 3.
ʿΥποτασσέσθω ἕκαστος τῷ πλησίον αὐτοῦ καθὼς καὶ ἐτέθη ἐν τῷ χαρίσματι αὐτοῦ. CLEM. *ad Corinth.*, p. 49 [CLEM. ROM. *Ad Corinthios*, Ep. I, cap. xxxviii, MIGNE, *Patrol. gr.*, t. 1, col. 284].
[7] CYP. *Ep.* X, *Ep.* XII, *Ep.* XXVII, *Ep.* LXV [MIGNE, *Patrol. lat.*, t. 4].
[8] [friend of Eustathius, ordained by him, later became his rival and taught that there was no distinction between presbyter and bishop. 4th C.]
[9] [history].
[10] [Macedonius, elected bishop of Constantinople by the Arian bishops in 314, became the leader of the Pneumatomachi, Macedonians or Marathonians.]

Novatians [1], *Donatists* [2], etc. maintained the distinction of Ecclesiastical orders among themselves, and acknowledged the duty of the inferiour Clergy to their Bishops : and no wonder, seeing it standeth upon so very firm and clear grounds ; upon the reason of the case, upon the testimony of Holy Scripture, upon general tradition and unquestionable monuments of antiquity, upon the common judgment and practice of the greatest Saints, persons most renowned for wisedom and piety in the Church.

Reason plainly doth require such subordinations ; for that without them it is scarce possible to preserve any durable concord, or charity in Christian Societies ; to establish any decent harmony in the worship, and service of God, to check odious scandals, to prevent or repress banefull factions, to guard our religion from being overspread with pernicious heresies, to keep the Church from being shattered into numberless Sects, and thence from being crumbled into nothing ; in fine, for any good time to uphold the profession, and practice of Christianity it self : for, how if there be not setled Corporations of Christian people, having bulk and strength sufficient by joint endeavour to maintain the truth, honour, and interest of their religion, if the Church should onely consist of independent and incoherent particles (like dust or sand) easily scattered by any wind of opposition from without, or by any commotion within ; if *Christendom* should be merely a *Babel* of confused opinions and practices, how I say, then could Christianity subsist ? how could the simple among so discordant apprehensions be able to discern the truth of it, how would the wise be tempted to dislike it, being so mangled, and disfigured ? what an object of contempt and scorn would it be to the profaner World, in such a case ? It needeth therefore considerable societies to uphold it ; but no Society (especially of any large extent) can abide in order and peace, under the management of equal and coordinate powers ; without a single undivided authority, enabled to moderate affairs,

---

[1] [Sect founded by Novatianus, a Roman presbyter, one of the earliest antipopes (beginning of 3rd cent.); he excluded from ecclesiastical communion all those who after baptism had sacrificed to idols (*lapsi*). Novatians later called themselves καθαροί or Puritans. See Epistles of Cyprian.]

[2] [Sect in N. Africa, of same character as the Novatians ; they believed that 'all sacerdotal acts depended upon the personal character of the agent' (*Enc. Brit.*) and therefore denied the elegibility for sacerdotal office of the *traditores*, i.e. those who had delivered up their copies of Scripture under Diocletian ; condemned by the synod of Arles (314) but restored under Julian.]

and reduce them to a point, to arbitrate emergent cases of difference, to put good orders in execution, to curb the adversaries of
order and peace; these things cannot be well performed, where there
is a parity of many concurrents, apt to dissent, and able to check
each other [1] : no *Democracy* can be supported without borrowing
somewhat from *Monarchy*; no body can live without a head ; an
Army cannot be without a General, a Senate without a President,
a Corporation without a Supreme Magistrate [2] : this all experience
attesteth ; this even the chief impugners of *Episcopal* presidency
do by their practice confess ; who for prevention of disorder have
been fain [3] of their own heads to devise Ecclesiastical subordinations of *Classes, Provinces* and *Nations*; and to appoint *Mode-
ratours* (or temporary Bishops) in their assemblies ; so that reason
hath forced the dissenters from the Church to imitate it.

If there be not inspectours over the doctrine and manners of
the common Clergy, there will be many who will say and doe any
thing ; they will in teaching please their own humour, or sooth the
people, or serve their own interests ; they will indulge themselves
in a licentious manner of life ; they will clash in their doctrines,
and scatter the people, and draw them into factions.

It is also very necessary for preserving the unity and communion
of the parts of the Catholick Church ; seeing single persons are
much fitter to maintain correspondence, than headless bodies.

The very credit of religion doth require, that there should be
persons raised above the common level, and endued with eminent
authority, to whose care the promoting it should be committed ;
for such as the persons are, who manage any profession, such will
be the respect yielded thereto ; if the ministers of religion be men
of honour and authority, religion it self will be venerable ; if *those*
be mean, *that* will become contemptible.

---

[1] Ecclesiae salus in summi Sacerdotis dignitate consistit, cui si non exors
quaedam, et ab omnibus eminens detur potestas, tot in Ecclesia efficiuntur
schismata, quot sacerdotes. HIER. *in Lucif.* [*Dialogus contra Luciferianos,*
MIGNE, *Patrol. lat.,* t. 23, col. 173].
   Nec Presbyterum cœtus rite constitutus dici potest, in quo nullus sit ἡγούμενος. BEZ. *de Grad. Min.,* cap. 22 [*Ad Tractationem De Ministrorum Evangelii
Gradibus, ab Hadriano Saravia Belga editam, Theodori Bezae Responsio,* Geneva,
1592, p. 132].
[2] Essentiale fuit, quod ex Dei Ordinatione perpetua necesse fuit, est, et erit,
ut presbyterio quispiam et loco et dignitate Primus actioni gubernandae praesit
cum eo, quod ipsi divinitus attributum est jure. BEZ. *de Min. Evang. Grad.,*
cap. 23, p. 153. [*op. cit.,* p. 153].
[3] [obliged].

The Holy Scripture also doth plainly enough countenance this distinction ; for therein we have represented one *Angel* presiding over principal Churches [1], which contained several *Presbyters* ; therein we find Episcopal ordination, and jurisdiction exercised ; we have one *Bishop* constituting *Presbyters* in divers *Cities* of his *Diocese* ; Ordering all things therein concerning ecclesiastical displine [2] ; judging Presbyters [3], rebuking, μετὰ πάσης ἐπιταγῆς, *with all authority* [4] (or imperiousness, as it were ;) and reconciling Offenders, secluding [5] Hereticks, and scandalous persons.

In the *Jewish* Church there were an *High-priest, Chief-priest,* a *Sanedrin,* or *Senate,* or *Synod.*

The Government of Congregations among God's ancient people (which it is probable was the pattern that the *Apostles,* no affecters of needless innovation, did follow in establishing ecclesiastical discipline among Christians) doth hereto agree ; for in their *Synagogues,* answering to our Christian Churches, they had as their *Elders* and *Doctours,* so over them an ἀρχισυνάγωγος [6], the *Head* of the *Eldership,* and *President* of the *Synagogue.*

The primitive general use of Christians most effectually doth back the Scripture, and interpret it in favour of this distinction ; scarce less than demonstrating it constituted by the *Apostles* ; for how otherwise is it imaginable, that all the *Churches* founded by the *Apostles* in several most distant, and disjoined places (at *Jerusalem,* at *Antioch,* at *Alexandria,* at *Ephesus,* at *Corinth,* at *Rome*) should presently conspire in acknowledgment and use of it ? how could it without apparent confederacy be formed, how could it creep in without notable clatter, how could it be admitted without considerable opposition, if it were not in the foundation of those Churches laid by the *Apostles* ? How is it likely, that in those times of grievous persecution falling chiefly upon the *Bishops* (when to be eminent among Christians yielded slender reward, and exposed to extreme hazard ; when to seek preeminence was in effect to court danger and trouble, torture and ruine) an ambition of irregularly advancing themselves above their brethren should so generally prevail among the ablest and best Christians ? How could those famous Martyrs for the Christian truth be some of

---

[1] *Apoc.* [*Rev.*] II, III, etc.
[2] *Tit.* I, 5.
[3] *1 Tim.* V, 1, 17, 19, 20, 22, etc.
[4] *Tit.* II, 15.
[5] [excluding].
[6] ראש הקהל

them so unconscionable as to affect[1], others so irresolute as to
yield to such injurious encroachments? and how could all the Holy
Fathers (persons of so renowned, so approved wisedom and integrity) be so blind as not to discern such a corruption, or so bad
as to abet it? how indeed could all God's Church be so weak as
to consent in judgment, so base as to comply in practice with it?
in fine, how can we conceive, that all the best monuments of
antiquity down from the beginning (the *Acts*, the *Epistles*, the
Histories, the *Commentaries*, the *Writings* of all sorts coming from
the Blessed *Martyrs*, and most Holy *Confessors* of our faith)
should conspire to abuse us; the which do speak nothing but
Bishops; long *Catalogues* and rows of *Bishops* succeeding in this
and that *City*; *Bishops* contesting for the faith against *Pagan*
Idolaters, and *Heretical* corrupters of Christian doctrine; *Bishops*
here teaching, and planting our religion by their labours, there
suffering and watering it with their bloud?

I could not but touch this point: but I cannot insist thereon;
the full discussion of it, and vindication of the truth from the cavils
advanced against the truth by modern dissenters from the Church,
having employed voluminous Treatises; I shall onely farther add,
that if any man be so dully, or so affectedly ignorant as not to see
the reason of the case, and the dangerous consequences of rejecting
this ancient form of discipline; if any be so overweeningly presumptuous, as to question the faith of all History, or to disavow
those Monuments and that tradition, upon the testimony whereof
even the truth and certainty of our religion, and all its sacred
Oracles do rely; if any be so perversly contentious, as to oppose
the custome[2], and current practice of the Churches through all ages
down to the last age; so self-conceitedly arrogant, as to condemn
or slight the judgment, and practice of all the Fathers (together
also with the opinion of the later most grave *Divines*, who have
judged Episcopal presidency needfull, or expedient, where practicable) so peevishly refractary as to thwart the setled order of that
Church, in which he was baptized, together with the law of the
Countrey, in which he was born; upon such a person we may
look as one utterly invincible, and intractable: so weak a judgment,
and so strong a will who can hope by reason to convert? I shall
say no more to that Point.

---

[1] [to aim at].   [2] *1 Cor.* XI, 16.

The ἡγούμενοι then, (the Guides and Governours) in our *Text* are primarily the *Bishops*, as the Superiour and chief Guides, each in his place according to order peaceably established ; then secondarily the *Presbyters* in their Station as Guides inferiour, together with the *Deacons* as their assistants ; such the Church always hath had, and such, by God's blessing, our Church now hath, toward whom the duty of obedience is to be performed.

To the consideration of that I should now proceed, but first it seemeth expedient to remove a main obstruction to that performance ; which is this ; a misprision [1], or doubt concerning the persons of our Guides and Governours ; for in vain it would be to teach or persuade us to obey them, if we do not know who they are, or will not acknowledge them : for as in religion it is *Primus Deorum cultus Deos credere, The first worship of God to believe God* (as *Seneca* saith)[2] so it is the first part of our obedience to our Governours to avow them ; it is at least absolutely prerequisite thereto. It was of old a precept of St. *Paul* to the *Thessalonians* ; *We beseech you brethren to know those, who labour among you, and preside over you*[3] ; and another to the *Corinthians* ; *Submit your selves* (saith he) *to such, and to every one that helpeth with us, and laboureth*—then he subjoineth, ἐπιγινώσκετε τοὺς τοιούτους, *acknowledge such*[4] ; there were, it seemeth, those in the *Apostolical* times, who would not know, or acknowledge their guides ; there were even those, who would not *admit* the *Apostles* themselves, (as St. *John* saith of *Diotrephes*)[5] who *resisted their words* (as St. *Paul* saith of *Alexander*)[6] to whom the *Apostles* were not *Apostles*, as St. *Paul* intimateth concerning some in regard to himself ; there were then *Pseud-apostles*, who excluded the *true Apostles*, intruding themselves into that high office[7] : No wonder then it may be, that now in these dregs of time, there should be many, who disavow, and desert their true Guides, transferring the observance due to them upon bold pretenders ; who are not indeed Guides, but seducers ; not Governours, but Usurpers, and sacrilegious invaders of this holy Office : The duty we speak of cannot be secured without preventing or correcting this grand mistake ; and this we hope to compass by representing a double character

---

[1] [failure to recognize as valuable].
[2] SEN. *Ep.* XCV, [50].
[3] *1 Thess.* V, 12.
[4] *1 Cor.* XVI, 16, 18.
[5] *3 John* 10.
[6] *2 Tim.* IV, 15.
[7] *2 Cor.* IX, 2 ; XI, 13 ; *Phil.* III, 2.

or description, one of the *true Guides*, another of the *counterfeits*, by comparing which we may easily distinguish them, and consequently be induced dutifully to avow and follow the one sort, wisely to disclaim and decline the other.

Those, I say, then, who constantly do profess, and teach that sound and wholesome doctrine, which was delivered by our Lord, and his Apostles in word and writing, was received by their Disciples in the primitive Churches, was transmitted and confirmed by general tradition, was sealed by the bloud of the blessed *Martyrs*, and propagated by the labours of the Holy Fathers ; the which also manifestly recommendeth and promoteth true reverence and piety toward God, justice and charity toward men, order and quiet in humane Societies, purity and sobriety in each man's private conversation :

Those who celebrate the true worship of God, and administer the Holy Mysteries of our religion in a serious, grave, decent manner, purely and without any notorious corruption either by hurtfull errour, or superstitious foppery, or irreverent rudeness, to the advancement of God's honour, and edification of the participants in vertue and piety.

Those who derive their authority by a continued succession from the *Apostles* ; who are called unto, and constituted in their office in a regular and peaceable way, agreeable to the institution of God, and the constant practice of his Church ; according to rules approved in the best and purest Ages : who are prepared to the exercise of their function by the best education, that ordinarily can be provided, under sober discipline, in the Schools of the Prophets, who thence by competent endowments of mind, and usefull furniture of good learning, acquired by painfull study, become qualified to guide and instruct the people : who after previous examination of their abilities, and probable testimonies concerning their manners (with regard to the qualifications of incorrupt doctrine, and sober conversation prescribed by the *Apostles*) are adjudged fit for the office [1] ; who also in a pious, grave, solemn manner, with invocation of God's blessing, by *laying on the hands of the Presbytery* [2] are admitted thereunto.

Those whose practice in guiding and governing the people of God is not managed by arbitrary, uncertain, fickle, private

---

[1] *1 Tim.* III, 7, 10.   [2] [*1 Tim.* IV, 14.]

fancies or humours, but regulated by standing Laws; framed (according to general directions extant in Holy Scripture) by pious and wise persons, with mature advice, in accommodation to the seasons and circumstances of things for common edification, order and peace.

Those who, by virtue of their good principles, in their disposition and demeanour appear sober, orderly, peaceable, yielding meek submission to Government, tendring [1] the Churches peace, upholding the communion of the Saints, abstaining from all schismatical, turbulent and factious [2] practices.

Those also, who are acknowledged by the Laws of our Countrey, an obligation to obey whom is part of that *humane constitution*, unto which we are in all things (not evidently repugnant to God's Law) indispensably bound to submit [3]; whom our Sovereign, God's Vicegerent and the nursing Father of his Church among us (unto whom in all things high respect, in all lawfull things entire obedience is due) doth command and encourage us to obey:

Those, I say, to whom this character plainly doth agree, we may reasonably be assured, that they are our true Guides and Governours, whom we are obliged to follow and obey: for what better assurance can we in reason desire? what more proper marks can be assigned to discern them by? what methods of constituting such needfull officers can be setled more answerable to their design, and use? how can it be evil or unsafe to follow guides authorized by such warrants, conformed to such patterns, endowed with such dispositions, acting by such principles and rules? can we mistake, or miscarry by complying with the great body of God's Church through all ages, and particularly with those great Lights of the Primitive Church, who by the excellency of their knowledge, and the integrity of their vertue have so illustrated [4] our Holy Religion?

There are on the other hand sufficiently plain characters, by which we may descry seducers, and false pretenders to guide us.

Those who do ἑτεροδιδασκαλεῖν, *teach otherwise* [5], or discost [6] from the good ancient wholsome doctrine, revealed in the Holy *Scripture*, attested by *Universal Tradition*, professed, taught, maintained to death by the Primitive *Saints*, and *Martyrs*; who affect novelties, uncouth [7] notions, big words, and dark phrases, who dote

---

[1] [having a tender regard for].   [2] [seditious].
[3] *1 Pet*. II, 13.   [4] [adorned].   [5] *1 Tim*. VI, 3; I, 3, 4.
[6] [depart].   [7] [strange, uncommon].

on curious empty speculations, and idle questions, which engender strife, and yield no good fruit [1].

Those [2] who ground their opinions, and warrant their proceedings not by clear testimonies of divine revelation, by the dictates of sound reason, by the current authority of wise and good men, but by the suggestions of their own fancy, by the impulses of their passion, and zeal, by pretences to special inspiration, by imaginary necessities, and such like fallacious rules.

Those who by counterfeit shews of mighty zeal, and extraordinary affection, by affected forms of speech, by pleasing notions, by prophesying *smooth things, daubing* and *glozing* [3], by various artifices of flattery and fraud attract and abuse weak and heedless people.

Those who without any apparent commission from God, or allowable call from men, or extraordinary necessity of the case, in no legal or regular way, according to no custome received in God's Church do intrude themselves into the office [4], or are onely assumed thereto by ignorant, unstable, giddy, factious people, such as those of whom St. *Paul* saith, that *according to their own lusts they heap up teachers to themselves, having itching ears* [5].

Those who are not in reasonable ways fitly prepared, not duly approved, not competently authorized, not orderly admitted to the office, according to the prescriptions of God's Word, and the practice of his Church ; not entring into the fold by the door, but breaking through, or clambering over the fences of sober discipline.

Those who in their mind, their principles, their designs, and all their practice appear void of that charity, that meekness, that calmness, that gravity, that sincerity, that stability, which qualify worthy and true Guides : who in the disposition of their mind are froward [6], fierce, and stubborn, in their principles loose and slippery, in their designs and behaviour turbulent, disorderly, violent, deceitfull : who regard not order or peace, but wantonly raise

---

[1] *Gal.* I, 9 ; *1 Tim.* I, 4 ; VI, 4, 20 ; *2 Tim.* II, 14, 16, 23 ; *Tit.* III, 9 ; 2 *Pet.* II, 18.

[2] Ipsorum ordinationes temerariae, inconstantes, leves. Tertull. [*De Praescriptionibus*, cap. xli, Migne, *Patrol. lat.*, t. 2, col. 68].

[3] [*Isa.* XXX, 10 ; *Ezek.* XXII, 28].

[4] Hi sunt qui se ultro apud temerarios convenas sine divina dispositione praeficiunt, qui se praepositos sine ulla ordinationis lege constituunt, qui nemine Episcopatum dante Episcopi sibi nomen assumunt. Cypr. *de Un. Eccl.*, p. 256 [Migne, *Patrol. lat.*, t. 4, col. 523].

[5] *2 Tim.* IV, 3.   [6] [evilly disposed].

scandals, create dissensions, abet and foment disturbances in the Church. Who under religious appearances indulge their passions, and serve their interests, using a guise of devotion, and talk about holy things as instruments to vent wrath, envy and spleen ; to drive forward designs of ambition and avarice : who will not submit to any certain judgment or rule, will like nothing but what their fancy suggests, will acknowledge no law but their own will ; who for no just cause, and upon any slender pretence withdraw themselves, and seduce others from the Church, in which they were brought up, deserting its communion, impugning its laws, defaming its Governours, endeavouring to subvert its establishment : Who manage their discipline (such as it is of their own framing) unadvisedly and unsteadily, in no stable method, according to no setled rule, but as present conceit, or humour, or advantage prompteth ; so that not being fixed in any certain judgment or practice, they soon clash with themselves, and divide from one another, incessantly roving from one Sect to another ; *being carried about with divers and strange doctrines* [1] *; like children tossed to and fro with every wind of doctrine* [2].

Those, the fruits of whose doctrine and managery [3] amount at best onely to empty *form of godliness, void of real vertue* [4] ; while in truth they fill the minds of men with ill-passions, ill-surmises, ill-will ; they produce impious, unjust and uncharitable dealing of all kinds, particularly discontentfull murmurings, disobedience to Magistrates ; schisms and factions in the Church ; combustions and seditions in the State.

In fine those, who in their temper, and their deportment resemble those ancient seducers, branded in the Scripture, those *evil men, who did seduce, and were seduced* [5] :

Whose dispositions are represented in these *epithets* : they were ἀνυπότακτοι [6] *unruly*, or persons indisposed and unwilling to submit to Government ; τολμηταί, αὐθάδεις [7], *presumptuous, and selfwilled*, or self-pleasing darers ; γογγυσταί, μεμψίμοιροι [8], *murmurers, complainers*, or conjunctly discontented mutiners ; αὐτοκατάκριτοι [9], *self-condemned*, namely by contradictious shufling and shifting, or by excommunicating themselves from the Church ; γόητες [10], *bewitchers*, inveagling [11] and deluding credulous people by dissimulation, and

---

[1] *Heb.* XIII, 9. [2] *Eph.* IV, 14. [3] [management].
[4] [*2 Tim.* III, 5.] [5] *2 Tim.* III, 13. [6] *Tit.* I, 10.
[7] *2 Pet.* II, 10. [8] [*Jude* 16.] [9] *Tit.* III, 10, 11.
[10] *2 Tim.* III, 13. [11] [deceiving, beguiling].

specious appearances ; *having a form of godliness, but denying the power thereof* [1] *; being wolves in sheeps cloathing* [2], *grievous wolves not sparing the flock* [3] *; deceitfull workers, transforming themselves into the servants of Christ, and Ministers of righteousness* [4] *; lovers of themselves, covetous, boasters, proud, revilers, truce-breakers, false-accusers, traytours, heady, high-minded, vain talkers, deceivers, ignorant* [5], *unlearned, unstable* [6] *:*

    Whose practices were ; *To cause divisions and offences contrary to received doctrine ; By good words and fair speeches to deceive the hearts of the simple* [7] *;—To swerve from charity—having turned aside to vain jangling, desiring to be teachers of the law, understanding neither what they say, nor whereof they affirm* [8]. *To beguile unstable souls* [9] *; To lie in wait to deceive* [10] *; To speak perverse things that they may draw disciples after them* [11] *; To creep into houses captivating silly women* [12] *; To dote about questions and strifes of words, whereof cometh envy, strife, railings, evil surmisings, perverse disputings* [13] *; To speak swelling words of vanity ; To admire persons because of advantage* [14] (or out of private design, for self-interest ;) *To subvert whole houses, teaching things which they ought not for filthy lucres sake* [15] *; To speak lies in hypocrisie* [16] *; To preach Christ out of envy and strife, not out of good-will, or pure intention* (οὐχ ἁγνῶς, *not purely ;)* [17] *To promise liberty* [18] to their followers ; *To walk disorderly* [19] (that is in repugnance to order setled in the Church ;) *To despise dominion, and without fear to reproach dignities* [20] *; To speak evil* (rashly) *of those things which they know not* [21] (which are beside their skill and cognizance) *To separate themselves* [22], from the Church.

    Such persons as these, arrogating to themselves the office of Guides, and pretending to lead us we must not follow or regard, but are in reason and conscience obliged to reject and shun them, as the Ministers of *Satan*, the Pests of *Christendom*, the Enemies and Murtherers of Souls [23].

---

[1] *2 Tim.* III, 5.   [2] *Matt.* VII, 15.   [3] *Acts* XX, 29.
[4] *2 Cor.* XI, 13, 15.   [5] [*2 Tim.* III, 2, 3, 4, etc.]; *1 Tim.* VI, 4.
[6] *2 Pet.* III, 16.   [7] *Rom.* XVI, 17, 18.   [8] *1 Tim.* I, 6, 7.
[9] [*2 Pet.* II, 14.]   [10] *Eph.* IV, 14.   [11] *Acts* XX, 30.
[12] *2 Tim.* III, 6.   [13] *1 Tim.* VI, 4.   [14] *2 Pet.* II, 18 ; *Jude* 16.
[15] *Tit.* I, 11.   [16] *1 Tim.* IV, 2.   [17] *Phil.* I, 16, 17.
[18] *2 Pet.* II, 19.   [19] *2 Thess.* III, 6, 11.
[20] *2 Pet.* II, 10 ; *Jude* 8, 16.
[21] *Jude* 10.   [22] *Jude* 19.
[23] *Tit.* III, 10 ; *2 Thess.* III, 6 ; *Rom.* XVI, 17 ; *1 Tim.* VI, 5.

It can indeed no-wise be safe to follow any such Leaders (whatever pretences to special illumination they hold forth, whatever specious guises of sanctity they bear) who in their doctrine or practice deflect from the great beaten roads of holy Scripture, primitive Tradition, and Catholick practice, roving in bye-paths suggested to them by their private fancies and humours, their passions and lusts, their interests and advantages : there have in all ages such counterfeit Guides started up, having debauched some few heedless persons, having erected some παρασυναγωγὰς, or petty combinations against the regularly setled Corporations ; but never with any durable success or countenance of divine providence ; but like prodigious *Meteors* [1], having caused a little gazing, and some disturbance, their Sects have soon been dissipated, and have quite vanished away ; the authours and abetters of them being either buried in oblivion, or recorded with ignominy : like that *Theudas* in the speech of *Gamaliel* ; who *rose up boasting himself to be somebody ; to whom a number of men about 400. joined themselves ; who was slain, and all as many as obeyed him, were scattered, and brought to nought* [2].

But let thus much suffice to have been spoken concerning the Persons, to whom obedience must be performed.

---

[1] *Jude* 13.   [2] *Acts* V, 36.

[a] I proceed to the duty it self, the obedience prescribed, which may (according to the extent in signification of the word πείθεσθαι) be conceived to relate either to the government, or to the doctrine, or to the conversation of the persons specified ; implying that we should obey their laws, that we should embrace their doctrine, that we should conform to their practice, according to proper limitations of such performance, respectively :

We begin with the first, as seeming chiefly intended by the words :

Obedience to ecclesiastical Government ; what this doth import we may understand by considering the terms, whereby it is expressed, and those whereby its correlate (spiritual government) is signified ; by examples and practice relating to it, by the nature and reason of the matter it self.

Beside the word πείθεσθαι (which is commonly used to signify all sorts of obedience, chiefly that which is due to Governours) here is added a word serving to explain that, the word ὑπείκειν, which signifieth to yield, give way, or comply ; relating (as it seemeth by its being put indefinitely) to all their proceedings in matters concerning their charge. In other places, parallel to our *Text*, it is expressed by ὑποτάσσεσθαι [1], the same term, by which constantly the subjection due to secular powers (in all the precepts enjoining it) is expressed : Ὁμοίως νεώτεροι ὑποτάγητε πρεσβυτέροις [2], *In like manner* (or correspondently saith St. *Peter*) *ye younger submit your selves to the elder* (that is, as the Context shews, ye

---

[a] I proceed ... may] *T.* ; *B.* I proceed to the duty itself.
The obedience prescribed may

[1] *Tit.* III, 1 ; *Rom.* XIII, 1 ; *1 Pet.* II, 13.
[2] *1 Pet.* V, 5.

inferiours in the Church obey your superiours ; ὁ νεώτερος both
there and otherwise [1] doth signify the state of inferiority, as ὁ
πρεσβύτερος importeth dignity and authority.) And, ὑποτάσσεσθε τοῖς
τοιούτοις, *Submit your selves unto such, and to every one that helpeth
with us, and laboureth* [2], saith St. *Paul* ; and ἀλλήλοις ὑποτασσόμενοι,
Submitting your selves to one another in the fear of God [3], that is,
yielding conscientiously that submission, which established order
requireth from one to another : whence we may collect, that the
duty consisteth in yielding submission and compliance to all laws,
rules and orders enacted by spiritual Governours for the due cele-
bration of God's worship, the promoting edification, the conserving
decency, the maintenance of peace ; as also to the judgments and
censures in order to the same purposes administred by them.

This obedience to be due to them may likewise be inferred from
the various names and titles attributed to them ; such as those of
Prelates, Superintendents, Pastours, Supravisours, Governours and
Leaders ; which terms (more largely touched before) do imply command and authority of all sorts, *Legislative, Judicial* and *Executive.*

Such obedience also Primitive Practice doth assert to them : for
what authority the Holy *Apostles* did assume and exercise, the
same we may reasonably suppose derived to them ; the same in
kind, although not in peculiarity of manner (by immediate commission from *Christ*, with supply of extraordinary gifts and graces)
and in unlimitedness of extent : for they do succeed to the Apostles
in charge and care over the Church, each in his precinct (the
Apostolical office being distributed among them all [4].) The same
titles, which the Apostles assumed to themselves, they ascribe to
their *Sympresbyters*, requiring the same duties from them, and prescribing obedience to them in the same terms; They claimed no more
power than was needfull to further edification [5], and this is requisite
that present Governours also should have ; their practice in government [6] may also well be presumed exemplary to all future Governours : As then we see them διατάσσειν, *to order* things, and frame
Ecclesiastical Constitutions, διορθοῦν *to rectify* things, or reform

---

[1] *Luke* XXII, 26.   [2] *1 Cor.* XVI, 16.
[3] *Eph.* V, 21 ; *1 Pet.* V, 5.
[4] Cujus in solidum singuli participes sumus. Vid. CYPR. *de Unit. Eccl.*
[Episcopatus unus est, cujus a singulis in solidum pars tenetur. MIGNE, *Patrol.
lat.*, t. 4, col. 516].
[5] *2 Cor.* X, 8 ; XIII, 10.
[6] To ordain Elders ; to confirm Proselytes ; to exercise jurisdiction.

defects, to *impose* observances *necessary*, or expedient ᵃ to the
time¹ ; to judge causes and persons, *being ready to avenge* or
punish *every disobedience*² ; to *use severity* upon occasions³ ;
with the spiritual *rod* to chastise scandalous offenders, *disorderly
walkers*, persons contumacious and unconformable to their injunc-
tions⁴ ; to reject hereticks⁵, and banish notorious sinners from
communion, warning the faithfull to forbear conversation with
them⁶ : As they did challenge to themselves *an authority from
Christ*⁷ to exercise these and the like acts of spiritual dominion
and jurisdiction, exacting punctual obedience to them ; as we also
see the like acts exercised by Bishops⁸, whom they did constitute
to feed and rule the Church ; so we may reasonably conceive all
Governours of the Church (the heirs of their office) invested with
like authority in order to the same purposes, and that correspondent
obedience is due to them ; so that what blame, what punishment
was due to those, who disobeyed the Apostles, doth in proportion
belong to the transgressours of their duty toward the present
Governours of the Church ; especially considering that our Lord
promised his perpetual presence and assistence to the Apostles⁹.

We may farther observe, that accordingly in continual succession from the first ages, the good Primitive *Bishops* (the great
Patrons and Propagatours of our Religion) did generally assume
such power, and the people readily did yield obedience ; wherein
that one did wrongfully usurp, the other did weakly comply, were
neither probable, nor just to suppose ; whence general tradition
doth also confirm our obligation to this duty.

That this kind of obedience is required doth also farther appear
from considering the reason of things, the condition of the Church,
the design of Christian Religion.

1. Every Christian Church is a Society ; no Society can abide
in any comely order, any steady quiet, any desireable prosperity

---

ᵃ to] *T.* ; *B.* for

¹ *1 Cor.* XI, 34 ; *Tit.* I, 5 ; *Acts* XIV, 23 ; XV, 28.
² *1 Cor.* V, 12 ; *2 Cor.* X, 6.
³ *2 Cor.* XIII, 10.
⁴ *1 Cor.* IV, 21 ; *2 Cor.* XII, 21 ; XIII, 2 ; *2 Thess.* III, 6, 14.
⁵ *Tit.* III, 10.
⁶ *1 Tim.* VI, 5 ; *Rom.* XVI, 17.
⁷ *2 Cor.* X, 8 ; XIII, 10.
⁸ Episcopi successores Apostolorum. CYPR. *Ep.* XXVII, LXIX, XLI, LXXV
(Firmil). [MIGNE, *Patrol. lat.*, t. 4.]
⁹ *Matt.* XXVIII, 20.

without government; no government can stand without correspondent obligation to submit thereto.

2. Again, The state of Religion under the Gospel is the Kingdom of Heaven; *Christ* our Lord is King of the Church; it he
visibly governeth and ordereth by the spiritual Governours as his
Substitutes and Lieutenants (whence they peculiarly are styled his
Ministers, his *Officers*, his *Stewards*, his *Legates*, his *Co-workers*.)
When he ascending up to God's right hand was invested with
entire possession of that royal State, he setled them to administer
affairs concerning that government in his place and name; *Ascend-*
ing up on high he gave gifts unto men—He gave some Apostles,
some Prophets, some Evangelists, some Pastours and Teachers;
He gave them, that is he appointed them in their office, subordinate
to himself, *for the perfecting of the Saints, for the work of the*
Ministery, for the edifying of the body of Christ[1]; As to him
therefore ruling by them, by them enacting laws, dispensing justice,
maintaining order and peace, obedience is due.

3. Again, For the honour of God, the commendation of Religion, and benefit of the People[2], it is needfull, that in all religious
performances things should, according to St. *Paul's* rule, be performed *decently, and according to order*[3], without unhandsome
confusion, and troublesome distraction; this cannot be accomplished without a determination of persons, of modes, of circumstances appertaining to those performances (for how can any thing
be performed decently, if every person hath not his rank and station,
his office and work allotted to him; if to every thing to be done,
its time, its place, its manner of performance be not assigned, so that
each one may know what, when, where, and how he must doe?)
such determination must be committed to the discretion and care
of some persons, impowered to frame standing laws or rules concerning it, and to see them duly executed (for all persons without
delay, strife, confusion, and disturbance cannot meddle in it) with
these persons all the rest of the body must be obliged to comply;
otherwise all such determinations will be vain and ineffectual. Such
order reason doth recommend in every proceeding; such order
especially becometh the grandeur and importance of sacred things;
such order God hath declared himself to approve, and love, espe-

[1] *Eph.* IV, 8, 11, 12.   [2] *1 Cor.* XIV, 23; *Tit.* II, 10.
[3] *1 Cor.* XIV, 40.

cially in his own house, among his people, in matters relating to his service ; for *He is not* (as St. *Paul* saith, arguing to this purpose) *the God of confusion, but of peace, in all Churches of the Saints* [1].

4. Again, It is requisite that all Christian brethren should conspire in serving God with mutual charity, hearty concord, harmonious consent ; that (as the *Apostles* so often prescribed) they *should endeavour to keep unity of spirit in the bond of peace* [2] ; That they should *be like-minded, having the same love, being of one accord, of one mind* [3], *standing fast in one spirit, with one mind* [4] ; *That they should walk by the same rule, and mind the same thing* [5] ; *That with one mind, and one mouth they should glorify God, the Father of our Lord Jesus Christ* [6] ; *That they should all speak the same thing : and that there be no divisions among them, but that they be perfectly joined together in the same mind, and in the same judgment* [7] ; (like those in the *Acts*, of whom it is said, *The multitude of believers had one heart, and one soul*) [8] *That there should be no schisms* (divisions, or factions) *in the body* [9] ; that all dissensions, all *murmurings*, all emulations should be discarded from the Church [10] : the which precepts, secluding [11] an obligation to obedience, would be impossible, and vain ; for (without continual miracle, and transforming humane nature, things not to be expected from God, who apparently designeth to manage Religion by ordinary ways of humane prudence, his gratious assistence concurring) no durable concord in any Society can ever effectually be maintained otherwise than by one publick reason, will and sentence, which may represent, connect, and comprize all ; in defect of that every one will be of a several opinion about what is best, each will be earnest for the prevalence of his model and way ; there will be so many Law-givers as Persons, so many differences as matters incident ; nothing will pass smoothly and quietly, without bickering and jangling ; and consequently without animosities, and feuds ; whence no unanimity, no concord, scarce any charity or good-will can subsist.

---

[1] *1 Cor.* XIV, 33.   [2] *Eph.* IV, 3.
[3] *Phil.* II, 2 (σύμφυχοι); *1 Pet.* III, 8 (ὁμόφρονες); *2 Cor.* XIII, 11.
[4] *Phil.* II, 2 ; I, 27.   [5] *Phil.* III, 16.
[6] *Rom.* XV, 5, 6 ; XII, 16.   [7] *1 Cor.* I, 10.   [8] *Acts* IV, 32.
[9] *1 Cor.* XII, 25 ; XI, 18 ; I, 11 ; III, 3.
[10] *2 Cor.* XII, 20 ; *Phil.* II, 14.   [11] [without, but for].

5. Farther, in consequence of these things common edification requireth such obedience : It is the duty of Governours to order all things to this end, that is to the maintenance, encouragement, and improvement of piety ; for this purpose their authority was given them, (as St. *Paul* saith[1]) and therefore it must be deemed thereto conducible : it is indeed very necessary to edification, which without discipline guiding the simple and ignorant, reclaiming the erroneous and presumptuous, cherishing the regular, and correcting the refractary, can no-wise be promoted.

Excluding it, there can be no means of checking or redressing scandals, which to the reproach of Religion, to the disgrace of the Church, to the corrupting the minds, and infecting the manners of men will spring up, and spread[2]. Neither can there be any way to prevent the rise and growth of pernicious errours, or heresies ; the which assuredly in a state of unrestrained liberty the wanton and wicked minds of men will breed, their licentious practice will foster, and propagate ; to *the encrease of all impiety*[3]; *their mouths must be stopped*, otherwise *they will subvert whole houses, teaching things which they ought not for filthy lucre sake*[4] ; *the word* of naughty seducers *will spread like a gangrene*[5], if there be no corrosive or corrective remedy to stay its progress.

Where things are not managed in a stable, quiet, orderly way, no good practice can flourish, or thrive ; dissension will choak all good affections, confusion will obstruct all good proceedings ; from anarchy emulation and strife will certainly grow, and from them all sorts of wickedness ; for *where* (saith St. *James*) *there is emulation and strife, there is confusion, and every evil thing*[6].

All those benefits, which arise from holy communion in offices of piety and charity (from common prayers and praises to God, from participation in all sacred ordinances, from mutual advice, admonition, encouragement, consolation, good example) will together vanish with discipline ; these depend upon the friendly union and correspondence of the members ; and no such union can abide without the ligament of discipline, no such correspondence can be upheld without unanimous compliance to publick order. The cement of discipline wanting, the Church will not be like a *spiritual house*,

---

[1] *2 Cor.* XIII, 10 ; X, 8.
[2] *1 Tim.* I, 19 ; VI, 5 ; *2 Tim.* II, 16, 17, 18.
[3] *2 Tim.* II, 16.   [4] *Tit.* I, 11.
[5] *2 Tim.* II, 17.   [6] *Jas.* III, 16.

compacted of *lively stones* [1] into one goodly pile ; but like a company of scattered pebles, or a heap of rubbish.

So considering the reason of things, this obedience will appear needfull ; to enforce the practice thereof we may adjoin several weighty considerations.

Consider obedience what it is, whence it springs, what it produceth, each of those respects will engage us to it.

It is in it self a thing very good and acceptable to God, very just and equal, very wise, very comely and pleasant.

It cannot but be gratefull unto God, who is the God of love, of order, of peace, and therefore cannot but like the means furthering them ; he cannot but be pleased to see men doe their duty, especially that which regardeth his own Ministers ; in the respect performed to whom he is himself indeed avowed, and honoured, and obeyed [2].

It is a just and equal [3] thing, that every member of society should submit to the laws, and orders of it ; for every man is supposed upon those terms to enter into, and to abide in it ; every man is deemed to owe such obedience in answer to his enjoyment of privileges, and partaking of advantages thereby ; so therefore whoever pretendeth a title to those excellent immunities, benefits and comforts, which communion with the Church affordeth, it is most equal, that he should contribute to its support and welfare, its honour, its peace ; that consequently he should yield obedience to the orders appointed for those ends. Peculiarly equal it is in regard to our spiritual Governours, who are obliged to be very solicitous and laborious in furthering our best good ; who stand deeply engaged, and are responsible for the welfare of our souls : they must be contented to *spend, and be spent* [4], to undergo any pains, any hardships, any dangers and crosses occurring in pursuance of those designs : and is it not then plainly equal (is it not indeed more than equal, doth not all ingenuity and gratitude require?) that we should encourage, and comfort them in bearing those burthens, and in discharging those incumbencies by a fair and chearfull compliance ? 'tis the *Apostle*'s enforcement of the

---

[1] *1 Pet.* II, 5.

[2] Tempus est, — ut de submissione provocent in se Dei clementiam, et de honore debito in Dei sacerdotem eliciant in se divinam misericordiam. CYPR. *Ep.* XXX. [MIGNE, *Patrol. lat.*, t. 4, col. 314].

[3] [equitable, fair].

[4] [*2 Cor.* XII, 15.]

duty in our Text : *Obey them* (saith he) *and submit your selves ; for they watch for your souls, as those, who are to render an accompt, that they may doe it with joy, and not with grief* (or groaning.)

Is it not indeed extreme iniquity and ingratitude, when they with anxious care, and earnest toil are endeavouring our happiness, that we should vex and trouble them by our perverse and cross behaviour ?

Nay, is it not palpable folly to doe thus, seeing thereby we do indispose and ᵃhinder them from effectually discharging their duty to our advantage ? ἀλυσιτελὲς γὰρ ὑμῖν τοῦτο, *for this* (addeth the *Apostle*, farther pressing the duty) *is unprofitable to you*, or it tendeth to your disadvantage and damage ; not onely as involving guilt, but as inferring loss ; the loss of all those spiritual benefits, which Ministers being encouraged, and thence performing their office with alacrity and sprightfull diligence would procure to you : it is therefore our wisedom to be obedient, because obedience is so advantageous and profitable to us.

The same is also a comely and amiable thing, yielding much grace, procuring great honour to the Church, highly adorning and crediting Religion : It is a goodly sight to behold things proceeding orderly ; to see every person quietly resting in his post, or moving evenly in his rank ; to observe superiours calmly leading, inferiours gladly following, and equals lovingly accompanying each other ; this is the *Psalmist's, Ecce quam bonum ! Behold, how* (admirably) *good, and how pleasant it is for brethren to dwell together in unity !* ¹ such a state of things argueth the good temper, and wisedom of persons so demeaning themselves, the excellency of the principles, which do guide, and act them, the goodness of the constitution which they observe ; so it crediteth the Church, and graceth Religion ; a thing which (as St. *Paul* teacheth) *in all things* we should endeavour ².

It is also a very pleasant and comfortable thing to live in obedience ; by it we enjoy tranquillity of mind, and satisfaction of conscience, we taste all the sweets of amity and peace, we are freed from the stings of inward remorse, we escape the grievances of discord and strife.

ᵃ hinder] *T.* ; *B.* impede

¹ *Ps.* CXXXIII, 1. ² *Tit.* II, 10, 5.

The causes also and principles, from which obedience springeth, do much commend it : it ariseth from the dispositions of soul, which are most Christian, and most humane ; from charity, humility, meekness, sobriety of mind, and calmness of passion ; the which always dispose men to submiss, complaisant, peaceable demeanour toward all men, especially toward those, whose relation to them claimeth such demeanour ; these a genuine, free, cordial and constant obedience do signify to live in the soul ; together with a general honesty of intention, and exemption from base designs.

In fine, innumerable and inestimable are the benefits and good fruits accruing from this practice ; Beside the support it manifestly yieldeth to the Church, the gracefulness of order, the conveniences and pleasures of peace, it hath also a notable influence upon the common manners of men, which hardly can ever prove very bad, where the Governours of the Church do retain their due respect and authority ; nothing more powerfully doth instigate to vertue, than the countenance of authority, nothing more effectually can restrain from exorbitancy of vice, than the bridle of discipline : this obvious experience demonstrateth, and we shall plainly see, if we reflect upon those times when piety and vertue have most flourished : whence was it, that in those good old times Christians did so abound in good works, that they burnt with holy zeal, that they gladly would doe, would suffer any thing for their Religion ? whence but from a mighty respect to their superiours ; from a strict regard to their direction and discipline ? did the *Bishops* then prescribe long fasts, or impose rigid penances ? willingly did the people undergo them ; did the *Pastour* conduct into danger, did he lead them into the very jaws of death, and martyrdom ? the flock with a resolute alacrity did follow ; did a *Prelate* interdict any practice scandalous, or prejudicial to the ᵃChurch, under pain of incurring censure ? Every man trembled at the consequences of transgressing [1] : No terrour of worldly power, no severity of justice, no dread of corporal punishment had such efficacy to deter men from ill-doing as the reproof and censure of a Bishop ; his frown could avail more than the menaces of an Emperour, than

---

ᵃ Church,] *B.* ; *1686* Church ;

[1] Neque hoc ideo ita dixerim, ut negligatur Ecclesiastica disciplina, et permittatur quisquam facere quod velit, sine ulla correptione, et quadam medicinali vindicta, et terribili lenitate, et charitatis severitate. AUG. *adv. Petil.* III, iv [*Contra Litteras Petiliani Donatistae*, MIGNE, *Patrol. lat.*, t. 43, col. 350].

the rage of a Persecutour, than the rods and axes of an Execu-
tioner : No rod indeed did smart like the spiritual rod, no sword
did cut so deep as that of the spirit ; no loss was then so valuable [1],
as being deprived of spiritual advantages ; no banishment was so
grievous as being separated from holy communion ; no sentence
of death was so terrible, as that which cut men off from the Church :
No thunder could astonish or affright men like the crack of a
spiritual *anathema* : This was that which kept vertue in request,
and vice in detestation ; hence it was that men were so good, that
Religion did so thrive, that so frequent, and so illustrious examples
of piety did appear : Hence indeed we may well reckon that
Christianity did (under so many disadvantages, and oppositions)
subsist, and grow up ; obedience to Governours was its guard ;
that kept the Church firmly united in a body sufficiently strong
to maintain it self against all assaults of faction within, of opposition from abroad ; that preserved that concord, which disposed
and enabled Christians to defend their Religion against all fraud
and violence ; that cherished the true vertue, and the beautifull
order, which begot veneration to Religion ; to it therefore we owe
the life and growth of Christianity, so that through many sharp
persecutions it hath held up its head ; through so many perillous
diseases it hath kept its life untill this day. There were not then
of old any such cavils and clamours against every thing prescribed
by Governours ; there were no such unconscionable scruples, no
such hardhearted pretences to tender conscience devised to baffle
the authority of superiours ; had there been such, had men then
commonly been so froward [2] and factious as now, the Church had
been soon shivered into pieces, our Religion had been swallowed
up in confusion, and licentiousness.

If again we on the other hand fix our consideration upon disobedience, (the nature, the sources, the consequences thereof) it
will, I suppose, much conduce to the same effect, of persuading
us to the practice of this duty :

It is in it self a heinous sin, being the transgression of a command in nature and consequence very important, upon which God
layeth great stress, which is frequently inculcated in Scripture,
which is fenced by divers other Precepts, which is pressed by strong
arguments, and backed by severe threatnings of punishment upon
the transgressours.

[1] [serious].   [2] [evilly disposed].

It is in its nature a kind of apostasie from Christianity, and
rebellion against our Lord ; for as he that refuseth to obey the
King's Magistrates in administration of their office is interpreted
to disclaim his authority, and to design rebellion against him ; so
they who obstinately disobey the Ministers of our Lord's spiritual
Kingdom, do thereby appear to disavow him, to shake off his yoke,
to impeach his reign over them ; so doth he himself interpret and
take it : He (saith our Lord) *that heareth you, heareth me, and
he that* (ὁ ἀθετῶν, *that baffleth*) *despiseth you, despiseth me* [1] ;
and, *If any man neglect to hear the Church* (or shall disobey it,
ἐὰν παρακούσῃ) *let him be to thee as a heathen, and a publican* [2] ;
that is, such a refractary person doth by his contumacy put himself
into the state of one removed from *the Commonwealth of Israel,*
he forfeiteth the special protection of God, he becometh as an alien,
or an Outlaw from the Kingdom of our Lord [3].

Under the *Mosaical* Dispensation those *who would doe pre-
sumptuously, and would not hearken unto the Priest, that stood
to minister before the Lord* [4], did incur capital punishment ; those
who factiously murmured against *Aaron,* are said to make an insur-
rection against God, and answerably were punished in a miraculous
way (*The Lord made a new thing, the earth opened, and swallowed
them up ; they went down alive into the pit.*) [5] It was in the
Prophetical times an expression signifying height of impiety ; *My
people is as those, who strive with the Priest* [6] : Seeing then God
hath no less regard to his peculiar Servants now than he had then ;
seeing they no less represent him, and act by his authority now,
than any did then ; seeing their service is as pretious to him, and
as much tendeth to his honour now, as the *Levitical* service then
did ; seeing he no less loveth order and peace in the *Church,* than
he did in the *Synagogue* ; we may well suppose it a no less heinous
sin, and odious to God, to despise the Ministers of *Christ's* Gospel,
than it was before to despise the Ministers of *Moses* his Law.

It is a sin indeed, pregnant with divers sins, and involving the

---

[1] *Luke* X, 16 ; *Matt.* X, 40.   [2] *Matt.* XVIII, 17.

[3] Nec putent sibi vitae aut salutis constare rationem, si Episcopis et sacer-
dotibus obtemperare noluerint ; cum in Deuteronomio Dominus Deus dicat, etc.
CYPR. *Ep.* LXI [MIGNE, *Patrol. lat.,* t. 4, col. 381].

[4] *Deut.* XVII, 12.   [5] *Num.* XVI, 11, 30.

[6] *Hos.* IV, 4. Quo exemplo ostenditur, et probatur obnoxios omnes et culpae
et paenae futuros, qui se schismaticis contra praepositos et sacerdotes irreligiosa
temeritate miscuerint. CYPR. *Ep.* LXXVI [MIGNE, *Patrol. lat.,* t. 3, col. 1192].

breach of many great commands, which are frequently proposed and pressed in the *New Testament*, with design in great part to guard and secure it ; *That of doing all things in charity* [1], of *doing all things without murmurings, and dissentions* [2], of *pursuing peace so far as lieth in us* [3], of maintaining unity, concord, unanimity in devotion, of avoiding schisms, and dissensions ; and the like ; which are all notoriously violated by this disobedience ; it includeth the most high breach of charity, the most formal infringing peace, the most scandalous kind of discord that can be, to cross our Superiours [4].

It is also a practice issuing from the worst dispositions of soul, such as are most opposite to the spirit of our Religion, and indeed very repugnant to common reason, and humanity ; from a proud haughtiness, or vain wantonness of mind, from the irregularity of unmortified, and unbridled passion, from exorbitant selfishness (selfishness of every bad kind, self-conceit, self-will, self-interest) from turbulent animosity, froward crosness of humour, rancorous spite, perverse obstinacy ; from envy, ambition, avarice, and the like ill sources, the worst fruits of the flesh and corrupt nature ; to such dispositions the rejecting God's *Prophets* of old, and the non-compliance with the *Apostles* are ascribed in *Scripture* ; and from the same the like neglect of God's Messengers now do proceed ; as whoever will observe, may easily discern ; do but mind the discourses of factious people, you shall perceive them all to breathe generally nothing but ill-nature.

The fruits also, which it produceth, are extremely bad ; manifold great inconveniences and mischiefs, hugely prejudicing the interest of religion, and the welfare of the Church.

It is immediately and formally a violation of order, and peace ; whence all the wofull consequences of disorder and faction do adhere thereto [5].

It breedeth great disgrace to the Church, and scandal to Religion, for what can appear more ugly than to see among the Professours of Religion Children opposing their Fathers, Scholars

---

[1] *1 Cor.* XVI, 14.   [2] *Phil.* II, 14.
[3] *Rom.* XII, 18 ; *2 Tim.* II, 22 ; *Heb.* XII, 14 ; *Mark* IX, 50.
[4] An esse tibi cum Christo videtur, qui adversus sacerdotes Christi facit ? etc. CYPR. *de Unit. Eccl.*, p. 258 [MIGNE, *Patrol. lat.*, t. 4, col. 529].
[5] Vid. CYPR. *Ep.* LV. Neque enim aliunde, etc. [haereses obortae sunt, aut nata sunt schismata, quam inde quod sacerdoti Dei non obtemperatur. MIGNE, *Patrol. lat.*, t. 3, col. 828-9].

contesting with their Masters, Inferiours slighting and crossing
their Superiours ? what can more expose the Church and religion
to the contempt, to the derision of *Atheists* and *Infidels*, of profane
and lewd persons, of wild *Hereticks*, and *Schismaticks*, of all
enemies unto truth and piety, than such foul irregularity [1] ?

It corrupteth the minds and manners of men ; for when that
discipline is relaxed, which was ordained to guard truth, and
promote holiness ; when men are grown so licentious, and stubborn,
as to contemn their Superiours, to disregard their wholsome laws,
and sober advice, there can be no curb to restrain them ; but down
precipitantly they run into all kind of vitious irregularities and
excesses [2] ; when those mounds [3] are taken away, whither will men
ramble ; when those banks are broken down, what can we expect
but deluges of impious doctrine, and wicked practice to overflow
the ignorant and inconsiderate people ?

Doth not indeed this practice evidently tend to the dissolution
of the Church, and destruction of Christianity ? for when the
Shepherds are (as to conduct and efficacy) *taken away*, will not
the Sheep be scattered, or *wander astray, like Sheep without a
Shepherd* [4], being bewildred [5] in various errours, and exposed as
a prey to any wild beasts ; to *the grievous wolves*, to *the ravenous
lions*, to the wily *Foxes* [6] ? here a fanatical Enthusiast will snap
them, there a profane Libertine will worry them, there again a
desperate Atheist will tear and devour them [7].

Consult we but obvious experience, and we shall see, what
spoils and mines [8] of faith, of good conscience, of common honesty
and sobriety this practice hath in a few years caused : how have
Atheism and *Infidelity*, how have profaneness and dissoluteness

---

[1] Inde Schismata, et Haereses obortae sunt, et oriuntur, dum Episcopus, qui
unus est, et Ecclesiae praeest superba quorundam praesumptione contemnitur.
CYPR. *Ep.* LXIX [*ibid.*, t. 4, col. 416].

Haec sunt initia Haereticorum, et ortus atque conatus Schismaticorum male
cogitantium ut sibi placeant, ut praepositum superbo tumore contemnant. Sic
de Ecclesia receditur, sic altare profanum foris collocatur, sic contra pacem
Christi, atque unitatem Dei rebellatur. CYPR. *Ep.* LXV [*ibid.*, t. 4, col. 409].

[2] Ecclesiae gloria praepositi gloria est. ID. *Ep.* VI [*ibid.*, t. 4, col. 241];
Ep. LV [i.e. *Ep.* XII Ad Cornelium Papam, *ibid.*, t. 3, col. 821].

[3] [fences, curbs].   [4] *Matt.* XXVI, 31.   [5] [lost in a maze].
[6] [*Acts* XX, 29 ; *Matt.* VII, 15.]

[7] Τοῦτο πάντων τῶν κακῶν αἴτιον, ὅτι τὰ τῶτ ἀρχόντων ἡφανίσθη, οὐδεμία
αἰδώς, οὐδεὶς φόβος, etc. CHRYS. *in 2 Tim.* [cap. i] *Orat.* 2 [MIGNE, *Patrol. gr.*,
t. 62, col. 609].

[8] [undermining].

of manners, how have all kinds of dishonesty and baseness grown up since men began to disregard the authority of their spiritual Guides? what dismal tragedies have we in our age beheld acted upon this stage of our own Countrey: what bloudy wars and murthers (murthers of *Princes*, of *Nobles*, of *Bishops* and *Priests*) what miserable oppressions, extortions and rapines; what execrable seditions and rebellions; what barbarous animosities, and feuds, what abominable treasons, sacrileges, perjuries, blasphemies; what horrible violations of all justice and honesty? and what I pray was the source of these things; where did they begin; where but at murmuring against, at rejecting, at persecuting the spiritual Governours, at casting down and trampling on their authority; at slighting and spurning ᵃat their advice? surely would men have observed the Laws, or have hearkned to the Counsels of those grave and sober persons, whom God had appointed to direct them, they never would have run into the commission of such enormities.

It is not to be omitted, that in the present state of things the guilt of disobedience to spiritual Governours is encreased and aggravated by the supervenient guilt of another disobedience to the Laws of our Prince and Countrey: Before the secular powers (unto whom God hath committed the dispensation of justice, with the maintenance of peace and order in reference to worldly affairs) did submit to our Lord, and became *nursing parents of the Church*, the power of managing Ecclesiastical matters did wholly reside in spiritual Guides; unto whom Christians as the *peculiar* subjects of God, were obliged willingly to yield obedience; and refusing it were guilty before God of spiritual disorder, faction, or schism; but now after that political authority (out of pious zeal for God's service, out of a wise care to prevent the influences of disorder in spiritual matters upon the temporal peace, out of gratefull return for the advantages the Commonwealth enjoyeth from religion, and the Church) hath pleased to back and fortify the Laws of spiritual Governours by civil sanctions, the knot of our obligation is tied faster, its force is redoubled, we by disobedience incur a double guilt, and offend God two ways, both as Supreme Governour of the World, and as King of the Church; to our schism against the Church we add rebellion against our Prince, and so become no less bad Citizens, than bad Christians; Some may perhaps

ᵃ at] *T.*

imagine their disobedience hence more excusable, taking themselves now onely thereby to transgress a political Sanction ; but (beside that even that were a great offence, the command of our temporal Governours being sufficient, out of conscience to God's express will, to oblige us in all things not evidently repugnant to God's Law) it is a great mistake to think the civil law doth any-wise derogate from the Ecclesiastical ; that doth not swallow this up, but succoureth and corroborateth it ; their concurrence yieldeth an accession of weight, and strength to each ; they do not by conspiring to prescribe the same thing either of them cease to be Governours, as to right ; but in efficacy the authority of both should thence be augmented ; seeing the obligation to obedience is multiplied upon their subjects ; and to disobey them is now two crimes, which otherwise should be but one.

Such is the nature of this duty, and such are the reasons enforcing the practice thereof ; I shall onely farther remove two impediments of that practice ; and so leave this Point.

1. One hindrance of obedience is this, that spiritual power is not despotical, or compulsory, but parental or pastoral ; that it hath no external force to abet [1] it, or to avenge disobedience to its laws : they must not κατεξουσιάζειν, or κατακυριεύειν (be imperious, or domineer) they are not allowed to exercise violence, or to inflict bodily correction [2] ; but must rule in meek and gentle ways, directly influential upon the mind and conscience, (ways of rational per-suasion, exhortation, admonition, reproof) *in meekness instructing those that oppose themselves ;—convincing, rebuking, exhorting with all long-suffering, and doctrine* [3] : their word is their onely weapon, their force of argument all the constraint they apply ; hence men commonly do not stand in awe of them, nor are so sensible of their obligation to obey them ; they cannot understand why they should be frighted by words, or controlled by an un-armed authority.

But this in truth (things being duly considered) is so far from diminishing our obligation, or arguing the authority of our Govern-ours to be weak and precarious, that it rendereth our obligation much greater, and their authority more dreadfull ; for the sweeter and gentler their way of governing is, the more disingenuous and unworthy a thing it is to disobey it ; not to be persuaded by reason,

[1] [urge].

[2] Μάλιστα γὰρ ἁπάντων Χριστιανοῖς οὐκ ἐφεῖται πρὸς βίαν ἐπανορθοῦν τὰ τῶν ἁμαρτανόντων πταίσματα, etc. CHRYS. de Sacerd. II [MIGNE, Patrol. gr., t. 48, col. 634]. ᾿Ενταῦθα οὐ βιαζόμενον, ἀλλὰ πείθοντα δεῖ ποιεῖν ἀμείνω τὸν τοιοῦτον. Ibid. [col. 634]. Matt. XX, 27 ; Luke XXII, 26 ; 1 Pet. V, 3.

[3] 2 Tim. II, 25 ; IV, 2 ; 1 Tim. III, 3.

not to be allured by kindness, not to admit friendly advice, not to comply with the calmest methods of furthering our own good, is a brutish thing ; he that onely can be scared and scourged to duty, scarce deserveth the name of a man : it therefore doth the more oblige us, that in this way we are moved to action by love rather than fear : Yet if we would fear wisely and justly, (not like Children, being frighted with formidable shapes, and appearances, but like men apprehending the real consequences of things) we should the more fear these spiritual Powers, because they are insensible [1] : for that God hath commanded us to obey them, without assigning visible forces to constrain or chastise, is a manifest argument, that he hath reserved the vindication of their authority to his own hand, which therefore will be infallibly certain, and terribly severe ; so the nature of the case requireth, and so God hath declared it shall be ; The Sentence that is upon Earth pronounced by his Ministers upon contumacious Offenders, he hath declared himself ready to ratify in Heaven, and therefore most assuredly will execute it [2] : As under the Old Law God appointed to the transgression of some laws, upon which he laid special stress, the punishment of *being cut off from his people* [3] ; the execution of which punishment he reserved to himself to be accomplished in his own way, and time ; so doth he now in like manner take upon him to maintain the cause of his Ministers ; and to execute the judgments decreed by them ; and if so, we may consider that *it is a dreadfull thing to fall into the hands of the living God* [4] : Ecclesiastical Authority therefore is not a shadow, void of substance or force, but hath the greatest power in the World to support, and assert it ; it hath arms to maintain it most effectual and forcible [5] (those of which St. *Paul* saith ; *The weapons of our warfare are not carnal, but mighty through God—*) [6] it inflicteth chastisements far more dreadfull, than any secular power can inflict ; for these onely touch the body, those pierce the soul ; these concern onely our temporal state, those reach eternity it self ; these at most yield a transitory smart, or kill the body, those produce endless torment ; and (utterly as to all comfort in being) [7] destroy the soul.

[1] [not to be perceived by the senses].
[2] *Matt.* XVIII, 18.
[3] [*Exod.* XXX, 33, 38 ; *Lev.* VII, 20, 21, 25, 27 ; XVII, 4, 9 ; XIX, 8 ; XXIII, 29 ; *Num.* IX, 13 ; etc.].
[4] *Heb.* X, 31.   [5] [powerful].   [6] *2 Cor.* X, 4.
[7] [with regard to all comfort in existence].

The punishment for extreme contumacy is called *delivery to Satan*[1]; and is not this far worse than to be put into the hands of any Gaolor, or hangman[2]? what are any chords of hemp, or fetters of iron in comparison to those bands, of which 'tis said, *Whatever ye bind on earth, shall be bound in heaven*[3]; which engage the soul [a] in a guilt, never to be loosed, except by sore contrition, and serious repentance? what are any scourges to St. *Paul's* rod, lashing the heart and conscience with stinging remorse; what any axes or faulchions[4] to that *sword of the spirit*[5]; which cutteth off a member from the body of Christ; what are any faggots and torches to that unquenchable *fire and brimstone*[6] of the infernal lake; what, in fine, doth any condemnation here signify to that horrible curse, which devoteth[7] an incorrigible soul to the bottomless pit?

It is therefore indeed a great advantage to this power that it is spiritual.

2. Another grand obstruction to the practice of this duty is, pretence to scruple about the lawfulness, or dissatisfaction in the expedience of that, which our Governours prescribe, that we are able to advance objections against their decrees, that we can espy inconveniences, ensuing upon their orders; that we imagine the constitution may be reformed, so as to become more pure, more convenient, and comely, more serviceable to edification; that we cannot fansie that to be best, which they enjoin[8]: For removing this obstruction let me onely propound some questions.

Were not any Government appointed in vain, if such pretences might exempt, or excuse from conformity to its orders? can such ever be wanting[9]? is there any thing deviseable, which may not be impugned by some plausible reason, which may not disgust a squeamish humour? is there any matter so clearly innocent, the lawfulness whereof a weak mind will not question, any thing so firm and solid, in which a small acuteness of wit cannot pick a

---

[a] in a guilt] *1686*; *B.* in a noose of guilt

[1] [*1 Tim.* I, 20].
[2] Spiritali gladio superbi et contumaces necantur, dum de Ecclesia ejiciuntur. CYPR. *Ep.* LXI [MIGNE, *Patrol. lat.*, t. 4, col. 382].
[3] [*Matt.* XVIII, 18].   [4] [broad sword].   [5] [*Eph.* VI, 17].
[6] [*Rev.* XXI, 8].   [7] [consigns].
[8] CYPR. *Ep.* L, LII (p. 97) [MIGNE, *Patrol. lat.*, t. 4].
[9] Φιλόνοις [, ὥς φησιν ἡ παροιμία,] οἶνος οὐ λείπει, οὐδὲ φιλονείκῳ μάχη. SOCRAT. *Hist.* [*Eccl.*] VII, xxxi [MIGNE, *Patrol. gr.*, t. 67, col. 807].

hole, any thing so indisputably certain, that whoever affecteth to cavil may not easily devise some objections against it?

Is there any thing here, that hath no inconveniences attending it? are not in all humane things conveniences, and inconveniences so mixt and complicated, that it is impossible to disentangle and sever them? can there be any constitution under Heaven so absolutely pure and perfect, that no blemish or defect shall appear therein? can any providence of man foresee, any care prevent, any industry remedy all inconveniences possible? Is a reformation satisfactory to all fancies any-wise practicable; and are they not fitter to live in the *Platonick Idea* of a Commonwealth, than in any real society, who press for such an one? to be facile and complaisant in other cases, bearing with things which do not please us, is estemed commendable, a courteous and humane practice, why should it not be much more reasonable to condescend to our Superiours, and comport with their practice? is it not very discourteous to deny them the respect which we allow to others, or to refuse that advantage to publick transactions, which we think fit to grant unto private conversation?

To what purpose did God institute a Government, if the resolutions thereof must be suspended, till every man is satisfied with them[1]; or if its state must be altered so often, as any man can pick in it matter of offence or dislike; or if the proceedings thereof must be shaped according to the numberless varieties of different and repugnant fancies?

Are, I pray, the objections against obedience so clear, and cogent, as are the commands, which enjoin, and the reasons, which enforce it? are the inconveniences adhering to it apparently[2] so grievous, as are the mischiefs, which spring from disobedience? do they in a just balance counterpoise the disparagement of authority, the violation of order, the disturbance of peace, the obstruction of edification, which disobedience produceth?

Do the *scruples* (or *reasons*, if we will call them so) which we propound, amount to such a strength and evidence, as to outweigh the judgment of those, whom God hath authorized by his Commission, whom he doth enable by his grace to instruct and

---

[1] Οὐ γὰρ μόνον τὴν ἀρίστην (πολιτείαν) δεῖ θεωρεῖν, ἀλλὰ καὶ τὴν δυνατήν. ARIST. *Pol.* IV, i [1288 b, 37].

Si ubi jubeantur quaerere singulis liceat: pereunte obsequio etiam imperium intercidit. TAC. I, p. 450. Otho [*Hist.* I, 83].

[2] [manifestly].

guide us [1] ? May not those, whose office it is to judge of such things ; whose business it is to study for skill in order to that purpose, who have most experience in those affairs specially belonging to them, be reasonably deemed most able to judge both for themselves, and us what is lawfull, and what expedient ? have they not eyes to see what we doe, and hearts to judge concerning the force of our pretences, as well as we ?

Is it not a design of their office to resolve our doubts, and void our scruples in such cases, that we may act securely and quietly, being directed by better judgments than our own [2] ? Are they not strictly obliged in conscience, are they not deeply engaged by interest to govern us in the best manner ? Is it therefore wisedom, is it modesty, is it justice for us to advance our private conceits against their most deliberate publick resolutions ? may we not in so doing mistake ; may we not be blind, or weak (not to say fond, or proud, or perverse) and shall those defects or defaults of ours evacuate so many commands of God, and render his so noble, so needfull an ordinance quite insignificant ?

Do we especially seem to be in earnest, or appear otherwise than illusively to palliate [3] our nauyhty [4] affections, and sinister respects [5], when we ground the justification of our non-conformity upon dark subtilties, and intricate quirks ; which it is hard to conceive that we understand our selves, and whereof very perspicacious men cannot apprehend the force ? Do we think we shall be innocent men, because we are smart Sophisters ; or that God will excuse from our duty, because we can perplex men with our discourses ? or that we are bound to doe nothing, because we are able to say somewhat against all things ?

Would we not doe well to consider, what huge danger they incur, and how massy a load of guilt they must undergo, upon whom shall be charged all those sad disorders, and horrid mischiefs, which are naturally consequent on disobedience ; what if confusion of things, if corruption of manners, if oppression of truth, if dissolution of the Church do thence ensue ; what a case then shall we be in, who confer so much thereto ? would not such considera-

---

[1] Dixisti sane scrupulum tibi esse tollendum de animo, in quem incidisti ; Incidisti sed tua credulitate irreligiosa, etc. CYPR. *Ep.* LXIX (ad Florent.) vid. optime et apposite de hac re disserentem [MIGNE, *Patrol. lat.*, t. 4, col. 417].
[2] Qui fidei et veritati praesumus. CYPR. *Ep.* LXXII [*ibid.*, t. 3, col. 1170].
[3] [to disguise].   [4] [evil].   [5] [motives].

tions be apt to beget scruples far more disquieting an honest, and truly conscientious mind, than any such either profound subtilties, or superficial plausibilities can doe; which Dissenters are wont to alledge? For needeth he not to have extreme reason (reason extremely strong, and evident) who dareth to refuse that obedience, which God so plainly commandeth, by which his own authority is maintained, on which the safety, prosperity, and peace of the Church dependeth, in which the support of Religion, and the welfare of numberless souls is deeply concerned?

Did, let me farther ask, the *Apostles*, when they settled orders in the Church, when they imposed what they conceived needfull for edification, and decency, when they inflicted spiritual chastisements upon disorderly walkers, regard such pretences? or had those self-conceited, and self-willed people (who *obeyed* not their *words*, but *resisted* and rejected them)[1] no such pretences? had they nothing, think we, to say for themselves, nothing to object against the Apostolick orders, and proceedings? they had surely; they failed not to find faults in the establishment, and to pretend a kind of tender conscience for their disobedience; yet this hindred not, but that the Apostles condemned their misbehaviour and inflicted severe censures upon them?

Did not also the primitive *Bishops* (and all spiritual Governours down from the beginning every-where almost to these days of contention and disorder) proceed in the same course; not fearing to enact such laws concerning indifferent matters, and circumstances of Religion, as seemed to them conducible to the good of the Church? did not all good People readily comply with their orders, how painfull soever, or disagreeable to flesh and bloud, without contest, or scruple? yet had not they as much wit, and no less conscience than our selves? They who had wisedom enough to descry the truth of our Religion through all the clouds of obloquy and disgrace, which it lay under; who had zeal and constancy to bear the hardest brunts of persecution against it; were they such fools as to see no fault, so stupid as to resent[2] nothing, or so loose as to comply with any thing? No surely; they were in truth so wise as to know their duty, and so honest as to observe it.

If these considerations will not satisfy, I have done; and pro-

---

[1] *2 Tim.* IV, 15; *1 Tim.* I, 20; *2 Thess.* III, 14, 6.
[2] [to feel].

ceed to the next Point of our duty, to which the precept in our Text may extend; concerning the doctrine of our Guides: In which respect it may be conceived to imply the following particulars, to be performed by us, as instances, or parts, or degrees thereof.

1. We should readily, and gladly address our selves to hear them; not out of profane and wilfull contempt, or slothfull negligence declining to attend upon their instructions: There were of old those, of whom the *Prophets* complain, who would not so much as hearken to the words of those, whom God sent unto them; but stopped their ears, *withdrew the shoulder, and hardned the neck, and would not hear* [1]; there were those in the *Evangelical* times, who did ἀπωθεῖν τὸν λόγον, *thrust away the word of God, judging themselves unworthy of eternal life* [2]; *who would not admit, or hear the word of life* [3], and overtures of grace propounded by the *Apostles*; There were *Gadarenes*, who beseeched our Lord himself to depart from their Coasts [4]; There have always been *deaf Adders, who stop their ears to the voice of the Charmer, charm he never so wisely* [5]; No wonder then if now there be those, who will not so much as allow a hearing to the Messengers of God, and the Guides of their soul: some out of a factious prejudice against their office, or their persons, or their way do shun them, giving themselves over to the conduct of Seducers; some out of a profane neglect of all Religion, out of being wholly possessed with worldly cares, and desires, out of stupidity and sloth (indisposing them to mind any thing that is serious) will not afford them any regard: All these are extremely blameable, offensive to God, and injurious to themselves: It is a heinous affront to God (implying an hostile disposition toward him, an unwillingness to have any correspondence with him) to refuse so much as audience to his Ambassadours; It is an interpretative [6] repulsing him; so of old he expressed it; *I* (saith he) *spake unto you, rising early, and speaking, but ye heard not, I called you, but ye answered not* [7]; so under the Gospel, *He* (saith our Lord) *that heareth you, heareth me*; and *he that despiseth* (or regardeth not) *you, despiseth me* [8]; and, *We are Ambassadours of Christ, as though God did beseech*

---

[1] *Neh.* IX, 29; *Prov.* I, 24; *Isa.* LXV, 12; LXVI, 4; *Jer.* VII, 13; VI, 10.
[2] *Acts* XIII, 46.   [3] *Matt.* X, 14.   [4] *Luke* VIII, 37.
[5] *Ps.* LVIII, 4, 5.   [6] [implicit].   [7] *Jer.* VII, 13.
[8] *Luke* X, 16.

you by us; we pray you in Christ's stead be reconciled to God [1].
It is a starving our souls, depriving them of that food, which God
hath provided for them ; It is keeping our selves at distance from
any means or possibility of being well informed and quickned to
the practice of our duty, of being reclaimed from our errours, and
sins ; it is the way to become hardned in impiety, or sinking into
a reprobate sense : This is the first step to obedience ; for *how
can we believe, except we hear?* this is that, which St. *James*
urgeth, *Let every man be quick to hear* [2] ; and which St. *Peter*
thus enjoineth : *Like new-born babes desire the sincere milk of
the word, that we may grow thereby* [3] ; We should especially be
quick and ready to hear those, whom God hath authorized and
appointed to speak ; we should *desire to suck the milk of the word*
from those, who are our spiritual Parents, and Nurses.

2. We should hear them with serious, earnest attention, and
consideration ; so that we may well understand, may be able to
weigh, may retain in memory, and may become duly affected with
their [a] discourses ; We must not hear them drowsily and slightly,
as if we were nothing concerned, or were hearing an impertinent
tale ; their word should not pass through the ears, and slip away
without effect ; but sink into the understanding, into the memory,
into the heart ; like *the good seed* falling into a *depth of earth* [4],
able to afford it root, and nourishment ; therefore we must attend
diligently thereto : περισσοτέρως οὖν δεῖ προσέχειν, *we should therefore give more abundant heed* (as the *Apostle* saith) *to the things
we hear, lest at any time we should let them slip* [5]. This duty the
nature and importance of their word requireth : *It is the word not
of men,* but *in truth the word* of the great *God* [6], (his word as
proceeding from him, as declaring his mind and will, as tendring
his overtures of grace and mercy) which as such challengeth great
regard and awe ; it informeth us of our chief duties, it furthereth
our main interests, it guideth us into, it urgeth us forward in the
way to eternal happiness ; 'tis the word that is *able to save our
souls* [7] ; to *render us wise unto salvation* [8] ; It therefore claimeth,
and deserveth from us most earnest attention ; it is a great indignity
and folly not to yield it.

---

a discourses] *1686* ; B. discourse

[1] *2 Cor.* V, 20.   [2] *Jas.* I, 19.   [3] *1 Pet.* II, 2.
[4] *Matt.* XIII, 5.   [5] *Heb.* II, 1.   [6] *1 Thess.* II, 13.
[7] *Jas.* I, 21.   [8] [*2 Tim.* III, 15.]

3. We should to their instructions bring good dispositions of mind, such as may render them most effectual and fruitfull to us ; Such as are right intention, candour, docility, meekness.

We should not be induced to hear them out of curiosity, (as *having itching ears*)[1] being desirous to hear *some new things*[2], some fine notions, some taking[3] discourse ; somewhat to fansie or talk pleasantly about ; (as the *Athenians* heard St. *Paul*)[4] not out of censoriousness, or inclination to criticize, and find fault (as the *Pharisees* heard our Saviour, *Laying wait for him, and seeking to catch something out of his mouth, that they might accuse him*)[5] not out of design to gratify our passions in hearing them, to reprove other persons ; or for any such corrupt and sinister intention, but altogether out of pure design that we may be improved in knowledge, and excited to the practice of our duty.

We should not come to hear them with minds imbued with ill prejudices, and partial[6] affections, which may obstruct the virtue and efficacy of their discourse ; or may hinder us from judging fairly, and truly about what they say ; but with such freedom and ingenuity as may dispose us readily to yield unto, and acquiesce in any profitable truth declared by them ; like the generous *Beraeans*, who *received the word* μετὰ πάσης προθυμίας *with all* alacrity and *readiness of mind, searching the scriptures daily whether these things were so*[7] ; ὡς ἀρτιγέννητα βρέφη, *like infants newly born*[8], that come to the dugg without any other inclination than to suck what is needfull for their sustenance.

We should be docile, and tractable ; willing and apt to learn ; shaking off all those indispositions of soul (all dulness, and sluggishness, all peevishness and perverseness, all pride and self-conceitedness, all corrupt affection and indulgence to our conceits, our humours, our passions, our lusts, and inordinate desires) which may obstruct our understanding of the Word, our yielding assent to it, our receiving impression from it : There were those, concerning whom the *Apostle* said, that he could not proceed in his discourse, because they were νωθροὶ ταῖς ἀκοαῖς, *dull of hearing*[9] (or sluggish in hearing,) who were indisposed to hear, and uncapable to understand[10], because they would not be at the pains

---

[1] [2 *Tim.* IV, 3.]
[2] [*Acts* XVII, 19.]
[3] [alluring].
[4] *Acts* XVII, 21.
[5] *Luke* XI, 54.
[6] [biased].
[7] *Acts* XVII, 11.
[8] *1 Pet.* II, 2.
[9] *Heb.* V, 11.
[10] *1 Cor.* III, 2.

to rouse up their fancies, and fix their minds upon a serious consideration of things : there were those, who had *a spirit of slumber, eyes not to see, and ears not to hear* [1] ; who *did hear with the ear, but not understand* [2] ; *seeing did see, but not perceive ; for their heart had waxed gross, their ears were dull of hearing ; and their eyes were closed* [3] ; Such indocile persons there always have been, who being stupified and perverted by corrupt affections became uncapable of bettering from good instruction : All such we should strive to free our selves from ; that we may perform this duty to our Guides, and *In meekness receive the engrafted word* [4].

These practices (of hearing, of attending, of coming well disposed to instruction) are at least steps and degrees necessarily prerequisite to the obedience prescribed ; and farther to press them all together upon us, we may consider, that it is strictly incumbent on them (under danger of heavy punishment and *woe*) *willingly*, earnestly, with all diligence and patience to *labour* in teaching and admonishing us [5] ; they must *give attendance*, and *take heed unto their doctrine*, that it may be *sound* and profitable ; they *must preach the word* [6], and *be instant* upon it *in season, out of season* (that is not onely taking, but seeking and snatching all occasions [a] to doe it) *reproving, rebuking, exhorting with all long-suffering, and doctrine* [7] ; they *must warn every man, and teach every man in all wisedom, that they may present every man perfect in Christ Jesus* [8] : as they are obliged in such manner to doe these things, so there must be correspondent duties lying upon us, to receive their doctrine readily, carefully, patiently, sincerely and fairly : As they must be faithfull dispensers of God's heavenly truth [9], and holy mysteries, so we must be obsequious entertainers of them : imposing such commands on them doth imply reciprocal obligations in their hearers and scholars ; otherwise their office would be vain, and their endeavours fruitless ; God no less would be frustrated in his design, than we should be deprived of the advantages of their institution.

[a] to doe it] *T.*

[1] *Rom.* XI, 8 ; *Isa.* XXIX, 10.
[2] *Isa.* VI, 9 ; *Acts* XXVIII, 26 ; *John* XII, 40.
[3] [*Matt.* XIII, 15].   [4] *Jas.* I, 21.
[5] *1 Cor.* IX, 16 ; *2 Cor.* V, 14 ; *1 Pet.* V, 2 ; *Rom.* XII, 3 ; *1 Tim.* V, 17.
[6] *1 Tim.* IV, 13, 16.   [7] *2 Tim.* IV, 2.
[8] *Col.* I, 28.   [9] *1 Cor.* IV, 2.

But farther, it is a more immediate ingredient of this duty, that

4. We should effectually be enlightned by their doctrine, be convinced by their arguments persuading truth and duty, be moved by their admonitions, and exhortations to good practice: We should open our eyes to the light, which they shed forth upon us ; we should surrender our judgment to the proofs, which they alledge ; we should yield our hearts and affections pliable to their mollifying, and warming discourses : It is their part to subdue our minds to *the obedience of faith,* and to subject our wills to the observance of God's Commandments (*Casting down imaginations, and every high thing that exalteth it self against the knowledge of God, and bringing into captivity every thought to the obedience of Christ*)[1] it must therefore answerably be our duty not to resist, not to hold out, not to persist obstinate in our errours, or prejudices ; to submit our minds to the power of truth, being willingly, and gladly conquered by it ; it must be our duty to subjugate our wills, to bend our inclinations, to form our affections to a free compliance of heart with the duties urged upon us ; we should not be like those *Disciples,* of whom our Lord complaineth thus : *O fools, and slow of heart to believe all that the Prophets have spoken*[2] ; nor like the *Jews,* with whom St. *Stephen* thus expostulates : *Ye stiff-necked, and uncircumcised in heart and ears, ye do always resist the Holy Ghost*[3]. They should speak with power, and efficacy[4] ; we therefore should not by our indispositions (by obstinacy of conceit, or hardness of heart) obstruct their endeavours ; they should be *co-workers of your joy*[5] (that is working in us that faith and those vertues, which are productive of true joy and comfort to us) we therefore should co-work with them toward the same end ; they should edify us in knowledge, and holiness ; we should therefore yield our selves to be fashioned, and polished by them.

5. We should, in fine, obey their doctrine by conforming our practice thereto ; this our Lord prescribed in regard even to the *Jewish* Guides and Doctours ; *The Scribes and Pharisees sit in Moses his seat ; all therefore whatsoever they bid you observe, that observe and doe*[6] ; the same we may well conceive that he requireth in respect to his own Ministers, the teachers of a better

---

[1] *2 Cor. X, 5.*
[2] *Luke XXIV, 25.*
[3] *Acts VII, 51.*
[4] *1 Cor. IV, 20 ; II, 4.*
[5] *2 Cor. I, 24 ; 1 Cor. III, 5.*
[6] *Matt. XXIII, 2, 3.*

Law, authorized to direct us by his own Commission, and thereto more specially qualified by his grace : this is indeed the Crown and completion of all ; to hear signifieth nothing ; to be convinced in our mind, and to be affected in our heart will but aggravate our guilt, if we neglect practice : Every Sermon we hear, that sheweth us our duty, will in effect be an enditement upon us, will ground a sentence of condemnation, if we transgress it : for, as *The Earth which drinketh in the rain that cometh oft upon it, and bringeth forth herbs meet for them by whom it is dressed, receiveth blessing from God, so that which beareth thorns and briers, is rejected, and is nigh unto cursing, and its end is to be burned* [1] : and, *Not the hearers of the law are just with God, but the doers of the law shall be justified* [2]. And it is a good advice, that of St. *James* ; *Be ye doers of the word, and not hearers onely deceiving your own selves* [3] ; 'tis, he intimateth, a fallacy some are apt to put upon themselves to conceit they have done sufficiently, when they have lent an ear to the word ; this is the least part to be done in regard to it, practice is all in all ; what is it to be shewed the way, and to know it exactly, if we do not walk in it, if we do not by it arrive to our journey's end, the salvation of our souls ? To have waited upon our Lord himself, and hung upon his discourse, was not available [4] ; for when in the day of accompt, some shall begin to allege, *We have eaten, and drank before thee, and thou hast taught in our streets ; Our Lord will say, I know you not, whence ye are, depart from me all ye workers of iniquity* [5]. And, it is our Lord's declaration in the case, *whosoever heareth these sayings of mine and doeth them, I will liken him unto a wise man, which built his house upon a rock ;—but every one that heareth these sayings of mine, and doeth them not, shall be likened unto a foolish man, that built his house upon the sand* [6].

Many are very earnest to hear, they *hear gladly*, as *Herod* did St. *John Baptist*'s homilies [7] ; they *receive the word with joy*, as the *temporary believers* in the Parable did [8] ; They doe, as those men did in the *Prophet, delight to know God's ways, do ask of God the ordinances of justice, do take delight in approaching God* [9] ; Or as those in another *Prophet ; who speak one to another,*

---

[1] *Heb.* VI, 7, 8 ; X, 26.   [2] *Rom.* II, 13.   [3] *Jas.* I, 22
[4] [of no avail].   [5] *Luke* XIII, 26, 27.
[6] *Matt.* VII, 24, 26 ; *John* XIV, 21.
[7] *Mark* VI, 20.   [8] *Matt.* XIII, 20.   [9] *Isa.* LVIII, 2.

*every one to his brother, saying, Come, I pray you, and hear what
is the word that cometh forth from the Lord ; And they come unto
thee as the people cometh, and they sit before thee as my people ;
and they hear thy words, but will not doe them ; for with their
mouth they shew much love, but their heart goeth after their
covetousness : And lo thou art to them as a very lovely song of
one that hath a pleasant voice, and can play well on an instrument ;
for they hear thy words, but they doe them not* [1] : They for a time
rejoice in the light of God's Messengers, as those *Jews* did in the
light of that *burning and shining lamp*, St. *John* the *Baptist* [2] ; but
all comes to nothing ; but they are backward and careless to perform, at least more than they please themselves, or what suteth
to their fancy, their humour, their appetite, their interest : Many
hearers will believe onely what they like, or what suteth to their
prejudices and passions ; many of what they believe will practise
that onely which sorteth with their temper, or will serve their
designs ; they cannot conform to unpleasant, and unprofitable
Doctrines : Sometimes care choaketh the word, sometimes temptation of pleasure, of profit, of honour allureth, sometimes difficulties,
hazards, persecutions discourage from obedience to it :

These particulars are obvious, and by most will be consented
to : there is one point which perhaps will more hardly be admitted,
which therefore I shall more largely insist upon : 'tis this,

6. That as in all cases it is our duty to defer much regard to
the opinion of our Guides, so in some cases it behoveth us to rely
barely [3] upon their judgment and advice ; those especially among
them who excell in dignity, and worth ; who are approved for
wisedom and integrity ; their definitions, or the declarations of
their opinion, (especially such as are exhibited upon mature deliberation and debate, in a solemn manner) are ever very probable
arguments of truth and expediency ; they are commonly the best
arguments which can be had in some matters, especially to the
meaner and simpler sort of people. This upon many accompts
will appear reasonable.

It is evident to experience, that every man is not capable to
judge, or able to guide himself in matters of this nature (concerning divine truth and conscience.) There are *children in under-*

---

[1] *Ezek.* XXXIII, 30, 31, 32.   [2] *John* V, 35.
[3] [entirely, without qualification].

standing [1], there are men *weak in faith* [2] (or knowledge concerning the faith,) there are *idiots*, ἄκακοι (men not bad, but *simple*) [3] persons *occupying the room of the unlearned* [4], *unskilfull in the word of righteousness*, who (as the *Apostle* saith) *need that one should teach them which be the first principles of the oracles of God* [5].

The vulgar sort of men are as undiscerning and injudicious in all things [6], so peculiarly in matters of this nature, so much abstracted from common sense and experience ; whence we see them easily seduced into the fondest conceits [7] and wildest courses by any slender artifice, or fair pretence ; *like children tossed to and fro, and carried about with every wind of doctrine, by the slight of men, and cunning craftiness, whereby they lie in wait to deceive* [8].

There are also some particular cases, a competent information and skill in which must depend upon improvements of mind acquired by more than ordinary study and experience ; so that in them most people do want sufficient means of attaining knowledge requisite to guide their judgment, or their practice [9] : And for such persons in such cases it is plainly the best, the wisest, and the safest way to rely upon the direction of their Guides, assenting to what they declare, acting what they prescribe, going whither they conduct.

The very notion of Guides, and the design of their office doth import a difference of knowledge, and a need of reliance upon them in such cases ; it signifieth, that we are in some measure ignorant of the way, and that they better know it ; and if so, plain reason dictateth it fit that we should follow them ; and indeed what need were there of Guides, to what purpose should we have them, if we can sufficiently ken [10] the way, and judge what we should doe, without them ?

---

[1] [*1 Cor.* XIV, 20].

[2] *Rom.* XIV, 1 ; XV, 1, etc. ; *1 Cor.* III, 2 ; VIII, 9.

[3] *Rom.* XVI, 18.   [4] *1 Cor.* XIV, 16.   [5] [*Heb.* V, 12].

[6] Vulgo non judicium, non veritas. TAC. [Neque illis judicium aut veritas. *Hist.* I, xxxii].

[7] ἄκριτον ὁ δῆμος. M. ANT. [*Comment.* IV, 3 : ἀπιδὼν... τὸ εὐμετάβολον καὶ ἄκριτος τῶν εὐφημεῖν δοκούντων. See Gataker's edition, Cambridge, 1654, Annotationes in Librum IV, p. 125].   [8] *Eph.* IV, 14.

[9] ᾿Αλλ᾿ εἰδότες ἑτέροις βέλτιον εἶναι τὰς ἑαυτῶν ἡνίας ἐνδιδόναι τεχνικωτέ- ροις, ἢ ἄλλων ἡνιόχους εἶναι ἀνεπιστήμονας, καὶ ἀκοὴν ὑποτιθέναι μᾶλλον εὐγνώ- μονα, ἢ γλῶσσαν κινεῖν ἀπαίδευτον. GREG. NAZ. *Orat.* I [*Apologetica*, XLVII. MIGNE, *Patrol. gr.*, t. 35, col. 456]. — fide calidus, et virtute robustus, etc. CYPR. *Ep.* XXIII de *Luciano* [MIGNE, *Patrol. lat.*, t. 4, col. 290].

[10] [to descry].

In the state of learning (in which the assigning us Teachers supposeth us placed) whatever our capacity may be, yet our judgment at least (for want of a full comprehension of things, which must be discovered in order, and by degrees) is imperfect ; in that state therefore it becometh us not to pretend exercise of judgment, but rather easily to yield assent to what our Teachers, who see farther into the thing, do assert ; *The learner* (as *Seneca* saith) *is bound to be ruled, while he beginneth to be able to rule himself* [1].

Δεῖ μανθάνοντα πιστεύειν, *A learner should in some measure be credulous* [2]; otherwise as he will often fail in his judgment, so he will make little progress in learning ; for, if he will admit nothing on his Master's word, if he will question all things, if he will continually be doubting and disputing, or contradicting and opposing his Teacher, how can instruction proceed ? He that presently will be his own Master, is a bad Scholar, and will be a worse Master. He that will fly before he is fledged, no wonder if he tumble down.

There are divers obvious, and very considerable cases, in which persons most contemptuous of authority, and refractary toward their Guides, are constrained to rely upon the judgment of others, and are contented to doe it, their conscience shewing them unable to judge for themselves ; In admitting the literal sense of Scripture, according to translations ; in the interpretation of difficult places, depending upon the skill of languages, grammar, and criticism, upon the knowledge of humane arts and sciences, upon histories and ancient customs ; in such cases all illiterate persons (however otherwise diffident, and disregardfull of authority) are forced to see with the eyes of other men, to submit their judgment to the skill and fidelity of their learned Guides, taking the very principles and foundations of their Religion upon trust ; And why then consonantly may they not doe it in other cases ; especially in the resolution of difficult, sublime, obscure, and subtile points, the comprehension whereof transcendeth their capacity ?

---

[1] Regi debet, dum incipit posse se regere. SEN. *Ep.* XCIV [51].
[2] [not identified].

But farther,

The more to engage and incline us to the performing this part of our duty (the regarding, prizing, confiding in the judgment of our Guides) we may consider the great advantages, both natural and supernatural, which they have to qualify them in order to such purposes.

1. They may reasonably be presumed more intelligent and skilfull in divine matters, than others ; for as they have the same natural capacities and endowments with others (or rather commonly somewhat better than others, as being designed and selected to this sort of employment) so their natural abilities are by all possible means improved : it is their trade and faculty, unto which their education is directed : in acquiring ability toward which they spend their time, their care, their pains ; in which they are continually versed and exercised (*having*, as the *Apostle* speaketh, *by reason of use their senses exercised to discern both good and evil*) [1] for which also they employ their supplications, and devotions to God.

Many special advantages they hence procure, needfull or very conducible to a more perfect knowledge of such matters, and to security from errours ; such as are conversing with studies, which enlarge a man's mind, and improve his judgment ; a skill of disquisition about things, of sifting and canvasing points coming under debate ; of weighing the force of arguments, and distinguishing the colours of things ; the knowledge of languages, in which the *divine Oracles* are expressed, of Sciences, of Histories, of practices serving to the discovery and illustration of the truth : exercise in meditation, reading, writing, speaking, disputing and conference, whereby the mind is greatly enlightned, and the reason strengthned ; acquaintance with variety of learned Authours, who

[1] *Heb.* V, 14.

with great diligence have expounded the Holy Scriptures, and with most accuracy discussed points of doctrine ; especially with *Ancient writers*, who living near the *Apostolical* times, and being immediately, (or within few degrees mediately) their Disciples may justly be supposed most helpfull toward informing us what was their genuine doctrine, what the true sense of their writings : By such means as in other *Faculties*, so in this of *Theology*, a competent skill may be obtained ; there is no other ordinary, or probable way ; and no extraordinary way can be trusted, now that men appear not to grow learned or wise by special inspiration or miracle ; after that all pretences to such by-ways have been detected of imposture, and do smell too rank of hypocrisie.

Since then our Guides are so advantageously qualified to direct us ; it is in matters difficult, and doubtfull (the which require good measure of skill and judgment to determine about them) most reasonable, that we should rely upon their authority, preferring it in such cases to our private discretion ; taking it for more probable, that they should comprehend the truth, than we (unassisted by them, and judging merely by our own glimmering light) can do ; deeming it good odds on the side of their doctrine against our opinion, or conjecture.

They have also another peculiar advantage toward judging sincerely of things, by their greater retirement from the World and disengagement from secular interests [1] ; the which ordinarily do deprave the understandings, and pervert the judgments of men ; disposing them to accommodate their conceits to the *maximes* of worldly policy, or to the vulgar apprehensions of men : many of which are false, and base ; by such abstraction of mind from worldly affairs together with fastning their meditation on the best things (which their calling necessarily doth put them upon) more than is usual to other men, they commonly get principles and habits of simplicity and integrity, which qualify men both to discern truth better, and more faithfully to declare it.

Seeing then in every *Faculty* the advice of the skilfull is to be regarded, and is usually relied upon ; and in other affairs of greatest importance we scruple not to proceed so ; seeing we commit our life and health (which are most pretious to us) to the *Physician*, observing his prescriptions commonly without any reason, some-

---

[1] *2 Tim.* II, 4.

times against our own sense; we entrust our estate, which is so
dear, with the *Lawyer*, not contesting his advice; we put our goods
and safety into the hands of a *Pilot*, sleeping securely, whilst he
steereth us, as he thinketh fit: seeing in many such occasions of
common life we advisedly do renounce, or wave our own opinions,
absolutely yielding to the direction of others, taking their authority
for a better argument or ground of action, than any which our
conceit, or a bare consideration of the matter can suggest to us;
admitting this *maxime* for good, that it is a more adviseable and
safe course in matters of consequence to follow the judgment of
wiser men, than to adhere to our own apprehensions[1]: Seeing it is
not wisedom (as every man thinks) in a doubtfull case to act upon
disadvantage, or to venture upon odds against himself, and it is
plainly doing thus to act upon our own opinion against the judgment of those who are more improved in the way, or better studied
in the point than our selves; seeing in other cases these are the
common approved apprehensions and practices; and seeing in this
case there is plainly the same reason, for that there are difficulties
and intricacies in this no less than in other Faculties, which need
good skill to resolve them; for that in these matters we may easily
slip, and by errour may incur huge danger and damage; why then
should we not here take the same course, following (when no other
clearer light, or prevalent reason occurreth) the conduct and advice
of our more skilfull Guides? especially considering, that beside
ordinary, natural and acquired advantages, they have other supernatural both obligations to the well discharging this duty, and
assistences toward it: For

2. We may consider, that they are by God appointed, and
impowred to instruct and guide us: it is their special office, not
assumed by themselves, or constituted by humane prudence, but
ordained and setled by divine wisedom for our edification in
knowledge, and direction in practice[2]: they are God's messengers

---

[1] "Ὃν [γὰρ] ἂν ἡγήσωνται περὶ τὰ συμφέροντα ἑαυτοῖς φρονιμώτερον ἑαυτῶν
εἶναι, τούτῳ οἱ ἄνθρωποι ὑπερηδέως πείθονται. Xen. *Paed.* I [*Cyropaedia*, I,
vi, 21].

᾽Εν μὲν τῷ πλεῖν πείθεσθαι δεῖ τῷ κυβερνήτῃ, ἐν δὲ τῷ ζῆν τῷ λογίζεσθαι
δυναμένῳ βέλτιον. Aristonymus *apud* Stob. Tom. II, Tit. 3. [Socrates, no. 41,
in Joannis Stobaei *Florilegium*, Lipsiae, 1838; the quotation from Aristonymus
is no. 40].

[2] *Jer.* III, 15. I will give you Pastours according to mine heart, which shall
feed you with knowledge and understanding. Cypr. *Ep.* LV [on *Jer.* III, 15,
i.e. *Ep.* XII. Migne, *Patrol. lat.*, t. 3].

purposely sent by him [1], selected and *separated* by his instinct [2] *for this work* [3]; they are by him *given for the perfecting of the Saints, and edifying the body of Christ* [4]: It is by God's warrant, and in his name that they speak, which giveth especial weight to their words, and no mean ground of assurance to us in relying upon them: for who is more likely to know God's mind and will, who may be presumed more faithfull in declaring them, than God's own Officers, and Agents? those whose great duty, whose main concernment it is to speak not their own sense, but the word of God? They are God's mouth, by whom alone ordinarily he expresseth his mind and pleasure; by whom *he entreateth us to be reconciled* [5] in heart and practice to him; what they say therefore is to be received as God's word, except plain reason upon due examination do forbid.

If they by office are teachers, or Masters in doctrine, then we answerably must in obligation be Disciples, which implies admitting their doctrine, and proficiency in knowledge thereby; If they are appointed Shepherds, then must we be their Sheep, to be led and fed by them; if they are God's messengers, we must yield some credence, and embrace the message uttered by them; so the *Prophet* telleth us: *The Priests lips should keep knowledge, and they should seek the law at his mouth, for he is the messenger of the Lord of hosts* [6]; so the Law of old enjoined;—*According to the sentence of the law, which they shall teach thee, and according to the judgment, which they shall tell thee thou shalt doe; thou shalt not decline from the sentence which they shall shew thee to the right hand, nor to the left* [7]; so our *Lord* also in regard to the *Scribes* and *Pharisees* saith, *The Scribes and Pharisees sit in Moses his chair, all therefore whatsoever they bid you observe, that observe and doe* [8]; upon accompt of their office, whatever they direct to (not repugnant to the divine Law) was to be observed by the people [9]; and surely in doubtfull cases, when upon competent inquiry no clear light offereth it self, it cannot be very dangerous to follow their guidance, whom God hath appointed and authorized to lead us; if we err doing so we err wisely in the way of our duty, and so no great blame will attend our errour.

---

[1] *Rom.* X, 15.   [2] [prompting].   [3] *Acts* XIII, 2.
[4] *Eph.* IV, 11, 12; *1 Cor.* XII, 28; *1 Tim.* I, 11, 12; II, 7; *Tit.* I, 3; *1 Thess.* II, 4.
[5] *2 Cor.* V, 20.   [6] *Mal.* II, 7.   [7] *Deut.* XVII, 11.
[8] *Matt.* XXIII, 3.   [9] *Ezek.* XXXIV, 16.

3. We may consider that our Guides as such have special
assistence from God ; to every vocation God's aid is congruously
afforded ; but to this (the principal of all others, the most important, most nearly related to God, and most peculiarly tending
to his service) it is in a special manner most assuredly and plenti-
fully imparted.

They are *stewards of God's various grace* [1] ; and they who
ᵃ dispense grace to others cannot want it themselves : they are
cooperatours with God [2], and God consequently doth cooperate
with them ; It is *God* who doth ἱχανοῦν, *render them sufficient to
be Ministers of the new Testament* [3] ; and they *minister of the
ability, which God supplieth* [4] ; Every spiritual labourer is obliged
to say with St. *Paul* ; *By the grace of God I am what I am—I have
laboured, yet not I, but the grace of God, which was with me* [5].

God's having *given them* (as St. *Paul* saith) to the Church,
doth imply that God hath endowed them with special ability, and
furthereth them (in their conscionable discharge of their ministery)
with aid requisite to the designs of *perfecting the saints, and edifying the Body* [6] in knowledge, in vertue, in piety.

As the Holy Ghost doth constitute them in their charge (according to that of St. *Paul* in the *Acts* ; *Take heed unto your selves,
and to all the flock, over which the Holy Ghost hath made you
overseers)* [7] so questionless he doth enable, and assist them in
administring their function. There is *a gift* (of spiritual ability,
and divine succour) imparted by their consecration to this office,
with *the laying on the hands of the Presbytery* [8], joined with humble
supplications for them, and solemn benedictions in God's name upon
them. The divine Spirit, which *distributeth, as he seeth good, unto
every member of the Church* needfull supplies of grace doth *bestow*
on them in competent measure *the word of wisedom*, and *the word
of knowledge* requisite for their employment [9].

God of old did in extraordinary ways visibly communicate his
spirit unto his *Prophets* and Agents ; the same he did liberally
pour out upon the *Apostles*, and first planters of the *Gospel* ; The

---

ᵃ dispense] *B.* ; *1686* dispence

[1] *1 Pet.* IV, 10.   [2] *1 Cor.* III, 9.   [3] *2 Cor.* III, 5 ; *Phil.* II, 13.
[4] *1 Pet.* IV, 11.   [5] *1 Cor.* XV, 10.
[6] *Eph.* IV, 11, 12 ; *1 Cor.* XII, 28.
[7] *Acts* XX, 28.   [8] *1 Tim.* IV, 14 ; *2 Tim.* I, 6.
[9] *1 Cor.* XII, 7, etc. ; *Eph.* IV, 16 ; *Rom.* XII, 5, 6.

same questionless he hath not withdrawn from those, who under the *Evangelical* dispensation (which is peculiarly the *ministration of the Spirit*[1], unto which the aid of God's Spirit is most proper and most needfull) do still by a setled ministery supply the room of those extraordinary ministers; but imparteth it to them, in a way although more ordinary and occult, yet no less real and effectual, according to proportions answerable to the exigencies of need and occasion; And by the influence hereof upon the Pastors of his Church it is, that our Lord accomplisheth his promise to be *with it untill the end of the World*[2].

Clavis scientiae, the key of knowledge[3] spiritual, is one of those keys, which he hath given to them, whereby they are enabled to open the Kingdom of Heaven.

Great reason therefore we have to place an especial confidence in their direction; for whom can we more safely follow, than those, whom (upon such grounds of divine declarations and promises) we may hope that God doth guide; so that consequently in following them we do in effect follow God himself? *He that heareth you, heareth me*[4], might be said not onely because of their relation unto Christ; but because their word proceedeth from his inspiration, being no other than his mind conveyed through their mouth.

4. We may also for our encouragement to confide in our Guides consider, that they are themselves deeply concerned in our being rightly guided; their present comfort, their salvation hereafter depending upon the faithfull, and carefull discharge of their duty herein: they must render an accompt for it; so that if by their wilfull, or negligent miscarriage we do fall into dangerous errour or sin, they do thence not onely forfeit rich and glorious rewards (assigned to those, *who turn many unto righteousness*)[5] but incur wofull punishment; this doth assure their integrity, and render our confidence in them very reasonable; for as we may safely trust a Pilot, who hath no less interest than our selves in the safe conveyance of the vessel to port; so may we reasonably confide in their advice, whose salvation is adventured with ours in the same bottom[6], or rather is wrapped up, and carryed in ours; It is not probable they will (at least designedly) misguide us to their own extreme damage, to their utter ruine: *If they do not warn*

---

[1] *2 Cor.* III, 8.   [2] *Matt.* XXVIII, 20.
[3] *Luke* XI, 52.   [4] [*Luke* X, 16].   [5] [*1 Cor.* XV, 34].
[6] [i.e. bottom of a ship; in the same boat].

*the wicked from his wicked way to save his life, God hath said
that he will require his bloud at their hands* [1] ; and is it likely they
wittingly should run such a hazard, that they should purposely
cast away the souls, for which they are so certainly accomptable ?
it is our *Apostle*'s enforcement of the precept in our *Text* ; *Obey
them that guide you* ; *for they watch for your souls, as they that
must give an accompt* ; which argumentation is not onely grounded
upon the obligations of ingenuity and gratitude, but also upon
considerations of discretion and [a] interest ; we should obey our
Guides in equity and honesty ; we may doe it advisedly, because
they in regard to their own accompts at the final judgment are
obliged to be carefull for the good of our souls.

Upon these considerations it is plainly reasonable to follow our
Guides in all matters, wherein we have no other very clear and
certain light of reason, or revelation to conduct us : the doing so
is indeed (which is farther observable) not onely wise in it self,
but safe in way of prevention, that we be not seduced by other
treacherous Guides ; it will not onely secure us from our own weak
judgments, but from the frauds of those *who lie in wait to deceive* [2].
The simpler sort of men will in effect be always led not by their
own judgment, but by the authority of others ; and if they be not
fairly guided by those, whom God hath constituted and assigned
to that end, they will be led by the nose by those, who are concerned to seduce them : so reason dictateth that it must be, so
experience sheweth it ever to have been ; that the people whenever
they have deserted their true Guides, have soon been hurried by
impostors into most dangerous errours, and extravagant follies ;
being *carried about with divers, and strange doctrines* [3] ; being *like
children tossed to and fro with every wind of doctrine* [4].

It is therefore a great advantage to us, and a great mercy of
God, that there are (by God's care) provided for us such helps,
upon which we may commonly for our guidance in the way to
happiness more safely rely, than upon our own judgments lyable
to mistake, and than upon the counsel of others, who may be
interested to abuse us ; very foolish and very ingratefull we are,
if we do not highly prize, if we do not willingly embrace this
advantage.

[a] interest] *B.* ; *1686* interests

[1] *Ezek.* III, 18 ; XXXIII, 2, 8.
[2] *Eph.* IV, 14.   [3] *Heb.* XIII, 9.   [4] *Eph.* IV, 14.

I farther add, that as wisdom may induce, so modesty and humility should dispose us to follow the direction of our Guides ; *Ye Younger* (saith St. *Peter*) *submit your selves unto the Elder* (that is, ye Inferiours to your Superiours, ye that are the Flock to your Pastours) *and* (subjoineth he immediately) *be cloathed with humility* [1] ; signifying ; that it is a point of humility to yield that submission ; Every modest, and humble person is apt to distrust his own, and to submit to better judgments : And *Not to lean to our understanding, not to be wise in our own eys* [2] ; *not to seem to know any thing, not to seem any body to ones self* [3], *in humility to prefer others before our selves* [4], are divine injunctions, chiefly applicable to this case, in reference to our spiritual Guides ; for if it be pride or culpable immodesty to presume our selves wiser than any man, what is it then to prefer our selves in that respect before our teachers ; as indeed we do, when without evident reason we disregard, or dissent from their opinion ?

It is then a duty very reasonable, and a very commendable practice to rely upon the guidance of our Pastours in such cases, wherein surer direction faileth, and we cannot otherwise fully satisfy our selves.

Neither in doing so (against some appearances of reason, or with some violence to our private conceits) do we act against our conscience, but rather truely according to it ; for conscience (as the word in this case is used) is nothing else but an opinion in practical matters, grounded upon the best reason we can discern ; if therefore in any case the authority of our Guides be a reason outweighing all other reasons apparent, he that in such a case, notwithstanding other arguments less forcible, doth conform his judgment and practice thereto, therein exactly followeth conscience ; yea in doing otherwise he would thwart and violence [5] his own conscience, and be self-condemned, adhering to a less probable reason in opposition to one more probable.

I do not hereby mean to assert, that we are obliged indifferently (with an implicite faith or blind obedience) to believe all that our teachers say, or to practise all they bid us : for they are men, and therefore subject to errour, and sin ; they may neglect or abuse the advantages they have of knowing better than others ; they may

---

[1] *1 Pet.* V, 5.　　　　　　　[2] *Prov.* III, 5, 7.
[3] *1 Cor.* VIII, 2 ; *Rom.* XII, 3, 10 ; *Gal.* VI, 3.
[4] *Phil.* II, 3 ; *1 Tim.* VI, 4.　　[5] [do violence to].

sometimes by infirmity, by negligence, by pravity fail in performing faithfully their duty toward us: they may be swayed by temper, be led by passion, be corrupted by ambition or avarice, so as thence to embrace and vent bad doctrines: We do see our Pastours often dissenting and clashing among themselves, sometimes with themselves, so as to change and retract their own opinions [1].

We find the *Prophets* of old complaining of *Priests*, of *Pastours*, of *Elders* and Prophets, who *handled the law, yet were ignorant of God* [2]; who *erred in vision, and stumbled in judgment* [3]; who *were profane, brutish, light and treacherous persons*; *who polluted the sanctuary and did violence to the Law* [4]; *and profaned holy things* [5]; who *handled the Law, yet knew not God* [6]; from *whom the Law, and counsel did perish* [7]; *who taught for hire, and divined for money* [8]; *who themselves departed out of the way, and caused many to stumble, and corrupted the covenant of Levi* [9]; *who destroyed and scattered the sheep of God's pasture* [10].

There were in our *Saviour*'s time Guides, *of the ferment of whose doctrine* good people were *bid to beware* [11]; who *transgressed and defeated the commandment of God by their traditions* [12]; who *did take away the key of knowledge, so that they would not enter themselves into the Kingdom of Heaven, nor would suffer others to enter* [13]; *blind guides* [14], who both themselves did fall, and drew others into the ditch of noxious errour, and wicked practice: the followers of which Guides did *in vain worship God, observing for doctrine the precepts of men* [15].

There have not since the primitive times of the Gospel wanted those who (indulging to ambition, avarice, curiosity, faction, and other bad affections) have depraved and debased religion with noxious errours, and idle superstitions; such as St. *Bernard* describeth, etc. [16].

---

[1] *Isa.* III, 12. O my people, they which lead thee, cause thee to err, and destroy the way of thy paths.
   [2] *Jer.* II, 8.   [3] *Isa.* XXVIII, 7.
   [4] *Jer.* XXIII, 11; X, 21; VI, 13; XII, 10; *Zeph.* III, 4; *Jer.* XVIII, 18; V, 31.   [5] *Ezek.* XXII, 26.   [6] *Jer.* II, 8; *Mal.* I, 6.
   [7] *Ezek.* VII, 26.   [8] *Mic.* III, 11.
   [9] *Mal.* II, 8, 9; *Jer.* XXIII, 10, 11, 12.   [10] [*Jer.* XXIII, 1].
   [11] *Matt.* XVI, 6, 12; *Luke* XII, 1.   [12] *Matt.* XV, 2, 6.
   [13] *Luke* XI, 52.   [14] *Matt.* XV, 14.   [15] *Matt.* XV, 9.
   [16] Vid. [JOHN JEWEL] *Apol. Eccl. Angl.* [Londini, 1562, sig. D 8 v: "Et quid mirum, si Ecclesia erroribus abducta fuerit, illo praesertim tempore, cum nec episcopus Romanus qui summae rerum solus praeerat, nec alius fere quisquam aut officium suum faceret, aut omnino officium suum intelligeret? Vix

We are in matters of such infinite concernment to our eternal welfare, in wisdom and duty obliged not wholly without farther heed or care to trust the diligence, and integrity of others, but to consider and look about us, using our own reason, judgment and discretion, so far as we are capable ; we cannot in such a case be blamed for too much circumspection, and caution.

We are not wholly blind, not void of reason, not destitute of fit helps ; in many cases we have competent ability to judge, and means sufficient to attain knowledge ; we are therefore concerned to use our eyes, to employ our reason, to embrace and improve the advantages vouchsafed us.

We are accomptable personally for all our actions as agreeable or cross to reason ; if we are mistaken by our own default, or misled by the ill guidance of others, we shall however deeply suffer for it, and *die in our iniquity* [1] ; the ignorance, or errour of our Guides will not wholly excuse us from guilt, or exempt us from punishment ; it is fit therefore that we should be allowed, as to the sum of the matter, to judge and chuse for our selves : for if our salvation were wholly placed in the hands of others, so that we could not but in case of their errour or default miscarry ; our ruine would be inevitable, and consequently not just : we should perish without blame, if we were bound, as a blind and brutish herd, to follow others.

We, in order to our practice, (which must be regulated by faith and knowledge) and toward preparing our selves for our grand accompt, are obliged to get a knowledge and persuasion concerning our duty ; *to prove* (or search, and examine) *what is that good, and acceptable, and perfect will of God* [2] ; for ignorance (if anywise by our endeavour vincible) will not secure [3] us : *He that* (saith our *Lord*, and *Judge*) *knew not, and did commit things worthy of stripes, shall be beaten with few stripes* [4] (few ; not in themselves, but comparatively to those, which shall be inflicted on them, who transgress against knowledge, and conscience.)

enim est credibile, illis otiosis et dormientibus, Diabolum toto illo tempore, aut dormivisse perpetuo, aut fuisse otiosum. Quid enim illi interim fecerint, quaque fide curaverint domum Dei, ut nos tacemus, audiant saltem Bernardum suum : Episcopi, inquit, quibus nunc commissa est Ecclesia Dei, non doctores sunt, sed seductores : non Pastores, sed impostores : non Praelati, sed Pilati (Ad Eugenium)". [Cf. BERN. *De Consideratione*. Ad Eugenium (MIGNE, *Patrol. lat.*, t. 182), though the words quoted by Jewel are not used there].

[1] *Ezek.* III. 18. [2] *Rom.* XII, 2 ; *Eph.* V, 10.
[3] [render us safe]. [4] *Luke* XII, 48.

We are bound to study truth, to improve our minds in the knowledge and love of it, to be firmly persuaded of it in a rational way ; so that we be not easily shaken, or seduced from it.

The *Apostles* do charge it upon us, as our duty, and concernment ; that we *abound in faith, and knowledge*[1] ; that we *be rooted and built up in Christ, and stablished in the faith*[2], *so as to be stedfast, and unmoveable*[3], not to *be soon shaken in mind or troubled*[4] ; *to grow up, and encrease in all divine knowledge*[5] ; that *the word of God should dwell richly in us in all wisedom*[6] ; that we should *be filled with all knowledge so as to be able to teach and admonish one another*[7] ; that *our love should abound more and more in knowledge and all judgment, that we may approve things excellent*[8] (or scan things different) that we *be enriched in all the word* (that is in all the doctrine of the Gospel) *and in all knowledge*[9] : that *we be filled in the knowledge of God's will in all wisedom and spiritual understanding*[10] ; that we should not be *unwise, but understanding what the will of the Lord is*[11] ; That we should *be perfect and complete in all the will of God*[12] (that is first in the knowledge of it, then in compliance with it) that *in understanding we should not be children, but perfect men*[13].

We are likewise by them commanded to *take heed of false Prophets*[14], to *try the spirits whether they are of God*[15], to *see that no man deceive us*[16], to *look that no man spoil us by vain deceit*[17], to *try all things and hold fast that which is good*[18] ; which precepts imply, that we should be furnished with a good faculty of judgment and competent knowledge in the principal matters of Christian doctrine, concerning both the mysteries of faith, and rules of practice. Our *Lord* himself, and his *Apostles* did not upon other terms than of rational consideration and discussion exact credit and obedience to their words, they did not insist barely upon their own authority, but exhorted their Disciples to examine strictly, and judge faithfully concerning the truth, and reasonableness of their

---

[1] *2 Cor.* VIII, 7.   [2] *Col.* II, 7.
[3] *1 Cor.* XV, 58.   [4] *2 Thess.* II, 2.
[5] *Col.* I, 10 ; *2 Pet.* III, 18 ; *1 Pet.* II, 2 ; *Eph.* IV, 15.
[6] *Col.* III, 16.   [7] *Rom.* XV, 14.   [8] *Phil.* I, 9, 10.
[9] *1 Cor.* I, 5.   [10] *Col.* I, 9.   [11] *Eph.* V, 17.
[12] *Col.* IV, 12.
[13] *1 Cor.* XIV, 20 ; *Heb.* V, 12.
[14] *Matt.* VII, 15.   [15] *1 John* IV, 1.
[16] *Matt.* XXIV, 4 ; *Eph.* V, 6.
[18] *1 Thess.* V, 21.   [17] *Col.* II, 8, 18.

doctrine : *Search the Scriptures, for they testify of me* [1]; *If I doe not the works of my Father, believe me not ; but if I do, though ye believe not me, believe the works* [2]: so our Lord appealed to their reason, proceeding upon grounds of Scripture, and common sense : and, *I speak as to wise men, judge ye what I say* [3]; so St. *Paul* addressed his Discourse to his Disciples ; otherwise we should be uncapable to observe them.

We are also bound to defer the principal regard to God's wisedom and will, so as, without reservation or exception, to embrace whatever he doth say, to obey what he positively doth command, whatever authority doth contradict his word, or cross his command : in such cases we may remonstrate with the *Apostles, If it be just before God to hearken unto you rather than unto God, judge ye* [4]: and *we ought to obey God rather than men* [5]; we may denounce with St. *Paul, if an angel from heaven preach any other Gospel, let him be accursed* [6].

We are obliged always to act *with faith* (that is, with a persuasion concerning the Lawfulness of what we doe) for *Whatever is not of faith, is sin* [7]: We should *never condemn our selves in what we try* or embrace [8].

These things considered, we may, and it much behoveth us, reserving due respect to our Guides, with humility and modesty to weigh and scan their dictates, and their orders ; lest by them unawares we be drawn into errour or sin ; like the ingenuous *Beraeans*, who did ἀναϰρίνειν τὰς γραφὰς, *search and examine the scriptures, if those things were so* [9]. [a] Our Guides are but the *helpers*, they are not Lords of our faith ; the *Apostles* themselves were not [10].

We may, and are bound, if they tell us things evidently repugnant to God's word, or to sound reason and common sense, to dissent from them [11] ; if they impose on us things evidently contrary to God's Law, to forbear compliance with them ; we may

---

a Our Guides ... helpers,] *T.*

[1] *John* V, 39. [2] *John* X, 37, 38 ; XV, 22, 24 ; XII, 48.
[3] *1 Cor.* X, 15. [4] *Acts* IV, 19. [5] *Acts* V, 29.
[6] *Gal.* I, 8. [7] *Rom.* XIV, 23. [8] *Rom.* XIV, 22.
[9] *Acts* XVII, 11. [10] *2 Cor.* I, 24.
[11] *Isa.* VIII, 20. Plebs timens Dominum separare se debet a peccatore praeposito. CYPR. [*Ep.* LXVIII, MIGNE, *Patrol. lat.*, t. 3, col. 1061 : " Propter quod plebs obsequens praeceptis dominicis et Deum metuens a peccatore praeposito separare se debet "].

in such cases appeal *ad legem et testimonium* ; we must not admit
a *non obstante* to God's law.

If other arguments (weighed in the balance of honest and
impartial reason, with cautious and industrious consideration) do
overpoise the authority of our Guides ; let us in God's name
adhere to them ; and follow our own judgments ; it would be a
violation of our conscience, a prevarication toward our own souls,
and a rebellion against God to doe otherwise : when against our
own mind, so carefully informed, we follow the dictates of others,
we like fools rashly adventure and prostitute our souls.

This proceeding is no-wise inconsistent with what we delivered
before ; for this due wariness in examining, this reservation in
assenting, this exception in practice, in some cases, wherein the
matter hath evidence, and we a faculty to judge, doth no-wise
hinder, but that we should defer much regard to the judgment of
our Guides ; that we should in those cases, wherein no light discovereth it self outshining their authority, rely upon it ; that where
our eyes will not serve clearly to direct us, we should use theirs ;
where our reason faileth to satisfy us, we should acquiesce in theirs ;
that we should regard their judgments so far, that no petty scruple
emerging, no faint semblance of reason should prevail upon us to
dissent from their doctrine, to reject their advice, to disobey their
injunctions.

In fine, let us remember, that the mouth of truth, which bid us
to *beware of the* bad *doctrine* of those who *sate in Moses's chair*,
did also charge us *to observe all they taught and injoined* [1] ; that
is all not certainly repugnant to the divine Law. In effect, if we
discost [2] from the advices of our sober teachers, appointed for us
by God ; we shall in the end have occasion to bewail with him in
the Proverbs : *How have I hated instruction, and my heart despised reproof ? And have not obeyed the voice of my teachers,
nor inclined mine ear to them that instructed me* [3] ?

To these things I shall only add one rule, which we may well
suppose comprised in the precept we treat upon ; which is that at
least we forbear openly to dissent from our Guides, or to contradict their doctrine ; except onely, [a] if it be so false (which never,

----

[a] if it be so false] ; *B, 1686.* if it be not so false [obviously a slip of Barrow's
pen].

[1] *Matt.* XXIII, 2, 3 ; XV, 14.   [2] [to depart].   [3] *Prov.* V, 12, 13.

or rarely can happen among us) as to subvert the foundations of faith, or practice of holiness. If we cannot be internally convinced by their discourses, if their authority cannot sway with us against the prevalence of other reasons, yet may we spare outwardly to oppose them, or to slight their judgment; for doing thus doth tend as to the disgrace of their persons, so to the disparagement of their office, to an obstructing the efficacy of their Ministery, to the infringement of order and peace in the Church: for when the inconsiderate people shall see their teachers distrusted and disrespected; when they perceive their doctrine may be challenged, and opposed by plausible discourses; then will they hardly trust them, or comply with them in matters most certain and necessary; than which disposition in the people there cannot happen any thing more prejudicial or banefull to the Church.

But let thus much serve for the obedience due to the doctrine of our Guides; let us consider that which we owe to them in reference to their conversation, and practice.

The following their practice may well be referred to this precept; for that their practice is a kind of living doctrine, a visible Law, or rule of action; and because indeed the notion of a Guide primarily doth imply example; that he which is guided should respect the Guide as a Precedent, being concerned to walk after his footsteps.

Most of the reasons, which urge deference to their judgment in teaching, do in proportion infer [1] obligation to follow their example, (which indeed is the most easie and clear way of instruction to vulgar capacity; carrying with it also most efficacious encouragement and excitement to practice:) they are obliged, and it is expected from them to live with especial regularity, circumspection, and strictness of conversation; they are by God's grace especially disposed, and enabled to doe so; and many common advantages they have of doing so; (a more perfect knowledge of things, firmness of principles, and clearness of notions; a deeper tincture, and more savoury relish of truth, attained by continual meditation thereon; consequently a purity of mind and affection, a retirement from the world and its temptation, freedom from distraction of worldly care, and the encombrances of business, with the like.)

They are often charged to be exemplary in conversation (as

---

[1] [imply].

we before shewed) and that involveth a correspondent obligation
to follow them. They must (like St. *John Baptist*) *be burning and
shining lights* [1] ; *Stars in God's right hand* [2] ; *lights of the world* ;
*whose light should shine before men, that men may see their good
works* [3] ; and by their light direct their steps.

They are proposed as copies, which signifies that we must in
our practice transcribe them.

We are often directly commanded to imitate them ; ὦν μιμεῖσθε
τὴν πίστιν, *whose faith imitate ye* [4] (that is their faithfull perseverance, in the doctrine and practice of Christianity) saith the *Apostle*
in this *chapter.*

Their conversation is safely imitable in all cases, wherein no
better rule appeareth, and when it doth not appear discordant from
God's Law, and the dictates of sound reason ; for supposing that
discordance, we cease to be obliged to follow them ; as when our
Lord prescribeth in respect to the Pharisees ; *Whatever they bid
you observe, that observe and doe ; but doe not after their works ;
for they say and doe not* [5].

It is indeed easier for them to speak well, than to doe well ;
their doctrine therefore is more commonly a sure Guide than their
practice ; yet when there wanteth a clearer guidance of doctrine,
their practice may pass for instructive ; and a probable argument,
or warrant of action.

---

[1] *John* V, 35.   [2] *Apoc.* [*Rev.*] I, 16, 20.
[3] *Matt.* V, 14, 16.   [4] [*Heb.* XIII, 7].   [5] *Matt.* XXIII, 3.

BIBLIOTHÈQUE
DE LA FACULTÉ DE PHILOSOPHIE ET LETTRES
DE L'UNIVERSITÉ DE LIÈGE

Président : M. Delbouille — *Administrateur :* J. Stiennon

Les prix s'entendent en N. F.
Les fascicules CLXI et suivants peuvent être livrés sous une reliure de toile :
le prix indiqué au catalogue est alors majoré de 6,00 N. F.

CATALOGUE CHRONOLOGIQUE
DES DIFFÉRENTES SÉRIES

Série in-4° (30 × 27,5) « Publications exceptionnelles ».
Cette série *n'est pas comprise* dans le Service des Echanges internationaux.

Fasc. I. — Rita Lejeune et Jacques Stiennon. *La légende de Roland dans l'art du moyen âge.* 1966. 411 + 405 pp., 63 pl. en couleurs et 510 pl. en noir (2 volumes) . . . . 2.900 Fb
(pour la Belgique)

Les commandes sont à adresser à : Editions Arcade, 299, avenue van Volxem, Bruxelles.

Fasc. II. — Pierre Colman. *L'orfèvrerie religieuse liégeoise du XV⁰ siècle à la Révolution.* 1966. 298 + 111 pp., 244 pl. en noir (2 volumes) . . . . 1.250 Fb

Les commandes sont à adresser à : Société Desoer, 21, rue Sainte-Véronique, Liège.

Série grand in-8° (Jésus) 27,5 × 18,5.

Fasc. I *. — Mélanges Godefroid Kurth. Tome I. *Mémoires historiques.* 1908. 466 pp. . . . . Epuisé

Fasc. II *. — Mélanges Godefroid Kurth. Tome II. *Mémoires littéraires, philosophiques et archéologiques.* 1908. 460 pp. . . Epuisé

Fasc. III *. — J. P. Waltzing. *Lexicon Minucianum.* Praemissa est *Octavii* recensio nova. 1909. 281 pp. . . . . . . Epuisé

Fasc. IV *. — Henri Francotte. *Mélanges de Droit public grec.* 1910. 336 pp. . . . . Epuisé

Fasc. V *. — Jacques Stiennon. *L'écriture diplomatique dans le diocèse de Liège du XI⁰ au milieu du XIII⁰ siècle. Reflet d'une civilisation.* 1960. 430 pp. 25,00

2

Fasc. XXV. — J. P. WALTZING. *Plaute. Les Captifs.* Texte, traduction et commentaire analytique, grammatical et critique. 1921. 100 + 144 pp. . . . .   Epuisé

Fasc. XXVI. — A. HUMPERS. *Etude sur la langue de Jean Lemaire de Belges.* 1921. 244 pp. . . . .   Epuisé

Fasc. XXVII. — F. ROUSSEAU. *Henri l'Aveugle, Comte de Namur et de Luxembourg.* 1921. 125 pp. . . . .   Epuisé

Fasc. XXVIII. — J. HAUST. *Le dialecte liégeois au XVII* siècle. Les trois plus anciens textes (1620-1630).* Edition critique, avec commentaire et glossaire. 1921. 84 pp. . . . .   Epuisé

Fasc. XXIX. — A. DELATTE. *Essai sur la politique pythagoricienne.* 1922. 295 pp. (Prix Bordin, de l'Institut) . . . . .   Epuisé

Fasc. XXX. — J. DESCHAMPS. *Sainte-Beuve et le sillage de Napoléon.* 1922. 177 pp. . . . .   Epuisé

MÊME SÉRIE (25 × 16).

Fasc. XXXI. — C. TIHON. *La Principauté et le Diocèse de Liège sous Robert de Berghes (1557-1564).* 1923. 331 pp. (Avec deux cartes). . . . .   Epuisé

Fasc. XXXII. — J. HAUST. *Etymologies wallonnes et françaises.* 1923. 357 pp. (Prix Volney, de l'Institut) . . . .   Epuisé

Fasc. XXXIII. — A. L. CORIN. *Sermons de J. Tauler. I. Le Codex Vindobonensis 2744, édité pour la première fois.* 1924. 372 pp. .   Epuisé

Fasc. XXXIV. — A. DELATTE. *Les Manuscrits à miniatures et à ornements des Bibliothèques d'Athènes.* 1926. 128 pp. et 48 planches   Epuisé

Fasc. XXXV. — OSCAR JACOB. *Les esclaves publics à Athènes.* 1928. 214 pp. (Prix Zographos, de l'Association des Etudes Grecques en France) . . . .   Epuisé

Fasc. XXXVI. — A. DELATTE. *Anecdota Atheniensia.* Tome I : Textes grecs inédits relatifs à l'histoire des religions. 1927. 740 pp. avec des figures . . . .   Epuisé

Fasc. XXXVII. — JEAN HUBAUX. *Le réalisme dans les Bucoliques de Virgile.* 1927. 144 pp. . . . .   Epuisé

Fasc. XXXVIII. — PAUL HARSIN. *Les relations extérieures de la principauté de Liège sous Jean d'Elderen et Joseph Clément de Bavière (1688-1723).* 1927. 280 pp. . . . .   Epuisé

Fasc. XXXIX. — PAUL HARSIN. *Etude critique sur la bibliographie des œuvres de Law* (avec des mémoires inédits). 1928. 128 pp.   Epuisé

Fasc. XL. — A. SEVERYNS. *Le Cycle épique dans l'Ecole d'Aristarque.* 1928. 476 pp. (Prix Th. Reinach, de l'Association des Etudes Grecques en France) (réimpression anastatique)   60,00

Fasc. XLI. — JEANNE-MARIE H. THONET. *Etude sur Edward Fitz-Gerald et la littérature persane, d'après les sources originales.* 1929. 144 pp. . . . .   Epuisé

Fasc. XLII. — A. L. CORIN. *Sermons de J. Tauler. II. Le Codex Vindobonensis 2739, édité pour la première fois.* 1929. 548 pp. .   Epuisé

Fasc. XLIII. — L.-E. HALKIN. *Réforme protestante et Réforme catholique au diocèse de Liège. Le Cardinal de la Marck, Prince-Evêque de Liège (1505-1538).* 1930. 314 pp. (Prix Thérouanne, de l'Académie Française) . . . .   Epuisé

Fasc. LXV. — M. DE CORTE. *Le Commentaire de Jean Philopon sur le Troisième Livre du « Traité de l'Ame » d'Aristote.* 1934. XXII-86 pp. . . . . Epuisé

Fasc. LXVI. — P. HARSIN. *Dutot : Réflexions politiques sur les finances et le commerce.* Edition intégrale publiée pour la 1ʳᵉ fois. Tome 1. 1935. LVI-300 pp. avec 9 tableaux . . . . .

Fasc. LXVII. — P. HARSIN. *Dutot : Réflexions...* Tome II. 1935. 324 pp. avec un tableau hors-texte. Les deux fascicules . . . Epuisé

Fasc. LXVIII. — FERNAND DESONAY. *Œuvres complètes d'Antoine de La Sale.* Tome I. *La Salade.* 1935. XLV-270 pp. . . . . Epuisé

Fasc. LXIX. — P. NÈVE DE MÉVERGNIES. *Jean-Baptiste Van Helmont, Philosophe par le feu.* 1935. 232 pp. (Prix Binoux, de l'Institut) . Epuisé

Fasc. LXX. —. S. ETIENNE. *Expériences d'analyse textuelle en vue de l'explication littéraire. Travaux d'élèves.* 1935. 145 pp. (réimpression anastatique) 40,00

Fasc. LXXI. — F. WAGNER. *Les poèmes mythologiques de l'Edda.* Traduction précédée d'un exposé général de la mythologie scandinave. 1936. 262 pp. . . . . Epuisé

Fasc. LXXII. — L.-E. HALKIN. *Réforme protestante et Réforme catholique au diocèse de Liège. Histoire religieuse des règnes de Corneille de Berghes et de Georges d'Autriche (1538-1557).* 1936. 436 pp. (Prix d'Académie, de l'Institut de France) . . . . Epuisé

Fasc. LXXIII. — ANTOINE GRÉGOIRE. *L'apprentissage du langage.* 1937. Tome I. 288 pp. (Prix Volney, de l'Institut de France) (réimpression anastatique). 40,00

Fasc. LXXIV. — J. DUCHESNE-GUILLEMIN. *Etudes de morphologie iranienne. I. Les composés de l'Avesta.* 1937. XI-279 pp. . . Epuisé

Fasc. LXXV. — HERMAN F. JANSSENS. *L'entretien de la Sagesse. Introduction aux œuvres philosophiques de Bar Hebraeus.* 1937. 375 pp. 15,00

Fasc. LXXVI. — AUGUSTE BRICTEUX. *Roustem et Sohrab.* 1937. 91 pp. . . . . Epuisé

Fasc. LXXVII. — JEAN YERNAUX. *Histoire du Comté de Logne. Etudes sur le passé politique, économique et social d'un district ardennais.* 1937. 250 pp. . . . . Epuisé

Fasc. LXXVIII. — A. SEVERYNS. *Recherches sur la Chrestomathie de Proclos. Première partie. Le Codex 239 de Photius. Tome I. Etude paléographique et critique.* 1938. 404 pp. et 3 planches (Prix Gantrelle, de l'Académie Royale de Belgique). Voir fasc. CXXXII.

Fasc. LXXIX. — A. SEVERYNS. *Recherches sur la Chrestomathie de Proclos. Première partie. Le Codex 239 de Photius. Tome II. Texte, traduction, commentaire.* 1938. 298 pp. Voir fasc. CXXXII.

Fasc. LXXX. — ROBERT DEMOULIN. *Guillaume Iᵉʳ et la transformation économique des Provinces Belges (1815-1830).* 1938. 463 pp. (Prix Chaix d'Est-Ange, de l'Institut) . . . . Epuisé

Fasc. LXXXI. — ARMAND DELATTE. *Herbarius. Recherches sur le cérémonial usité chez les anciens pour la cueillette des simples et des plantes magiques.* 1938. 177 pp. . . . . Epuisé

Fasc. LXXXII. — JEAN HUBAUX et MAXIME LEROY. *Le mythe du Phénix dans les littératures grecque et latine.* 1939. 302 pp. . Epuisé

Fasc. LXXXIII. — MARIE DELCOURT. *Stérilités mystérieuses et naissances maléfiques dans l'antiquité classique.* 1938. 113 pp. . Epuisé

CATALOGUE PAR MATIÈRES

PHILOSOPHIE

HISTOIRE

PHILOLOGIE CLASSIQUE

14

Fasc. LXXXI. — ARMAND DELATTE. *Herbarius. Recherches sur le cérémonial usité chez les anciens pour la cueillette des simples et des plantes magiques.* 1938. 177 pp. . . . . Epuisé

Fasc. LXXXII. — JEAN HUBAUX et MAXIME LEROY. *Le mythe du Phénix dans les littératures grecque et latine.* 1939. 302 pp. . Epuisé

Fasc. LXXXIII. — MARIE DELCOURT. *Stérilités mystérieuses et naissances maléfiques dans l'antiquité classique.* 1938. 113 pp. . Epuisé

Fasc. LXXXVIII. — ARMAND DELATTE. *Anecdota Atheniensia et alia.* Tome II : Textes grecs relatifs à l'histoire des sciences. 1940. 504 pp. avec 5 planches . . . . Epuisé

Fasc. XCIII. — LOUIS DELATTE. *Textes latins et vieux français relatifs aux Cyranides.* 1942. x-354 pp. 17,50

Fasc. XCIV. — JULIETTE DAVREUX. *La légende de la prophétesse Cassandre d'après les textes et les monuments.* 1942. XII-240 pp. avec 57 planches . . . . Epuisé

Fasc. XCVII. — LOUIS DELATTE. *Les Traités de la Royauté d'Ec-phante, Diotogène et Sthénidas.* 1942. x-318 pp. . . . . Epuisé

Fasc. CIV. — MARIE DELCOURT. *Œdipe ou La légende du conquérant.* 1944. XXIV-262 pp. 17,50

Fasc. CVII. — ARMAND DELATTE. *Les Portulans grecs.* 1947. XXIV-400 pp. . . . . Epuisé

Fasc. CXVI. — LÉON LACROIX. *Les reproductions de statues sur les monnaies grecques. La statuaire archaïque et classique.* 1949. XXII-374 pp. et 28 planches . . . . Epuisé

Fasc. CXVII. — JULES LABARBE. *L'Homère de Platon* (Prix Zographos de l'Association pour l'encouragement des Etudes grecques en France). 1950. 462 pp. 22,50

Fasc. CXIX. — MARIE DELCOURT et J. HOYOUX. *La correspondance de L. Torrentius.* Tome I. *Période liégeoise (1583-1587).* 1950. XXII-544 pp. 25,00

Fasc. CXXV. — ALFRED TOMSIN. *Etude sur le Commentaire Virgilien d'Aemilius Asper.* 1952. 160 pp. 10,00

Fasc. CXXVII. — MARIE DELCOURT et J. HOYOUX. *La correspondance de L. Torrentius.* Tome II. *Période anversoise (1587-1589).* 1953. XIX-633 pp. 27,50

Fasc. CXXVIII. — LÉON HALKIN. *La Supplication d'action de grâces chez les Romains.* 1953. 136 pp. 10,00

Fasc. CXXXI. — MARIE DELCOURT et J. HOYOUX. *La correspondance de L. Torrentius.* Tome III. *Période anversoise (1590-1595).* 1954. XIX-634 pp. 25,00

Fasc. CXXXII. — ALBERT SEVERYNS. *Recherches sur la Chrestomathie de Proclos.* Tome III. *La Vita Homeri et les sommaires du Cycle.* I. *Etude paléographique et critique.* 1953. 368 pp. avec 14 planches. Avec les fasc. LXXVIII et LXXIX, les 3 fascicules . Epuisé

Fasc. CXXXVIII. — ROLAND CRAHAY. *La littérature oraculaire chez Hérodote.* 1956. 368 pp. . . . . Epuisé

Fasc. CXLI. — LOUIS DEROY. *L'emprunt linguistique.* 1956. 470 pp. (réimpression anastatique). 60,00

Fasc. CXLIII. — JULES LABARBE. *La loi navale de Thémistocle.* 1957. 238 pp. . . . . Epuisé

Fasc. CXLV. — JEAN HUBAUX. *Rome et Véies.* 1958. 406 pp., 10 figures hors-texte . . . . Epuisé

Fasc. CXLVI. — MARIE DELCOURT. *Héphaistos ou la légende du magicien*. 1957. 244 pp., 1 carte et 6 figures hors-texte . . .   Epuisé

Fasc. CXLVII. — GILBERT FRANÇOIS. *Le polythéisme et l'emploi au singulier des mots* θεός, δαίμων *dans la littérature grecque d'Homère à Platon*. 1957. 374 pp. . . . .   Epuisé

Fasc. CLI. — MARIE DELCOURT. *Oreste et Alcméon*. 1959. 113 pp.   Epuisé

Fasc. CLVI. — ROBERT JOLY. *Recherches sur le traité pseudo-hippocratique du régime*. 1960. 260 pp. (Prix Reinach de l'Association pour l'encouragement des Etudes grecques en France, 1961) .   17,00

Fasc. CLXV. — MARCEL DETIENNE. *La notion de daïmon dans le pythagorisme ancien*. 1962. 214 pp.   15,00

Fasc. CLXX. — ALBERT SEVERYNS. *Recherches sur la Chrestomathie de Proclos*. Tome IV. *La* Vita Homeri *et les sommaires du Cycle*. II. *Texte et traduction*. 1963. 110 pp.   15,00

Fasc. CLXXIV. — MARIE DELCOURT. *Pyrrhos et Pyrrha. Recherches sur les valeurs du feu dans les légendes helléniques*. 1965. 130 pp.   15,00

Fasc. CLXXVI. — A. BODSON, *La Morale sociale des derniers Stoïciens*. 1967. 148 pp.   15,00

PHILOLOGIE ROMANE

Fasc. XIV. — ALBERT COUNSON. *Malherbe et ses sources*. 1904. 239 pp. . . . .   Epuisé

Fasc. XXVI. — A. HUMPERS. *Etude sur la langue de Jean Lemaire de Belges*. 1921. 244 pp. . . . .   Epuisé

Fasc. XXVIII. — J. HAUST. *Le dialecte liégeois au XVIIe siècle. Les trois plus anciens textes (1620-1630)*. Edition critique, avec commentaire et glossaire. 1921. 84 pp. . . . . . .   Epuisé

Fasc. XXX. — J. DESCHAMPS. *Sainte-Beuve et le sillage de Napoléon*. 1922. 177 pp. . . . .   Epuisé

Fasc. XXXII. — J. HAUST. *Etymologies wallonnes et françaises*. 1923. 357 pp. (Prix Volney, de l'Institut) . . . .   Epuisé

Fasc. XLIX. — M. DELBOUILLE. *Le Tournoi de Chauvency, par Jacques Bretel* (édition complète). 1932. CII-192 pp. avec 11 planches (18 figures) . . . .   Epuisé

Fasc. L. — CH. FRANÇOIS. *Etude sur le style de la continuation du « Perceval » par Gerbert et du « Roman de la Violette » par Gerbert de Montreuil*. 1932. 126 pp. . . . .   Epuisé

Fasc. LIV. — S. ETIENNE. *Défense de la Philologie*. 1933. 73 pp. .   Epuisé

Fasc. LVII. — E. GRÉGOIRE. *L'astronomie dans l'œuvre de Victor Hugo*. 1933. 246 pp. . . . .   Epuisé

Fasc. LX. — CLAIRE WITMEUR. *Ximénès Doudan. Sa vie et son œuvre*. 1934. 150 pp. avec 5 planches (Prix biennal Jules Favre, de l'Académie Française)   10,00

Fasc. LXI. — RITA LEJEUNE-DEHOUSSE. *L'Œuvre de Jean Renart. Contribution à l'étude du genre romanesque au moyen âge*. 1935. 470 pp. . . . .   Epuisé

Fasc. LXVIII. — FERNAND DESONAY. *Œuvres complètes d'Antoine de La Sale*. Tome I. *La Salade*. 1935. XLV-270 pp. . . .   Epuisé

Fasc. LXX. —. S. ETIENNE. *Expériences d'analyse textuelle en vue de l'explication littéraire. Travaux d'élèves*. 1935. 145 pp. (réimpression anastatique)   40,00

Fasc. LXXIII. — ANTOINE GRÉGOIRE. *L'apprentissage du langage.* 1937. Tome I. 288 pp. (Prix Volney, de l'Institut de France) (réimpression anastatique).   40,00

Fasc. LXXXVI. — ANTOINE GRÉGOIRE. *Edmond-Puxi-Michel. Les prénoms et les surnoms de trois enfants.* 1939. 188 pp. . . .   10,00

Fasc. LXXXIX. — FERNAND DESONAY. *Antoine de La Sale, aventureux et pédagogue.* 1940. 204 pp. . . . .   Epuisé

Fasc. XCII. — FERNAND DESONAY. *Œuvres complètes d'Antoine de La Sale.* Tome II. *La Sale.* 1941. XXXVII-282 pp. . . . .   Epuisé

Fasc. XCVI. — LOUIS REMACLE. *Les variations de l'h secondaire en Ardenne liégeoise. Le problème de l'h en liégeois.* 1944. 440 pp. avec 43 figures (Prix Albert Counson, de l'Académie Royale de Langue et de Littérature Françaises)   20,00

Fasc. CIII. — PHINA GAVRAY-BATY. *Le vocabulaire toponymique du Ban de Fronville.* 1944. XXVIII-164 pp. avec 10 cartes . . .   12,00

Fasc. CVI. — ANTOINE GRÉGOIRE. *L'apprentissage du langage.* Tome II. *La troisième année et les années suivantes.* 1947. 491 pp. (réimpression anastatique). . . . .   sous presse

Fasc. CVIII. — RITA LEJEUNE. *Recherches sur le Thème : Les Chansons de Geste et l'Histoire.* 1948. 256 pp. . . . . .   Epuisé

Fasc. CIX. — LOUIS REMACLE. *Le problème de l'ancien wallon.* 1948. 230 pp. . . . .   Epuisé

Fasc. CXX. — JULES HORRENT. *La Chanson de Roland dans les littératures française et espagnole au moyen âge.* 1951. 541 pp.   Epuisé

Fasc. CXXII. — JULES HORRENT. *Roncesvalles. Etude sur le fragment de Cantar de gesta conservé à l'Archivo de Navarra (Pampelune).* 1951. 261 pp. . . . .   Epuisé

Fasc. CXXIII. — MAURICE DELBOUILLE. *Le Lai d'Aristote de Henri d'Andeli.* 1951. 112 pp. . . . .   Epuisé

Fasc. CXXVI. — LOUIS REMACLE. *Syntaxe du parler wallon de La Gleize.* Tome I. *Noms et articles. Adjectifs et pronoms.* 1952. 402 pp., 19 cartes   17,50

Fasc. CXXIX. — *Essais de philologie moderne* (1951). 1953. 252 pp.   17,50

Fasc. CXXXV. — LÉON WARNANT. *La constitution phonique du mot wallon. Etude fondée sur le parler d'Oreye.* 1956. 409 pp. . .   20,00

Fasc. CXXXIX. — LOUIS REMACLE. *Syntaxe du parler wallon de La Gleize.* Tome II. *Verbes. Adverbes. Prépositions.* 1956. 378 pp., 15 cartes   20,00

Fasc. CXL. — PAUL AEBISCHER. *Les Versions norroises du « Voyage de Charlemagne en Orient ». Leurs sources.* 1956. 185 pp. . .   12,50

Fasc. CXLI. — LOUIS DEROY. *L'emprunt linguistique.* 1956. 470 pp. (réimpression anastatique).   60,00

Fasc. CXLVIII. — LOUIS REMACLE. *Syntaxe du parler wallon de La Gleize.* Tome III. *Coordination. Subordination. Phénomènes divers.* 1960. 347 pp., 9 cartes   20,00

Fasc. CL. — *La technique littéraire des chansons de geste.* Colloque de Liège, 1957. 1959. 486 pp. . . . .   Epuisé

Fasc. CLVIII. — JULES HORRENT. *Le Pèlerinage de Charlemagne. Essai d'explication littéraire avec des notes de critique textuelle.* 1961. 154 pp. . . . .   Epuisé

18

Fasc. CLIX. — SIMONE BLAVIER-PAQUOT. *La Fontaine. Vues sur l'Art du Moraliste dans les Fables de 1668.* 1961. 166 pp. (Prix Bordin de l'Institut) . . . . Epuisé

Fasc. CLXI. — *Langue et Littérature.* Actes du VIIIᵉ Congrès de la F. I. L. L. M., Liège, 1960. 1961. 448 pp. 25,00

Fasc. CLXII. — JEAN RENSON. *Les dénominations du visage en français et dans les autres langues romanes. Etude sémantique et onomasiologique.* 1962. 738 pp. et 14 hors-texte, en deux volumes 40,00

Fasc. CLXIII. — PAUL DELBOUILLE. *Poésie et sonorités. La critique contemporaine devant le pouvoir suggestif des sons.* 1961. 268 pp. 17,50

Fasc. CLXVIII. — ALAIN LEROND. *L'habitation en Wallonie malmédienne (Ardenne belge). Etude dialectologique. Les termes d'usage courant.* 1963. 504 pp. et 3 cartes 30,00

Fasc. CLXXV. — *Méthodes de la Grammaire. Tradition et Nouveautés.* Actes du colloque de Liège, 1964. 1966. 196 pp. . . 17,50

Fasc. CLXXVII. — L. REMACLE. *Documents lexicaux extraits des archives scabinales de Roanne (La Gleize).* 1967. 439 pp. . . 32,00

Fasc. CLXXVIII. — M. TYSSENS. *La geste de Guillaume d'Orange dans les manuscrits cycliques.* 1967. 474 pp., 2 hors-texte . . 38,00

PHILOLOGIE GERMANIQUE

Fasc II. — HEINRICH BISCHOFF. *Ludwig Tieck als Dramaturg.* 1897. 128 pp. . . . . Epuisé

Fasc. III. — PAUL HAMELIUS. *Die Kritik in der englischen Literatur des 17. und 18. Jahrhunderts.* 1897. 214 pp. . . . . . Epuisé

Fasc. IV. — FÉLIX WAGNER. *Le livre des Islandais du prêtre Ari le Savant.* 1898. 107 pp. . . . . Epuisé

Fasc. XX. — T. Southern, *The Loyal Brother,* edited by P. HAMELIUS. 1911. 131 pp. . . . . Epuisé

Fasc. XXXIII. — A. L. CORIN. *Sermons de J. Tauler. I. Le Codex Vindobonensis 2744, édité pour la première fois.* 1924. 372 pp. . Epuisé

Fasc. XLI. — JEANNE-MARIE H. THONET. *Etude sur Edward Fitz-Gerald et la littérature persane, d'après les sources originales.* 1929. 144 pp. . . . . Epuisé

Fasc. XLII. — A. L. CORIN. *Sermons de J. Tauler. II. Le Codex Vindobonensis 2739, édité pour la première fois.* 1929. 548 pp. . Epuisé

Fasc. XLVI. — A. L. CORIN. *Comment faut-il prononcer l'allemand?* 1931. 164 pp. . . . . Epuisé

Fasc. LXII. — M. RUTTEN. *De Lyriek van Karel van de Woestijne.* 1934. 305 pp. (Prix des Amis de l'Université de Liège, 1935 ; Prix de critique littéraire des Provinces flamandes, période 1934-1936) . . . . Epuisé

Fasc. LXIV. — S. D'ARDENNE. *The Life of Sᵗ Juliana.* Edition critique. 1936. XLIX-250 pp. . . . . Epuisé

Fasc. LXXI. — F. WAGNER. *Les poèmes mythologiques de l'Edda.* Traduction précédée d'un exposé général de la mythologie scandinave. 1936. 262 pp. . . . . Epuisé

Fasc. LXXXIV. — JOSEPH WARLAND. *Glossar und Grammatik der germanischen Lehnwörter in der wallonischen Mundart Malmedys.* 1940. 337 pp. avec 2 cartes . . . . Epuisé

PHILOLOGIE ORIENTALE

Fasc. LXXVI. — Auguste Bricteux. *Roustem et Sohrab*. 1937.
91 pp. . . . . Epuisé

Fasc. XCV. — Abbé Robert Henry de Generet. *Le Martyre d'Ali
Akbar*. Drame persan. Texte établi et traduit, avec une Introduction et des Notes. 1947. 144 pp. 7,50

Fasc. CXLI. — Louis Deroy. *L'emprunt linguistique*. 1956. 470 pp.
(réimpression anastatique). 60,00

Fasc. CXLII. — J.-R. Kupper. *Les nomades en Mésopotamie au temps
des rois de Mari*. 1957. xxxii-284 pp. . . . . . . Epuisé

Fasc. CLV. — Henri Limet. *Le travail du métal au pays de Sumer
au temps de la IIIᵉ dynastie d'Ur*. 1959. 313 pp. 18,00

Fasc. CLXXIX. — Ch. Fontinoy. *Le duel dans les langues sémi-
tiques* . . . . sous presse

Fasc. CLXXX. — H. Limet. *L'Anthroponymie sumérienne dans les
documents de la 3ᵉ dynastie d'Ur* . . . . sous presse

Fasc. CLXXXII. — *XVᵉ Rencontre Assyriologique Internationale*.
1967. 175 pp. 20,00

VARIA

Fasc. XV. — Victor Tourneur. *Esquisse d'une histoire des études
celtiques*. 1905. 246 pp. . . . . Epuisé

Fasc. LXXIII. — Antoine Grégoire. *L'apprentissage du langage*.
1937. Tome I. 288 pp. (Prix Volney, de l'Institut de France)
(réimpression anastatique). 40,00

Fasc. LXXXVI. — Antoine Grégoire. *Edmond-Puxi-Michel. Les
prénoms et les surnoms de trois enfants*. 1939. 188 pp. . . . 10,00

Fasc. XC. — Eugène Polain. *Il était une fois... Contes populaires
liégeois*. 1942. 371 pp. . . . . Epuisé

Fasc. CVI. — Antoine Grégoire. *L'apprentissage du langage*.
Tome II. *La troisième année et les années suivantes*. 1947. 491 pp.
(réimpression anastatique). . . . . sous presse

Fasc. CXXIX. — *Essais de philologie moderne* (1951). 1953. 252 pp. 17,50

Fasc. CXXXIII. — Albert Husquinet. *L'adaptation scolaire et
familiale des jeunes garçons de 12 à 14 ans d'après le test socio-
métrique et le test d'aperception thématique*. 1954. 202 pp. . . Epuisé

Fasc. CXLI. — Louis Deroy. *L'emprunt linguistique*. 1956. 470 pp.
(réimpression anastatique). 60,00

Fasc. CXLIX. — *Ars Nova*. Colloques de Wégimont. II-1955. 1959.
275 pp. . . . . Epuisé

Fasc. CLVII. — *Les Colloques de Wégimont : Ethnomusicologie II -
1956*. 1960. 303 pp. et 4 hors-texte 20,00

Fasc. CLXXI. — *Les Colloques de Wégimont : Le « Baroque »
musical*. IV. 1957. 1963. 288 pp. 20,00

Fasc. CLXXII. — *Les Colloques de Wégimont : Ethnomusicologie*.
III. 1958-1960. 1964. 280 pp. 20,00

Les fascicules marqués d'un astérisque : I*, II*, III*, IV*, V* appartiennent
à la Série grand in-8° (Jésus) 27,5 × 18,5. Les fascicules I-XXX appartiennent
à la Série in-8° (23 × 15), les autres à la même série (25 × 16).

**Association Intercommunale
de MECANOGRAPHIE
88, rue Louvrex — LIEGE**

Imprimé en Belgique